OF ALL THE ASPECTS OF RECOVERY IN POSTWAR GERMANY perhaps none was as critical or as complicated as the matter of dealing with Nazi criminals, and, more broadly, with the Nazi past. While on the international stage German officials spoke with contrition of their nation's burden of guilt, at home questions of responsibility and retribution were not so clear. In this masterful examination of Germany under Adenauer, Norbert Frei shows that, beginning in 1949, the West German government dramatically reversed the denazification policies of the immediate postwar period and initiated a new "Vergangenheitspolitik," or "policy for the past," which has had enormous consequences reaching into the present.

ADENAUER'S GERMANY AND THE NAZI PAST chronicles how amnesty laws for Nazi officials were passed unanimously and civil servants who had been dismissed in 1945 were reinstated liberally—and how a massive popular outcry led to the release of war criminals who had been condemned by the Allies. These measures and movements represented more than just the rehabilitation of particular individuals. Frei argues that the amnesty process delegitimized the previous political expurgation administered by the Allies and, on a deeper level, served to satisfy the collective psychic needs of a society longing for a clean break with the unparalleled political and moral catastrophe it had undergone in the 1940s. Thus the era of Adenauer devolved into a scandal-ridden period of reintegration at any cost. Frei's work brilliantly and chillingly explores how the collective will of the German people, expressed through mass allegiance to new consensus-oriented democratic parties, cast off responsibility for the horrors of the war and Holocaust, effectively silencing engagement with the enormities of the Nazi past.

ADENAUER'S GERMANY AND THE NAZI PAST

ADENAUER'S GERMANY AND THE NAZI PAST

The Politics of Amnesty
and Integration

Norbert Frei
Translated by Joel Golb

COLUMBIA UNIVERSITY PRESS
New York

Columbia University Press
Publishers Since 1893
New York, Chichester, West Sussex
Publication of the Institut für Zeitgeschichte
Vergangenheitspolitik © 1997 Verlag C. H. Beck, München
English Translation Copyright © 2002 Columbia University Press
All rights Reserved

Library of Congress Cataloging-in-Publication Data
Frei, Norbert.
    Adenauer's Germany and the Nazi past : the politics of amnesty and
    integration / Norbert Frei; translated by Joel Golb.
        p. cm
    Includes bibliographical references and index.
    ISBN: 0-231-11882-1 (cloth : alk. paper)
    1. Denazification.   2. Germany (West)—Politics and government.
3. Germany—Politics and government—1945–1990. I. Title
DD259.4 .F72413 2002
940.53/144/0943–dc21   2002073502
                                              CIP

Columbia University Press books are printed on permanent and durable
acid-free paper
Printed in the United States of America

c 10 9 8 7 6 5 4 3 2 1

CONTENTS

FOREWORD

Most people know two things about modern Germany: that Hitler's Germany, the most popular tyranny of the last century, initiated an unprecedented slaughter, the Holocaust, and that today's Federal Republic is a democratic polity, peaceful and responsible. But we know or remember less about the process by which the country managed the transition from a state of horror to a state of constitutional order and stability.

How Germans dealt with the legal and political legacies of the Nazi past remains an important and instructive issue. We live in a world in which questions about how to make the transition from a criminal regime occupy nations in many parts of the world, from Eastern Europe to South Africa and Latin America. We could assume that Germany provides an extraordinary example of a successful transition. And on the whole it does—with a most tortured and ambiguous beginning.

It is precisely that beginning, by now forgotten and hitherto not fully explored, that Norbert Frei, a German historian of the postwar generation, reconstructs with admirable thoroughness, political insight, and moral sensitivity. His study begins with the establishment of the Federal Republic in 1949—when the three Western occupying powers granted partial sovereignty to the newly elected government in Bonn, reserving for themselves certain formal and informal rights. The new state had to assume the task of denazification, of dealing with the multiple legacies of Nazi criminality and German complicity. The most memorable effort at justice had been at the several Nuremberg trials of the Third Reich's principal leaders on charges that included the planning of incursionary war and genocide; sentences ranged from prison terms to death, whereas a few of the accused—amidst public controversy—were acquitted. By 1949, some of the convicted remained in jail, a few still under sentence of death. After the creation of what came to be known as West Germany, much of the remaining burden of dealing with the Nazi past devolved on Germans themselves. (Frei does not treat developments in the German Democratic Republic, or East Germany, which remained under Soviet tutelage.) The new political authorities had to deal with the past in specific political and legal contexts: who should be prosecuted and for what offenses, who should be compensated for losses or for penalties the Allies had imposed earlier, and who should be barred from public office in light of what acts in the past. These matters dominated politics in the early years of the Bonn Republic: they had to be decided collectively by the executive and parliament, by political parties whose existence depended on popular suffrage, and by a judiciary that was largely a carryover from the Third Reich.

Frei examines the vast political-cultural space in which the decisions concerning amnesty and integration were taken: he analyzes the government initiatives and the party responses, all political moves made with an eye to organized lobbies and popular opinion. The prevailing mood favored a hasty end to prosecution, seen by some Germans as Allied retribution, "victors' justice," and by a few even as a symptom of the vindictiveness of world Jewry. West Germans, including millions of resentful expellees from Polish and Czech lands, had no desire to delve into the past, to try and punish compatriots who had served the Nazi state to the last. More, many of them were uncomfortable with the few Germans who had actively resisted Hitler, most notably those connected with the July 20 coup against him, traitors in the eyes of all too many.

The two major parties—the Christian Democrats and the Social Democrats—realized that, as Frei correctly states, "they would have to fish for their votes from a people whose overwhelming majority some ten years earlier would have voted for Hitler in a free and secret election." Hence both parties—with differences between them—recognized the political need for leniency, for virtual amnesty, for condoning continuities in political careers. Even forthright democrats recognized the force of what one prominent and irreproachable writer of the time propounded: a person's right to political error or faulty judgment. This view

could be read as a plea for exculpation: supporters of Nazism had committed an "error," not a crime. West Germany's political class came to
think that a genuine or radical purge of all those who had been implicated in the Third Reich, individuals and organizations, would result
in massive alienation and an anti-Bonn mood, just as there had been a
fatal anti-Weimar mood.

Frei carefully considers the non-German players in the ongoing
struggle: among them were the three Allied high commissioners with
their reserve powers. The American, John J. McCloy, mindful that the
Korean War and the cold war generally made eventual German support
of the United States an imperative, often enough acceded to Chancellor
Konrad Adenauer's pleas for leniency or clemency, especially toward
industrial leaders. But there were limits, and German politicians as well
as the German public had to reckon with the continued rights of the
high commissioners; they also had to heed warnings from German commentators that yielding all too frequently to nationalist truculence
would arouse a critical "foreign response." Jeering comments from the
putatively antifascist East Germany about the many ex-Nazis in West
German political life were regarded as a nuisance in the propaganda
war between the two states. (We now know that the East German regime
covertly sanctioned the use of former high-ranking Nazis.) Bonn also
had to contend with and separate itself from large numbers of organized
extreme right-wing elements, people filled with contempt for the Allies
and with disdain for the West. So the "brown" past was more than a
smudge on the new landscape; there was no tabula rasa for Bonn, no
Stunde null, no total break with elements of the previous regime.

The great achievement of this book is to trace for the first time in
meticulous detail the debates and decisions, the motives and compromises, that Germans made in this initial period of transition. Author and
subject are splendidly matched: Frei has an eye for complexity. He casts
his historic net widely and shrewdly; he depicts in depth the emergent
political culture in which these issues were tackled; he has drawn on a
vast array of sources, some hitherto untapped, both from the public
sphere and from private papers of the leading actors. This is an astound-
ing and successful work of scholarship, leaving the reader with a mounting unease about the lack of a radical cleansing but with a clearer grasp
both of conditions at the time and the success of later efforts to correct
or abandon certain soothing distortions, such as the notion that a small
gang around Hitler was solely culpable while most Germans were innocent or ignorant. We can now appreciate the great achievements of later
generations, most notably perhaps Frei's own, and the courage and candor of men such as Willy Brandt or Richard von Weizsaecker.

Frei's themes are of riveting relevance as other countries coming to terms with their own past go beyond the facile division between resisters and collaborators and face the issue of retroactive justice. Adam Michnik, the renowned Polish dissident and critic, once advocated a policy of "amnesty, not amnesia." By and large, and more perhaps by good fortune than design, the Federal Republic came to live and ultimately prosper by this precept.

Fritz Stern

INTRODUCTION

> The general feeling is that we need to create a
> positive new order, hence to be bighearted, offer
> many opportunities, and tolerate many people
> who were our enemies yesterday.
>
> —*Dolf Sternberger, June 1949*[1]

Germany's question of how to deal with the Nazi past is older than the West German republic. Again and again over the decades, it has been the object of heated public controversy, leading repeatedly in turn to alterations of both intellectual and political perspective. But the history of what became known as "overcoming the past" itself only became an independent subject of historical research in the 1990s—a development running more or less parallel to the emergence of great public debates over the Holocaust and the Germans, the Wehrmacht's crimes in World War II, slave labor and reparations, as well as over the forms and appropriate degree of social-historical memory.[2] The present study is framed by that context. Concerned with the opening years of the West German state, it focuses on a chapter in the early Adenauer period's political history considered very important when it unfolded—put pointedly, a sustained effort at "overcoming" earlier attempts to confront, legally and morally, the immediate Nazi past. On the one hand, the chapter's importance was related to the need for short-term stabilization of a society that, following years of occupation, had to take increasing responsibility for its own well-being. On the other hand, it was related to the need to produce more sustained political, judicial, and intellectual standards for confronting that same past.

In the first years following the defeat of Germany, the Allies had carried out a campaign of political purging that was initially upheld and supported by Germany's democratic, legally sanctioned political parties. But in the fall of 1949, immediately after the inauguration of the West German parliament (the Bundestag), all the parties initiated efforts to end the purging—in part, even to revoke it. In its totality, the policy of purging had not been ineffectual; a series of parliamentary initiatives, legislative acts, and administrative decisions aimed at its vitiation. These measures have barely been considered in the older historical research except in a different, mostly social-political, context. While there is little evidence of strategic planning behind the measures, retrospectively there is much that argues for their amounting to a unified body, and their linkage to specific forms of anti-Nazi normative legislation points in the same direction.

Throughout this book—and following its original German title, *Vergangenheitspolitik*—I refer to the sum total of such political-legal measures as the Adenauer era's "policy for the past." This phrase—which is not to be found in any of the documentary sources—is both less sweeping and much more precise than the commonly used phrase "overcoming the past," itself part and parcel of the old West German republic's political discourse. Unlike the latter phrase, it is not meant to be basically applicable to all political activity understood as a reaction to the Third Reich.

Rather, a "policy for the past" signifies a political dynamic that extended over half a decade and was characterized by a high degree of societal acceptance—indeed of collective *expectation*. At stake, in the first place, was both an annulment of punishments and integrative measures on behalf of an army of millions of former Nazi Party members. Virtually without exception, these people regained their social, professional, and civic, but not their political, status—which they had lost in the course of denazification, internment, and requital for "political" deeds. At stake in the second place (as it were, flanking the amnesties) was political and judicial border demarcation vis-à-vis remaining groups of ideologically committed Nazis. The postwar democracy's foundational anti-Nazi consensus was here selectively recodified according to needs of the moment. The basic elements of the policy for the past discussed in these pages are thus amnesty, integration, and demarcation.

When it comes to analytic precision, the term's advantages are underscored by the identity of the policy's beneficiaries: not the victims of Nazism, but those considered the "victims" of its overcoming. A list would include, above all, the previously dismissed officials and the large number of "fellow travelers." But it would also include the remaining individuals referred to as *Entnazifizierungsgeschädigten*—"those damaged by denazification"; tens of thousands of formerly interned persons; and in fact most war criminals convicted by the Allies, along with Nazi criminals condemned in German courts. With their social advancement, the reproach of German moral guilt conveyed by the original denazification project naturally faded. For this reason, those who had never personally been held accountable could consider themselves symbolically exonerated.

There was another factor contributing to such collective self-awareness: in part already since the occupation period, in part through compensatory linkage with measures on behalf of former Nazis, certain groups of those they had persecuted were receiving reparations. Such minorities were hardly in a position to publicly oppose the policy for the past that had emerged in the early 1950s—and this not only on grounds of the prevailing power structure, but also of legitimate self-interest. As a result, the "concept" of extensive pardoning—never systematically defined as one of the new beginning's foundations, but clearly present to anyone with Dolf Sternberger's insight—went practically uncontested. The wish for such pardoning had already made its way through German society before the Bonn republic's founding; but it could only become reality after this had taken place.

Beginning as early as 1945, the course of purgation, "reeducation," and "reorientation" set out on by the British and Americans had sparked private expressions of unease and half-loud demands for fundamental changes; very soon, there were also widely publicized explicit critiques of denazification. At some point in 1947 or in 1948 at the latest, these critiques gained the upper hand. Parallel to this intensifying opposition, and roughly at the same pace as the Allied enlistment of the Germans in West European economic and political reconstruction, was a lessening of German readiness for the basic attitudinal change that had been demanded of them. While imposed from the outside, a preoccupation with the national past had also been considered a necessity by many Germans. Increasingly, this necessity dissolved into a shared engagement for a post-national future.

In the "new beginning" of 1949, demarcating the present from the period of foreign control played a central role in the German need for a sweeping past-political inventory. The radical dismissal of measures for purging and punishment was thus in part meant as a symbolic break with the period of direct occupation. It was also meant as a break with the war years: reflecting a historical myopia unintentionally aggravated by the war crimes trials, public awareness of the Third Reich's unjust nature (an awareness itself quite feeble from the start) was now widely limited to those years alone.

Toward the end of 1949, Dolf Sternberger could critically diagnose a triumph of "vital forgetting" that followed a short phase of moral "thin-skinnedness" among his fellow Germans.[3] In the course of the following years, the forgetfulness went much further than the "certain silence" that Hermann Lübbe would later discover in relation to the thematizing of individual Nazi pasts.[4] At first, there had been a discretion practiced en masse and by no means exhausting itself in the sphere of the private and personal; eventually, the discretion evolved into a *triumph of silence* whose meaning has long called for extensive study. The present book is meant to set the groundwork for research into the political-historical framework of this evolving public consensus.

The book's approach is necessarily skeptical regarding a historical functionalism often advocated in Lübbe's wake—a functionalism disposing of the problem before its analysis. At the same time, it is in full harmony with an insight Eugen Kogon formulated—no less clearly than Lübbe—long before West Germany's founding[5]: that the political amnestying and social reintegration of the army of "fellow travelers" was as necessary as it was unavoidable. But it likewise adheres to a basic scholarly imperative: that of carefully probing the social and political framework of such measures, confronting their political-moral costs and inquiring into the extent to which we can draw distinctions. The backdrop to this analytic endeavor is formed by one particular thesis regarding the increased currency of demands for amnesty and reintegration—along with the deepening sense of both their urgency and inevitability—in Germany at the end of the 1940s. The thesis is that such a development was only possible because the young democracy wished to purchase political legitimation through granting services with—particularly in the case of the reintegrated officials—a thoroughly financial dimension.

In the 1980s and early 1990s, historical studies of the Adenauer period[6] generally neglected the widespread readiness—indeed appeals—to extend such services to groups not falling under the "fellow traveler" rubric, even with the most generous interpretation; this phenomenon points beyond the above-mentioned pragmatic motives. At the beginning of the 1950s, both politicians and the public intervened sweepingly—and as if doing so were a self-evident thing—for war criminals and Nazis condemned by the Allies. They demanded their release from prison and pressed for their reintegration. This is perhaps the most dramatic aspect of the history laid out in the following pages; it is certainly the most unsettling. More research is needed on the societal experiences and mental structures underpinning such support for even the most heinous individuals. But much speaks for understanding it as, to no small extent, a reflex and consequence of Nazism's powerful capacity for social binding.

In West Germany of the early 1950s, past-political pressure groups, some of them highly professionalized, managed to realize aims sometimes running against general public interest in their lack of scruples; very likely, these aims would have been rejected by most of a better-informed public. The success of such groups was made easier by the persistence of "national" solidarity among the defeated *Volk* (the post-Nazi national community), the large areas of the recent past that were unprocessed and unilluminated, and the refusal of any serious acknowledgment of what had happened—a refusal evident on various levels. For this reason, it is important to closely consider the activities of these past-political lobbies, along with their surrounding social constellations—as it is to take steady account of media positions and publications playing an essential and active role in the past-political process.

Crucially, formulating the Adenauer years' policy for the past was never an entirely German affair. It not only was bound up with directives of and measures taken by the Allied occupation authorities, but also depended on Allied cooperation. At the start, to the extent legislation was in question, Allied permission was mandatory. The Allies' shifting options and reactions, on occasion—still—their actions, thus also play a key role in this book's unfolding history. Alongside examples of realpolitik-based flexibility, we here also repeatedly find episodes in which the Allies rejected past-political measures desired by the Germans as exceeding the reasonable or acceptable—for instance, their rejection of swollen demands for the pardoning of war criminals— or at least the years' long deferral of conclusive action on those demands. An advantage of studying the close interaction between German room for maneuver and Allied claims of control is that the German policy for the past is not isolated from basic influences: a shifting geostrategic situation; evolving West European security interests.

The Allied withdrawal from the business of direct administration and the founding of the West German state thus mark the point at which older past-political claims and expectations by the Germans entered the realm of the realizable. The active phase of that state's policy for the past began with the "fresh beginning" in Bonn and lasted until the mid-1950s. It stands at the center of this study, whose narrative unfolds the same chronological sequence from three separate perspectives: first, a look at Germany's past-political legislation in the early postwar period; second, a consideration of the core political-symbolic problem of the Nazi war criminals; third and finally, the process of past-political border demarcation and the establishment of corresponding legal norms.

PART I

A Legislation for the Past

Parliamentary and Administrative Junctures

The German parliament, or Bundestag, has never been the scene of a general debate concerning the Nazi past—a debate held independently of specific legislative goals. Nevertheless, policies concerning that past were being shaped there from the very beginning. A taste of what would come was offered by the reactions to the short speech Social Democrat Paul Löbe delivered to open the new parliament on the afternoon of 7 September 1949: on two occasions hecklers interrupted the president—chosen by virtue of seniority—as he carefully broached the Nazi period. No one took special exception to Löbe's mention of the "massive weight of guilt" on the German side—this was far enough removed from any "collective guilt" tonalities and was cloaked with the standard distinction between the Nazi leadership, on the one hand, and the German *Volk*, on the other. Presumably, Löbe was not only convinced on this particular occasion that "a criminal system" had piled guilt "on the shoulders of our *Volk*." For memory had drawn him back to the Reichstag's dramatic meeting on 23 March 1933, when the Social Democratic Party (SPD) alone voted against the Authorization Act, which destroyed the constitution and in effect ceded power to Hitler. The perspective furnished by this early act of resistance (the "patriotic deed") appeared to rule over Löbe's entire approach to the

1

"Third Reich." A single catcall came from the ranks of the Communists; among the legislators from the "bourgeois" parties, more than a few had offered Hitler carte blanche after the torched Reichstag had been relocated to the Kroll Opera House. Correspondingly, the bourgeois ranks maintained their silence—surely less out of decorum than discomfiture. But real disorder burst forth shortly after Löbe once more cited the Social Democratic opposition to the Authorization Act, this time recounting that it had cost the party 24 lives—the erstwhile Reichstag president's attempt to answer the charge leveled by "outside critics" that the German people had offered no resistance to the Nazi terror. "The other parties also had victims—we don't want to draw up any accounts here" was one of the complaints voiced from the right-wing parties. The 73-year-old Löbe, in fact, had simply been too slow in proceeding with his line of argument, that "the Communists also had many victims, as did members of the earlier Center and other representatives extending to the right-wing parties"—all these victims demonstrating the unfounded nature of the "outside" charges.[1]

Very touchy when it came to internal matters, but ready for practical consensus and displaying solidarity toward the outside world: this was the face to be shown for years by the Bundestag whenever the past became a legislative theme. A striking shyness was revealed when it came to looking back accurately on the dark facts, not to mention showing the courage to confront them in vivid detail. But despite all the self-imposed "duty to be objective," all concord in resolving difficulties, and all the efforts at verbal discretion, such confrontations could not always be avoided. This was the case whenever the issue was collective amnesty, or managing the political purging, or rehabilitating the officials and military men affected by it—in short, whenever a policy for the past was meant to be constructed. On such occasions it was necessary to discuss the past, at least through intimations.

The first direct debate emerged mere days after the Bundestag's convening: from every corner calls were already sounding for both amnesty and an end to denazification. The smallest political factions struck the most strident tones, with the German Party from Lower Saxony struggling most vociferously for a past-political profile. As early as 8 September 1949 the party's 17-member team had succeeded in formulating the interests of all so-called lesser offenders and simple fellow travelers. They did so through an emergency motion, directed at a not-yet-existent federal government, requesting a placing on the agenda of "laws for the immediate cessation of denazification and an amnesty for all members of groups 3 and 4,[2] or similarly situated groups affected by the consequences of previous denazification."[3] A week later, the Catholic-based Center Party drafted an amnesty law of its own; the draft envisioned impunity for those convicted of crimes, committed during the occupation period, "linked to enthusiasm for the democratic idea or opposition to surmounted National Socialism"—or (space now being offered for less worthy motives) other crimes "that were determined or favored by the troubles and insecurity of the times."[4] On 20 September, Alfred Loritz's right-wing populist Economic Reconstruction Association demanded an immediate amnesty "for all crimes that can be qualified according to the penal laws as infractions and misdemeanors"; this included transgressions that the Nazi wartime economy laws had defined as crimes but that were not perpetrated out of "especially crude self-interest," thus causing no "especially heavy damage to the *Volksgemeinschaft*."[5] The next day Loritz added a request for a "general amnesty for all fellow travelers and lesser offenders."[6]

That both the Christian Democrats and the Liberals refrained from such requests almost certainly reflected, above all else, a lack of desire to take the initiative away from the emerging West German government.[7] For, at least since an official statement of Adenauer's on 20 September, it was perfectly clear that the alliance formed between the Christian Democratic Union and Christian Social Union (CDU-CSU), together with the Free Democratic Party (FDP) and the German Party, would not remain inactive in this sphere for long. As the chancellor explained it, "much misfortune and mischief" accompanied "denazification"; while those "truly guilty" of crimes during the National Socialist period had to be punished with appropriate severity, the distinction between "two classes of human beings in Germany," namely the "politically objectionable" and the "politically unobjectionable," now needed to "vanish as fast as possible." The confusion caused by the war and its aftermath, Adenauer declared, had imposed great trials and temptations on many people. For this reason, understanding was called for in the case of many lapses and transgressions. The federal government had thus decided to "let bygones be bygones" whenever it seemed justifiable. Making his voice heard through the cheers of his party supporters, the chancellor now announced that as part of the amnesty question the possibility of "applying to the High Commissioners for a corresponding amnesty for punishments imposed by the Allied military courts" was being examined.[8]

Despite the lackluster impression made by Adenauer's assessment as a whole,[9] at crucial points it lacked neither careful precision nor a certain artfulness. Showing restraint in his choice of words, the chancellor had captured the hopes of many: those schooling themselves in self-pity as the *Entnazifizierungsgeschädigte*—individuals "damaged by denazification." Without promising something outside his powers, he had awakened hopes among condemned war criminals and those close to them. With energetic polish he rounded off his remarks in this direction—they had all been placed in his speech's second half—with the promise "to draw the necessary lessons from the past, in the face of all those undermining our state's existence, whether they can be classified as radicals of the right or left." The brief condemnation of "anti-Semitic endeavors manifest here and there" that directly followed was apparently meant to strengthen that tone of resolution, but as Kurt Schumacher complained the day after, its effect was in fact all too "flat and weak."[10] It was left to the leader of the opposition to make the halfway clear statement that "the Hitlerian barbarism"—*Hitlerbarbarei*—had dishonored the German *Volk* through the extermination of 6 million Jewish human beings." It is remarkable that the SPD chairman laid so much stress on the "dishonor" experienced by the Germans, declaring that "we will have to bear its consequences for an unforeseeable period." To be sure, this formulation needed to be understood against the background of Schumacher's particular form of nationalism—of his persistent emphasis on German duty and responsibility, now taking the form of a demand for concrete help for the survivors, "mostly older and sick individuals."[11] But it would seem to reveal as well a partiality quite similar to that prompting Adenauer's statement that he considered it "unworthy, indeed in itself incredible, that after everything occurring in the National Socialist period, there are said to be people in Germany who still persecute or despise Jews because they are Jews."[12]

With his rather skewed pronouncement, the chancellor here hinted at much that would emerge and reemerge over the following months, and following years, in public debates. This amounted to a readiness to aid those former *Volksgenossen* and party members who were, to varying degrees, guilty—indeed to an enthusiasm for the process. Such enthusiasm stood in stark contrast to the somewhat understandable inhibitions and uncertainties regarding the few Jewish survivors—but also to manifestations of overt distancing from those survivors, often less easy to grasp. Adenauer's governmental address omitted any liberating word—for which many were waiting[13]—regarding the Jewish victims: an omission that was perhaps no coincidence, but rather an augury of this intercession on behalf of both perpetrators and "nominal" Nazis. It was quite clearly the case that an intrepid engagement on behalf of a persecuted minority was a far less pressing task than shaping a policy for the past benefiting a German majority—one whose actual suffering (e.g., through expulsion and bombing) and false claims to victim status (through denazification or "military conviction") had only begun with the crumbling of Hitler's regime.

CHAPTER 1

The Amnesty Law of 1949

The German Federal Republic, depicted as an innocent swaddled baby, is handed by the Western powers to a distinctly grandfatherly Mr. Germany. In 1949 this caricature illustrated the widespread view of the founding of the West German state as a totally new beginning.[1] The counterpart to this view was an equally widespread, fervently felt desire for a wholesale eradication of the huge number of guilty verdicts pronounced since 1945 in the framework of denazification. In the autumn of 1949, a fixed notion on the collective horizon of expectations was that the expiatory measures imposed by the Allies—measures accepted strictly because of the Allied presence—would generally end with the restitution of German statehood. Put somewhat differently, in the beginning—even before Adenauer—was the idea of amnesty.[2]

Certainly this wish for a tabula rasa did not involve a consistent expression of moral indifference or a deliberate apologetics. Often (perhaps for the most part) it was grounded in the complicated circumstances surrounding postwar guilt and punishment—circumstances often experienced as unjust. Examples of such experiences were the gradually abating rigor of the denazification process, accompanied by a shift from penalizing to promoting many heavily implicated individuals; unequal access to ration coupons; periods of internment that were often haphazard; and the simple feeling of having atoned *enough* through aerial bombardment, flight, and expulsion. An additional factor was the increasing German familiarity with the role of amnesty as a political-legal instrument, which reflected an increasing recourse to it. In order to tidy up the denazification process, the occupation authorities had in fact declared many amnesties.[3] Similarly, to disencumber a judiciary whose ranks had been highly thinned through the purging of Nazis, between 1947 and 1948 amnesty laws had been passed in the German states (the *Länder)* controlled by the Americans and British, as well as in those controlled by the French; these sometimes covered prison sentences of up to one year. To be sure, such amnesties were directed first and foremost at crimes committed in the hunger years for survival's sake—they expressly excluded all crimes motivated by a desire to "maintain Nazi rule," by "militarism," and by an intent to spread Nazi ideology. A June 1947 regulation issued by the Central Judicial Office of the British zone makes it perfectly clear that the intent was in fact not to provide relief for Nazi criminals: it exempts from punishment all deeds previously declared punishable by the Third Reich alone (e.g., "racial" transgressions), along with crimes committed either in opposition to Nazism or in order to escape Nazi persecution.[4] In addition, in the spring of 1949 the British-American zone's economic council decided on amnesty for tax-related offenses.[5]

Nevertheless, as early as the summer of 1949, different plans being considered by the justice ministries of the various West German Länder all nurtured the hope for a broad "federal amnesty"[6]; called on the occasion of the state's foundation, such an amnesty was quite clearly meant to extend beyond the limited realm of economic offenses. The recommendation of the minister of justice "not to speak separately of crimes against humanity and organizational offenses," but rather to quietly integrate them with other types of crime reveals the direction things had taken[7]: the longing for amnesty no longer stopped short of judgments passed by the Allied military courts and German *Spruchgerichte*—the inquest courts set up in the British zone. In this manner, the conceptual step toward including genuine Nazi crimes had now been taken. What remained open, for a time, was the extent to which the federal legislators would be able to elaborate on this concept under the critical gaze of the Allied High Commissioner.

In any case, when the fresh-faced cabinet met on 26 September 1949 to initiate discussion of an amnesty law, its desirability went without saying.[8] Adenauer appeared to capture the widely shared viewpoint succinctly: "In view of the confused times behind us, a general tabula rasa is called for." Still, the extent to which the federal government was authorized in the matter was unclear. Looking back on standard recent practice, Thomas Dehler, justice minister of the new German state and a Free Democrat, voiced the opinion that any amnesty law had to be passed in collaboration with the Länder. He was here adhering to the stance taken in the "Frankfurt Plan" formulated by Walter Strauß, his unloved Christian Democratic Union (CDU)-appointed state secretary— a plan that Strauß had already submitted on 12 September.[9] Strauß's proposal itself reflected the debate unfolding in previous months among the justice ministries of the different Länder.

Dehler's reservations in light of possible sensitivity on the part of the Länder were shared by his cabinet colleagues Fritz Schäffer, Gustav Heinemann, and Franz Blücher: a circumstance sparking Adenauer's instinct for power. It seemed the issue at hand might also offer a chance to demonstrate the proper relation between the Länder and the federal government. In any event, without beating around the bush, the chancellor indicated the situation resembled that "in a monarchy when a king ascends the throne. The federation has now been born and the President is on the scene. In light of this event, within the German *Volk* the broadest possible circles expect an amnesty." Dehler was given the task of clarifying the legal situation.

On account of clearly courageous behavior during the Third Reich, Dehler had little fear of being sullied by contact with those who were politically tainted.[10] Only a week later the federal justice minister presented his colleagues in the Länder with a draft of a "Law for Granting Exemption from Punishment." Dehler's position now was that the federal government's authority "was not to be doubted"; in view of the matter's urgency, he was requesting that things "such as comments and suggestions" regarding this "thoroughly" considered plan be tabled within a week. What the draft envisioned was an amnesty for all past and pending sentences of imprisonment up to a year and all fines up to 10,000 German marks, so long as the deed was committed before 15 September 1949. In this manner, offenses from the Nazi period were incorporated without any reservations. As Dehler explained, subjective preconditions (e.g., support for democracy or the absence of a "criminal disposition") had been intentionally omitted in order to minimize the judiciary's investigative requirements. Granted, the "generally very mild verdicts passed by the courts over recent months" spoke against an amnesty for punishments extending beyond six months' imprisonment. But, Dehler observed, it was also unmistakable that in "certain cases between 1946 and 1948"—he of course meant the trials of Nazis, initially prompted by the Allied denazification process—"verdicts were passed ranging between six months and one year, such verdicts no longer appearing suitable." The liberal politician thus deemed a more generous amnesty to be defensible as a "one-time special measure," "drawing a close to the past with its misery, confusion, and a savagery born of war and the postwar period."[11]

In a cabinet meeting a few days later, Dehler conceded, again, that his proposal was very far-reaching, now justifying it as "probably necessary to mark the new beginning offered by establishment of the Federal Republic." It seems that on this occasion as well the ministers dispensed with a discussion of the extent and consequences of an amnesty—and even a basic consideration of its true necessity. The short minutes, at least, contain only Adenauer's renewed indication that "this matter is in itself suited for a thorough discussion of the constitutional situation." An agreement did emerge from the meeting to wait for the results of the contacts initiated with the justice ministers—after which Dehler's bill would be debated once again.[12]

The various reactions from the Länder arrived by mail; they reflected little enthusiasm. There were the expected doubts regarding the federal government's authority to declare such amnesties. Beyond this, several of Dehler's colleagues, familiar with the basic material from the amnesties declared by individual Länder, criticized the inconsistencies at work in the proposal. But above all, there were strong objections to the planned extent of the amnesty: Hesse and Lower Saxony opted for an upper limit of six months; Württemberg and Bavaria considered three months sufficient, economic crimes excepted. Bavaria's justice minister Josef Müller reproached Dehler—his personal friend—with the fact that many "pronounced criminals" would profit from an amnesty for sentences up to a year. Reservations regarding "countenancing serious criminals" also came from the other political direction; but "Joe the Oxman"—Müller's nickname in Bavaria—was the only minister to overtly address what others must also have observed: namely, that such a generous amnesty would exempt most criminals "either already sentenced or facing sentencing for grave acts of Nazi violence, particularly for serious breeches of public peace and similar offenses resulting from the anti-Jewish measures of 1938." Not least of all because of his wartime connections to Allied and German resistance circles, Müller was a controversial figure in the Christian Social Union (CSU) and would be dismissed as chairman in 1949. He considered the prospects of such an amnesty "legally and politically untenable."[13]

The records reveal nothing about the way Dehler arrived at one-year sentences as the amnesty's proposed limit. What is clear is that he was impressed enough by the protests of his colleagues in the Länder to back off somewhat at their meeting in Frankfurt on 17 October 1949. Reasonably accurately, the German Press Agency reported that the "great amnesty" was on the agenda.[14] Still, instead of the sweeping one-year amnesty, the representatives of the Länder proposed various limits ranging from three to six months, depending on the nature of the criminal and economic offenses. The vast majority of participants were also in favor of the federal government being limited to recommending specific amnesty legislation to the Länder; Württemberg, Bavaria, and Hamburg were bluntly opposed to a "federal amnesty."[15]

Presumably such demurring undertones had meanwhile reached the chancellor's ears—at the cabinet meeting the next morning it was agreed to send a message to the justice ministers of the Länder: The distinction between criminal and economic offenses was acceptable, but the penal limits, which needed to be twice as high as what was proposed in Frankfurt, were not. More precisely, the federal government insisted on a one-year upper limit for economic offenses, simply shortening the general impunity by six months.[16] The formal decision in favor of the altered bill was made at the cabinet meeting of 28 October.[17] The tug-of-war then began in earnest.

Alarmed through press reports, Friedrich Meyer-Abich, "General Inspector of the Central Judicial Office of the British Zone," now turned to Dehler.[18] Meyer-Abich's protest concerned a single regulation drafted into the government's plan. According to this regulation, judgments passed by the Spruchgerichte were not to be part of the amnesty, since such a decision needed to be made in conjunction with what the substantiation referred to as a *Bereinigung der Entnazifizierung*—a "cleaning up" of denazification. According to Meyer-Abich, this argument revealed a complete misunderstanding of the proceedings of the Spruchgerichte, which for the most part had already come to an end. (These Spruchgerichte in the British zone served as full if special courts and were in fact consistently confused by the public with the *Spruchkammern,* or denazification tribunals in the American zone of occupation.[19]) What was at stake in the British zone's Spruchgerichte was not denazification but rather, exclusively, legal requital for so-called organizational crime. As Meyer-Abich explained, the punishment these courts meted out was for "conscious membership in organizations determined to be criminal at the Nuremberg trials," that is, the SS, Gestapo, SD (the SS's security division), and the Nazi "Corps of Political Leaders." Having been judged criminal perpetrators, these "organization members" were now not to be treated in a harsher manner than other miscreants. A good two-thirds of the roughly 24,000 trials in Spruchgerichte had ended in guilty verdicts.[20] In view of the large number of prison sentences, this recommendation also seemed called for "because a generous amnesty would strengthen the will to cooperate in a democratic state and in construction of the fatherland."

Clearly indignant at not having been consulted from the start, the general inspector informed the justice minister concerning the "impossible consequences" that would result from exclusion of those condemned by the Spruchgerichte: "in the case that his punishment did not exceed the amnesty-limit, a perpetrator sentenced because of personal participation in a crime against humanity would qualify for the amnesty; but the organization member, simply punished for belonging to the organization and for an awareness of its criminal activities imparted through a knowledge of the said deed, would not share the amnesty's benefit. The personal perpetrator could thus emerge scot-free, while the man in the know ... would still be subject to punishment." Meyer-Abich was in no way arguing that individuals who occupied "prominent positions" and who "strengthened the organization's criminal potential to particularly strong degree" should be spared; on the contrary, he was objecting to a potentially more far-reaching amnesty "inspired by circles of former organization members or stemming from their defenders." But he considered an amnesty for punishments extending to six months as suitable, since most Spruchgericht sentences of that length had already been served.

Not least because of his title, Meyer-Abich was not especially beloved by a Bonn administration bent on sovereignty; his appeal had been rather urgently phrased. If people in the Federal Justice Ministry needed a reason for leaving the appeal unanswered, it was furnished by Meyer-Abich himself two weeks later through an article in the Hamburg newspaper *Die Welt*. Here as well he did not argue against amnesty in a basic manner. He did warn against giving in to demands exceeding all reasonable measure: "the young Federal Republic must not let amnesty be wrested from it by force." For the initiated it was easy to recognize whom the general inspector was aiming at by insisting that the proposed law should "be understood only as a generous state-gesture to which there is no moral claim whatsoever. Whoever attempts to demonstrate the opposite, surrounds the guilty with a halo of martyrdom and inflicts damage in the sphere of foreign affairs."[21] This was directly addressed to Friedrich Grimm, star counsel for the political right and expert in amnesty questions—already—during the Weimar Republic. Grimm's "Memorandum Concerning the Necessity of a General Amnesty" had been circulating in Bonn for some weeks.[22]

At least because of this public intercession, it was clear that Meyer-Abich would accomplish little in Dehler's ministry. His concerns nonetheless had an impact—by way of the Länder. On 23 November 1949, the *Bundesrat* (the federal council for the Länder) announced a series of changes to the amnesty plans now in its purview. Among such changes was the request for inclusion of Spruchgericht sentences in the amnesty. The Bundesrat now also agreed to the federal government's proposed amnesty limits, at the same time acknowledging federal authority by a vote of 25 to 18.[23] The time had come for the Bundestag to take up the plans.

Meanwhile, however, quarrels had broken out within the ruling coalition. By all appearances the German Party—a party that systematically catered to the needs and wishes of former Nazis out of a desire to move beyond its Lower Saxon base—was particularly unhappy. In the course (or on the periphery) of a coalition meeting on 29 November, that is, the day before the presentation of the plan to the Bundestag, it became the subject of one more discussion.[24] This was the context for adding, as it were underhandedly, another important dimension to the amnesty project. The Legal Committee of the Bundestag was meeting at the same time as the coalition. While the committee members waited for Justice Minister Dehler to arrive for a talk on basic policy, State Secretary of Justice Strauß attempted to divert them with various matters worth being informed of but not yet ripe for decision. Simultaneously Dehler himself was discussing the special question of "illegals," dear to the heart of the German Party, possibly alone with Adenauer and German Party delegate Hans-Joachim von Merkatz. Already at the time only initiates had any idea of what was meant by the "illegals." Behind the concept hovered the problem of "persons with false names,"[25] a problem with uncertain—and, as was later disclosed, exaggerated—dimensions. "Illegals" were individuals who had gone underground in 1945 for political reasons and who played no role in the amnesty plans in their present form. Once it became clear that Dehler and committee member Merkatz were both still occupied elsewhere, the delegates split up. Considerably annoyed, they expressed the firm intention of seeing the amnesty through the Bundestag before Christmas.[26]

The speed with which the government was itself proceeding was reflected in the raw nature of the bill passed on to the Bundestag the next day.[27] Since the last arrangements agreed on had made their way neither through the cabinet nor the Bundesrat, the government presented the amnesty law's draft in several versions, with an accompanying substantiation only applying to the first version. The plans, the legislators were informed, were aimed at drawing to a close "years of distress, moral abasement, and legal confusion"; indeed, "especially" in the economic sphere, "many persons who under normal economic conditions would have done nothing against the law became liable to prosecution." Such an introduction evoked, above all, offenses linked to the black market, offering little hint of the project's *past-political* significance. This was all the less so as the individual substantiations did not contain one word regarding what was largely at issue: amnesty for Nazi criminals. Although it was only by default, the omission—not yet reversed—of those sentenced in the Spruchgerichte did point in that direction.

It was thus no wonder that the amnesty law's basic political content escaped even the journalists who had a chance to study both the document—now containing either ten or twelve paragraphs, depending on the version—and its substantiation. Following the Bundesrat's discussion, the *Süddeutsche Zeitung* thus expressed regrets that the draft was less "general" than Dehler wished to have it believed; "against the wishes of broad circles of the populace," it was concerned "not with the political but simply the criminal side of the great 'forgetting' signified by every amnesty, as the word itself states."[28]

In itself, juridical parlance hardly accounts for the strikingly discrete language of the amnesty law's substantiating arguments. The same goes for the banishment of the extra, informally approved amnesty of "illegals" to the end of the Bundestag publication's appendix, which dealt with the government's position regarding the Bundesrat's proposed changes. This seems less the reflection of a lack of experience with the new legislative machinery than the result of a hastiness intimately bound up with a bad conscience. As if out of a procedural void, an additional paragraph, numbered 6a (later 10), emerged here, prompted by "various ideas ... raised in the Federal Justice Ministry following passage of the plans by the cabinet."[29] Dehler would never become less vague in this matter.[30]

Without taking account of the degree of expected punishment, the extra paragraph anticipated impunity for "offenses" and "misdemeanors" taking place since 10 May 1945 "for the purpose of hiding one's civil status on political grounds," so long as the perpetrator repudiated the false information with the police by 31 March 1950. The only offenses not covered by this special proviso were those classified as "crimes" in the penal code—that is, "actions subject to punishment by penitentiary or incarceration of more than five years." As explained in the attached substantiation, the proviso's purpose was "to offer an opportunity for starting a law-abiding life, and for the laying aside of a highly undesired illegal status, also in the interest of public order and safety, to many persons who, because of their former ties to National Socialism, have been living in the Federal Republic under a false name, with false papers, or without having reported to the police as duly required." But this could be realized—so the argument went—only through a supplementary regulation, since such offenses "exist until the moment of active repentance," thus not falling under the general amnesty, limited as it was to a fixed term. This special problem, not soluble in any other way, was in fact the reason for the government being compelled to spell things out more clearly, as it saw it, in the proviso. Through the above described procedure, Dehler had at least been able to keep an unavoidably even clearer explanation out of the amnesty proposal's official substantiating section.

Undoubtedly there had been many reasons to strive for verbal chastity in the document. One might have been to assure the solid prospects for speedy passage of the amnesty law. That was gratifying to the chancellor, since the bill clearly had the weight that, at the time the cabinet was established, he had directly described as desirable for the first law to be seen through under his governmental stewardship.[31] It was also, however, somewhat delicate. After all, it was not a good idea to spell out too clearly in the book of history—and perhaps more urgently, before the eyes of the High Commissioners and the international public—that the new democracy found nothing more pressing than making things easier for an army of minor and not all that minor Nazi criminals. In retrospect, it appears that the fact was smoothed over with remarkable ease.[32]

On 2 December, the Bundestag debated the law for the first time.[33] The absence of the printed text until the session's start made impossible any serious debate over what had now become three versions (government plans, desired changes of the Bundesrat, the justice minister's "personal" draft with the extra amnesty for "illegals"). Hence more than basic responses to the amnesty question could not be expected— responses that, however, turned out to be very eloquent indeed. Dehler managed the rhetorical finesse of explicating his plan without a single reference to the Nazi period. All "the confusion behind us" appeared to have begun with the occupation in one way or another; all desire for amnesty appeared limited to those "years of transition and years of economic convulsion." August Martin Euler, a Bundestag member from Hesse and an attorney, took up the words of his party colleague Dehler. His lament over the "period of massive confusion" was followed by that of Christian Democrat Eduard Wahl, former defense attorney at Nuremberg and initiator of the jurists' lobby group for war criminals known as the Heidelberg circle.[34] Wahl expounded on the "history of the suffering of the German *Volk*" in the "apocalyptic years" since the capitulation "that lie behind us." In comparison, the reference by Alfred Loritz, delegate for the Economic Reconstruction Association, to the "fearful recent years since 1945" sounded rather colorless. And attorney Bernhard Reismann, speaker of the Center Party, himself left no doubt that in vividly describing the "evil period"—*unheilvolle Periode*—"of recent German history" from which a clean break was called for, what he had in mind was not the Third Reich but rather the occupation period. Reismann did suggest that what was at stake was not only "clearing up affairs that followed 1945." But his only example was the case of a man—undoubtedly eminently worthy of amnesty, both politically and morally—now being prosecuted because "in the Nazi period he falsely denied high treason when under oath as a witness."

Not a single speaker openly indicated that the amnesty was meant to cover crimes extending to involuntary manslaughter and to less grievous forms of homicide; nor did any indicate that such offenses—until then neither amnestied nor declared lapsed—had in fact been rather frequent after *Kristallnacht*. Instead, considerable verbiage was expended drawing attention to the need (which no one disputed) for amnestying postwar economic and property offenses; that such amnesties already existed in the different Länder, and needed simply to be unified, was passed over in silence. Not a shred of consideration was given to either the clear-cut movement beyond such economic crimes or—above all— the political meaning of this effort to break with past events. The motive for this rather glaring omission was not the same for all political factions; by the same token, knowledge of the amnesty law's concrete consequences had probably not reached every last delegate. Finally, there were various special interests at work on behalf of different clients.[35] Nevertheless, some additional words by Reismann at the first debate's conclusion were right on the mark: "all parliamentary parties," he observed, shared "the basic idea of a need to cover the past with forgetting."

With the amnesty being considered something like a Christmas present, it is clear that none of the delegates wanted to be thought of later as having spoiled the fun. Precisely a week after the first session— that is, more quickly than Dehler had hoped—the second and third sessions had already taken place. The Bundestag's Legal Committee had spent a full day scrutinizing the government's draft, the Bundesrat's desired changes, and the proposals of the parties, which had been available since September. The committee now presented a revised version that had been approved unanimously.[36] In some basic aspects, this version went beyond the government's draft. As long as the perpetrators had not acted "out of cruelty, dishonorable sentiments, or greed" and had not committed a crime or deliberate misdemeanor in the past three years the amnesty for prison sentences up to a year plus fines up to 5,000 marks was now meant to cover not only economic offenses but, once again, offenses in general. The committee accepted the government's proposal of an extra amnesty for "illegals," as well as the Bundesrat's demand to include those sentenced by the Spruchgerichte. But at the same time, the delegates had added something entirely new: a ninth paragraph exempting "sentences for actions taken on a political basis after 8 May 1945 and that can be attributed to the special political circumstances of recent years." Despite the exclusion of murder, homicide, and several other capital crimes from this exemption, the new paragraph basically left open the type of crime along with the degree of sentence; as later interpretations would show,[37] it in fact introduced an extraordinarily far-reaching regulation.

The impetus for this massive extension of the amnesty was Reismann's declaration that without its supplementation in the spirit of the Center Party's proposal of 15 September (amnesty for offenses "related to enthusiasm for the democratic idea or opposition to surmounted National Socialism") the party might vote against the law. The Legal Committee seems to have been surprised by this demand. And if the session's minutes are not misleading, the shock-tinged objection that accepting the demand of the Center Party would mean burdening the amnesty law with the all-too-familiar "idea of crimes motivated by conviction" led to the apparently innocuous solution of amnestying crimes committed "on a political basis." It is unclear whether Reismann was responsible for this formulation or it emerged from the ad hoc editorial committee, which, along with Reismann, again included the German Party delegate von Merkatz and a representative of the justice ministry. The fact is that the commission's additional paragraph went far beyond the Center Party's original intentions. And a significant difference between that party's wishes and the actual results continued to exist after the addition, at least, of a fixed time span—unanticipated by those who devised the paragraph—and the removal of crimes resulting in death. More specifically, the phrasing worked in favor of not only democratically inclined "political perpetrators" but also those who sympathized with Nazism—as long as the crime occurred after 8 May 1945. Very possibly this was sensed by many members of the committee: those who approved the law only with reservations.

In any event, in the parliamentary debate the next day, committee member Hermann Kopf (CDU) saw it as perfectly clear "that these specifications—'political basis' and 'special political circumstances'—are elastic specifications possessing a certain vagueness that jurists are not fond of."[38] The lawyer offered solace by assuring himself and his audience that it was "surely" the wish of all the parties represented in the law committee—the CDU-CSU, Social Democratic Party (SPD), Free Democratic Party (FDP), German Party, Bavarian Party, German Communist Party, and Center Party—that in juridical praxis the new paragraph would "not in any manner be treated as a law protecting National Socialism." In actuality this by no means corresponded to the wishes of the entire parliament, as a certain "Dr. Franz Richter" made amply clear in arguing that "no temporal limit whatsoever should be set here—an even broader stroke through the past should be drawn instead." To this delegate of the National Right[39]—later unmasked as former Nazi official Fritz Rößler—not only the termination date of 8 May 1945 seemed unsuitable. As he saw it, the question of how the word *dishonorable* was to be understood needed answering, "after a truly remarkable lack of clarity in that regard has prevailed over recent years." Richter-Rößler spoke for those who basically wanted a total amnesty for Nazi crimes.

Such forces stood no chance of getting very far in the Bundestag. But in light of their very existence, the serenity with which even the communists approved the law is remarkable. German Communist Party member Robert Leibbrand, for instance, had been present at the Legal Committee's deliberations. With a disarming lack of guile he indicated that the new paragraph's expandable formulation resulted from "the majority of the committee being very timid about spelling out the baby's proper name and saying that actions committed from opposition to National Socialism will be declared exempt." Leibbrand stressed the committee's agreement that when such actions had already occurred before 8 May 1945 they needed no amnesty; unfortunately, he explained, this view was not always shared by "our judges and prosecutors." There was thus a need to ask the Federal Justice Ministry to clarify the situation.

In toto, the course of the second debate—conducted mainly by lawyers—casts doubt on the idea that the delegates had a sense of the full consequences of the "Law for Granting Exemption from Punishment." Before the law's summary approval in the third debate, not a single delegate addressed its *past-political* implications. The only delegates who did not vote in favor were from the Bavarian Party and the CSU—but they themselves made clear beforehand that the sole reason was not accepting the federal government's authority. No delegate spoke out against amnesty.

The Bundesrat took up the amnesty law a few hours later. In this forum the tricks lurking in the putatively urgent bill were seen much more sharply, and not simply out of a sense that amnesty was the states' purview.[40] Hans Ehard, minister-president of Bavaria—who was in any case strictly against the law because of the authority question—saw it as "a straightforward reward for what people have done over recent years, sometimes in unheard of fashion, and indeed without taking account of whether it was done for the Nazis or against them." Ehard took the text apart with all the skills of a jurist. He had only sarcasm for the formulation of the freshly added ninth paragraph ("actions taken on a political basis"): "I can commit a deed from political motives. But what is a political basis? I have no idea where this concept may have ever appeared in legal precedent." For Ehard, anyone could construct such a "basis," the possibility thus being opened up for an "utterly vast and unlimited extension of the amnesty ... amounting to everything being forgiven and forgotten ... with the exception of murder, arson, and crimes using explosives." Whoever wanted this should "say it honestly" rather than keeping it silent. Ehard's remarks were seconded by Gebhard Müller, president of Württemberg-Hohenzoller and also a jurist: he had seldom seen a law formulated so effectively "to produce such unforeseeable results." The ninth paragraph, Müller indicated, was a "complete impossibility." Against the backdrop of such clear-cut language, it must have been surprising that ten days later the Bundesrat passed the law without any changes.

In the meantime, the Bundesrat's Legal Committee had met to discuss the law; despite strong reservations—mainly regarding the limited amnesty for prison sentences up to a year and the "general amnesty of paragraph nr. 9"—most members were in favor of not appealing to the Mediation Committee. For considering the large majority of Bundestag delegates who favored the plans, handing the matter to that committee would probably slow things down in an unpopular manner, without any changes being produced in the end.[41] Despite this decision, Gebhard Müller once again battled against the law. Without mincing words he now ascribed an intent of concealment to the Bundestag, predicting that "when after the amnesty's passage the German people are informed about everything covered by the ninth paragraph, a mood that has been so amnesty-friendly will turn into its opposite." Müller did not shy away from illustrating his discomfiture with an example: perjury by an "old fighter" from the Nazi Party in a denazification tribunal to the detriment of a guiltless "*Volk*-comrade," with the innocent man then serving a sentence of forced labor while the perjurer, meanwhile unmasked and sentenced for his deed, receives amnesty. Müller could not agree with "that sort of far-reaching amnesty," despite all considerations of timing and expediency. It was properly pointed out that the month-long discussion was bad for the judicial system. This underscored the advantages of

Württemberg-Hohenzollern's approach: issuance of an administrative decree interrupting all sentences that fell into the framework of the original amnesty bill proposed in the Bundesrat. Württemberg-Hohenzollern thus approved both of Bavaria's motions to convene the Mediation Committee; doing so on constitutional grounds was rejected in a vote of 25 to 18; on substantive grounds the vote was only 22 to 21. Five days before Christmas the amnesty law had passed the penultimate hurdle.

On 20 December 1949, the West German government submitted the law to the Allied High Commission, which according to the occupation statutes had three weeks to raise objections. The chancellor's office was urging a quick decision,[42] which meant additional pressure to that already implicit in the broad Bundestag majority behind the law—itself a source of pressure on the Bundesrat. Moreover the newspapers gave a substantial spread to both the Bundestag and the Bundesrat debates, underscoring the Christmas deadline in the process.[43] The High Commissioners' sense of having been placed in a tight spot was thus not groundless, and the law's lack of precision must have strengthened their suspicion that something like a surprise attack was in the works. While on 23 December arrangements were being made in Dehler's ministry in case the High Commissioners did signal their approval before Christmas Eve, nobody really believed they would.[44]

In fact, a response was received only after the holiday. On 27 December, at the High Commissioners' hotel headquarters on the hill above the Rhine known as the Petersberg, a delegation from the French High Commission met with two officials from the Justice Ministry and the liaison team of the chancellor's office to review objections to the proposed law. The French delegation also announced an official meeting with the British and Americans for the following day.[45] Along with this step, "Allied circles"—themselves now wishing to generate a certain degree of public pressure—leaked hints to the press agencies that a remanding of the law to the West German government was entirely possible; above all, the ninth paragraph was "unclear and formulated imprecisely," offering, "in the absence of an unambiguous reading," grounds for freeing all war criminals."[46] While this was actually inaccurate, it did demarcate positions and draw attention to the real balance of power.

The 28 December Petersberg meeting led to neither a correction nor a rejection of the law. The event nevertheless had considerable political value. It confronted the government—represented by State Secretary Walter Strauß—with pointed disapproval of both the circumstances in which the amnesty law was presented to the High Commission and the law's contents. And it made clear that the Allied claims to control over

West German legislation were not to be misunderstood as merely for-mal. To be sure, no one down in Bonn seemed interested in acknowl-edging as much; instead Dehler spent days trying to demonstrate to his colleagues and the press that all the complications were a result of poor translation and a certain slowness on the part of Allied personnel.[47]

On the diplomatic front, the discord was ended through an exchange of notes between the High Commission and the chancellor. On 29 December, Adenauer received a note from the Allies affirming the wish "to recognize the greatest possible degree of freedom for the German legislative bodies"—while also expressing the (not unfounded) fear that the proposed law could amnesty perpetrators "who stood trial and were found guilty by German courts ... as a result of legislated Allied conditions and on account of offenses against Allied armed forces." The note suggested that in order to avoid such an "unsuitable interpretation and application" of the law, the ninth paragraph in par-ticular needed an "interpretation from a higher instance" making clear that it did not apply to "offenders against the public, free, and demo-cratic order." Such a step might be taken in the framework of a meeting between the justice ministers of the various Länder and their federal counterpart. And should the government offer assurances in this mat-ter, the Allied High Commission would be prepared to approve prom-ulgation of the law before expiration of the objection period.[48]

Upon reading this request, Dehler promptly suggested that the con-tents of the amnesty law were not affected; for the period in question, actions against the free and democratic order were as yet unheard of, and the future discovery of such a deed was "most improbable." Besides, Dehler argued, the ninth paragraph was specifically not meant to cover deeds directed "against the common good as such," and a con-ference with the justice ministers of the Länder "in any case" harmo-nized with his intentions. In addition, the Allies had already been informed by word of mouth that the interpretation of the law they feared would "in no way be binding." Dehler thus saw no reason to take issue with the High Commission's request.[49] After Adenauer's signing of an appropriate note of answer,[50] the law took effect on 31 December 1949. It was one of the first laws of the German Federal Republic.[51]

Quite likely a little tired of the subject as a result of the recent slugfest, the press now limited itself to brief reports. There were next to no commentaries or extensive reports on the amnesty's consequences. It was not spelled out, either approvingly or disapprovingly, that along-side black market delinquents and petty criminals a diverse group of Nazi offenders could now look forward to amnesty. One exception to this general rule was an evangelical weekly published in Stuttgart called *Christ und Welt*. This journal had devoted much energy since its foundation to supporting those who—to paraphrase the Gospels—were weary and whose load was heavy.[52] It compared the amnesty law to amnesties offered on official jubilee days and royal births. But, the Christian journal declared, this step did not mark an end "to the state of civil war under which we suffer." Now as before, what was necessary—if also not without its hazards—was a "true and comprehensive amnesty." It remained the case, *Christ und Welt* conceded, that in light of the ongoing "political proceedings" and "hierarchization of citizens into classes"—namely the expiatory denazification measures[53]—such an amnesty's dimensions could only be hinted at. The appeal was followed by an equally bold German formulation: *Wir wagen zu raten, das Wagnis zu wagen,* translatable as something like "we venture to counsel to enter on the adventure."[54]

Naturally writers for the professional legal journals could not have it so simple; their views were clashing. Writing in the *Neue Juristische Wochenschrift,* Frankfurt criminal jurist Erich Schmidt-Leichner spoke of a plethora of unclear points and "editorial errors" in the "federal amnesty," expressing his strongest doubts about the law's constitutionality.[55] In contrast, SPD Bundestag delegate Adolf Arndt maintained in the *Süddeutsche Juristen-Zeitung* that the law was "an extraordinary and highly generous step in the effort to regain civil peace." Arndt was convinced of the law's validity, a view that was hardly surprising considering his presiding chairmanship of the Legal Committee's decisive meeting.[56] The two commentators agreed in their assessment of the exchange between Adenauer and the High Commission. Schmidt-Leichner made the lapidary observation that "so long as the contents correspond to the law, this agreement has merely declaratory significance; so long as they deviate from it, the agreement is not binding." Arndt named the arrangement "inessential" and announced his strongest objections in the event the law should be subject to Adenauer's intended "official interpretation."

But the notorious Nazi "judges' letters"—a vehicle for massive manipulation of the judiciary—were not only on the mind of Adolf Arndt (himself forced to abandon his vocation as judge in 1933[57]). Immediately after the Christmas break, in conversations with representatives of the legal administrative bodies of the Länder, Dehler and Strauß had made two things clear: that no meeting with the Länder justice ministers would result from the amnesty law and that the law would not be followed by an implementing order.[58] What was offered instead was a circular letter—its motive lying, for a start, in a need to at least formally maintain one's word vis-à-vis the Allies. This was the vehicle for Dehler's version of the ninth paragraph's etiological history, in order, he explained, "to counteract an excessively broad understanding of the provision." In fact, the Justice Minister's obligatory essay constituted an exemplary legal smokescreen. On the one hand, Dehler invoked the legislative intent behind the original Center Party proposal: an amnestying of punishable actions "that following the collapse were inflicted on advocates of National Socialism out of bitterness at injustice experienced at the hands of National Socialism." On the other hand, he referred to actions that "have their origin in the National Socialist–generated political and human tensions between the National Socialists and their opponents [or] in the political collapse caused by National Socialism." Implicitly present here is an assertion that in its generosity the ninth paragraph could indeed, and very easily, be applied to Nazi crimes—so long as these occurred after 8 May 1945. What remained was simply a vague exclusion: "all actions on a political basis" not representing "a direct consequence of National Socialism."[59]

To the extent legal commentators knew of this ministerial circular, they revealed themselves to be rather negatively impressed. From their perspective, clarity of interpretation was not all that compatible with sensitivity to Allied feelings—which Dehler was in any case obliged to register again a year later, in the form of a complaint from the American High Commission.[60] As long as Dehler meant what he had written, Schmidt-Leichner's remarks on the ninth paragraph could only appear as a slap: the "objective" notion of a "political basis," he observed, allowed "no differentiation of cases according to political value or lack of value attached to them in the present." According to the law, it was one and the same "whether it was a matter of crimes committed by former National Socialists against anti-fascists or vice versa." Whoever bribed an official in order to be denazified more quickly or in better fashion had acted on a political basis—but the same was true of whoever beat up a worker in the Allied-imposed industrial dismantling program, or whoever got even with a Nazi *Ortsgruppenleiter* (a communal head). In the circumstances following the collapse, even crimes without a political character could have a political basis, "since life in general unfolded then on a political basis."

For his part, Adolf Arndt entirely approved such a broad interpretation. In particular, it was hoped that vengeful nationalists would no longer press the judicial system into proceedings involving plots and perjury, "in which political events are on trial." Nonetheless, Arndt explained, after "full reflection" the Bundestag had declined to give the amnesty a stamp "that would have limited this good turn to democrats." In "sobering recognition" that to a great extent the period after 8 May 1945 had the "marks of a civil war," the individuals meant to be amnestied were those who had attempted to evade their political or penal responsibility through criminal deeds. Arndt did not shy away from pathos à la *Christ und Welt:* "what must cease in Germany is the chase after human beings."

It is important to note that such juridical generosity of spirit was narrowly linked to the democratic determination of Arndt the politician. In this capacity, he cautioned that what mattered would be not only the spirit in which the law was applied but also whether "otherwise than in the Weimar Republic" the courts would be willing "to punish all attacks on democracy's free order with the entire force of the law." In regard to interpreting the amnesty law, the Social Democrat's hopes would soon be disappointed. He had maintained that "so-called 'political' offenses," in particular those offenses prosecuted in the Spruchgerichte as "crimes against humanity," were virtually always of a "dishonorable" or "cruel" nature, hence excluded from amnesty even when the sentence was no more than a year. But a criminal court in the British zone came to an opposite conclusion. The court was considering the case of a Nazi political leader. Following the November 1938 pogrom, he had struck a Catholic in the face with his fist on account of the latter's remark that the churches would now probably also be persecuted. The Nazi had then denounced the Catholic to the Gestapo and to his public employers, after which he was punished by transfer. The same judge who had previously sentenced the Nazi functionary to a year in prison now amnestied him: dishonorable sentiments or cruelty were not to be assumed; rather, the accused had acted "in the heat of the moment, and prompted by the ideology of his times." The *Neue Juristische Wochenschrift* considered this interpretation an exemplary rectification of the sentencing praxis in the supreme court of the British zone: there, perpetrators who had acted from conviction were "constantly prevented" from invoking their ideology; but "here this must be allowed them. Only those who were pitiless or inhuman receive no mercy."[61]

A similar case involved a party functionary who had personally beaten up a suspected communist during a hearing before handing the man over to two SA (Storm Trouper) thugs. The Higher Regional Court of Hesse provided the following ruling: since the original judgment referred to an "offense on political grounds" and referred to nothing that pointed to "signs of torture," neither "cruelty" nor "dishonorable sentiments" were presumable, and the perpetrator was to be amnestied. The conclusion of the lawyer who reported the case in the *Neue Juristische Wochenschrift:* when political deeds were in question, action from "dishonorable sentiments" was of course not completely out of the question—but it was not "frequent."[62] Even a deed unmistakably motivated by "dishonorable sentiments" and subjectively having no political grounding could indeed be grounded objectively in "political circumstances" fulfilling the appropriate passage in the ninth paragraph ("actions taken on a political basis"); because what was at issue was a misdemeanor and not a crime, it was eligible for amnesty as well. For instance, according to a decision of the Higher Regional Court of Düsseldorf, this was the case with perjury from personal enmity or desire for revenge in the framework of denazification proceedings.[63]

A look at the judgment column of the legal journals suggests one conclusion: that the "generosity" so emphatically recommended as a "basic interpretive rule" by Schmidt-Leichner in his authoritative first assessment of the amnesty law was indeed practiced—at least in the case of offenses committed by Nazis.[64] However, it is not easy to judge the number of amnestied Nazi perpetrators. The reason for this lies in the methodology of the statistical surveys provided by Dehler: while they followed a unified schema, they contained no breakdown of the time the deed occurred.[65] In toto, as a result of the amnesty law, no fewer than 792,176 persons benefited from what the jurists called "privileging" (*Vergünstigung*) in the period leading up to 31 January 1951.[66]

Most of these exemptions from punishment—virtually half a million—were offered in the framework of the general amnesty (remission of prison sentences extending up to six months, along with fines of up to 5,000 marks); somewhat more than 250,000 cases were disposed of in this manner. A good 35,000 persons who had received sentences of up to a year were likewise released on parole. In comparison, the number of persons amnestied on the grounds of the ninth paragraph (actions on a political basis) was relatively small—516. The number of those benefiting from the tenth paragraph was even smaller: despite the Federal Justice Ministry's declaration that an extension of the deadline could not be counted on, by that date (31 March 1950) only 241 "illegals" had taken advantage of the chance to reveal their identities without punishment.[67] Quite likely, the others were less afraid of the still-ongoing formal denazification procedure than of indictment for Nazi crimes that were too serious to fall under the amnesty.

These statistics do not reveal very much about the amnesty's impact on punishment for violent Nazi crimes. They in fact inherently obscure the relation, since for the sake of simplicity the judiciary naturally subsumed deeds defined by the ninth and tenth paragraphs under the general amnesty, so long as they fell within the penal limits of six months and one year respectively. The figures for the two paragraphs account for only the "hard" cases that "required" an amnesty with no penal limit (in the case of the tenth paragraph, an extended deadline as well).

A second set of statistics, incomplete but divided into type of offense, allows somewhat more precise conclusions.[68] We are here informed of an amnesty for more than 3,000 persons either charged with or sentenced for crimes and misdemeanors "against personal freedom"; in roughly a tenth of the cases, the sentence was imprisonment up to a year. It is a solid assumption that the amnestied individuals were rarely "normal" kidnappers—and that they were in fact functionaries in the SA, SS, and party who had dragged their victims off to concentration camps and cellars. Chances are also good that Nazi perpetrators made up a portion of the more than 20,000 amnestied persons who had been sentenced for deeds "directed against life," the approximately 30,000 amnestied persons who had been sentenced for causing bodily injury, and the approximately 5,200 amnestied persons who had been charged with "crimes and misdemeanors in office." Finally, a number of the 180-odd persons enjoying amnesty for crimes "related to religion" must have been in the same category; cemetery desecration was one of the most frequently represented of such crimes. We are in any event offered no basis for judging the—presumably—considerable number of amnesties granted individuals for offenses committed against Jews, especially on Kristallnacht.

It is impossible to adequately reconstruct the distinction between Nazi crimes and the other offenses, criminal and economic in nature, that the law benefited. The true number of these exemptions must thus remain an open question. We can nevertheless assume that tens of thousands of Nazi offenders profited from the law. Regarding the equally unresolved question of the offenses' nature, let us simply note that in less severe cases the law allowed amnesty for involuntary manslaughter (minimum sentence: three months) and homicide (minimum sentence: six months). For this reason, we cannot exclude the possibility that among the Nazis who were amnestied a number indeed had bloody hands.

The will toward amnesty revealed by the German Bundestag in the first weeks of its existence, and the palpable impatience for an amnesty's passage that ran through all the political coalitions, went far beyond what was objectively called for. Doubtless, in the case of hundreds of thousands of otherwise blameless citizens guilty—often unavoidably— of property and economic offenses during the recent hunger years but still lacking amnesty from one of the Länder, placing mercy before justice furthered both social peace and relief of the criminal courts. And even a limited "classical" amnesty for petty criminals, under the sign of a new republican beginning, may have had a certain justification. But amnestying other offenses was disputable—at least politically so. It was possible not only to view that decision from Adolf Arndt's perspective, as a generous step on the way to legal peace, but also to view it as a fresh and grievous encroachment on a legal structure that had been only tentatively restored after twelve years of legal debasement—as something that damaged a sense of justice only tentatively regained. But in the parliamentary debate, not a single politician spoke up for the latter perspective.

As a political signal, the amnesty law's impact was hard to exaggerate. Already discussed in the German Federal Republic's formative phase, set into motion by a broad majority straight after establishment of the Bundestag and the federal government, the law constituted an act of high political symbolism. Superficially the amnesty was a simple sign of a new beginning. But through its partially open, partially masked relation to both Nazi rule and its occupation aftermath, it advanced the struggle for a recuperation of historical-political identity and political self-determination in regard to the past. The amnesty marked a first confirmation on a federal level of the "just leave it behind us" mentality that had already emerged in parts of Germany's postwar society in 1946–47—and that had continued growing. Regardless of postulates to the contrary voiced by the democratically inclined parties, the amnesty law meant entering on a progressive delegitimation of prosecution for Nazi crimes. It also meant the prospect of ever broader demands for amnesty, culminating in a point-blank call for a "general amnesty" covering even the worst sorts of crime.

Such tendencies were aggravated through a connection drawn—despite its objective absence—both by many politicians and by the general public between an amnesty and the end of denazification. Inversely this purported connection was bound to further aggravate the judgment passed on denazification, faced as a collective experience still being played out—albeit fragmentarily—in a real present. This judgment's apogee was an almost universally shared conviction that the political purge imposed on the Germans by the occupation authorities had failed monstrously, was unjust in virtually every respect, and needed to be ended as quickly as possible.

CHAPTER 2

The "Liquidation" of Denazification

From its very inception, the Bundestag entertained the notion that discarding all remnants of denazification constituted an urgent political task. Nevertheless, nearly half a year went by before a chance to openly acknowledge the notion arose in the plenum. Proposals of this sort had already been tendered in September 1949 by the German Party, the Economic Reconstruction Association, and the FDP. But these remained on the back burner for some time in the Legal Committee—which was preoccupied with the amnesty law, considered top priority, and wished to clarify the question of authority in the matter of denazification.[1] Now suspecting deliberate procrastination, FDP members roused themselves to action: against the clear opinion—expressed in the cabinet and elsewhere—of a justice minister from their own party, and against the opinions of his counterparts in the Länder as well, they found a federal law ending denazification both possible and politically necessary.[2] They offered a draft in this regard on 23 February 1950, thus forcing a parliamentary conference.[3]

A few days earlier, the National Right had offered a draft of its own.[4] Although a similar contribution from the German Party arrived too late for the debate, it was still timely enough to document the independence of this smallest of coalition partners in a question central to the party and its supporters.[5] For the smaller right-of-center parties, a campaign to end denazification was a way to gain political profile. They were manifestly unimpressed by the fact that a number of Länder had already either passed or prepared laws to wind up denazification—indeed that anyone halfway informed politically considered the entire process most easily ended on the Länder level, since denazification had been carried out on the levels of both the zones and the Länder.

This simply serves to confirm something already evident in the debate over amnesty: when it came to formulating a proper policy for the past, it was relatively easy for the small parties to place the big parties in a no-win situation. Neither the CDU-CSU nor the SPD were willing to adopt a fawning stance, meaning a tough plenum debate was on the horizon, with harsh voices raised against denazification. As things turned out, the marked differences over particulars emerging in the good two-hour-long debate were indeed accompanied by a basic conflict of principle: Despite all reservations concerning the process and its results, some representatives considered the political purging to be correct in essence; others retroactively denied any justification to even the initial considerations behind the Allied measures.[6] On the one side stood a large group of moderate CDU and SPD members, joined by the Center Party; they faced a phalanx of radicals in which the FDP and the German Party naturally played a special role as part of the government.[7]

Anyone listening only to the radicals would have gained the impression of witnessing a competition to find the most pejorative epithet describing an in-any-event defunct venture: "national misfortune" (Euler, FDP), "crime" (Richter, National Right), and "tumor on the body of the German *Volk*" (Etzel, Bavarian Party) were a few of the invective phrases. In the name of the German Party, Hans-Joachim von Merkatz fired an entire salvo: "a modern witch-hunt," "a monstrous birth engendered by totalitarian thinking and an orientation toward class warfare," "an insidious weapon." Beneficently, the speakers of the two largest political factions refrained from such insults.

Speaking for the SPD, Fritz Erler confirmed the historical-political need to have at least attempted a comprehensive purge after the Allied liberation. To be sure, he indicated, "setting about the task" as "a kind of" revolutionary gesture would have been preferable to a bureaucratic procedure, and he further asserted that "a line needs to be drawn through the whole chapter of political purging." At the same time, preventive measures had to be taken so that such a step "did not simultaneously mark the start of renazification." In relation to the broad context of Germany's unfolding political debate about how best to approach the past, Erler's observations concerning the social reality of Nazism and the motives of its adherents are highly illuminating: according to Erler, a large portion of the people favored the regime out of "error"; others went along out of delusion, or greed, or complacency in imitating seemingly cleverer people; and more than a few "indeed truly out of authentic idealism." The Social Democrat was not satisfied with the usual explanatory schema—here the criminal leadership, there the duped citizenry. "Very many decent people," he suggested, "must have positively worked together with the National Socialist state and its organizations. Otherwise, despite all its terror, National Socialism would not have been able to last nearly so long." But in attributing simple "error"—or even what Eugen Kogon so effectively termed "the right to error"—to so many people, Erler avoided having to ask how extensively their earlier behavior was grounded in *conviction*.[8] In this manner, for Erler as well, the "fellow travelers" simply appeared as a "large mass" that was peculiarly lacking certain qualities: a mass "of those individually truly harmless persons who consequently are unaware of any guilt and experience any contact with a denazification tribunal's procedures as virtual persecution."

With his reflections on Nazism's socially integrative power, Erler went somewhat beyond what had been said in the Bundestag until then about the "Third Reich." He did not, however, transgress the interpretive limits set by a political pragmatism regarding the past: limits the large parties could ignore only at the risk of damaging their voting base. Speaking for the CDU-CSU, Eugen Gerstenmaier displayed a similar reverence before that pragmatism. Still, Fritz Richter's previous immoderate remarks gave him a chance to effectively distance himself from the radicals: neither an "exemption for main offenders" nor a "carte blanche for political bandits" was tolerable. Keeping in mind the audacious public remarks made by a number of Nazis over recent weeks, this statement was applauded more strongly by the SPD than by Gerstenmaier's own party.[9] He was particularly rankled that such activities had already drawn the attention of the American press and that they had prompted American High Commissioner John McCloy to warn publicly of a "revival of Nazism."[10] Gerstenmaier was torn between a demonstratively emphasized awareness of national adherence and a Protestant love of the truth; both of these dimensions were at work as he evoked his participation in the "July Plot" (culminating on 20 July 1944) to kill Hitler. On the one hand Gerstenmaier pleaded with the outside world to understand "that the German people is gradually entering an epoch of consciousness in which it [wishes to] confront its own history ... with the greatest possible freedom, and if possible, without foreign standards of value being imposed on us." On the other hand, he conceded,

expressing regret, that "under the influence of an irresponsible dema-
gogy, among a broad strata of our people there is a gradually vanishing
awareness of the formative context ... within which our national misfortune is embedded, and in which it will remain embedded in the
awareness of other peoples." In spite of—certainly more than as a result
of—this finding, Gerstenmaier considered an end to denazification necessary, not only because "political conviction as such" was not meant
to be punished, but also because "in the reconstruction of the German
fatherland" his party was not willing to do without people numbering
"in the millions" who had been seduced by Nazism.

With these words, Gerstenmaier clarified—in a reasonably sovereign fashion—the absence of any alternative to a policy of extensive
integration on the government's part. If both the CDU-CSU and the SPD
adopted the policy in a very similar way, this was not merely on
grounds of party strategy. Naturally both sides wished to draw on the
potential of the "fellow travelers" while placing a check on any
strengthening of special interest parties in their vicinity.[11] But at the
same time, a more serious consideration was that the continued denial
of citizenship rights to larger groups of denazified individuals would
implicate the legitimacy of the constitutional order. With all the frivolity at his disposal, Eugen Kogon had already observed in 1947 that
"fellow travelers" could be either killed or won over to democracy.[12]
Three years later hardly a politician could be found still willing to deny
the necessity of such integration. Gerstenmaier was aware that this path
was by no means risk-free—and that political costs would come with
an integration by no means practically limited to "unpolitical" "fellow
travelers." For this reason the "warning" he referred to, expressly citing his parliamentary faction's permission, was not issued haphaz-
ardly; linked with his plea for integration, it was a "warning that a
revival of old politically violent games and criminal instincts in German Länder is—as we consider to be proper—a mortally dangerous
activity, and that we would even like to render punishable any *playing* with such ideas."

Gerstenmaier was alluding to ongoing preparations for a "Law to
Protect the State"; according to the Union's plans, this was also meant
to regulate an end to denazification on a federal basis.[13] It thus seemingly would have been logical to reject not only the National Right's
plans but also those of the FDP, instead of passing the latter on to the
Bundestag's Committee for Protection of the Constitution. But this
would have weighed down the coalition climate more than was necessary; more important, it would have increased the risk of the Union
being seen by the general public as advocates of continued denazifica-

tion. This was probably the reason the Social Democrats gave their approval to passing on the FDP's plans. Several speakers did attack the plans' central demand—that no new denazification proceedings were to be opened, and ongoing proceedings were to be terminated. But only Reismann from the Center Party dared to point out the connection between this demand and the amnesty still being tendered to the "illegals": "people who are now coming out of their mouse holes protected by amnesty [are meant] to be generously freed from the difficulties they have justly earned!"

Within the FDP leadership, the most energetic champion of denazified persons was August Martin Euler.[14] He of course did not include one word about the above connection in his substantiation accompanying the proposal, and in his concluding remarks he showed just as small an inclination to take up Reismann's questions concerning morality, justice, and the feelings of the victims. For years to come, one quality in particular would mark the policies formulated to overcome the past by a substantial majority of Free Democrats: intransigence.

Since September 1950, the Committee for Protection of the Constitution had been the only parliamentary body responsible for the question of denazification. Euler here found a congenial opponent in German Party delegate Hans-Joachim von Merkatz. That neither figure was in fact a committee member, both participating as representatives of parliamentary factions, simply underscores their special role: for the sake of each of their parties' glory the two jurists were determined to do everything possible to set in motion a federal law ending denazification; both were also flexible enough to make do with strongly worded recommendations for termination. Making use of vigorous postulates embellished with juridical jargon, Merkatz and Euler largely determined the course of the negotiations.[15] In the first working session, Merkatz detailed the reasons why the termination laws of the Länder were not sufficient to meet the German Party's demands for a "liquidation" of a denazification process that had "sources in foreign law." Albeit only through intimation, he even raised the question of whether a kind of "compensation" might not be arranged for those who had been denazified at an early point, hence according to relatively strict criteria, to balance the "favoring of the very last persons." To be sure, when Christian Democrats and Social Democrats expressed their indignation, Merkatz—supported by Euler—denied ever having more in mind than a reinstatement in public service of "fellow travelers" and exonerated persons: a step in any case long since counted on in conjunction with pending legislation regarding those covered by Article 131 of the Basic Law (see chapter 3).

As was his habit in the Bundestag, Euler opened his remarks to the committee with a couple of crudities about the Americans. "Under the influence of the Morgenthau Plan," the Americans had undertaken a completely misguided denazification program in the style of the "purging operations following the Civil War." It was now time "to let the past be buried" and to "shore up" the German people so that they could face the "dangers from the East." The clearest rebuff to this ressentiment-tinged nationalism was offered by Matthias Mehs, a CDU delegate and innkeeper from the Eifel. Mehs declared for the record that "the German people did not defeat Hitler; Hitler was defeated by General Eisenhower." He was also for putting the past behind, but it was important to see that denazified persons "were already reemerging with a certain brazenness and making demands." Walter Menzel, Social Democratic recorder for the committee and a man not known for polemics, noted gratefully that Mehs's rebuff had "cleared the atmosphere somewhat." The FDP and the German Party delegates themselves saw to even more clarity by requesting a vote over the federal government's authority in the termination issue. The results were clear: only 4 of 14 voting members believed in such authority. It was thus decided to establish a four-man subcommittee responsible for compiling a summary of federation-wide recommendations in place of the law being demanded by the right-wing rigorists. In their role as party representatives, Euler and Merkatz were naturally included in the subcommittee.

At the time of the full committee's next meeting, the subcommittee had not yet completed its task. Euler—meanwhile its referee—had nonetheless prepared a clear "guideline": "Applications for political investigation can no longer be filed after 1 January 1951, to the extent this was still possible under legislation of the Länder." Such a regulation would have meant an end to the entire denazification process in a couple of weeks. But for most committee members this was too fast—and too far-reaching. What they were most strongly opposed to was the possibility that the circle of main offenders and incriminated persons—becoming increasingly small as a result of "downgrading"—would enjoy the same beneficence as the much larger group of lesser offenders, as well as the multitude of "fellow travelers" (among whom even Alfred Hugenberg, national press czar and former backer of Hitler, now numbered). In light of such eroding standards, most committee members considered it called for to differentiate between, on the one hand, groups 3, 4, and 5 (lesser offenders, "fellow travelers," and exonerated persons) and, on the other hand, groups 1 and 2 (main offenders and incriminated persons). At least the biggest fish, they reasoned, should suffer the expiation imposed on them a while more —or, if the fish had not yet surfaced, the chance should be left open to net them later.[16] But since Euler insisted on a "decision" concerning his proposal, a formal vote became unavoidable—and now only a single colleague in his parliamentary faction spoke up in his defense.[17] This new defeat moved the FDP delegate not to something like seeing reason but simply to a shift of tactics. In the following sessions, he tried to extract the allowances he desired for groups 1 and 2 in bits and pieces.[18] While he did manage to dominate the debate through ever new proposals, he also drew his opponents together. In the end, he had changed very little.

The suggestions that the Committee for Protection of the Constitution presented to the Bundestag at the start of October 1950 were unmistakably more restrained than the demands of the FDP and the German Party. At the same time, the suggestions clearly showed the tenacity of both parties. The CDU-CSU and the SPD—certainly prompted partly by the approaching series of Landtag (state legislature) elections—had agreed on a list of recommendations meant to offer the Länder the most unified possible regulation. The unstated yet obvious goal of the bill was to take the wind out of the sails of political agitators who had been exploiting denazification's extreme unpopularity with great virtuosity— but to do so without throwing overboard all the principles prevailing until then.[19]

In line with the above-mentioned concerns of most committee members, the paramount difference between their recommendations and the demands of the German Party and the FDP was the presence of certain distinctions. Above all, the termination of proceedings planned for 1 January 1951 would now apply only to groups 3, 4, and 5. At the same time, pending proceedings against main offenders and inculpated persons were to be allowed to continue, and limitations on their professional and other activities, as well as the exclusion from voting eligibility, were to be maintained. On the other hand, the committee called for all restrictions on lesser offenders and "fellow travelers" to be lifted by 1 July 1951 at the latest; fines and court costs were to be dispensed with as early as 1 January 1951, and work camp sentences were to be "extensively" amnestied.[20]

As was to be expected after Euler's above-mentioned appearance in the committee, in discussions of the bill held on 18 October 1950, the Free Democrats expressed disappointment. They nevertheless attempted to bargain. They expressed readiness to abandon the demand for a federal law and to accept the committee's recommendations applying— alone—to groups 1 and 2. But a "final and radical" end was necessary to the "unfortunate" denazification proceedings, declared Ludwig Schneider, reiterating his parliamentary group's standpoint. In the

American zone, the "colossal expense" of maintaining the tribunals spoke against doing so for only a few cases. And in the British zone, where denazification of main offenders and guilty persons had been left to the military government and no information on the number of those so classified was available, it was necessary to avoid "new and zealous" denazification after transfer of responsibility to German hands. The German Party seconded the new FDP demand, which had been offered on grounds that approached the ridiculous. Since the FDP had tied its critique of the bill to corresponding suggested alterations, and since the National Right was demanding its own changes, the Bundestag approved the SPD's motion to have the matter referred back to the committee.[21]

Two months later, in its last session before the Christmas break, the Bundestag took up the theme anew. The series of Landtag elections had meanwhile taken place, the FDP registering considerable success.[22] With its majority of CDU-CSU and SPD members, the committee had basically rejected the proposed changes, while now adding several new points to their own bill. First, there was a request to the federal government for statistics on the number of political victims of Nazi justice and "persons who died in concentration camps and other camps on the territory of the Federal Republic."[23] Next, the government was asked to prepare a report on the prosecution of Nazi criminals by German courts, those of the military governments, and those abroad. Finally, the executive branch was asked to prepare a reparations law for individuals persecuted on political, racial, or religious grounds, intended to "supplement in timely fashion" the legislation of the Länderrat.[24]

These additions had their source in SPD recommendations.[25] Formulated like a compensatory moral injunction, they reflected the by now hardly disputable fact that the original goal of the committee's proposal had practically been realized. In all the Länder located within what had been the American zone, laws terminating denazification— with the exception of the main offenders and incriminated persons—had been passed, and the last work camp sentences were to be ended before the month's end. Termination regulations had been issued in the British zone and in Rhineland-Palatinate, and Württemberg-Hohenzollern followed at the start of 1951.[26] The entire idea of federal "recommendations" in this domain—recommendations that in any case could not address the different requirements of different Länder—was patently obsolescent. Denazification nevertheless remained a highly provocative theme.

This was all the more the case since in the second meeting to discuss the committee's proposal neither the FDP nor the German Party gave any thought to forgoing a chance to increase their political profile. Once again their spokesmen insisted on a formal termination of denazification that covered main offenders and incriminated persons.[27] Under such circumstances, a collision with CDU and SPD speakers could hardly be avoided.

The Free Democrat and physician Richard Hammer saw to the proper prelude—one stamped by his own abstruse ressentiment toward the Allies. Hammer's critique was directed at the "grotesque" nature of denazification, a process that would be treated "for centuries" in "seminars for history and law not without smirks." In 1945 the Allied "police troops" had forbidden the "natural emotional impulses of a healthy person"—meaning "a revolution with murder and homicide." And Hammer knew the reason for this: In the leading circles of the occupation powers, a group of people was to be found "in whose world death was conceivable only in connection with the electric chair." The complaint of German Party delegate Hans Ewers concerning the parliamentary majority's rejection of federal authority to pass a termination law was hardly less shrewd: "Because Nazism was the most totalitarian and centralized thing anywhere," its "consequences" could in fact "be canceled out only in a totalitarian and centralized manner."

The remarks offered by committee member Matthias Mehs had a refreshing clarity—and not only in contrast to such muttering: "Without a doubt, we are for drawing a line. But this ... cannot mean letting the chief sinners from the pre-1945 period once more run about in world history unshorn." Whether or not the fact he was doing so had actually occurred to him, the Christian Democrat in any event had no objections to following up on words that Social Democrat Hermann Brill had hurled back at the National Right's Adolf von Thadden in the last committee session: Amnesty for groups 1 and 2 would "actually signify that the Third Reich never existed."

The basis for a palpable stir—naturally registered by the press—had now been laid.[28] The FDP's state chairman for Schleswig-Holstein, attorney Fritz Oellers, felt called on to instruct tavern owner Mehs concerning the special injustice of the Spruchgericht proceedings, which he wished to see included in the termination recommendations. As Oellers described it, on account of the simple accusation of membership in a criminal organization, these courts would even condemn "some sort of harmless—using quotation marks here is fine with me—man who had belonged to the SS at some time or other." In this manner, Oellers explained, Nuremberg's postulation of a "collective guilt" on the part of the SS, the Gestapo, the SD, and the leadership corps of the Nazi Party had found its way into the denazification process.

Oellers here assiduously ignored the amnesty that had gone into effect the previous year, with its explicit inclusion of those sentenced by the Spruchgerichte. He also passed over the committee's stipulation, included among its recommendations from the start, offering even main offenders and inculpated persons the possibility of applying for reclassification in a more favorable group, as long as the earlier classification had been based "simply on a legal presumption." With seeming generosity, the Free Democrat attributed to his Christian Democratic colleague a lack of awareness of the facts, then continued adroitly in the subjunctive: "For if it were otherwise, the CDU would have been confirming collective guilt through its spokesmen." A storm now broke out among the Union's members, the agitation increasing as the German Party's Ewers sprang to colleague Oellers's assistance with the call that now the "truth had emerged." The already closed list of speakers had to be reopened; a CDU delegate protesting Oellers's remarks in the name of his parliamentary faction declared that the party had already "offered much proof that we reject collective guilt."

This in turn evoked a word from the German Party's Margot Kalinke. Unlike the jurists who had dominated the debate, Kalinke presented herself as a "German woman"; she was greeted by the Social Democrats with the call "here come the Nazis!" Above all, she explained, it was necessary "that we create peace among our own *Volk*." Reconciliation, Christianity, community, peace were concepts that needed to be not simply talked of when Christmas bells sounded. Kalinke then expressed her shame at Berlin's denazification legislation—for which, she confirmed, the Social Democrats were responsible; it forced "the wife of a German officer or the wife of a soldier ... to have the dead man denazified if she wants to file a claim."

Werner Jacobi, an SPD delegate, now tried to calm the newly approaching argumentative tide. He called for exercising "a bit of care," despite the Christmas season, with a "chapter" "appearing to constitute a danger for all our accumulated political credit." "For months, indeed for years," Jacobi observed, the Social Democrats had "the feeling that in the defense even of a Nazi perspective and in not recognizing the still existing danger posed by a whole row of Nazi activists, things have in fact gone a little too far." Jacobi had been a long-term prisoner of the Gestapo and the concentration camps. As an example of what he meant, he named Oswald Pohl, chief of the SS's Central Office of Economy and Administration—"one of the most heinous murderers in German history," "responsible for the abhorrent crimes committed in the camps," now awaiting execution in Landsberg. Jacobi noted that Pohl had "suddenly rediscovered Christ via lip service," moving his visitors with "purported penitence."[29] "No one's protecting him," came the call directed at Jacobi from the ranks of the German Party: a brazen inversion of the facts, which the Social Democrat immediately refuted.[30] He also stood by his critique of the widespread "generalizing" intervention in favor of all those feeling themselves affected by denazification.

As was to be expected from all this preliminary activity, the Bundestag now took up the committee's recommendations point by point—without the new proposals for changes tendered by the FDP and the German Party. The "black-red coalition," confirmed with as much indignation as perspicacity by Adolf von Thadden at the time of the vote, had a clear majority. But in the repeated debates it had become clear that the radical minority enjoyed rhetorical dominance over the theme of denazification; that minority set the tone. Both the arguments of its political representatives and their appearance on the scene contributed significantly to the public's increasingly negative assessment of the political purging's value. Beyond that, it contributed to the fact that many convinced democrats found nothing more worth defending in the denazification process.

"Liberation from the law of liberation" was thus the title of an editorial in the *Frankfurter Allgemeine* commenting on the Bundestag's recommendations the day of their release. Still, Thilo Bode explained, these recommendations in no way amounted to the "magic word" "bringing the denazification machinery to a halt": whoever wanted to make the Germans into "inwardly free people" had to tear up the "special law," which took revenge for political error and political conviction. As long as this did not happen, Bode asserted, the world was not to be amazed that even in the face of the Korean War, the Germans "showed such a preference for political neutrality."[31]

Such a perspective paid no attention whatsoever to denazification's original purpose. Correspondingly, the value had vanished from what ought to have been a central fact: that already in the first version of the committee's recommendations, at the SPD's suggestion, the large parties had agreed to an addition—now passed through their majority—specifying that the end of denazification "in no manner" effected the "completion of judicial procedures in the case of individual crimes." The value had likewise vanished from the committee's request that the federal government press the public prosecutors "to move forward decisively with such procedures, using all available means of search and investigation."[32] Much in any case speaks for seeing the request less as a sign of political determination than as an effort to save face before the foreign opinion evoked with such persistence.[33] It is hard to judge the extent to which, beyond such tactical maneuvering, concrete disappointment was already hovering behind the scenes. Committee member Jacobi could in any event declare, without being contradicted, that he knew of "a slew of examples" of people who had evaded the denazification process. As the protocol put it, "and while he is in fact completely uninterested in these people continuing to be caught up in the denazification mill, he still believes that in such cases the public prosecutors had cause to determine whether prosecution was necessary for crimes against humanity or other criminal offenses. Not the smallest step had been taken in that direction—something looked at highly negatively abroad."[34] Unmistakably such sentences convey a fear that what the committee had more or less directly demanded would not take place.[35]

Over recent years, denazification had ceased to be the straightforward and not inconsequential procedure for political purging it had been at the outset. It was now a machine for political rehabilitation, its main product being an army of "fellow travelers," accompanied by many cases of undeniably unjust treatment.[36] In light of this fact, the clearly expressed demand in the three Bundestag debates for an end to the procedure is not all that surprising. Much more so is the tenacity with which the two smaller coalition partners—the FDP and the German Party—stood up for the interests of Nazi potentates classified, now as before, as part of groups 1 and 2, or who at least had good cause to fear being placed in these categories—all in all a very limited number of people. And just as remarkable is the ensuing rapprochement— indeed the closing of ranks—between the CDU-CSU and the SPD when it came to formulating a policy for the past. Perhaps here we already find a sign of an emerging—middle- and long-term—dividing line in West German society: on the one hand a pragmatic politics aimed at attracting a plurality, promoted (out of both capacity and necessity) by parties staking a claim to broad national status; on the other hand the lobbyism of right-wing nationalist political interest groups, along with a lunatic fringe hoping to suppress all the atrocities of the Nazi era.

Corresponding to their sense of democracy, when it came to denazification both the Union and the SPD desired to—and in light of their drive for votes, were able to—limit themselves to intervening for lesser offenders and the mass of "fellow travelers." Such individuals could be counted on to adapt to the new political circumstances. If the FDP and the German Party went beyond this to support the small group of main offenders, all of whom had by no means abjured either Nazi practice or—even less so—ideology, then the question of motivation would become central. A glance at the statistics makes clear that simply accumulating voters could not have been at stake here: up to 1949–50, of the approximately 3.66 million denazifications proceeding in the Western zones, only around 25,000—that is, not even 1 percent—led to classification in either of the higher categories. In contrast, around 150,000 persons were classified as lesser offenders, and around a million as "fellow travelers."[37]

In the course of the legislation to terminate denazification undertaken by the various Länder (either the second or third round), persons in groups 1 and 2 had been given back their voting rights, starting in 1951–52.[38] Nevertheless, the above figures mean that even for the smaller parties, gaining votes among these groups could have been of only limited interest. One motivating factor may have been the consideration that specially radical demands to close down the proceedings could produce more credibility among the lesser offenders than the Union and the SPD had managed. But in the end, deliberations grounded in principle best explain the FDP's and the German Party's aggressive rejection of all remaining political purging—a rejection that despite all duty-bound protests would have distinct consequences for the continued prosecution of Nazi criminals.[39]

In this respect, awareness of one factor in particular stood behind the intercession for both a sweeping end to denazification and its political proscription, as well as for the most comprehensive possible amnesty: the individuals profiting from such measures would belong to the bureaucratic, economic, and military elite that had been corrupted in the Third Reich. In such members of the middle and upper middle class, the FDP saw something like born advocates of the great, nationally conscious, economically liberal, and anticonfessional party they hoped to be. Speaking at a meeting of the party's board, August Martin Euler made perfectly clear the connection with both the German Party and the right-wing splinter parties in many regions, as did the FDP's competition. Euler was referring to the Hessian communal elections of May 1952: "In Wiesbaden, we received 23 seats, the German Party only two . . . . The trump was that the chief mayor from the Nazi period had run as second on our list. In Offenbach, we had the reverse results. An earlier denazification tribunal chairman, an entirely decent man, was not tough enough to stand up against the SPD's machinations. Many crass decisions were made in the tribunal for which the guiltless chairman was held responsible . . . . The German Party entered the fray with the chief mayor from the Nazi period, an excellent man whose reappearance caused no objections whatsoever. Neither the SPD nor the German Communist Party could say a word against him. We would have been able to win this man for ourselves if our local chapter had not been so foolish as to give prominence to the tribunal chairman. These two examples show what we have done right and wrong."[40]

CHAPTER 3

The Rehabilitation and Pensioning of the "131ers"

With the amnesty law and the symbolic verdict against a denazification process that was in any case dying, the political expectations confronting the first German Bundestag in regard to the recent past were by no means fulfilled. For, since 1948 at the latest, the decision had gradually evolved in the realms of politics and administration to annul another highly unpopular element of Allied occupation policy: the politically grounded dismissal of large sections of the public administration in place at the war's end. From the German (bureaucratic) perspective, this sweeping measure was marked by a fatal mix of purgative aims and reformist zeal. As the British and Americans saw it, the measure was the first step in a far-reaching transformation of the civil service.[1] While the resistance to such an alteration of the system had always been strong, it only gained a firm footing in the deliberations over the constitution by the Parliamentary Council, where civil servants held half the mandates. Through this lobbying venue, they would manage to become the only group in West German society enjoying claims to financial and legal compensation inscribed in a special article of the Basic Law. More specifically, the claims were on behalf of colleagues forced to retire because of—as the euphemism had it—"postwar events."[2]

Article 131 would become a bulwark against the efforts at reform that the Allies had not yet abandoned. True, it did not guarantee reinstatement to "displaced" officials, professional soldiers, and other state employees. But its sheer existence signaled a certain political obligation on the part of the legislators, especially since it contained references to individuals with a right to a pension. The article's key sentence was as follows: "Federal law shall regulate the legal status of persons, including refugees and expelled persons, who were public employees on 5 May 1945, left service for reasons other than regulations regarding public officials and salaries, and until now have not been reinstated, or have not been reinstated in their earlier positions."[3] Formally, this statement of course left all possibilities open to the Bundestag; it did not take sides in the dispute over whether, with the unconditional surrender of the Third Reich, the public officials' "well-earned rights" were or were not at an end. But politically the Parliamentary Council had now set things in motion in favor of the same officials; and thanks to the indefatigability and effectiveness of their lobby, their situation would quickly be on the government's agenda.

At the start, no one knew precisely how many people had been dismissed and had not been reinstated since 1945. To gain a clearer idea, the government distributed forms at the beginning of 1950. By the late summer, after the due degree of coalition wrangling, plans for a law were ready. In presenting these plans to the Bundestag, Gustav Heinemann would describe the main concern as a "regulation of the existential question facing several hundred thousand persons and their family members." The Interior Minister avoided citing the—meanwhile reported—total number of dismissed persons. Instead, he cited the number qualified according to his bill: 265,000 persons, two-thirds being public officials and one-third from the military.[4] This was in fact only around 60 percent of the 430,306 individuals who had filled out a valid form.[5] Including family members, the total number of people involved would have been roughly 1.3 million.

For most such people—especially those formerly employed in the eastern regions or in the territory of the Soviet occupation zone–German Democratic Republic—material survival was certainly the main thing at stake. Their difficult situation was naturally no different from what generally faced refugees and people expelled from their homes at the war's conclusion. But beyond survival the increasingly loud demands for reinstatement and benefits had an eminently past-political dimension: as much as anyone else, Article 131 of the Basic Law covered individuals removed from their posts in the course of denazification. According to the forms, the number of such persons was precisely

55,368, or a good quarter of the "civil 131ers"—thus the terminus technicus that had gained circulation.[6] For most of these people, what was at stake was not merely money but the restoration of an "honor" purportedly damaged after the war's end. In addition there were the individuals who had not been formally dismissed but had simply lost their employers: career soldiers, chief officials in the Reich Labor Service, and officials in the Gestapo. The motives of those pressing for a regulation such as Article 131 were thus consistently economic but often went beyond that. The skirmishing over passage of a law in the Bundestag was duly complicated, the arguments brought into play duly multilayered.

The cabinet itself hardly grappled with the issues at stake—this despite the proposed article's appearance five times on the roster in 1950, and the focus it received in sessions held in early summer, rendered less formal by the ill chancellor's absence.[7] The same neglect typified the Bundestag's review of the proposed law in 1950–51. Rather, since 1949 the war of words was unfolding in brochures, newsletters, and memoranda of the different special interest groups, as well as in the Bundestag's Committee on Civil Service Law. Taking up the issue at the start of March 1950—a step, parallel to the government's own activities, that lacked authorization from the plenum—the committee started things out with an invitation to the "131" lobbyists. The guest list for these two-day hearings reveals how well organized the lobby had in fact become; it included not only the German Union of Employees, the Union for Public Services, Transport, and Traffic, and the German Civil Service Association—that is, the general West German unions for public service employees—but also the Association of Officials and Public Administration Employees from the Eastern Regions and the Sudetenland, the General Association for the Protection of Officials, the Association of Pension Entitled Former Wehrmacht Officers and their Surviving Dependents, the Alliance of Former Officials in the Wehrmacht and Officers of the Special Service, along with the Alliance of Former Directors of the Reich Labor Service.[8]

The committee also, however, offered a hearing to the president of the Bavarian Regional Office of Compensation, Philipp Auerbach, representing the Alliance of Individuals Persecuted on Grounds of Religion, Politics, and Race."[9] For alongside the claims of persons "displaced" after the war, those of public officials dismissed during the Third Reich were supposed to be addressed. For a time, it seemed this would be taken care of through a single law. Still, an unambiguous answer was never furnished to the question of where the priority lay in this tactless "coupling business."[10] The moral weight apparently fell on the side of a few hundred people who had been persecuted by the Nazis; the "131ers," however, enjoyed the weight of vastly greater numbers.

The most vigorous propaganda on behalf of "displaced" Germans from the east was undertaken by the Association of Officials and Public Administration Employees from the Eastern Regions and the Sudetenland and the General Association for the Protection of Officials: the former with Hans Lukaschek, federal minister for expellees, as honorary chairman; the latter focused entirely on the interests of denazified persons. But more than the commotion these groups excited, the arguments of Hans Schäfer, chairman of the German Civil Service Association, demonstrated the breadth of the front and the clear vision of its members. Forcefully stirring the conscience of the Bundestag delegates, Schäfer ("myself never a party member") reminded them that "you have recently agreed on the amnesty law, thus making clear that within certain limits even criminally liable citizens are to have their past sins forgotten. But in the long term, you cannot apply two separate standards and judge those who erred politically, were forced by circumstances, and were deceived, more harshly than a truly guilty criminal offender."[11] Schäfer had no doubts that the burden of "denazifying" was born chiefly by civil servants, and he believed the reason for this lay in the "idea" held by the occupying powers "that the civil service, whose members indeed largely formally belonged to the Nazi party or one of its affiliates, had been a standard-bearer and willing tool of the Hitler-regime." In this respect, Schäfer was clever enough to avoid confronting this "misguided theory of collective guilt" with a call for a blanket amnesty. On the contrary, he maintained that considering "every last party comrade as taboo" would amount to "an irresponsible whitewash." To be sure, for Schäfer as well, hardly any brown-shirts remained in the end: the only public officials he deemed out of bounds were those "classified in categories 1 and 2—there are not very many."

In fact, the civil servants classified as main offenders and incriminated persons added up to less than half a percent.[12] Aside from what thus amounted to virtually insignificant concessions, the strategy of the "131" lobby involved obliterating, or at least impeding, all conceivable distinctions—including the distinction between persons who had been "displaced at home" (i.e., those dismissed during denazification) and persons expelled from the eastern territories. The lobby's basic premise was the implacable thesis that the rights of civil service workers ought to have survived the 1945 "change of state form" unimpaired; its principal goal was the most far-reaching possible work reinstatement for those who had been dismissed, along with benefits equal to those of persons who had retained their jobs or had gotten them back after the war.

Remarkably the maximal demands regarding retirement and survivors' benefits and receipt of half pay did not damage the prospects of successfully seeing through reinstatement. To the contrary, they furnished an additional supporting argument: for Schäfer and colleagues, "reemployment" represented "in any case the cheapest solution" for the authorities—this leaving aside the fact that most former party members had "for decades" been "proven public officials in both profession and character." As their advocates argued, letting their "valuable administrative experience" lie fallow was hardly an economical option.

Along with this threat of national economic decline, the standard repertoire of the "131ers" included warnings of the horde of agitators that might emerge one day from an army of disgruntled former state servants: an army suddenly discovering politics as a result of its existential plight. With his usual tact, the chairman of the Civil Service Association encapsulated this notion as follows: especially younger people, who had joined the Nazi party at the advice of older colleagues in order not to end up on the street, and who then "had to bear the greatest sacrifice of blood in the war," might now "not gain the necessary respect for the idea of the democratic state" if they remained unassisted.

In the case of the Association of Officials and Public Administration Employees from the Eastern Regions and the Sudetenland, so much subtlety was not at hand. With the government's law draft lagging behind the demands of those public officials expelled from the eastern territories, the South Baden chapter issued a statement referring to a "constitutional breach" going beyond anything "that the fascist system of National Socialism had accomplished in its civil service policies." To the extent such formulations on the part of functionaries reflected the opinion of ordinary members, radicalization was in fact no longer a danger but already a reality. It was manifest in the government's draft merely prompting a form of "bitter recognition": "that all the inhumanity inflicted on us in the East is to be crowned by a capricious act of our own leadership."[13]

To conjure up such blundering, what form did the draft need to take? After a long behind-the-scenes scuffle, mainly between finance minister Schäffer and minister for expellees Lukaschek, the federal government had offered to make an annual sum of 350 million marks available for "131ers." It was hoped that a 3 percent cut in the income of "Western officials" and "Western pensioners" would bring in another 120 million marks. If Fritz Schäffer's repeated avowals are to be believed, this exhausted the government's possibilities.[14] Despite a substantial narrowing of the circle of eligible persons, legislation corresponding to this framework would have satisfied only two-thirds of the financial claims being tendered for persons who could be reemployed, and only one-half of those being tendered for the pensioners.[15] For this reason, at the time of the draft's presentation, it was clear a number of things still had to be taken care of before the Bundestag could give its approval. It was also evident that the association's maximal demand, which according to Schäffer amounted to 1.7 billion marks, had in no way been cleared from the table.[16]

A serious problem developed for the Bundestag from the uncompromising manner in which the attorneys for the "131ers" presented their—putatively indisputable—case. But no one perceived more clearly than Adenauer that the lobbyists' stubbornness opened room for maneuver on neighboring turf, where the question of reforming civil service law was being played out. Now as before, the government was under pressure in regard to such reforms—though the pressure was abating. Stated pointedly, the obvious complications in resolving the problem of the "131ers" offered a superb alibi for procrastination in the basic civil service reorganization that the Americans in particular had been demanding for years. The demands would end in 1953 with the Federal Civil Service Law, a resounding confirmation of the status quo ante.[17]

Adenauer himself considered both complete equality between the expelled eastern civil servants and those working in West Germany and a deduction from the latter's pay as unacceptable. The limited will of the government to see through its own "131" draft, and the extent of the dilatory tactics that were being employed, was apparent in the chancellor's delay in meeting a delegation of the Soldiers' League until 25 August 1950, only a week before the bill's presentation to parliament.[18] Adenauer used the occasion to accept the league's demands—which inevitably further complicated matters. But the executive branch's lack of decisiveness comes through even more clearly in a remark of the interior minister regarding the first Bundestag debate of the proposed law: the "entire vexing business, which for months has pressed itself on the various departments and the central government, will now slide over to you."[19]

Heinemann's rhetorical pity for the parliamentarians mirrored a general shyness regarding clear-cut words. No one wanted to make the dismissed public officials and officers into enemies. Instead of accepting responsibility for a few definitive excisions, everyone tried to shove the bogey onto his neighbors and to continue basking in the favor of the "131ers."

It is thus not surprising that the Bundestag's three debates of the proposed law turned into something like a collective effort to treat the theme from an exclusively sociopolitical vantage, as much as this was possible. Almost all the speakers avoided any reference to the theme's past-political import. It is true that some did so in language amounting to a downright entreaty making quite clear what was at stake: Heinemann, clearly affected by the "manner of fighting of those representing the interests of persons covered by Article 131," confirmed the "greatest possible consideration"—this even facing the invective offered by the South Baden chapter of the Association of Officials. But he asked the critics to be kind enough to stick to the main culprit: "If displeasure is to be expressed—and I say once again, in view of the distress at work in these circles, I have a great deal of understanding for such displeasure—then let it be directed at the responsible party, and now as before that is Adolf Hitler." The lively applause with which both the governing parties and the SPD responded marked the extent of opposition to the "131ers" in this two-hour first parliamentary debate (13 September 1950). Apparently no thought was given, for instance, to the possibility of discussing the political complicity of both top public officials and the generals, let alone the complacency of the entire bureaucracy. Instead, distinguished merely by sharpness and degree of dosage, there was a critique of the "defamation" (Richter alias Rößler, National Right) and "discrimination" (Fröhlich, Economic Reconstruction Association) inflicted on the Wehrmacht, along with a plea on behalf of the noncommissioned officers, the prisoners of war, and the "late repatriates" (Menzel, SPD). And by turns, delegates promised to support an improvement (generally considered necessary) of the legal draft, for the sake of the "honor and right of the German soldiers" (Farke, German Party).[20]

When, in April 1951, the law was finally ready for the second and third debates, the circumstances surrounding it had been fundamentally altered.[21] For, through a surprising statement, the chancellor had placed himself at the head of those defending former Wehrmacht members (who were no longer attacked anywhere simply for being such). Two recent events had forced him into a certain balancing act: (1) scarcely granted an early release from custody in Brussels, the former commander in chief of the Wehrmacht in Belgium, General Alexander von Falkenhausen, had publicly accused several Belgian politicians (among these, former prime minister Paul-Henri Spaak)—of attempting to collaborate in 1940; (2) in France, former paratroop general Bernhard Ramcke, who in January had used his parole to flee the country but had returned at Bonn's advice, had just been condemned as a war criminal. In both cases, the courts apparently decided to limit the sentence—or, at least, the part that had to be served—to the period of pretrial detention.[22] Despite all due consideration for the feelings of the French and Belgians (duped as they had been through both generals' actions), Adenauer wished to offer a signal to circles whose support he considered necessary for future German rearmament, circles that had long considered such foreign trials for German soldiers incarcerated abroad to be unbearable.[23] In the Bundestag, the chancellor thus reassuringly declared that the government would do all in its power "to ease the burden of men who have been imprisoned and arrange their restored freedom as quickly as possible." Naturally the government could not intervene for those "who were really guilty." But the percentage they constituted was "so extraordinarily minimal and so extraordinarily small" (sic) that "there has been no breach in the honor of the former German Wehrmacht."

The chancellor's well-calculated "word to the members of the former Wehrmacht" promised care and protection: "No one may reproach the career soldiers on account of their earlier activities and, so long as they are to be employed in public service, place them behind other applicants if they have the same personal and professional qualities. The chapter of collective guilt for militarists [sic] alongside activists and beneficiaries of the National Socialist regime must be ended, once and for all."[24] For the *Frankfurter Allgemeine* this declaration meant nothing less than the "end of a legend." As military expert Adelbert Weinstein observed in that publication, Adenauer's remarks simply confirmed what had already been said at the start of the new year by West Germany's president, Theodor Heuss, thus needing "little commentary."[25] Weinstein nonetheless did choose to establish the remarks' connection with the planned rearmament a bit more clearly: "The top echelons of the young republic have rehabilitated a group of men who were the victims of unhealthy fantasies. That will supply democracy in Germany with manpower that will strengthen not only the Federal Republic but the entire West."[26]

With his opening words, Adenauer had fixed the course of the Bundestag's second debate over the "131" law. Virtually no speakers could now refrain from remarks full of praise and encouragement—and that waxed downright poetic whenever a party colleague was in question. The keenest of such eulogies to the Wehrmacht was offered by CDU delegate Franz-Josef Wuermeling on the debate's second day. Accompanied by cheers from the governing parties, Wuermeling expressed "heartfelt joy" at the chancellor's "pronouncement of honor," before proclaiming, in the name of his parliamentary faction, that "the age of collective guilt is now at an end." He then continued the idea as if hoping to raise Adenauer's ante: "The honor of the German soldiers was never lost, and thus needed no restoration through yesterday's declaration of the chancellor, but mere confirmation."[27] "Very good!" resounded from the Union's benches—but also from the SPD. This prompted Carlo Schmid, the SPD's speaker for foreign affairs, to admonish the somewhat gushing Wehrmacht enthusiasts in his own and the opposition's ranks as follows: "I do not believe this house will end up praised for this competition to have the honor of being the first to defend the honor of German soldiers."[28]

This loud, extended hymn of praise for the Nazi military—it lacked a line dedicated to the Waffen SS on quite obvious grounds—was doubtless an expression of a drastic alteration in perceptions and perspectives regarding security policy, as a result of the Korean War. At the same time it was one aspect of an overriding effort (one leaving its stamp on virtually all political realms) to come up with a bearable interpretation of the past. But to some degree, it also revealed the bad conscience of the parliamentarians regarding the so-called simple soldiers: Many such soldiers were still enduring piteous circumstances and were now being forced to observe the rather generous arrangements being made for their professional superiors.

Compared to the government's original offer, the package arranged, after tedious negotiations, in the offices of the Committee on Civil Service Law—a package comprising both promises of pensions for the "131ers" and commitments for their reemployment—had become much larger. First, nearly 15,000 professionals who formerly worked in the Reich Labor Service now belonged to the circle qualified for claims. Also, at the suggestion of the governing parties, the career soldiers had been granted an additional improvement in the second debate. (Out of obvious motives, the FDP and the German Party claimed this suggestion as a result of their own policies.) With few dissenting votes, the Bundestag had decided to exempt requests submitted on account of "documented personal courage in face of the enemy" from the general qualifications, with a maximum of two requests admitted for the period 1933–45.[29] The law now also assured normal retirement benefits to all "displaced" pensioners and people expelled from the east.[30] Every ex-official fit for service who had a right to file a claim now qualified as "to be reemployed"; he could maintain his former official title, with the addition of the German initials indicating the qualification (z. Wv.). As long as he could demonstrate ten years of service, he was to receive a transitional salary scaled to the previous service until permanent reemployment by the state. This applied expressly to those who had been dismissed during denazification: while the law had declaimed their exclusion from any right to reemployment, they in fact widely enjoyed priority when it came to being rehired, since it was not the state but their previous departments that had to pay the transitional salary—

and the departments naturally wished to save money.[31] In addition, there was no longer any talk of a 3 percent cut in the salaries of "domestic" public officials.[32]

In practice, the "131" law benefited all dismissed career soldiers and public officials from the "Greater German Reich" who were now living in West Germany, including those from the Bohemian and Moravian protectorates but excluding Austria. Through a supplement to the opening section of the government's proposal, the Committee on Civil Service Law had made a point of excluding Gestapo members from the proposed legislation—as well as, until the law's first amendment in the summer of 1953, former employees of Göring's extended central monitoring office, camouflaged as the "Air Force Research Office." But even this ostentatious exclusion turned out to be worth little, since simultaneously the final chapter included an important disposition of exception. It stipulated that both Gestapo officials and members of the "Research Office" were indeed covered by the law—so long as these persons had simply been transferred there "ex officio." The exception also applied to career soldiers in the Waffen SS, otherwise unmentioned in the law. And in "special exceptional cases" those who had been transferred "ex officio" could even have their period of service in the new positions recognized.

But ex officio transfers had in fact been the rule and were in no way identical with transfers "against one's will," something that Josef Ferdinand Kleindinst (CSU), the committee's recorder, nevertheless insinuated in his defense of the bill. He did this when facing a motion for emendation by the German Communist Party; avowing their own support for consideration of the claims of any individual Gestapo member "who remained a decent human being despite everything," the Communists had proposed deleting the paragraph in question and instituting an appropriate implementing measure in its stead. In offering this proposal, they actually made Kleindinst's job easy. Without an authorization anchored in law, he argued, the "guiltless party" could not be helped.[33] While this may well have been true, such an authorization would have needed formulation as a real legal derogation—something precisely not signified by the proposed word choice, contrary to what Kleindinst suggested. The gist of what was finally decided was that whoever had, for instance, been transferred from the police to the incipient Gestapo—the sort of procedure that was common in the first years of Nazi rule—had an automatic claim to placement in a position and, in the case of ten years' service, to the transitional salary or pension. Verification by the employers was required only for requests to also recognize years spent with the Gestapo.[34]

In any case, independently of these regulations, the authorities had another, more expedient way to accommodate former members of the Gestapo and the SD: to employ them in public service "anew." It was mostly younger public officials who profited from this method—officials excluded from the "131" legislation because they had begun their careers with the secret police. The substantial amount of both "new" employment and reemployment—including, in particular, police service on both a Länder and local level—is reflected in the frequent unmasking of Nazi criminals accompanying the more consequent prosecutions inaugurated in the late 1950s. Some of the persons now accused of mass murder or complicity in mass murder had even gained prominent positions with the criminal police and the security police.[35]

Parliament's nearly unanimous generosity toward the former public officials and professional soldiers left the individual parliamentary factions with little room for gaining profile. Not only the radical fringe parties—those wishing to more or less systematically stir up resentment, capitalizing on unfulfilled hopes—now faced difficulties. This was also the case for the FDP, which thus set about showing its special concern for the "denazified 131ers." In the legislation's very last hours, during the third debate's point-by-point vote on 10 April 1951, the Free Democrats attempted to document their fighting spirit in favor of persons who had quickly advanced their careers "on account of narrow ties with National Socialism." To this end, the party repeated its proposal, already rejected in the second debate, that the intended nonrecognition of such appointments and promotions be unconditionally scrapped. As Herwart Miessner argued, anything else would mean "preferential law" and a violation of the principle of equality. (Miessner was a board member of the General Association for the Protection of Officials. In 1950 he moved from the German Rightist Party to the FDP; he had already made a name in the plenum through his aggressive stance regarding the "professionally untrained"—Berufsfremde—now employed in public service.[36]) Miessner predicted that nonrecognized Nazi promotions would become "a constant obstacle to establishing inner peace," since they "would reveal an intent of renewed denazification." At this point, months had gone by since the Bundestag's delayed recommendations to terminate the denazification process. Miessner's words thus amounted to the laborious evocation of a specter and most likely filled no one outside the FDP with fear. At least one party member also thought the scare tactics went too far: To the applause of the CDU and SPD, Berlin delegate Hans Reif, longstanding critic of pandering to the "onetimes," succinctly declared "that if I had the right to vote I'd vote against the proposal that has just been defended." The large majority of parliament then did just that.[37]

The FDP had in any case made clear its desire to be surpassed by no one in pronounced sympathy for the "years-long plight" and "embitterment" of the "131ers," a sympathy expressed once again during the committee's final deliberations. The party did express the hope that the law's enactment would result in "this circle finding its way back to work upholding the state."[38] But the FDP always stressed its view that the law reflected a duty, indeed a necessity, to correct injustice—and not, for example, a voluntary social and political accomplishment—one that was now estimated to cost the young democracy the massive annual sum of 750 million marks.

Confirming this was left to the larger parties, as was tying the fact to certain things being expected of those the legislation had in mind. Such was the context for an open admission by Fritz Erler, speaking on behalf of the Social Democrats: "in their own difficult circumstances, a great many people may be filled with envy when observing individuals benefiting from this law." But, Erler indicated, rather than envy, what present circumstances called for was a mutual promise "that we will also intercede with the same amount of good will on behalf of the other injured groups who find themselves in need." By the same token, speaking for the CDU-CSU, Franz-Josef Wuermeling stressed that the great extent to which the law met the demands of the "131ers" meant "that for many, it will not be easy to convince ... other sections of the nation of its propriety"; for this reason, the benefited persons were "fully obligated to utmost personal exertion in rebuilding our homeland and working together with all the democratic forces."[39]

Undoubtedly one factor present in the calculations of all the parliamentary factions was the Landtag elections in Rhineland-Palatinate and Lower Saxony, scheduled for the period from the end of April to the start of May 1951. But we should also note that in the initial years, a basic characteristic of West Germany's social-political legislation was a high degree of consensus between the leading forces in government and the opposition.[40] Against this backdrop, the tacit understanding of the "131" law as, above all, an element of social policy, and the tacit agreement to publicly present it as such, formed something like a bridge over which parliament could march in unison[41] With such a bridge, it was possible to largely avoid confronting all the other motives and implications of the legislation—themes over which there was far less consensus between the parties. Such themes included the general political implications of the law in relation to the Nazi past; the question of how to reintegrate, politically and mentally, the provisionally déclassé portions of the old elite; and, not least of all, the law's military-political implications. But however expedient, the absence of these considerations pointed to one thing in particular: that the consensus, with two abstentions, in the Bundestag's passage of the "Law Regulating the Legal Status of Persons Falling under Article 131 of the Basic Law" on 10 April 1951 rested on a kind of collective self-deception.[42]

Nevertheless, the process of "rearranging the landscape for the future"—*Flurbereinigung für die Zukunft* (Bundestag president Ehlers's expression, offered in relief after the vote)—was now under way; the legislative assembly had now done its job.[43] It had in fact been possible to synchronize the generous alimentation of the "131ers" with the pensioning of those public officials who had been dismissed during the Third Reich on political or racial grounds: a confluence perhaps easing the perspective of one or another individual who might have considered the approach to the "131ers" as, indeed, very generous. For similar optical reasons, the "Law Regulating Reparations for National Socialist Injustice against Public Officials" was passed—likewise unanimously— a few days before the "131" law and was announced simultaneously with its counterpart.[44]

The informal linkage of the two laws was continued in the payment supplements regularly offered before the Bundestag elections until 1965. But with time, the linkage became less of an "alibi" for the "131" law and more of a routine.[45] After four amendments, complete equalization of pay and pensions had been achieved between "displaced" public officials and those either left in office in 1945 or employed since then; the right of the "131ers" to reemployment (promoted through fixed minimum quotas) had already been established with the second amendment.[46]

Now privileged, all the public officials formerly occupying the directors' floors of the Reich's various ministries and still unemployed in mid-1951 began pressing themselves on Bonn. Already by the summer of 1950 more than one quarter of the section managers of the new federal ministries were former Nazi Party members, and in three ministries even the personnel managers had been so.[47] During this period Interior Minister Heinemann repeatedly tried to prevent such appointments through a cabinet decision, but he was supported only by Jakob Kaiser, the minister for German affairs, who was himself critical of the chancellor. The most outspoken opponent of any "lockout" rule was Vice Chancellor Franz Blücher, who in February 1951 convinced the cabinet to install a former party member as personnel manager in the ministry specially founded for the Marshall Plan. Adenauer put an end to the months-long power struggle between his ministers in typical fashion. Focusing entirely on the rehabilitative function of denazification, he even managed to make do without the concept of incriminated persons: "the Federal Chancellor maintains the standpoint that so long after the collapse of the National Socialist regime, the distinction between politically exonerated and nonincriminated persons should be ended."[48]

Soon afterward the "advance of ex-party comrades" even reached the state secretary level, and by February 1953 a good 60 percent of section managers appointed over the past two and a half years were such individuals—in part as a consequence of the "131" law.[49] To be sure, many had only entered their Nazi positions in 1937 or later, sometimes through a "collective notification," and often claimed to have been simply "nominal" party members rather than real adherents. According to the statistics, in 1953 almost 15,000 posts in the federal administration's ministerial realm, amounting to 30 percent, had been filled with "131ers." There was a markedly higher percentage of such persons in the Foreign Ministry (40 percent), the Interior Ministry (42 percent), and the Ministry for Expellees, where three-quarters of the public officials— in any event merely sixty-three—were "131ers."[50]

No hitches accompanied the integration of the "131ers," or at least there was no noticeable resistance to the process. But setting in motion the other aspect of Ehlers's "landscape rearrangement," reemployment in conformity with the reparations law, certainly had its problems. Already over recent years, inviting interested emigrants back to their posts had turned out remarkably difficult for many people involved in the process, in different venues—not least the universities.[51] At present, administrators often seemed to consider the presence of former party members a detriment to the employment of those who had been persecuted.[52] It is true that the reparations law for public service had furnished the public officials dismissed in the Third Reich with a privileged status in comparison with other persecuted groups. However, nothing had changed in regard to a structural asymmetry with so many implications for the praxis of reemployment; in basically offering the same legal treatment to the great number of "fellow travelers" and the relatively small group of persecuted persons, those formulating public service legislation prolonged the possibility of de facto discrimination.

The difficulties manifest in reintegrating public officials dismissed by the Nazis was a sign of one thing in particular: the reality of public service was only slowly coming to approximate the Bundestag's democratic postulates—and the path to an equality of circumstances in the official apparatus led over deep breaches, swerves, and stumbling blocks. Over the following years there was plenty of evidence of such rough passage, although for a long time not all the injustices and scandals publicly believed to be linked with the "131" legislation in fact had much to do with it.

This became clear in the course of the recurring debates over Adenauer's chancellery head, the previous official commentator on Nazi racial law, Hans Globke, as well as through a series of articles published by the *Frankfurter Rundschau* a few weeks after the "131" law's passage.[53] Highly unwelcome because of their factual richness, these articles illuminated the circumstances prevailing in the Foreign Office: long before the law took effect, public officials who had served under Nazi foreign minister Ribbentrop occupied almost all of that venue's leading positions.[54] Three-quarters of them were former party members—a fact Adenauer himself would later confirm before the Bundestag: "But I believe that if you ever consider the matter quietly, you will not be able to say that it would have been *possible* to proceed otherwise. It is in fact impossible to erect a foreign ministry without having, at least at first, people who understand something of the earlier history in the important posts.... I think we now need to finish with this sniffing out of Nazis."[55] And indeed, things quickly quieted down following this debate over the report—itself to be practically ignored, despite its mild tone—of the parliamentary investigative committee formed in October 1951 at the SPD's behest. Indirectly, this confirmed the view of all the critics who argued that from the start the opposition's attacks were aimed less at the return of Ribbentrop's personnel than at the chancellor, at what was termed his "Catholic foreign policy," and at his continuing grip on the Foreign Ministry. (Meanwhile even a portion of the CDU-CSU had begun to doubt the wisdom of his refusal to appoint a foreign minister.)[56]

Among the widespread errors in assessments of the "131" legislation is the view that all those reemployed were incriminated persons.[57] As explained above, this was not the case. But it would also be incorrect to assume that the group of incriminated Nazis among the reemployed individuals was identical to the approximately 55,000 "displaced" persons listed at the start of 1950. In reality, around a tenth of the public officials removed in the course of the political purging now passed as exonerated, and another tenth were either unaffected or unclassified.[58] On the other hand, a good portion of the roughly 100,000 public officials expelled or displaced from the eastern territories were quite likely more or less incriminated persons—although not even 1 percent of them was classified as such. Around a third of the "displaced easterners" were forced to endure a classification as "fellow travelers," the large majority of the remainder passing as exonerated, unaffected, or unclassified. We may assume that, given a background check similar to the checks originally carried out in the western zones, many of them would have been removed from public service, or even interned.

In 1945–46, considerable numbers of "domestic" public officials were subject to such internments, as well as to summary dismissals. For a time in the American zone everyone who had joined the Nazi Party before 1 May 1937—the date was simply fixed by the Allies—was asked to clear his desk. But the "backflow"[59] of such persons, dismissed in more or less wholesale fashion, had already begun in 1947–48, and by the start of 1950 30 percent of "displaced" public officials had found a new position in public service—albeit few with full rights and privileges.[60] For this reason—and this was widely recognized—anyone still on the street because of his denazification notice a year and a half later, when the "131" law had taken effect, must have been quite strongly incriminated.

But such conclusions were far too obvious to require extensive discussion (either written or spoken)—at least not generally and abstractly. Both inside and outside the Bundestag, the overwhelming majority of West Germans were clearly in favor of "normalization"—put otherwise, for more or less forgetting everything having to do with Nazism. As it pertained to the realm of public service in particular, this included the annulment of all sanctions felt to have been imposed wholesale and the recovery by those affected of their former rights—in short, the most extensive possible restoration of personal continuity. Not a single political party disputed the necessity and legitimacy of such a massive reintegration process.

Against this backdrop, negative attention was reserved for the special case that violated normal expectations, amounting to an obvious abuse of the principle of integration. Occasionally a concrete example would offer the small number of critical observers a chance to spark some indignation, but even then, in view of the special favors being dispensed in hard times, naked envy regarding the bureaucracy (in both its traditional and present form) may have lurked behind that response. But, more important, with the uncovering of such major and minor scandals, the gap had not been bridged between identifying the symptom and naming its source.[61] The unappetizing special cases that did come to light did not alter a climate in which scrupulousness increasingly flourished. Both individuals and groups that considered their reemployment or pensioning to be proceeding too slowly or inadequately were emerging with increasingly hard-edged and brazen demands. In the end even the "born" professional officers of the Waffen SS—a group that had remained outside the "131" legislation on solid grounds—got what it wanted.[62] It was a sign of the reigning mood that the term

Wiedergutmachung, commonly being used to designate reparations for persecuted persons, was now increasingly applied to the "131ers." (Note that from the perspective of the persecuted, if not of the "131ers," the term's literal sense of "making things good again" was certainly problematic.)

Among the professionals raising complaints, precisely the jurists found it entirely in order to see themselves damaged by the fact that—whatever its constitutional basis—there had been a change of "circumstances" for the state to whose Führer they had been bound by a special oath. They also found it in order to sue for "reparations"—*Wiedergutmachung*—for this damage. Such juridical steps naturally did not exclude a very pronounced "sense of honor." This is exemplified in the case of the earlier president of the Provisional Court of Appeal in Darmstadt, Ludwig Scriba, who filed a complaint against the state of Hesse for denying him full retirement benefits in the framework of the "131" law. Scriba had "already openly professed loyalty to the Nazi party before the seizure of power." After 1933 he rose quickly from director to president of the court. Since Hesse's regional personnel office had—accurately—seen a close connection between this and Scriba's narrow party ties, it had not included his later promotions when fixing benefits. The Administrative Court offered a settlement: recognition of the promotions up to the level of president. Scriba rejected the settlement, declaring that it "clashes with my sense of honor." Perhaps his added argument, cited in the *Frankfurter Rundschau,* is more suggestive: as a reward for directing the Provisional Court of Appeal for nine years "without reproach," he "was forced to spend two and a half years in a concentration camp." When the state representative interceded that he surely meant an internment camp, Scriba replied that the internment camp in Darmstadt had "little to distinguish it from a concentration camp."[63]

Without a doubt, the former chief judges and Nazi functionaries considered themselves victims—with a right to *Wiedergutmachung.* The "object lesson" that internment had certainly meant to much of the state and societal elite had long since faded; personalities such as Scriba had replaced all such lessons with a notebook full of ressentiment.[64] The assumption that Scriba the pensioner was not alone in his opinions is supported by the repeated references, coming from all sides in the "131" debate, to "bitterness" among the public officials. Scarcely anyone ventured to raise questions about its factual basis. It thus seems that for many people the pedagogic effects of "collapse" and internment had already exhausted themselves in a retreat to the virtue of doing one's duty, a process closely connected to the apologia of the unpolitical public officials.[65]

In the middle of the 1950s, legal cases of the above sort were by no means rare, although little information circulated about them. With their regard for harmony, the local papers considered it a matter of "tact" to ignore such "strictly personal" affairs. By the same token, the individuals involved needed to be of some prominence if the national press, the illustrated weeklies, and the radio were to show interest in any complaints.[66] This explains how an impression could emerge that it was the (in the end relatively small) group of outspoken "Nazi bosses" who profited most of all from the blessings of the "131" law, and not an alternative group bringing with it far more serious structural implications: the totality of compromised officialdom in justice and administration, along with the "displaced easterners" and professional soldiers.

During this period the avid desire for sensation on the part of the reader of *Der Spiegel* (Germany's postwar equivalent to *Time*) was being sated by reports on the pension claims filed by widows of important Nazi fanatics like Heydrich, Himmler, and the jurist Roland Freisler, the tricks through which they saved their fortunes from the Federal Republic's claws—doubtless far more readily and comfortably sated than could ever be the case with a clear analysis of the "131" law's effects, say in light of the virtually complete rehabilitation of the old judiciary.[67] The more well known the name and notorious the crimes, the less important was precision. It no longer seemed important even to keep straight the various statutes used to justify satisfaction of their pension claims. In the shadow of the scandals surrounding prominent "brown"—that is, Nazi—families, much was seen in shades of gray. (The Bundestag would end up trying to get around the proprietary favoring of such families through an alteration of the Basic Law.[68]) Even the distinction between those reemployed by virtue of the "131" law and those "merely" receiving a pension dissolved into haze; both were "131ers"—hence something like natural antipodes to people brought into public service after the war—the "45ers"—but also to the "33ers" and many other persecuted individuals waiting for payment through the reparations law.

The "131" law would be accompanied by a large number of implementing regulations and executive decrees—by 1954, the figure was over a hundred.[69] Linked—specifically in their bearing on the fate of the highly incriminated ex-Nazis—with the complexities of the regulatory moves by the Länder to end denazification, these decrees and regulations in fact did not make it easy for the public to raise reservations or objections at the right place and time. This was the case, for instance, with Franz Schlegelberger, former secretary of state in the Reich Ministry of Justice, sentenced at Nuremberg in 1947 to life imprisonment for war crimes and crimes against humanity. For health reasons, Schlegelberger was released from prison in 1950, and in July 1951 he emerged as "exonerated" from delayed denazification proceedings. Until 1959 he was able to enjoy his "131" pension undisturbed, until, following repeated inquiries in the Bundestag, the Social Democrats managed to have the pension rights terminated. Schlegelberger naturally moved up the appeals ladder, finally reaching a settlement with the Federal Administrative Court involving financial compensation for agreeing to forgo his rights under the "131" law.[70]

Such tepid and nontransparent procedures were not the rule but were certainly common enough—as seen, for example, in a list drawn up in the "Jewish Almanac" for 1958–59.[71] Clearly, many of those who reacted to the situation with anger and indignation lacked an understanding of the binding nature of pension claims based on federal law. But abuses did not merely result from imbroglios and legal holes. Rather, "in the application of this law, administrative offices and courts often proceed in a manner that can only be considered absurd"—this from Eugen Gerstenmaier, then West German president, speaking on the radio in February 1956; Gerstenmaier also referred to "criminal cynicism."[72] As a result, it was precisely sensitive, critical spirits who tended toward a distaste for close scrutiny of what was transpiring, a distaste often translated into discovering a "restoration" where actually, to a great extent, a (bitter) outcome of the constitutional state was in fact at work.[73]

Among the possibilities inherent in such a state—possibilities to which people were still unaccustomed in the 1950s—was breathtaking political controversy. Such a controversy over the "131" law now broke out between the Constitutional Court and the Federal High Court, the supreme body for civil cases.[74] Its starting point was the fact that in connection with this legislation, the Bundestag (as beforehand the parliamentary council) had avoided deciding whether the public officials' legal status had or had not "vanished" in 1945. The overwhelming number of professional jurists considered this question as settled with the Bundestag's generous accommodation regarding pensions and reemployment; according to their interpretation, the "change of state form" had not affected the "situation of the public officials." The Constitutional Court, it turned out, had a very different opinion. On 17 December 1953, having been asked to consider almost 2,000 appeals, it rejected the thirty-four complaints it had admitted for consideration from public officials and pensioners who felt that their basic rights had been violated by the "131" law in different ways. The main point of the wide-ranging judgment was as simple as it was sensational: "On 8 May 1945, the civil service's status was fully canceled."[75] The decision was greeted with shock by West Germany's jurists; it sparked the most hard-bitten possible opposition.

For its critics, the most provocative aspect of the so-called civil-service judgment was its outspoken historical-political reasoning. Over many pages and with the use of extensive citations, the constitutional judges documented the ideological indebtedness of the civil service toward a state that had degenerated into a mere "apparatus of power in the service of the Nazi Party": a state that, as the Allies had rightly seen, needed to be completely defeated militarily, its legal organization destroyed, in order to "sever its ties to the National Socialist movement and build it anew from top to bottom in a democratic manner." The Constitutional Court did not wish to take a firm position regarding the repeated doubts, in light of that situation, "whether following 8 May 1945 the German Reich actually still existed as a state." But it flatly denied that "the legal status of the public officials, who not only are tied economically to the state to the utmost degree but also are the primary legal embodiment of the state's power, could survive ... a collapse of the state's entire organization." The judges—members of the court's First Panel—saw the reason for this as lying above all in the "fact that in the 'Third Reich,' the status of the civil service itself experienced a deep transformation, one affecting its very nature"—through the "carefully planned work of Hitler and the Nazi party," begun right after the seizure of power, "to destroy the party-politically neutral professional civil service"; through laying aside the constitutional protection of the public officials vis-à-vis the legislator; through the introduction of a personal oath of allegiance to Hitler; and through the relation of dependency with "the party that ruled the state."

One of the very few commentators to wholeheartedly approve the "boldness" of this judgment was Reinhold Kreile, a 24-year-old starting lawyer writing in the *Frankfurter Hefte* in the late summer of 1954. While the legal literature was referring to "recklessness," Kreile spoke of a "Magna Charta of introspection." The young jurist stressed the political import of the judgment's concern with the past—the court's intention to tear away "the veil of forgetting": "For Germany has suppressed the memory of its National Socialist past to such an extent that the Kaiserreich and Weimar Republic seem closer and more vivid than the Nazi regime." The court succeeded in introducing the "theme of Germany's downfall, Kreile explained, into a public discussion otherwise ostensibly concerned with "the German miracle and German ascent." "What the Constitutional Court has basically said (now detached, to be sure, from the judgment's careful legal formulation) is this: the civil servants in National Socialist Germany were Adolf Hitler's civil servants. The conclusion follows from itself: the German people was Adolf Hitler's people."[76]

The legal establishment was naturally not blind to this interpretive possibility. Quaking with indignation, it nevertheless avoided openly citing such clear words, even for the sake of refuting them. Five months after the Constitutional Court's judgment, on 20 May 1954, the Federal High Court voiced its own opinion; the occasion was the demand of a "displaced eastern" pensioner for payment of retirement benefits.[77] Notably, the Constitutional Court had in no way materially tampered with the legislative regulation encoded in Article 131 of the Basic Law; to the contrary, they had directly confirmed it—a fact not mitigating the Federal High Court's critique. The most aggressive reproaches of the court's president, Hermann Weinkauff, and his colleagues were prompted precisely by the historical-political spirit of the "official's judgment" that Kreile had pinned down so accurately. The main charge leveled at the court's putatively "red" and inexperienced First Panel was not to have pronounced a legal judgment, but rather to have delivered an—in any event false—"historical value judgment."[78]

This conclusion, however, did not restrain the Federal High Court itself from using a historical argument to defend the continued rights of the public officials, an argument purporting to show how things really stood for German officialdom in the Third Reich. "Now as before, despite the disgraceful, illegal pressure weighing upon them, the over-whelming majority of German officials felt duty-bound first and fore-most to the state and its legitimate business, perceiving their offices in such a spirit. At the start and for a certain time after, the tie to Hitler's person could be understood as a tie to the highest organ of the state ... the tie to the party as, at the beginning, maintenance of respect for a political decision by the national majority. But as the criminal goals and methods of National Socialism gradually revealed themselves more and more, this imposed tie was predominantly of a merely involuntary nature, endured with acute inner disapproval and under the most acute form of terror." As the court wished to have it, the Nazi "ideal" of a civil service devoted to its cause was "predominantly in conflict with real-ity"—the evident conclusion being that the Constitutional Court had succumbed to the Nazis' illusion. Whereas the "civil service judgment" had cited Nazi laws and ordinances, underscoring their characteristic qualities, the Federal High Court saw effective continuity in the offi-cials' "professional labor." Even in the Third Reich, the "legal core" of the civil servants' status rested in their possession "of administrative and jurisdictive functions, not however those to be considered political functions in the true sense; that is, they had functions that the state as such always practices and that are independent of its various manifestations," hence the legal status's outlasting of the "change in state form." Were the status null and void, the Federal High Court reasoned, the officials—as individuals widely affected by the "terror"—would have to bear the consequences of unjust measures of which they were in fact "victims," and "in its practical results that leads to a collective liability, even extending to women and children with a right to benefits, irreconcilable with thinking that is governed by law."

In these few lines, the judges had managed to more or less encapsulate all the provocative phrases then common currency in the conservatives' defensive battle against a thesis of political-moral complicity—a thesis certainly central to the "civil service judgment." With its ruling, the Federal High Court hoped to basically force the constitutional judges into a volte-face. But the judges would not be put off. The complaint, on constitutional grounds, of a former assistant criminal investigator offered a basis—obviously highly welcome—for a sharp settling of accounts with their critics. The former official had begun his career with the Gestapo, thus being excluded from reemployment on the basis of the "131" law, and maintained that this situation was a violation of his right to freedom of opinion as stated in Article 3 of the Basic Law. In an opinion that was once again very wide-ranging, the court defended the "civil service judgment" while rejecting the complaint.[79] While expressly disinclined to respond to either "attacks of a primarily political bent or indeed expressions of suspicion," it in fact responded to the polemics of the specialized law journals, which had sometimes been downright base.[80]

The judges were confronting a critique that treated alterations to Germany's civil service law during the Third Reich as an insertion of "National Socialist embellishments." Along with citing the "professional labor" supposedly flying in the face of such embellishments, the critics maintained that "the National Socialist rulers would soon have learned to respect the reality of a modern rationally administered state." In fact, as Otto Koellreutter, emeritus professor of public law, indicated, until well into the war things proceeded "far more lawfully" than in the "post-1945 communist-democratic cold civil war." In face of such opinions, it was incumbent to once more clearly demonstrate that, in the constitutional judges' words, "to an in any case considerable extent" the civil service had "taken seriously and confirmed," "on its own behest," its legal duty to always intercede for National Socialism."

The first evidence the judges offered in this regard was the example of teachers and professors in the Third Reich. What followed—not without rhetorical effect—was a catalog of misdemeanors extending from judges and prosecutors to officials in financial and municipal departments, doctors in public service, policemen, and customs officials; the catalog's practical effect was to demonstrate a pattern of collaboration in discriminating against Jews and others "alien to the *Volk*" taking in the entire civil service. In the judges' opinion, even assuming that individual officials "did their best to mitigate onerously unjust provisions," this did not alter the underlying judgment: "If the officials cognizant of the execution of such provisions had really considered the provisions of civil service law regarding their duty toward National Socialism as mere National Socialist 'embellishment' in an otherwise duly legal civil service law ... then they would have had to consider themselves legally prevented ... from collaborating with such measures; before every pertinent official action, they would then have had to inform their employers, in other words the state, that an irresolvable legislative contradiction was here apparent." Naturally, the judges agreed, such an expectation "would have been unfair"—but just this indicated that the civil servants could not escape the effects of a "perverted administration." It indicated that the "effort to distinguish a realm of 'purely professional administrative activity' within the greater purposive realm of the National Socialist state" by the Federal High Court and authoritative jurists "is not only methodologically incorrect but simply impossible."

Confronting the notion of "National Socialist embellishment"—a notion that had become common currency in West German legal doctrine—also offered the Constitutional Court occasion for an effective swipe at the personal continuity within university law departments. "The wish, in itself understandable, of individual authors to disavow earlier statements they themselves no longer approve of must not lead to a diminishment of the impact of such statements *at the time*." The judges were unmistakably disinclined to temper their realistic assessment of the reality of officialdom in the Third Reich. "Hitler's ideal of all civil servants becoming convinced National Socialists in fact remained an ideal. The extent of dependence on National Socialist ideas may have differed widely within the different administrative branches, as well as—depending on the system's outer success—within individual periods of National Socialist rule. But Hitler nevertheless realized his intent of legally and effectively binding the *institution* of the civil service to the state in its entwinement with National Socialism. And for this reason the fate of the institution must be evaluated in relation to the collapse of the system."

With these words, the Constitutional Court powerfully confirmed its earlier decision regarding the demise of the civil service's status at the moment of capitulation. In a parallel decision given on the same day, the judges expressly declared the Federal High Court's submission of 20 May 1954—the source for that confirmation—as inadmissible.[81] But measured against the reaction to the "civil service judgment" delivered more than three years before, the "Gestapo judgment" and the overturn of the submission was now almost completely ignored by the legal community. In view of the well-advanced pensioning and reemployment of the "131ers," there was really no more cause for engaging in a fight with the constitutional guardians; and for the present, a self-critical reception within the civil service was unthinkable—particularly on the part of the jurists. The Constitutional Court remained a "voice in the wilderness."[82]

Nevertheless it would be inaccurate to describe the unprecedented conflict between that body and the Federal High Court as without theoretical and political consequences. The Constitutional Court's imperturbability in upholding the demise of German officialdom's legal status was by no means rash—not even in face of the fact that it had simultaneously upheld the "131" law's individual regulations. First, in confirming the law the court had also sanctioned important limits that had been placed on legal claims. Second—and more important—at least the judicial branch had now put it on record that the singular benefits accorded the "displaced" officials did not represent something to be expected, but were in actuality a generous act of integration on the part of the new state. In retrospect, against the backdrop of the massive presence of the officials' lobby on all political and juridical levels, the impression even arises of a division of labor—certainly not intended, but practically effective—between the Bundestag and the Constitutional Court: a court that many people actually believed they could discredit with the appellation "political."

In 1945 there had been individuals in Germany who looked forward to the permanent dissolution of the corrupted elite structures and a basic democratization of state and society. To many—particularly those who had been persecuted by the Nazis—it must have been very depressing a few years later to observe the return en masse of the civil servants. For hardly ten years after it was all over, the same people who, as it were, made Hitler's state were back at work, if not tidily pensioned. "All too many 131ers have already thoroughly triumphed over all too many 45s," wrote a copiously resigned Eugen Kogon in the fall of 1954.[83] But was this really the "victory of the men from yesterday"? In this often cited portion of a famous essay, Kogon diagnosed a "quiet, gradual, creeping, implacable return of that which was," suspecting it to be "the fate of the Federal Republic." But little attention has been given his explanation of the meaning of "that which was": it included "unimaginative, litigious old hands at democracy," along with haughty "nationalists" laying claim to their old privileges and inwardly unreformed "National Socialists"—individuals "who have adapted somewhat in reason but have remained entirely unchanged in feelings." Strikingly, a historical explanation both pointing past and canceling out the contemporary diagnosis seems concealed within this sweeping definition. What Kogon could not know in his time (and what, in distinction to a growing number of optimists, he did not dare hope) was that in the long run reason that had adapted would come to dominate feelings that had not—indeed would perhaps even vanquish such feelings.

Whether or not someone was ready in the mid-1950s to believe that over time the army of "men of the past" would become a mere troop of nostalgists for the good old Nazi days was a question not only of political standpoint but also of personal temperament and individual experience.[84] Many signals were open to different interpretations. But what was always clear and direct, imposing a special obligation on the civil servants, was the state's normative break with Nazism. By the same token, the fact that the "131ers" were forced to proceed with their "struggle" by strictly constitutional means, and to define their interests as economic and social in nature, must have had its effect. The feverish zeal with which they pushed from one amendment to the next (i.e., from election to election) was basically a symptom of an increasingly materialist orientation, and, connected with it, an increasing depoliticization. We can understand this as intensifying a "political indolence" that Theodor Eschenburg has pointed to as the old officialdom's reaction to the previous "enforced hyperengagement" with the Nazis.[85] Reinforced by the generosity of the "131" legislation, the tendency to turn from politics would increasingly take in those who, as a result of their temporary exclusion from the civil service, had maintained a strong dose of Nazi resentment.

Undoubtedly there is much accuracy in the widespread sense that a corps of civil servants duty-bound to the democratic state emerged at the end of a highly costly reintegration process.[86] Their oft-praised professional competence was not a postwar accomplishment and should not be chalked up as such. The price for this competence, however, was a complex of political-moral deficits, particularly glaring in the realm of justice and law enforcement. Without question, the virtually complete absorption of the "131ers," together with a deliberate retention of traditional officialdom, meant a quick increase in political stability. But it also meant a long-term loss of moral credibility. While the reality of this diminished moral status may not have weighed particularly heavy in everyday administrative life, elsewhere its effects were telling: frequently the political efforts at reparation for Nazi injustice in fact encountered certain "mental reservations" on the part of the responsible officials, and the prosecution of Nazi crimes was subject to the most egregious neglect.[87]

CHAPTER 4

The Amnesty Law of 1954

At the start of the 1950s, efforts to legally redress crimes of the Nazi period decreased drastically. In searching for an explanation for this fact, we should not overlook another—that alongside legal proceedings before the Allied military courts, West German courts initiated 17,000 preliminary investigations and obtained 5,500 convictions between 1945 and 1951.[1] Such statistics do not, however, explain the tempo and extent of the ensuing decrease: barely a decade later, facing an expiration of penalties for homicide and involuntary manslaughter (taking effect on 8 May 1960), the number of investigations would markedly rise—and this despite the long-standing amnesty or penalty expiration covering all lesser misdemeanors.

One of the reasons for this unmistakable collapse of punitive morale, so soon after the emergence of the Federal Republic, was the high degree of personal continuity in the judicial system; for the officials it favored, this continuity seemed to grant the system its political justification. As many delayed investigations, suspended proceedings, and extraordinarily mild judgments show, when it came to Nazi crimes quite a few prosecutors and judges were increasingly reluctant to duly apply the law. Undoubtedly they could feel their reluctance to be in harmony with the prevailing public and political mood, as manifest in the discussions concerning both the amnesty law of December 1949 and the Bundestag's recommendation to end denazification. The willingness to prosecute Nazi crimes was further weakened by the first early releases and pardons of Germans condemned as war criminals by Allied military courts, as well as by the loudly voiced demands for a general amnesty.[2] Finally, the passage of a second, expanded amnesty law in the summer of 1954 increased the political and social delegitimization of such prosecution once again. In that year, the number of new investigations plunged to a record low; the following year, merely twenty-one people were sentenced—a nadir that would be exceeded only once (in 1959) up through the 1960s.[3] The new law thus placed a check on prosecuting unpunished Nazi crimes extending considerably beyond its—in any event spacious—formal application framework. Its effect on judicial praxis resembled paralytic poison.

Even more than its predecessor of 1949, the 17 July 1954 "Law Concerning Release from Punishments and Fines and the Cancellation of Punitive and Fining Proceedings" contributed to a general "clearing up" of the judicial system; along with the regulations concerned with the penal effort to confront the Nazi period, a series of additional paragraphs addressed an assortment of current political needs. There was, for instance, a new version of a special amnesty, already agreed on by the Bundestag the year before but not passed because of the justice minister's constitutional reservations, meant to help save the necks of some Bonn officials: these had supplied news and documents to Robert Platow, editor of a political news service, and thus were being threatened with prison sentences for corruption and breach of confidence.[4] There was also an amnesty—not yet passable in 1949 because of the occupation authorities' law—for tax offenses, and one for infractions against rules governing trade between the occupation zones. Lastly, all those who had made themselves liable for punishment by asserting "facts touching on honor" were to receive mercy rather than justice—something of more than small interest to Adenauer himself, since in the last parliamentary elections he had falsely charged two SPD officials with having accepted contributions from the Eastern zone.[5]

These additions played a significant role in the second amnesty law. But its essence involved, as the new federal justice minister, Fritz Neumayer, put it, "making a break with crimes directly or indirectly connected with circumstances prevailing in a chaotic period."[6] When introducing the bill with these words to the Bundestag at the end of February 1954, Dehler's party colleague and successor was presumably unaware—at least in detail—of the long time span over which demands for the second "break with the past" had been presented to his predecessor, and of their motives and remarkable tenacity. He would also not have known the opinions on the matter held by Dehler, Secretary of State Walter Strauß, and the ministry officials over the preceding years. But this backdrop was of considerable importance for understanding the ensuing course of the deliberations—particularly since the Bundesrat had already rejected the government's bill, and the CSU had offered a different version far less generous to Nazi criminals.

As early as 1952, proposals to supplement the 1949 amnesty law with another amnesty had begun to make the rounds in Bonn's Ministry of Justice. At this point, the Constitutional Court had not even ruled on the legality of the first "federal amnesty." Still, the signing of both its basic text and its supplements in Bonn (26 May 1952) prompted new expectations from many quarters. Such expectations shared a single underlying premise: that the government could and was obliged to display more generosity than it had been allowed to until now as a result of Allied law.

One of the first people to express such views to Dehler was Robert Kempner—acting chief prosecutor for the Americans at Nuremberg, before the war a Prussian ministerial official and now head of a law office in Frankfurt am Main. Kempner had insisted that he did not wish "to get involved in the question of an amnesty for war criminals, since this was the concern of the American government."[7] At the same time, he pleaded for an amnestying of those receiving "relatively high" sentences from the occupation courts for minor property crimes and economic crimes—sentences that had not even been suspended in the case of first offenders. But Kempner also maintained that something needed to be done for individuals condemned or sentenced by German courts because of similar offenses "in connection with the postwar troubles." For in the meantime activities such as foreign exchange were no longer punishable—this while legal action for such foreign exchange dealings was facing members of the insolvent Jewish restitution bank in Frankfurt. The attorney thus considered an appropriate amnesty in order; it would, he predicted, not only promote "general public peace" but "also have a positive effect on the negotiations between Germany and Israel."[8]

In August 1952, Karl Marx, the editor of the *Allgemeine Wochenzeitung der Juden in Deutschland* (the "General Weekly for the Jews of Germany"), conveyed similar opinions—in any case without touching on the ongoing reparation negotiations—to President Theodor Heuss. Marx had good contacts with both Heuss and a number of cabinet members, including Dehler. He confidentially informed the chief of state about recent decisions of the Jewish Central Council aimed at an "inner purging" of Germany's Jewish community. But the "help of the federal government" was necessary—an amnesty was required for those people who, having had trouble coping after being released from concentration camps, found themselves on the "crooked path" for a while and feared being prosecuted for foreign exchange or black market activities, or even falsification of documents. Meant here, although (as with Kempner) not directly named, were Eastern European Jews—survivors of the "Final Solution" whom the Nazis had "evacuated" to the Reich's interior shortly before the war's end, or who had fled west after the war under American protection. Several thousand of these displaced persons had not emigrated to Israel or America but had constructed a new existence for themselves in West Germany, under precarious circumstances.[9] It was clear that others possessing false papers would profit from an amnesty for this particular group—Marx offered the concrete example of German "refugees from the east who should also in fact regain some peace." But, he indicated, in view of the "amnesty for war criminals being called for from all sides," one for the displaced persons was only just and proper.

A bitter polemic Marx handed over to Heuss went in the same direction. Scattered with reproaches of latent anti-Semitism and inequality of treatment, it was meant to demonstrate the deeply critical nature of the Jewish vantage point in face of both public support for war criminals and the judiciary's actions. At the end of the text, Marx noted his refusal to publish its contents: a reflection of his view of his own, rather controversial role, in a particularly bleak and painful period for German-Jewish relations, as that of well-meaning mediator.[10]

Marx's initiative was met by reserve in the Justice Ministry. For its own part, the Jewish Central Council appeared uninfluenced by the initiative as it proceeded with its own deliberations. At the end of September 1952, Marx was able to inform the president's office of an amnesty law draft drawn up by a jurist on the council. The draft relied heavily on the 1949 amnesty law.[11] Two months later, a printed version of the draft was officially delivered to the chancellor. In this context, the chairman of the Regional Conference of German Rabbis voiced the opinion that it was "an act of equity, that at the moment when the prison doors are being let open for those who committed crimes as representatives of power in the years of National Socialist rule, the people who then numbered among the oppressed and committed misdeeds after the war should also gain their freedom." And while Zwi Harry Levy's depiction of the situation facing many Jews "in the twilight of the postwar years" was similar to Marx's, Levy added an indirect reference to the activities of the war criminals' lobby: "no committee, no political party, no member of parliament, no organ of the press" had spoken up for the individuals he was discussing.[12]

THE AMNESTY LAW OF 1954

In that respect, nothing much would change in the future. Instead of understanding, what increased was annoyance, as irregularities in benefits to Jewish DPs became public knowledge. The Central Council's decision to seek an amnesty may have reflected both the concern—certainly not unfounded—that such reports might serve as an impetus to anti-Semitism and the general pressure now being placed on reparation policies.[13] The amnesty plans involved the remission of prison sentences extending to one year and fines of up to 10,000 German marks, the dismissal of pending cases for the period before 15 September 1952, and the amnestying of "actions taken on a political basis or in relation to economics or refugee matters" after 1 July 1948, regardless of the degree of punishment—this so long as such actions had their source in "circumstances of the occupation period, limitations resulting from currency and trading policies, and the involuntary resettlement of individuals." The plans also anticipated a second amnesty for "illegals," so long as they fulfilled the same conditions.

The reaction of the Justice Ministry to these plans was on the cool side. State Secretary Strauß saw no "pressing reasons" for an amnesty tailored to the needs of the DPs. The remark he attached to his answer to Rabbi Levy was in any case somewhat careless: "It seems very questionable whether a new comprehensive amnesty law can be justified after only three years."[14] Strauß was fully aware that an amnesty for economic crimes was being called for from very different quarters—and that Justice Minister Dehler was in no way strictly opposed to the idea.

During those weeks, Dehler was in fact being lobbied intensely by party colleague Ernst Achenbach, formerly head of the political section of the German embassy in occupied Paris, since 1946 a lawyer in Essen, in 1947–48 defense attorney at Nuremberg for both the I. G. Farben industrial cartel and the Nazi Foreign Ministry. In the spring of 1952 Achenbach announced the formation of a "Preparatory Committee for a General Amnesty."[15] Extending his influence rightward far beyond the FDP, he had gained the reputation as a prominent player in an amnesty movement aimed chiefly (though certainly not exclusively) at freeing war criminals condemned by the Allies. The committee's declared goal was the quickest possible "liquidation" of the legal prosecution of all Nazi crimes inside and outside Germany. In an ambitious memorandum, Werner Best—Reinhard Heydrich's chief deputy in the Reich Central Security Office, and eventually Deputy of the Reich in occupied Denmark—had developed a special argument favoring such a process.[16] Best knew Achenbach from Paris; after his release from Danish imprisonment he directed the appropriate matters in Achenbach's law offices. Best's argument centered on the figure of the "political crime," which he contrasted with common, privately motivated crimes carried out for personal advantage.[17] Intending to gain recognition for this apparently compelling distinction, Achenbach mobilized all the political and legal means at his disposal through his qualities as lawyer, Landtag delegate, and chairman of the FDP's Committee on Foreign Affairs. In his endeavor, he was backed up by corporate funds, and he was certainly also motivated by his own complicity in the deportation of France's Jews.[18]

One step in the endeavor was the late autumn 1952 "proposal" that the justice minister try to induce "restraint" regarding Nazi crimes on the part of the legal administrations of the Länder, it being "illogical and politically unwise" to see through trials in West Germany while simultaneously requesting mercy from the Allies for Germans condemned as war criminals.[19] Using carefully coached language, Dehler turned down Achenbach's demand, while making clear his readiness to discuss other possibilities for amnesty.[20] To no small degree, concern over the continued stability of the FDP seems to have informed this ambivalent response. More specifically, Achenbach operated in the knowledge of having the party's large, wealthy North Rhine-Westphalian chapter behind him—including its chairman, Friedrich Middelhauve, who was preparing to lead the FDP into a crucial test of cohesion at the pending party conference in Ems through a right-wing nationalist "German program."[21]

In fittingly self-assured style, Achenbach confronted the justice minister in December 1952 with the draft of a "Law for Amendment of the Law Granting Exemption from Punishment of 31 December 1949." This included a proposed new version of the ninth paragraph in the old amnesty, now widened to benefit " 'economic offenders' involved in East-West trade." As Achenbach explained it, in the export crisis of 1950, his own industrial friends from the Ruhr had "acted entirely in the interests of the West German economy" when they organized "business toward the east" in defiance of occupation regulations. Following the "reacquisition of German sovereignty," punishment of deeds "that damaged no German interests" had to be "terminated." But, Achenbach indicated, the law's substantiation needed to "disregard the politically inappropriate fact that to a large extent occupation law did not correspond to German interests." Instead it was to stress the confusing variety of regulations and the "frequent vacillations in administrative praxis."

At the same time, the draft proposed a second amnesty for the "illegals." To be sure, here as well the striking parallelism with the wishes of the Jewish Central Council ended with the proposal's substantiation: it contained a flat declaration that hardly anyone could take advantage of the first amnesty since "almost everyone had taken on a false name to evade being handed over to foreign states"—*fremde Staaten*—"on account of alleged war crimes." As the proposal had it, such a risk constituted an "emergency" in the juridical sense, which "excused the avoidance of being handed over for the commission of punishable deeds." Since the risk was no longer present, an additional amnesty in this domain would spare the judiciary "unnecessary work."[22]

As the responsible departmental minister, Dehler found it impossible to simply swallow such brazen reasoning. This was particularly the case since the proposals were clearly the tip of an iceberg of demands that his party's right wing had made ready. Dehler thus simply explained that he was already in contact with the Ministry of Economics regarding an amnesty for interzonal trade. However, when it came to an amnesty for "illegals," caution was called for: on the one hand, until ratification of the General Treaty governing relations between West Germany and the Allies, "intervention by the occupying powers" remained a possibility. But on the other hand, it was important to keep in mind "that many of the persons concerned are being sought from the German side on criminal grounds."[23]

In Essen, Best and Achenbach were not impressed by this advice. Although with severely damaged standing as a result of the Naumann affair, Achenbach did not refrain from reiterating the amnesty demands in a communication of 20 March 1953.[24] A day earlier, the Bundestag had ratified the treaties of Bonn and Paris (to Achenbach's annoyance, with only one dissenting vote from the FDP—that of Karl Georg Pfleiderer). Ghostwriter Best had never formulated his juridical motif with as much simplicity and sweep as in this renewed effort to move Dehler. The desired law should furnish amnesty for all "past crimes" that "were not committed for personal motives"; in other words, de facto it should furnish the general amnesty that was desired—and that neither Best nor Achenbach could seriously consider likely to receive the approval of the chancellor and his party. Nevertheless, with a view to the Bundestag elections in the fall, they declared the demand for such a law as in itself helpful. Namely, its "determined champions" could be assured of the sympathy of "hundreds of thousands of Germans," since "the circle of those in the populace sympathetic with an amnesty" was much larger than the number of those "directly and indirectly affected by the political penal proceedings." For this reason, Best and Achenbach explained, Dehler should have an appropriate draft prepared for discussion "without delay." In addition, the two jurists demanded a reinstatement of the amnesties and related laws enacted by the Nazis to benefit their violent functionaries and supporters and revoked by the occupying powers.[25]

Naturally Dehler's officials recognized the scope of the proposals. But their reference to the difficulty of clearly demarcating the concept of "political crime" (already present in Best's earlier memorandum) suppressed an acknowledgment that it was precisely this interpretive maneuvering room for which the former second in command in the Reich Central Security Office was aiming: with a suitable interpretation, every crime committed in service or uniform could then be defined as "political," as well as every ideologically motivated deed. The responsible Justice Ministry official left this salient objection unmentioned. Instead, clearly bent on a "constructive" assessment of the submission, he relativized his own finding that numerous crimes were "simply not worthy of amnesty" with a purely utilitarian argument: "Today we have rightfully ascertained that the sentencing of war criminals through foreigners was a mistake, since they could not be sufficiently familiar with German circumstances; but an amnestying of the relatively few criminal proceedings that have been seen through, as compared with the countless number of crimes that were committed, would necessarily awaken the impression abroad that such a reasoning process on the German side springs, in reality, from no true sense of justice."[26]

At least along official paths, neither Achenbach nor his political alter ego in the amnesty question, Werner Best, were informed of such reflections. Over recent days, the ties between the Essen law offices and the Bonn ministry had become frayed. Already in 1953, following the spectacular arrest of the squad of Nazi functionaries surrounding Werner Naumann and Achenbach's emergence as Naumann's defense attorney, State Secretary Strauß issued an internal recommendation to keep substantial distance from Best.[27] Since then it had become increasingly clear that Achenbach himself was part of the old Nazi coterie, to which he had opened the doors of the FDP in the Rhine and Ruhr regions. Hardly anyone was more in the know concerning this matter than Thomas Dehler. For not only did the justice minister have information at his disposal distributed to the cabinet, but also as head of an internal party three-man commission he had collected many facts demonstrating the distressing extent of Nazi infiltration of the FDP chapters in North Rhine-Westphalia and Lower Saxony.[28] By nature Dehler was no principled opponent of "reintegrating" former party members; nevertheless he now emerged as a bitter critic of the above-mentioned Friedrich Middelhauve, whom he blamed exclusively for Achenbach's rise to prominence and the FDP's entanglement in the Naumann affair. In his concluding statement as commission head, Dehler laid out an ultimatum for Middelhauve's withdrawal from all party functions, incontrovertibly declaring that "Herr Dr. Achenbach never was one of us and is not so now."[29]

Still, the basic conflict within the FDP was not to be swept away with verbal displays of power and wishful thinking. In practice, Dehler, the party's weak chairman Blücher, the traditional liberals from the southwest, and the left-leaning liberals from Hamburg and Berlin were rather helpless—at least for now—in the face of the party's right wing and its concept of a "national gathering." Achenbach was not booted out of the party, and Middelhauve did not give up his functions. Achenbach did have to abandon the chairmanship of the Committee on Foreign Policy, a source of relief for Blücher in view of the lawyer's stubborn critique of the treaties with the Western powers.[30]

In contrast to the palliative nature of the official party line, behind party doors Dehler continued to refer to the dramatic developments along the Ruhr and Rhine in terms of "subversion." Remarkably, the developments appear to have had no substantive influence on the justice minister's policies regarding amnesty—at least not in the sense of any fresh distance from the efforts to amnesty Nazi perpetrators. There were certainly obvious reasons to view such efforts as sending the wrong signals: Inside West Germany (and naturally inside the FDP in particular), a second amnesty law a few months before the Bundestag elections would have inevitably offered heart to the "onetimes"—at present, Adenauer in particular seemed no longer completely convinced of their lasting insignificance.[31] Outside in the West, an amnesty would furnish new evidence to those skeptics doggedly searching for signs of "renazification" and opposing both a General Treaty and a European Defense Community on the grounds of German untrustworthiness.

But in the amnesty question as elsewhere, personal convictions were evidently more important than such overriding political factors for the stubborn and impulsive Dehler. And Dehler was convinced that the special amnesty devised for those officials implicated in the Platow affair—initiated in December 1952 by an all-party coalition, and since then being considered by the Bundestag's Legal Committee—was incompatible with the principle of equality inscribed in the Basic Law. Nevertheless, following the Constitutional Court's confirmation of the federal government's right to legislate amnesties on 22 April 1953, the parties proceeded to accelerate their plans for the special amnesty, against the minister's advice. What emerged as a response in the Justice Ministry was the "plan" to incorporate the Platow amnesty into a general amnesty law, thus amnestying "certain offenses from the National Socialist period."[32] A hastily prepared referee's draft referred to a general halving of the penalties for Nazi crimes committed in a state of "extraordinary mental conflict" or out of a "falsely understood sense of duty."[33] It is difficult to say whether Dehler himself considered the proposal well founded. Possibly, he thought of it as bait for luring the parliamentarians away from their special law. His offer in any event came too late: before the cabinet could be confronted with the draft, the Legal Committee had adopted the draft of a law focusing entirely on one offense—the unauthorized distribution of official documents.[34] While Dehler was adamant in his opposition to the "lex Platow," he could not stop the Bundestag from passing the bill on 18 June 1953 and then rolling over the Bundesrat's objections in July.[35] It was now clear that a second general amnesty law would not be passed in the first legislative period.

Dehler's subsequent steps are not entirely easy to understand. It would seem that stubbornness and wounded pride played a substantial role in his decision to simply not sign the new law. Be this as it may, a concern that the "lex Platow" would not survive the Constitutional Court's scrutiny appears *not* to have been his central motive. Possibly he was more concerned that the Platow amnesty would ruin the chances for speedily passing an amendment of the 1949 amnesty law. At any rate, this latter consideration would definitely endow his refusal to sign the law with a deeper meaning. For, while generating no great affection on the chancellor's part, the obstinacy with which Dehler blocked this law approved by parliament rendered the solution he was pointing to—passage of a second, general amnesty at the start of the next legislative period—more plausible from week to week.[36]

Two days after the 6 September 1953 elections to the Bundestag, Dehler distributed a lapidary press release: "The federal minister of justice is preparing the draft of a law for general exemption from punishment."[37] This amounted to announcing a momentous commitment that at best had been only touched on in the morning cabinet meeting: the ministers had basically lent their ears and homage to Adenauer, towering over everyone by virtue of his electoral victory.[38] For weeks, Dehler had been skeptical regarding his chances of serving in a new government; most likely he now considered the chances as next to nil.[39] It is true that as the only cabinet member from the—now badly mauled—FDP, he could lay claim to having maintained his electoral profile in face of Adenauer. But the liberal Franconian had also become embroiled in a quarrel with the Würzburg bishop Julius Döpfner—something the Catholic conservatives knew how to use against him. Behind the scenes, Dehler's colleagues Theodor Heuss and Hermann Höpker-Aschoff were pressing for his replacement.[40] But even under such circumstances, publicly announcing an amnesty law was an extremely tricky matter, particularly since Dehler himself was convinced that a new draft was needed—and that the draft needed to be discussed and agreed upon by the ministers of justice of the Länder.[41] This meant the country would have to endure many months before possible passage of the law—months in which the criminal justice system would come under growing pressure as a result of awakened expectations.[42]

Despite all lack of color, Dehler's eventual successor Fritz Neumayer had adhered to his part colleague's position in the Platow amnesty issue, himself refusing to sign the law. When Dehler finally handed his ministry over to Neumayer on 22 October 1953, the preliminary work had in fact advanced substantially.[43] Barely two weeks after the elections and in the course of the new government's formation, the Justice Ministry arranged a departmental conference from which ideas emerged that were fraught with consequences for the amnestying of Nazi crimes. Prompted by some probing remarks on the part of Josef Schafheutle (conference chairman and head of the ministry's Criminal Justice Division), Max Güde, a former District Court judge, now head of the Political Division of the Federal Public Prosecutor's office, and the office's deputy at the conference, repeatedly raised the theme of *Befehlsnotstand*—of having acted under binding orders. From the perspective of the appeals instance, Güde explained, an amnesty in such cases was "expedient." For the courts were inclined to use new findings of fact to circumvent principles laid down by the Federal Court of Justice, in a series of decisions since 1950, whose effect had been to limit the possibility of assuming the presence of such binding orders.[44] Güde did express considerable skepticism regarding a general amnesty covering the postwar period, but he emphatically recommended a "clearing up" of criminal proceedings when it came to two "case complexes": so-called crimes of denunciation and summary court-martial judgments, both these complexes lying outside the legal system's purview.[45]

Güde considered incorporation of the appropriate regulations into the new amnesty law to be a pressing matter. Back in Karlsruhe he had a variety of suggested formulas telexed to Bonn's ministerial officials. With some closer consideration Güde believed he had come up with a definition making possible an incorporation, not of the "case-complex" of denunciations (he had in fact fallen victim to the process in 1933), but of binding orders: the limits to those meriting amnesty seemed to lie with deeds committed out of cruelty or base intention, deeds including murder. As an alternative he suggested a limitation to deeds not punishable by more than three years' imprisonment. Finally, he raised the possibility of limiting the historical time span for which the judge would have discretion to uncover and amnesty crimes on account of "the collapse of state order because of a situation of conflict, and especially because of a command."[46]

Without naming a concrete time span, Güde had managed with his last alternative, as it were incidentally, to offer a concept pointing the way forward. It would quickly offer Dehler's referees a way out of an impasse: under Best's terminological spell, they had until now been struggling to define the real meaning of a "political deed," thus persistently arriving at the very brink of a general amnesty.[47] The extent of the impasse is apparent in the discussion of the amnesty plans—taking place on the same day Güde cabled his suggestions to Bonn—with representatives of the judicial administrations of the Länder. In presenting the problem of binding orders, the officials from the Justice Ministry used Güde's arguments without being aware of his own suggestions for a solution. Most of their Länder colleagues were strongly inclined to tackling the problem seriously; but after a long debate they concluded it could be dealt with only in the framework of an amnesty law at the risk of abetting "heinous deeds." The parties thus agreed on a vague recommendation: "in suitable cases magnanimously to withdraw the state's appeal in agreement with the Chief Federal Public Prosecutor." Only the representative from Berlin—an all-party government headed by Ernst Reuter had a few days to go before relinquishing power—expressed categorical rejection of any amnesty in this domain. He explained that in the Berlin Senate there was an "aversion ... to covering violent National Socialist acts with a cloak of love."[48]

The Justice Ministry received the suggestions from Karlsruhe with more enthusiasm than it did the reservations from Berlin. The suggestions were already taken up in the next provisional referee's draft.[49] This could no longer have been surprising, the matter lying as it did in the hands of officials who were politically highly motivated—and at times highly incriminated. One of these officials, Ministerial Advisor Ernst Kanter, had not simply read Werner Best's memorandum but had enjoyed his personal trust since his own time as chief justice for the Wehrmacht in Denmark.[50] Another official deemed it in order to "finally dispense with" cases of *Befehlsnotstand* on account of "the mood abroad": "precisely the constantly repeated unfolding of the individual proceedings," he explained, gave "ever new opportunities to discuss the problems connected with Nazi rule."[51]

Apparently not influenced by the change at the head of their ministry, the responsible officials in the Criminal Justice Division—almost without exception former members of the Reich Ministry of Justice, military judges, or special judges—moved forward with the particulars of the law draft.[52] They brought Güde's ideas together in a new paragraph, entitled "Deeds Committed During the State's Collapse," which declared an amnesty for both sentences up to three years and fines for acts "that the perpetrator committed between 1 October 1944 and 31 July 1945 under the influence of the extraordinary circumstances prevalent in the state's collapse, in a state of real or imagined conflict of duty characterized by the belief that he had to either obey an order or fulfill an official or legal duty." The amnesty was also meant to cover expected future punishments within the same limits; the only excluded offenders were those who had "unconscionably leaped over their higher legal duty."[53]

In view of this massive widening of the law draft's past-political dimension, the ministerial officials considered it advisable to arrange additional confidential preliminary discussions with representatives of both the other governmental departments and the legal administrations of the Länder. Having gotten wind of a supplementation project aimed at the Nazi period, the German Bar Association's criminal law committee had already issued a statement to the effect that "*regardless* of the arrangement and wording of the stipulation," an offer of amnesty in this sense was "appropriate under all circumstances," and was "urgently approved."[54] But still, a careful integration of the official experts and a precise test of their reactions to the unusual formulation were highly advisable, if only for one reason: in the framework of a federal administration that had meanwhile become consolidated, haphazard procedures such as those still at work with the first amnesty law were not sure of success.

In fact, the Justice Ministry found itself confronted with substantial objections in the second departmental meeting. These objections, however, did not mainly involve the new suggestion to amnesty sentences up to three years for deeds committed during Germany's collapse. Rather, they focused on the proposed general amnesty for sentences up to three months—a proposal located outside the past-political context. Federal High Court president Eberhard Rotberg subjected the draft to severe scrutiny: in view of the many amnesties and laws to end denazification passed over recent years, it was to be feared that an additional amnesty law would cause considerable harm to the general perception of the law; in addition, the fact that the project began at the start of a new legislative period would suggest a "portentous rhythm"—and all this "on account of the difficulties of the Platow matter." Rotberg considered the general amnesty for sentences up to three months especially dubious, and amnesty for economic crimes as unnecessary or at least replaceable with case-by-case pardons. The only aspects of the draft he favored were the amnesty in currency exchange matters—and the paragraph dealing with the German collapse, which he even found temporally and substantially too restrictive.

Public Prosecutor Güde basically agreed with Justice Rotberg. Quite unsurprisingly, he shared Rotberg's approval of the "collapse" paragraph, while likewise considering it "more auspicious to completely dispense with the general amnesty and simply clear up the special complexes." The departmental representatives also approved the "collapse" paragraph. The emissary from the office of Theodore Blank (later to be defense secretary) pointedly praised the idea for its potential to "favorably influence" the populace "in the question of rearmament" through the state's demonstration of "generosity." In order to ensure that the "clearing up" was "generous," it was advisable, he explained, to even extend the amnesty limits to five years—while also ensuring that particularly serious cases not benefit from the process. A representative of the Foreign Ministry then spoke up against this suggestion: in "really serious cases" it was necessary to think about other countries and keep in mind that such an extension might have a negative influence on the willingness to release war criminals imprisoned abroad.[55]

The political effect of the "collapse" paragraph abroad was also discussed at the second meeting with the judicial administrations for the Länder on 24 November 1953. In this venue, ministerial director Schafheutle once more chose to nourish the legend of a tight spot imposed by the press on a helpless Federal Justice Ministry. Beyond this, he attempted to play down the real role of his ministry in the amnesty plans, instead favoring that of broker for diverging desires and interests, hovering, as it were, above party politics. But running across party lines, most of the Länder representatives were unimpressed by such putative modesty, speaking out against the "collapse" paragraph. To no small degree, their uneasiness was due to the amnesty's temporal limits, whose pragmatic basis was now clarified by Schafheutle for the first time: any proximity to the "events of 20 July 1944" had to be avoided, since this might end up bestowing amnesty on individuals who helped crush the act of resistance.[56]

At the same time that the Länder representatives were critically scrutinizing the law draft, State Secretary Walter Strauß—remaining with Justice Minister Neumayer as watchdog from the Union's ranks—informed the cabinet of his intent to present a draft of the completed law at the next session (1 December 1953). Since the Platow amnesty was still hovering in the air, there was considerable pressure for action; Neumayer's declared goal was to persuade the Bundesrat to adapt a formal position before Christmas.[57] In the face of principled objections by the minister for special affairs, Franz Josef Strauß, Neumayer did have the draft approved at the cabinet session.[58] But the haste would take its revenge. Since there had been no time to react in any fashion to objections from the representatives, their raising the objections once again in the Legal Committee of the Bundesrat became inevitable.[59] On 18 December 1953, the Bundesrat provisionally turned down the draft as "questionable from the view of legal policy and dangerous from that of criminal policy"; at the same time it postulated the duty to obtain the Bundesrat's consent.[60]

At this session, State Secretary Strauß reached the limits of what a legal policy maker can say without unsettling the idea of law and justice. In defending the "collapse" paragraph, he declared that he could not "help feeling that many events from that time cannot be mastered with standards belonging to a stable order, that time has a healing effect, and that it is not useful for the administration of justice to endlessly continue such proceedings."[61] Unsuccessful despite this solemn legal-political affidavit, Strauß tried to push aside the Bundesrat's rejection in the next cabinet session with the comment that it had simply resulted from "unfortunate circumstances." Approving the suggested reply to the Bundesrat, the cabinet maintained its support of the law draft without any changes.[62]

The tenor of the government's reception of the Bundesrat's objections repeated itself in the substantiation with which Justice Minister Neumayer presented the draft to the Bundestag at the end of February 1954.[63] The guiding maxim seems to have developed into calling as little attention as possible to the matter. As compared to Strauß's approach before the Bundesrat and the draft of a talk that was laid aside, the minister's actual words were markedly restrained.[64] Most telling of all in this respect was his omission of any remarks on the "collapse" paragraph—part of his general effort to give an impression that the law was intended as "merely an amendment to the old amnesty law," filling in some "gaps" that had been commonly acknowledged for years. With obvious calculation, Neumayer played down the enormous past-political significance of the amnesty plans through reminders of the "acquisition of so-called black [i.e., illegal] coal in the time of the Korea crisis in the winters of 1950–51 and 1951–52" (because of the changed economic situation, criminally prosecuting such activity was now in fact undesirable). "All in all," the minister indicated in an astonishing gesture of laissez-aller, "the means at the criminal justice system's disposal would not offer a possibility of realizing the goal of a total cleaning up"—Gesamtbereinigung—"of the situation prevailing in the war and the postwar period." In reality, what was being proposed was an abandonment of any attempt at legal redress in some crucial realms.

Otto-Heinrich Greve commented on the law draft on behalf of the SPD. He cast clear light on this tendency, leaving no doubt that the planned "collapse" paragraph went too far for the Social Democrats. In individual cases, placing mercy before justice was certainly appropriate, "but not every last person who committed an offense in this period and now can look forward to no more than three years' imprisonment should be granted amnesty." Considerable mistrust of the judiciary was not the least of the reasons raised by Greve—himself a lawyer—in rejecting so broad an amnesty: "I would like to see the judge who is then not in the position of being able to fit everything he considers worth amnestying into the framework of three years' imprisonment." Greve was the first and only speaker willing to concretely name the deeds that would fall within the amnesty: "the killing and abuse of prisoners of war, members of East European nations, Jews, the killing of soldiers and civilians, unlawful summary courts martial, etc."[65]

An alternative draft prepared by the CSU in connection with Franz Josef Strauß's remarks in the cabinet made one thing clear: in the Union as well, enthusiasm regarding amnesty for crimes committed during the "collapse" period was not unanimous.[66] The alternative draft did call for the general amnesty now omitted from the government draft; through its limit of three months of imprisonment, such amnesty was meant to replace a variety of special amnesties. But at the same time, the alternative got rid of the "collapse" paragraph, offering no replacement. Similarly to the SPD, CSU delegate Hermann Höcherl recommended mercy when there was doubt; at the same time, the principle of the "judicial clarification" of serious crimes committed in the war's final months was not to be abandoned. Since meanwhile "distinctive, well-grounded high-court adjudication" was present in this domain, doing so was in any case unnecessary.[67]

Höcherl was touching on the muddle being generated around the concept of "binding orders"—a concept that would be evoked repeatedly to both support and attack the "collapse" paragraph in further, intensive discussions of the law by the Bundestag's Legal Committee. Within this venue, State Secretary of Justice Strauß would reveal himself as an ardent defender of a specific amnesty for deeds committed during the "collapse." Falsely presenting himself as the "originator of the idea" of this amnesty and spurred forward by a feeling of intellectual superiority, Strauß struggled to demonstrate his special technical competence (this disregarding the Justice Minister's presence). "Already very early," he indicated—in 1951–52, in connection with support for the war criminals sentenced abroad—he had realized "that these things cannot be completely solved by subsumption to legal norms." Later, he asserted, the "gentlemen in the Federal Public Prosecutor's office and the Federal High Court" confirmed his belief "that these acts committed out of the confusion of the time, out of the terror inflicted on the perpetrators by their superior instances, are simply no longer subsumable to normal legal measures." For this reason, a dispensation from punishment "attempting to focus" on the problem of "conflict of duty, and indeed both real, objective conflict of duty and the putative conflict of duty present more in the perpetrator's subjective imagination," had now become a "central element of the entire bill." There was no desire, Strauß declared, to offer amnesty for "deeds directly committed by National Socialists" (sic), "although some National Socialists will certainly fall under it"—but rather for actions "that had been committed on behest of the National Socialist state leadership in the execution of orders." Criminal Justice Division chief Schafheutle seconded State Secretary Strauß's remarks; many examples over recent years showed that high-court adjudication concerning binding orders and errors regarding prohibition had not been sufficient to prevent "the files wandering back and forth for years between the lower courts and the Federal High Court."[68]

When it came to opposing this thesis in the Legal Committee, SPD delegate Greve had to shoulder the chief burden once again. (He did receive support from the Bundesrat representative, who conveyed the states' reservations.) On the basis of precise knowledge of the situation in Lower Saxony, Greve explained, he was aware that difficulties in passing sentence emerged with very few Nazi crimes. But it was precisely such cases, he argued, that ought not be amnestied, since a large portion of the offenders had not suffered from conflict of duty, but rather "claimed the deed as their own." This was the case, for instance, with Gauleiters, Kreisleiters, and other Nazi party officials. Greve saw the case of "soldiers from the ranks, noncommissioned officers, and officers ... who disregarding the political system believed in the need to obey an order" as different. But at all events it had to be certain "that the regulation does not serve primarily as a way of furnishing former National Socialists with impunity." Rather, Greve maintained, it needed to be applied to persons who "at an earlier time inwardly professed allegiance to National Socialism but later turned from it" and who at the time of the deed found themselves in a "genuine conflict of duty." Greve declared himself ready to help shape the "collapse" paragraph in this direction; with the FDP's representatives now signaling their interest in a solution acceptable to all the parliamentary factions, an agreement emerged to give the paragraph one more try.

At the beginning of April, the Legal Committee spent almost an entire session on this problem alone.[69] While the SPD delegates did stress somewhat different matters than, for example, Hans-Joachim von

Merkatz of the German Party, the results of the remarkably focused discussion demonstrated how little room for definitional maneuver actually existed, as long as either the temporal or sentencing framework could not be altered. The first option, however, was out of the question (and thus not even raised) because setting back the amnesty's starting point would have meant covering still far more genuine Nazi crimes than was the case for the period of October 1944 onward, crimes connected to the "Final Solution" and Mobile Killing Unit (*Einsatz* group and *Einsatz* squad) murders, and to the crushing of the July 20 plot. On the other hand, narrowing the sentencing framework—an idea the Social Democrats were flirting with—would have meant leaving out many more serious crimes that the SPD itself had no objections to amnestying, so long as they were committed by, as Greve put it, "little people," from whom "the burden of a possible 'they've in fact made themselves guilty' ought to be removed."

There was also a startling strong consensus that the time had indeed passed for continued legal confrontation with the violence and terror of Nazi Germany's final phase. Caught up by the general mood, the SPD's Adolf Arndt—himself deeply burdened by the weight of so many inadequate judgments he had been collecting for years in a "horror cabinet"—let slip the following observation: it was "in any case bad that ten years after the fact, there is a desire to pronounce judgment without any capacity to reconstruct the circumstances and mentality of the time."

The possibilities for an "improvement" of the draft were thus somewhat limited. In the end, they involved the effort—pursued by the Social Democrats with greater intensity than the ruling parties—to keep the judges' room for discretion as narrow as possible. But all the objective and subjective conditions that theoretically could be—and sometimes actually were—tied to amnesty (binding orders, capacity for judgment of the offender, his "fear, consternation, or confusion") did not change the basic situation. When it came to those deeds that had not yet been decided on, the prosecutors and judges retained enormous practical leeway. For an exact determination of a deed's circumstances and motives would have required precisely the proceedings that the new amnesty law was going to make impossible.

The Legal Committee naturally could not and did not wish to tamper with the principle of equal treatment according to which every amnesty covered not only sentences that had already been passed but also sentences that were expected to come. The version of the "collapse" paragraph the committee finally adopted—unanimously with three abstentions—was identical with that passed by the Bundestag: "for crimes committed under the influence of the collapse's extraordinary circumstances in the period between 1 October 1944 and 31 July 1945, in compliance with an official or legal duty, especially a command, amnesty will be granted extending beyond paragraphs 2 and 3, so long as the offender could not have been expected to abstain from the crime, and so long as no heavier punishment than incarceration for up to three years plus fine, alone or together, has been legally imposed or is expected to be so at the time of the law's effective date."

In the course of the Bundestag's second and third debates over the amnesty law on 18 June 1954, it became obvious that now as before, an amnesty for "deeds committed during the collapse"—at Adolf Arndt's behest, the reference to the "state" had been removed)—represented the touchiest point of the entire project.[70] In this respect Justice Minister Neumayer was very accurate in observing that the "collapse" paragraph had received "more precise and thorough" scrutiny than any other. Meanwhile the SPD had in fact submitted a proposal for a revision involving a reduction of the sentencing framework from three years to one year; during the debate, Hannsheinz Bauer, one of the party's speakers, underscored the proposal with a speech that was both full of facts and forceful.

Using a series of judgments handed down for Nazi crimes as his examples, Bauer presented the plenum with the full dimensions the amnesty would take on, should the sentencing framework not be narrowed. The cause for this was the ubiquitously manifest mildness of the judges, in connection with the "collapse" paragraph's expressly stated amnestying of crimes of homicide, this contrasting with all other provisions of the proposed law. With a sentencing framework of three years, it could be assumed that, for instance, the murder of the American-appointed mayor of Aachen by an SS squad at the end of March 1945 would be amnestied; likewise with the crimes committed by the summary courts that left a bloody trail across southern Germany in the spring.[71] In these cases, sentences were handed down of two and a half and three years, respectively. Cases of the lynching of American pilots caught after parachuting into the Reich in 1944–45 were now receiving sentences of a year in jail—thus even falling inside the modified framework the SPD was suggesting. "Despite all will to mildness," Bauer declared, "and the wish we also share to gradually draw a line under the sad events of an uncanny era," the Social Democrats nevertheless thought it important "to leave untampered certain absolute standards in legal theory."

Following this impressive appeal, a majority of delegates voted, surprisingly, for the opposition's proposed changes. But this was the result of a strategic failure in the government's camp and had no lasting significance. In the third debate that followed immediately, the CDU-CSU, All-German Block-Union of Expellees and Victims of Injustice, and the German Party factions voted together for a restoration of the "collapse" paragraph's original version. Some left-leaning FDP liberals did support the Social Democrats, but most of that party's delegates now duly displayed their faith in their justice minister's insistence that any "abuse" of the three years' amnesty had been prevented through the general absence of amnesty for acts "motivated by greed or for which the manner or grounds of execution reveals a base intention."[72]

While in its final form, the second amnesty law contained more than thirty paragraphs, the Bundestag's final vote again made clear that in the end the "collapse" paragraph alone produced dissent. Most Social Democrats, along with some Free Democrats and a single CDU delegate, stuck with their "no" or abstained from voting; most members of the Union voted "yes." One distinguishing characteristic of the first legislative period had been the great coalition in political issues having to do with the Nazi past. The coalition was now beginning to crumble.

The amnesty finale had, however, one more prolongation. The Bundesrat's appeal to the Mediation Committee forced a fresh round of work on the law. This offered new room for maneuver to the few Social Democrats who had sided with the government—including, it is true, both party head Erich Ollenhauer and his deputy, Wilhelm Mellies.[73] While the provisions of the law with past-political relevance remained unchanged, the SPD coalition finally signaled its approval.[74] Adolf Arndt presented the argument for the party's gradual relenting with strong pathos and weak substance: it was "simply no longer tolerable, here and today, for the reputation of the legislative bodies, the credibility of democracy, an orderly judicial system, and not least law itself, to further prolong passage of this law."

Dissatisfaction with the tedious proceedings had in fact spilled beyond the circle of experts. Even before the new complication, *Der Spiegel* had for example observed that "the indecisiveness of the Bonn parliament has already blocked the Federal Republic's entire criminal justice system for over half a year. On the one hand, in many proceedings legal steps have been taken to block a legal decision before passage of the amnesty; on the other hand, in many cases the courts have failed to start the main hearing out of an awareness they would be covered by the amnesty even before their conclusion."[75] The government was clearly responsible for this situation—especially former Justice Minister Dehler, with his public announcements of an amnesty—and not the opposition. Arndt, however, did not broach the subject, instead expressly claiming "coresponsibility for the law" as his parliamentary faction's due. True, the jurist did maintain his "grave reservations" regarding the amnesty law, but the outcome of such reservations was an appeal to the courts "to weigh, precisely in these cases, the eligibility for amnesty with special care and all deliberation, with a view to the victims of these crimes." Most members of the SPD coalition appeared satisfied with this admonishment to justice, pronounced by a leading legal policy maker; in any event virtually all of them now also favored the law. The records show only one abstention and three opposing votes in the entire Bundestag.

The extraordinary past-political import of the amnesty law passed on 17 July 1954 lay in the above-depicted, very far-reaching amnesty for "deeds committed during the collapse" (it would henceforth be known as paragraph 6). But the law did contain other provisions that would affect the confrontation with the Nazi period:

• Paragraph 3 ("Crimes Committed from Necessity") offered amnesty to the offender with no previous convictions in the case of acts committed "as a result of wartime or postwar events, in an emergency situation not due to his own fault," when a sentence not higher than a year's imprisonment had been passed or was expected. In a way, this meant a half year's extension of the amnesty framework over the 1949 amnesty law, though clearly specified in terms of both time and substance.

• Paragraph 7 ("Hiding One's Civil Status") introduced the renewed amnesty for "illegals" demanded from many quarters. Drawing on the law of 1949, persons living under a false name were once more offered a chance "to voluntarily report untrue information regarding personal circumstances" before the end of 1954 without incurring legal consequences; "crimes that had been committed to hide one's civil status on political grounds" but that were not disclosed by the offender himself were also amnestied, so long as no more than a three-year sentence had been passed or was expected. But other than paragraph 6, all the provisions of exclusion, including those for crimes of homicide, remained in play here.

• Paragraph 20.2 eradicated the record of convictions by the *Spruchgerichte,* as long as the sentence was no more than five years. De facto, this meant the erasure from the books of virtually all the convictions resulting from membership in one of the Nazi organizations declared criminal at Nuremberg.[76] But since these courts, and along with them condemnations on account of "organizational crime," had existed only in the British zone, the German specialists considered this erasure as serving "simple justice."[77]

The symbolism was certainly more palpable with this last provision of the second amnesty law than with any other; whoever wished to could indeed view it as a "liquidation" of "occupation injustice" and a further political-moral devaluation of "foreign" efforts at political purging. Still, in a fundamental manner the law's general past-political meaning lay in the confirmation of collective attitudes and expectations promoting the termination of much more than simply the legal confrontation with Nazi crime. This point should not be lost in considering the amnesty statistics (which at the time were withheld from public access).

According to the data of the justice authorities of the Länder, a total of approximately 400,000 persons benefited from the amnesty law—of these, all but a few thousand from the general amnesty for sentences extending to three months' imprisonment (paragraph 2).[78] It was hardly possible for many of these cases to involve Nazi crimes, since sentences extending to six months had already been amnestied in 1949. The small group of persons whose amnesty was covered by one or another of the law's remaining provisions included those accused or sentenced because of interzone transactions or in the context of the Platow affair. The number of amnestied Nazi criminals was thus relatively small. Amnesty for deeds committed during the "collapse" (paragraph 6) also played a negligible statistical role: in the first year of the law's effect, remittances or discontinued proceedings were granted in only seventy-seven such cases—although forty-four of these involved manslaughter, including less serious cases. When the law was being debated, the Justice Ministry had offered estimates of up to 80,000 for the total number of those living "underground."[79] In this light, the figures for the amnestying of "illegals" were particularly surprising. At the end of 1954, 954 cases had been registered; over the next six months another 97 cases were recorded. The majority of persons amnestied in this category had committed "transgressions" (814 cases, mainly in North Rhine-Westphalia), and there were scarcely any crimes or misdemeanors. Lacking any substantial information, but quick to toss forth palliating jokes, both politicians and ministerial bureaucrats had let themselves be misled by general amnesty propagandists into greatly overestimating the "illegals" problem.[80]

It is also the case that the import of such raw statistics is limited. The most serious objection to considering them in isolation is that the law's immediate impact is thus being addressed, not its long-term consequences. As already indicated, these involved a further weakening of the public expiatory morality—that is, a political and social delegitimation of efforts at criminal prosecution. An additional sign of the growing laxity, indeed inaction, of the judicial system regarding Nazi crimes is the dramatic decline in the onset of new proceedings. In 1954 these sank to a record low of 183 cases; the figure would rise significantly only at the end of the decade, with limitation periods about to expire. (From the end of the 1950s until the end of the 1970s, the number of new proceedings would not fall under the 1954 figure.[81])

While it is no longer possible to quantitatively fix the judicial paralysis resulting from the second amnesty law, this does not allow any doubt regarding the paralysis. No later than 1960, there were references in the Bundestag to the second half of the fifties as a period of extremely "hesitant" investigation of Nazi matters; with the approach of the first debate over temporally limiting prosecution, a representative of the Justice Ministry admitted as much to members of the Legal Committee.[82] And in fact, beyond provisions of the amnesty law concretely referring to the Nazi period, the paralysis resulted from a basic past-political leaning of the parliamentarians themselves—a leaning that would eventually be acknowledged as such by some of them.

An additional factor coming into play was a particular sort of doubt regarding the amnesty's logic and justice. Tied in to the harsh critique leveled by West German juridical specialists, a set of questions was being posed by many, certainly including prosecutors and judges.[83] What were the grounds for the plausibility of a regulation that did not amnesty particular crimes simply because they had been committed on 30 September instead of 1 October 1944? Had not the "collapse"—for a long time now, a facile metaphor masking individual responsibility—in fact begun much earlier? And had not those who committed crimes in the exercise of an assumed "official or legal duty" *before* the amnesty's starting point been "politically blinded" or "confused idealists"? Were they really so very different from the later perpetrators? The fact was that practically speaking only murder and collaboration in murder could be prosecuted; starting at a basically arbitrary moment, virtually all those guilty of manslaughter could go scot-free, since sentences of more than three years for their crimes were virtually nonexistent. In relation to the Nazi past, this fact led to a fatal obscuring of the general sense of justice—or better said, injustice.

The "collapse" paragraph also had grave consequences for the controversy surrounding so-called binding orders. Through the paragraph, the law opened the door not to the literal concept but nevertheless to the *motif* of crimes committed on account of a superior's orders—and this encouraged the spread of one or another brand of apologetics in both courtrooms and taverns. Tales concerning the incapacity of this or that individual to evade criminal orders without risking life and limb would now flourish over the next few decades—this despite numerous high court judgments tending to have a corrective impact, and the unambiguous results of historical-criminological research.[84] For a time, such tales would figure in the standard repertoire of defense attorneys in trials for violent Nazi crime. And the constant claim to have *subjectively felt* oneself under "binding orders" was more difficult to refute than their objective presence. Put pointedly, in its amnestying of deeds expressly committed in the *assumption* of an official or legal duty, paragraph 6 of the amnesty law extended an open invitation to violent Nazi criminals to take recourse to such "binding orders."[85]

Undoubtedly a recognition of this facet of the amnesty hardly ever made its way beyond a narrow circle of experts, nor beyond those the law affected who happened to be savvy. For the general public the 1954 amnesty law at best represented—perhaps more so than the law passed five years before—a natural "clean break" with the wartime and postwar confusion, a break with little specific content, running parallel to the termination of many efforts unfolding throughout West Germany to "clear up" the past. At worst, it represented nothing more than an unseemly favor granted those Bonn officials who had engaged in illicit business with Platow the news trader—something suggested in a juicy *Spiegel* cover story a few months later.[86]

One looks in vain for an account of the amnesty law's past-political implications even half as thorough and probing as the above article. There were of course tactical factors weighing against a piece of serious investigative reporting—especially concern at the prospect of offering the West arguments militating against efforts to free the last war criminals. But the uniform journalistic silence contained a wider message: in the end it was the expression of an enormous social "aversion"[87] to any fundamental, criminal-legal confrontation with Nazi atrocities and a continued political-moral discussion of what was commonly termed the "twelve ill-fated years."

The amnesty law of summer 1954 marked the end of a specific past-political developmental sequence from the first West German amnesty of 1949 to the recommendations of both the Bundestag and the Länder for an end to denazification, to the practically total reinstatement of the officials dismissed in 1945. For most West Germans this meant the termination of any squaring off with personal Nazi pasts—a process imposed on them after the capitulation. In any case, they were no longer to be bothered by court and state. It is true that the externally prompted effort at comprehensive political purging had already been converted into a process of individual rehabilitation under the eyes of the military governments. But with the founding of the Federal Republic, the effort to politically, socially, and mentally "reintegrate" former Nazis was drastically intensified by the various political parties. One of the most important instruments in this integrative enterprise was an effective amnesty policy, which now reached a certain closure. There was, in fact, remarkable consensus between the larger parties on one point: for the foreseeable future, more than had been achieved was untenable, and this in terms of both foreign policy considerations and the prospects for parliamentary support.

For to the same degree that the concept of "integration through amnesty"—to be sure not explicitly defined as such—had become reality, the reserve of agreement between the CDU-CSU and SPD regarding policy toward the past had become exhausted. Especially the FDP and the smaller bourgeois right-wing parties were engaging in an obvious effort to extend the concept—they had, after all, done much to promote it and push it through. For this reason, additional common steps between the government and the Social Democratic opposition were practically excluded. In the face of excessive sentences handed down to communists and excessive legal indolence regarding right-wing radicals, we thus find Walter Menzel admitting, in the 1955 budget debate, something akin to remorse at his coalition's support of the second amnesty law a year before: "Through this amnesty, all those who had so murderously and bestially assaulted helpless and defenseless people before 1945 were pardoned, so long as no more than three years in prison were to be expected. This is what most deeply wounds our sense of justice: that individuals were treated so differently and unequally before the courts."[88]

The bitter words of the chairman of the Committee for Protection of the Constitution make clear that a rather deep-reaching sobering process had taken hold in the SPD. But meanwhile, any additions to the politics of amnesty had become more or less unnecessary. This is because, in contrast to the victims, by the mid-1950s only a tiny minority of perpetrators still suffered directly on account of their pasts, a remainder of those the Allies had condemned for war crimes and crimes against humanity. For years, a battle had been waged with unheard of energy for their release; not least of all, this represented a symbolic battle over the past. Mere shards of a memory understood as blocking a brighter future still needed to be shoved aside.

PART II

A Past-Political Obsession: The Problem of the War Criminals

Well before the weapons fell silent, the determination of the Allies to pass judgment on the Hitler regime and its accomplices after the war had been viewed with considerable apprehension by the potentially accused—and not by them alone. In the war's final phase, Goebbels had begun to incorporate Allied warnings of future punishment into his "steadfastness"-centered propaganda, the goal being to mobilize Germany's last remaining readiness for combat; as a result, even among those Germans who personally had little to fear, a kernel of suspicion had been planted that any justice meted out by the victors was bound to be triumphalist and vengeful. Hence a ressentiment arose ("just getting even with a loser on his knees"), even making itself manifest in regard to the Nuremberg trials: the American, British, and Soviet prosecution, through a specially created International Military Tribunal, of twenty-four leading figures in the Nazi party, state, and army, as well as six Nazi organizations. But the intensive coverage of the proceedings furnished by the occupation-controlled media and the shock felt at horrific crimes now being exposed to the clear light of day meant that—at least at first—the condemnation of the "major war criminals" did receive general approval.

Quite the contrary with all remaining trials the occupying powers initiated on the basis of the Moscow Declaration of 30 October 1943 and law no. 10 of the Allied Control Council (20 December 1945): from the beginning, they were greeted mainly with rejection and protest.[1] This was the case for the 489 trials of more than 1,600 individuals—for the most part concentration camp personnel—conducted under American army jurisdiction, mainly on the site of the former camp at Dachau, starting in the summer of 1945.[2] It was the case for the twelve subsequent trials at Nuremberg (mainly in 1947–48, with 184 accused), conducted by the Americans alone after the breakup of the anti-Hitler coalition. And it was the case for the numerous proceedings that the British (roughly 1,000 accused) and the French (roughly 2,100 found guilty) supervised in their respective zones. Let us note that little is known concerning the German reaction to the military trials in the Soviet occupation zone (presumably 30,000–40,000 condemned).[3]

At least in the Western zones, the trials were marked by a clear desire to serve justice on both individual offenders and the groups they belonged to, but crucially, particularly the subsequent trials focused on the former military, state bureaucratic, and economic elite. Precisely this selective juridical procedure implicitly rebutted the notion of Allied orientation toward a principle of collective guilt. Nevertheless, among the German population the trials soon fell into the same basic disrepute as had denazification. Already toward the end of the 1940s, the term *war criminal* was heatedly contested—not, however, because it was actually misleading, insofar as many of the suspected crimes were not linked to the German military campaign, references to *Nazi* criminals thus being more appropriate. Rather, the sense here was strictly apologetic. Even then, it was thus becoming clear that the prisons in Landsberg am Lech, in Westphalian Werl, and in the Eifel's Wittlich, where those condemned, respectively, by American, British, and French courts were serving their sentences or awaiting execution, would become the objects of a harsh political tug-of-war.

At this time, the proverbial man on the street tended toward a more or less diffuse sense of dissatisfaction. In contrast, at a very early point a formidable portion of Germany's old elite—at first it was above all the church—began working with great determination for an end to the war-crimes trials. Since the founding of the West German republic, a well-organized and highly effective network of groups and individuals, with the previous Nuremberg defense attorneys at its center, saw to the theme's political topicality. Within a short time, one thing alone remained at stake: paving the way as quickly as possible for as many of the condemned as possible—quite a few former Wehrmacht members among them—to gain their freedom from "Allied prisons."

This enterprise was encouraged by the shift in Western security interests, in the framework of a sharpening East-West conflict—most concretely, by the outbreak of the Korean War. Against the backdrop of the Federal Republic's integration into the Western camp, Adenauer was himself spurred forward by the need to see through a West German contribution to Western defense, and with it, the restoration of a degree of national sovereignty. From then on the chancellor himself would fight for the "rehabilitation of German soldiers." To the general German public, nothing seemed to besmirch the soldiers' collective honor more profoundly than the fact that a small and dwindling number had been condemned as war criminals or were—mainly in France—still awaiting trial.

CHAPTER 5

The War Crimes Issue Preceding the Bonn Republic

Western Europe is longing for the benefits
of the much-promised *Pax Americana*. One of its
cornerstones should be an impeccable judicature.

—*Alfried Krupp, prisoner in Landsberg,*
27 October 1948[1]

Americans were the strongest proponents of the idea that
the Third Reich kingpins responsible for war, plunder, and genocide
should not simply receive perfunctory trials, that rather they should be
held to account before an international court subject to scrutiny by the
world's public, thus pointing the way to an evolution of international law.
Without the engagement of the United States, the Nuremberg tribunal
would never have been established.[2] And as indicated, with the subsequent trials at Nuremberg and at Dachau, it was also the Americans who
attempted to extend this idea of juridical punishment for Nazi crimes systematically. The idea had a strong pedagogic element, reflecting as it did
a belief in the possibility of historical-political enlightenment.

But the Americans not only articulated an especially strong commitment to the "Nuremberg system"; at the same time, the system's earliest critique emerged from American ranks. Namely, a small but significant segment of U.S. public opinion had already expressed doubts
concerning the legal fairness of the proceedings against the "major war
criminals" before their November 1945 onset. Proponents of the stern
approach to the occupation advocated by Henry M. Morgenthau maintained that the agreed-upon strategy was far too gentle. But they had
been on the defensive since the spring, with a journalist as prominent

as Dorothy Thompson expressing her reservations concerning a trial in which the judges were simultaneously accusers and "executioners." Likewise, with a view to the Soviet Union, William H. Chamberlin of the outspokenly pro-German, zealously anticommunist *Chicago Tribune* voiced doubts concerning the persuasive powers of an indictment whose standards could not be enforced on a worldwide basis.[3]

This internal American critique would soon form an important starting point for Germans hoping to see a turn from the principles that guided Nuremberg.[4] But in 1945–46, the critique hardly made its way over the Atlantic—reflecting the will of its Allied creators, the legal German press had found nothing to complain about in the tribunal's ten-month existence. The American press officers had devoted a great deal of energy to steering the new German papers in the direction of a reportage that was both extensively documentary and affirmative in nature.[5] For this reason, public opinion was at first strongly dominated by published opinion. Opinion surveys regarding the Nuremberg trials clearly suggest such was the case. The extraordinarily affirmative responses registered for 1945–46 proved fleeting; four years later, almost a third of all those surveyed considered Nuremberg and the subsequent trials as unjust.[6] But such views had virtually no chance of being acknowledged, let alone accepted, in a press duty-bound to the anti-Nazi postulate. Likewise, politicians in the newly approved parties showed little inclination to squander the trust invested in them on behalf of war criminals. For both these reasons, a central role here accrued to the church—a role it gladly accepted.

Constituting the only presumably uncompromised elite, both Catholic and Protestant dignitaries enjoyed the military government's special esteem in the period following the war's end. This fact quickly vaulted the church's self-confidence to remarkable heights; an array of prominent clerics now considered it a duty to intervene with the occupying powers on behalf of those fellow Germans accused of or condemned for war crimes. On the Catholic side, the most active figures in this enterprise were Josef Frings, cardinal of Cologne and chairman of the Bishops' Conference in Fulda, and Johann Neuhäusler, auxiliary bishop in Munich. On the Protestant side, the engagement was broader: along with the state bishops serving as council chairmen of the German Evangelical Church—until the beginning of 1949 Theophil Wurm (Stuttgart), then Otto Dibelius (Berlin)—and Dibelius's deputy, Hanns Lilje (Hannover), state bishop Hans Meiser (Munich) invested particularly striking energy in the war criminals question; but church president Martin Niemöller (Wiesbaden) and prelate Karl Hartenstein (Stuttgart) were also active.

Similarly to their approach to denazification, which they did their best to mitigate and alter through extensive whitewashing, the dignitaries first concentrated on speaking up for individually accused and condemned war criminals.[7] Fidelity to the church and a "Christian way of life" took argumentative priority—the reason why at Nuremberg only Konstantin Freiherr von Neurath, former foreign minister for the Reich and then "Reich-Protector" of Bohemia and Moravia, could count on the (Evangelical) church's support.[8]

In any event, since 1946–47 such ad personam pleas for compassion and mercy, apparently grounded entirely in Christian precepts, were increasingly bound up with overtly political motifs. From the beginning, in the discussion of the subject unfolding on both inner-church and interchurch levels, principled reservations regarding the Allied expiatory efforts were not unusual[9]; this was no secret to the occupying powers.[10] But now they were being forced to confront the reservations with increasing frequency, and sometimes directly. Thus, in September 1946 Bishop Wurm wrote to the British president of the International Military Tribunal, Sir Geoffrey Lawrence, to express his incomprehension that at Nuremberg only the German role in the attack on Poland was granted attention. The Evangelical Church's council chairman closed his allusion to the Soviet Union with the following warning: "it would be something dreadful if the Nuremberg judgment let to a strengthening of the sense that there is no longer any justice on earth, but that justice is dictated only by power."[11]

The church also did not abstain from criticizing the trials at the Dachau concentration camp and those held on account of the murder of imprisoned Allied soldiers (including the so-called pilots' cases). Both directly and indirectly, such criticism reached the occupation authorities. In the spring of 1947, for example, a plaintive monthly report from the Catholic pastor serving those interned at Dachau was first transmitted to Alois Muench, the archconservative anti-Semitic bishop of North Dakota, now apostolic visitator in Bonn.[12] Through Muench, it was passed on to Robert Murphy, political advisor to Lucius D. Clay, commander in chief of U.S. forces in Europe, likewise the military governor of the U.S. zone. (Clay had presided over the army-directed Dachau trials in the former capacity, over the subsequent trials at Nuremberg in the latter capacity.) The report spoke of the "corrosive force" of "the fact that the camp's detainees are sentenced to prison in assembly line trials simply because they were assigned guard duty in a concentration camp."[13] Evangelical Länder bishop Meiser conveyed a critique of the Dachau trials to the director of Bavaria's military government that was couched in very similar terms—though

Meiser also found the proceedings flawed from a constitutional perspective.[14]

Among the subsequent trials at Nuremberg, the church dignitaries'
principled objections were directed above all at the trials of ranking
Wehrmacht officers. In February 1948 the director of the chancellery of
the German Evangelical Church, Hans Asmussen, considered the
moment ripe to ask the influential Lord Bishop of Chichester, George
Bell, and a number of other non-German high church officials "if it is
not now time to set out on a new path and thus put an end to these trials." All of the individual criticisms of the way the proceedings
unfolded, the treatment of the prisoners, and the passing of sentences
did not hide the fact that for Asmussen more was at stake here than correcting abuses: "Fundamental misgivings need to be addressed. No
rational person, let alone a Christian, can doubt that crimes committed
in war ought to be expiated through courts and punishment. But we
now have to confront the undeniable fact that public opinion, not only
in Germany but also in other countries, says, 'Today the generals are on
the dock; with a shift in the power balance it would be the generals of
the former victorious nations.' No power in the world can presently pass
equal judgment on *all* those who have committed crimes against humanity over recent years. The legal basis for the trials differs from one country to the next. But without exception, the proceedings are directed at
the vanquished. While the intent of the war crimes trials was to render
the world's conscience more acute, the result has been the opposite."[15]

In March and April, accommodating responses and promises of
support arrived in the Swabian town of Gmünd, which housed part of
the church chancellery.[16] But by then, the trial opponents in the church
already felt themselves to be in a distinctly improved position. For one
of the Nuremberg judges had himself seen to it that the war criminals'
horizon had begun to brighten. On 19 February 1948, the presiding
judge in the so-called hostage murder trial, Charles F. Wennerstrum,
delivered the sentences handed out against ten Wehrmacht generals
who had been stationed on the southeast front. They had been accused
of ordering the mass execution of both large numbers of captured Balkan
partisans and persons who had nothing to do with the fighting, especially gypsies and Jews. Field Marshall Wilhelm List and General Walter Kuntze received life sentences, six other generals were sentenced to
between seven and twenty years in prison, and two were freed. Three
days after the trial's end, Wennerstrum, a judge on the Iowa Supreme
Court, returned to the United States. But before his flight home, a correspondent for the *Chicago Tribune*—which was becoming increasingly
polemical in its opposition to the Nuremberg proceedings—managed to

coax him into an interview; the interview was a bombshell not only in Nuremberg.[17] If he had known seven months previously what he knew now, Wennerstrum explained, he would never have come to Nuremberg. It was not just that the proceedings he was presiding over had proved badly flawed—for instance, the defense attorneys had been granted access to only a portion of the documents of indictment. Beyond this, Wennerstrum indicated, the entire idea behind the trials was "vindictive" and stamped with "personal ambition." It was telling, the judge observed, that the staff of the Nuremberg prosecutor's office, including a number of individuals "who became Americans only in recent years, whose backgrounds were embedded in Europe's hatreds and prejudices," and who were thus not inclined to grant the Germans any justice, a situation reflected in the absence of any appeals process.[18]

Transparently, this critique was laced with a strong dose of anti-Semitism. Brigadier General Telford Taylor, the forty-year-old chief prosecutor at the subsequent Nuremberg trials, responded in a way revealing that Wennerstrum had touched on a raw nerve: the accusations were absolutely untenable, malicious, probably the expression of a psychopathic disturbance. Taylor was a left-wing firebrand with the self-assuredness of a Harvard Law School graduate.[19] His eagerness to damn the twenty-year older, conservative-leaning judge's opinions meant that what amounted to more than a small scandal could not lie sleeping. In the American headquarters in Frankfurt, anyone who wished to could secretly read articles by correspondents accredited there when they were cabled to the States. This discovery emerged from Taylor's reply having gone to the press before Wennerstrum's interview was published in the *Tribune*.[20]

In this manner, Taylor had naturally aggravated rather than lessened the damage done by the departed judge—particularly since aside from disparagement of one's country, the only real charge being thrown at him was that his nonsensical attack constituted welcome material for propaganda by "all the worst elements in Germany." By contrast, Taylor's nigh-imploring remark that the Nuremberg trials stood "for justice and not vengeance" went almost unnoticed. One person who sensed the episode's calamitous nature was the correspondent in Germany for the *New York Herald Tribune*. The sobering gist of his front-page article was as follows: "This whole development is surprisingly revealing that [*sic*] the Nuremberg trials have become a greater and more controversial issue among Americans themselves in Germany than between the occupation forces and the Germans."[21]

In fact, the journalist's conclusion reflected only part of the truth. There was a great amount of tension not only between the Americans who were working in Germany—a situation revealed by the Wenner-strum affair—but over recent years, home-based American critics of the proceedings had themselves gained considerable ground. At the same time, no one could maintain that in regard to Nuremberg the differences in opinion between occupiers and the occupied were unimportant. Over the coming months this situation would gradually become public.

In the wake of the Wennerstrum episode, both Catholic and Protestant critics of the trials increased their pressure on the Americans. Germany's politicians continued to avoid the theme of Nuremberg, limiting themselves to doing their best for the mass of ordinary soldiers still being held by the Allies, in cooperation with the relevant charitable organizations. (This was the context for the 1947 establishment of a committee for war prisoner questions in Stuttgart's Länder council.[22]) But the leaders of both churches were focusing in an increasingly direct manner on the war criminals. In the process they handily glossed over the fact that the persons in question were by no means all "soldiers" but rather included ranking party functionaries, ministerial officials, SS members, and civilians implicated in heinous deeds. One particular factor here added to the growing obfuscation: the *war criminal* champions' placement of the so-called Malmédy trial at the center of their increasingly strident critique, in an exploitation of the German public's highly emotional identification with the *war prisoners.*

The Belgian town of Malmédy had come to signify one of the largest—and soon one of the most controversial—of the 489 trials held by the American army between 1945 and 1948. The trial was concerned with the murder of American soldiers during the German offensive in the Ardennes in December 1944—more particularly with the massacre of seventy-two disarmed Americans by the First SS Tank Division (the last form taken by the "Bodyguard Regiment Adolf Hitler") at a Malmédy crossing. These cold-blooded murders had moved the American public more strongly than any other news from the war; even the later revelations of concentration camp mass murder did not palliate the indignation at the Belgian episode. With the crime's punishment now invested with high symbolic meaning, and with seventy-three perpetrators and responsible persons firmly established, the trial's outcome was hardly surprising. All the accused were found guilty, including the division commander and SS colonel Joachim Peiper, leader of the "battle group"—named after him—to which the guilty men belonged. Forty-three of them were sentenced to death.[23]

None of these—doubtless severe—death sentences would be carried out. To a great extent this was the result of the stubbornness of American defense attorney Col. Willis M. Everett, but it was also the result of the susceptibility of the Washington establishment. Through constant assertions of dubious interrogation methods and other flaws in the prosecution's procedure, Everett succeeded in cultivating doubt in Washington regarding the trial's fairness. In 1948, Everett submitted a plea of habeas corpus to the Supreme Court. While the plea was rejected, it did lead to Secretary of the Army Kenneth Royall ordering a new investigation by the theater judge advocate, General James L. Harbaugh. Already two months earlier Harbaugh had recommended mitigating the sentences, which reduced the number of persons facing execution to twelve and led to the release of thirteen similarly sentenced SS men.[24] Well aware that the critics of the Malmédy trial would not find this outcome satisfying, Lucius Clay ordered an additional internal review.[25]

The German newspaper reader learned next to nothing about any of this. At the same time, figures belonging to the appropriate church circles were very much in the know—and determined to exploit the clear differences at play on the American side. Whereas they received their information on the Nuremberg trials from the very helpful defense attorneys there, much of the information on the Dachau trials came from the defendants themselves, being mediated by those charged with shepherding souls in internment camps and prisons. In writing to five American congressmen in March 1948, on account of purported pretrial mistreatment of Malmédy defendants, to press for additional legal proceedings and a suspension of the death sentences, (Protestant) Auxiliary Bishop Neuhäusler relied on documents delivered to him by the (Catholic) priest at Landsberg, Karl Morgenschweis.[26]

The Americans had chosen the Landsberg fortress as "War Crimes Prison No. 1" not only for reasons of historical symbolism—that is, as the site of Hitler's early imprisonment and Nazi education—but also on security grounds. In Landsberg men condemned at Nuremberg would meet men condemned at Dachau. It is the case that the British maintained a special prison in Werl for war criminals, as did the French in Wittlich. It is also the case that Spandau served as the central symbol of the overall Allied effort to prosecute the major war criminals. But over the coming years, the growing lobby for the war criminals would target none of those places with as much intensity as they did the Landsberg fortress.

Within this process, the determining factor was not nostalgia, but rather something that could not be overlooked. With the Dachau and (above all) Nuremberg trials, the Americans had emerged as the political and moral leaders of the effort to punish Nazi war crimes and crimes against humanity. What distinguished American military justice from that of the French and British was not so much the number of sentences as the demonstrative nature of its confrontation with Germany's implicated military, bureaucratic, and economic elite—or at least with a significant part of it.[27] There was, to be sure, cause enough to criticize the American trials. And if the Americans could be swayed from their punitive program, this would almost certainly have had a beneficial impact on Britain—and even France, where some German soldiers suspected of war crimes were still being detained. (Other states holding on to such prisoners were Belgium, Holland, and Luxembourg, as well as the Soviet Union.)

The task the two confessions had set themselves was thus no small one. But it is also true that support for their cause was most readily available. If we put aside the escape aid organized for various Nazi criminals in the same period by German clerics with links to the Vatican, then it appears that activity in the Catholic camp centered mainly around Auxiliary Bishop Neuhäusler.[28] Especially for the "Dachauians," he represented the ideal attorney, since from 1941 to 1945 he had himself been a Dachau inmate.[29] He could now proceed with the determined energy of the morally unblemished—although this was in fact far from entirely justified.[30] When necessary, the Catholic engagement could receive the backup of Cardinal Frings, who argued in a more moderate tone than Neuhäusler. Still, in general the Evangelical engagement unfolded on a higher hierarchical level than that of the Catholics and was more clearly motivated by considerations of national policy. It revealed a close connection between political decisiveness and administrative professionalism on the one hand and a precise knowledge of the juridical situation on the other.

A first important example of this was the chilly anti-Nuremberg petition submitted to Lucius Clay on 20 May 1948 by the American zone's Evangelical church leaders, a group of bishops headed by Bishop Wurm.[31] Depicting specific incidents that could have been learned of only from the defendants themselves, these clerics cited the "defense's handicap in face of the prosecution," the "influencing of witnesses," and the "conflict between the court's name and character." It was characteristic of the approach taken by Wurm and his colleagues that the working conditions of the (German) defense attorneys—they in fact steered the clerical pens—figured prominently among the complaints.[32] These gentlemen found both their rooms and their honoraria (3,500 German marks monthly) too small. Their displeasure, conveyed by the bishops, was also directed at the "institute of witness detention, alien to German legal praxis," particularly since it had been applied—in fact only rarely—"under the pressure of extradition to the eastern states."

In the context of an unhesitatingly paraded confusion over the Nuremberg court's status ("after the other victorious states withdrew from the proceedings"), Wurm and his colleagues submitted a protest already heard in regard to the International Military Tribunal—that the judgments were passed "on the basis of a new international law, until now lacking all normative status." But the conclusion drawn from this had unprecedented clarity: "If the exclusive application of such law to the defeated has already raised suspicion that what is here at work is less justice than the exercise of power and use of a political instrument, the Nuremberg court's refusal to consider evidence of unexpiated inhumane acts on the part of the victorious states, evidence submitted to exculpate the excused, has even further diminished the already shaken trust in this tribunal's justice."

The Evangelical spiritual shepherds' judgment of the ongoing trial of the Wehrmacht High Command was even harsher. With the use of "civilian judges in the sentencing of officers held as war prisoners, the Nuremberg court has distanced itself from the practice in use up to now, determined according to principles of international law. The approach taken to this end, removing the officers' military rank beforehand, has its last historical example in Adolf Hitler's treatment of the German officers of 20 July 1944." At a time, the bishops indicted, when the denazification process was being wound up at an accelerated pace, Nuremberg represented an "anachronism." The creation of a possibility for appeal was an "undeniable need." "Should the American government deny the establishment of an appeals body," they continued, "despite the fact that the Interallied Military Court[33] has become an American court in the eyes of public opinion, then we call for support in establishing an international court of appeal."

At the very end of their petition, the shepherding clerics returned to a more theological language. At this point they also confirmed "that criminal deeds must be expiated." But here as well complaints over the "injustice" of the Nuremberg proceedings occupied center stage: their "psychological effects impair the health of public opinion most severely, preventing the establishment of new trust in law and justice. The love of Christ presses us to work for the regaining of trust in state order by a despairing, skeptical, and nihilistic humanity, an order in which the principles *suum cuique und audiatur et altera pars* are maintained as well as is possible among human beings."

Wurm asked Charles M. LaFollette, director of Württemberg-Baden's military government and an attorney, to pass on the petition. LaFollette had himself taken part in the subsequent trials of Third Reich jurists as the acting prosecutor and had a highly precise knowledge of the Nuremberg procedures. He did not allow himself to be fooled by the bishop's more gentle concluding pirouettes. In clear annoyance, he commented on each of the cleric's points, underscoring the nigh ideal nature of the working conditions deplored by the defense attorneys, when measured against postwar Germany's general circumstances,[34] and even against those normally prevailing in American courts. In principle, LaFollette indicated, he had nothing against the appeals body the bishops were demanding, although the available possibilities of review seemed sufficient to him, and honoring the demand at the present time would have been interpreted as an acknowledgment of improper juridical procedure. LaFollette added the suggestion that Clay read between the lines: for after all, the bishops' petition came at a time "when prominent industrialists such as Farben and Krupp and really big militarists such as the general staff generals and really important political figures such as [former Deputy Secretary of the Foreign Office] Weizsäcker are facing the end of their trials. The people previously convicted, although prominent in their fields, almost uniformly belonged to a class not previously revered by the German people. That is to say, they were doctors or lawyers or civil servants or people from the middle classes, such as defendants in the [Oswald] Pohl [the SS general in charge of concentration camp slave labor], Rsha [the SS Central Office for Race and Resettlement], Einsatzgruppen cases. It is true that the South East Generals were convicted and Milch was convicted, but Milch was an interloper, a man from the middle class and not part of the traditional German army class; and the South East Generals, while of a class revered by the Germans, were not as important to the revival of militarism and the conviction of members of the general staff. In other words, there is a possibility now of people being convicted who comprise those elements in Germany which have always made it militaristic and nationally arrogant. We cannot forget that the Protestant Church of Germany was always the State church of Prussia and certainly unless we are blind we can see a connection between this sudden rushing of the Church to the defense of those with whom it had such close ties in the past."[35]

LaFollette was clearly not prepared to hide his feelings; he did not, however, harbor great hopes that Clay would find the time to read his five-page letter. He was mistaken. The general not only studied the arguments but also indicated his intent to make them the basis of his office's reply to the church leaders. He took the matter so much to heart that he personally dictated some passages. Openly indignant at the bishops' unhesitating adoption of unverified, second-hand information as the basis of their complaint, Clay cited the sense of "solemn responsibility" with which he personally verified the evidence before approving a sentence. Certainly, he indicated, there had been irregularities, and practices he did not approve of. But these were always present in legal proceedings and would be even more frequent if an appeals body were set up. These considerations placed aside, the evidence in the cases reviewed up to now was overwhelming. "I cannot but feel, in all conscience, that the sentences thus far awarded have been just and frequently lenient. Never in history has evidence so convicted those in high places for their actions. It is difficult to understand how any review of the evidence of those yet to be sentenced could provide a basis for sentimental sympathy for those who brought suffering and anguish to untold millions.[36]

These sentences, formulated with unveiled emotion, found their way unchanged into the reply to Bishop Wurm that Clay signed a few days later. His staff merely toned down the closing remarks somewhat. Whereas Clay had attributed a desire to discredit the Nuremberg court to Wurm ad personam, the final version read thus: "I regret that an effort is now being made to discredit a court which with high intent is endeavoring to establish precedents in international law which may serve to prevent again a world being plunged into chaos."[37]

In light of ongoing events, it was in fact perhaps more proper to have made the reproach on a nonpersonal level—particularly since Wurm immediately made the exchange of views public.[38] The bishop had realized that bringing in the press could increase the pressure on an occupying power whose hegemony was starting to crumble, and which could simply no longer afford to strictly regulate the legitimate press.[39] Beginning in the early summer of 1948, the manner in which Wurm exploited his insight rendered him something like the war criminals' star defense attorney for Germany's general public.[40] For the American headquarters' War Crimes Branch, it rendered him the guiding force behind a "planned and concerted attack on American occupation policies." [41]

The perception on both sides was both true and false. For despite the intense public focus on Stuttgart's Bishop Wurm, his Munich colleague Meiser was scarcely less devoted to the cause of the war criminals. In the course of 1948, Meiser also bombarded the Americans with petitions, thus causing another internal review committee to be set up by the American army—albeit probably without Meiser learning of this himself.[42]

All in all, the intercession for the war criminals was far more concerted than the Americans having to wrestle with the bishops probably realized. Based deep within occupied Germany's emerging political structures and old elite social grouping, the chorus of sympathizers would become audible only after a certain hesitation. Still, a reflective observer might have been struck by the fact that—despite inevitable personal rivalries and various kinds of desire for profile—there was absolutely no critique of Wurm's engagement inside the church, and none in the press.[43] Quite to the contrary, the latter realm now became a venue for the first extended negative reports on "Nuremberg," as a result of Wurm's harsh confrontation in May and June 1948 with Robert Kempner, now serving as chief prosecutor in the Nuremberg trial of the Nazi Foreign Ministry's high officials (the most long-lasting of the military tribunal's cases).

As a previous Prussian official, Kempner was a preferred interlocutor for German petitioners. On Easter 1948 he offered Wurm an opportunity to visit the Nuremberg prison. The bishop returned home from his visit with an awareness "that my fears that the care and treatment of the prisoners was cause for great concern were groundless."[44] But a few weeks later, in an open letter to Kempner, Wurm launched a massive and sweeping attack on both the Nuremberg and Dachau proceedings. He had, he indicated, been forced to recognize "that in trial preparations in those cases thus far ending with death sentences, criminal methods and repellent tortures"—abscheuliche Quälereien—"have been applied in order to extort statements and confessions."[45]

Kempner's reply was that he could not say anything concerning the Dachau proceedings but that in Nuremberg the accused were convicted not on the basis of confessions but, virtually without exception, on the basis of documentary evidence, and that in addition Wurm had furnished "no evidence" to accompany his communication.[46] The reply was not particularly persuasive and perhaps could not be so. Kempner had in fact himself just experienced an embarrassing and not irrelevant courtroom episode marked by a defense attorney in the Foreign Ministry trial citing an interrogation transcript in which Kempner threatened the prosecution witness Friedrich Gaus with delivery to the Russians. Kempner's colleagues were horrified by this fiasco—especially Charles LaFollette, since the chief prosecutor had chosen to lay all responsibility for the matter on the shoulders of a subordinate who was now working elsewhere.[47] LaFollette did publicly defend Kempner's reply to Wurm, but when speaking with Clay he minced no words. Kempner's "foolish, unlawyer-like method of interrogation was common knowledge in Nuernberg all the time I was there and protested by those of us who anticipated the arising of a day, just such as we now have, when the Germans would attempt to make martyrs out of the common criminals on trial in Nuernberg."[48]

In the meantime, Bishop Wurm had himself heard about Kempner's lapse and promptly opened a new round of slugging. Supplied with fresh material by the Nuremberg defense attorneys, he both denounced the Gaus interrogation and cited a series of additional interrogation records said to document related abuses.[49] In a position to observe Wurm at close hand, LaFollette recognized that the explosiveness of the old Evangelical leader's attacks was not to be underestimated. The strategy Wurm had come up with was to link reproaches aimed at Nuremberg with those aimed at Dachau in order to demand a review of all sentences by a review body—and this strategy was in fact as clever as it was dangerous. For it threatened to bring the entire expiatory program into disrepute. Wurm was now creating the impression that the putative mistreatment of prisoners being investigated for the Malmédy trial—mistreatment he had begun referring to as "crimes against humanity"[50]—was an established fact. He also implied knowledge that innocent men had been sentenced, in other words, "knowing" individuals for whom it was "most improbable that they really committed crimes."[51]

The Württemberg Synod greeted these bishoply words with deep gratitude. This was particularly so since they were linked—albeit in a somewhat coquettish manner—with a reference to reproaches made against the church on account of its passivity in face of Third Reich injustice. "It would not be suitable to remain silent at present out of fear and caution. I would like not to abandon the hope that those now in power are more ready than was the Third Reich to hear such words, pleas, laments. This will most certainly have rewards for the entirety of the German people, and the entire political development of [other] peoples."

To be sure, the gesture of powerless petitioner was becoming ever less suitable to Wurm's campaign, being carried out with persistence and increasing shrillness. When Robert Kempner tried to defend himself by actually citing LaFollette's reference, at the South German Congress of Jurists, to those wishing to discredit Nuremberg as "enemies of the German people,"[52] Wurm answered with utmost severity. "Apparently Dr. Kempner is of the opinion that the remark has something to do with him." "I put that aside," Wurm continued, "and merely recall that I was once a traitor to land and *Volk* in the eyes of the Nazis. Naturally the reproach's echo by the Americans leaves me as cold now as it did then. But there are perhaps Americans who believe that such sorts of argument are not compatible with the honor of the American nation." Wurm was not at a loss for any argument—or any argumentative tenor. "It would not only be more clever but also much more democratic to speak openly about the Nuremberg trials instead of letting the subject be taken over by nationalist and anti-Semitic whispering campaigns. The Germans cannot be blamed for asking why only Germans can be accused of war crimes. Every honest person knows that in this war, war crimes were committed not only by the Germans."[53]

In the weeks-long controversy between Kempner and Wurm, it is remarkable to see an influential paper such as *Die Zeit* (in the person of its lead journalist, Richard Tüngel, then drifting further and further into nationalist waters) vehemently taking Wurm's side and not even avoiding anti-Semitic undertones.[54] Equally remarkable is the virtual silence of the politicians—a singular exception being Erwin Schoettle, chairman of the Württemberg SPD, who offered the bishop a gentle rebuke: his arguments were being appropriated "with pleasure" by that—substantial—portion of the populace still ready "to consider the originators and agents of murderous National Socialist orders as unlucky persons who would have been named heroes had Hitler won the war."[55]

In the summer of 1948, the Catholic bishops backed the demand for an appeals body introduced into the debate by Wurm and his Evangelical colleagues. To this end, Johann Neuhäusler—supported, if not instrumentalized, by former Nuremberg defense attorney Rudolf Aschenauer, lawyer for (among others) the infamous Otto Ohlendorf in the Mobile Killing Unit proceedings and generally considered part of the right-wing scene—had compiled more and more claims of abuse in the Dachau trials, presenting them at the episcopate convened in Fulda. On 26 August, Cardinal Frings mailed a memorandum to General Clay from that venue itself. While somewhat milder in language, it did not lag behind the Evangelical demands in content.

According to the Catholic bishops, over the past three years "much additional shattering of the faith in justice" had taken place; as a result, the initial ready willingness, of youth in particular, "to start a new life in which not force but law prevails" was in danger of turning into disillusion. If the conviction were to win out "that even those presently in power only speak of law while in fact engaging in power politics, the demoralization of our people will become unstoppable." For that reason it was crucial "that at least the trials meant to represent propitiation for injustice in solemn form be carried out without any defects involving injustice and power-political abuse." But the "moral standing" of these trials seemed "gravely threatened." As the bishops saw it, contributing to this situation was the fact that the trials had taken on the "hated characteristics" of the [Nazi] special courts. "The Nuremberg courts thus tried German individuals on the basis of a law previously unknown in Germany, and which the same nations applying it against Germany are unwilling to follow." Placing aside, they indicated, the still entirely unresolved question of whether, "against the command of one's legal superior," a person "is obliged to follow [either] his own judgment or norms superior to the state," incidents of unequal treatment had occurred that rendered the absence of an appeals body incomprehensible. In fact, the American federal court system was eminently suited for reviewing the Nuremberg and Dachau sentences. "Let it punish the truly guilty and give the feeling back to both the German people and the entire world that victors and vanquished are subject to the same law, just as they will eventually face the same divine judge."[56]

The exalted tone of the Catholic shepherds' memorandum evoked respect from the Americans.[57] Presentation of the detailed complaints was left to Auxiliary Bishop Neuhäusler—doubtless an adroit move. The day after seeing to this duty, he promptly presented the military government with a new complaint over "career witnesses": in the Flossenbürg trial the accusations rested on the testimony of homosexuals, child molesters, pimps, communists, and hoodlums.[58]

Less than a week later, on 31 August 1948, Neuhäusler had the opportunity to repeat his complaints before the Texan judge Gordon Simpson. At the behest of Secretary of the Army Royall, Simpson had been in Germany with two colleagues since the start of the month as head of a commission reviewing various criticisms voiced over the war crimes trials, in particular the Malmédy trial. Describing himself as a former concentration camp inmate, Neuhäusler emphasized his complete awareness that in general every accused person maintained full innocence and that doubtless much of what those sentenced in Dachau said about the court proceedings was false. He also did not wish to vouch for the material that was being presented—while adding that "many of the witnesses, perhaps 90 percent, were paid professional witnesses with criminal records ranging from robbery to homosexuality."[59] As had been the case with a delegation Bishop Wurm sent to Munich a week earlier,[60] Neuhäusler suggested (to no effect) that Judge Simpson might use the chance to directly contact the Landsberg prisoners.

According to the records of both meetings, it seems that the Munich auxiliary bishop and colleagues had a better sense than their Stuttgart counterparts of how to gain favor with the army secretary's representatives. This may well be linked to one fact: Neuhäusler conveyed the expressed wish of the Fulda Bishops' Conference that any mitigation of sentences be carried out quietly and that the bishops' memorandum likewise not be made public. In contrast, the Stuttgart emissaries had repeated Wurm's brusque demands for public review, going beyond them to insist on the exclusion of those involved in the earlier proceedings— their behavior having generated "a new wave of anti-Semitism."[61]

In the report it presented on 14 September 1948, the Simpson Commission confirmed that mistakes had been made in connection with the Dachau trials, not all investigators being up to their tasks, their methods "questionable." But this was the three judges' most negative finding. Despite all efforts to please the report's instigator, Kenneth Royall—his distaste for the trials in general had long since become common knowledge—they confirmed that the proceedings were essentially "fair." The commission did propose commuting 29 of the 139 death sentences still pending, including 12 from the Malmédy proceedings. But this did not reflect any doubt regarding the guilt of the condemned men. Rather, the peculiar justification offered was compensation for earlier possible injustices.[62]

For Clay, the report opened the way to ordering a resumption, on 15 October 1948, of the execution in Landsberg of those condemned at the Dachau trials, suspended since June. Immediately before the executions resumed, a member of the Simpson Commission went public in the United States with the claim of having evidence that Malmédy prisoners had been mistreated and that the commission chairman had suppressed the evidence.[63] Starting then, the debate about the war criminals took on greater impetus in the United States, caught up as the country was in election fever—but not only there. Clay's execution orders were now being issued on a weekly basis, and this naturally allowed the clerical advocates of the condemned no rest. They tried to stop the process with additional protests of principle and a flood of individual petitions.[64] The executions were set to continue until February 1949, and Clay was obliged to personally issue execution orders for each condemned criminal. None of his bishop opponents seem to have noted the extreme psychic burden this represented for the general[65]—and none seem to have argued against the death penalty on theological or moral grounds.

Since Clay's September 1948 response to their memorandum, the Catholic bishops could nurture no doubts regarding his determination to see through the punishment of the war criminals. In a friendlier tone than that adopted vis-à-vis the Evangelical bishops, but no less decisively, and presenting the same arguments, Clay had defended the punitive program's intention and praxis. Once more, he had rejected the thesis—to be repeated often over the coming years—that an unprecedented "special law" had been used to pass sentences in Nuremberg (and Dachau). In Clay's view, both the London treaty of 8 August 1945 and Allied Control Council law no. 10 simply codified long-standing legal principles with supranational status.[66] Once more he rejected the argument that the defendants had carried out the orders of superiors or followed prevailing law: While these factors could be grounds for mitigating punishment, they could not free anyone from responsibility for criminal deeds. And once more he rejected the assertion of differing legal interpretations and evaluation of evidence in different courts, along with the calls for an appeals body—this with a reference to the U.S. practice of automatic review of sentences, as well as to the charter of the International Military Tribunal, which did not designate any appeals process.[67]

Despite Clay's thoroughly negative answer, the bishops had still hesitated in going public with their demands, quite clearly a reflection of the assumption that such silence could at least lead to concessions in individual cases. With news of the resumption of executions, they were forced to conclude that their strategy had failed. Accordingly, the Catholic leaders now joined their Evangelical counterparts in public protest. Over the following days the *Christlicher Nachrichtendienst*'s teleprinters went into overdrive, keeping pace with a massive volume of telegrams: to Royall (from Neuhäusler and Wurm), Clay (from Frings and Neuhäusler), the latter's deputy, General Hays (from Neuhäusler), and even President Truman (once more from Neuhäusler).[68] While these petitions did not result in a sweeping extension of the halt to executions, Clay responded, already, on 25 October to the pressure exerted by their publication, ordering a new suspension of the remaining Malmédy death sentences, along with a number of additional such sentences.[69]

During this large-scale political-journalistic offensive of the two German churches—Wurm and Neuhäusler had also begun to hold press conferences—Neuhäusler conceived the apparently pioneering idea of placing the term *war criminals* (*Kriegsverbrecher*) in quotation marks.[70] (In fact, since crimes against humanity were the particular focus of the Dachau trials, the term really applied only to a portion of the Nazis condemned there.) This palliative gesture soon became a standard German practice. That it first made itself manifest in a telegram to Truman virtually excludes the possibility of a pen slip.[71]

By now, Bishop Wurm had begun to play ball with Bishop Neuhäusler. In a letter to John Foster Dulles, foreign policy advisor for Republican presidential candidate Thomas Dewey, he in turn revealed his thoughts more clearly than had previously been the case. "I cannot hide from you, and all the many citizens of the USA honestly striving for a restoration of European order, as well as a rescue of Germany from its frightful situation, that we are presently grappling with one question: whether in your country things are the way they once were in the Third Reich, where individuals possessing clear understanding and good will could not prevail against those benefiting from particular political calculations. It is my firm conviction that the positive course the USA has embarked on can only achieve victory over the powerful troublemakers on all sides if the Hitlerian spirit is also fully expelled from its own shores—and if law and justice are meted out to no one's favor or detriment, but only according to the facts."[72]

In the awareness of acting both in harmony with, and, as it were, in the place of, "millions of Germans and non-Germans who wish for the best,"[73] Neuhäusler proceeded to confront the military government with ever more petitions, sprinkled with statements from the Landsberg prison's Catholic shepherds, as well as lawyers and relatives of the accused. In the months that followed, his correspondence with Clay continued (Clay left none of the auxiliary bishop's letters unanswered). In one letter Neuhäusler styled himself as a mouthpiece of the German people, in another, as a lone warrior, and in yet another he cited the bishops' memorandum—and then again a plea that had now even been tendered by the Holy Sea.[74] Being much more adroit psychologically than eighty-year-old Wurm, sixty-year-old Neuhäusler attempted to build curious bridges between himself and the general and to flatter his ego. "I know it is difficult to reopen so many trials, in order to gain the ultimate clarity and security in every case, to the extent this is humanly possible. But Herr General, you have already shown that difficulties a thousand times greater cannot keep you from helping justice triumph: the 100-day long Berlin airlift with its nigh unimaginable achievements, maintained, indeed steadily strengthened, in the face of storm and rain and other obstacles, is a shining example of this. In their striving for truth, clarity, and justice, demand the same tenacity and backbone from your judges as you have from your tireless pilots and all their helpers! Do not scorn the possibility of German assistance in this regard—just as Germans are now gladly contributing their emergency relief for Berlin." Whatever persons, the bishop indicated, were found guilty after a "new joint investigation" should "suffer the appropriate penalty"—as long as they were not to "deserve clemency to any great extent on special grounds."[75]

So much compassion might well have sparked mistrust—hence following longer expositions, Neuhäusler rarely omitted asserting something to the effect that his intervention was inspired not by "personal" factors but by "pure humaneness"—*reiner Menschlichkeit*—"and a love of justice." He believed himself above any "suspicion regarding this my struggle."[76] Whatever the motivational mix at work in the bishops' defense of Nazi criminals, the element of injured national pride was doubtless stronger in the Evangelical than in the Catholic camp. In any case, ever since—despite the suspended Malmédy sentences—the executions in Landsberg had picked up their pace, the bishops' voices had become more agitated from week to week. Admittedly, the Americans also revealed an increasing degree of nervousness. Petty matters became a source of tense correspondence.[77] With every advance in preparations for a West German state, with every mutation in occupation policy and loosening of the military government's control, the executions appeared increasingly awkward. Clay knew this. Desiring to free his successor from being associated with the process, he did his best to bring it to a timely end.[78]

Since the bishop's telegram offensive, critical opinion in the press had also become increasingly outspoken. Announced only now, the drastic mitigation of the sentence imposed on Ilse Koch, "the witch of Buchenwald"—as the wife of that concentration camp's commandant, she had been charged with gruesome and sadistic acts in the Buchenwald trial and sentenced to life in prison—furnished wind to the critics' sails.[79] Likewise with the self-assured sallies of the defense attorneys in the Nuremberg trial of the Wehrmacht High Command, now drawing to an end, and with the debate, sparked by the presiding judge, over the fairness of the long sentences imposed on steel industrialist Alfried Krupp and his managers in their just-finished trial.[80] The readiness of the media to support American policies in the war criminal issue was palpably abating.

One particular article in *Der Spiegel* was symptomatic in this regard. Framed by a stirring account of the efforts by the bride of an SS captain facing execution to have her husband spared, it furnished a detailed description of the Landsberg execution process. At the same time, it wasted no words on the nature of the deeds committed by the offenders—for whom the term "Landsbergers," smacking of civic uprightness, had now been chosen. A veneer of distance from the condemned persons' interests, still maintained by the news magazine, was cut through in a citation from a report (no more precise identification offered) suggesting that "so-called sound popular opinion"—*sogenannte gesunde Volksempfinden*—"is very clearly inclined toward charitable leniency." The magazine considered the church leaders' petitions—as opposed to the usual "inflationary material" at play in sworn affidavits—as pointing to the justice of suspending the death sentences.[81]

In contrast, voices raised to publicly defend the executions or even question the church's engagement had become very rare indeed. Characteristically that role was now left to the American-run *Neue Zeitung*— albeit here as well clarity was most often found in the letters column. At any rate, a Munich resident could express his amazement there at the talk of pardons: "If these criminals and a large number of their accomplices had been hanged in 1945, everyone would have considered it self-evident." True, a letter from someone who had been interned by the Allies came next, using catchwords such as Dresden and Hiroshima to cite Allied "crimes against humanity" that no one apparently intended to punish. Clear-cut words regarding the two churches were reserved for Ludwig Bergsträsser, though the *Neue Zeitung* did not identify him for its readers as head of Darmstadt's regional government or as a Social Democratic member of the Parliamentary Council. "Why does the church place itself protectively before those who committed murder and other crimes? In a period in which human beings—even simply on grounds of having expressed a free opinion—were tormented and murdered in concentration camps, a voice from the church was hardly heard, and then very lightly, raised for an arrested pastor and almost no one else. . . . I thus believe that today as well the church should leave such matters to more authorized persons, instead of attempting to alleviate the need of this age's victims, impeding a reemergence of such barbarity through Christian educational labor."[82]

By the start of 1949, the general current of opinion outside Germany as within had long since moved against the gist of Bergsträsser's remarks. In the United States, the signs pointed to appeasement—as they did in England, where Winston Churchill would demonstratively donate twenty-five pounds for the defense of General Field Marshall Erich von Manstein, whom the British had put on trial in Hamburg in August 1949.[83] In the United States, both the increasing intervention of the Senate and the creation of ever more investigative commissions revealed how politically difficult it had become to resist the pressure of a small but effective pro-German lobby, a lobby that promoted its cause by evoking the German bishops' protests and the prisoners' assertions, unhesitatingly promulgated by their attorneys. The difficulty was compounded by an injection into such protests and assertions of one insinuation in particular: Communist machinations in the war crimes trials of the early postwar period.

In this context, it was perhaps not astonishing that Joseph McCarthy, with his acute awareness of media potential, got himself appointed to the three-man Baldwin Subcommittee, established in March 1949 by the Armed Services Committee to once more review the Malmédy trial.[84] Meanwhile, the number of pending executions had dwindled to six (from an original forty-three). The apparent purpose of the new subcommittee was to come up with reasons for commuting these last sentences. Its members, however, took their duties far more seriously than anticipated. After only four weeks, McCarthy quit, protesting that the chairman, Republican senator Raymond Baldwin, wished to exculpate the U.S. army. In fact, the only thing perhaps casting doubt on that charge was the refusal by Baldwin and his two Democratic colleagues to have former interrogators at the Dachau trials, attributed by McCarthy with "Gestapo-like methods," strapped to lie detectors.

At the start of September 1949, preparations for parliamentary activity began in Bonn. At the same time, the Baldwin Subcommittee convened in Germany. The senators' 108 interlocutors included members of the army who had participated in the investigation and trial, the lawyers for those who were condemned, and the church activists. But the subcommittee also paid considerable attention to witnesses for the defense—whoever could know something or claimed to do so was heard. Among other things to emerge in this manner was that the chief witness attesting to the prisoners' claimed abuse was a court-identified swindler. A medical team working for the subcommittee took the members to Schwäbisch Hall, site of claimed torture. The senators ended up concluding that many of the accused had been shoved about during the investigation, and there may have been isolated cases of beating, but there was not a scrap of evidence of torture. There had been staged trial scenes meant to break the pact of silence between SS men, but conclusions about their propriety had long since been drawn, to the advantage of the condemned persons. "The subcommittee is impressed by the thoroughness of General Clay's final review. [It] believes that the use of the mock trials so prejudiced the thinking of all who reviewed this case that they resulted in otherwise guilty men escaping the death sentence or perhaps going entirely free. It is the considered opinion of the subcommittee that the Army in reaching its final conclusion in these cases ruled out any evidence secured by improper procedures during the pretrial interrogation, or as a result of procedural errors made by the court."[85]

As a result of such conclusions, the senators saw no basis for commuting more sentences. In general, they did express regret at the lack of experience in criminal law of many trial participants, a surprising number of whom were Americans who had only recently been naturalized. The senators' effort to avoid promoting any prejudice regarding these mostly Jewish emigrants, volunteering as they had to serve the army, is manifest in the formulation of one passage in their closing report. "This subcommittee wants to make it clear that it is not condemning the efforts or the loyalty of any group of persons or individuals, but it does feel that it is unfortunate that more native-born, trained American citizens were not available to carry out this most important function. The natural resentment that exists within a conquered nation was aggravated by the fact that so many of the persons handling these matters were former citizens of that country."[86]

But the Baldwin Commission also came to a very different conclusion: namely, that the agitation directed at the Malmédy trial was merely the tip of a comprehensive attack on the program for punishing the war criminals. And this, the senators maintained, served in turn to discredit U.S. occupation policies in their entirety, the aim being to drive the Americans out of Germany and resuscitate German nationalism. "There is evidence." they averred, "that at least a part of this effort is attempting to establish a close liaison with Communist Russia."[87] In other words, the struggle against the war crimes trials was part of a plot.

This was of course a sensational thesis, but in the autumn of 1949, when the Baldwin Report was published in Washington, the general sensibility was not open to such a critique.[88] The truth is that despite its likely underestimation of German nationalism's anti-Bolshevist stamp, the senators' conclusions were by no means as absurd as public opinion would have had it. In the course of 1949, the cartel supporting the war criminals would reach organizational and political dimensions actually rendering it impossible *not* to see it as at least a potential problem for democracy. The senatorial prognosis was in all events rather cautious: "In the event of the withdrawal of the American occupation forces, it is quite probable that there would be efforts made to have a general amnesty program to release these former Nazis and SS officers." It would soon become clear that such efforts in no way presumed a U.S. withdrawal.

The two leading bishops' reaction to the report underscored that in many respects the Baldwin Subcommittee's fears were not exaggerated but in fact restrained. The report had expressly attributed honorable motives to the two denominations, simply speaking of the danger that their Christian efforts could be abused by others. Nevertheless, the bishops felt called on to offer sharp rebuttals. "It is all too easy to throw dirt in order not to admit light where darkness reigns," indignantly exclaimed Neuhäusler; and Wurm scornfully observed that "one does not know whether to laugh or cry at such suspicions. I am more inclined to laugh."[89] Wurm's proposal "to investigate what agreements have been made between Auxiliary Bishop Neuhäusler and myself" was meant sarcastically. But his next sentence revealed more than he could have liked: "The investigation would lead to the finding that there was neither oral nor written communication between us, but that independently of each other, simply on grounds of the material that reached us, we both concluded that in the investigation of war crimes American justice has not proceeded conscientiously enough."

Although somewhat hidden between his sallies against U.S. investigative officers he qualified as "executioners" ("their deeds do not lag behind those of the Nazis in sadism"), Wurm here had actually confirmed that he and Neuhäusler were drawing from the same murky well. His mention of attorney Rudolf Aschenauer was a similar confirmation—not only had Aschenauer been continuously feeding Neuhäusler (and in the United States, from time to time, McCarthy) with horror stories; he also naturally found a receptive listener in Wurm.[90] The impression of a complexly synchronized interactive venture between church officials and lawyers for the war criminals has meanwhile become so compelling that even the U.S. intelligence services were taking it seriously.[91] At the same time, one would have searched the German press in vain for a critical word.

CHAPTER 6

The Politicization of the War Criminal Question (1949-50)

Nuremberg is a regression to barbarity.

—*Attorney Robert Servatius, September 1949*[1]

By the spring of 1949, the struggle to free the war criminals had already been elevated to a new organizational level. In Heidelberg, a "jurists' circle" had been formed that, on account of its high-caliber membership, would soon emerge as a central coordinating body. The immediate reason for its founding may have been the termination of the subsequent trials at Nuremberg, with a concomitant dissolution of important institutional connections and a threatened rupture of the steady information exchange between the defense attorneys.[2] In this situation, Eduard Wahl, defense attorney in the I. G. Farben trial and, since 1941, professor of international law at Heidelberg University, offered to establish a "coordination site" in Heidelberg and to take care of conference possibilities.[3]

The Heidelberg circle met about every three months. From the lists of participants and the session summary, we can observe how quickly this private group slipped into the role of a quasi-official body—one whose decisions were even adhered to by public authorities.[4] The group's core members were leading defense attorneys from the Nuremberg trials: the adept Rudolf Aschenauer (meanwhile the legal adviser to nearly 700 Landsberg prisoners[5]); Hellmut Becker (Ernst von Weizsäcker's lawyer in the Foreign Ministry trial); Georg Fröschmann (lawyer for euthanasia program organizer Viktor Brack in the doctors' trial, and for SS *Hauptamtchef* Gottlob Berger in the Foreign Ministry trial); Justus Koch (Foreign Ministry again); Otto Kranzbühler (former naval judge and lawyer in the Krupp trial and trial of industrialist Friedrich Flick, as well as lawyer for Saar industrialist Hermann Röchling before the French military court in Rastatt); Hans Laternser (lawyer for the Wehrmacht General Staff in the International Military Tribunal, as well as in the High Command and "hostage murder" trial of generals who served in the Balkans); and finally, lawyers Rudolf Müller, Heinrich von Rospatt, and Helmut Henze, who worked with Wahl on behalf of I. G. Farben. The circle's regular guests also included the long-standing Nuremberg defense attorney Hans Gawlik, meanwhile director of the "Coordination Bureau for the Advancement of Legal Defense for German Prisoners Abroad" at the Länderrat in Stuttgart, the organizational basis for the Central Bureau for Legal Defense that would be established, also under his direction, at the Justice Ministry in Bonn.[6] Alongside the "ex-Nurembergians," some Higher Regional Court presidents were always to be found in Heidelberg; they were led by Hodo Freiherr von Hodenberg (Celle), an uncompromising opponent of the Allied trials, and according to Kranzbühler the circle's second "leading figure" after Wahl.[7] Two of Wahl's university colleagues, both dismissed from their positions by the Nazis, were also present: law professors Gustav Radbruch (who would die in November 1949) and Karl Geiler, who had now become the rector of Heidelberg University. They were, however, usually represented by conservative specialist in international law Erich Kaufmann (Munich), yet another member of the Foreign Ministry defense team and soon to be appointed the chancellery's first "Legal Adviser for Matters of International Law."[8] Finally, the two church denominations were represented: the Catholic through attorney Heribert Knott, chancellor of the Cologne Archdiocese and delegate for the chairman of the Fulda Bishop's Conference; the Evangelical through High Consistory members Rudolf Weeber, based in Stuttgart, and Hansjürg Ranke, an experienced church official responsible for the war criminal issue in the church chancellery since his return from British incarceration as a war prisoner[9]—as well as through Fritz Flitner of the "Office for Legal Protection" of the Evangelical Relief Association in Stuttgart. And once the Federal Justice Ministry came into existence, official Alfons Wahl would arrive regularly from Bonn to take part in the meetings.

Because of the relatively large interludes between the meetings, from the start it seemed sensible for this circle of academics to limit itself to strategic questions and coordinative goals; detail work was hardly possible. To this extent, the circle did not constitute, for instance, competition with the imposing—and ever growing—number of organizations and groups devoted in a concrete way to the war criminals. Rather it was something like a clearing center intent on tying interests together, setting priorities, and placing a check on activities that seemed counterproductive.[10]

At least as telling as the names and institutional affiliations of the circle's members were the names of those who were absent: to start with, Ernst Achenbach and Friedrich Grimm, whose presence might well have been expected, owing to their intense activity on behalf of the war criminals. Referring to relevant experiences from the early Weimar period, Grimm, for instance, had published his ambitious legal-theoretical "Memorandum Concerning the Necessity of a General Amnesty" as early as the summer of 1949.[11] And Achenbach, Grimm's indirect successor in Essen—in the 1920s already the seat of an amnesty committee for Germans accused of war crimes in World War I—was battling on all political and juridical fronts against the Allied prosecutorial effort.[12] Likewise unrepresented (at least directly) in the Heidelberg circle was the "Quiet Help for War Prisoners and Interned Persons" of Helene Elisabeth Princess of Isenburg, named the "Mother of the Landsbergers." On the surface, the absence of "Quiet Help" can be explained by the fact that even traditional charitable organizations (the German Red Cross; Caritas) were connected to the circle only through the Länderrat's coordinating office. But the group by no means limited itself to quietly distributing parcels to the "incarcerated ones"; to the contrary, as its name itself suggests, it linked such activity with a highly specific past-political mission. And precisely this mission precluded, not contacts with individual "Heidelbergians," but the invitation of figures like Princess Isenburg, Grimm, and Achenbach to the circle's meetings. For the circle's policy toward the past was stamped by an effort to avoid, as much as possible, any profession of historical weltanschauung—and to apparently form no value judgments. What was preferably conceived and coordinated there was past-political legal positivism, with a claim to "objectivity" and the goal of fully doing away with the war criminal problem—no more, but also no less.

This strategy was especially manifest in the circle's relationship with representatives of the Evangelical church. Many of the latter figures were not, of course, subject to the same explosions as Theophil Wurm, but quite a few could hold their nationalist propensities in check only with difficulty—or else had no wish to do so. The largely sober jurists did their best to counteract the clerics' desire for self-revelation. One example of this emerged in connection with the creation and presentation of the German Evangelical Church's so-called war criminal memorandum.

The authors, signatories, and catalysts of the memorandum were aiming at nothing less than a comprehensive modification of America's war criminal policy. Preliminary work on the text had begun in the summer of 1948.[13] At that time, Hansjürg Ranke had prepared the preliminary version of a rather lengthy article systematizing the objections to the Dachau and Nuremberg trials raised over preceding months. It was meant to be delivered to Senate President Vandenberg as a text coauthored by all the bishops in the American zone, other recipients being Secretary of State Marshall and Secretary of the Army Royall.[14] It appears that a memorandum from the Catholic Bishop's Conference issued at the same time and possessing the same thrust caused this step to be postponed.

Through the emergence of the Heidelberg circle, the plans once more took on currency. Since their inception, Ranke had carefully kept up with developments and collected additional information.[15] The matter could thus already be discussed over the course of the first meetings. From the discussions, an agreement emerged to, in Otto Kranzbühler's contented formulation, "have the church alone produce the memorandum."[16] Kranzbühler predicted a "weakening" should the "Heidelbergians" step forward as cosignatories. Most likely this prediction—to the extent that it was not simply meant to flatter the churchmen and did not simply mirror rivalry between the lawyers—was connected with a suspicion that deploying large numbers of previous Nuremberg defense attorneys would spark unnecessary American mistrust. The memorandum could have an optimal effect only if it presented as many legal objections as possible alongside the main proposal, and did so in an impressive form. In this respect, Kranzbühler and his colleagues desired to help with both legal knowledge and money—but from the background. A certain amount of money (around 5,000 marks) was necessary since the text, 164 pages long in printed form, needed translation into English; the I. G. Farben lawyers volunteered to cover these costs.[17]

Although not envisioned as such from the start, in the course of its planning the memorandum increasingly turned into a secret project. Undoubtedly a contributing factor was the fact that the only printed version was in English—and that its 1,000 numbered examples represented the "original" version.[18] And another contributing factor was the eventual recommendation of Prelate Hartenstein—along with Wurm and Niemöller, he had designated himself as the text's editor for the German Evangelical Church—that the "entire business" "be kept completely confidential, indeed secret."[19] In fact, this undertow of portent would turn out a skillfully prepared ingredient for evoking expectations and curiosity, a necessary ingredient in light of the memorandum's basic identity with what Wurm and colleagues had been publicly pushing for all along. While certainly having an effect on survey-measured public sentiment, their enterprise had not managed to budge those who mattered to any great degree. But now, furnished with stiffer backbones by the Heidelberg circle, the churchly shepherds were freshly determined to achieve results by all possible means—their main target in this respect being John J. McCloy, the new American High Commissioner in Germany.

On 21 February 1950 Hartenstein and the two authors of the final memorandum, Ranke and Weeber, had the opportunity to deliver McCloy a copy of the text.[20] The delivery took place in a "very relaxed and open manner," following a supper in the High Commissioner's Bad Homburg villa—perhaps not as much a coincidence as the three visitors believed.[21] In any event the deeper reason for the good atmosphere was that McCloy himself had something to communicate. He could thus sit back and listen to Karl Hartenstein's remarks, delivered in English, describing the memorandum's genesis and essential points. The material, he heard, was assembled entirely without any assistance from the church, which simply served as an honest broker for many individuals not in a position to speak for themselves. The church was concerned with nothing other than peace and justice, but it had also come to realize that a false solution would conjure up dangers for both sides. The presentation of testimonies was meant to prevent the problem being inflamed by a misguided and furtive nationalism. Hartenstein emphasized a protective proviso also included in the memorandum: the church had neither the ability nor the duty to examine the truthfulness of the complaints in toto. He concluded by presenting the demands of the German Evangelical Church: all proceeding needed to be reviewed by an independent body, including German judges, and this without any time pressure. Such a review would need to furnish both the condemned and their lawyers with a hearing; the lawyers would have to be supplied not only with the trial documents but also with the review records. At the same time, the credibility of the evidence on which the original guilty verdict was based had to be examined, and the sentence substantiated. Furthermore, until the sentence review, the punishment was to be suspended with probation, as provided for in U.S. regulations, and in appropriate cases mercy was to take precedence over justice.[22]

High Commissioner McCloy did not show any great surprise at these demands. In the nine months since his arrival in Germany, the war criminal theme had quickly moved to the top of his list of priorities. He himself had come to consider "reaching an intelligent, objective, and just decision" in regard to the Landsberg prisoners as "one of the greatest problems" facing him in Germany[23] During the previous months, he had run the matter over in his mind with corresponding intensity—and made ready a basic plan that he now presented to his guests with remarkable openness. McCloy began by reminding them of the intent behind the "Nuremberg system" he had helped prevail (against Morgenthau), a system that had in part been conceived with a view to the negative lessons of the war crimes trials following World War I.[24] The American public, McCloy indicated, would not accept a general amnesty for those condemned in Nuremberg, and general attacks on the soundness of the sentences were actually improper; especially the sentences passed in the SS cases were "faultless." There were, however, some cases in which the punishment seemed too severe. McCloy had thus decided to review all the cases, and to this end he had proposed the establishment of an independent three-man judicial committee to the State Department—its task would be to have enough recommendations on the table in sixty days for McCloy to arrive at final decisions quickly. The participation of German judges was in any case not practicable. But McCloy indicated he was planning a "permanent parole board" to regularly decide on releases owing to good behavior.

As far as the Dachau trials were concerned, jurisdiction lay not with the High Commissioner but with General Handy, commander in chief of the U.S. army in Europe (the two functions had meanwhile become separate). McCloy explained that Handy had not been able to agree to establishing a judicial committee, instead opting for one more internal review. McCloy left no doubt he considered the general's motives sound: incessant repetition of the same reproaches against the army courts had resulted in increased skepticism regarding a fresh full review of the sentences—a sentiment compounded by the fact that a review of the Malmédy trial had produced only one witness claiming to have been coerced into a false statement. And after all, thirty-seven shackled U.S. soldiers had been murdered at Malmédy by shots in the base of the skull.

The productive nature of the conversation clearly surprised the German Evangelical Church's delegates. But in conclusion, the High Commissioner did offer some words of warning. Doubtless aimed not only at Bishop Dibelius, whom McCloy named directly, they expressed "some unhappiness" at a stance condemning "*everything* that has transpired before the military courts" as "unjust." As attested by their own notes, the three gentlemen left McCloy's final remarks unanswered.[25]

The detail with which McCloy initiated the churchmen into his plans—if only under a seal of confidentiality—was all the more startling in that he was still waiting for a green light from Washington.[26] McCloy biographer Thomas Schwartz has interpreted this approach as a sign of political independence, and this is doubtless correct.[27] At the same time, his decision to make "Landsberg" into his most urgent concern—hence a decision over the fate of fifteen persons still on death row—underscores his special feel for the necessities of realpolitik. A political professional, McCloy had realized that more was at stake here than punishment or mercy for a handful of criminals. Through his encounters with various Germans, the centrality the theme had taken on over recent months had become clear. Most likely, his conversations with Adenauer contributed to such insight. For ever since Bonn had embarked on politics, the political world had itself discovered the war criminal question.

Put more precisely, the discovery had already been registered in the ranks of the Parliamentary Council—true, not in the sense of open backing for the war criminals (either on an individual or collective basis), but in the sense of a subsurface attentiveness to, and partial support for, specific interests linked to this group. It is in any case clear that, although not addressed head on, the war criminal question was present in the concerns of at least some of the delegates. In appropriate contexts, the theme seems to have been placed on a secret agenda—this is particularly manifest in discussions of the death penalty and extradition law. Against the backdrop of an Allied expiatory will that was by no means exhausted, the significance of both these issues was transparent. That nobody overtly made the connection is no less remarkable than the manner in which the demand to abolish the death penalty was placed on the agenda.

Over recent years, German criminal law had displayed an understandable insecurity when it came to passing and—more so—carrying out death sentences.[28] The constitutional convention held in Bavaria's Herrenchiemsee castle had expressly recommended that the Parliamentary Council address the issue, but no one near the council's political center offered a motion to this effect.[29] Rather, Hans-Christoph Seebohm did so in December 1948, in the council's steering committee speaking for the right-wing German Party. And since Seebohm was certainly not fulfilling any heart-filled humanistic impulse on the part of his constituency, the motive for his proposal needs to be looked for elsewhere. In fact, Seebohm's argument did contain an illuminating remark, albeit embedded in all sorts of humanistic rhetoric. Rejection of the death penalty would "signify in a very basic manner the German people's turn away from any system based on violence and its abhorrence at the large number of death sentences carried out over the past fifteen years."[30] The "Thousand-Year Reich" had lasted a little more than twelve years. Anyone who was able and willing to calculate could thus have no doubt that Seebohm wished to see the past three years' occupation, with its substantial number of death sentences and executions, included in his characterization.[31]

At first, no plurality could be mustered for the German Party proposal.[32] But this changed with a corresponding motion by the SPD in the third debate. Where the Social Democrats appealed to human progress, evoking their traditional rejection of the death penalty as something "barbarous," even against the backdrop of the most terrible crimes, Seebohm could not resist the chance to toss another heavy hint: "Looked at in terms of weltanschauung, especially the experience of recent years, which is to say not only the period up to 1945 but also that after, has made it an absolute necessity to speak out against the death penalty."[33] All other participants in the debate stuck to a level of ethics and criminal policy. On 5 May 1949, after nearly three months' adjournment that allowed enough time for consultation among the different party factions, the steering committee approved the proposal with no further discussion, and by a large majority. The following day, the plenum approved the plans after a short debate.[34]

It is certainly the case that the past-political motives at work in the parliamentary decision to abolish the death penalty were not limited to a narrow calculation of—at least indirect—aid to the war criminals facing Allied execution. Communist Party delegate Renner, for example, explained his assent with the remarkable observation that "in light of its composition and National Socialist past," the judicature should not be furnished with the death penalty, since it would then be used as a "political weapon against the progressive-democratic forces."[35] But the argument that it was inadmissible to execute "German individuals" on West German soil, where the Basic Law had abolished the death penalty, would prove very useful indeed in the heated debates of the coming years.[36]

Also anchored in the Basic Law, the extradition ban was less useful for purposes of agitation—although in itself it had some import. In the steering committee debate, it went unmentioned that the occupying powers had repeatedly extradited Nazi criminals to states previously under German occupation to face trial for their deeds in situ. Nevertheless, it would have been inappropriate to utterly deny the discussion's participants access to such considerations. And indeed, at least one person emerged who was willing to reveal his thoughts in that direction: once again, it was Hans-Christoph Seebohm. From the vantage point of the German Party delegate, the formulation suggested by the council's editorial committee ("no German may be extradited abroad") revealed a grave flaw; but instead of spelling it out, Seebohm first offered a semantic argument. The reference to "abroad" could be omitted, since where else would people be extradited? The response was that such an omission could render impossible the usual practice of delivering ordinary criminals to the Eastern zone. Only now, Seebohm found himself forced to speak more clearly. "Remanding a prosecuted person to another part of Germany not presently federal territory is not extradition. In contrast, I can imagine the concept of 'extradition' being used to cover procedures also carried out within federal territory, namely when later, on the basis of occupation statutes, the order is issued to hand over German individuals to the occupation authorities, who themselves extradite them. Just here, I would like to have the sense of that being expressly prevented through excision of the term *abroad*. If something of that sort is forced on us in occupation statutes or by another means, then it should be an encroachment on the basic human rights of the Germans, one for which the opposing side is expressly responsible."[37]

Without question, the "German individuals" Seebohm had in mind were above all persons suspected of serious war crimes. It was only in their case that political interest would be strong enough to allow the occupation authorities to intervene despite the Basic Law. But apparently such efforts were removed from the thoughts of most of the delegates. Despite Seebohm's repetition of his proposal before the Parliamentary Council's plenum,[38] both steering committee and plenum opted for the original version of the extradition ban. It offered a high degree of security to yet undiscovered war criminals and Nazis guilty of crimes against humanity. But at least, as long as occupation law prevailed, it did not constitute a blanket guarantee.

This was shown in spectacular fashion in the case of Erich Koch, former *Gauleiter* of East Prussia and Reich Commissioner for the Ukraine. At the end of May 1949, Koch emerged from his hiding place—apparently, to cite *Christ und Welt*'s speculation, because he intended "to claim the protection of the just-enacted Basic Law, which forbids both extradition and the death penalty." Koch, the speculation continued, "may be prepared to be placed before a German court and in the worst case sentenced to life in prison." Koch was in British detention, and the British had to consider the extradition requests of Poland and the Soviet Union. In February 1950 they handed this "German individual," charged with the most brutal crimes, to Warsaw. For *Christ und Welt,* the decision has a "political aftertaste"; despite all the author's efforts to avoid undertones suggesting anything like support for the

British, it remained clear that his reservations were not simply formal-legal in nature. The decision's entire direction made him uneasy. But his closing argument skillfully packaged his criticism: "We regret that the opportunity has been denied Germany to judicially disapprove in belated form what its citizens already condemned with indignation at the time of the deed."[39]

A few weeks earlier in *Die Zeit,* Marion Gräfin Dönhoff—stemming from East Prussia, she would become that liberal Hamburg weekly's leading voice over the following decades—had already demanded, very similarly, that Koch "first of all" be brought before a German court. Details concerning the man's atrocities were meant to shore up the demand. In contrast to *Christ und Welt, Die Zeit* raised no objections in principle to the extradition of this "major political henchman": no one "has so earned, a thousand times over, the sure death awaiting him in the east—and that our penal code no longer provides for—as Erich Koch." At the same time, Countess Dönhoff implicitly erected a hierarchy of victims, precedence being granted Koch's punishment for the death and torment inflicted on the East Prussian populace in the winter of 1944–45 over that for his complicity in the mass murder of Poles and Jews. And rather directly she revealed a distaste for the Allied punitive effort, expressed in her journal for a long time now with scarcely less sharpness than *Christ und Welt:* "We are fed up with observing men such as Weizsäcker and others who fought against people of Koch's stamp under constant risk to their own life being sentenced by Allied courts—as if all that was of no concern to us—while figures such as East Prussia's head of the police and SS, Hellwig, and Koch's dirty right hand, Herr Dzubba, run around free."[40]

In fact, German justice would certainly have not left an unpleasant character like Koch go scot-free and might well have punished the man with demonstrative severity. Be that as it may, nobody was preventing the state prosecutors from taking up the cases Countess Dönhoff referred to—and this is not the only reason her regrets over German justice not being granted a trial were somewhat strained. Another reason involves the regrets being belied by the basic tendency emerging more and more in the West German political-journalistic debate over the war criminals. Subject to some sharp permutations since mid-1949, the debate was at all events distinguished by a scrambling together of very different problems: war crimes and Nazi crimes against humanity; political purging and criminal prosecution; bureaucratic responsibility and the exercise of physical violence. From this perspective, Dönhoff's apologia for Weizsäcker in an article on Erich Koch can be understood as not only simply—and obviously—misplaced but also symptomatic: both the symptom and outcome of a policy toward the past whose threads were increasingly coming together in Bonn.

As things turned out, Bonn was not the venue of the first open political broadside against the "Nuremberg system," but rather neighboring Düsseldorf—or more precisely, the Paderborn marketplace. This was the scene for a speech on intellectual freedom, Christian faith, and state power, delivered in July 1949 by Karl Arnold, the CDU minister president of North Rhine Westphalia, to an audience of 10,000.[41] While the formal occasion was a celebration in honor of the cathedral's patron saint, the speech was actually part of the campaign leading up to the first Bundestag elections, then in full swing. The state's exercise of power had to be "morally grounded," Arnold explained, and Christianity had always struggled for such a foundation. The anti-Hitler conspirators of 20 July 1944 acted on the same principle; at least the "great majority" of the resistors were motivated by a duty to show "that the sense of right and justice had in no way died out in Germany."

Some of those who took Arnold's words at face value and then considered the parallel he proceeded to draw must have shuddered at the present circumstances. In one breath with 1944, the minister president lamented the "spiritual confusion of our time"—something "not shown more resoundingly than through the fact that in Nuremberg, alongside genuine war criminals, men were also sentenced to prison whose concern was preventing World War II by risking their lives, and after Hitler nonetheless got it started, ending it through the violent criminal system's downfall." Finally Arnold let the cat fully out of the bag: it was inadmissible "that a man such as the former state secretary of the Foreign Ministry, Ernst von Weizsäcker, should be held in his innocence as a war criminal in Landsberg." "Miscarriages of justice" by the military courts had to be corrected, and beyond this a "statute for the continued pacification of the German people" had to be issued; through the latter, "those circles still standing apart from the state will be led toward it once again."

Among those sensitive to the nuances of political language, some may have found Arnold's words, with their tenor of "bringing together" the *Volksgemeinschaft*, rather unpleasant. It did, however, quite precisely strike that chord understood by voters standing to the right of the CDU. But comparing the sentence passed on Ernst von Weizsäcker with the "case of the French captain Dreyfus, condemned despite his innocence," was more than a venial election sin. Things were not made better by citing "state omnipotence and its supposed interests" as the comparison's linking element, while at the same time omitting any mention of the basic fact that Dreyfus was a Jew.

How did it come about that a representative of the CDU's left wing, speaking in the heartland of political Catholicism, could intervene so massively on behalf of precisely Weizsäcker, a man seeming to emerge straight from the storybook of old Protestant-nationalist leadership? What was it that moved a former Christian trade unionist, himself surviving the "Third Reich" uncompromised and at some cost,[42] to offer such a preposterous analogy? We can best arrive at an answer by inquiring into "who": Arnold's committed speech was the reflection less of a personal need than of a preoccupation of its actual author, Theo Kordt, since December 1948 adviser on international law in the Düsseldorf state chancellery. Kordt had not hesitated to attribute the role of Emile Zola to Arnold, his "very juristically inclined present boss."[43] In 1939— but before the war's outbreak—Theo Kordt had been a diplomatic counselor in the German embassy in London; his younger brother Erich was serving then as bureau director of the Foreign Ministry. Both that year and the year before, the brothers tried to warn the British about German intentions and move them toward a tougher policy. Since the arrest of Weizsäcker in July 1947 as a central defendant in the planned Foreign Ministry trial, Theo Kordt had been doing everything in his power to help his former boss. Naturally, these efforts contributed to casting a little light on the specific service of the Kordt brothers in the resistance to Hitler. But the more far-reaching intent was to stylize the former state secretary—he had been shifted to the Holy See ambassadorship in 1943—into an anchor and starting point of numerous efforts by an "authentic" Foreign Ministry (or by its "youngsters") to prevent the war.[44]

At a certain point in the Foreign Ministry proceedings at Nuremberg, it became clear that beyond Ribbentrop's condemnation in the main trial, plans had been laid for a trial of the office's bureaucratic elite. But even long before this—indeed, since the point when traffic and postal service had begun to function again in Germany—efforts were at work among that same elite to develop the most shadow-free possible image of the past shared by its members. For example, in March 1947, shortly before Weizsäcker was "invited" to Nuremberg for "file work," he wrote Erich Kordt to the effect that his remarks on the London activities of both Kordts in the summer of 1939 had been "soothing."[45] "It seems," he observed, "that I also played some sort of role in your brother's excursion. I hope that if necessary my memory is the same as your brother's, so that no contradictions emerge."[46]A half year later it had become "necessary"; summoned to Nuremberg for questioning, Theo Kordt wrote Weizsäcker as follows: "I have put my memory through a very probing examination of conscience and believe that I am going to the consultation well prepared. I have recently had a very detailed conversation with Master [Hellmut] Becker and hope to be able to contribute something useful. These lines are meant simply to assure you that Erich and I are attached to the good, just cause with the old devotion, and that we do not lack the determination to do our part."[47]

And in fact, in the interrogation by Robert Kempner, Kordt did not shy away from brazen assertions. He thus declared that his brother Erich had kept Weizsäcker "constantly" informed about the London communications with the British and that he himself brought the state secretary up to date each time they met in Berlin. Theo Kordt to Kempner: "It is certain that Herr von Weizsäcker was at the center of opposition in the Foreign Ministry. Without his agreement, I would have had much more difficulty taking the steps I did to save the peace and, later, to end the war as quickly as possible through the downfall of National Socialism."[48]

Nothing better reveals the self-understanding and self-assuredness of the Foreign Ministry's dispersed cadre than the name they gave Chief Prosecutor Robert Kempner in their private correspondence: "Dr. Sixtus Beckmesser"—the reference being to the character in Wagner's "Meistersinger" whose last name has become a standard German term for a pedantic philistine or petty complainer. Occasionally Ernst von Weizsäcker also phrased things through a diction of camouflage and superciliousness. Long since having reached the age of retirement, he more often met the efforts on his behalf by his younger diplomatic colleagues, and even his younger defense attorney, with a certain detachment whose origin was most likely partly religious. In face of the rampant reinterpretation of the historical events and the inflation of the resistance, he leaned toward reserve.[49]

Becker consistently coordinated and quite often inspired the declarations on behalf of Weizsäcker.[50] They serve as impressive evidence of the enormous energy with which at least some members of the old official elite were striving toward an acceptance of their reading of the recent past by both the occupying powers and the new German political decision makers. The hoped-for result of such a development was by no means limited to continued employment in one's chosen vocation. Rather, it was nothing short of moral rehabilitation, and the acknowledgment of a putatively widespread struggle to preserve distance from the Nazis. In the case of the pre-Nazi Foreign Ministry cadre (which in any event had almost entirely joined Nazi Party ranks at the end of the 1930s), another factor was also in play: seeing to it that the claim to a substantial influence on Germany's foreign policy—a claim already being voiced in the "German Bureau for Questions of Peace"[51]—

not be threatened by standing back and watching a more or less representative condemnation of figurehead Weizsäcker. From this perspective, the state secretary's eventual condemnation, despite all the contrarily invested energy, to seven years' imprisonment meant that everything needed to be done to shorten the prison term. For if it indeed proved possible to spring him early, then the cadre's reading would have been at least *partially* vindicated: Weizsäcker as a "man of peace"; the legitimacy of a German striving for great-power status cleanly distinct from a Nazi racial imperialism that no one had liked or indeed even supported.

In essence it was now becoming clear, in the summer of 1949, how right Charles LaFollette had been in his prediction that once "really important political figures such as Weizsäcker" had to enter prison, the moment would have arrived when people other than church leaders were willing to take up the war criminal issue.[52] The development was favored by a Bonn-based political centralization that had now gathered steam. But its deeper source was the fact that with the new Federal Republic old structures of influence could reconsolidate—structures that could make very good use of a talent like Hellmut Becker. As would be expected, this busy lawyer and family friend of Weizsäcker, himself from the best of families (his father was the liberal Prussian culture minister Carl Heinrich Becker), spared no effort to mobilize all available political and journalistic connections, direct and indirect, that could help his client. In this manner, the Weizsäcker case became a catalyst for a politicization of the war criminal problem.

Few of the defense lawyers had Becker's ability to combine a sure sense of public effect with political imagination. When, for instance, in May 1949, a month after his sentence was delivered, Weizsäcker was brought in handcuffs to Landsberg to serve his term, Becker immediately considered the possibility of "gaining as much capital as possible" from the "shackling episode" "through press and voice." Becker had pleaded for Weizsäcker's acquittal. Disappointed by the trial's outcome and convinced that the episode "very clearly" demonstrated "the impossibility of trying to criminally prosecute political guilt, even when it has already been assumed," Becker now began to seek help for Weizsäcker on overlapping individual and political levels.[53]

On the individual level, Becker undertook a careful information campaign involving a large circle of friends, patrons, and former colleagues of Weizsäcker, along with important journalists. Having already reported on the trial in an extremely friendly spirit, the journalists would now supply the accompanying music, in Germany and abroad, to the many private petitions being delivered to the highest U.S. officials.[54] On the political level, Becker pushed for a strategy similar to the Heidelberg circle's (albeit before its existence). He thus urged Theo Kordt to convince his boss, Karl Arnold, that action on his part was called for in the moment the "government of West Germany" was being formed. "In my view, the new government should absolutely demand an amnesty from the occupying power as a kind of birthday present. Naturally this should not mean an amnesty for Nazis and war criminals, but a statute for the continued pacification of the German people, through which all the nation's circles now standing apart will be led toward the state . . . . The goal of such an amnesty would have to be seeing to it that from now on only the truly criminal criminals"—*die wirklich kriminellen Verbrecher*—"are stuck away in prison."[55]

Perhaps even more remarkable than this proposal's virtually word-by-word echoing in Arnold's later talk is the actual source of Arnold's Weizsäcker-Dreyfus comparison: Theo Kordt's brother Erich.[56] In its founding period, Bonn was characterized by short paths of influence; adept individuals had a rich range of interesting possibilities at their disposal. One evening at the start of October 1949, for instance, Erich Kordt had an opportunity to place Federal President Theodor Heuss in the picture regarding Weizsäcker. Kordt's former Foreign Ministry colleague Hans von Herwarth ("Jonny") had spotted him in the Bonn-Munich night -train and invited him for a nightcap in the attached presidential wagon. Heuss revealed himself to be not only open to the subject at hand but also well informed; he was ready "to stubbornly pursue the case of our friend W." Kordt learned that Heuss had already "emphatically" intervened on Weizsäcker's behalf with John McCloy. He had even spoken on that occasion of a "miscarriage of justice," the High Commissioner then remarking that he had already been contacted to that effect by others, but that as far as he understood there was "truly incriminating" material in the Weizsäcker files.[57] The episode dramatically illuminates the extent to which things had begun to move, despite the Bonn government's still very brief existence.

This was apparent in the cabinet meetings from the very beginning, in the consultations over the 1949 amnesty law. With the remark that requests related to an amnesty had "been delivered to us on many occasions," Adenauer opened the door to a ministerial discussion of the options available to encourage a softening of sentences passed already by the military courts. No one present doubted there was good cause, and Labor Minister Storch could maintain without being contradicted that the military courts had imposed heavy punishments "on account of trifles." With such a mood being evident even in the cabinet, it was clear to Adenauer that any tackling of the amnesty problem by Parliament had to be carefully prepared and demarcated. "How are we to prevent a debate over the Nuremberg judgments immediately breaking out in the Bundestag? Until now, I have searched in vain for such a possibility." The ministers liked his idea of only addressing the war criminal issue in a concluding remark and of having the Standing Advisory Committee agree that following the chancellor "no one else takes the floor." But in the end, it apparently seemed too risky to the chancellor.[58]

Adenauer in any case refrained from publicly repeating his cabinet statement promise to lodge a protest with the High Commissioner regarding the military court judgments. Meanwhile he had been forced to recognize that in such cases the right to grant mercy was entirely in Allied hands; he was also in the process of recognizing that his role in the business lay behind the scenes. To the dismay of observers at the Petersberg High Commissioner headquarters, enough people were assembling on the Bonn stage anyway, their activities more or less unchecked. Over the following months, the chancellor's tactic thus mainly involved groundwork, which is to say measured sallies during his regular meetings with the Allied High Commission and various encounters with the High Commissioner. Such occasions could be used to plant the seeds of one central idea: that the mitigation of sentences, or better yet a basic correction of the entire expiatory program, benefited not only the condemned individuals but also, with appropriate public presentation, the internal prestige of the new democratic state.

The cabinet debate ended somewhat confusedly. Three days later, the CDU and CSU stepped forward with a proposal very likely based on middle-term considerations such as Adenauer's. Under the rubric "measures on behalf of Germans being detained abroad," the two parties demanded what basically was imminent in any case, a move of the "Coordination Bureau for the Advancement of Legal Protection for German Prisoners Abroad" from the Stuttgart Länderrat to Bonn.[59] Naturally no one in Parliament wished to turn down this initiative; hence a hastily established subcommittee of the Committee for Occupation Law and Foreign Affairs had already made ready a draft resolution at the start of November 1949. It was unanimously passed by the plenum on 1 December.[60]

Passage was preceded by a short but instructive debate, opened by CDU delegate Eugen Gerstenmaier. As head of the Evangelical Relief Association, Gerstenmaier possessed a knowledge of details doubtless rendering him specially suited for the role of reporter on committee affairs. But in view of his expertise, it was all the more portentous that even he was doing his part to sponsor the increasing rhetorical amalgamation of the war criminal problem with that of the war prisoners—the latter actually no longer present in the West. Despite certainly being aware he was making an entirely false connection, he thus opened his report with an estimation of the number of war prisoners held in the Soviet Union: 300,000 to half a million, with another 15,000 estimated for Poland.

It was clearly the case that in both Poland and the Soviet Union, many Germans were being held as war criminals after the passage of peremptory judgments. But precisely this rendered invalid any real comparison with the situation in the rest of Europe, where there were also far fewer prisoners. Gerstenmaier summed up the statistics as follows: Holland—200 condemned or accused German war criminals, Belgium—100, Luxembourg—50, Denmark—55, Norway—60, Italy—20, Greece—8, Yugoslavia—the more substantial figure of 1,400, and France—1,200. Gerstenmaier explained that legal work on behalf of these persons had previously been at the initiative of independent aid organizations; it now needed to be taken over by the government.

In contrast to his remarks on the communist countries, Gerstenmaier's critique of the West was formulated in restrained terms, as if performed out of duty. He remained uninterrupted as he asked his colleagues to turn their attention "still once again, but now from this venue—which as far as I am aware has not yet happened—to the questionability of the entire procedure used up to now against these accused individuals abroad. I believe that beyond the German borders, the conviction is growing that the procedure ... is more than problematic." Above all, the sentences passed in the first postwar years had to be considered "entirely excessive." But it was "not our intention here to add up everything which has been neglected in these proceedings." On the one hand, Gerstenmaier described the situation of the prisoners in Yugoslavia in thoroughly graphic terms—thus drawing a protest from the communist delegates that he was a defender of war criminals. On the other hand, he preferred to criticize the French situation only indirectly. To this end, he cited a "prominent French expert in criminal law" serving as a defense lawyer for accused German war criminals. The jurist, he explained, had referred to the law passed by the French National Assembly on 15 September 1948 as "a kind of legal 'genocide' "—*Völkermord*.[61] At this point in the Bundestag minutes, "hear, hear! in the middle and right" is registered.[62]

Apparently Federal Justice Minister Dehler considered this too gracious a way out for Gerstenmaier. He chose to paint the French picture in sharper contours.[63] What was at play there, he declared, was granting those accused "the most primitive possible legal guarantees, at least on our side." For while the Germans were denied the right to "evoke higher military orders," "members of the maquis" could take advantage of precisely that principle. Once he had got going, Dehler illustrated the French law's import through those "difficult cases whose tragedy we wish in no way to deny, but that to the contrary represent a heavy moral weight for us Germans": the "executions carried out against civilians in Oradour, in Tulle, in Ascq."[64] Every member of an SS, SD, or military police unit was considered an accomplice, the result being death sentences passed on "the unit's translator, the clerk, the truck driver, the cook." And this showed "how necessary it is that the accused men receive help from us over here."

When Dehler declared that his ministry had already been instructed to initiate such legal defense, cries of "bravo" echoed from the governing parties' ranks. That Dehler's illustration had basically been rather vague did not even disturb the German Communist Party speaker, the only delegate who found it necessary to explain in detail why his faction would approve the draft resolution. The Communists' promise that no underhanded tricks would be tolerated in the new Central Bureau for Legal Defense, and that it would not be allowed to become a propaganda center, rang correspondingly hollow.[65] How, precisely, did the German Communist Party intend to control, from one case to another, the choice of paths upon which Dehler's legal defenders would choose to wander—including those abroad?

In one decisive point the communists were already being led by the nose—and with them, presumably, a majority of the delegates. From the start, the Justice Ministry had not intended to limit the Central Bureau to help for condemned and accused Germans abroad—this in contrast to both the proposal's wording and Gerstenmaier's explanation. So much was guaranteed by Hans Gawlik alone.[66] Gawlik was the director of the Coordination Bureau in Stuttgart and was slated to become the future director of the Central Bureau. As a former defense attorney at Nuremberg, he as it were automatically had the interests of war criminals jailed in Germany in mind, along with their lawyers.[67] It was also the case that for the time being none of those in the know wished to draw public attention to this situation—and with it, the attention of the Allies.[68]

The degree of the occupation powers' attention when the Bundestag addressed the war criminal theme was revealed six weeks after the Central Bureau decision, when Justice Minister Dehler once again took up the French "war prisoner" theme—this time at length. The occasion was prompted by an SPD interpellation, the party apparently wishing to make up for having missed the opportunity of demonstrating its solidarity in the debate of 1 December 1949. But whereas the SPD and CDU speakers chose their words with care—there was, after all, agreement on the basic issue—the Free Democrat Dehler tested French feelings to the utmost: in the Oradour case, he asserted, "things" had "occurred" that "go beyond the humanly bearable."[69] Dehler was not referring in any way to the massacre of 642 men, women, and children carried out by members of the "*Reich*" Tank Division.[70] (His only remarks in that respect were that he did not wish to gloss the event over and that it burned as a "stigma in one's soul.") Rather, he meant the situation of the incarcerated Germans. His trial scenario was presented under the sign of pure apologia: "Where are the guilty men? As far as it has been possible to ascertain, they are dead or vanished; five unimportant people remain, five young men who were mostly minors at the time of the event, had been inserted into a squad through an order, and—aside from one—have not been shown to have been participants. And the one who has been charged is an Alsatian. This is how things actually appear."

The justice minister's summary term for the French law in question, which appeared to threaten the SS men with a sentence, was "the Lex Oradour."[71] "It establishes a presumption of guilt that in praxis is not refutable. One can only have pity with accused men who end up in this painful situation." Dehler knew what the solution was to the problem of such "last throes of the evil times under which many innocent people must still suffer": a new Treaty of Westphalia that would mutually bury "all injuries, all acts of violence and hostility" in an "eternal forgetting."[72]

Over recent weeks, Dehler had made himself noticeable through many presumptuous requests—for instance, publicly forwarding a recommendation in mid-December to the American High Commissioner that old and sick war criminals like Weizsäcker and Krupp be amnestied.[73] In the face of his latest brazen gesture, an indignant French reaction could hardly be avoided; twenty-four hours later—12 January 1950—Adenauer bore the brunt during a scheduled Petersberg meeting. "I would have understood it if Dr. Dehler's remarks had been made by a minister in the Third Reich," exclaimed French High Commissioner André François-Poncet—he was accompanied by both his administrative colleagues in his confrontation with the chancellor. François-Poncet expressed his surprise and dismay at Dehler's repeated reference to 1,200 accused Germans in France.[74] Already on 7 December 1949, in response to the chancellor's cautious initiative,[75] he, François-Poncet, had indicated that the number of open cases stood at 234 and that they involved approximately 600 suspects. Dehler's doubling of the number and his critique of French justice could only have a "grave effect" on the atmosphere between France and Germany. "In such cases, the term used in Germany is *Brunnenvergiftung*"—"well poisoning," indicating calumny or defamation—the High Commissioner explained to a clearly surprised Adenauer. All the latter could do was apologize and state he would speak with Dehler the next morning.[76]

The vexation caused by the remarks of his—thoroughly obtuse— justice minister must have served the chancellor as a sign of how tactically correct it was to keep the war criminal theme out of public discussion.[77] Loud complaints were utterly ineffective—and they had the side effect of quickly enticing many countrymen into nationalistic waters. Likewise, as long as it was impossible to wrest any demonstrable concessions from the Allies, it was at least doubtful that blatant gestures would impress right-wing voting groups. Dehler evidently believed the contrary; acting on his belief, he had incurred the permanent mistrust of the Americans, while sparking McCloy's drastic warnings of a resuscitated nationalism.[78] What seemed more likely was that such actions demonstrated precisely that absence of state sovereignty with which "national circles" reproached Bonn's "licensed democrats."

One factor in particular points to the skeptical stance of many German "experts" regarding the government's chances of making headway with the "war prisoners" question: the difficulties following fast on activation of the Central Bureau in mid-March 1950. The German Red Cross, Evangelical Relief Association, and Catholic Caritas showed very limited willingness to give up their responsibilities (which in part were legal in nature) for looking after the prisoners. This is true above all for the legal office of the Evangelical Relief Association, directed by Fritz Flitner, the politically ambitious and rigidly nationalistic former president of the Naumburg High Court in eastern Germany. Flitner would have himself loved to take over the Central Bureau.[79] As late as the summer of 1950, the jurist Margarethe Bitter, who to Flitner's sorrow had been given responsibility over the corresponding Justice Ministry departmental section ("Legal Protection for Germans Abroad"), had to inform the justice minister that until then, the legal aid cases previously taken care of by the charitable organizations had not by any means been "generally" handed over to the Central Bureau.[80] But Bitter could count on an "abating" of such organizational work "through a lack of means." Whereas the charities had received 400,000 marks from the state in 1949, Bonn now directly took care of all the bills—including, most importantly, those of the defense attorneys.[81] The phase of widely uncontrolled activity by the attorneys, especially those working for Germans imprisoned in France—thus came to an end; but the business waiting beyond the Rhine remained lucrative and desirable.[82]

Despite the initial tension with the charity organizations, by the middle of 1950, the seventeen members of the Central Bureau's staff were already working on 2,784 individual cases, mostly prisoners in France. A degree of self-satisfaction is audible in director Hans Gaw-lik's remark, in his first progress report, that in the "Western countries as well as Italy and Greece" there was meanwhile "not a single German prisoner involved in criminal proceedings who lacks the services of a foreign attorney."[83] To the extent, then, that one could trust in the existence of a fair judicial system beyond German borders, as well as in the possibility, five years after the war's end, of fair trials being offered defendants in the same countries as their alleged crimes, there would have seemed no further cause for any great concern. But the same individuals who might have brought the public around to such a position—above all the justice minister—preferred nurturing ressentiment, or at best—as with Adenauer—keeping silent. In general, the absence of any effort in Bonn to end the burgeoning legal and conceptual confusion is unmistakable. Without a doubt, one of the main reasons for this was a lack of oversight. But such a lack resulted less from difficulties in receiving precise information than from an instinctive refusal to take it into account. The view of many officials was clouded through discomfort with the facts at hand.

By 1950, the German effort to help war prisoners, "Germans imprisoned abroad," war criminals in Allied military prisons, persons condemned in *Spruchgerichte,* interned persons, "fellow travelers," and "minor Nazis" had thus resulted in a high degree of rhetorical and legislative confusion. This state of affairs was reflected in the failure of even critical and juridically educated individuals to fulfill their duty both to inform the public and to make clear distinctions. A good example of this was offered by Ernst Müller-Meiningen Jr., a lawyer and a member of the *Süddeutsche Zeitung*'s editorial staff, in a mid-December 1949 commentary. The occasions were the amnesty law that had just been passed and the end to denazification clearly on the horizon.[84] There was nothing particularly remarkable in Müller-Meiningen's embrace of both occasions as, respectively, a "break with the past" and a "detoxification of our political life." On the other hand, the direct linkage of the measures to the war criminal question was astonishing for an enlightened and thoughtful jurist: "The word *amnesty* is also steadily gaining actuality for those Germans sentenced by *Allied courts,* especially in the *Nuremberg* and *Dachau* war crimes trials. There is a general formal movement in this direction, after the legal principles behind the trials being surrounded by controversy before their start—these principles certainly not having been rendered more stable through developments in the meantime. It is true that an 'amnesty' is here especially problematic, since not common crimes are being judged but primarily political-historical responsibility." It is difficult to say what moved Müller-Meiningen to align himself with such an apologetic viewpoint. In any case, his normal tendency to differentiate here proved no major burden: since it was impossible to begin the "massive trials" afresh, it would "be necessary to annul, so to speak, on the administrative path what took place on the 'legal path.' "

The spur furnished by the Bundestag's amnesty law to public support for more far-reaching efforts was unmistakable. Alongside *Die Zeit*—the most important West German weekly—the newly founded *Frankfurter Allgemeine* now emerged as a vociferous opponent of "Nuremberg"—published daily, that national paper was clearly tied to the tradition of the old liberal-conservative *Frankfurter Zeitung*. "Landsberg must be expunged" could be read on the front page at around the same time as the *Süddeutsche Zeitung* commentator was demanding "a break with the past." The heading encapsulated the arguments of Professor Erich Kaufmann and Dr. Justus Koch—both, it will be recalled, defense attorneys in the Foreign Ministry trial—during a meeting of Düsseldorf's Rhine-Ruhr Club of conservative industrialists. Although the remarks were in quotations, the newspaper's sympathy with them was evident. In Koch's viewpoint, whoever fought against "Nuremberg's unjust cases" promoted "democratic development along with a true reconciliation with the occupying powers." A somewhat oracular observation then followed: "Nothing would be better than Landsberg being crossed off the list of facts constituting sins for the political thinking of the Germans." Koch was perhaps himself a little frightened by this sentence: on the one hand, he now limited its implications by explaining that with "Landsberg" he did not mean those who were "guilty in a truly disgraceful and criminal sense"; on the other hand, he explained that a final stay in the execution of men already condemned to death was a "specially pressing request." Erich Kaufmann and Justus Koch were meant to become Adenauer's advisers on international law. Both men conveyed an impression, according to the *Frankfurter Allgemeine,* "that things have already advanced a great deal. We may hope that the occupying power responsible for carrying out these trials will be prepared for a solution that is simultaneously practical and just."[85]

In actuality, as Kaufmann learned while active in a Heidelberg circle delegation that had met with McCloy, the Americans were in the process of realigning their approach to the war criminal question.[86] The U.S. army's European command had already decided on a War Crimes Modification Board, meant to offer another internal review of the

Dachau trial verdicts and serve as a permanent body for decisions on pardons and shortened sentences.[87] At the same time, it had become clear to the High Commissioner's office that something needed to happen regarding the Nuremberg judgments—but not yet what that should be. Shortly before Christmas, McCloy and General Handy agreed on a common intermediate step: for each month of "good behavior" five days would be removed from prisoners' sentences. This was a very common practice in the American penal system, encouraging prisoner discipline. It was already being used by the British and French in regard to the war criminals imprisoned in Werl and Wittlich. A practical result of the decision was the early release over the coming days of sixty Landsberg prisoners, including five sentenced at Nuremberg.[88]

In a meeting of the Allied High Commission on 16 October 1949, McCloy announced the new, rather hastily prepared procedure. He also expressed the intent to establish a planning commission to deal with the pardon and probational release of more prisoners sentenced at Nuremberg (hence under his jurisdiction). But at this point the High Commissioner himself did not appear to have a clear sense of how things would develop.[89] The only sure thing was that the parole system now in place was not meant as the final word.

"In Landsberg things are better" was the headline of the *Frankfurter Allgemeine* article on the releases, appearing three days before Christmas. Without explaining or commenting on the grounds for the early freedom, the article went on to depict various "mitigations" in the prisoners' daily life—including visits by the town's youth choir on holidays.[90] Anyone capable of reading between the lines could draw only one—indeed accurate—conclusion: that the Americans' punitive program at Landsberg was unusually generous and liberal.[91] This was, however, not said directly.

The release program did not remove any of the anticipatory weight on McCloy's shoulders. It is the case that, for the time being, no high-pressure demands were being made in public.[92] But a mood could also be set through little things, as a *Frankfurter Allgemeine* report on "Christmas in Landsberg" showed. According to a note of thanks from the Evangelical prison chaplain, enough packets had been received to bestow on 350 prisoners. The paper paraphrased the chaplain: "The joy was especially great on the part of men condemned to death for years whose cell doors had finally been opened for a few hours." Länder Bishop Meiser had also been moved; he had held a prayer service with his imprisoned coreligionists, described by the chaplain as having "to suffer here, to no small extent, in place of our people" (*unser Volk*). The article closed on a highly political rather than pastoral note, indicating that many "Landsbergers" were very bitter "at still being designated 'war criminals' in most journalistic articles, although they are in fact simply hostages for other groups among the German *Volk* who have been spared that lot."[93]

Such sentences were naturally not formulated to make McCloy's business easier. At the same time, a separate factor complicated his intention of convincing Washington that some action was still needed in the "Nuremberg" matter. The British announcement, running nearly parallel to the Landsberg releases, of the verdict in the trial of Erich von Manstein, ongoing before a military court in Hamburg since the summer. Former Field Marshall von Manstein was the mastermind of the blitzkrieg against France and conqueror of the Crimea and Sevastopol and the eastern front. He had been accused, among other things, of issuing orders for the implementation of Hitler's so-called Commissar Decree, calling for the murder of Soviet army commissars in the eastern campaign. Manstein's sentence was eighteen years—a decision whose severity was criticized not only in the German but also in the British press.[94] Within such a context, McCloy felt it necessary to discourage both exaggerated hopes among the Germans and false fears regarding his intent at home. To this end, he made public a letter to Apostolic Visitator Muench, warning against expectations of a "general amnesty."[95] What he planned, McCloy explained, was a procedure "in which individual appeals for mercy, if sufficiently clear and substantiated, are weighed objectively by an appropriate committee of responsible persons."[96]

The range of perspectives that the High Commissioner was willing to consider from various quarters—extending from the Heidelberg jurists to the Allied High Commission, the American press, and the church's leaders[97], most recently and concretely the German Evangelical Church delegation that had brought him the above-discussed memorandum— was certainly a sign of his outward self-assuredness. But it was also a sign of his inner struggle. McCloy knew that a significant step was needed if the war criminal issue was not to become a disturbing factor in German-American relations. But what remained uncertain at the start of 1950 was precisely how large this step needed to be in order to avoid frustrating the Germans while simultaneously not infuriating the Americans.

It would nevertheless be a mistake to assume that McCloy's sole concern was finding an optimal political solution. The matter was important to him personally, and this for at least two reasons: on the one hand, now as before he considered the "Nuremberg system" he had helped create to be the politically and morally most suitable and procedurally most proper response to the atrocities of the "Third Reich"; on the other hand, he believed that the Germans wished to forget their crimes as quickly as possible—and that precisely such forgetting was not to be allowed.

When McCloy left for a two-week trip to the United States on 20 January 1950, the war criminal question stood rather high on the list of things he hoped to tackle. His firmness when it came to basic questions would prove of great help here. To a considerable extent the trip had been conceived as a promotional tour for a newborn West German state that might well need to be incorporated into the Western defense community, and throughout the two weeks McCloy was bombarded with skeptical questions that might well have made his intentions seem misplaced. How safe, in fact, was democracy in Germany? How strong were the new forces in play, how durable the old ones? Was German nationalism once more on the march? Was something like "renazification" actually taking place? It was not only the east-coast press that was posing such questions—now as before it was quite uneasy when it came to West Germany, its correspondents steadily reporting troubling developments both in Bonn and in the country's grass roots[98]—but also influential figures in politics and commerce. Day after day McCloy gave speeches and stood up to the questions, not evading the difficulties, but not dramatizing them either.[99] The quiet confidence he displayed in the process, along with the conviction of his arguments, had their source in a strong sense of vigilance. When it came to this point, McCloy had no desire or need to reproach himself with anything, and thus had no hesitations in raising the war criminal problem in Washington, along with asking for advice from friends and former colleagues in New York.[100]

Complete success was nevertheless impossible. McCloy found no support for his proposal, laid out most recently at the State Department and for the secretary of the army, for the German High Commissioner's office and European Command together to speedily form a three-man team of American jurists to review cases from both Nuremberg and Dachau. Back in Germany, he thus decided to establish a board only active on behalf of the High Commissioner's office, while nonetheless coordinating its decisions with those of the European Command's War Crimes Modification Board.[101] In March 1950, McCloy could announce the formation of his Advisory Board on Clemency for War Criminals. It consisted of the presiding judge for the New York Appeals Court, David W. Peck; the chairman of the New York Board of Parole, Frederick A. Moran; and the State Department's assistant legal adviser, Brigadier General Conrad E. Snow. The three experts began their work in July 1950.

Meanwhile, the Korean War had begun, the international political situation thus changing in a way that could not help influencing the "Landsberg" question. However, contrary to what has sometimes been argued, the war was not the main axis in the development of the war criminal question.[102] As we have seen, the origins of the struggle to free the Germans condemned by Allied military courts lay much earlier, and the basic motives were primarily related not to defense policy but to devising a specific policy for the past. What was at stake was the political and moral rehabilitation of a military, administrative, and economic elite whose honor and influence had been, as it were, collectively damaged by the condemnation of some of its members. To echo the traditional claims to leadership and representation of this elite, what was at stake was a "national question."

In contrast to this overriding concern, policies regarding security merely played a marginal role between 1947 and 1949–50—and then mainly, of course, among former Wehrmacht members. But they hardly needed "Korea" to remove the plaintive aura from their call to free their condemned comrades. A clear-cut juncture emerged fast on the heels of the initial talk outside West Germany of bringing the country into the defense of the West. As stated by retired Senior General Heinz Guderian to the right-wing-leaning German-American journalist Karl von Wiegand in the spring of 1950, before he would be willing to accept a command in a new German army, "generals and other officers, statesmen and diplomats imprisoned in Spandau and elsewhere" would need to be free.[103] But for a long time now, those in officer circles were tested more in talking themselves into an awareness of utter guiltlessness and talking the former enemy into a new sense of posing problems than in drawing up such preconditions. We thus find the British star reporter Sefton Delmer offering, mere days "before Korea," what was said to be the favorite witticism of Field Marshal Albert Kesselring, condemned to death in 1947 on account of the execution of partisans and now waiting (in highly comfortable conditions[104]) to be released in Werl: "No soldiers can be sent into the next war as officers—they will need to be jurists."[105]

In the light of so much sarcasm, it could only be expected that "after Korea" the Americans would promptly face the argument that their methods against partisans there were indistinguishable from the Wehrmacht's methods on the eastern front. But the argument only demonstrated that, with a German rearmament seemingly on the horizon since September 1950, the war criminal issue had a long way to go before running its course.

CHAPTER 7

The Debate Under the Sign of Rearmament (1950-51)

> For me, the gallows of Landsberg are the most concrete
> superlative of "crimes against humanity." ... Let the East
> descend upon us (I don't hope for that!)—I'll never do
> my part to prevent it.
>
> —*Letter of a former soldier to the West German president,*
> *7 June 1951.*[1]

Around 1948, former Wehrmacht officers began to discuss the possibility of a future German army; by the summer of 1950,
the subject had made its way into quasi-official memorandums. In all
such deliberations, restoring "military honor" played a central role. The
officers' essentially unanimous conviction was that not the Wehrmacht's military campaign but rather the organization's treatment by the
victorious powers in the postwar period had deeply damaged this honor.
For the dismissed professional soldiers, an awareness of sociopolitical
demotion was as distressing as the material difficulties they now were
facing.[2] The source of this awareness was, on the one hand, the internments and military court trials, on the other hand, the unusually critical public discussion in the first postwar years, framed as it was by anti-
military norms. Without a principled change in a situation felt to
constitute "defamation," there was a general inclination to refrain from
participating in a new army meant to be tied to the Western defense system in one way or another. The concrete rallying cry emerging from virtually all relevant private conversations and planning papers was this:
freedom for all comrades being held as war criminals.

At the start of August 1950, a working group directed by retired lieutenant general Hans Speidel produced a paper titled "Ideas Regarding

the Federal Republic's External Security." In the weeks that followed, Adenauer would draw in basic ways on this paper, which laid considerable emphasis on the war criminal question, in his exploratory discussions of military policy.[3] The same emphasis was present in the notorious "Himmeroder Memorandum" of October 1950—but even more so.[4] The memorandum was prepared in cloistral solitude a few miles from the French war criminal prison in Wittlich in the Eifel. Both its opening and its conclusion took up the war criminal issue; along with a "rehabilitation of German soldiers through a declaration of governmental representatives of the Western powers" and a corresponding "declaration of honor" by the Bundestag and federal government, the military authors of the memorandum demanded the "freeing" of Germans condemned "as 'war criminals,'[5] to the extent they had merely been obeying orders and had not been guilty of punishable deeds according to earlier German laws." This goal included a suspension of pending trials; it would be attainable, the authors indicated, only through a series of steps: "before the beginning of the activation a *visible* start [in that direction] needs to be made. The question of those condemned in Spandau (especially the two soldiers) needs to be addressed."[6] Only after such steps, they continued, would it be possible to gain "the truly valuable elements indispensable for the construction of a reliable and superior corps of troops."[7] Considered soberly, the message here was even nastier than something like the offer of a package deal. Rather, it amounted to a naked threat: with further intransigence, the Allies would find an army of unreliable and dishonorable men at their disposal.

For a long time now, Adenauer had been aware that such politically rather thoughtless statements reflected the mood of many former Wehrmacht officers. The situation had meanwhile become extremely complicated, with the apparently serious external threat to the new West German state simultaneously representing, it seemed, a chance for negotiating a return of German sovereignty, as recompense for a deployment of German troops. In light of such a situation, an insistence on such peripheral factors could in fact only have a disturbing effect. In both of Adenauer's top secret memorandums offering a West German contribution to the Western defense effort, dispatched to the Allies on 29 August 1950, not a single word was devoted to the war criminal question.[8]

The extent to which the question clashed, at present, with Adenauer's planning is revealed by one incident in particular: his sharp-toned admonishment of Karl Arnold, North Rhine Westphalian minister president, a party colleague and favorite opponent. "In the interest of the idea of Europe" Arnold had just publicly renewed the call for the release of Ernst von Weizsäcker, as well as General Alexander von Falkenhausen, at the same time offering a critique of the French war criminal trials.[9] Arnold had to endure being told that he had "broached questions of foreign policy in a most unsuitable manner"—one "that according to the Basic Law is exclusively within the federal domain and is federal responsibility."[10] Adenauer's effort to muzzle Arnold was as absurd as it was revealing.[11] At the same moment when the chancellor had inwardly accepted the juncture between the war criminal and rearmament issues, hoping to resolve the matter in his own way, he was insisting on nothing being publicly said about it. He even deleted any reference to it in his letter to Arnold.[12]

Such rebukes of course fail to hush those motivated by political conviction. The press was even less inclined to being controlled, despite Adenauer's repeated efforts in that direction.[13] In the middle of the exploratory discussions, we thus find Paul Sethe, associate editor of the *Frankfurter Allgemeine,* publishing a lead article on, precisely, the connection between rearmament and the war criminal question.[14] Sethe considered it "natural" that the professional soldiers in particular "inwardly never accepted" most judgments in the war criminal trials. Reflecting, down to the level of word choice, the arguments being voiced in former Wehrmacht officer circles, he posed a rhetorical question: "Does anyone believe that a man of honor will put on his uniform while convinced that his comrades are unjustly sitting in jail?"[15] Whoever desired a German army had to "unravel this completely tangled knot."

In actuality, Sethe's corresponding apology for the "novel circumstances of the most fearful of all wars," circumstances that "destroyed the inherited legal perspective held by both sides," pointed to one fact: the confusion he claimed to find everywhere was above all his own. This became particularly clear in his article's closing passage, where he referred wholesale to the "more recent series of war criminal trials." The nation, he declared, "came to understand its purpose very quickly: through the sudden branding of many industrialists, officers, and high officials as criminals, the leading strata of the *Volk* was to be struck to the core—but the Germans' simplest sense of self-worth was also to be wounded. A sort of refined Morgenthau policy was here in play. This, and only this, explains how a man such as Krupp could be condemned. His fate was sealed not by his deeds but by his name. This, and only this, explains how a man such as Ernst von Weizsäcker could be condemned. For years, he risked both his freedom and his life to block Hitler's paths and make the war impossible, and he now sits in prison as a war criminal—a case bordering on madness. What is a company to think, marching by the walls of Landsberg when such men sit on the other side?" The idea of German soldiers marching by Landsberg (or Werl) soon developed into one of the most popular metaphors of the war criminal rearmament juncture. It was even considered acceptable by many who also considered the unvarnished demand for political barter—"soldiers in turn for war criminals"—repellent.

As a result of the remilitarization debate swinging into full play "after Korea," as well as the arrival of McCloy's pardon commission in Munich, rather far-reaching expectations took root in relevant circles in the summer of 1950.[16] The press was now creating an impression that a comprehensive solution to the war criminal question was imminent. Papers such as the *Frankfurter Allgemeine, Christ und Welt,* and *Die Zeit*—the latter represented above all by Marion Gräfin Dönhoff— seemed to be trying to summon up the result they were hoping through the commentaries they were offering.[17] Hope-laden reports even appeared in the provincial journals.[18] As part of this process, various details nourished the notion that the three-man commission headed by Judge Peck was reviewing the sentences passed against the Landsberg prisoners with special benevolence. For example, word got out that a commission member had visited the prison and personally formed "a picture" of the prisoners. The newspapers also reported that the lawyers for each of the roughly 100 cases received a half-hour hearing and that the large quantity of petitions in the commission's hands were being carefully studied.[19]

The signals pointing to mercy seemed so strong that, prompted by a concerned query from the New York-based German-Jewish émigré paper *Der Aufbau,* McCloy felt compelled to clarify matters. He had never considered a "general amnesty" for German war criminals, and there would be none.[20] At the same time, the High Commissioner indicated that he had recently agreed with General Handy on an extension of the remission for good behavior from five to ten days a month. For all those not sentenced to death or life behind bars—such persons were not included in the arrangement—this meant, in reality, a shortening of the punishment by a third. Nineteen prisoners were released as a result at the end of August; these included industrialist Friedrich Flick, former Nazi "Agricultural Leader" Richard Walter Darré, and former Nazi press chief Otto Dietrich.[21]

In any case, in mid-October 1950, which is to say only a few weeks after announcement of the new regulation, McCloy strayed from its substance by indicating the intent to grant Ernst von Weizsäcker an early release. In February, his sentence—along with the sentences being served by his former Foreign Ministry colleagues Ernst Woermann and

Gustav Adolf Baron Steengracht von Moyland—had been reduced from seven to five years by the military court that had condemned him.[22] As the *Frankfurter Allgemeine* reported in detail, with account taken of good behavior—in view of the rather untypical inmates, not exactly a crucial factor in securing Landsberg discipline—Weizsäcker would only have had a right to release on 2 December.[23] According to the newspaper, the source of the former state secretary's additional six weeks' bonus was "many letters from many countries" attesting to "measures taken to protect Jews and mitigate the harshness of the German occupation in Norway."[24] Beyond this, McCloy was cited to the effect that in civilized lands it was usual to exercise mercy when the condemned man deserved it. What the press did not report and McCloy did not bother mentioning was the effort of Germany's top politicians and officials, stretching out over a number of months, to convince him and his closest associates of Weizsäcker's worthiness for mercy. To this end, Hellmut Becker had kept the former state secretary's ex-"youngsters" who now occupied influential posts in Bonn very busy.[25] After Adenauer became active "on his own initiative," Becker convinced President Heuss to plead once again on Weizsäcker's behalf.[26]

In light of the massive nature of the intervention by German politicians, journalists, and church figures, McCloy must have been relieved he had pardoned Weizsäcker when he received the news of the former state secretary's death in the summer of 1951. Even retrospectively the image of the man dying in "dishonoring incarceration" (Bishop Wurm) would have made anyone concerned with the rise of right-wing German sentiment shudder.[27]

Be that as it may, in the fall of 1950 the early release of a prominent "Landsberger" did not simplify matters—especially since from month to month McCloy was putting off his decision regarding the Peck Commission's recommendations, handed to him on 28 August.[28] Through the delay, German impatience was steadily increasing, with rumors sweeping the Bundestag and even Adenauer starting to apply pressure. On 8 November 1950, the chancellor faced Parliament in a first debate over foreign policy principles, posing the "Question of a Contribution of the German Federal Republic to the Defense of the West."[29] He did not intend to discuss his top secret activities over the past ten weeks, but rather the recent New York conference of Foreign Ministers, the Pleven Plan that France was proposing, and Moscow's suggestion of a meeting of the Foreign Ministers of the Four Powers. But Adenauer—himself not being kept fully up to date regarding consultations between the Western powers[30]—was mainly concerned with testing the Plenum's mood regarding rearmament.

Despite such intentions, a number of delegates insisted on also addressing the war criminal theme; unsurprisingly, both right-wing and radical right-wing delegates were less shy in this respect than speakers for the ruling coalition, struggling as they were to preserve an appearance of restraint. Known for his rhetorical unpredictability, the German Party's Hans-Joachim von Merkatz was already clear enough. Amid applause and cries of "bravo" from the government's benches, he declared that, while no "reparation"—*Wiedergutmachen*—had been offered for the "defamation of the German soldiers," their honor could not be impaired "by anything": "We view the honor of German soldiers as firm and irreproachable." But, he explained, the "effort to keep *honorable men in prison* in at times demeaning conditions" demanded a response. Merkatz's explanation for the "energetic action" needed "to remove this burden from the soul of the Germans" was illuminating. "Men such as Manstein, Kesselring, and others, sitting in Landsberg and Werl, these men and ourselves are one. For we have also born the burden placed on them, who have stood in for us."[31]

The contribution of Johann Schuster (Economic Reconstruction Association) was even more drastic, its basic dynamic being an enumeration of demands. Regarding the "honor of German soldiers," he managed to encapsulate the bulk of the current slogans in a few sentences: "We cannot expect a single German man to again place himself in a uniform while those ... who removed theirs five years ago still ... languish in other countries' dungeons"—*Kerker*—"although it can be shown that they have themselves committed no crimes and are only suffering because a sort of *collective criminal law* has been created there. My ladies and gentlemen, I believe that such an approach can also be considered a *crime against humanity*. Namely, more than a few people are still languishing in dungeons on the basis of this collective criminal law."[32]

An interpellation raised shortly afterward by the CDU-CSU, SPD, FDP, German party, Bavarian Party, and Center Party factions clearly points to one conclusion: that with his words, Schuster was not marking out a minority position—that in truth, if it were not for party reasons, he would have been greeted by applause from all quarters. The interpellation was sprinkled with the standard reproaches and prejudices directed at Allied justice. The occupying powers' repeated extradition of Germans ("in one case even to Poland") was deplored as a contravention of the Basic Law's ban on extradition; Schuster also declared that the German public was very distressed by "rumors of imminent executions in the Landsberg prison, under the control of the American occupying power."[33] Finally, he conceded it was "not to be disputed that crimes worthy of death should receive an appropriate punishment," but in the same breath he sowed doubt on "whether executions for war crimes only take place when murder, in the sense of common law, has been indisputably proven. Rather, the concern emerges that now as before persons condemned for war crimes are subject to special laws, and that as a rule the deeds they have been charged with would not justify a guilty verdict according to common law."[34]

Caritas director Heinrich Höfler (CDU) substantiated the interpellation.[35] As he explained it, he was under an obligation to speak of a "deep dissatisfaction" running through the German nation—and this in "a question also ... directed at the German and European future." Justice Minister Dehler wholeheartedly supported Höfler, declaring that since the start of its work, the government had tried to prevent the carrying out of legally valid death sentences. Alongside the Basic Law and the fact that the sentences rested on retroactive "special laws," the effort was grounded in the conviction, acknowledged in all "cultured nations," that executions had to follow judgments without unreasonable delay. In Landsberg, so much time had passed that carrying out the sentences would clash with one's "sense of justice." For this reason, the government would again raise "serious remonstrations."[36]

Two days later (16 November 1950), Adenauer had an opportunity to remonstrate at the Petersberg seat of the High Commissioners. In urgently coached words, he described to McCloy how concerned he was "with the inner attitude of the German people" and its lack of readiness to defend its own freedom. A "psychological transformation" of majority opinion was absolutely necessary.[37] With this in mind, the chancellor had put together a list (as he explained, conceived by himself alone, and not meant as a means of pressure) of necessary measures and concessions on the Allies' part; at the meeting's end, he handed over the list.[38] Two of the items it contained were concerned with the war criminal theme—treated in Adenauer's earlier, verbal comments at some length, albeit, then as afterward, with considerable caution. For the High Commissioners needed to gain the—not inappropriate—impression that the chancellor was only grappling most unwillingly, and as gingerly as possible, with the entire issue. Again and again, he related his objections regarding extraditions and death sentences to the German public's criticisms. The objections only became concrete in the matter of General von Falkenhausen, whose trial had now begun in Brussels—but a representative of Belgium was not sitting across the table.[39]

Of course, the High Commissioners immediately understood that with his paper—he had already deleted the term *aide-mémoire* during the session—Adenauer was presenting a bill (some of its touches highly personal[40]) meant to be settled by the occupying powers in return for a German defense contribution. The subsections "Revision of Occupation Statute," "Occupation Costs," and "Individual Problems" could leave no doubt in this respect.[41] In their lapidary terseness, the demands regarding war criminals were completely clear: extraditions were to be generally halted, all the war criminal trials suspended or ended as quickly as possible, and pardons granted in the widest possible framework.[42]

If Adenauer had really presented his demands as brusquely as his notes imply, and if McCloy had not just complained to François-Poncet about the apparent French procrastination in trying extradited Germans,[43] then the High Commissioners would probably have reacted somewhat more harshly than they did. McCloy explained that the American Board of Extradition examined every extradition request with "unusual care"; for a long time now, the only extraditions to the West were for suspected murder (in regard to eastern Europe, the extradition standards were in any case extremely rigorous). Sir Ivone Kirkpatrick, Brian Robertson's successor for the British at the table, seconded McCloy: "murder according to German law!"[44] François-Poncet, directly involved in the matter through the ongoing French extradition request aimed at three Württemberg residents, now spoke up in a way offering little hope that his government would abandon such efforts anytime soon. Many criminals had hidden themselves away for a long time and were only now reemerging "because they believe that either by virtue of the circumstances or the German authorities they are now protected." Those affected were neither "innocent lambs" nor "victims of French malice," but persons who had committed "horrifying crimes" in France. French public opinion was no less sensitive then German; the French public would not understand it if, only halfway through to the limitation statute's onset, the judicial "made a break with these things and pardoned everyone." Germany, François-Poncet asserted, needed to remind itself from time to time that regrettably, the war crimes were no invention.[45]

It is the case that McCloy shared Adenauer's concern over the labile West German mood, as well as over Kurt Schumacher, the Evangelical Church, and the church's influence on "confused" public opinion; he had long since learned to think of Adenauer as a stroke of fortune.[46] But he was still irritated by the imperious tone and extraordinary quibbling connected to the war criminal theme and dominating much of the meeting. "I do not wish this aide-mémoire or what it contains to be considered so to speak an object of exchange for a German troop contingent," he let slip out toward its conclusion. And regarding the Landsberg decision that Adenauer had called to mind, McCloy's nerves had already become rather raw: "It can be on January 1; it can also not be on January 1."[47]

At that moment, McCloy probably was not even aware yet that the previous evening Adenauer's two most important military-political advisors, the retired Lieutenant Generals Adolf Heusinger and Hans Speidel, had intervened for their imprisoned counterparts with considerable vigor in a raidlike visit to the Bonn offices of the German High Commission.[48] In the wake of the Bundestag's interpellation of 14 November and the subsequent press attention,[49] the pressure applied by Speidel and Heusinger on the 15th, and Adenauer's aide-mémoire— not meant to be one—of the 16th, McCloy could only gain the impression of an offensive planned in general staff fashion but without political insight. In any event, in the late fall of 1950, the fact that the High Commissioner had to consider American public opinion was playing no role in Bonn's calculations.

What was the case in Bonn was even more so in a town like Bad Boll, where 200 former Wehrmacht soldiers convened between 18 and 22 November for "days of reflection." This first meeting of "men who were so long branded as scapegoats inside and outside the country" had been prepared by retired tank commander Heinrich Eberbach, director of the newly founded Evangelical Academy, "long before the question of rearmament gained topicality."[50] The event welcomed "everyone from the senior general to the lance corporal," "from the director to the master carpenter to the unemployed person"; it had been conceived as a statement leaping over chasms of politics and weltanschauung. The main group Eberbach was targeting was the young officers; the main purpose was "to clear up the undigested experience of the war and the postwar period, as an inner precondition for every additional step."[51]

Not least of the undigested matter was the July 1944 anti-Hitler plot, with the former adjutant to Major Otto Remer, the Nazi antiresistance hero who played a central role in suppressing the plot, vehemently defending that course of action. There were other controversies, as well, with still convinced Nazis and former SS officers confronting individuals who were looking for a new political orientation.[52] But there was unity in a "decisive rejection of Adenauer's rearmament plans"—something that former Wehrmacht colonel and present housing minister Eberhard Wildermuth, leading the occasion's not-so-small team of prominent persons, could not prevent. The basis for this rejection was naturally not pacifism but rather a suspicion that new German troops would be limited to "small, operatively nonindependent units" and the continued failure to "lay aside any defamation of German soldiers."[53] In the excited words of one young officer, "I can't have become a soldier in order to see sentries before the dungeon door of Field Marshal von Manstein!"[54]

The longer the delay in McCloy's Landsberg decision, the more compelling this line of argument appeared to many Germans. Not only was it a highly suggestive argument, but it also steered things away from the questions of guilt and atonement that people wishing to support the war criminals had to confront "before Korea." The pressure on the High Commissioner thus constantly increased over the coming weeks. Sometimes it took grotesque forms:

• On 25 November, the Heidelberg jurists' circle—informed about the Landsberg matter down to the most minute detail—decided to prevail upon either McCloy or his associates so "that there is no wait for all cases to be finally settled by the Nauheimer authorities [the High Commission's Administration of Justice Division], but that some Nurembergers are released beforehand, if possible already for the Christmas holiday."[55]

• On 27 November, Justice Minister Dehler suggested checking "whether a step can be taken by the federal president on behalf of the persons sitting in Landsberg condemned to death." The idea stemmed from one of the defense lawyers active in Nuremberg, who remembered a passage in the judgment at the Nazi Foreign Ministry trial describing as a sadistic "crime against humanity," typical of the Nazis, a situation in which "a man condemned to death learns nothing about the suspension of execution for months or even years and must live in the unbearable anxiety and spiritual oppression of not knowing if the next day is to be his last on earth."[56]

• On 6 December, the German Evangelical Church's council delivered two memorandums to fifteen Länder governments and churches. The memorandums made an appeal for the most extensive possible "commutation or ... repeal by an act of pardon of the punishment" for persons who seemed in retrospect to have received excessive sentences or to have been judged on the basis of dubious principles, "especially in cases where sentence of death has been passed."[57] When handing the texts over to one of McCloy's associates, High Consistory member Ranke remarked that while the church had "never spoken out on behalf of true war criminals," it was still the case that "the conscience of all responsible church agencies was weighed down by the situation in Landsberg. The church's bureaus have been receiving steady appeals from different congregations to speak up against carrying out death sentences that have been postponed for a long time now. . . . In this point, the German sense of justice differs from the Americans' sense of justice."[58]

• On 7 December, *Christ and Welt* published an article by Swiss-American journalist Robert Ingrim. Having previously intervened fervently for Ernst von Weizsäcker, Ingrim now demanded a "general amnesty"; anything else would simply only help Stalin, who understandably highly valued "not letting the wall between the Germans and the Western powers crumble."[59]

• On 16 December, the *Mannheimer Morgen,* a paper that was Social Democratic in orientation, produced an extensive report that included Friedrich Grimm's memorandum, written the previous year but until then unpublished.[60] The report then rhetorically queried, "How do things stand?" before responding, "Legal equality must not be withheld from the German people."[61]

• On 20 December, Adenauer's international law adviser, Erich Kaufmann reported to the president's office that according to one of the Nuremberg defense attorneys, himself supplied with the information in strictest confidence by Frederick Moran (the "most well disposed" member of the pardon commission), the Landsberg matter was once more in McCloy's hands, and he was taking advice from his legal adviser. "The limited friendliness of Mr. Bowie toward the Germans is known." Perhaps, he indicated, this information would be useful to the president in his New Year's address.[62]

• Finally, on Christmas 1950, retired Admiral Gottfried Hansen, chairman of the Association of Pension-Entitled Former Wehrmacht Officers and Their Surviving Dependents, demanded a "general amnesty" from the Allies for former Wehrmacht members condemned as "so-called war criminals."[63]

John McCloy's hope of at least preserving the holiday spirit by postponing the decision until January had turned out to be an illusion. Meanwhile, both he and his family were being terrorized with murder threats; bodyguards now protected his children.[64] On 2 January 1951 he had a long conversation with Adenauer that partly concerned the Landsberg decision once again.[65] A week later, in the I. G. Farben House in his Frankfurt headquarters, he was visited by a Bundestag delegation, steered by Carlo Schmid, that hoped to dissuade him from a rumored confirmation of some of the death sentences.[66] The idea for this step had originated in the Committee for Foreign Affairs, and the delegation made McCloy feel distressed enough to declare that "if our relations depend on these individual cases, then our friendship is really hanging by a thread."[67] The Germans had to finally understand the "enormity" of what happened, as well as what the rest of the world thought of these horrific Nazi deeds."[68]

Possibly the High Commissioner's unusual display of emotion was connected with the audience he had granted the "arguments" of self-appointed Landsberg activists twenty-four hours earlier.[69] It was possibly also connected with events transpiring the previous Sunday (7 January) in Landsberg am Lech: a loud demonstration for sparing the lives of the "doomed men" by at least 3,000 people, with speakers from various parties unanimously demanding American respect for the Basic Law's abolition of the death penalty.[70] (The most outspoken speaker in this respect was the CSU's Bundestag delegate Richard Jaeger, later to become a fervent champion of restoring the death penalty.) Gebhard Seelos, delegate from the Bavarian Party, declared Helgoland—still being used by the Royal Air Force for target practice—and Landsberg to be a "beacon of the German *Volk* in their struggle for justice, peace, and the reconciliation of nations" [*Völkerversöhnung*]. As the German Press Agency reported, he then spoke up "against the crime inflicted by the National Socialists on five million Jews and against the inhumane waiting [suffered] by the Nazis condemned to death"—this accompanied by strong applause from the crowd.[71]

But with this breathtaking parallel between victims and perpetrators, the highpoint of the past-political drama in the Landsberg marketplace had not yet been reached: three-hundred counterdemonstrators now arrived on the scene, identified by the *Frankfurter Allgemeine* correspondent as "foreigners brought over with seven omnibuses from the Lechfeld camp for displaced persons." Their effort to upset the proceedings was "repressed by the police and the German populace."[72] In the *Allgemeine Wochenzeitung der Juden in Deutschland,* chief editor Karl Marx would report on what both the *Frankfurter Allgemeine* and the news agencies would shroud in silence: the fact that the Landsberg mayor began his talk by announcing the "time of silence" to be over.[73] Action, he stated, was finally needed; the protesting Jews had to go back where they came from. Marx also reported that meanwhile the Bavarian interior minister had ordered an investigation of whether the mayor was to blame for "the words 'Jews get out' "—*Juden raus*—"resonating from the throats of hundreds of chanting people."[74]

The Bonn delegation visiting McCloy on 9 January included Walter Strauß, state secretary in the Justice Ministry. The day before, he had visited army commander in chief Handy in Heidelberg in order to also influence him as forcibly as possible, since parallel to McCloy, he was about to announce his own decisions regarding outstanding death sentences—these from the Dachau trials. Strauß focused his arguments totally on the Malmédy proceedings, curtly gainsaying the general's precise knowledge of the material through a reference to its extensive nature. Strauß then suggested that in case the European Command confirmed the judgments, this would be above all to "save face" and because of a conviction by the "highest authorities" that "a shooting to death of prisoners contrary to international law," had occurred—something he did not consider proven.[75]

Strauß pressed his arguments on Handy for an hour and fifteen minutes.[76] The general limited himself to restrained asides and did not appear particularly impressed when Strauß moved into presumably momentous political terrain. The West German government was aware that the Malmédy discussion had been partly steered by circles unavoidably appearing "suspicious" to the Americans. "Now, however, outspoken *anti-Nazis* were standing up for a pardon," noted Strauß. The "popular mood" was "*very clearly*" against further executions. If they still took place, there was imminent danger. It remains unclear whether the state secretary offered the following remark precisely as he noted it down, but whatever conditions or palliations characterized its spoken form, it must have inclined anyone hearing it to brooding: "Should the sentence be carried out, the government, indeed the Federal Republic, is in danger!"[77]

Compared with this seemingly strong argument—in reality a political oath of allegiance—Strauß's added warnings could be considered harmless: New executions could endanger the effort at Western integration and encourage communist designs, since the Russians might demonstratively decide to suspend their pending mass executions in Waldheim. Both on public occasions and in private meetings, no idea appeared too misguided in face of a decision palpably close at hand— one presumably not delivering the desired general pardon for Nazi war criminals sitting on death row.

In the middle of January, President Heuss felt obliged to once more enter the fray. "My silence over the present weeks," he wrote with disarming openness to "dear Mr. McCloy" (who, Heuss indicated, should pass his comments on to General Handy), "runs the risk of being misinterpreted by people unaware of my past efforts—the letters and telegrams are piling up with suggestions that I should abandon my 'reserve'—which in reality is none at all—for open appeals etcetera. That is not my way of tackling such matters." To be sure, Heuss indicated, he was aware that many of the condemned persons "have even earned the maximum sentence according to the law," but there were also cases in which individual guilt had remained "entirely questionable." "With the psychological situation in which the dialogue between the states is presently proceeding," the "arguments"—with a touch of frivolity, Heuss himself put the word in quotes—that would henceforth count were "evident." And now Heuss demonstrated his own embrace, at last, of the above-described junctures—presented, naturally, in well-crafted statesmanlike words: "My concern is great that something like the execution of the Landsberg prisoners might do sore damage to our mutual discussions regarding West German incorporation into a European and Atlantic community."[78]

The High Commissioner's return letter to Heuss came a few days before he announced his decisions. The answer was a serious one. For weeks, McCloy had been preoccupied not only with the recommendations of his pardon commission but also with the individual cases.[79] He could only hide his disappointment over recent developments with difficulty. Both the manner in which he had been imposed on by all sides and his examination of the case files had been depressing experiences. "I believe there is no subject on which I have spent so much time and thought since I have been in Germany. I am very glad to be able to say that I have found as a result of these continuous studies a basis for very extensive grants of clemency. In some cases, fortunately a very few, I have come up against a stone wall. There are some crimes the extent and enormity of which belie the concept of clemency. They involve murder of helpless women and children by the tens of thousands under circumstances which we would not credit were it not for the contemporaneous reports of the perpetrators themselves and their own admissions. I do not feel that the German people can possibly associate the interests of such criminals with their own."

McCloy emphasized that he not only bore responsibility to his own government and the Germans. Rather, his duty was international, since many of the crimes had been committed outside Germany against non-Germans. He had also explained this to the Bundestag delegation. At the end of his letter, he offered a politely formulated yet unmistakable critique: "I do wish that the German government and the German people had a wider concept of the crimes which are represented by many of those at Landsberg. I find from my mail the most abysmal ignorance of both the offenses and the character of the proof of the guilt which prevails in respect of them. I hope to improve this situation to some degree by issuing a rather complete report on the matter simultaneously with my decisions. To some extent this will not make pleasant reading, but I feel the current misunderstandings compel it."[80]

Among the recent "misunderstandings" was, for instance, the press attention enjoyed by a certain Baron von Stauffenberg, cousin of the anti-Hitler plotter, speaking in the name of the right-wing splinter group called the German Union. (This attention cannot have simply been a result of the speaker's name.) According to the baron, "The fate of the 'red jackets' "—the reference was to the prison clothes of those on death row in Landsberg—"was the measure of a time in which there is an intent to call the Germans to join ranks on the front of freedom and justice against Bolshevik imperialism."[81] Another example was the invitation extended by the *Frankfurter Allgemeine* to Tübingen theologian Helmut Thielicke to offer one more castigation of the Malmédy sentences in its pages: the sentences represented "storm centers"—*Brandherde,* literally "burning hearths"—of the worst legal depravity in the center of Western civilization"; above all, for the younger generation caught up in a debate about remilitarization, a confirmation of the sentences might represent the drop "that brought the vessel of their often so bitter and renunciatory thoughts to overflowing. For this reason, we do not wish to abandon the hope that General Handy does not only know where things now stand"—*was die Stunde geschlagen hat,* more literally, "what bell has now tolled"—"but above all that the Heavenly Judge watches over earthly judgments."[82]

A last example was the launching of fresh appeals by Bishops Neuhäusler and Meiser, the two church shepherds responsible in a regional sense for Landsberg. On the Evangelical side, Meiser organized an urgent letter on behalf of "all the church leaders in the west" of Germany to McCloy demanding that he "in no case allow a resumption of executions but place mercy before justice and commute the death sentences to imprisonment." As in all the church's earlier petitions, any objections of principle to the death penalty were here lacking. Meiser's line of argument was in fact not theological but purely political—and martial to boot: "Germany's relationship with the Allies will certainly be burdened most seriously if blood once more would appear to flow between both peoples [*sic*]."[83]

Meiser attempted to distance himself from the related Catholic efforts. He did not wish to cooperate with the dubious, above-mentioned "Working Group for Truth and Justice," linked through Helene Princess of Isenburg to the even more dubious "Action to Prevent the Carrying Out of the Death Sentences," steered by Rudolf Aschenauer.[84] Still, the arguments the latter organization offered journalists in Munich in mid-January 1951 were hardly distinguishable from Meiser's arguments.[85] And their tactic of warning against the dangers of a new German nationalism was rather the same: things had reached the point where there was no rightward limit on use of that particular trick. When Auxiliary Bishop Neuhäusler appealed to McCloy on 24 January—naturally not without failing to place the press in the picture—he basically hit the mark dead center: "I wish that your advisers and judges could listen in on ordinary people the way I can. From all circles, strata, and parties, you would then hear that no one can muster any understanding for executions three or four years after sentencing."[86]

The fact was that over recent weeks German newspapers and magazines had not published a single commentator speaking out against the general public trend. While one or another of them may have urged a little understanding for the American perspective, no one dared doubt the basic propriety of a sweeping act of pardon. There was no call for even the simplest distinctions. People whose word mattered or who wanted to still be heard kept any reservations quiet. The few people willing to speak up had nothing to lose when it came to public regard: the communists, for example, but also the anticommunist "Working Group for Freedom, Justice, and Human Dignity," composed of the groups of formerly persecuted people that had split off from the Association of Victims of the Nazi Regime. Referring to the Pohl and Ohlendorf cases in its publication, that group did express regret over the willingness of "political and church authorities ... to generally plead for a pardoning of criminals." But even the one-time victims hastened to add that they were "not interested in taking revenge."[87]

In face of the imminent decision, the *Frankfurter Allgemeine* also cited Pohl and Ohlendorf. But the paper was now marking a modest move toward drawing distinctions, after weeks of carefully reproducing any and all protests for the "Landsbergers." For meanwhile, confidential information from the chancellor's office had suggested that not all the "red jackets" would, in fact, be pardoned.[88] Obviating bitter political disappointment and excessive nationalist reactions was thus called for; no one who considered Adenauer's approach as essentially well founded, and the nationalism uniting the heterogeneous troop of rearmament opponents as an ominous factor, could have had an interest in such a response. "Landsberg has become modern" was the title of Thilo Bode's lead article signaling the change of course.[89] Bode spoke out firmly against the sorts of opinions being expressed by Gebhard Seelos and Hans Christoph Baron von Stauffenberg: "Those are all unfortunate judgments" (*fatale Sprüche*). "They are based on the fact that Landsberg—not always to the advantage of those imprisoned there—has become positively modern. A sign of our times is making collective judgments, and these collective judgments and collective demands— '*no* more people should be executed in Landsberg'—threaten to obscure the question to the point of being unrecognizable."

Bode tried to fix the distinction between a man condemned in the Malmédy trial, like SS major Peiper, commander of the combat group that did the killing but himself not proven to be directly implicated, and men like Ohlendorf—having admitted responsibility for the extermination of "95,000 people in the east behind German lines"—and Pohl—standing "at the head of the administrative organization of all the concentration camps." "We find no grounds for pleasure in the idea of Ohlendorf and Pohl one day running about free. We do not wish to read revelations in the style of 'I murdered 95,000 men'—such a thing cannot be expected of the very clever Ohlendorf—nor something rather more likely, philosophical justifications and depth psychological explications on this man's part. We wish him to give up his life as atonement for the 95,000 people he did away with in cold blood. For him the life of others was no great matter; his own life is no greater matter for us and ought not be for him." According to Bode, pity for the wrong person was of little use for the "German cause." In this way, he implicitly criticized parliament's sweeping demand in November for a halt to executions. If the Germans drew careful distinctions, they could "demand all the more justly that the unhappy chapter of the war criminal trials be finally closed according to the immutable principles of the law."

With these remarks, the quasi-official *Frankfurter Allgemeine*—let us take note: not the parliament, and not the West German government—had in a certain way traced out the line demarcating the place where what might be considered past-political extremism began. From now on it would be up to more or less camouflaged Nazis to fight for the lives of managers of the mass murder of the Jews. These people gathered in circles such as Princess Isenburg's, but the scene sympathetic with their aims extended deep into the bourgeois conservative camp, receiving support, not least of all, from circles in the church.[90] For the princess, in the emergency situation she was faced with in the late fall of 1950, all the assurances she had been offered—to the extent they had been—were now in tatters. After a visit with Otto Ohlendorf, she wrote her "fatherly friend" retired bishop Wurm that there was no longer room for a day's hesitation if "the most grievous injustice" was to be prevented. "through wicked propaganda the Ohlendorf case has been completely distorted. No upright thinker can let the obvious miscarriage of justice pass. . . . So many horrifying mistakes have become manifest that I make myself personally guilty if I do not do everything to shed light on this case. I have traveled out to see Mrs. McCloy and succeeded in receiving a promise from Mr. McCloy to personally study the matter."[91]

In part as a result of the many letters reaching him daily, McCloy had become well aware of the hazy boundaries between apologists, unrepentant Nazis, and those seeking clemency out of Christian conviction or on humanitarian grounds. And he was also aware that from the perspective of the West's security policies, the problem of the condemned military men had a very special weight—that it needed to be cleared up or at least neutralized as quickly as possible.

On 22 January 1951, a meeting took place between the just-appointed commander in chief of NATO in Europe, General Dwight D. Eisenhower, and Adenauer's military advisers, Heusinger and Speidel. Arranged by McCloy and held in his Bad Homburg villa, the meeting almost perfectly suited the above-stated purpose.[92] In the last weeks of the war, both Malmédy and the uncovered horrors of the death camps had rendered Eisenhower into a bitter opponent of the Germans, identifying the Wehrmacht with Nazism and demanding severe retribution. For the sake of American *raison d'état,* he was prepared to put aside his feelings. After drinks and dinner, an agreement was reached in McCloy's library on a text that had been prepared in advance by Speidel and Heusinger.[93] The next day, Eisenhower paraphrased it in the Frankfurt airport for the press: "For my part, I do not believe that the German soldier intrinsically lost his honor....As I said to the chancellor and the other German gentlemen with whom I conversed yesterday evening, I have come to the conviction that a real distinction can be drawn between German soldiers and officers in themselves and Hitler and his criminal group."[94] Over the following months, other versions of these remarks would make the rounds among former Wehrmacht officers.[95] Drawing more attention to both the moment of pardon and the shared anticommunism, these versions would not fail to have their effect.[96]

On 31 January 1951, the information services for the High Commissioner's office and for the European Command published the results of the review of the request for pardon by a total of 102 Landsberg prisoners.[97] McCloy had made the decision concerning the fate of 89 remaining prisoners from the subsequent trials at Nuremberg, General Handy for the 13 remaining prisoners sentenced to death at Dachau.[98] Handy had commuted all but two of the death sentences to life in prison, including the remaining Malmédy prisoners awaiting execution; in this way the lives of all the men convicted on account of Malmédy were spared. The general had confirmed the death sentence handed down to Georg Schallermair, former chief duty officer for the guards in the Dachau annex camp at Mühldorf-Inn, and to Hans Schmidt, adjutant to the Buchenwald camp commander.

McCloy's decisions were more complex. In fifty-two out of fifty-four cases, he had reduced the length of fixed prison terms, in thirty-two of these cases to time already served (i.e., immediate release). Of the twenty life sentences, seventeen were reduced, most of these to fifteen or twenty years. Of the fifteen death sentences, he converted four to life and six to periods between ten and twenty-five years. Five death sentences were confirmed: the sentence against Oswald Pohl, as well as those passed against leaders of the Mobile Killing Units, Paul Blobel, Werner Braune, Erich Naumann, and Otto Ohlendorf.[99] In this manner, the lives of twenty-one of the twenty-eight Landsberg "red jackets" were spared. A striking aspect of McCloy's decision was his refusal to approve any mitigation for a series of persons sentenced in both trials concerning the Wehrmacht, the "hostage murder" trial and that of the Wehrmacht High Command. This was especially remarkable in that seven Mobile Killing Unit leaders had been granted pardons.[100]

More than a third of those pardoned could already leave Landsberg in the first days of February 1951.[101] Among them were all persons still imprisoned as a result of the Krupp trial: the photo of the greeting scene between the hollow-cheeked head of the firm, Alfried Krupp von Bohlen und Halbach, and his younger brother, resplendent in fur-lined winter coat, went around the world.[102] Without a doubt, the surprising pardon issued Krupp and eight of his managers brought McCloy much support on German industry's management level—the industrialists had been trying for years to shed the stain placed on them at Nuremberg for complicity with Hitler's regime and its war of aggression. With the freeing of the Krupp personnel, the problem of "industrial war criminals" (Theodor Heuss[103]) was in fact now as good as resolved, since those condemned in Nuremberg's Flick and I. G. Farben trials had already been largely freed in the summer of 1950. It is a fact that, measured against their comparatively large original punishment (between six and twelve years), Krupp and his directors got off lighter than most of the leading industrialists, but they, as well, had served more than a minute part of their sentences, almost all having been incarcerated since 1945.

For the international public, the dismissal of a convicted war criminal whose name epitomized the German armaments industry was hard to swallow—particularly in the form served up by McCloy.[104] In France and England, as well as in the United States, the criticism focused above all on the freeing of Alfried Krupp, especially since that gesture was linked to the return of his firm's confiscated property.

The general pardoning process was criticized most severely in the United States. Telford Taylor referred to a heavy blow against international law and against the principles "for which we entered the war." Much of the U.S. local press and many radio commentators voiced extremely negative reactions; both the *New York Times* and the *Washington Post,* however, saw the process as a "compromise between justice and utilitarianism," thus acknowledging the imperatives of realpolitik.[105] In congress, McCloy's decision was greeted with considerable mistrust, but a committee then formed to investigate the matter ended up expressing only cautious criticism.[106]

As would be expected, the West German reaction was rather different.[107] The only expressions of regret came from the two Krupp trial prosecutors, Joseph W. Kaufman and Robert Kempner; otherwise, it was these pardons in particular that garnered the most praise. On 1 February "Landsberg" dominated the headlines of the entire German press[108]—the government's efforts to play down the news preemptively through contacts with correspondents in Bonn having thus failed miserably.[109] According to High Commission observations, editorial departments devoted a page to the theme on average, and often took the trouble to directly name all those affected. The thoroughness of the explanations McCloy and Handy offered for their decisions was generally appreciated, being seen as a sign of the review process's careful nature.[110]

At the same time, very few West German commentators were fully satisfied. An exception was Stuttgart's *Deutsche Zeitung,* which observed that the curtain had now fallen in Landsberg and the decisions now needed to be accepted, nationalist ressentiment avoided. To the contrary, there were rather frequent demands for a commutation of the seven remaining death sentences, if only because of the Basic Law. Most Bonn politicians who spoke out on the issue took a similar line, for instance, Social Democrats Carlo Schmid and Erich Ollenhauer.[111] The government itself abstained from any official statement, indicating that the decisions were taken on the basis of American rather than German law.[112] For months, Adenauer remained silent on the matter—the silence encouraging a new campaign, chiefly promoted by the sensational press. The campaign, criticized by the chancellor only from behind the scenes, took over a maxim first promulgated in *Die Zeit:* "It is too late to kill!"[113]

The line that the *Frankfurter Allgemeine* took was closer to views being expressed in government circles than the line taken by *Die Zeit,* or by *Die Welt,* where Hellmut Becker cautioned that McCloy had not created a tabula rasa. The Frankfurt paper having already disposed of Ohlendorf and Pohl before the decision, an article by Thilo Bode now designated the three additional decisions against Mobile Killing Unit heads as "probably uncontroversial." However, when it came to General Handy's confirmation of the death sentences imposed on Schallermair and Schmidt, Bode asserted that "doubt cannot be suppressed." But what troubled the paper most of all was "McCloy's striking restraint in the question of the condemned soldiers"; in unmistakable fashion, this was the deeper source of the article's title: "Landsberg—Penultimate Act."[114]

The general approach of McCloy and his advisory committee had been to show clemency whenever there were any grounds at all (as Judge Peck put it, "if we have erred, we have erred on the side of leniency").[115] In the case of the condemned Wehrmacht officers, the approach carried complications: For everything that could be interpreted as extraordinary generosity, the High Commissioner could count on being reproached at home and by U.S. allies as having bowed to the German juncture; for everything pointing in the contrary direction, he could count on being reproached by the Germans as having wished to demonstrate conscious severity. In the face of this dilemma, McCloy's procedure can be considered highly adept. By not revoking five judgments (while offering two of those convicted a prospect of a review of their fitness for prison), he demonstrated firmness; and by immediately releasing five prisoners (including Wilhelm Speidel, brother of the Adenauer adviser), he demonstrated flexibility. Something else was meant to be accomplished by directly raising the theme of "the honor of German soldiers" in the written comments on his decision: "The suggestion has been made that condemnation of individual officers is a reflection on the German military profession as a whole. To condemn those who were not faithful to their professional obligations is not to condemn the whole profession any more than to condemn the doctors and lawyers who participated in the medical experiments and in the administration of the people's courts under the Nazis is to condemn the medical and legal professions as a whole."[116]

According to High Commission surveys, most Germans had expected a greater degree of mercy.[117] They were not ready to be convinced by such arguments any more than was the mass of former professional soldiers. When it came to the latter group, the reaction of retired admiral Gottfried Hansen, chairman—as indicated above—of the Association of Pension-Entitled Former Wehrmacht Officers and their Surviving Dependents (and from the end of 1951, of the "League of German Soldiers") was characteristic: he called on the chancellor to intervene with McCloy for a "generous clemency project"—the cases of soldiers condemned to jail should once more be reviewed, this time by "German courts."[118]

If the fate of the generals nevertheless received little attention over the following months, this was because the Landsberg discussion focused entirely on the seven remaining candidates for death. From the government's perspective, this meant a certain relief in the rearmament debate—though it would be exaggerated to say that Bonn welcomed the latest agitation concerning the "red jackets." Still, the government did not neglect anything that could have saved the lives of the seven Nazi criminals.

The atmosphere was typified by the following events: a renunciation by the town of Landsberg of all its carnival balls, and the offer by a Catholic priest there to replace the condemned men at the gallows;[119] the emergence of all sorts of protest placards and the threat of "actions"—*Aktionen*—by the clandestine Nazi organization *Bruderschaft* ("Brotherhood") in the case of the sentences being carried out;[120] the appeal of Princess Isenburg to her "Working Group for Truth and Justice" to "come to Bonn" ("You will receive more specific details after arrival at the Hotel Stern").[121] In such an atmosphere, the government did not want to have to be reproached for harming the delinquents through neglect.

Once again it was Thomas Dehler who took the initiative in the matter. Having plagued the Americans over Landsberg practically since the start of his term, the justice minister suggested a German role in the consultations over the remaining death sentences as early as April 1950: carrying out the sentences would have a "shocklike" effect on the public.[122] Indisputably the Justice Ministry had the most to do with the matter at hand, but the chancellor's comparative restraint was nonetheless striking. At first he only expressed agreement that the Justice Ministry "get in touch" with the Allied High Commission's officials "on account of apparent miscarriages of justice."[123]

Dehler's legal referees considered the judgments passed on Schallermair and Schmidt to constitute such "miscarriages"; even they could discover no additional exculpatory material in the other cases.[124] The Heidelberg jurists' circle saw the situation in even less hopeful terms. The day after the cabinet meeting, a decision had indeed been reached in a full meeting of the circle to send a delegation to General Handy's legal advisor, in order to express "reservations concerning carrying out the death penalty" in both cases under the European command's purview. But while according to Justice Ministry official Margarethe Bitter, an argument based on procedural flaws was at least possible in the case of Schmidt, any grounds for an argument was lacking in the case of Schallermair; as the confidential meeting record conceded, the case was "more difficult." It thus seems that the three Justice Ministry representatives needed, as it were, to impose the démarche in favor of the two concentration camp killers on the remaining circle participants as a solemn obligation. In any case, the circle apparently also felt obliged to confirm "that General Handy showed great generosity in pardoning eleven of the condemned men." When it came to the cases that were under McCloy's purview, those present could only propose asking "the churches (Cardinal Frings and Bishop Wurm)" to underscore "irregularities" in the substantiation of two sentencing confirmations. The meeting record shows no doubts being raised as to the fairness of the verdicts. Rather, the focus was now on what would happen later— although waiting a while was necessary before "having to do something for the [remaining] Nurembergers."[125]

Justice Minister Dehler had his problems with so much composure. To be sure, shortly after the meeting, the Heidelberg delegation—and separately, Frau Bitter, supported by the condemned men's lawyer— had been able to express their united "concern" regarding the fates of Schallermair and Schmidt to Handy's legal adviser.[126] But this was not enough for Dehler. Backed up by the arrival of the Princess Isenburg in Bonn on 13 February he promptly raised the Landsberg matter once again at the next cabinet session. As if himself a member of the "Working Group for Truth and Justice," he solemnly reported its proposal that the government "or even the president" appeal to President Truman. Opinions, however, were "divided" on the "utility of such a step." It was thus decided that the chancellor and the justice minister should clarify the matter between them.[127]

Apparently, Adenauer had nothing against the FDP being a bit of a nuisance to the Americans. He in any case did not prevent Dehler from prompting Heuss to write a fresh letter to Handy. (The general had only just answered Heuss's sweeping war criminal plea from January.) With the true ring of conviction, Dehler explained to Heuss that carrying out the sentences again Schallermair and Schmidt would "mean grave, irreparable injustice." Both cases, he declared, were designed "to again most heavily shake the German people's trust in law and justice." "In the shortest possible time" after the executions, Germans would "necessarily ... become tools of agitation for extreme circles." Since the ministry's own representations had failed, all that remained was the "final path—the federal president adding his own voice."[128]

To this end, Dehler now presented the exculpatory arguments that the Central Bureau for Legal Defense had been able to muster, supported by the defense attorneys.[129] Measured against General Handy's substantiation of the decision to maintain the death sentences handed down to Schallermair and Schmidt, distinct from all the other condemned men, the arguments were rather shabby. Handy focused on one of Schallermair's crimes in particular, beatings "which he personally administered" that resulted in the death of a large number of prisoners. And furthermore: "He visited the morgue daily with an inmate dentist to extract the gold teeth from the dead bodies from the camp."[130] As numerous former concentration camp inmates attested, Schallermair was a prototype of the brutal beater. In the Justice Ministry's protocol this was reformulated as follows: "It may be correct that in the last months before the collapse, apparently under the pressure of the sharp orders directed against loosening of discipline in the camp, Schallermair beat prisoners. However, no testimony from any witness conclusively demonstrates that mistreatment on the part of Schallermair caused the death of prisoners. As a study of the trial records shows, the testimony of the prosecution witnesses rests on hearsay or suppositions." In contrast, for the Justice Ministry, more credence should have been granted the statements of three Jewish ex-prisoners whom the defense had meanwhile managed to discover. These individuals claimed "that Schallermair certainly now and then beat a prisoner, but that [sic] they are sure Schallermair never mistreated a prisoner to the point of death from the mistreatment."

In the case of Schmidt, the Central Bureau experts presented nothing but alleged procedural errors. As a result of a serious illness (put more precisely, as a result of mistreatment in the pretrial period, although this was said only off the record), Schmidt could not participate in the proceedings for a long period; he also could not appear as a witness on his own behalf. In the various later reviews of the verdict, "as thorough as they may have been," this basic flaw could not be rectified. The Justice Ministry did not waste any words on the fact, stressed by Handy, that Schmidt had been responsible for all the executions in Buchenwald, including those carried out by Special Unit 99, which had slaughtered hundreds of war prisoners with the help of an insidious device.

Well-meaning parties had just managed to keep Heuss from receiving Princess Isenburg.[131] Nevertheless, the president did not place the task presented him by Dehler onto the back burner. Already the next day, he had a personal letter sent to Handy. In this letter he first offered warm words of thanks for the general's use "of the lovely privilege of pardon, above all in cases where the confusion of military engagement led to nasty excesses"—*bösen Ausschreitungen*—in which the "question of guilt" is too difficult to reconstruct on an individual basis." Apparently Heuss was referring especially to the Malmédy pardons. "Nothing can be further from my intentions," he added, "than glossing over perpetrated crimes—crimes *were* perpetrated and must be expiated." Heuss attached a proviso to his concrete intercession for Schallermair and Schmidt: he could not judge the exculpatory argumentation in detail. On the other hand, he pointed to the statements in that direction offered by "Jewish witnesses." Even his closing remarks skillfully straddled a fence: He was not drawing attention to the two cases "because I take a special interest in these persons, who filled a repulsive professional function. But the utmost must be done to assure a sense of careful legal finding—a feeling destroyed so horribly in Germany in 1933 and only slowly built up again after 1945."[132]

In Handy's answer to Heuss's first intervention in the Landsberg affair, he had candidly admitted trusting in God's help to see things through. This time around, his terse reaction showed that his capacity for German interference had been exhausted.[133] Still, Dehler and his referees persisted. In the wake of the Landsberg decisions, important past-political differences within the governmental coalition now became manifest. On the one hand, Chancellor Adenauer, and with him the majority of politicians from the CDU and CSU, were inclined to accept the verdict confirmations of both McCloy and Handy.[134] There was no reference to Landsberg prisoners in a message delivered that week from Adenauer to the pope, asking him to intercede for an end to the West European war criminal trials and a commutation of the death sentences passed in that context.[135] On the other hand, the majority of FDP and German Party members were not ready to abandon the struggle.[136] It was highly obvious that the smaller governmental parties, under pressure from a massive rightward public opinion trend reflected in an 11 percent result for the neo-Nazi Socialist Reich Party in the Lower Saxon Landtag elections, believed it necessary to watch out for anything that smacked of acknowledging "American interests"—or, inversely, abandoning "German interests."

This did not mean that the leaders of the FDP and the German Party went as far as defending the crimes of the Mobile Killing Unit heads as a necessity of the anti-Bolshevik struggle—the perspective of freshly consolidated Nazi circles. In an abstract sense, the fact of the murder of the Jews was not denied. But it appears that the parties thought it incumbent to align themselves behind popular right-wing doubt regarding the condemned men's concrete guilt. For apologists, when such doubt made no sense, as in the case of Ohlendorf (the only man accused at Nuremberg who openly admitted and even tried to justify his deeds), then grotesque stylization and mystification of the criminals was in order[137]—and here, as well, it was not thought wise to raise strenuous objections. But not only the German Party and the FDP, with their past-politically motivated clientele, refrained from tearing away the apologetic veil—especially when it could be strengthened with the favored argument of "binding orders."[138] Rather, in the rule, the CDU-CSU and the SPD adopted a similar procedure.

The efforts of the Central Bureau for Legal Defense need to be understood against this backdrop. Even in the entirely hopeless case of the Mobile Killing Unit leaders, the bureau furnished massive technical and financial support until the end. Toward that end, there was a delay in the execution of the seven condemned men, despite the intention of proceeding as speedily as possible. In a confidential 24 May 1951 conversation with *Die Zeit*'s Robert Strobel, the bureau's director, Hans Gawlik—who himself now fully expected the executions to take place—explained the delay as follows: at the last moment, the defense lawyers had submitted pleas for mercy to President Truman and habeas corpus appeals to the U.S. Supreme Court. "The pleas for pardon," noted Strobel, "were submitted in secret agreement with the Federal Justice Ministry, which supported them through legal advice and the offer of material in its possession. Gawlik told me there is a suspicion in the American High Commission that the Federal Justice Ministry had stepped into the process in this way. But no proof to this effect is available. In case this should be asserted, the Federal Justice Ministry would dispute its quiet participation in any form."[139]

A few days later, the suspicions of the German High Commission became a certainty. The Associated Press reported that Warren Magee, once Weizsäcker's attorney, had received 50,000 marks for his work on behalf of the condemned "Landsbergers." And contrary to what Gawlik had predicted, Dehler did not even bother issuing a denial. In the AP's words, " 'We are willing to answer for what we did at any time,' emphasized the Federal Justice Ministry. Without intervention of the Legal Protection Bureau, no defense of the Landsberg prisoners would have been possible. The Justice Ministry maintains the position that in at least two of the seven cases, carrying out the death penalty 'even contravenes American law.' "[140] As things actually stood, there was in fact no point in denying the Justice Ministry's entanglement in the Landsberg issue's end phase. (The situation manifestly wounded McCloy in a deeply personal way—particularly since his leniency had come to mean being forced to endure accusations of opportunism from various quarters, including the British.)[141] As a final phase of this entanglement, following the Supreme Court's rejection of the habeas corpus pleas, Gawlik once more called on McCloy's political adviser, Samuel Reber, directly interceding on 21 May for Pohl, Ohlendorf, and the latter's three associates. (Gawlik was especially qualified for this task as Ohlendorf's attorney at Nuremberg—although choosing him here was perhaps not the brightest idea.) Even in this final intercession, Reber felt obliged to demonstrate how painstakingly the High Commission had scrutinized the files, citing from them by heart to make his point.[142]

Unsurprisingly the parallel visit to General Handy turned out to be equally demanding. The FDP strategists assigned the task to both Dehler's referee, Margarethe Bitter, and Vice Chancellor Blücher's adviser, Georg Vogel, who handed the general a letter from Blücher, purportedly containing fresh exculpatory evidence. As a result it became clear that the European command had meanwhile taken the time to review the belated witness testimony on behalf of Schallermair. Likewise Handy promptly countered the argument that Schmidt had missed two-thirds of his trial because of illness with the observation that "Schmidt fully participated in the portion of the proceedings that concerned him." Handy was also unimpressed by Vogel's confirmation that "the fact that the Herr Vice Chancellor has written to General Handy in his capacity as chairman of one of the great democratic parties in no way meant that what was involved here was a purely private initiative. The intervention had the full approval of the Herr Federal Chancellor. It was only a question of finding a new 'approach,' since the Federal Republic had already officially intervened through its highest organ, the federal president." Handy only raised his voice slightly in response to Bitter's objection that "radical right-wing" views could "appropriate the theme." "You are moving on dangerous ground," he commented. Vogel noted later that "in a very kind and serene tone, the general made it clear that he was completely familiar with the political side of the problem."[143]

For the two condemned men from the Dachau trials, the end of all tactical moves had arrived. "Each additional step at this moment would be an excess" was the way Vogel closed his report. At the same time, lawyer Magee was using the last legal possibilities available in the United States: new habeas corpus appeals lodged in the Washington, D.C., district courts led—as had already been the case in mid-February, "literally in the last hour"—to a postponement of the executions.[144] On 26 May, Magee requested the original petition lists collected by the Landsberg activists, supposedly containing 610,280 signatures, for presentation to the White House.[145] On 6 June, all legal means had finally been exhausted; once again the Supreme Court had decided. In the early hours of 7 June, the seven Nazi criminals were hanged in the Landsberg prison courtyard. Blücher and Finance Minister Schäffer were present.

After the nationalistic uproar and apologistic propaganda of recent weeks—"history is certainly being rewritten these days," wrote the steadily critical *Manchester Guardian*[146]—it could hardly be expected that the German public would leave the executions uncommented. While the chancellor maintained an iron silence, Franz Blücher considered it appropriate to make use of his information advantage. On the morning after the executions, the FDP chairman declared that "in this truly somber hour, the fate of the condemned Landsbergers and our attitude toward it requires one final word," then laying due stress, among other things, on his intervention for Schallermair and Schmidt. Striving to place the liberals and himself in the proper light, he paid the price of ambivalence. "What was at stake was the higher principle: preserving belief in the immutable norms of a law without whose presence human coexistence is not possible."[147]

To the relief of the Americans, most of the German press reacted with more equanimity.[148] "A start of fright has moved through the German populace," observed the "Spotlight" column of the *Süddeutsche Zeitung*, "but also, in a certain sense, a sigh of relief."[149] Similarly to Karl Gerold in the *Frankfurter Rundschau*, a number of commentators now raised their voices against "fascists of a new stripe" who, following the example of Bundestag delegate Franz Richter, hoped to exploit Landsberg to the fullest.[150] "These gallows were no cross at Golgatha" was the comment of the *Hannoversche Presse* a few days later. Placed above an appropriate excerpt from Ohlendorf's Nuremberg cross-examination, it was meant as an answer to those who "attempted to make a national manifestation out of the laying to rest of the earthly remains of the executed men—to compare the life and death of Ohlendorf with that of Christ and to glorify it as an Easter revelation."[151] Even the editors of *Christ und Welt*, so highly generous to the Landsberg lobby over the past months, struck a reconciliatory tone. "Quite likely there is hardly another example in world history of so lengthy and dogged a struggle for the lives of human beings—one undertaken by so many different departments and with such different means—as the struggle for the lives of the seven death candidates," began the evangelical paper's lead article. The motives of those engaged in the struggle, the editors explained, were highly varied, and much was simply a consequence of the American judicial system. All in all, the paper saw "far less a form of political ressentiment and far more a spontaneous expression of simple human empathy" in the German campaign for the "Landsbergers"—thus rejecting all criticism of the campaign from abroad. In conclusion, however, there was a warning for *Christ und Welt*'s own readers: "It is certain that no heroes or martyrs ended up on the Landsberg gallows. It is certain that such an end has not marked the tragic finale to a great hour of German history, but the dismal aftermath to a bitter end of one of Germany's historical epochs. We have full empathy with those who are now bereaved. But there is not the least ground for any glorification now or in the future."[152]

Steered by adaptable "former ones" (the commonly if misleadingly applied term) like Klaus Mehnert and Giselher Wirsing, *Christ und Welt* was very well aware that the future did not lie in gazing backward at a corrupted right-wing nationalism, but in the Western defense community. There would be continued interventions for anyone who could be useful in this context—meaning that even after the last executions on German soil, the struggle for the war criminals was not at an end.

The *Frankfurter Allgemeine* had already been making open efforts in recent weeks to shift attention from the "red jackets" to the military men—from Landsberg to Wittlich and Werl.[153] In Thilo Bode's commentary on the executions, this was now announced in point blank fashion—as, in fact, the very *sense* of the executions. "The death of the seven Landsberg prisoners can in the end prove a service in a good cause. The reproach standing between the Germans and the other nations [*sic*], to the effect that individuals with tens of thousands on their conscience still lived and were indeed national heroes, has lost its substance since yesterday night. We are thus offered the hope that the path is now open for a passion-free, sober, legal consideration of the war criminal complex—a complex that unfortunately still exists. No one will wish to maintain that it has been resolved to full satisfaction. Catchwords like Werl, Landsberg, Wittlich, and the German war prisoners in France are on everyone's mind. It has hopefully now become easier to correct injustices and give law precedence over unpleasant feelings"—*ungute Gefühle*.[154] As opinion surveys indicated, Bode's hope was shared with at least half his countrymen: 55 percent of men and 46 percent of women had meanwhile come to agree that rearmament was out of the question "as long as the German soldier is still considered a war criminal." Of all the opinions being voiced on the defense contribution theme, this was the most popular.[155]

CHAPTER 8

A "General Treaty" Instead of a "General Amnesty" (1951–52)

Accoording to the Central Bureau for Legal Defense, the "number of Germans domiciled with the Western powers" was slightly less than 1,800 in the spring of 1951.[1] Such deliberately strained terminology had now become much more than an official legal tool—since the hysteria surrounding Landsberg, a willingness to call the war criminals by their name had dissipated throughout West German society. A prime example of the new euphemism was an interpellation, prompted by the Central Bureau's tally, that Herbert Wehner formulated for the Social Democratic parliamentary faction: "German war prisoners in the West" read the extremely vague heading to this otherwise highly precise document. While without exception Wehner's questions were related to persons accused and condemned by the Western powers, he completely avoided use of the—now-disreputable—term *war criminal*."[2] For its part, the press was becoming increasingly inclined toward use of the formula "so-called war criminals," and the Heidelberg jurists' circle had suddenly taken to placing the term in quotation marks.[3] Toward the end of 1951, the *Times* of London took note of the term appearing this way in the government's press office bulletin.[4]

Correspondingly, increasing favor was being granted distinctions between "political war criminals" and "real" ones, "condemned sol-

177

diers" and "genuine criminals"—and paraphrases such as "actions connected with the war events." Such diction certainly reflected the basically sweeping application of the term *war crime*. The term covered offenses against codified laws of war (e.g., the execution of war prisoners and hostages). It covered crimes against humanity and peace condemned at Nuremberg (although we should note that no one—Spandau residents Rudolf Heß and Baldur von Schirach aside—served time on account of these supposedly abstract crimes alone). And it covered Nazi crimes in the narrower sense—in particular, those of the concentration camps and death camps. Nevertheless, the term's lack of precision was an artificial and corollary, in no way causal "argument" of critics struggling to create complications.

The increasingly small number of incarcerated war criminals resulting from the pardons and assorted dismissals was accompanied by an increasingly intense, transparent desire to eradicate the notion itself—indeed, to leave none of its traces.[5] The psychic need to once and for all dispense with the war criminal theme grew in inverse proportion to the theme's factual significance. For, whereas in the spring of 1950 there were still around 3,400 such incarcerated persons, a year later the figure had dropped to almost half that amount, and in the course of 1951 it would again substantially diminish, reaching precisely 1,258 persons on 31 January 1952. Slightly fewer than 700 of these war criminals were being kept in Landsberg, Wittlich, and Werl. Around half as many were in France; the rest were distributed among the Benelux countries (above all), as well as Norway, Denmark, and Yugoslavia (the latter country now holding 46 prisoners, in comparison with 1,000 in the spring of 1950).[6]

Despite all the propaganda about "dungeons," for a long time now the defense and general legal assistance offered this prison population could only have been considered optimal.[7] But it remained the case that although the number of prisoners being held in Werl and Wittlich had been reduced to the same extent as in Landsberg—that is, by around a third—neither the French nor the British had managed to convince themselves of the need for a major pardoning project of their own.[8] And it was also the case that precisely on account of McCloy's generosity, the situation at Landsberg seemed stable for the foreseeable future. This meant, however, that six years after the end of a war that had generally been shoved into a much more distant past, no end to the punitive measures against war criminals was in sight. Indeed, as was underscored by the political and journalistic commotion surrounding the flight of the celebrated Bernhard Ramcke from French imprisonment and the (mild) military court sentence he received after his return in March 1951, the only thing that could be counted on was new trials and new sentences.[9]

In such a context, once could hardly have not expected additional demands to terminate the proceedings once and for all. At the same time, most of the politically influential protagonists had learned from the events surrounding the Landsberg decision. On the one hand, three weeks after the executions, the *Sonntagsblatt*—edited by Hannover's state bishop Lilje but apparently without authorization from the church's experts—announced that the "time for a general amnesty, for a truly great act of forgetting" had "arrived for both sides."[10] On the other hand, the strategists in the Heidelberg jurists' circle were now focusing more than ever before on the search for solutions that excluded the public.

Looked at closely, the entire whirlwind running through the press had been of use to the radicals alone, while offering foreign observers a painful picture and weakening rather than strengthening any readiness for generosity. Instead of furnishing properly inclined journalists with material and arguments as had earlier been the case, the legal experts now counseled restraint, while themselves doing their best to restrain the right-wing loudmouths. This is the case, for instance, with High Consistory member Ranke, who devoted much of his energy in the Bonn branch of the German Evangelical Church to the war criminals, cooperating there as easily with CDU Bundestag delegate Eduard Wahl, head of the jurists' circle, as with leading Social Democrats. In the fall of 1951 Ranke praised himself for having put a stop to the increasingly uncontrolled actions of Princess Isenburg and her circle. All further steps, Ranke explained to Wahl, would have to be taken in such a way that "political radicalization through this problem complex is avoided." This meant avoidance of a "stirring up of nationalist instincts through a public campaign" that he considered "extremely dangerous," "now as before."[11]

This was no abstract warning. Ranke was touching on latent differences within the Heidelberg circle—differences always present but now surfacing.[12] Typically they had emerged precisely when possibilities for having a direct political say were opening for the circle. An invitation in this direction had been extended by State Secretary Walter Hallstein, just back from Adenauer's vacation retreat in the Swiss Alps. Working from there at the start of August 1951, the chancellor and his advisors had drafted the plans for a comprehensive "security treaty" with the Western allies.[13] Such plans were bound up with a desired recuperation of national sovereignty—in which context the war criminal problem also needed to be settled. Representatives of the West German government and the Allied High Commission had achieved that much concord in their preliminary discussions, ongoing since May, over an agreement "to terminate occupation law."[14] There had even been discussions concerning the need to come up with a new pardoning process should the agreement bear fruition.[15] It was thus all the more remarkable that the state secretary's question considering the anticipated form of a "general resolution of the war criminal problem" found the Heidelberg jurists rather unprepared.[16]

For just that reason, seven leading members of the circle prepared a priority list for Hallstein in a hastily convened special meeting. Its participants evidently had information from the preliminary negotiations at their disposal. Since "certain advances" had been achieved in the past, there were no prospects now for additional advances "unless basic organizational changes, and with them a shifting of responsibility, are attained."[17] Consequently "for all 'war criminals' incarcerated in Germany, authority to exercise the right to pardon and to enforce sentences must be transferred to German agencies.... Should he give his consent, the federal president might be suggested as the German pardoning authority." In the exercise of pardons, the president would "naturally" consider suitable individuals. In addition, the jurists had come up with another idea, in case this one proved impracticable. Its realization, as well, implied the circle's collaboration. Corresponding to the peace treaty with Japan, the West German government would have to be granted the right to make proposals in all matters related to pardons; in that case, however, "deviating from the Japanese solution, a mixed authority for decisions regarding the proposals should be formed. We conceive this as one Allied member, depending on the country involved, and one German member; the chairman, the third member, should be appointed through mutual agreement." If neither the presidential model nor the mixed pardon commission were to be approved, then "under all circumstances" sentence enforcement would need to remain in Allied hands in order to demonstrate their final responsibility.

The Heidelberg experts also came up with a proposal regarding the war criminals held in Spandau: that in the future, their pardoning should not require unanimous agreement of the four powers represented on the International Military Tribunal, but only a majority decision. This idea would have required what amounted to the Russians canceling themselves out. Undoubtedly it reflected considerable political naïveté—along with a fair share of audacity, already apparent in the proposal to make the West German president chief commissioner of pardons. In contrast, the second solution, the establishment of a "mixed authority," held much promise. But before the promise could be realized, this solution would be a source of conflict within the jurists' circle.

In the circle's next general meeting, most members approved the results of the special session, while aligning themselves with the position of Eduard Wahl and Hellmut Becker that no measures posing a threat to the government's negotiations should be taken. However, a minority around Celle's Regional Court president Baron von Hodenberg pressed for publicity; he considered it imperative to "support" the government's efforts through a public resolution. But in a formal vote— unusual for the circle—he lost out, most members deciding against bringing in the press. Instead, they opted for another arrangement: submitting the circle's proposals to the Bundestag's Committee on Occupation Law and Foreign Affairs—or more precisely, its Subcommittee on War Prisoners.[18]

This subcommittee was steered by Evangelical Relief Association director Eugen Gerstenmaier. In the beginning it had actually concerned itself with the problem of war prisoner repatriation, trying to aid prisoners in the Soviet Union in particular.[19] But since mid-1951 the chief focus of its work had increasingly shifted toward helping war criminals sentenced by the Allies, which did not signify neglect of the simple war prisoners, since there was a separate Committee for War Victims and War Prisoners.[20] Significantly Eduard Wahl now attended the meetings regularly, and Herbert Wehner showed up increasingly often as well. Both men were thus present on 17 September 1951 when Gerstenmaier, looking ahead to the pending German-Allied negotiations, raised the question of whether an effort to bring about a "general act of pardon" was called for, then probingly adding, "in that case, what will happen with the genuine criminals?" With no apparent scruples, Wehner pleaded for doing as much as possible to establish a "compensatory policy" favoring "sentenced persons in the hands of foreign powers." Wahl, on the other hand, clarified the proposal for a mixed commission made that morning in the jurists' circle.[21] By the next meeting three weeks later, Gerstenmaier had overcome any of his own reservations; what was at stake was abandoning the previous "defensive approach" and working for a "total settlement"—more literally, a "total cleaning up" (or "clarification"), a *Gesamtbereinigung*.[22]

A further three weeks later, the Heidelberg jurists had given shape to the proposals sketched by Wahl; for the sake of the higher degree of solemnity, they had them undersigned mainly by church figures.[23] The subcommittee now gave an audience to several former Nuremberg defense lawyers. After repeating the familiar objections to the Dachau trials, Kranzbühler and colleagues offered the opinion that at most 10 percent of the "Landsbergers" had been "truly liable to punishment." Animated in this direction, the parliamentarians promptly declared that among those not sentenced to life imprisonment, "it is certain that no more guilty persons" were to be found, "in the sense of international and national jurisdiction." During the discussion of the proposals, this radical refusal to acknowledge any guilt whatsoever made it possible, indeed necessary, to leave behind the apparently optimal demand for a "general pardon" or "general amnesty." Instead of pardon, the desired solution was now actually "correction of injustice"—although this was not explicitly formulated. The committee in any case could not agree on whether, alongside the recommendation of a mixed commission, there should also be a demand for the immediate interim release of all those who had served a third of their sentences. Concerning the reservations expressed by Wahl, Kranzbühler, Bitter, and others, Wehner opined that in practice it would prove completely inconsequential if the releases were interim or not.[24] Over recent months, the war criminal issue had been exploited by the right with great effectiveness. It was clear that Wehner now wished to clear it from the table at virtually any price.

In the late summer of 1951, thanks to the excellent connections of its head, Eduard Wahl, the Heidelberg circle succeeded, within a period of a few weeks, in making its own ideas regarding a "settlement"—again, *Bereinigung*—"of the war criminal problem" into the conceptual platform of West German policies regarding the problem.[25] This success was sparked by Adenauer's negotiation preparations—although the much more narrowly conceived Allied plans for a General Treaty had diminished their momentum.[26] Both the government and the Committee on Foreign Affairs took up the circle's demands; in particular, the idea of a mixed commission quickly became a fixed concept.

At the end of October 1951, following provisionally final discussions in the Subcommittee on War Prisoners, the Central Bureau formulated a set of "proposals for the future treatment of interrogation and trial proceedings against Germans on account of actions connected with wartime events." This fifteen-point catalog marked the first official specification of German wishes. It had been put together in collaboration with Heinz Trützschler von Falkenstein, negotiating head of the Foreign Ministry, and Wilhelm Grewe, coordinator of the diplomatic tug-of-war—it had just begun and would last for months—over supplements to the General Treaty.[27]

At the start of the new catalog stood maximalist demands similar to those raised by the chancellor to the High Commissioner in November 1950[28]: no further legally enforceable death penalties should be carried out; sentences up to twenty years should be remitted; new investigative proceedings should be abandoned; and pending proceedings should be suspended when a sentence of more than twenty years was not expected or pretrial custody had lasted more than a year with no preferring of charges. For cases in which a sentence of more than twenty years could be counted on, the proceedings were to be concluded within nine months or else discontinued. At the same time the occupying powers were to fully abandon new extraditions. The desired procedure of the mixed commission was new and had implications for the small group of persons incurring heavy punishment. Alongside the chairman, envisioned as a qualified jurist and member of a state that had been neutral during the war, both a German and an assessor from the "detaining state" were to be present. "All records related to the pretrial proceedings and trial" kept in the "detaining state" were to be furnished, and the defense attorneys for the condemned men were to be allowed full inspection of the records. Imprisonment was to be "separate from prisoners of other sorts," in Germany, but under a director from a neutral foreign country.[29]

The catalog was signed by Justice Minister Dehler. Its tone was more suitable for an armistice treaty than an agreement meant to place relations between the West German state and the Western powers on a new cooperative footing. The text's contents were barely distinguishable from the demands for a general amnesty and total break with the past that had recently been passed at the FDP convention in Munich.[30] Indisputably, starting with the emergence of the General Treaty on the political horizon, champions of the tabula rasa principle had gathered new momentum. More or less well meaning party colleagues and Bundestag delegates obliged to the war criminal theme were pressing Dehler with sarcastic queries and baseless complaints (for instance, concerning the "inhumane treatment" of those imprisoned in Werl).[31] Attorneys—some inspired by a radio broadcast of Beethoven's "Fidelio," with its selfless rescue of a dungeon-dwelling hero—mailed in eccentric proposals,[32] and the above-mentioned new and potent lobby was organized in connection with the FDP's Westphalian chapter: Ernst Achenbach's "Preparatory Committee for a General Amnesty."[33]

As was the case at the year's beginning, a public mood was looming that could only weigh down the dialogue with the Allies. This was particularly the case since the nationalist and historico-apologetic tenor emerging under the sign of rearmament was now being harmonized with war cries from the numerous blossoming soldiers' organizations.[34] In this respect, two November 1951 interpellations submitted in the Bundestag by the CDU-CSU faction—but later to be withdrawn—were clearly meant to cover the negotiating chancellor's back: one spoke up against "political efforts" in the newly formed "League of German Soldiers"; the other against the "amalgamation of former SS members," seen as an attempt to revive the "demons of a calamitous past."[35] But it was equally clear that the FDP and German Party coalition partners wished to have nothing to do with this relief operation. Quite to the contrary, a few days later they offered a showpiece motion "regarding the freeing of Germans in foreign custody." The request it contained could not have been formulated more sweepingly: "The Federal Government is authorized to approach the governments of those countries still holding Germans in custody on account of wartime actions with the request to free the prisoners before the coming Christmas holiday or, in case release should appear impossible because of being charged with heavily punishable offenses, to approve placing the proceedings under German jurisdiction." The government was expected to approach the Soviet Union and the other Eastern Block states in the same manner.[36]

In fact, a gesture from the Russians—who, it would turn out four years later, were still holding 10,000 Germans[37]—was not on the horizon. But something could be hoped for from the Western powers, particularly after the request by Cologne's Cardinal Frings for a generous Christmas amnesty became public knowledge.[38] The motion's tactical purpose was thus to steer public satisfaction regarding the anticipated year's-end act of pardon in the direction of the governing parties' apparatus; once this seemed assured, the motion vanished from the parliamentary agenda without a whimper.[39] The day before Christmas Eve, the AP counted 259 early releases, although most involved only a few weeks being cut from the full sentencing period.[40] These Christmas gestures, however, revealed nothing about the willingness of the Three Powers to come up with a definitive answer to "the old problem of the war prisoners" (Marion Gräfin Dönhoff's renewed demand in *Die Zeit* at the end of 1951): to take up the problem with the Germans "finally and without prejudice."[41]

Into November, all German plans were being formulated without participation of the Allies. The Committee for Occupation Law and Foreign Affairs had now tackled the proposals formulated in its subcommittee by the Heidelberg jurists, the Central Bureau, and the SPD alliance, handing the package on to the chancellor with hardly any changes.[42] In their mid-September Washington conference, the foreign ministers of the Three Powers had discussed the theme but come to no conclusions.[43] Adenauer—well aware of the anticipatory pressure in the parliament, among the public,[44] and, just as important, within Bonn's ministerial bureaucracy—considered raising the problem in his first, highly prestigious conference with the foreign ministers (scheduled for 22 November 1951 in Paris). He believed the chances were good of more generosity being displayed there than had been by the High

Commissioners, who were all tired of the theme after the years-long quibbling, and who had all become very fastidious. But in a preliminary meeting, the ministers made it clear to Adenauer that they did not like the idea of the issue being raised at this conference. In formal fashion, McCloy asked Adenauer to first convey his "views" to the High Commission.[45] And shortly before the conference's start, the three commissioners notified their foreign ministers that, despite much discussion, the war prisoner proposals were not ready. This, it was agreed, was an important matter needing to be settled before conclusion of the various agreements—but first the chancellor had to announce his position.[46] It consequently became clear that the theme would not be on the Paris agenda.

The theme's absence notwithstanding, the day before the beginning of the conference Adenauer used a meeting with Dean Acheson, U.S. secretary of state, to raise the "war prisoner and war criminal question." In doing so, he spoke up on behalf of the Spandau prisoners—especially seventy-seven-year-old Konstantin von Neurath, "who on account of his old age and extremely bad health has to especially suffer."[47] Beyond this, he asked Acheson if he "would be willing to discuss the possibility of a quicker settlement of the war prisoner question with Herr [Robert] Schuman [the French Foreign Minister].[48] The same naturally also applies to those imprisoned in the British zone in Werl." Acheson consented to put in a word with his French colleague for reaching a "rational arrangement."[49] When it came to the British, Adenauer would soon have a chance to broach the matter for himself.

Adenauer's visit to London had been planned in the fall. Taking place at the start of December 1951, it lasted five days, during which he was granted the whole gamut of statesman's honors. In their reports on the visit, the German press repeatedly raised the clarion call of Werl—this certainly not without governmental encouragement.[50] And in fact, the "prisoner problem" (foreign policy aide Herbert Blankenhorn, writing in his diary) formed the central theme of a discussion between Adenauer and Britain's foreign minister, Anthony Eden.[51] In confidence, Eden informed the chancellor that thought was being given to a three-man pardon commission consisting of an Allied representative, a German, and a representative of a neutral country. On the condition that the latter individual acted as chairman, the proposal seemed acceptable to Adenauer. London had also anticipated his wish to bring something concrete back home with him: henceforth the period of pretrial imprisonment would be counted in the condemned men's favor, so that the release of around 30 of the 200 prisoners was pending even before Christmas.[52] But in regard to Manstein, the year's outstanding soldierly icon, "the chancellor encountered great restraint on the English side" (Blankenhorn again).[53] Churchill did speak proudly of his donation to the field marshall's defense—but as was observed in the (seventy-five-year old) chancellor's delegation, the prime minister had already become a little unusual in certain ways at seventy-seven.

Adenauer could have no interest in proclaiming his visits' results to be the early release of a number of prisoners from Werl—and this not only because London had requested discretion. Any even remotely martial tone of the sort the military activists would have loved would have been counterproductive. Now as before, the matter was delicate, the Allied attitude far from clear. It remained to be seen whether the Americans and French could also be pinned down to the three-man commission model discussed with Eden, and the extent of such a commission's authority was also uncertain. In such a situation, a public discussion of the possibility would actually in itself have had an unsettling impact—all the more so a critique declaring the commission model excessively complicated, a general amnesty the hour's dictate. Once again, the *Frankfurter Allgemeine* grasped this most quickly.

"The War Criminals' Halo" was the title of Thilo Bode's article in that paper, appearing in the first days of January 1952. Not without a struggle with his own ressentiment, Bode here attempted to fix the line of political rationality and define what appeared feasible.[54] The "humanly understandable but deeply regrettable echo" of the "grotesque accusations" leveled in the war crime trials was now "no one is guilty!" An example of this stance was the recent transfer of a prisoner who by the end of his train ride through northern Germany had no idea where to stick the cigarettes and drinks other travelers had slipped him. Granting this unidentified war criminal the now standard quotation marks, Bode still then raised objections to the "industrious circles" adeptly using the Landsberg decision "to set nothing less than a wave of national indignation in motion (at least on paper) for the entirely wrong people— a wave that has caused Germany endless harm, that has unnecessarily hardened a good-willed, open man like the American High Commissioner, and that in addition has certainly contributed to a pair of men being executed despite the fact that they should not have been under any circumstances. Their names are Schmidt and Schallermair."

The mention of the two concentration camp executioners is startling, since in the next sentence Bode located his "wrong people" above all in the ranks of camp guards, many of these persons having been previously convicted. The fact, he observed, that many Germans tossed such figures "together into one pot with a Manstein or an unfortunate innocent man lacking a great name is simply the result of the Allies having previously placed a Raeder, a Speer, and a Dönitz on the same bench as Frank, Kaltenbrunner, and Streicher."

Without stating it directly, this editorial writer for the *Frankfurter Allgemeine* had here mapped out a demarcating line that amounted to a line of class: as long as they were firmly determined by the Allies, Nazi crimes were to be expiated by the violent murderers and bullies who, corresponding to the popularly desired picture, came from the lower societal stratum, along with, perhaps, a pair of arrivistes who had bloodied their hands. But the bourgeois "desk murderers" and political perpetrators and the members of the bureaucratic elite, as well, of course, as soldiers in general, were to be finally freed from the stain of complicity and released from custody. With this approach, the *Frankfurter Allgemeine* was offering a variation on a basic idea of the chancellor's. For quite some time now, he had been speaking of the "real criminals"; and in dialog with the Heidelberg jurists and others, he was suggesting publication at the right moment of a list designating the previously sentenced persons among the condemned war criminals in order to counter their "general glorification."[55]

In any case, "under no circumstances acceptable" was the *Frankfurter Allgemeine*'s comment on Adenauer's supposed readiness—it would be promptly denied by the chancellor's office—to recognize the "legal validity" of the Allied sentences, in return for transfer of penal administration to German hands.[56] In raising his objections, Bode was not content with simply evoking Weizsäcker's sentence, but also repeated the old slogans regarding Malmédy—now given an aggressive edge with remarks directed at the—Jewish—investigating officers: "Is it a German concern to offer shelter to those dark elements whose conscience ought actually be weighed down by the Malmédy trial—and to do this by granting a certificate of 'legality' to judgments arrived at through all forms of extortion, mistreatment, and sabotage of the law? This would be a vicious lie."

Following such words, unmistakably rising above any doubts regarding national staunchness, Bode could conclude by speaking out directly against a general amnesty and for "mixed courts of law," entirely in Adenauer's sense. But here as well, he managed to bring in an argument that would have done honor to the hardest of the hard-liners: a general amnesty was not desirable because "people who are not guilty would be amnestied," and "amnesty cannot be granted those who are innocent." The following, second part of the argument revealed just how little need was generally now being felt for adequate punishment, and the widespread nature of a basically instrumental distancing from Nazi crimes: "But should the truly guilty—and that they exist must repeatedly be made clear—be amnestied? That cannot be useful for Germany's reputation."

As a "solution to the war criminal question" entered the vortex of negotiations on security and foreign policy, the psychological hurdles grew higher and higher—for both sides. It was no accident that Adenauer's initial reaction to Otto Kranzbühler's overview of the Heidelberg circle's demands—the chancellor received a delegation from the circle on 25 January 1952—was that the Allies' room for maneuvering was limited, since any step they now took would "consist of an at least indirect admission of having previously committed injustice."[57] But at the same time, the chancellor was interested in dispelling the impression being generated by the *Frankfurter Allgemeine* that the government was contemplating a recognition of the judgments. As he explained it, he had only recently discussed the arrangement adopted in the U.S.-Japan treaty with McCloy, who at one point had "spontaneously remarked, 'I cannot require that you recognize these judgments as justly grounded.' " According to Adenauer, McCloy had also spontaneously "suggested the possibility of pardon commissions consisting of three German judges and three from the Western allies, with a neutral chairman." At this point, Grewe remarked that McCloy had "some time ago" stressed the unacceptability of a neutral chairman. Adenauer, however, insisted on the new information's validity.

It is difficult to say how much wishful thinking was at play here and how much cold calculation. One thing is certain: The most difficult point of conflict between West Germany and the Allies lay precisely in the questions of recognizing the judgments' validity and the pardon commission's makeup. Much speaks for the assumption that in the context of the pending major defense debate in the Bundestag, the chancellor wished to somewhat underplay the conflict. All in all, the foreign policy situation remained fragile. The European Defense Community was by no means over its hurdles, the Saarland question was unresolved, since 10 March Stalin's note about German reunification was on the table. Adenauer had absolutely no need for shrill voices from the government camp intruding on consultations over central issues, and doing so out of excitement over a matter he considered secondary. In this respect, the defense debate (7–8 February 1952) unfolded in a markedly calm manner, something certainly due, above all else, to a clever steering of the war criminal issue (at least to the extent it was the governing alliance's concern) to a single, separate speech. With Eduard Wahl, the Union had the most qualified of men for the task.

Combining an academic bearing with the knowledge of a political insider, the Heidelberg professor focused on the Hague Convention, now and then introducing an allusion for the initiated, and remaining as generally moderate as a chancellor facing difficult negotiations could ever expect.[58] The only figure from the ranks of the governing parties daring something more direct than Wahl was August-Martin Euler, who would not suffer any muffling of his own version of the old, fearful image: German soldiers marching by Werl. "I cannot imagine," he vividly proclaimed, "that new German troops march beneath the Werl prison while many worthy officers and ordinary people are kept there, alongside General Field Marshalls von Manstein and Kesselring—people of whom it can only be said that they exploited possibilities of warfare that must be present—and that are present in international law—to save one's bare life in face of an insidious, gruesome form of warfare."[59]

With the exception of Euler, the reticence regarding the war criminal matter was in fact striking. To be sure, this reticence was not only a sign of well-held discipline within the alliance. Rather, it was also connected with a draft resolution apparently conjured out of a hat by the governing parties on the debate's second day. According to the resolution, the Bundestag considered it necessary "that those Germans charged with war crimes and either already convicted by Allied courts or still held without a verdict be released, so long as what is at issue is not a crime as the word is ordinarily understood, that is, for which a single individual is responsible. An objective examination of the individual cases must follow without delay."[60] Approved by a large majority of delegates, this statement was almost equal to squaring the circle—a clear signal to the Allies and a forceful resolution for the chancellor, soberly formulated and yet radical enough for the old soldiers. More could hardly have been attained with so few words.

The coalition thus stood resplendent, and Herbert Wehner had to recognize that the governing parties had succeeded in outmaneuvering the SPD in an important side issue—one where there was in fact no argument. For as a sign of their rejection of a defense contribution "under current conditions," the Social Democratic delegates had turned down wholesale the coalition motions hammered out at the end of the two-day defense debate.[61] Suddenly it seemed that the delegates were abandoning the fight in favor of the war criminals (although in their ranks, as well, they were scarcely still considered to be such). And yet, with its euphemistic spring 1951 interpellation concerning "German war prisoners in the West," it was precisely the SPD that had seized the early initiative—so at least Wehner saw things, and not without reason. It had only been State Secretary Hallstein's reservations concerning a "public discussion" that induced the party to accept handing the matter to the Committee on Foreign Affairs (and eventually to the subcommittee),

where combined forces had arranged the package now ready for negotiations with the Allies. Wehner undertook a detailed written explanation of this matter for the Bundestag records.[62] Practically speaking, the
SPD had nonetheless suffered a setback, especially since even by the
party's own account, it had failed to clearly explain its complicated position of a "qualified yes" regarding a defense contribution.[63]

With the Bundestag resolution, the Germans had thrown a tough
problem at the foot of the Allies. The death of King George VI meant it
could be discussed a week and a half later in London. Before and after
his burial on 15 February 1952, the French, British, and American foreign ministers had a series of conversations concerning the stalled
Defense Community project, and Adenauer was brought in toward the
end. Of the three points predicted as posing difficulties in a preparatory paper of the High Commissioners, the Bonn parliament's demands
regarding the war criminals was seen as the most difficult. As the paper
described the status of the negotiations, the chancellor had been
informed of the Three Powers' willingness to hand the prisoners over
to the Germans. The precondition: Adenauer's recognition of the sentences and readiness to have them carried out. The chancellor, the paper
indicated, had also been told of the consideration being given a mixed,
expanded pardon commission consisting of three Germans and three
Allied representatives.[64] When it came to everything else, the Allies
themselves had differing opinions before the London meeting. More
precisely, John McCloy had become increasingly annoyed by developments over recent months and had now put his foot down.[65] In contrast
with Ivone Kirkpatrick, he believed that the pardon commission should
only make recommendations, not carry out pardons. François-Poncet
concurred but went further by maintaining that the commission should
always be fully activated in order to prevent an agreement being reached
between the Germans and one of the Three Powers over the heads of
the other two.

As became clear in London in the course of an initially strictly bilateral Anglo-American working session, McCloy was also firmly opposed
to a British suggestion that the six-man commission prevent stalemates
by taking on a seventh, neutral member.[66] During the war, efforts to
enlist support from neutral quarters regarding the problem of war crimes
had been fruitless; to now invite neutral parties on board might be taken
as an admission that mistakes had been made in the trials. In addition,
McCloy explained, the French were themselves strictly against a neutral commission member.

Other than Acheson, who was markedly restrained vis-à-vis the war
criminal issue, thus allowing McCloy to maintain his relatively rigid

position, British Foreign Minister Anthony Eden was manifestly engaged. Only a month before, he indicated, he had in fact offered Adenauer the prospect of a neutral member participating—as part of a three-man commission. In the process, he had occasion to hear how important precisely this point was to the chancellor. He was thus rather certain "that the present British position was the least the Germans would accept," nevertheless agreeing to the American idea—that is, a six-man commission without a neutral party—being presented to the Germans as a first proposal. In the case of a German rejection, Sir Ivone had the idea of suggesting that the neutral party be replaced with a representative from one of the smaller Allied countries, say Belgium or Holland.

McCloy could also not be easily budged regarding the other contentious point. The background of painful experience was not entirely muffled in his outspoken objections to granting decision-making authority to the commission: "If we did we ran the risk that the entire war criminal program might be washed out by a single vote in which one of the Allied members was soft and supported a German clemency proposal." At the suggestion of his foreign minister, it was agreed that at least unanimous commission votes should be seen as binding, while those reached by a majority would serve as recommendations for the different governments. Over the weekend, a group of referees prepared a proposal to that effect.

On 17 February (a Sunday), Acheson and Eden informed Schuman of developments and received his consent regarding the bilateral position.[67] Next, Adenauer was invited to a four-man meeting that took place on Monday morning; at that point, the German delegation was already aware of the new Allied proposal.[68] Prompted by host Anthony Eden to raise the war criminal question at the start, the chancellor opened with a typical suggestion that the High Commissioners had often heard: the question was "not materially but psychologically significant." No one in Germany wished "unjustified pardon for genuine criminals." Among the "so-called war criminals" were "a number of people who already had previous sentences on the German criminal register"; it would be desirable to enlighten public opinion regarding these authentic criminals through suitable publications.[69]

More astonishing than such remarks, untrammeled as they were with much knowledge of the facts, was the absence of any effort on the chancellor's part to raise the idea of the three-man commission with a neutral chairman discussed in his earlier London visit, as an alternative to the six-man commission with no neutral member that was now being proposed. Likewise, he offered no comment in the morning session on the plan's call for recognition of the sentences' legal validity.

He did broach the subject in the afternoon meeting, thus getting entangled in a dispute with Robert Schuman regarding the meaning of the term *Rechtskraft,* "legal validity" or "legal force"—the term that Schuman wished to see used.[70] Basically, Adenauer simply continued stressing what he had both tried for and achieved in the morning session: cosmetic operations such as not mentioning the German assumption of penal administration at the very start of the agreement, and likewise avoiding the word *Gnade,* "mercy," which implied acknowledgment of a sentence's validity.[71]

At Eden's suggestion, the commission was thus not named "Mixed Clemency Board" but simply "Mixed Board." If Adenauer's negotiating partners showed flexibility in such details, this was certainly due in part to the fact that really drastic suggestions for changes were absent, an impression consequently prevailing in the end that the main problem had been solved.[72] Dean Acheson, at least, contentedly reported to the president as follows: "We also reached full agreement with Adenauer on the future handling of war criminals in Germany. We cannot, of course, maintain prisons of our own on her territory after the new arrangements go into effect. The solution here was quite similar to that in the case of Japan."[73] But in regard to both the side question of the war criminals and the main question of West Germany's military integration, this optimism—the outcome of generally difficult negotiations—would prove premature.

Measured against the expectations conveyed to the chancellor for his London trip by referees for the Central Bureau for Legal Defense (through Justice Minister Dehler) and the Heidelberg jurists (through the *Frankfurter Allgemeine*), what he returned with to Germany was rather meager.[74] Worse yet (although not to be learned then by either professional grouping), the chancellor had not even mentioned any of the clever provisos that both the official and freelance defenders of the war criminals had come up with over recent months. The only such thing he decided to venture was bringing the war criminal trials pending in France into the negotiations—and here he failed miserably.

There was an appropriate reaction by the Justice Ministry officials let into the picture by Grewe.[75] Undoubtedly the anticipated review of the war criminal sentences by a Mixed Board represented progress and was hence to be welcomed, opined Margarethe Bitter following her first look at the London draft.[76] "In all events," she continued, "this progress seems purchased at a very high price, which lies in the fact that it implies an acknowledgment of the validity of the judgments on the German side." This was manifest above all in the anticipated assumption of penal administration. While in both Werl and Wittlich such administration was already a German responsibility—Landsberg, to the contrary, being fully under American control—this was itself based on occupation law dictate. In contrast, a freely concluded agreement would conjure up a conflict with the ban on special courts (Article 101 of the Basic Law) and on retroactive punishment (Article 103); it would at least require an implementing law per Article 104 (legal guarantees accompanying denial of freedom). And whether a majority could be found for this in the Bundestag was doubtful.

The requirement of the board's unanimity for binding decisions was the particular object of expert Bitter's critique. This, she observed, would give the state that imposed the punishment de facto veto rights. She also expressed skepticism regarding the length of the review process, should only a single board be appointed, as after the agreement took force no other possibility of dispensing pardons would exist, and there would thus be a long initial period of complete inaction. Finally, Bitter warned against the limitations placed on the circle of individuals envisioned as qualified for the Mixed Board; as the formulation stood, all officials were excluded, meaning no judges or university professors could be nominated. "But on account of their specialized knowledge, precisely the contribution of these persons cannot be dispensed with," protested the jurist. In doing so, she was offering a clear sign of where the Central Bureau hoped to see the German role on the board heading—into the hands of the Heidelberg circle and its associates.

Bitter's arguments had touched on practically all the points of criticism that were to be wrestled over in the negotiations over the coming months—literally until the day of the signing in Bonn, 26 May 1952. While the results of all this haggling for improvements were meager, the engagement it involved was highly telling.

It was not difficult for Dehler's legal referees to provoke heated opposition to the London agreement on his part. Annoyed in any case by the chancellor's failure to respond in any way to his premeeting suggestions, the justice minister now once more donned his beloved robe of "guardian of the constitution." "In various respects the sentences, whose execution is now to be taken over by the Federal Republic, conflict with the basic rights of the Basic Law," he wrote Adenauer, at the same time requesting a meeting. Other than was still the case in January, Dehler now indicated what was filling him with so much concern: the fact that sometimes even more far-reaching reservations regarding the plan were being expressed "in other circles as well."[77]

Presumably, Dehler was referring not so much to the Heidelberg jurists—even before London, they had begun to plan appointments for the "larger number of commissions" that they desired[78]—as to the team assembled around his Essen party colleague Ernst Achenbach. Namely, a few days earlier Achenbach had gone public with a large-scale "call for support for nonpartisan measures to bring about a general amnesty." Half-page advertisements in the *Welt am Sonntag* and the right-wing Düsseldorf weekly *Der Fortschritt* ("Progress") explained the allegedly noble goals of the preparatory committee.[79] The twelve signatories included seven Landtag delegates, among them the mayor of Essen Hans Toussaint (CDU), FDP North Rhine-Westphalian state party chairman Friedrich Middelhauve, and the CDU politician Josef Hermann Dufhues. In the name of the SPD, Wehner had immediately distanced himself from the appeal.[80]

"Pacification at home and abroad" was the group's motto. Intent on the semblance of party-political neutrality, it's markedly historical line of argument began with the 1648 Treaty of Westphalia and ended with the pacification proposal that amnesty expert Friedrich Grimm had addressed to Hitler in September 1933. Sandwiched between these historical moments was the Essen amnesty commission of 1929, when "responsible German men" like Adenauer, Cuno, Lehr (now the new interior minister), von Seeckt, and Pater Muckermann, prompted by the pending evacuation of the Rhineland, had interceded for a general pardon—one then granted in the amnesty law of 24 October 1930.

Historical analogizing—more perfectly mastered by no one—was the specialized past-political strategy of both Achenbach and his alter ego, Werner Best, and pacification via discretion each man's credo. Not the individual interest of the condemned men but the common national interest was the legal rationale of a general amnesty; the somewhat less noble conclusion: "the persons and cases per se are not interesting. The goal is that precisely for the sake of general peace they are no longer discussed and debated."

Naturally, there was no mention in the appeal of the deeds and perpetrators that were meant to be systematically veiled in silence; on the other hand there was frequent mention of breaking with the past, ressentiment, counterclaims, and political cleverness, understood as a challenge for the "other side." And although formulated in the diction of benign intent ("dangerous" and "illogical" were the harshest epithets), anyone not wearing nationalistic blinders must have recognized remarks like the following as brazen threats: "It is disquieting when without objective necessity—for no one on earth has any use for the continued punishment of hundreds of condemned Germans—the feelings of millions of Germans are excited and made accessible to negative or radical agitation."

If people such as Dehler could scarcely stand up to such warnings about radicalism from radicals masked as upright citizens, this was above all because the borderline separating such views from what they themselves considered proper had long since become hazy.[81] Perhaps nothing characterizes the mood inside the ministerial bureaucracy more drastically then the Foreign Ministry notations containing "suggestions for a final solution"—*Endlösung*—"to the so-called war criminal problem."[82] In essence, a majority of the Bonn professionals had probably come to favor a general amnesty. They simply knew better than did outsiders that such a demand was politically inopportune, indeed counterproductive. This was not the least of the reasons that in the secret specialized negotiations over three appendix agreements to the General Treaty—these negotiations would keep the German and Allied experts busy through March and April—the war criminal problem hardly played a role.[83] Its place was fixed as Article 6, paragraph 1, of one of these appendixes, the comprehensive "Convention on the Settlement of Matters Arising Out of the War and the Occupation" (shortened as the Transition Treaty).

Still, the main reason that for some time after the London conference it could seem as if the theme had been checked off the list was the systematic policy of secrecy surrounding the treaty, at Adenauer's insistence.[84] Even the specialized departments were only brought into the negotiations when necessary for specific points, and other than Adenauer, State Secretary Hallstein, and—acting as general manager—Professor Grewe, nobody on the German side had a total political overview. As a result of pressure from Dean Acheson, the signing date being aimed at was mid-May 1952. Around three weeks before this, the chancellor and foreign minister had to face up to the fact that they would not be able to push through the treaty as an isolated pair. Both in the cabinet and the coalition party factions, a dangerous protest was brewing. Its source was unhappiness at bad treatment mixed with political unease regarding individual clauses known through hearsay.[85]

It was of course the case that the unease was not related to the war criminal theme alone, but it was also certainly true that the theme was more than marginal. In that respect, one event in particular helped sabotage a relaxed atmosphere: while the treaty's war criminal article was being kept carefully off limits in Bonn, in March already, the State Department divulged its basic contents to a congressman, and this was followed by the *Frankfurter Allgemeine*'s publication of a corresponding AP report. The concern the report generated was in fact considerable, since it pointed to hopes for a total settlement not being fulfilled. There was, as well, a direct reference to West German obligations: "proceeding with execution of the sentences and preserving the conditions of incarceration with no changes."[86]

In contrast, the aspect of the treaty that would soon emerge as the most controversial, acknowledgment of the sentences' validity, could only be gleaned from the report by specialists.[87] It would not become general knowledge in Bonn until 25 April 1952. This was the date of two meetings: on the one hand, the third of a round of consultations by cabinet members and important coalition members set in motion through pressure by liberals threatening revolt; on the other hand, the first meeting for months of the Subcommittee on War Prisoners. In both settings, Article 6, part 1, of the Transition Treaty was high on the agenda, and the mood that Hallstein encountered after summing up the London results was the same in both: an "acknowledgment" of the sentences was completely out of the question.

Supported by Herbert Wehner, Eduard Wahl—a man whose omnipresence was as great a his usual reserve—spoke up in the subcommittee against "taking over the prisoners." "In general popular opinion, and in their own opinions," so long as these people remained incarcerated by the Allies, they basically had "the status of something like war prisoners, while, if we introduce them to our criminal prisons, they are suddenly criminals under German law." In response to the question of what procedure was intended for those imprisoned in France, Hallstein stressed that the chancellor favored inquiring into the wishes of those affected. Wehner now exploded: this was a "shattering thought"; the prisoners would be "horribly disappointed."[88]

The tone in the special coalition meeting—it was held in the König Museum—was even harsher. Weeks earlier already, when in the company of like-minded spirits, Justice Minister Dehler had not hesitated to qualify the "London agreement" as "cause for great concern."[89] Neither he nor his state secretary—himself, we will recall, a Union man—now minced their words.[90] Walter Strauß made it perfectly clear that as far as the Justice Ministry was concerned, the chancellor and his negotiators in the Foreign Ministry would have done better to follow the referees' suggestions. This meeting's four-hour debate was also consumed by the penal administration theme. If, Strauß declared, the Germans were to take over incarceration and hence sentence execution, they would also have to enjoy the right to issue pardons. Anything else was "political extortion." As the secret protocol then summarized, "We ought not be frightened by Allied threats to transfer prisoners abroad to serve their sentences, should the Germans refuse to take over execution of punishment. Just let the Allies try it; he ... could not imagine that a ratification of the treaty by the German parliament would then come into question."[91]

As the discussion chairman, Vice Chancellor Blücher wished to see moderation prevail. At the same time, his own feelings had been sharpened as the discussion proceeded. He thus eventually offered his own declaration that "it is more tolerable to accept international detention on German soil than to establish an independent German judicial authority over the accused."[92] Finally, Lieutenant General Heusinger, mindful of the latest demands for amnesty by the "League of German Soldiers,"[93] referred to the issue's "psychological side," then stressing that the Allies had to agree to a solution "before the first German soldier puts on his uniform." Hallstein was aware of what had to be done: the coalition members insisted on fresh negotiations with the goal of getting rid of the duty to take over incarceration, hence acknowledgment of the sentences. Beyond this, corresponding to the old demands of the "Committee for Occupation Law and Foreign Affairs," as many prisoners as possible were to be released before the Mixed Board began its work.[94] All that remained, then, was returning the entire matter to the executive level.

And indeed, only three days later a now nervous chancellor tried to convince the High Commissioners to make concessions regarding a range of points. The risk of a shipwreck in the effort to get the General Treaty through parliament could no longer be overlooked. Adenauer thus pressed for a removal from the supplementary agreements of anything that could mean required approval by the Bundesrat.[95] What counted, he argued, was limiting things to what was "essential" and putting aside matters that were "peripheral."[96]

Among the Allies, as well, word had gotten around that the war criminal question was actually anything but peripheral. For this reason, Adenauer did not have to explain at great length to the High Commissioners why the "idea" had suddenly "occurred" to him that every Allied prison should simply be supplied with a "German director without specific function." As McCloy and (even more so) Kirkpatrick immediately understood, behind this proposal lay the refusal by Adenauer's coalition partners to accept German responsibility for sentence enforcement, a refusal that was only thinly cloaked in constitutional doubts and was in fact motivated exclusively by political considerations. Without voicing complaints over Adenauer's backpedaling from what had been agreed in London, the two High Commissioners now showed readiness to cooperate with a negotiating partner who had run into difficulties. At Kirkpatrick's suggestion, an agreement was reached that the Three Powers would reserve the right to hold all war criminals in detention until the West German government felt ready to do so (i.e., through passage of an appropriate law). Kirkpatrick also tried to dispel the chancellor's concerns that the pardoning policy would stand still until the Transition Treaty took effect.

The matter, however, was once more high on the agenda at the next meeting between Adenauer and the High Commissioners. As the experts concluded in their subsequent meeting, Kirkpatrick's idea would be very difficult to realize, especially since the Germans wanted at all costs to avoid major adjustments to the treaty arrangements.[97] The chancellor reacted with downright horror to McCloy's suggestion of incorporating an additional proviso guaranteeing the Allies the right to maintain their own prisons in West Germany; every reservation injected into the main text would simply strengthen its critics.

In the course of these drawn-out negotiations, it was repeatedly evident how difficult McCloy found it to maintain his calm in regard to the war criminal issue. During the discussion of the prisons' administrative expenses, which the Allies wished to help cover once the treaty took effect, Adenauer reminded his interlocutors that German personnel also had to be hired for Landsberg. "If he were himself a prisoner," the protocol has McCloy shooting back, "he would prefer Landsberg because of the prevalent cleanliness and many other modern facilities." Adenauer responded that "he had spent several months in prison. In his opinion, every judge should have spent some time in prison. Much depends on the prisoners hearing a friendly word now and then."[98] Clearly, the incessant give and take had not done much to soothe the nerves of the sorely pressed negotiators. And three more weeks of it were meant to follow.

There could be little talk at this point of "secret" negotiations. Since 29 April, Adenauer had been regularly informing the cabinet about the negotiations, at least in general terms.[99] And on 30 April, a relieved Walter Roemer—a department head in the Justice Ministry serving as mediator in the prison administration question—informed a reconvened special meeting of the coalition that the Allies were now ready to retain responsibility for carrying out the sentences.[100] Twenty-four hours later, Blücher had his referees clarify the General Treaty before the FDP's directorship,[101] which on 8 May took up the negotiation status of the war criminal question in all its details. Apparently, Adenauer's furious protest against Blücher's procedure had produced no effect.[102] It did not escape the chancellor that it was none other than Ernst Achenbach who set the tone of this working session.[103] Citing the "daily" increasing approval of his campaign for general amnesty, he frequently put both Blücher and Dehler on the defensive through precisely formulated objections. Achenbach, the self-appointed legal advisor to the war criminals, was particularly indignant about the specification in Article 6—

Dehler had read the full article to the directorship—that pardons were to be issued only on the Mixed Board's recommendation: "That is a pernicious clause, introduced with cunning." As he himself openly declared, he was concerned about no longer being able to appeal to the "individual powers" directly and "with pathos."[104]

Without a doubt, Adenauer's unhappiness owed much to Dehler: while the negotiations were still proceeding, the Justice Minister had shown perfect willingness to inform the public of the government's reluctance to take over administering the Allied sentences—and of the Allied inclination to show understanding.[105] For as was to be expected, an informal corrective from the High Commissioners was not slow in coming; it made clear enough that problems, in fact, very much persisted in this regard.[106] Meanwhile, in all superfluousness, Hans Mühlenfeld, chairman of the German Party parliamentary faction, had been cited to the effect that no consent would be given a "second Versailles."[107]

A few hours after the meeting of FDP heads broke up, John McCloy met with seven representatives of the coalition parties; he was aware that they were especially opposed to particular points of the treaty. The comprehensive war criminal article was naturally discussed in this evening meeting, but the High Commissioner ended with the impression that the reservations formulated by the FDP and the German Party were in fact only feebly supported by the Union and could be overcome.[108] McCloy's perspective had become more optimistic; like the chancellor, he now pinned his hopes on the war criminal question losing its centrality once the entire treaty package was signed.

The hectic negotiations over details went forward in this framework. They were only interrupted by cabinet meetings now held almost daily, in which mainly FDP and German Party representatives incessantly retapped the war criminal issue.[109] But essential changes in the article were proposed neither in consultations between officials nor in the two meetings between Adenauer and the High Commissioners that again took up the subject.[110]

At the end of the concluding foreign ministers' consultations in Bonn on 24–25 May, Adenauer made one last effort, not to alter the relevant clauses of the treaty, but at least to reduce the problem. Immediately before the start of the four-man conference, Acheson, Eden, and Schuman had agreed that in case the chancellor should raise the theme he would receive the assurance that, once the treaty came into effect, each of the Three Powers would continue with the previous process of reviews and releases.[111] This concession was nothing more than what had been added to the treaty text two weeks previously upon German insistence; based as it was on Allied good will, it was in the end a matter of course. As things turned out, Acheson decided to offer a statement to this effect on his own initiative. In doing so, he offered Adenauer an opportunity to issue a more far-reaching plea—one that clearly surprised his negotiation partners—for a "very wide-ranging act of pardon shortly after the signing of the treaty." According to the records, which reproduced the typical diction used by the chancellor in this matter, Adenauer left no doubt concerning how important he considered such a gesture: "He is here not referring to the pardoning of authentic war criminals. But the atmosphere in which the war criminal judgments were passed in 1945 has preoccupied the German public to an extraordinary degree. Formerly, the birth of a king was cause for acts of pardon. If the birth of the General Treaty stood under the same sign, public opinion in Germany would certainly react to it in a more positive fashion. The present treaty arrangements would then be seen as genuine progress; otherwise certainly not, since too much from the past would remain there."[112]

As a response, all three of Adenauer's interlocutors stressed that they had already done much to reduce the prisoner population, and intended to do more. They promised no special measure.[113] Adenauer's follow-up was as concrete as the response was vague: it was important to let the German people see "that with the signing of the treaty, another, new situation had come into being than what had been in effect since 1945." And less on humanitarian than on political grounds, he needed to draw attention to those incarcerated in Spandau, among whom were "especially sad cases" such as Neurath.[114] With these words coming at the end of negotiations lasting months, and with only the next day's formal signing of the—historically not exactly unimportant—treaty remaining, it would be difficult to conclude that Adenauer had underestimated the weight of the war criminal question.

Measured against what might have been hoped by those whose sense of shame had not entirely vanished, Adenauer and his helpers had achieved a great deal. First, in London, they had seen to establishment of a Mixed Board that was balanced in composition. While not annulling the discretionary authority of the individual powers over the condemned war criminals in their custody, it still made the authority accessible to input from a multilateral consultative body. Then, in Bonn, they obtained the concession (if only under the pressure of a governmental right-wing armed with dubious constitutional arguments) that the judgments did not have to be even implicitly acknowledged. The proviso necessary to this end had been hidden in an inconspicuous section of the General Treaty,[115] the cession of the prisons to the Allies banished to a letter.[116] Whenever applying cosmetics had been possible, the Allies had complied.

Could all of this not have been read as a program for, as it were, automatically ending the war criminal problem? In fact, the nationalists and apologists viewed it as an *institutionalization* of the problem. They did so despite the shrinking of the number of imprisoned persons by another hundred since the start of the year, and despite the fact that in May 1952 only around 600 condemned men were still locked up in Landsberg, Werl, and Wittlich. But cause for dissatisfaction remained for whoever was not inclined to trust a process that was from now on firmly regulated and irrevocable, instead desiring an immediate, total settlement. This situation could not be altered by the official commentary to Article 6, part 1, of the Transition Treaty, which stressed the "political significance" of the final agreement—and ascended to a perspectivist self-reflective statement not very common in texts of this sort: "In order to achieve a solution that in the end is satisfactory for all the participating states, one circumstance in particular will be necessary: that even in cases of majority decisions that are not unanimous, the envisioned commission—whose members are independent and not bound to instructions of their governments, but rather are meant to act as representatives of their national legal conscience—will exert the required influence on the different governments through the personal repute of its members and the persuasive powers of its recommendations.[117]

CHAPTER 9

The Windup of the War Criminal Problem

In spring 1952 the exact measures specified in the Transition Treaty for winding up the war criminal problem became public knowledge. It is true that no widespread cries of joy could be expected in response. But it is also true that the absence of a single influential voice being raised in appreciation of the Allies, or at least in respect for their concessions, was not a good sign. It did fairly reflect the West German political climate around a year before the general elections: sniffing a distinctly auspicious wind, the extreme right (which to a large extent still operated outside parliament) was worrying both the governing parties and the Social Democratic opposition. That opposition had hardly any maneuvering room in which to further sharpen the flatly anti-Allied, outspokenly nationalistic stance being cultivated by Kurt Schumacher. In contrast, efforts by the smaller governmental parties and the Union's right wing to gain more profile now markedly increased. In the FDP, a quarrel had flared up over a "German program" that had been devised with the aid of ex-Nazi experts. The program was intended as the overture to a drastic "opening to the right"—the slogan being used by many party members.[1] And in the German Party, the number of those advocating a "large party of the right" was multiplying. The hope was that such a party could win over hardened old Nazi cadres still inhabiting the political wilderness, in the process putting the brakes on Adenauer's all-too-insistent orientation toward the Western powers. In such a context, expressing satisfaction with those powers or even praising their policies passed for a major tactical error. Many Bundestag delegates saw such moves as equal to political self-mutilation.

Even among those fully supporting Adenauer's orientation, few individuals were willing to speak up openly and clearly against the spreading nationalist tendencies: a situation that had come to thoroughly irritate the chancellor, leading him to fear for the structural solidity of the bourgeois governmental majority.[2] His state secretary viewed things very similarly. In Adenauer's first governmental team, Otto Lenz was perhaps the only politician already possessing a "modern" outlook. He was also a man not overly modest about what he knew, and perfectly willing to cultivate a relaxed relationship with the Allies. In background conversations with German correspondents, he conceded growing concern about "the nationalism reawakening everywhere"—a nationalism proceeding "as if Nazi crimes did not exist." As someone well acquainted with the media, Lenz here ascribed a high degree of complicity to the press; most of the illustrated magazines, for instance, were speculating about the nationalist mood prevailing "among wide circles of the population." Recently, "from the fact that with the arrival of Allied troops somewhere or other five Germans were killed," *Stern* magazine "drew conclusions plainly in the direction of gaining moral compensation for the Hitler regime's murdered millions from such trespasses by individuals on the opposing side."[3] Such an attitude, noted one of Lenz's journalistic interlocutors, "damages us enormously on the Allied side." Among the Allies there was great understanding for the fact "that Schäffer and Adenauer fight hard over every considerable sum, every important formulation. That is even considered their inherent right. But there is no understanding for the Germans again acting as if they were merely innocent lambs."[4]

These remarks do not, of course, indicate a need to analytically dissect the soul of the new West German state. (Lenz was an adept political operative who had organized a splendid campaign for Adenauer, not someone struggling to really get at the bottom of things.) But Lenz's remarks nevertheless hit home as a description of the political landscape in Bonn—and beyond.

As soon as the ink had dried, dissatisfaction, indeed protest, emerged throughout West Germany over the war criminal arrangement initialed by Adenauer and the Three Powers' foreign ministers. In Hannover and Dortmund, organizations of soldiers and repatriated POWs held regular mass rallies under the motto "no General Treaty without a general amnesty."[5] Based in Kiel, retired Admiral Gottfried Hansen spoke out at steady intervals.[6] While possessing less than imposing political skills, the admiral was now chairman of the "League of German Soldiers" and a spokesman for ten soldiers' organizations in toto with, putatively, 2 million members; he thus had institutional clout. In the middle of July, he was able to personally explain his viewpoint to the chancellor.[7] In Essen, Achenbach's "Preparatory Committee for a General Amnesty"[8] prepared an ambitious new PR campaign, headed by "office director" Werner Best, under the slogan "Now even more: a strengthened amnesty movement!"[9] In Frankfurt and Wiesbaden, local branches of the committee, spurred on by a Hesse-wide collection of signatures said to number 33,000, planned public demonstrations explicitly intended as pressure on that state's government.[10] Bernhard Ramcke was now residing in Wuppertal-Sonnborn, aware since his flight from France and subsequent return of having fulfilled a mission and shaken up "world public opinion." From that location he directed an "urgent appeal" to the "Reich-Chancellor" and all the Bundestag delegates "to reject all consultations over a defense contribution as long as a single German still is to be found in a prison of the Western allies."[11]

It is thus apparent that in the summer of 1952, Adenauer's hopes for an easing of the problem had not been realized.[12] The demand for a general amnesty had become more widespread, the impatience of Achenbach and his cohorts greater than ever. And now, from the ranks of the Bundestag, an elegant young former eastern-front major by the name of Erich Mende reported for duty. In mid June, the *Freie Demokratische Korrespondenz* published an essay of his presenting the West German government and the Allies with a crystal-clear ultimatum. "If," Mende explained, "by the third debate over the General Treaty, the supplementary agreements, and especially the agreement on the European Defense Community, the problem of the former soldiers still being held in and out of Germany has not been fundamentally altered, then despite a basic approval of the underlying approach to foreign policy, various delegates from the war generation will have to deny their consent to these agreements."[13]

Mende was different from the right-wing radical propagandists for general amnesty not only in tone and tactics but in strategy as well. While not dispensing with the standard emotive vocabulary (from "Malmédy" to "Korea"), the newcomer did reveal himself flexible enough to incorporate the treaty arrangements aimed at by the government into his own proposals. Mende's central demand was as follows: the proceedings of the Mixed Board, which in their presently anticipated form were bound to be protracted, needed to be speeded up through a generous preliminary amnesty. As Mende pointed out to his readers, he had already offered the Allies (albeit regrettably in vain) a proposal to this end in the spring, "to release," on 8 May, "all those being held who are over sixty or under twenty-eight, as well as those who are sick or weak, in a symbolic gesture of the victors on the occasion of the seventh anniversary of the 'capitulation.' " Mende had often distinguished himself militarily but had not been implicated politically.[14] His formulations were impressive. "We do not underestimate the aftereffects of everything unfortunately perpetrated in the name of Germany on yesterday's enemies. But in the end, seven years have passed and the will to a European Defense Community is inalienably tied to psychological premises. An army is not simply an accretion of officers, enlisted men, and equipment. Rather it is a living organism whose deciding element is the spirit inhabiting it. But this spirit, in the sense of a readiness for European solidarity and defense, cannot manifest itself in any German division knowing its former commanders and comrades to still be in Allied prisons, without a general conviction of their guilt being present."

As spectacular as Mende's ultimatum appeared to the public (and as out of place to many ministerial officials[15] and colleagues in parliament[16]), the truth is it did not amount to the eloquent and earnest gesture of a lone individual.[17] In February, already, the young delegate had been granted an audience with Adenauer; he had come away with the impression of having received "full agreement" on one point in particular, "that as the only formerly active officer from the German Wehrmacht in the German Bundestag, I had the duty to intercede for the freeing of those soldiers still in prison, whose misfortune is greater than their guilt. In the end, we agreed in all confidence that I should calmly persist in indicating that approving the Defense Community agreement is impossible for me as long as soldiers of whose guilt I am not convinced are being imprisoned in Werl, Wittlich, Landsberg, and elsewhere."

The chancellor may have prevailed on Mende to concede the experience of inexcusable "crimes and abominations" on the eastern front (on "both sides"). But the distinguished civilian politician certainly did not object when the holder of the Iron Cross forcefully stressed the need to distinguish between the "cold and gruesomely executed crimes that we only learned about in part after the war" and "entanglement through binding orders." And, Mende explained, "many lapses committed in the severe circumstances of war and the mercilessness of a dictatorship, especially on the part of young soldiers," needed to be considered in a milder light.

What Adenauer seems not to have informed Mende was that for a long time now, the war criminal problem had only marginally represented a problem of soldiers: at the time of the signing of the Transition Treaty, merely 88 of the 603 prisoners in Landsberg, Werl, and Wittlich were former Wehrmacht members. In contrast, nearly half were "concentration camp cases," the remainder "pilot cases" and those involving the police, the Gestapo, and accomplices in crimes of euthanasia.[18] The proportion of soldiers was a little higher in France: 90 of 299 prisoners.[19]

In other words, the entire commotion concerning "former soldiers ranging from privates to field marshals" did not, as Mende maintained, concern "one thousand [men] with many family members living for seven years in hardship and distress." Rather, taking into account the Benelux countries, Denmark, Norway, and Italy, at most 300 people were in question. But whoever publicly cited statistics referred, now as before, to the total number of war criminals. One basic reason for this was that any effort at differentiation, however carefully formulated, ran up against the resolute opposition of those affected, as well as their many-branched lobby.[20]

More substantive differentiating efforts by Adenauer and parts of the Union were themselves repeatedly staved off by the apologists and a populist press.[21] They were also rejected by the ministerial bureaucracy's referees. When, for example, before the parliamentary debate over the General Treaty, the head of the CDU-CSU faction, Heinrich von Brentano, asked his party colleague Walter Strauß how many people "actually have no right to claim our political or moral support," Margarethe Bitter offered the following assessment for the state secretary's signature: "A distinction between those persons for whom one can and cannot intervene is generally very difficult. Doing so would involve precise knowledge of the facts on which the accusation or judgment was based. This is almost never possible. The efforts at legal defense have regularly been based on the premise that Germans accused abroad under especially unfavorable conditions must still have the possibility of a sufficient and effective defense. Reputable defense attorneys who have participated in many trials maintain that something like 10 percent of those condemned have committed punishable deeds according to German law, with the question still being open of whether the sentences delivered against them were much too hard."[22] The fewer the number of war criminals sitting in Allied prisons, the more uncompromising the solidarity being expressed for them; public pronunciations in the opposite direction were hard to find.[23]

The German Party had an allergic reaction to Mende's idea of a priority list of the young, old, and ill, a reflection of the party's belief that they could force a wholesale freeing of the war criminals in return for initialing the General Treaty. Naturally once again the desire for political profile played a role here—something promptly demonstrated in a "Major Interpellation of the German-Party Parliamentary Faction and Colleagues."[24] But a letter regarding the Mende matter that Heinrich Hellwege, German Party chairman and minister for Bundesrat affairs, addressed to Adenauer demonstrated something a little different: the extent to which the smallest of the coalition parties stood under the influence of "notable prisoners in Werl" and their families, which is to say under the anticipatory pressure of a considerable portion of its clientele. "A ranking list would be seen by those lagging behind as something like a sharpening of the punishment," predicted Hellwege. "I have cause to presume that it could come to hunger strikes and acts of despair, if not to suicides. I know that the imprisoned men are at the end of their rope and that even their family members can simply no longer bear such things. To my knowledge, the sense that *everyone* must be released from their cells, as long as those involved are not common criminals who deserve a longer sentence, is shared not only by the most widespread public circles, the prisoners, and their relatives, but also, for example, those caring for them and those shepherding their souls."[25] Who, specifically, counted as common criminals was clarified as little by Hellwege as anyone else.

Chancellor Adenauer could only welcome differences of opinion between coalition partners when they contributed to weakening the ranks of those struggling for a general amnesty. From his perspective, there was thus even something to be said for Erich Mende's proposal, as long as it reflected personal initiative and not a general FDP effort.[26] In a second "conversation" at the end of June, Adenauer thus directly asked the alert political recruit for the names of those who should be pardoned under the agreed-on conditions. Three weeks later, despite Hellwege's reservations (and, of course, not without notifying the press), Mende supplied Adenauer with the list.[27] It contained the names of over 140 prisoners; more than two-thirds were meant to be released for illnesses ranging from "stomach irritation" to high blood pressure.[28]

Shortly after, armed with a new certainty of journalistic attention, Mende proceeded with a fresh sally: "He himself would have to say 'no' to the treaty if his own generals, Manstein, Kesselring, and Hoth, remained in prison."[29] While he publicly stressed that "professional criminals and 'camp-kapos' " were not contained on the list, he had also informed the chancellor that examination of the "legal and guilt question" had been "consciously" avoided. But Mende could in fact not have vouched for either assertion, since the list had been put together by referees at the Central Bureau for Legal Defense.[30]

In this context, the Heidelberg circle's decision to try out a new proposal before the High Commissioners could have created little real surprise. The proposal's purpose was "to achieve comprehensive pardoning measures before ratification of the General Treaty." It differed from Mende's proposal only in its inclusion, along with old, sick, and youthful persons, of those who had completed a third of their sentence, account taken of the total period already spent in prison.[31] It was the case, however, that Cardinal Frings had now met Walter Donnelly, and what had emerged from their conversation was that the new High Commissioner argued in scarcely less "orthodox" a fashion than John McCloy. In his final press conference, the latter figure had once more spoken up strongly against a general amnesty.[32] These were probably among the factors for the Heidelberg jurists deciding to leave a new initiative to the government.[33]

Actually, over the previous weeks Adenauer had been doing everything he could in this regard. On 9 June he had taken an hour to clarify his position on the war criminal question with influential military commentator Basil Henry Liddell Hart, an ardent admirer of the German generals. During the course of the meeting the chancellor calmly picked up the journalist's offer to make use of his connections. What was needed was not the House of Lords debate Liddell Hart had mentioned, but "visible evidence of clemency." According to the minutes, Adenauer explained "the situation" to his visitor as follows: "Social Democracy was using all means to stymie ratification. But if he had real evidence of clemency at hand, he could appear before the German people and influence the mood in a way favorable to ratification. There was, however, no time to be lost, since the first debate on the treaty was scheduled for the start of July."[34]

A few days later, Robert Schuman reminded the chancellor of the willingness he had indicated, in the framework of the Bonn conference of foreign ministers, to tackle the problem of the German war criminals being held in France. To this end, Adenauer now once again proposed the "earliest possible establishment of a French-German experts' commission," since as was well known the question "was of very great political and psychological significance" for the government.[35] At the same time, he used every opportunity to press the Americans on the matter, and at the start of July McCloy assured him that despite words to the contrary neither he nor General Handy had canceled the regular sentencing reviews; what he rejected was simply one more general review.[36]

The first debate over the General Treaty took place on 9 and 10 July 1952. The debate made clear how precarious the situation facing the right wing of the coalition, and with it the entire government, actually was.[37] On the one hand, from concern over the "honor of former German soldiers," the SPD was demanding "justice," holding both a general amnesty and the form of pardon anticipated by the treaty to be "unjustifiable."[38] On the other hand, Adenauer and the other speakers for the Union dealt with the war criminal theme as briefly as possible. Franz Josef Strauß was demonstratively at ease as, interrupted by gales of laughter, he made short shrift of the opposition.[39] At the same time, the unease of the FDP and German Party speakers was unmistakable; both Mende (FDP) and Merkatz (German Party) did their best to at one and the same time demand, emphatically, a resolution of the problem before ratification and remove all doubt regarding their "yes" to a path promising sovereignty and rearmament. Free Democrat delegate Margarete Hütter showed little sign of being troubled by this dilemma. Active for ages in support of German war victims and war prisoners, she displayed much past-political adeptness in her use of the right wing's rhetorical armor. She also showed herself firmly anchored in the corresponding communicative circle, recounting the rumor that at the end of July a "high American official" had offered the "imprisoned ones" at Landsberg a few words of advice: "first sign up." Before treaty ratification, he had indicated, there would be no releases. To applause not limited to the FDP, the war widow now countered with the classic right-wing threat: the "problem of the so-called war criminals" must not be allowed to "poison the path to a new Europe." It had to be resolved "before the nationalists appropriate it in the next elections and misuse it for their own ends. We need to keep in mind that from day to day the political weight of every single guiltless prisoner increases, and that one day this question can conjure up a frightful political reaction which those of us approving the principle of cooperation with the West will no longer be able to control."[40]

In midsummer 1952, words of this sort—naturally coined more flexibly in taverns, back rooms, and soldiers' newsletters than in the Bundestag—were making the Americans increasingly uneasy. To be sure, the attacks were not being leveled at them alone, but it was a fact that roughly two-thirds of the war criminals still incarcerated by the Allies on West German soil were in Landsberg. Hence in Heidelberg and Frankfurt, U.S. army headquarters and those of the American High Commission, there was a feeling of being singled out for special treatment. Finally, when the West German media— long since incapable of offering an even halfway objective account of the matter—began to take shots at Walter Donnelly for not having promptly offered a prospect for the desired change of course, the quasi-official *Neue Zeitung* hit back with a potentially explosive lead article.[41]

The article's title ("A Necessary Clarification") itself made clear that what was being presented did not involve the usual effort to glean sympathy for the dominant Western power and its worldview. In forcefully couched words, the American mouthpiece warned the Germans against trying to make the war criminal question into a "political business." With virtually unprecedented clarity, the *Neue Zeitung* reminded its readers "that during World War II things took place in the German Wehrmacht that until then had been absent from the armies of all civilized countries." And against the ever more widespread myth of guiltless soldiers, or at least soldiers who had only been obeying orders, the article indicated that "the individual field marshals, generals, officers, and remaining military personnel were not sentenced as a collective entity but as individually responsible people who could be held accountable for the murder of war prisoners, the 'liquidation' of Jews and other 'undesirable' population groups, and the transference of both war prisoners and civilians in their hands to concentration camps and other forms of 'special treatment.' " Before Germans carried the matter too far, they needed to take account of the fact "that none of the future partners of Germany in the Western defense community will be prepared to deviate from the principle of voluntarism adopted by all democratic political structures in order to purchase the contribution of some community member." Now as before, the reader was reminded, the dictum that John McCloy had registered for the Germans in October 1950 prevailed: "We neither 'buy' allies nor force anyone to be our partners."

There could be no doubt that the article, appearing in a Munich paper, was written with a view toward Bonn. It was in fact received in government circles with considerable concern,[42] as it was by the soldiers' organizations.[43] It did not, however, produce any concrete changes. Rather, the verbal attacks on the occupation powers even seemed to intensify. And naturally, the brand new West German version of the old paramilitary Stahlhelm would not even think of shoving its demonstratively elected president, Albert Kesselring, released from Werl in October 1952 following commutation of his death sentence, into anything like the second rank.

On 16 September, a day before the tensely awaited Bundestag consultations over the German Party's "major interpellation," the *Neue Zeitung* issued another warning: the Allies were not holding anyone without a reason and were not willing to purchase a German contribution to Western Europe's defense.[44] But the sharpness of the earlier article was missing. There was a significant current of self-justification running through the piece now—including, precisely, the passage recalling the mass murder, with its insistence that most of those condemned were "common criminals" with no military status. At an earlier point, such an assertion, scarcely to be found in the German press, would have been highly appropriate. But in this context it must have seemed like a transparent maneuver to the mistrustful reader, a maneuver meant to make it easier for "soldierly" Germans to back off from the demand for a general amnesty.

In a certain manner, the same could be said for the German Party interpellation, particularly as revealed in one passage: "A resolution of the question of the so-called 'war criminals' corresponding to the imperatives of justice and political reason is a precondition for the possibility of honorably approving the German defense contribution." Close consideration of the passage would have revealed no direct talk of a resolution ratification juncture, nor any demand for a sweeping release of all the war criminals; the concept of a general amnesty was also absent. There were no less than thirteen appended questions, themselves based on the premise that the Mixed Board referred to in the Transition Treaty would indeed be established. The declared goal of the German Party was, however, "the release of the greatest possible number of prisoners" before the treaty took effect, followed by the fastest possible start to the board's work.[45]

In the end, the two-hour war criminal debate turned out to be a fairly lame affair.[46] This came as a bit of a surprise to journalistic observers who for weeks had been constantly reporting on various soldierly demonstrations (most recently the assembly of 7,000 Africa Corps veterans in Stuttgart[47]). Above all, of course, this development disappointed the nonparliamentary right. In the previous day's cabinet meeting, Adenauer had warned that the matter "could only be taken care of without much noise," and that the most important thing was taking account of public opinion abroad. This warning seems to have born fruit, and it was certainly no harm that shortly before, Hallstein had even taken Erich Mende to task.[48]

In the plenum, Hans-Joachim von Merkatz had the duty of substantiating the "interpellation" for the German Party. In doing so, he gave ample latitude to his talent for well-formulated and sweeping pronouncements.[49] Although more knowledgeable in this domain than virtually anyone else, he avoided almost anything concrete. The only thing clear was that the German Party did not wish to play the role of "tip of the battering ram," meaning they had no desire to take on the business of those still demanding an uncompromising tabula rasa. It is also the case that whoever was attentive to Adenauer's replies would have found little cause for continuing such an effort.[50] Over the past two and a half years, almost three quarters of the original "German prisoners held in foreign incarceration under the charge of war crimes" had been released; and thanks to the relentless efforts of the West German government, the others—so long as they did not belong to the "small percentage of absolutely asocial elements" (now Adenauer's preferred replacement for "genuine criminals," to the distress of Achenbach and friends)—had good chances of being "brought home" soon.[51]

Chancellor Adenauer did not only make use of a highly discrete terminology; he also declared his "full" understanding for the "unease in broadest circles of the German people, indeed almost the entire German public, concerning the questions we are grappling with." He doubtless offered the remark in view of its widespread circulation throughout the world on the radio's diplomatic network—it was also hurried into print in the government press office's bulletin on the same day.[52] What had been signaled here was that the governmental camp had decided to counter the propagandists of general amnesty with their own offensive. Steered by Otto Lenz, the "Working Alliance of Democratic Circles" was now also active in that direction; the organization had been founded to pave the road for the CDU and had until then not lost its somewhat dubious aura.[53]

The conclusion to CDU delegate—and Heidelberg circle head— Eduard Wahl's learned excursus before the plenum was delivered with an eye on the self-appointed experts who were his juridical colleagues.[54] Although painstakingly prepared, the balance of Adenauer's activities may have still seemed wanting to them. Wahl, in contrast, offered a dazzlingly positive account. Without specifying the context more closely, he informed the plenum with deep gratitude of a meeting between the circle and the chancellor a few months previously. He had then realized the energy with which Adenauer had quietly devoted himself to the "problem of the war-condemned"—the *Kriegsverurteiltenproblem.* "There was something imposing," Wahl declared, "in the self-evident manner with which the government chose the path of silence regarding these successes, in the interest of those who could not yet be helped. The visitors had been nothing short of deeply moved by this courage to be unpopular in the interest of the basic issue."[55]

While not as profoundly moved as Wahl, Pastor Hans Merten, SPD speaker and specialist in matters regarding present and repatriated war prisoners, did reveal himself as inclined toward consensus. Merten— since 1949 a referee in the Ministry for Expellees—distanced himself from the "juncture between the question of German war prisoners and the question of ratification of the General Treaty and the European Defense Community treaty." His explanation was that his party did not see the resolution of such a "heartfelt matter for the entire German peo-

ple" as something that could be linked with "any other political questions."[56] Without much difficulty, the explanation could be read as follows: the SPD believed it could afford a rejection of the two treaties; it
did not believe it could afford a failure in the war criminal question, a
question long since simply conflated, of course, with that of the war
prisoners.

Erich Mende also raised the theme of linkage, but considered it perfectly justified—or at least no less moral than the linkage of the two
treaties. Wishing to escape from the soldiers' organizational milieu,
Mende was willing to venture a mild rebuke. Through "competition of
the different groups," things had become "all too overstated." While
thus rejecting "ultimative demands," he also linked his approval of the
Defense Community to "common psychological presumptions and to a
resolution of the war criminal problem." He demonstrated his collegial
competence by indicating that in the military court in Bordeaux a "German emigrant" was preventing "any correspondence of the German
defense attorneys with their clients."[57] The discussion had sufficiently
made clear that it was no longer thought appropriate to term these
"clients" war criminals. Still, the German Party's Hans Ewers felt called
on to explicitly make the point himself: "I would request that the term
'war criminal' be generally avoided; these are in fact basically not criminals but innocent condemned men."[58]

The debate's most striking aspect was the extent to which the stand-
points of the various parties had merged. This was doubtless linked to
the fact that in all the parliamentary factions the experts were doing the
speaking and exchanging compliments. (The exceptions were the Communists and the Center Party, which had no such experts.) The main
reason, however, may have been quite different. Anyone who had carefully studied the material and was capable of putting resentment on the
back burner for the sake of realpolitik could discover a solution already
on the horizon. And this solution virtually amounted to a general
amnesty. In other words, in the late summer of 1952, the champions of
such an amnesty had not so much lost a battle in Bonn as experienced
their Waterloo. Many of them had simply not noticed. The soldiers'
groups were convinced of their new indispensability—seen as a result
of rearmament. Born forward on a wave of public approval,[59] they continued to behave as if the nation's fate depended on a few generals
behind bars. And this despite a basic reality: since the last Bundestag
debate, anyone could see that the longed-for sweeping gesture alone
restoring, in their eyes, the honor of German soldiers would not take
place. There would be no devastating blow against the "Nuremberg system" to heal the wounds of 1945–46. Instead, there would be further

partial solutions and compromises—albeit with a foreseeable termination. Little symbolic capital could, of course, be gained from such an approach, and not much else that might be useful for new momentum.

Persons like Achenbach had naturally understood this. In contrast to the old soldiers, they had always chiefly viewed the war criminal issue as a way of stoking nationalist fires. With the treaties signed and the bureaucratic pardoning process under way, it could now be assumed that many such fires would die down. But Achenbach and colleagues could hardly speak up against the demand being made by virtually the entire Bundestag: that as many releases as possible be carried out before the treaties' ratification.[60]

The dilemma was unmistakably in the air in a common session of the FDP's directorship and Committee on Foreign Policy held a few days later.[61] The war criminal debate had not improved the tactical position of the party's right wing vis-à-vis the treaties. For months, Achenbach had been bent on delaying ratification. He now piously averred no desire to see the treaties fail on account of the war criminal problem; were the ratification to be held off until January 1953, a "satisfactory solution" would be a good way closer. In truth, Achenbach—as we will recall, the Free Democrat's foreign policy speaker—was interested in a chance to once again raise the demand for a "comprehensive pacificatory amnesty," and thus to scatter sand in governmental machinery set on a Western course.

Compared with such shady motives, the concerns of the chairman of the FDP's Committee on Security, retired Tank Commander Hasso von Manteuffel, seemed almost movingly simple. What spoke against accelerated ratification, he explained, was the fact that the "mass of voters" attached importance to the question of a general amnesty, and "this debt needs to be settled from the moral vantage." Manteuffel—whose high decorations were not only military but included an oak cluster with swords and brilliants alongside the Nazi Party's Golden Badge of Honor—now proclaimed that agreeing to the Transition Treaty meant "the German *Volk* losing its face." Dehler could easily counter such concerns by pointing out that in "questions of the fate of our *Volk*" making the "best possible decision" was what counted—not election tactics. But Manteuffel's remarks did indicate the sorts of feelings with which the FDP was tormenting itself, even on the leadership level. The unanimous renewed demand passed at the meeting's end for a "resolution of the problem of the war-condemned" apparently reflected such torment. But rather than referring to a general amnesty or—in line with Achenbach's recent word choice—a "comprehensive pacification," the demand merely spoke of "the most wide-ranging releases"—these naturally to be carried out "before the meeting of the Mixed German-Allied Board."[62]

What was actually being implicitly stated here was that the FDP would not refuse to approve the treaties on account of the war criminals. The tough battle over West Germany's foreign policy orientation—between both opposition and government and government and parliament, as well as within the governing coalition itself—did continue into the spring. By dint of the Constitutional Court's clever inclusion in the process—this was in relation to the *Bindungsklausel:* Article 7.3 of the General Treaty, which asserted its validity in the case of German reunification—the gaping public was here offered a spectacle at least as confusing as it was entertaining.[63] But the battle mainly concerned that clause, along with (intermittently) the "Saar question" and the economic burdens ensuing from the treaties. Nothing was any longer being linked to regulating the war criminal problem.

This, to be sure, still had to be conveyed to the public, above all the soldiers' organizations. While the Justice Ministry and the Heidelberg jurists' circle had already managed to largely agree on the Mixed Board's composition,[64] the stirred-up advocates of a general amnesty still believed in the power of protest. "Who are the real war criminals?" asked Bernhard Ramcke at the first postwar get-together of the Waffen SS, attended by about 3,000 former members in the last October weekend of 1952 in Verden. The question not only annoyed Adenauer intensely, but had considerable resonance both among the Germans[65] and in London, Paris, and Washington.[66] In the eyes of the parachute general the question's answer was clear: the guilty ones were those "who without tactical justification destroyed whole cities, bombed Hiroshima, and now are manufacturing new atomic bombs." In the future, he declared, the "black list" upon which the SS was registered might again become a "list of honor."[67] Meanwhile, activists in the Association of Former POWs had made plans to stage "fire demonstrations" before the Allied prisons; on the occasion of the annual "remembrance week for the war prisoners," for instance, "fires of exhortation" were to be lit on the Fallerberg in the Eifel, their "glow lighting the cells of the political prisoners in the Wittlich prison and telling them they have not been forgotten."[68]

As a result of its sociopolitical responsibilities and interests, an association like that for the repatriated POWs depended on functioning contacts with the government; Bonn could thus more or less bring it to reason by edict. But things were not so easily taken care of when a radical engagement for the war criminals was fused with concrete extreme right-wing and Nazi reorganizational efforts. The Office for Protection of the Constitution could observe, but not alter, what unfolded in the

Socialist Reich Party's meetings before its banning in October 1952. And clearly the war criminals were a great theme for Otto Ernst Remer, that party's star speaker.[69] For its part, the "Working Group for Truth and Justice" continued to agitate: along with the Princess Isenburg and her coterie, its supporters now included people such as Otto Kranzbühler, Theodor Oberländer—old Nazi fighter and cofounder of the Union of Expellees, he would become federal minister of expellees in 1953—Karl Cerff from the Mutual Aid Association of Former Combat SS Members, as well as Bundestag delegates Erich Mende (FDP) and Helene Wessel (Center Party).[70]

Finally, from taverns in Lower Saxony up to the Bundestag, the German Party did not miss an opportunity for gaining profile. Upon the flight of two war criminals from Werl and the issuing of an arrest warrant, the party waxed indignant in the latter venue (a "small interpellation") over the reference to "lifelong convicts." Interior Minister Lehr was able to deny an official use of this term. In his reply, he saw it incumbent to take up the German Party's formula to the effect that the Federal Criminal Bureau had "not rendered itself an executory organ of foreign justice." Rather, he explained, following acquaintance with the "closer circumstances," the arrest request had been immediately expunged from the German wanted persons file.[71]

"Closer circumstances" here referred to the fact that the local criminal police would probably never have even initiated a search for the escapees if the request to do so had come from the British and not, as was the case, from the German director of the Werl prison. On the threshold of constituting official complicity in the flight, this abstention from official assistance was rather remarkable. Even more so was what then transpired in the East Frisian town of Aurich—an incident the interior minister did not bother mentioning: one of the two men, Wilhelm Kappe—serving a life term for murder of a Russian war prisoner—had shown up there at his relatives. Wilhelm Heidepeter, a fish dealer and SPD chairman in the Aurich senate, learned about this and informed the police. They managed to arrest the escapee, but not to hold him long enough for the arrival of a British officer from Werl. Kappe escaped a second time and henceforth both he and his comrade Hans Kuhn—sentenced to twenty years for murdering four Canadian pilots—could rely on the solidarity of both press and public.[72] In contrast, Heidepeter found himself pursued as an "informer." Armed with clubs, citizens of Aurich gathered before his house, shattered the picture window, and stuck up a poster: "The traitor lives here." Fortunately, the man had already fled; he was thus not forced to watch as his party colleagues— corrupted by a struggle in the communal elections to garner the votes of former members of the now-banned Socialist Reich Party—removed him from all his duties and took measures to remove him from the party. Not only the CDU was of the opinion that Heidepeter had made himself guilty of "betrayal of a German man."

Outside of Germany, some newspapers (mainly English, but one Swiss as well) voiced great dismay at this incident in East Frisia.[73] The German papers offered virtually no support for Heidepeter. Not only the sensational glossy magazines but also *Der Spiegel* described the incident with manifest sympathy for the *"war criminals."*[74] And in Bonn two months later there was an obvious effort to avoid aggravating popular feelings in the matter; it was only with utmost hesitation that, when requested to do so by the British High Commission, officials of the Interior Ministry agreed in December 1952 to a—concealed— revival of a joint effort by the criminal bureaus of the Länder to hunt down the two men. The confidential records offer the following summary: "(1) On the German side, there was an expression of willingness for loyal cooperation. In view of passive resistance from the populace, success cannot be guaranteed. (2) On the British side, there was an assurance of absolute discretion and the most far-reaching measures to prevent press publication."[75]

That in fact the British had, slowly but surely, become a bit fed up could not have been very surprising. But the severity of Kirkpatrick's response to one particular campaign for the war criminals was remarkable. The campaign was launched in November 1952 by the *Abendpost,* a Frankfurt tabloid, and was evidently catalyzed by a new round of criticism being directed at Werl.[76] Citing a "strong movement" in that direction among its readers, the paper had proposed a "hostage operation" (*Geiselaktion*). In response, more than 200 persons offered to act as guarantors behind bars, in order that "seven years after the war's end" the prisoners be allowed to spend "the Christmas holiday with their families."[77] The British High Commissioner did grant the volunteers "good faith," but he also named them "victims of ignorance and, indeed, of confusion of thought."[78] Interestingly, the paper published his response on its title page. It would be an error, Kirkpatrick indicated, to believe "that the prisoners could maintain justifiably that they only carried out military orders that were later rendered into crimes by Allied law. To the contrary, almost all the men and women here in question were convicted for having participated in either the murder of helpless war prisoners or the murder or mistreatment of Allied nationals in slave labor camps or concentration camps." He firmly rejected the charge of injustice or a "lack of generosity."

Similar remarks were naturally not to be expected from the Germans. But most likely not only the British were startled by the West German government's willingness, even after the appearance of Kirkpatrick's remarks, to praise the foiled guarantors for their "especially high-minded motives," as the *Abendpost's* Herbert Blankenhorn put it in the name of the chancellor.[79] Already the war prisoner expert for the SPD, Hans Merten, had confirmed in the tabloid that the "operation" had "not failed to make its mark abroad." The former pastor meant this positively; as a sign of his support he also furnished the paper with the name of a volunteer from the Ministry for Expellees.[80]

Despite such lack of instinct, the political significance of the war criminal question now abated. In the Bundestag's second debate over the two treaties at the start of December 1952, only a few delegates voiced objections to the arrangement described in the Transition Treaty.[81] The "no" Erich Mende offered in the corresponding vote remained the exception.[82] The SPD did try to gain a shred more capital from the theme: this by demanding a treaty addition specifying that the ratification papers could only be deposited once the West German government had signed a treaty with the French regarding the treatment of the "condemned and legally prosecuted war prisoners" there. But the government brushed this aside as counterproductive. Konrad Adenauer now laid out the basic line as follows: the Western powers had shown "steadily increasing" understanding, and the "representatives of former soldiers" themselves did not want an "amnesty for asocial and criminal elements."[83]

With the reprint of an article from the quasi-official *Diplomatische Korrespondenz,* the governmental bulletin even ventured something like a final word. The remarkable thing here was the concession coming at the end of a summary of success (as Adenauer saw it). Until this point, the concession's clarity had been very rare indeed: "One thing here needs to be particularly underscored and brought to the awareness of the German public: according to the government's own inquiries, many of the charges are grounded in facts that are truly shocking." At the same time, it could be expected that with the approaching passage of the treaties, the "files from an unfortunate chapter of war and postwar history [*sic*] will be closed."[84]

Another three months would pass before the third, concluding debate on the treaties. Adenauer's effort, against all advice to the contrary, to see things through straight after the second debate had failed miserably.[85] If the ugly war criminal toad had now shrunk to generally manageable proportions, this was to a considerable extent due to the chancellor's steady plugging away behind the scenes. Stronger from week to week, he was now already acting with a view to the Bundestag elections set for the summer of 1953.

It was not only that he now again and again demonstratively received symbolic military figures: from former Generals Hans Georg Reinhardt (condemned at Nuremberg to fifteen years in prison for the shooting of war prisoners) and Hans-Jürgen Stumpff (acquitted in 1947 on war crimes charges), to Kesselring (released on parole in October— ostensibly on grounds of illness—and considered innocent by two-thirds of polled Germans), to a delegation from the "Working Alliance of Military Associations" led by retired General Kurt Linde.[86] At the same time, he did everything in his power to wrest yet more prisoners from the Allies in the months before ratification. And such efforts were complimented by the government's try at capturing a little limelight from a measure deemed standard by the "incarcerating powers": the Christmas release, together, of those due to be let loose in a few weeks anyway. (In 1952, the French made particular use of this policy, with fifty-seven pardons and thirty-seven reductions of sentence.[87])

But Adenauer himself seized the initiative. In doing so, he did not need to fear a paucity of suggestions from any quarter regarding opportunities waiting to be seized. In January 1953, John Foster Dulles, the new American secretary of state, announced a forthcoming visit to Bonn. As to be expected, the Foreign Ministry prepared an appropriate file for the chancellor.[88] But parallel to this, Bundeswehr planner Heusinger spoke up—albeit to the president. His reason: former comrades were directing "much very bitter criticism at the Herr Chancellor and State Secretary Hallstein," and this had started to spill over onto him and Speidel. Heusinger thus urged the president to raise the war criminal problem with his guest. If the Americans were ready to apply their standard parole procedure at home, the "great majority of all those imprisoned" could "regain their freedom."[89]

The fact of the matter was that recently little had happened in Landsberg. But Adenauer had already contacted Dulles in mid-December 1952 on just that subject, the intermediary being Samuel Reber, the acting High Commissioner and a man viewed favorably in Bonn. The chancellor's message was that a "far-reaching gesture toward a solution" would be very important—and it would be even better for the gesture to simultaneously come from all three Allies.[90] Because nothing resulted from either this idea or Dulles's visit, Adenauer again contacted the High Commission at the end of March 1953—albeit with a new interlocutor, since James P. Conant had now taken over from the unsuccessful Donnelly. The third debate over the treaties had meanwhile taken place with little discussion of the war criminals—even Mende remained silent on the subject and offered his "yes" vote.[91] Since then, no one could maintain that the chancellor was interested in advance concessions. What he did want, in recognition of his efforts, was a solution he could clearly point to in the elections. The thing that mattered, he explained to Conant, was setting the "pardoning machinery" into motion immediately; this could be either through the Mixed Board anticipated in the Transition Treaty or through the special interim bilateral commissions that, according to the treaty, each of the Three Powers had a right to install.[92] In order to underscore the urgency of the entire process, the cabinet had named the German board members even before the final Bundestag debate; it was to be headed by Hodo Freiherr von Hodenberg, one of the most intransigent spokesmen for the war criminals.[93]

Adenauer's meeting with Conant served as preparation for his approaching first trip to the United States.[94] Not least of the trip's purposes was to demonstrate the chancellor's international repute to the German electorate. If Adenauer had hoped to inject the war criminal theme, via Conant, into his Washington discussions in a manner leading to concrete results, then the hopes were disappointed. The theme did occupy a prominent place on the agenda of the two official negotiation sessions (7 and 8 April), but reaching an understanding proved difficult. Adenauer came prepared with figures for the French and British prisons meant to demonstrate the hesitant pardoning policies of the Americans. For their part, the Americans proved rather unprepared. Once more, Adenauer stressed the need to activate the Mixed Board before completion of the entire ratification process. (With the French National Assembly rejecting the European Defense Community, prospects for such ratification were becoming increasingly murky in France). And in spelling out the connection with German rearmament, he revealed the purposeful distance that, in the context of the war criminal issue, always emerged from evocation of third parties, here the "chairmen of the soldier's organizations": "It would ... render future recruitment difficult if people who cannot be proved to have committed war crimes continued to sit in prison."[95] But Dulles could only offer a promise to review the pardoning practice of the U.S. army (legally responsible for most of the Landsberg prisoners) in the direction of greater liberality; he also expressed the intention of contacting the other Allies in this regard. Conant simply confirmed the hope of establishing the Mixed Board or some other procedure. When it came to time limits, he was almost coquettish: "in the near future, and certainly before the September elections in Germany."[96]

Things were indeed dragging, even after the Bundestag ratified the various conventions and agreements making up the General Treaty on 15 May 1953, thus finally concluding the West German role in the proceedings. At the start of June, Adenauer found himself facing the seeming certainty of a Four-Power conference over Germany that might endanger the entire process of Western integration, given the right Soviet offer. Driven by such a concern, he dispatched Herbert Blankenhorn to President Eisenhower with top secret papers urgently requesting a preliminary Western conference and West German participation, should the threat become reality.[97] In delivering the papers, Blankenhorn added a pair of additional requests from the chancellor, as important, he explained, as they were pressing: that the American High Commissioner be promoted to the rank of ambassador, and that a pardon commission be established, if need be on a bilateral basis. The second measure, Blankenhorn remarked, "would be extremely helpful to the chancellor in the forthcoming electoral debate." Eisenhower's response to both points was very open: personally, he wished "that the whole war crimes business could be settled." Nevertheless, he indicated, French reservations regarding an early putting into force of individual treaty portions had to be considered.[98]

In any case, Adenauer's tenacious appeals—in mid-May even to Churchill, at the start of July again to Conant[99]—had begun to sharpen an awareness on all sides that something really had to move before the elections.[100] In mid-July, the foreign ministers of the Three Powers actually did meet in Washington (the Germans were not invited to participate). The Americans now placed the theme of "German war criminals" on the agenda. Dulles and Great Britain's representative, Lord Salisbury, had a clear preference for the idea of a shared pardon commission, but they also displayed understanding for French foreign minister Georges Bidault's indication that he had to avoid allowing a new public uproar in France resembling the recent response to the Oradour judgments.[101] Bidault thus appealed for separate commissions and for a certain amount of waiting, since it was still too early for any favors to Adenauer that could influence the voters. In any event, Bidault argued, the matter had to be handled in a way not suggesting any sort of triumph for the war criminals. In the end, there was an agreement to recommend establishing separate commissions to the High Commissioners—but ones that would function according to the most uniform possible guidelines.[102]

Naturally the French-inspired effort to keep the Allied arrangement under wraps for a while failed. A few days after the foreign ministers' conference, the first information started leaking; a little later the facts had already made the rounds of the German papers, resulting in friendly comments from governmental quarters.[103] Herbert Wehner did try his best to depict the establishment of three bilateral commissions as inadequate.[104] But for anyone who had even observed developments over recent years from a distance, it could be clear that the war criminal problem was now speedily moving toward a de facto solution. In the remarkable diction of the right-wing agitators, the problem was "ripe for a final solution."[105]

About three weeks before being presented with the expected Allied election gift, the chancellor had resorted to a little supplementary self-help: through a visit to Werl. Part one of his Münsterland appearance involved a pilgrimage of 50,000 Silesians to the miraculous portrait of the Holy Mother in Werl.[106] Part two involved the "war criminal prison." There had been many recent complaints over conditions in the prison, and while Kirkpatrick had offered the credible assurance that "latrine gossip" was involved here, Adenauer now had a certain basis for his wish to gain his own sense of the picture.[107] Since the military prominents (Kesselring and Manstein, along with former general Eberhard von Mackensen, sentenced in Rome to twenty-five years in prison by a British military court for his involvement in the massacre in the Ardeatinian caves) had already been released, the chancellor had to settle for SS general Kurt Meyer and Colonel General Nikolaus von Falkenhorst, but he also spoke to one freed prisoner.[108] His excursion report to the cabinet: the prison food was good and the accommodations "very comfortable"; the two generals even had an extra living area and their cells were unlocked. (The latter arrangement represented a contrast with that made for the other prisoners—they had remained locked in since the two above-mentioned escapes.) All the "imprisoned ones" had access to a radio, newspapers, and books; they were allowed one cinema visit weekly; and two hours daily were set aside for walks.[109]

It is unknown if and how the chancellor's ministers responded to his inspection account. Likewise with the reaction of the man steering the complaints, Erich von Lewinski (called von Manstein), whom Adenauer received in the Schaumburg Palace a few days later. For the chancellor, simply meeting Manstein meant gaining ground in the military area. The benefits were certainly increased by the public speculation that began circulating shortly after concerning the political future of the "greatest surviving army leader of the German Wehrmacht" (*Der Spiegel*).[110]

It cannot be said for sure how much Adenauer's courting of the generals and the precisely scheduled institution of the German-Allied pardon committees—the instructions of the three High Commissioners were dated 31 August and 1 September 1953[111]—contributed to his resounding election victory a week later.[112] But it is quite clear that his ostentatious engagement on behalf of the war criminals over recent months, together with the news of the early application of the procedures agreed on in the Transition Treaty, inclined more than a few people from the soldiers' milieu toward reconciliation. Undoubtedly, as a Rhenish-Catholic civilian Adenauer had not been able to influence the hard core of the war criminal lobby—something that presumably not even Free Democrats of Erich Mende's stamp had been able to really manage. But the smaller coalition partners had succeeded in sucking in anything on the right that was capable of some kind of integration.[113] Agitators like Achenbach were left empty-handed, without a capacity for continued use of the war criminal issue to stoke a political resentment going further right than the bourgeois, conservative coalition. In other words, their own partial success would now force them to accept a certain "return to the bourgeois order."[114]

In October and November 1953, the three bilateral pardon commissions took up their tasks.[115] Alongside the Foreign Ministry and the Central Bureau for Legal Protection, the most effective members of the Heidelberg jurists' circle, lawyers Wahl, Kranzbühler, and Becker, had taken up the "organizational and material preparation for the proceedings necessary on the German side."[116] But their chances of making a real impact were limited. Smoothing over the Allied regulations' "not insignificant" discrepancies in favor of the war criminals proved impossible; likewise an installment of their longstanding hand-picked commission candidates.

In contrast to the Mixed Board anticipated for the period following the commencement of the treaties, there was no equality principle in appointments to the bilateral commissions, which had only an advisory function. Both the American zone's Interim Mixed Parole and Clemency Board and the British zone's Mixed Advisory Board consisted of five persons, two of whom could be named by the West German government. The chairman was in the first case one of the Americans, in the second one of the British. The French zone's "Mixed Consultative Commission" had seven members, three of them German. The regulations governing the American-German commission were the most complicated, consisting of eight dense pages. The reason for this was that to a great extent the releases from Landsberg were meant to follow the American system of parole—that is, to take place in the framework of a lasting supervision of the prisoners through parole officers.

Despite many minute details and formalities—insisted on by the Allies in view of domestic public opinion—the pardon commissions made speedy progress. In the autumn of 1953, the Americans had still held a good 300 war criminals—the largest group among the Allies. Within a year, around 200 of these had been released, almost all on parole after having served a third of their sentence.[117] Among themselves, the French and British had by now expressed some strong doubt regarding the quality of their earlier legal proceeding.[118] They had also pardoned more than half their prisoners now, so that at the end of 1954 there were only 173 war criminals in Allied custody on West German soil.[119]

To be sure, such generosity did not prevent additional pressure being exerted on the German side. In the fall of 1954, this was demonstrated in a new "major interpellation," vexatious for Adenauer, submitted by the German Party together with the All-German Block Union of Expellees alliance.[120] A half year later came new stirring on the part of Admiral Hansen and Erich Mende.[121] Still, the war criminal theme had now unmistakably turned into a special theme for minority interests.[122] This was all the more the case after the arrangement Adenauer arrived at in Moscow, in September 1955: release of the 9,626 Germans still being held in the Soviet Union—among them, as Bonn was perfectly aware, numerous justly convicted war criminals and perpetrators of crimes against humanity—in return for diplomatic relations between the USSR and the West German state.[123] This did furnish Mende with an opportunity to once again appeal to the Western powers.[124] But another sort of opportunity, its earlier strategic value manifest in the "prayer weeks" held for the war prisoners, was now absent: that to effectively conflate the numerically still relatively large problem of the war prisoners with the relatively small problem of the war criminals.[125]

In August 1955, the unified Mixed Board finally took up its work. Following the collapse of the European Defense Community treaty, the newly negotiated Paris treaties, including the Transition Treaty, had taken effect on 5 May 1955. A total of 94 war criminals, as compared to 433 at the start of the entire process, now sat in the three Allied prisons.[126] There was thus not much left for the new body to do (its three Allied and three German members had been recruited from the old bilateral commissions). But because those still imprisoned could repeat their applications for pardoning or parole in six-month intervals, the Mixed Board would review no fewer than 513 such applications in the course of its existence. On average, the Landsberg prisoners submitted between four and five applications, the prisoners in Werl and Wittlich only one. The difference underscored the fact that the Americans found it most difficult of all to completely abandon the principle of punishment. U.S. public opinion played a major role here—something demonstrated in the release early in 1956 of SS general Sepp Dietrich, sentenced in the Malmédy trial to life imprisonment. Stress on the fact that Dietrich was only out on parole did not mute the criticism; in the end the American commission member had to be replaced as a scapegoat. It was in any case also striking that even rejections by the commission were often unanimous, the cooperation of German members creating considerable German disquiet for a time.[127]

By the summer of 1957, the French and British had emptied their war criminal prisons. That it took the Americans a year longer was a reflection not only of their painstaking parole system but also of the presence in Landsberg of some very nasty characters: doctors who had experimented on human victims and SS leaders of Mobile Killing Units. Such individuals constituted a special group of prisoners—and the whole group had in fact already received one form of pardon. This was in 1951, when John McCloy decided to commute their life sentences and death sentences. Freeing horrendous Nazi criminals ten years after their trial was hard for the Americans to stomach.

The far milder scruples persistently prevailing on the German side in regard to the same sort of criminals is exemplified in the case of Martin Sandberger, Doctor of Law, former leader of Mobile Killing Unit 1a and responsible in that capacity for rendering Estonia *judenfrei* as well as for the murder of many communists in the fall and winter of 1941–42.[128] For almost two years, Sandberger had been commander of the security police and the Security Service of the SS (the SD), first in Estonia and later in Italy; he ended up as group leader in the Reich Central Security Office with the rank of regimental leader. In April 1948, in the course of the Nuremberg Mobile Killing Unit trials, he was sentenced to death by hanging. Military Governor Clay confirmed the sentence in March 1949, but a short time later the formal legal measures of Sandberger's defense team came into play. Parallel to this, his Stuttgart-based family—his father was a retired production director at I. G. Farben whom President Theodor Heuss referred to as "a very ardent member of the Democratic Party"[129]—organized high-powered political help.[130] Along with Ernst Mayer, managing director of the FDP's directorship, and William Langer, the zealously anticommunist North Dakota senator of German origin,[131] Carlo Schmid—now vice president of the Bundestag—spoke up for a commutation of the death sentence. Schmid was known to Sandberger from the latter's days as an ambitious Nazi student leader (party member since 1931) at the law faculty of the University of Tübingen. He had already received his doctorate in 1934, at the age of twenty-three, for a dissertation on "Social Security in the National Socialist State."

Before the judges, Sandberger had admitted direct responsibility for the shooting of "around 350" communists and had not denied the murder of Jews by his Mobile Killing Unit.[132] Nevertheless, he was one of nine condemned men from the Mobile Killing Unit trials whom McCloy granted life in January 1951. At the prompting of Carl Friedrich von Weizsäcker (who was acquainted with Sandberger's sister), Helmut Becker now concerned himself with the further fate of the life-term prisoner—and he did so with great application. Following the 1953 establishment of the American-German pardon commission, Becker submitted petitions on behalf of (like-aged) Sandberger at regular six-month intervals; the petitions were always supported by notables from Württemberg, including Justice Minister Haußmann, Gebhard Müller, and Länder bishop Martin Haug.[133] In December 1953, he again contacted Carlo Schmid; if, he explained, the sentence could now be reduced to twenty-five years, "then parole can be achieved in another half year."[134] Becker well understood that as former chairman of the SPD's foreign affairs committee, Schmid knew a great deal about war criminal matters; Schmid responded with a request for sentence reduction that he deemed optimally suited to American requirements.

At the start of his petition, Schmid remarked that he neither could nor wished to "call into question the justice of Sandberger's conviction—as little now as in my earlier effort to have the original death sentence mercifully commuted to life in prison." He then explained why "this man cannot have been a raving fanatic." At Sandberger's own behest, he had been assigned Schmid as director for his probative period as a jurist; Sandberger had then seen to it that measures taken against Schmid by the Gestapo were brought to a stop. The source of these measures, Schmid explained, was that "following the first harassment of Jewish students I let it be known that those students given notice to leave their rooms could live in my house."[135]

Carlo Schmid's character sketch of Martin Sandberger was dialectically impressive. "I can still remember good things about him. He was an industrious, intelligent, and gifted jurist who on the one hand had succumbed to the spiritual nihilism of the epoch while on the other hand clinging desperately to the formal bourgeois world comprising his family's tradition. Without the intervention of National Socialism, Sandberger would have become a diligent, industrious, assiduous official like many others; he would have tried to build his career upon special and striking accomplishments, since he was very openly ambitious. This ambition also prompted him to join the SS and SD. He saw these party organizations as offering him the best prospects of quickly rising to positions in which he could distinguish himself. I often warned him about taking this path; as a young man already, the temptations of an at least superficially illustrious career were stronger than the persuasive powers of my arguments.... Martin Sandberger should be offered a chance to prove himself anew in life. I am convinced that Landsberg has purged him. Perhaps outside prison walls he will be able to do more to dismantle what remains of Nazi sentiment and thinking than if he remains in his cell forever."[136]

Despite Schmid's eloquence, the Americans remained firm. In the summer of 1955, with the establishment of the Mixed Board on the immediate horizon, the father of the condemned man appealed to President Heuss, presumably at the urging of Hellmut Becker. Despite long-standing personal contact between the men, Heuss was hesitant to engage himself with the matter too closely. He did, however, decide to consult Becker—as the latter had certainly hoped. In a detailed presentation, Becker expressed the conviction "that the judgment is so confused, the evidence so difficult, and the deciding legal questions of 'complicity' and 'higher orders' so unclarified, that today a serious legal examination might simply not be possible." Regarding the shooting murder of Estonia's Jews, Becker explained, "Sandberger's name is connected to the horrific event at a specific point; this necessarily led to a condemnation according to the special definition of complicity at work in Nuremberg law, but it would not represent complicity in a homicide according to German law."[137]

Instructed in this manner, Heuss decided to write an elaborate appeal to James Conant, now U.S. ambassador in Bonn, during his vacation. In his intercession for Landsberg's "young man" as an exemplary learner and teacher, Heuss evoked, among other things, both Carlo Schmid and Sandberger's "family circumstances" (illness of the old mother).[138] As he had in fact often done already in such cases, Heuss emphasized his nonjurist status in order to pronounce legal judgments or transmit them to others. He thus spoke of "graded direct legal responsibility" and offered the opinion that "according to the basic juridical theses of Allied and German legal procedure," the matter was "subject to dispute" [sic]. His closing formula was also typical. "I believe that in turning to you in this matter I am safe from any suspicion on your part that I wish to make light of the outrages and injustice committed by German men. But ten years without freedom can—I only say can—have brought a purging, and mercy is the most beautiful thing allotted the law."[139]

Federal President Heuss's intervention was not crowned with success. His advisers might have told him it would not be, since in line with the Transition Treaty establishment of the Mixed Board meant the Allies

were no longer allowed to intervene directly; all pardons had to be recommended by that body.[140] The sole solace the American embassy could
offer in the summer of 1955 was that only around three-dozen war criminals were still being held in Landsberg. The interim American-German
commission had paroled over 250 men over the last two years.[141]

Martin Sandberger belonged to the small group of prisoners still sitting in Landsberg after the military prisons in Werl and Wittlich had
already been closed down. In December 1957, the institution—for a long
time now the object of a populist press claiming to be concerned with
costs[142]—housed only four inmates, all serving life terms. Three of them
were Mobile Killing Unit leaders originally condemned to death (Ernst
Biberstein, Martin Sandberger, and Adolf Ott); the fourth (Otto Brinkmann)
had been sentenced to life for crimes against humanity. Informal sound-
ings of the Americans with the aim of transferring the remaining Landsbergers to German custody—a possibility expressly anticipated in the
Transition Treaty—led nowhere for one reason: the lack of any willingness by the West German government to pass an appropriate law. This
reflected an absence of any desire to have to recognize the judgments so
late in the game. Instead, the Foreign Ministry filed parole applications
for the remaining prisoners in January 1958. These were turned down,
but now solely on practical grounds: the filing coincided with the Mixed
Board's American-prompted effort to dispense with the complicated
parole system altogether. The system had always been criticized by the
Germans with the argument that those freed on parole from Landsberg
were no "American gangsters,"[143] an argument that was in fact not inaccurate in view of the favorable social prospects of virtually all those
affected. In the end, it had turned out to be something like a form of occu-
pational therapy for fifty official "parole workers" along with one American and one German full-time "parole commissioner."[144] In theory, the
supervision of many of those paroled needed to be continued into the
1970s—a meaningless torture for all concerned.

Gradually and in all silence, the great majority of those paroled
since 1953 had thus already been definitively released over the preceding months. Precisely this had to transpire now for Sandberger and
his three jailhouse colleagues. To such an end, the Mixed Board unanimously (hence bindingly) recommended reduction of the sentences to
time already served. At the same time, the decision was made to release
the remaining parolees from supervision. Using this procedure, the
board had dispatched its duty in a way conforming to the system. On 9
May 1958, the gates of the Landsberg fortress were opened for the last
members of the circle of Nazi criminals who had been tried by the Allies
on German soil a decade earlier.[145]

Rudolf Heß, Albert Speer, and Baldur Schirach remained incarcerated in Spandau. Aside from these men, "war-condemned" Germans were now being held only in Holland, France, Belgium, and Italy. Their number had once again dropped substantially since 1955—the total was now fewer than thirty persons.[146] It is the case that some of them could not count on being freed anytime soon—Herbert Kappler, former police chief in Rome and the sole remaining Italian prisoner, would manage to escape in 1978, and two German war criminals would only be released from Holland's Breda prison at the start of 1989. Such—limited—severity must be understood against a backdrop of continued prosecution of criminal collaborators, especially in France and Holland: the prosecution furnished something like moral justification for punishing the atrocities of security police leaders and other Nazi functionaries to the full. Following the war criminal debates, but also in view of a parallel process involving the virtual end to prosecution of Nazi crimes, it can hardly be surprising that little understanding was expressed for such a policy within West Germany.[147]

In the mid-1950s, the Allied project of punishing German war criminals thus wound up in humble fashion—an endgame contrasting almost tragically with the project's beginning ten years before. Little was now left of the moral sweep implicit in a decision to expiate crimes of the "Third Reich" according to principles of elementary law. What had begun in the name of a better future, one illuminated by an imposition of international law, ended on the low ground of political opportunity. The fast transformation of the geostrategic situation—the Cold War and partition of Germany, its rearmament and Western integration—had played its role in this development. But alongside these international political factors, there were endogenous processes at work in both West Germany and among the Allies, especially the Americans, processes gradually leading to the project ending. In any case, the most important factor of all was the determined German resistance to the legal efforts nigh from the beginning.

Undeniably the project revealed a certain lack of legal-theoretical acumen, along with some defects in the military court proceedings—particularly at the start, and remedied through steady corrections and modifications. And yet, despite such failings, and despite a wave of pardons soon starting to relativize the initial program, it would be mistaken to simply declare the Allied punishment efforts a failure.[148] It is true that the punishments actually meted out cannot be elevated to sole measure of the "success" of the war criminal trials. At the same time, despite a widespread sense to the contrary, the punishments were not insignificant. There were many executions in the first postwar years, and—calculated from the time of their internment (usually 1945)—most of those who escaped with their lives spent ten years behind bars. The last four of the Landsberg prisoners saw freedom thirteen years after the end of the "Third Reich." The outcome of the Allied trials was notable—and this not only when compared with the quick disaster ensuing from the early postwar German prosecution of Nazi crimes.

It is also the case that the trials' past-political meaning lay beyond the expiation demanded from criminal individuals. When it came to illuminating the criminal nature of the "Third Reich," the judicial reckoning with its personnel—with those who placed themselves at the service of its inhumane goals and those who profited from its system—as well as the public confrontation with its ideology and methods, was of inestimable long-term value. Without the trials, the criminal dimensions of Nazi rule and the Nazi military campaigns might have remained obscure for a long time.

Remarkably the enlightening impact of the trials—their central role in exposing the atrocities for perpetuity—also comprised the deeper ground for the massive collective resistance that faced the Allies. In this or that case, feelings of injustice may have been at play, but the chief motive for declining recognition of the judgments was political. More specifically, it was past-political. In the end, the tug of war unfolding over many years was not over individual perpetrators; this remained so despite the suggestive image of "German men in the hands of foreign powers," linked as the image was to the very patterns of thinking that had to be overcome. What was at stake was the question of the guilt and responsibility of an entire nation.

Although not the most important element, the war criminal issue played a decisive role in a specific struggle over interpreting the past. Barely unfolding in German society itself since the late 1940s, the struggle was all the more central to relations between the Germans and the Western occupiers. Its early fruits were mostly bitter; the stubborn fight to have the "war-condemned" released led to a fatal solidarity emerging between broad circles of the population and the thoroughly nonrepresentative interests of criminals and political apologists. In a certain manner, the Nazi *Volksgemeinschaft* thus received a second confirmation. Readiness for an open, self-critical debate about both the Nazi past and individual political failure was not merely not strengthened. At least when measured against the situation immediately after the war's end, it basically evaporated over a long period.

It was especially the punishment of crimes committed in the context of warfare that was rejected by the vast majority of Germans, not simply former soldiers. These crimes had been defined as such on the basis of the international legal stigmatization, codified at Nuremberg, of Germany's war as a war of aggression. In highly transparent fashion, many people experienced the prosecution of these crimes as a calling into question of the war's highly personal meaning—as a devaluation of their own, often self-sacrificing participation. What until now has been wrapped in the cloak of the "necessity of war" was now suddenly meant to pass as common crime, while the atrocities of the "other side" remained unpunished. Most likely, the successful collective denial of this interpretation was the most portentous result of the war criminal debate. In the struggle to free the imprisoned soldiers at the start of the 1950s, the legend of the Wehrmacht's "unstained shield"—of the "normal war" it waged in contrast to (in any event all-too narrowly defined) portions of the SS—received its impetus. And it did so in a way rendering refutation through historical research very difficult well into the 1980s.[149]

Already emerging during the political purging, the phenomenon of "neighborly" solidarity was also apparent in the war criminal trials. Whenever there was any possibility of intercession, even Mobile Killing Unit leaders were portrayed in their normal, bourgeois civic circumstances, in other words separated from crimes "in the east" whose monstrosity was certainly not easy to imagine. Such mechanisms were, of course, all the more common and simple in the case of so-called desk murderers. And this serves as an important touchstone for the (doubtless exaggerated) sense of a prevalence in 1950s Germany of a crime without perpetrators, a Nazism without Nazis.

Hence, at the time it transpired, the controversy over the war criminals did not contribute to the formulation of a measured historical-political discourse over the Nazi period. In the long term, the enlightening potential of the trials may have born fruit; in the short term, the various conflicts with the Allies at best led to a strengthening of the democratic parties' normative distance from Nazism and its crimes, a distance that offered, as it were, the initial legitimation of the democrats' past-political demands. But this distancing increasingly involved set phrases, which furnished welcome space for argument and competition with nationalist splinter parties and populist agitators. The intention of absorbing their followers served as a justification for terminological concessions such as the distinction between real and purported war criminals or the manipulation of the (never substantiated) notion that most of those sentenced were innocent. The larger parties' skill in adapting to the right increased the political pressure on the Allies; it certainly also helped wear them down over the years. Beyond this, it led for a time to a conservation of that past-politically grounded, self-reflexive nationalism constituting a basic, still barely researched mental propensity of the Germans at the start of the fifties.

It is an open question whether on its own the early West German republic's political class would have consistently been able to control such nationalism—which partially and occasionally conflated itself with a vociferous neo-Nazism. Regardless of their growing acquiescence in regard to the war criminal issue, the occupying powers, above all the British and the Americans, had no intention of allowing any test of this nationalism's political mettle.

PART III

Fixing Past-Political Limits: Judicial Norms and Allied Intervention

From its very onset, public political discussion in postwar Germany established a clear-cut normative demarcating line regarding the ideology and practice of Nazism. An important aspect of this demarcation involved legitimizing and correcting a set of policies for the past otherwise marked by amnesty and (re)integration. Against the twin backdrop of an extraordinarily wide-ranging effort at integration and an amnesty policy that cannot be considered anything but generous, the question of the nature and effectiveness of the norm-fixing process takes on special weight. The basic anti-Nazi consensus of the constitutions of the Länder and the Parliamentary Council offered a point of departure for the process; virtually the entire Bundestag, extending with diminished conviction toward the right-wing edges, relied on this consensus. At first, it amounted to little more than a general distancing that stemmed from Allied peremptory measures and political directives—a specific past-political praxis thus still needing formulation. What concrete form, then, did this praxis end up taking? Was their a particular strategy for demarcating past-political borders? And if so, how seriously was it taken? What were its basic premises and its protagonists? What was its outcome?

In the 1950s, most past-political demarcation measures were reactive in nature. This fell within the logic of the anti-Nazi self-understanding shared by the West German authorities. It corresponded to their political perception—in a certain manner already intended as normative—of the "Third Reich" as an oppressive system never desired by the Germans, and of the restored parliamentary democracy as the expression of general popular will. Beyond this, for a body politic defining itself, part and parcel, as a direct antithesis to the defeated regime, there was no need of any further demarcating lines vis-á-vis the past.

Still, already in the summer of 1949, first signs had emerged that it might be incumbent to modify this (unstated) position. Several of the parties now vying for Bundestag seats had made it unmistakably clear that they did not feel bound to the anti-Nazi consensus of the "approved" parties. Above all in the crisis-ridden regions of Lower Saxony and Schleswig-Holstein, marked as they were by large groups of refugees and high unemployment, but also in Bavaria, political groups were on a vote hunt involving a well-aimed exploitation of antidemocratic resentment—the feeling focused, of course, upon the occupation authorities.[1]

The reaction to this development by public opinion abroad was quick in coming. Particularly in the American press, fears of "renazification" and "new nationalism" were becoming increasingly prevalent.[2] True, not much inclination was apparent on the part of serious Western journalists to make a political tragedy out of the entry of a handful of right-wing radicals into the Bundestag and the acceptance of the German Party into the coalition government.[3] But it was also clear that there was a general expectation of determined resistance by the German government to (neo-)Nazi and nationalist agitation—and that in its absence intervention of the occupying powers was seen as called for.

As much as possible, Germany's democratic parties did not make a theme out of latent Allied threats of intervention. They did, however, register the anticipatory pressure from "abroad" with extreme attentiveness; playing a central role in their general past-political argumentation, this pressure carried particular weight in combating political activity of a more or less openly Nazi nature. The young West German state's political class felt a special obligation—going beyond the "normal" antinationalist guiding principles—to ostracize the relatively rare efforts at justifying Nazi anti-Semitism.[4] Bonn experienced its first substantial challenge in this regard a few months after the parliament first convened. A Bundestag delegate from the German Party stood at the affair's center.

CHAPTER 10

The Hedler Affair and the Establishment of Criminal-Legal Norms (1950)

I was amazed that it was once more possible to say everything.
—*A witness in the Hedler trial, February 1950.*[1]

Fifty-year-old Wolfgang Hedler was a former Stahlhelm man, then a Nazi Party member; before the war he had been a bank manager, after the war an employee of the church's relief organization in Rendsburg. On 26 November 1949, he gave a speech in the Einfeld "German House" (near Neumünster) articulating more or less all the slogans and resentments current in radical right-wing circles. Contrary to what Paul Löbe had indicated at the Bundestag's opening, the German *Volk* had by no means loaded a "massive weight of guilt" onto its shoulders; rather, it bore merely "minimal guilt," since "supranational powers" had been responsible for the war's outbreak. The resistance fighters were "national traitors," and contrary to what Kurt Schumacher had indicated, Germany would not be better off if it could now rely on the "strengths of the Jewish spirit and Jewish economic capacity." After the *Frankfurter Rundschau* carried a report on the speech on 12 December, Hedler expressly and wholeheartedly affirmed all these statements. He did not, however, confirm the most noxious of the remarks he was quoted as making: "It is possible to have differing opinions about the question of whether gassing the Jews was the means of choice. Maybe other ways could have been found to get rid of them."[2]

The day after the article's appearance, the Bundestag's advisory committee agreed to lift Hedler's parliamentary immunity.[3] The Public Prosecutor's office in Kiel began an investigation, its starting point being the notes taken by a Social Democratic delegate from the Schleswig-Holstein Landtag who had heard the speech and notified his colleagues. The SPD-led state government had already pressed Schleswig-Holstein's judicial authorities to take up the matter as quickly as possible, but things only began to unfold with the *Frankfurter Rundschau* article. The paper's editorial writer had not minced words, but interestingly he also maintained that in view of a "bad effect abroad" that was to be expected, the publication of "inadmissible remarks" needed justification. The boldness of "various demagogues greedy for followers" had to be diminished by proceeding against Hedler "with all the rigor of the available legal possibilities."[4] In retrospect, the journalist's detailed legal recommendations—a legal charge against Hedler in line with Article 18 of the Basic Law (misuse of the right to free speech for the sake of opposing the underlying free and democratic order) and removal of his delegate's mandate through the Constitutional Court, convened in the speediest possible manner—seem to contain a hint of suspicion that the matter would not turn out so simple.

On 31 January 1950, Hedler's trial began in the Fourth Criminal Panel of the Kiel district court.[5] Hedler was charged with having disparaged the memory of "German resistance fighters," insulted "members of the Jewish race" [sic], and "spurred different classes in the population to violent acts against each other in a manner threatening public peace." He was also charged with having insulted Theodor Steltzer, former minister-president of Kiel and a member of the resistance group known as the Kreisau Circle, as a "traitor to the *Vaterland*" by designating his policies as "national treachery." One charge was separated from the main proceedings: that Hedler had designated Bavarian SPD chairman Waldemar von Knoeringen a spy for the English secret service. The list of coplaintiffs read like an honorary citation of figures in the German resistance; Steltzer and Schumacher of course both signed the complaint.[6] In addition, SPD Bundestag delegate Jacob Altmaier and Hynek Lewitt from Eutin were admitted as coplaintiffs, the former "as a German Jew," the latter "as a member of the Jewish community."

Over an eight-day period, the court heard thirty-seven witnesses of Hedler's speech. The question of the accuracy of the SPD delegate's notations stood at the center of the proceedings—and here again especially the question of whether the witnesses had the "impression" that Hedler approved the Nazi "methods," which is to say the gassing. This focusing was more than problematic, since no one had asserted that Hedler had directly voiced approval of the mass gassing.[7] Two of the three judges were former Nazi Party members; through the chosen approach, the court arrived at the results it apparently desired: none of the witnesses (interrogated according to present party membership) wished to assert approval of gassing on Hedler's part. The German Party members—clearly propped to play the same tune[8]—even declared that Hedler had "distanced himself in the sharpest manner from the gassing." In this way, space was created for the judges' assertion in their verdict delivery, delivered on 15 February 1950, that a "grievous insult to the German Jews" would have been committed if Hedler had indeed literally expressed himself in the manner indicated by the opening witnesses, and over which the foreign press had been justifiably excited. "For the appearance has thus indeed been created that once again something like agitation against the Jews"—*eine Judenhetze*—"has been grasped in the making. It is clear that the sorts of statements the defendant has been charged with in fact also have the effect of doing extraordinary damage to our reputation abroad. Every individual who renders himself culpable of such irresponsible statements thus incurs a great deal of guilt, and the court wishes to leave no doubt that it would have punished the accused man with an exemplary prison sentence if his guilt had been demonstrated. This is, however, not the case." On account of the numerous witness statements, the judges explained, the presence of an insult to the Jews had to be denied.

At the same time, the court found sufficient evidence to support the charge of endangering the peace (paragraph 130 of the German Penal Code). The expert testimony of the Hamburg Jewish legal defense bureau's Hendrik van Dam had demonstrated that a "distressing effect upon the class of Jewish citizens" had resulted from Hedler's remarks. Nevertheless, the judges continued, the remarks constituted neither incitement to violence nor, intentionally, to "class warfare." For in that case, Hedler would have needed to be aware that his remarks were prone "to spur the class of non-Jewish citizens to one day use violence against the class of Jewish citizens. He would furthermore have to have inwardly sanctioned the possible onset of such an effect, and desired that eventuality (*dolus eventualis*). It is the court's conviction, however, that the witness testimony does not lead to such a finding." It followed that in the "Jewish matter"—*im Punkte Juden*—Hedler could be acquitted on grounds of insufficient evidence. When it came to all the other charges, the Kiel judges even managed to acquit him on grounds of proved innocence. The public prosecutor had asked for ten months in jail.

The trial had been held in Neumünster's city hall. When Hedler left the building after the delivery of the judgment, he was greeted by a cheering crowd. German Party functionaries handed him a bouquet with a black, white, and red bow, and the newly fledged hero's acquittal was celebrated in an adjacent tavern.[9] The satisfaction of Hedler's soul mates was all the greater because party head Heinrich Hellwege, forced, as a government member, to place more weight on Hedler's transgression of norms than on the German Party's sweeping integrative strategy, had already seen to his exclusion from the party.[10] Four days after the announcement of the verdict, the Schleswig-Holstein delegates' assembly formally severed its links with five of its twenty-one local chapters—those who had expressed their solidarity with Hedler and (distinct from the others) had not revoked it afterward. Having been placed by Hellwege under massive pressure, the state party chapter had thus renounced 1,200 of its members. For the time being, Hedler and his followers affiliated themselves with the German Reich Party.[11]

The immediate reaction to the Neumünster judgment had been forceful, and the long-term consequences were even stronger. As the Americans observed with relief, much of the press made no secret of its outrage at the acquittal.[12] One example was Heidelberg's *Rhein-Neckar-Zeitung*, a paper cofounded by Theodor Heuss, which indicated that the proceedings were a test of German justice.[13] But there were, of course, other opinions expressed as well—including that in the *Frankfurter Allgemeine* by Paul Sethe, to the effect that demanding a man's condemnation by a court "simply because he has dangerous ideas is actually the deep[er] source of disquiet." In any case, there were certain undertones to the manner in which Sethe evoked constitutional principles, warning of the danger of landing "once more in the midst of National Socialism" out of zeal in the fight against it. "Since particularly outside Germany distorting the true image of the Germans is one of the main occupations of many politicians, once again we will hear 'Germany is still completely contaminated by Nazism.' The matter is no negligible foreign policy concern to us, and we know how to track down such an attitude. But however great the necessary awareness of these dangers by delegates, ministers, and other politicians, day and night—when a man who is not a politician but a judge begins to consider political consequences in his judgments, justice has already disappeared."[14]

Writing for *Die Zeit*, former exile Ernst Friedländer ended up in the same corner as Sethe. The limits of what could be litigated in a constitutional state had to be respected; the courts were powerless against a speaker "who for instance declares he can feel no sympathy for the Jews and considers the way the July Plotters acted as mistaken." Under the motto "there are more important things than Hedler," Friedländer tried, in for him typical fashion, to make principles the focal point. In doing so, he did not avoid leaving himself open to misinterpretation—above all through the ominous sentence "it can turn out to have been good for Germany not to have won under Hitler." The notorious nonconformist's basic message was that the oft-decried "so-called German nationalism" emerging in the critique of the July Plotters was, in truth, mainly a "counterressentiment" against many "foolish actions by the men ruling since 1945"—and against the occupying powers.[15] Friedländer was especially rankled that John McCloy had himself spoken up regarding the Hedler scandal and had done so in a way that was not even awkward. If, McCloy had observed, Hedler had actually said the things he was charged with, then "I doubt that he can or will ever be acquitted morally by public opinion of the world, or indeed, of Germany."[16]

Subliminally and perhaps entirely unintentionally, the High Commissioner had formulated a position that, while certainly not recognized as such by most people, had long been suspected by many: that there would be no acquittal for the Germans; that for a long time to come they need not hope to be rid of their most recent past. It was probably also this suspicion that moved political pundits like Sethe, Friedländer, and Richard Tüngel, chief editor of *Die Zeit*, to harsh rebuttals and to steady demands for a normality they themselves finally knew had to evolve and could not be conjured up through print.[17]

The wishful journalistic images of normal treatment for West Germany—something understood as a wholly justified demand—was not the expression of conscious apologetics. Rather it emerged from a perspective that, in the end, had little contact with reality: from a belief in a completely new German beginning, tied to sweeping evocations of the larger world political picture, leading in turn to an exaggerated sense of the geostrategic importance and political esteem enjoyed by the new West German state. Such a self-image seemed to allow, for instance, angry references to the "obstinate radicalism"—for the most part nothing more than past-political sobriety—of many High Commission officials, understood as posing a danger to German-American relations, as if political symmetry prevailed here.

Among those in Bonn with political responsibility and direct contact with the Allies, such ideas were fading more quickly than among publicists of the old school. In this respect, the government's strikingly dry comment on the Neumünster judges' decision was highly revealing: The proceedings were not yet terminated, since the public prosecutor had filed an appeal. The cabinet, the Bonn spokesman indicated, had an official stenographic account of the judges' oral opinion at its

disposal; it showed that they had "tried" to arrive at an objective decision.[18] Interpretations with a different thrust were unfounded and
undermined trust in German justice[19]

Basically the government's reaction was nothing more than a weak
effort at damage limitation. The chief beneficiary of the domestic and
foreign protests arriving over recent days was the SPD, whose leaders
had to endure being insulted by a right-wing radical and had then not
even received judicial satisfaction. Were the courts still blind in their
right eye? Was a repeat at work here of what the Social Democrats had
experienced in the 1920s—traumatically so in the case of Friedrich
Ebert?[20] In the name of "free speech," did resistance members and exiles
from Nazism have to endure calumniation by incorrigible Nazis?

Naturally, such questions were now in the air. They nourished the
edginess with which, twenty-four hours after the judgment, the Bundestag discussed a statement read by Erich Ollenhauer as acting head of the
SPD parliamentary faction: in Neumünster, judges "who had undergone
the same party-political development as Hedler" had identified with
the accused man both substantially and politically. This meant
"renewed heavy damage and dishonor for the German people"; the SPD
demanded punishment of the guilty judges for legal miscarriage.[21] Without a doubt, this was heavy ammunition at a time when most of the delegates were only sketchily familiar with the oral opinion, when the written opinion was still pending, and when the public prosecutor had
already announced an appeal. But the SPD (not least of all its leaders)
felt deeply wounded; more level-headed figures in the party—men such
as Fritz Erler, who wished "no acclamation" from the Communists—
could not prevail.[22]

Under these circumstances, the admonition of CDU delegate Kurt
Georg Kiesinger not "to be swept toward precipitous, emotionally
grounded decisions" could have little effect. Despite his own deep reservations regarding Ollenhauer's statement, Kiesinger's tone remained
moderate; he expressly indicated his assent "in the essential question,
meaning the position taken against that with which you are reproach-
ing delegate Hedler."[23] Other coalition party representatives, as well as
the Center Party's Bernhard Reismann, also warned about hasty remonstrations. Reismann's remarks carried the most conviction, since he
combined a recommendation to wait until the appeal had been decided
with an admission of concern that "with the courts, a Trojan horse may
have stepped into [our] democracy"; in addition, he observed, a new
law might be called for.[24]

Despite such rationality, there was tension in the plenary hall.
Those speaking for the coalition's right-wing parties, Euler (FDP) and

Merkatz (German Party), saw to the tension being released. That precisely such men felt called upon to issue reminders about the lessons learned through Nazism and chastisements regarding insufficient respect for constitutional principles was simply too much for the Social Democrats. "Nazi advocate," Herbert Wehner and Franz Marx flung at Euler (thus receiving a call to order), and Rudolf-Ernst Heiland informed Merkatz that his membership in the Nazi party "at a time we were in jail" would not be forgotten.

It was clear that as a result of the Hedler judgment, the SPD had lost its composure. It was possible for someone like Carlo Schmid, a judge with a bourgeois-academic background who only became an SPD member in 1945, to clearly recognize the problems tied to the accusations of judicial miscarriage and to call for a milder approach in his remarks during the debate. For born SPD members, however, the point had come to confront their own perhaps all too halfhearted stance regarding the political purging—and their own possibly all too great generosity toward the old elite. What made things doubly bitter was having to be presented with pertinent statistics by, precisely, Heinz Renner, the eloquent speaker for the Communists: 80 percent of all judges and prosecutors serving in the previous British zone were former Nazis or had been "members of fascist corollary organizations."[25]

The turmoil in Social Democratic circles caused by the fact that the Neumünster judges had, in Carlo Schmid's words, "favored a proven liar over honorable witnesses," was reflected on a grassroots level.[26] Many party chapters spontaneously delivered protests to the West German president and to the chancellor. Already on the afternoon of the judgment announcement, for instance, the Hildesheim SPD telegraphed Heuss that the "judgment signifies belated acceptance of the Third Reich's crimes," and the Social Democrats in Helmbrechts, Upper Franconia, wrote Adenauer that "we know precisely that Hedler is only the straw man for Stinnes, Schröter, Pferdmenge & Co. and demand that the federal government immediately dismiss the judges who issued this verdict.[27] If the government continues to display such impotence, we shall take recourse to appropriate measures of self-help."[28]

Some thirty Jewish congregations also sent Heuss protests concerning the "disgraceful judgment," seen as representing a "collective insult" to the Jews. In addition, there were protests from the Association of Victims of the Nazi Regime, as well as, spilling beyond the leftist spectrum, scattered protests from all the factions in a community council, all the members of a district magistrate's office, and various labor councils.[29]

At the same time, a few hours after the Bundestag debate, there were union-sponsored demonstrations in Kiel and Neumünster attended by about 14,000 people. Seemingly the main motive here was sheer indignation over the course the ship of state seemed set on, combined with a deep distrust regarding the role of capitalism in a democracy that had, in fact, turned out thoroughly bourgeois. The main slogan in Neumünster was "never again Hitler, never again Hedler." The strong police presence there did not entirely prevent scuffles between demonstrators and counterdemonstrators.[30] In Kiel and Hannover, both manual and clerical workers in some of the larger firms stopped working for a short time. The German Trade Union Congress announced an extraordinary meeting of its national board, its president declaring, in the name of the Bavarian assembly, that the judgment was incomprehensible; the manner in which Hedler presented himself before the court evoked "the appearance of the accused in the trial of Hitler and Ludendorff in 1924."[31]

After all of this, it was quite clear that the Social Democratic parliamentarians could not simply resume their regular agenda—or simply wait for the appeal decision. Even the question of how to react if Hedler reappeared in the Bundestag was politically loaded. The decision was reached to "remove him promptly" should the president fail to take the "necessary measures."[32] Three weeks later, after being expelled from the plenary hall, Hedler moved to the delegate's rest area and began to give interviews.[33] At this point a group of Social Democrats led by Wehner and Heiland forced him out of the parliament building, in the process of which he took a dive on the back stairs. Hedler would make political capital from this incident for many months to come—along with financial capital via a suit for damages.[34] Despite the self-evident nature of parliamentary repercussions for such actions, the SPD's Council of Elders indicated no understanding for them. When Bundestag president Köhler nonetheless banished Wehner from parliamentary deliberations for ten days and Heiland for six, the SPD parliamentary faction demonstratively left the hall, followed by the Communists.[35]

But the Social Democrats had not wished to settle for scuffles and protest gestures. The same day as the Neumünster judgment, they introduced two bills in the Bundestag, each meant to draw the proper, specific, and concrete lessons from the Hedler case.[36] The "Law against the Enemies of Democracy" envisioned incarceration between three years and life for those using either threats or direct force "to attack the constitutional basis of the Federal Republic of Germany or that of one of its Länder." A minimum term of between three and six months was designated for anyone—including, specifically, public officials—who "out of enmity to democracy" attempted to "render the republic's flag contemptible or impugn the dignity of a group of people formed on the basis of race, belief, or weltanschauung." Whoever insulted the memory of victims of Nazism or denied the "reprehensibility of the genocide and racial persecution" was also to receive a minimum three-month sentence, a clause unmistakably meant as a comment on Hedler's acquittal. Finally, anyone "publicly or secretly working in favor of armed violence against other peoples" was to receive a minimum five-year sentence.[37]

The second bill was a "law for the reparation of National Socialist injustice in the realm of criminal law." It first postulated the legality (more precisely, the non-illegality) of resistance to both Nazi rule and the German war effort based on "conviction," in order to then declare all legal judgments based on politically or racially discriminatory Nazi laws as null and void.[38] The connection here with the radical right-wing propaganda against the July Plotters and others who resisted Hitler was fairly apparent; in face of a population still harboring substantial doubts regarding the legitimacy of the assassination attempt, such a normative act—still not seen through today—would doubtless have had considerable impact.[39]

It was already clear from the short opening debate of 16 March 1950, when the SPD submitted both its bills, that there were objections of legal principle to the second bill, which is to say to a systematic annulment of unjust legal rulings. Sensing this, Georg August Zinn—formerly justice minister of Hesse and soon to have the post back, along with that of Hessian president-minister—placed primary emphasis on the need to unify laws in his substantiating arguments. The bill, he explained, went beyond both the invalidation of Nazi laws and the sorts of amnesties that had already been adopted, in different ways, in the individual occupation zones. Zinn expressly rebutted the notion that the "legal, political, and moral rehabilitation" of those who had resisted Nazism out of "conviction" was a pressing political question. In his concluding words, he rejected any linkage with the Hedler case as a "manifest error," stressing that the bill collected "intellectual material" from different sides of this house."[40]

That may well have been the case, but in the end, those who hoped for the establishment of past-political norms proved too weak in face of a cross-party assembly of positive-law purists—an assembly led by no one other than Dehler. For within the Social Democratic initiative, the justice minister discovered a lurking danger for the "entire structure of our legal order"; he based his categorical rejection on the lack of any real need for action—when such a need arose, it would always be possible to do something. Adolf Arndt, who had helped shape the bill's substance and must have become certain of its impending failure, now called out that each occasion Dehler spoke was a "national misfortune."[41] But such sharp words (certainly reflecting a dose of professional rivalry) did not prevent the Legal Committee from in fact burying the bill a short time later.[42]

The SPD would hardly turn out more successful in its proposed "Law Against the Enemies of Democracy." Although it was not indicated by the title, there could be no doubt from the context that what was here being offered was a defensive package aimed anxiously at the right. It was tied to Arndt's preliminary work in 1947 for a Hessian state "law for the protection of democratic freedom" that had been discussed but never passed.[43] To a great extent it was born along by an awareness of the lack of will shown by Weimar democrats when facing the republic's enemies. In presenting the bill, Otto Heinrich Greve thus referred to the last weeks' experience as showing, precisely, "that certain political manifestations are the same as after 1918."[44] It was nigh macabre that when depicting the right-wing terror of the early 1920s, Greve was forced to endure uninterrupted heckling from right-wing delegates—and even declare, in response to Bundestag vice president Hermann Schäfer (FDP), that he had not wished to designate any members of the house as enemies of democracy.

Although it was not an ideal way of increasing his popularity, Greve was willing to openly assert his sympathy with the most recent American analyses of West German neo-Nazism. In addressing the issue of the return of former Nazis to public service, he directly reviewed the past career of Ernst Kutscher, Economy Minister Erhard's personal aide, who in 1944, as legational secretary at an advanced training meeting for "experts on Jews" in the Foreign Service, had among other things declared that "with this war, the Jew has dug his own grave." Clearly the proposed law—which Greve described as an "open declaration of war against all enemies of democracy"—could not prevent scandals of the latter sort, since Kutchner was not, at present, active in any antidemocratic sense, having slipped into the ranks of those who had become politically unobtrusive.[45] Still, with the Kutcher case raising the issue of anti-Semitism, none of the coalition speakers dared to rebut Greve, settling instead for silence.

Kurt Georg Kiesinger—himself not without a problematic past—voiced his support for an "offensive" protection of democracy, seeing Hedler's remarks as suggesting cause for "alarm."[46] The CDU, he indicated, would "not allow itself to be reproached by anyone for not seeing these danger signals." But he considered the SPD bill as insufficiently thought through. Speaking for the Union, he thus proposed handing it on to the Committee for Protection of the Constitution along with simultaneous scrutiny by the Legal Committee.[47] Those further right in the Union had little inclination to see the Social Democrats escape wholly unchastised: The FDP's August Martin Euler found himself impelled to warn of a possible "democratic terror" resulting from excessive interpretation of the planned regulations," and the German Party's Hans-Joachim von Merkatz attested to the "Jacobin spirit" from which he believed them to emerge.[48] Nobody was surprised by the National Right's Adolf von Thadden referring to both of the SPD's legal projects as having "a desperate resemblance to other ones from past periods.[49] While this argumentation was both grotesque and perfidious, from the perspective of a dogmatist like Thomas Dehler it was not entirely false.

Two weeks before, the justice minister had come out with an apologetic defense of the Neumünster court and German judges in general that was felt to be painfully embarrassing across party lines.[50] At the very start of the debate, he had made it clear that he had no intention of seeing the initiative being taken over by the Social Democrats. He would, he explained, soon submit his proposal for protecting the young democracy, but he would not make the mistake of adapting "ideas belonging to a police state." He added that neither a muzzling law nor another special law was needed—the appropriate provisions simply had to be added to the penal code "to give these threats of punishment the criminal character" that would scare off potential perpetrators.[51] With this it was already clear that nothing would come of the idea of sending a strong, fast signal to the right.

This ensuing political tug-of-war would last a year and a half.[52] Its results would prove the above impression correct: a "promotion" of the SPD bill, in a First Supplementary Penal Law passed in July 1951 with—in the end—SPD approval, that moved the original bill to a locus far beyond its original intent. At the beginning, Dehler maintained that the SPD had too little respect for the citizen's right to democratic freedoms; in contrast, at the time of the governmental bill's presentation in September 1950, he maintained that a "sacrifice of freedom" had to be accepted as the price for defending the state against threats.[53] Dehler's bill stood, in fact, entirely within a specific German tradition of authoritarian state protection, something making perfect sense since the bill's authors and champions had their roots in the same tradition. One could hardly imagine a stronger personal continuity of such a sort than that offered by Josef Schafheutle, coauthor and commentator of the Nazi German code of "criminal-legal state protection" and now involved decisively in the preparation of the First Supplementary Penal Law.[54]

Under the sign of the Korean war, the basic motivation had altered for adding politically related penal statutes to the young West German state's (in this respect still pristine) criminal law.[55] This process took place over a period of several months; in the end, the main concern was no longer containing the right-wing radical tide, but battling a communist threat defined as dire. Conceptually the process was manifest in an inverted sense of legal interests. The original SPD bill was meant to protect the principle of individual rights and democratic freedoms from denigration; in place of such rights and freedoms, the state had now emerged upon the scene. The special protection for the anti-Hitler resistance had now vanished. Instead, the focus was on the "classic" statutory offense of high treason—the concept of "endangerment to the state," introduced by the Nazis in 1933, was back on the books with a startling absence of terminological scruples. Put pointedly, the principle of state defense had now superseded that of civil rights.

On a purely theoretical level, this reconstituted political dimension of criminal law offered certain possibilities for moving decisively against *both* left-wing and right-wing extremists. But the legislators had neglected supplementary signals pointing in such a direction, and left to their own devices, the German courts of the 1950s honed a one-sided sword. Unmistakably, their procedure was not simply a reflex of new external and internal dangers. The rigorous, indeed unrestrained proceedings undertaken against Communists[56] contrasted all too drastically with the familiar old inhibitions in protecting democracy against its right-wing enemies for this to be the case. The consequences of the inadequate purging of West Germany's judicial system now revealed itself in a way going beyond the failure to adequately prosecute Nazi crimes: as a reluctance to move against Nazism's new-old protagonists and propagandists. For the most part, the double antitotalitarianism conjured up by the politicians thus produced only one reflection in the politics of the courtroom—a move against the left.

In view of West Germany's growing right-wing radical scene of the early 1950s,[57] there was hence an unmistakably scant contribution of the courts, on their own volition, to demarcating normative boundaries with Nazi positions and reorganizational efforts. When such criminal-legal demarcation did take place, it was usually as a result of political or public pressure—the Hedler case here being merely an early example.[58]

Around a year and a half after Bundestag delegate Hedler's Neumünster acquittal, the verdict was freshly considered in the appeal proceedings the public prosecutors had requested. The Higher Regional Court in Kiel had referred the matter to the First Criminal Panel of the

Regional Court. On 20 July 1951—a mere seven years after the July Plot—Hedler was sentenced to nine months in prison for "publicly insulting and denigrating the memory of dead individuals, conjoined with defamation." Specifically the court saw Hedler's denigration of the July Plotters in several speeches as proved; applying standard criminal law, the court also found him guilty of insulting the Jews, along with members of the Kreisau Circle and Waldemar von Knoeringen—not, however, Kurt Schumacher and Theodor Steltzer.[59]

As was to be expected, Hedler now lodged an appeal of his own, which was rejected by the Federal High Court in May and by the Constitutional Court in October 1952. Meanwhile, he had turned his back on the German Reich Party and set up his own National Reich Party. But as of the Constitutional Court rejection, Hedler was no longer running around free. A few days earlier, the Kiel public prosecutor had issued an arrest warrant on grounds of danger of flight; Hedler was taken into custody as he left the Bundestag building. His forced absence from parliament would last until April 1953, meaning that he had to serve two-thirds of his sentence.[60] In the second Bundestag elections a few months later, he would participate in the radical right's campaign to return to parliament and revive fortunes that were now flagging badly.

A few years earlier, the prospects of Nazi sympathizers had seemed far less deplorable than in the summer of 1953. By 1951–52, some of their opponents' optimism, sparked to a degree by the Hedler case, had dissipated. This optimism was evident in a provisional assessment by the ordinarily highly critical Eugen Kogon, directed first at a foreign audience and published in the *Frankfurter Hefte* in the spring of 1950. The reaction to the acquittal, he argued, had shown "that the German public is very awake in face of democracy's enemies."[61] A year later, this confidence had become murkier. "The Return of National Socialism" was the title of his analysis of the elections in Lower Saxony on 6 May 1951, in which the Socialist Reich Party (SRP) emerged as the fourth strongest parliamentary faction in the Hannover Landtag, with sixteen delegates.[62] Despite all the regional particularities at work in the radical rightists' success here, Kogon saw no cause to shrug the matter aside. His concern centered less on the return of Nazism itself than on the democratic parties' response. "They can master the danger if they want to. To do so, they need in any event to act, occasionally even together, and must neither flirt with the nationalists nor try to get the better of them on a false level and false path."

Kogon was afraid that in their conflict with the radical right, the parties and politicians could themselves turn rightward. He added a warning about the effects abroad: "as a result of increased insecurity over the course of Germany's political development, there will be a tendency in the world to very carefully mull things over." This was precisely the interpretation of the neo-Nazi problem receiving the easiest hearing in Bonn. It constituted one basic source of the measures at past-political demarcation taken to confront the SRP—measures culminating in the banning of the party in the fall of 1952. "Foreign opinion" here functioned as something like the visible third force in a process dominated by the executive and judicial systems.

CHAPTER 11

The Rise and Banning of the Socialist Reich Party (1951-52)

> I will not stand for being called a Nazi. I was, I am, and I
> will remain a National Socialist.
>
> —*Otto Ernst Remer in Braunschweig, 15 March 1951*[1]

In the first German Bundestag, there was little disagreement among the larger parties about the need, in case of doubt, to prescribe sanctions against organized right-wing extremism. As had already been made clear at the start of the debate over the reintroduction of criminal-legal statutes for political offenses, the SPD and the CDU were in wide agreement about interpreting the principle of a "defensible democracy" postulated in the Parliamentary Council[2] above all in terms of appropriate punishment. The readiness for administrative and policing measures increased under the pressure of rallies led by radical agitators, with crowds that had been growing since the spring of 1950, along with a hesitant criminal justice system and inadequate Constitutional Court jurisdiction. The SRP, in particular, would feel the weight of such measures; this organization was attempting to profile itself as the Nazi Party's successor with special directness, provocativeness, and success.

Outer impressions were enough to make the intentions clear: uniformed hall guards, red flags with black Reich eagles replacing the forbidden swastika, marching music (preferably Hitler's signature melody, the "Badenweiler"), and so on, accompanied by scarcely masked terminological echoes: *Reichsredner* ("Reich orator"), *Führungsprinzip* ("leadership principle"), *völkische Gemeinschaft* ("community of the

Volk"). The identity was not only apparent in such matters of style, but, of course, in both ideological underpinnings and personnel.[3] The SRP did indicate vague distance from Nazism and the "Third Reich" in certain points involving "mistakes" that could not be justified to a broader public—above all points related to the "Jewish question."

The party had been founded at the start of October 1949 by former middle-level Nazi functionaries.[4] Its organizational and agitational center was Lower Saxony. This was the base from which its chairman, Fritz Dorls, entered the Bundestag, on the list of the German Reich Party—shortly before first becoming an "independent," then a member of the Economic Reconstruction Association parliamentary faction. But the SRP's real star was retired Major General Otto Ernst Remer, who had gained desultory fame for his role in crushing the July Plot as commander of the *Großdeutschland* guard battalion, stationed in Berlin. Following a period of internment during which he received training as a bricklayer, Remer—now thirty-seven—again began grabbing headlines in the summer of 1949.[5] In gatherings of the Association of Independent Germans, a precursor of the SRP, he justified his own earlier role with sharp attacks against the "traitors" of 20 July. A few weeks before the fifth anniversary of the failed attack, the Friesland denazification board classified Remer as a nonincriminated person, their reasoning being that he had only done his military duty (as a career officer, he had never joined the Nazi Party). This produced a journalistic outcry, Remer becoming the main target of those who had hoped to see a positive West German interpretation of the anti-Hitler resistance take hold on the anniversary's occasion.

Following his successful electioneering intercession for Dorls—himself a rather disappointing speaker—the SRP systematically sent crowd-pleasing Remer out on agitational tours through northern Germany. His words and political convictions appeared to be wholeheartedly embraced among several social groups: former members of the Wehrmacht and the party; refugees and expellees who had experienced the years of denazification, internment, and camp life as an ongoing, multifaceted process of social and economic downgrading—often as a violent collapse of meaning. Gatherings with more than a thousand supporters were not exceptional. Taking place in many districts, this influx drew counterdemonstrations in its wake; riots were becoming increasingly frequent, with members of the Association of Victims of the Nazi Regime and the German Communist Party participating alongside Social Democrats and union activists.

Following an all-out brawl in Wolfsburg, the Lower Saxon interior minister (SPD) issued a ban on speeches by Remer in February 1950, basing the step on the Prussian Police Administration Law of 1931. A similar measure had been taken a few days earlier in Schleswig-Holstein, where elections for a new state parliament were meant to take place in July.[6] The governments of Hamburg and North Rhine–Westphalia also tried to put a stop to the spreading "Remer myth." But such measures did not promise much long-term effectiveness—some district heads were already refusing to carry them out on constitutional grounds. During the Lower Saxon elections in spring 1951, SRP gatherings were consequently forbidden because of the danger to public order posed by counterdemonstrations. In Emsland, the district government even issued a ban on Remer's presence that was not based on any statute.[7]

In 1950, the SRP was thus well on its way to shedding its "public nuisance" status.[8] The most troubling aspect of this development was the greater rather than reduced vigor and cohesion the afflicted states' administrative measures seemed to give the party. Its members simply considered themselves persecuted individuals, once again, following their "discrimination" in the first phase of the occupation. Nevertheless on 19 September 1950, the federal government decided to remove everyone from public service who was actively working "against the order of the democratic state." This was on the initiative of Interior Minister Gustav Heinemann, who had already ventured on a "law regulating order at public meetings" in the spring.[9]

The Bonn cabinet discussed the incompatibility resolution on two occasions.[10] If the sequence recorded in the minutes is significant, then the SRP followed the Association of Victims of the Nazi Regime (thought to be infiltrated by communists) as the second most important organization meant to be affected. Two other communist front organizations were spoken of in both meetings, but not the German Communist Party itself—and no other extreme right-wing factions.[11] A rather undigested effect was generated by a prompt forwarding of the resolution to the different Länder (with the request for "unified regulation") and hasty calling of a press announcement. It was otherwise with a corrected version worked out in a small circle and read to journalists by Heinemann, in the presence of Adenauer, Dehler, and Blücher, a few hours after the second meeting. Its basic direction was clear: first place among the organizations (now clearly identified) considered "incompatible with official duties" was assigned "the German Communist Party with all its subsidiary organizations," followed by no fewer than nine more factions considered to be on the extreme left. The SRP merely had eleventh place, and the only other radical-right factions on the list were the National Front and the Black Front—a faction composed of "dissident" Nazi Otto Straßer's disciples.

The next day's headlines corresponded with Adenauer's explanatory pronouncement that what was at stake was "preventing infiltration by the SED" (i.e., the East German regime) and "struggling against the communist zone with all decisiveness." There was no mention of the SRP; the Nazi successor organizations were mentioned only together with Heinemann's indication that experience pointed to the "interplay" between left-wing and right-wing radicals.[12]

In contrast to the public, the SRP's leaders were, naturally enough, very interested indeed in the government's incompatibility resolution. The day after its publication, party chief Dorls delivered a long complaint letter to President Heuss. It contained words of praise for the decision to do something about "communism's work of subversion," along with a protest at the SRP, "which probably rejects communism most clearly and distinctly of all present West German political organizations, finding itself named in one breath with the German Communist Party and its front organizations." The SRP, delegate Dorls explained to Heuss, was principally a party for "the last war's young soldiers"; it felt itself "far too much the moving force behind the anti-Bolshevist struggle"— *Kampf*—to accept the interior minister's unheard-of insinuation. Dorls then performed something like a reverse operation on Heinemann's press conference remark that the Constitutional Court alone would decide on banning parties. As long as the court did not yet exist—it would finally begin functioning in the fall of 1951—Heuss was obliged through his oath to intervene as "trustee" against the government's "flagrant breach of the constitution." Beyond this, he announced the intention to eventually file a complaint with the court.[13]

In the following day's exchanges, it became clear enough that the government's vigorous resolution would have to pass through the needle's eye of the constitutionally governed state—that is, the concrete decisions regarding dismissals would end up in the disciplinary and labor courts. Heinemann conceded as much, adding the observation that part of the damage done by SRP partisans to their special duty of allegiance stemmed from considering "former Admiral of the Fleet Dönitz to be the soul custodian of legitimate governmental power."[14] Dorls now believed he could afford a touch of sarcasm: "In itself alone, this might not be anticonstitutional; rather, through the variability of legal procedures and multiplicity of adjudicating bodies, one and the same material would itself result in the most variable legal decisions, thus producing complete legal chaos."[15]

Dorls had also contacted Thomas Dehler. His reaction revealed the government's insecurity in this matter—or at least the considerable wavering of one of its most important members. The justice minister was not above receiving the SRP leader in his office for the sake of some advice: the reproaches being leveled in the press, "essentially the foundation for the government's decision as well," needed to be refuted. In one of the "notes" with which his officials had become familiar, Dehler explained that in case the arguments offered "appear solid," he had offered Dorls the prospect of the matter being taken up by the cabinet.[16] Dorls now wrote a five-page "sketch" of the "nature and purpose" of his party; its rhetoric perhaps conveyed adequate information about the conceptual distress of its "*völkisch* author"—none, however, about the constitutional conformity of his troops. Regarding democracy, for example, he explained that the SRP had never held a debate over the state form it desired but that there was a shared "opinion values can be embodied in every form of state, as long as those responsible for state affairs see themselves as expressing values. Why not, then, in a democracy born out of European thinking as well?"[17]

Dehler's referees spent almost a month brooding over this easily perusable loyalty statement, handed the thing to Adenauer and Dehler, and settled for responding to Dorls, who was eagerly awaiting an answer, with their own question: "How many former members of the Nazi Party and its offshoots are now members of the SRP?"—as if, in the face of the presence everywhere of former party members, not least of all in the Justice Ministry, this could really explain anything at all. In all superfluousness, Dehler now shared a little more information with the SRP chief: he saw "no other possibility at present but having the justification and constitutionality of the government's decision considered by the Constitutional Court. I am doing everything I can to see to it that this court can assume its functions as quickly as possible."[18]

To Dehler's distress, Dorls brought their peculiar dialog to public attention.[19] The dialog did, at least, make one thing clear: The problem of the political reappearance of believing and organizationally capable Nazis could not be resolved through banning from specified professions. For those meant to be affected were, it seemed, usually part of the group (its size now certainly small) of those who had been "deprived of rights" in 1945 and who still had nothing to lose in 1950—least of all governmental employment. If this was the case (and a glance at the radical right's assemblies indicated it was[20]) then two remedies could be hoped for: above all, further economic upswing, offering many of the déclassés a chance, and in a way corrupting them for the new order; and a high-court banning of their principal party—this serving to separate those who turned to the SRP out of diffuse ressentiment and clear dissatisfaction with their situation from the hard core of convinced Nazis. But some difficult terrain had to be crossed before this could happen, including a jungle of conflicting interests inside the Bonn coalition.

In a cabinet meeting on 30 January 1951, exactly eighteen years after the German catastrophe's onset, Heinemann's successor, Robert Lehr, warned that the SRP required "special attention."[21] Himself of conservative-authoritarian temperament, the new justice minister had been a member of the German National People's Party in the Weimar period. But he lacked any sympathy for the Nazis.[22] He had been furnished with alarming reports from the newly formed Federal Office for Protection of the Constitution, according to which the party now had at least 6,000 members, being on the march above all in the rural areas of Schleswig-Holstein and Lower Saxony, but also of Westphalia.[23] The next point on the agenda demonstrated that the SRP's sharp attacks on the West German government were unabated; it involved criminal charges against Remer (for the second time in six weeks) and the former Nazi "general work leader" Ulrich Freiherr von Bothmer. Both men had argued that a federal cabinet composed of "traitors" had already arranged escape quarters in London.[24]

Aside from complaints filed against such insults, which simply could not be ignored, the government held back from any action for the time being. As justice minister, Dehler was responsible for reviewing potential criminal charges; unlike Lehr, Dehler was prone to—occasionally odd—forbearance.[25] Nevertheless, the sheer mass of slander tossed forth by SRP speakers meant that its leaders were soon wrapped in a web of civil and criminal proceedings.[26]

About a month before the early May Lower Saxony elections, things came to a head. SRP propaganda had meanwhile taken forms that observers in the government's press office viewed as directly comparable with the Nazi Party's pre-1933 election methods.[27] Spurred on by the strong reception their blustering party hero Remer was sure of everywhere, second-tier orators were now persistently shedding their reserve: threats against the "licensed democrats" and "rabble" in Bonn were becoming par for the course. But, perhaps unexpectedly, the individuals being attacked in this way revealed themselves as anything but sissies. Above all the CDU and SPD took up the fight against the "Remer Party" without gloves on. In the Chancellery, State Secretary Otto Lenz coordinated the propagandistic employment of various quasi-government organizations. Lenz also took responsibility for shots aimed below the neo-Nazi party's belt.

For a start, he had an aggressive sixteen-page "Response to Remer" printed in approximately a quarter million copies.[28] On the one hand, this brochure considered the former major general and his retinue from the perspective of 1923—when "a few obsessed individuals" began their "fateful agitation." On the other hand, under the motto "exactly like [Otto] Grotewohl"—the reference was to the Social Democratic politician who had approved the forced fusion of the SPD with the Communist Party in the Soviet occupation zone—it placed them in the vicinity of the Russian Communists. Karl Feitenhansl, the dubious founder of the radical-right Union of the Fatherland, now arrived from Munich and promised Lenz revelations concerning "Remer's ties to the Eastern zone in return for cash."[29] For the Union, but also for the Social Democrats,[30] this seemed the key to diminishing Remer without offending the career soldiers who sympathized with him.[31]

Until the point of the SRP's banning, the CDU and the SPD stuck to a single line: the party was to be located in a continuum of defeated Nazism and present-day communism to virtually the same degree. This decision not only made sense against the backdrop of German rearmament but was also very clever from a past-political vantage point. Without directly taking on Remer's dichotomy between those who "broke" and those who "upheld" their oath of allegiance to the Nazi regime, it could serve to demonstrate a readiness to defend democracy against "totalitarianism of the left and right"—or at least to tie the fight against Remer with traditional anti-Bolshevism. In this way, the delicate question of the Hitler-led military effort's moral qualities could remain unaddressed—as could the question, menacing for both the former soldiers and West Germany's present defense policies, of the actual sense of any defensive war against the Soviet Union.

Despite all propagandistic efforts, those governing in Bonn were increasingly uneasy as the 6 May 1951 elections in Lower Saxony drew closer. On 24 April, the cabinet allowed itself the rare luxury of a longer discussion held outside the regular agenda, centered on the "domestic situation and the elections." What emerged in the meeting was agreement that the coalition's successes were not being recognized enough in face of the clamor from right and left—and disagreement on virtually everything else. Distinct differences were apparent precisely in regard to the SRP. Supported on this point by Jakob Kaiser, Adenauer was in favor of "measures against right-wing radicalism" being taken that "corresponded" to the planned banning of the communist-steered "Central Committee for a Plebiscite Against German Remilitarization"; representing the German Party at the meeting, Hans-Joachim von Merkatz demurred. But Otto Lenz also maintained that a parallel approach was not in order since, "to a far greater extent" than with the communists, the case of the right-wing radicals involved "confused and bitter men who should not be rendered martyrs."[32]

Lenz's argumentation may have been based on the observations of his PR experts, but it certainly contained a grain of truth.[33] Merkatz's motives were purely tactical: his party's chairman, Heinrich Hellwege, harbored hopes of becoming Hannover's minister-president; if necessary for realizing this ambition, he was ready to extend the desired "civic block" to include the SRP (the CDU and the German Party had already come together to form the Lower German Union).[34] The Free Democrats' Lower Saxon chapter was sailing in a sharply right-wing direction,[35] and the party as a whole would probably have had few objections. In any event, the Free Democrat cabinet members were strikingly guarded during the exchange of views.

Two days later, with the interpellation of the governing coalition and Bavarian Party regarding the "Committee Against Remilitarization" on the agenda, Interior Minister Lehr duly raised the threat of similar steps against "neo-fascist rabble-rousers."[36] But the rest of the government camp remained remarkably monosyllabic when it came to the matter of right-wing extremism. Merkatz simply offered an ambiguous pronouncement about a "suicide of democracy" whose repetition had to be avoided, and August-Martin Euler (FDP) could only refer obliquely to the SRP's alignment with the antiremilitarization "Wiesbaden Proclamation" of the neutralists around Heinemann.[37] The party was using "the political innocence of a broad strata of our populace to furnish the German Communist Party with support that is perhaps not desired but is nevertheless real."[38]

This was inadequate for Lehr. Visibly distressed, he announced an immediate inspection tour of Lower Saxony.[39] Three days later, after his return to Bonn, he made clear his disinclination to be held in any further check by his calculating coalition partners. Stunned by the extent to which the SRP "has impressed people in northern Lower Saxony and successfully stirred them up against the state," he pleaded with Adenauer for an immediate banning, in a letter marked "strictly personal." It made no sense, he indicated, "to passively observe the day-to-day increase in the government's undermining and the establishment of an antistate organization of the old school," simply because the Constitutional Court did not yet exist. Lehr thus did not wish to invoke Article 21.2 of the Basic Law, which designated the court as sole arbitrator in the question of a party's constitutionality. Rather, he wished to declare an immediate ban on the SRP, based on Article 9.2, which outlawed organizations directed against the constitutional order. "Certainly," the interior minister indicated to the chancellor, "with this resolution we run the danger of it being annulled. But the worst thing possible for the federal government is to do nothing and wait around. Isolated measures have little chance of success."[40]

As Lehr saw things, in Lower Saxony, the Social Democratic minister-president Hinrich Wilhelm Kopf was hoping to increase the SPD's electoral chances through a "greatest possible splintering in the center and right-wing camps."[41] For this reason, he was himself in doubt that Kopf would carry out a decision to forbid all SRP activities at the "very last minute." Lehr nonetheless managed to win Adenauer over to this course of action before his trip to Strasbourg for the European Council. But then, in a cabinet meeting held without the chancellor on 4 May, it encountered passionate resistance: the dispute over Lehr's draft resolution went on for two hours, and Lehr's citation of Adenauer's assent made no difference.[42] Dehler, Seebohm, Schäffer, and Lenz, along with Blücher and the "parliamentary faction leaders" Merkatz (German Party), Kunze (CDU), and Schäfer (FDP), all firmly rejected proceeding in line with Article 9.2 of the Basic Law. The only ally Lehr could find was Hans Lukaschek, who believed "that a state emergency existed— and this not only in relation to domestic political circumstances, but rather also in light of the effects abroad." In the end, Dehler ended up seeing to it that the draft was truncated.[43]

The interior minister appeared before the press a few hours later, chaperoned by Seebohm and Blücher.[44] Compared with his plans, what he was now able to announce was a minimal program: forbidden on the basis of Article 9.2, Basic Law, was the SRP's "activistic" wing, meaning the Nazi SA–modeled *Reichsfront*. The Lower Saxon government was directed to "battle any form of electoral terror with the sharpest possible means." When it came to the SRP itself, Lehr could only state that the government would "apply for determination of unconstitutionality with the Constitutional Court as soon as it had taken up its duties."[45]

Delivered twenty-four hours before the opening of the polls on 6 May, it is hard to say how much influence this warning shot had on the election results. A tinge of the forbidden had always clung to the SRP, and it seems somewhat doubtful that—granted he even heard about it—the abstract threat of the Constitutional Court would have led a young Lower Saxon farmer to suddenly alter his voting choice. But it is also true that the 11 percent results achieved by the neo-Nazi party (with only four direct mandates) were below what many observers had feared.

From Adenauer's perspective, the damage was great enough. It was not only that the Lower Saxon Union had been able to attract less then a fourth of the voters, practically excluding an overthrow of the governing Social Democrats.[46] At the same time, the results were having a drastic effect abroad, the "Remer party" now suddenly becoming a theme for both headlines and politicians.[47] Before the elections, Adenauer's instrumentalizing of his "very serious concern" about the SRP's activities in Lower Saxony before the Allied High Commission had been quite nonchalant. The "extraordinarily close ties" between the right-wing radicals and the East German Communists,[48] he had explained, made a strengthening of the Allied military presence in West Germany absolutely necessary.[49] Three days after the elections in a Petersberg meeting, little trace of such an approach remained.[50] Naturally, the chancellor continued playing on the argument he and his interior minister had been pressing home for weeks, to the effect that the Lower Saxon government bore the blame for the unhappy situation. But apparently knowing it would be inadequate—most likely he himself did not entirely believe it—Adenauer premised the argument with a somewhat self-contradictory summation: While the SRP "is at the time not dangerous, it merits the most serious possible observation by the government and the broad public." The chancellor also left no doubt concerning his determination "under no circumstances to allow a repetition of the events leading to a strengthening of Nazism in the twenties." "If," he declared, "the legal means at our disposal prove insufficient, then we will introduce bills in the Bundestag furnishing us with the power to suppress a revival of National Socialism with force if necessary."

All such assurances could not keep Adenauer from receiving serious words of warning. They were delivered by John McCloy, and this not only because he chaired the meeting. The nationalist reaction to his Landsberg decision had frayed the American's trust, now replaced, to a degree, by bitterness. McCloy's tone was not unfriendly, but his remarks were focused; he explained that Remer and his consorts had been closely observed and that the Allies were "very worried." Certainly, he continued, the "core of the danger" was "small for the moment" and not typical for the political situation in the Western zones. But the situation had to be dealt with. It went without saying, he added, that the Allies preferred it being dealt with by the West German government—its "enthusiasm" would lead to "mastery" of the affair. But McCloy did not refrain from informing the chancellor point-blank "that we will intervene" if it "should ever prove necessary." And he then drew the British and French directly into the threat of intervention: "I am convinced that I do not only speak for myself but for my colleagues as well when I say that we are at your disposal to work with you at any time, either through consultation or direct assistance." The "old Nazi adventure" was not to be repeated.[51]

It is true the chancellor did not need such warnings to understand that the Lower Saxony elections had decisively changed things. In the cabinet, the day before the Petersberg visit, he had announced the intent to proceed against the SRP "with all available means"—as well as a complaint before the Constitutional Court. As he explained, it was necessary to already start collecting evidence. He added a remark addressed to the legalistic prevaricators: the situation must not be allowed to once more arise where "democracy dies from democratic principles, as in 1933." It seems that Dehler responded to this remark with silence, as he did to Adenauer's request for an explanation of "who is responsible for the court not functioning after all this time."[52]

The FDP and the German Party did not exactly respond enthusiastically to Adenauer's new plans for a speedy banning of the SRP. Neither party wanted, of course, to be seen as harboring sympathy for the neo-Nazis. But the German Party's parliamentary faction chief, Hans Mühlenfeld, did feel called on to inform the chancellor that "creating something like a lex SRP" was considered "nonviable." If at all, a "special law" could be considered by his party only when "extended to every totalitarian group or party, whether right or left."[53] This, however, was less a declaration of faith in a well-balanced democracy and more an indirect delaying tactic. Everyone knew that the possibility of unified free elections in East and West Germany—a possibility that needed to be kept open and would naturally have to include the Communists— militated against banning the German Communist Party.[54]

The extent of Dehler's enthusiasm for Adenauer's plans is shown by the fact that two months passed after the cabinet session before he dictated the following "remark": "I request that, together with the Interior Ministry, the complaint be prepared for the Constitutional Court in order to determine the unconstitutionality of the SRP, and in the process to extensively investigate whether the material at hand is sufficient."[55] The justice minister in fact invested considerably more time and energy in trying to confuse the insistent interior minister. In the middle of July 1951, he sent Lehr a letter marked "personal" expressing serious doubt that the SRP's unconstitutionality could be proven before the court.

Namely, this "could not be accomplished by showing that some months ago in the course of the election contest, a number of its prominent functionaries abused the government and its policies in the worst manner. It requires establishing that the party's real goals—which are mostly kept secret and not proclaimed openly—and the behavior of its followers—not merely a minority, however excessively loud!—are directed at the diminution or elimination of the basic democratic order."

Putatively to increase the complaint's chances, Dehler proposed establishing "forfeiture of the basic right to free expression of opinions," in accordance with Article 18 of the Basic Law. Once the SRP's "heads" were sentenced, it would be easier for the Constitutional Court to ban the party. For this reason, Dehler went on, the complaint against the communists would need to be submitted together with that against the SRP: the former case was clearly justified, whereas in the case of the SRP "at the moment" such clear justification was "absent." With a veneer of earnestness, Dehler suggested that Lehr present the "proposals" in one of the coming cabinet sessions. Because establishment of the Constitutional Court proved to be impossible before the summer break, enough time was available to prepare the complaint "with the necessary care and thoroughness."[56]

Lehr would not be put off any longer. Perfectly ready to consider an additional complaint based on the Basic Law's Article 18, he directly declared Dehler's proposal to "take distance" from an effort to ban the party as "out of the question." [57] Over the following months, supplied with a steady stream of reports from the Office for Protection of the Constitution (which had meanwhile taken to making inspection tours), the Interior Ministry put together a banning request under top secret conditions. But the theme only made its way back to the cabinet's agenda[58] with the results of the elections for the Bremen city parliament (7 October 1951), the SRP receiving 7.7 percent of the votes and eight mandates. In the intervening period, the virtually routine filing of complaints against SRP speakers had been considered sufficient, and the political-propagandistic fight had been allowed to peter out.[59]

At the same time, since the start of the treaty negotiations in the summer of 1951, Adenauer's interlocutors abroad had been repeatedly trying to ensure his vigilance. Adenauer was well aware that in France and England there was a "holy terror of individuals like Remer"[60]— accompanied by a tendency to place him a bit on display. The chancellor was thus himself now afraid of an instrumentalization of the party's success in the negotiations over the abolition of the occupation regime. The presence of such a danger was manifest.[61] On the American side, along with growing coverage by the press, concern about right-wing radicalism had even made its way into the official quarterly report of the High Commissioner.[62]

In a long letter to French Foreign Minister Robert Schuman, Adenauer acknowledged "many voices abroad that, referring to certain right-wing radical tendencies in Germany, warn against granting the Federal Republic too much sovereignty." He then repeated his appeal from Strasbourg that the extremists' significance not be exaggerated. The government was determined, he declared, "to proceed against enemies of the republic with all severity." Adenauer's concluding argument in this regard was entirely typical—and by no means honed solely for Schuman, the convinced European. He believed "that the nationalist tendencies stirring again among all the Western European peoples can best be overcome by moving toward European unification as speedily as possible."[63] In place of efforts at historical clarification and political pedagogy, Adenauer viewed functioning European collaboration—put more directly, economic upswing—as the recipe for freeing the Germans from their transfigured memories of material glory and national greatness. In view of the fact that more than half the SRP's followers gave improvement of the economic and social situation as their main aspiration, the chancellor's approach was certainly not false.[64]

Against this backdrop, much speaks for the assumption that the Allies were the main reason for the West German government trying to stamp out right-wing radicalism by banning, that otherwise they would have allowed it to play itself out via economic growth. Taken in face of the Lower Saxon elections, Adenauer's late-April decision to go along with Lehr's suggestion to ban the SRP presumably was tactically based— a result, that is, of the hope of more votes for the bourgeois parties. His readiness to crack down on the party six months later reflected similar tactics: a desire to please his now alert Allied negotiating partners.[65] But nothing indicates he considered the party's banning urgently necessary, now or before.

Preparations now proceeded in an appropriately businesslike manner. On 11 October 1951, Lehr presented the justice minister and chancellor with his thirty-five-page draft bill. He added a note indicating that the Bremen elections had offered especially strong evidence to be furnished later.[66] The comment revealed something about the paper's substance and structure: basically Lehr's officials had compiled citations that seemed incriminating in one way or another from the press, radio recordings, and reports of the Office of Constitutional Protection.[67] In addition they furnished names of witnesses and evidence. Frequently, the only explanation was a lapidary "Nazi Party ideas." The summarizing substantiation was not even four pages long and was so flat that the next day Lehr was given to understand—presumably by Dehler— that he needed to "complete and supplement" the complaint—together with that against the German Communist Party.[68]

A month later, an expanded version was ready to be approved by the cabinet. This version was not only free of tactically awkward passages, but also supplied with a firmer conclusion.[69] A "concrete danger to the "free, democratic order was already present "if, through its goals, the behavior of its members, and its political activities, a party attempts to realize an idea suitable for shaking authentically free democracy, and that above all serves to defame the values of authentic democracy within the German nation, in order to pave the way to an authoritarian-dictatorial form of state." Lehr expressly invoked the "experiences of the last three decades" and confirmed that the SRP's emergence had already done severe damage to the republic. He placed the foreign relations argument on practically the same level as that focused on domestic policy: "Within the country, wide circles of our people are deeply worried about a political movement of a totalitarian character once more rearing its head. Abroad, trust in the steady democratic development of the German people has suffered a strong setback."[70] The interior ministers of the Länder spoke out in precisely the same vein on 15 November, when they met to discuss the "resuscitation of National Socialism"; they concluded that the danger could not be dealt with through police measures alone. A resolution to ban the party had to be submitted "without delay."[71]

This was taken care of in the cabinet the next day, outside the framework of the normal agenda. A motion to ban the German Communist Party was passed at the same time, despite the fact that, as Lehr explained, documentary evidence was still not available. The government's right wing was apparently still feeling uneasy, and the politically inopportune anticommunist move served as a useful therapeutic device for parts of the coalition.[72] The Social Democrats were naturally in favor of the anti-SRP move but feared that a banning of the German Communist Party could make reunification more difficult. But for the sake of peace within their own coalition, the cabinet members shoved the SPD's reservations aside.[73]

From the moment the motions to ban the SRP and the German Communist Party—almost always mentioned together by the government in that order—were submitted to the now established Constitutional Court, Dehler abandoned his previous reservations. Instead, he revealed considerable concern with optimizing the agreed-on course. Naturally a certain rivalry with Lehr was at work here—but the dominant concern was shaping policy, the dominant motive making as much political capital from the new course as he could. This was manifest, for example, in Dehler's insistence that alongside Hans Ritter von Lex, Lehr's state secretary, other high-ranking government jurists should represent the government, rather than ordinary lawyers. It was manifest in his suggestion that the possibility of searches and seizures be explicitly called to the court's attention and that the way to ensure enforcement of its judgments be considered well in advance.[74] And it was manifest in his appeal, now, for complaints to be filed as quickly as possible against both parties in line with Article 18 of the Basic Law (forfeiture of basic rights).[75]

Such demonstrative engagement on Dehler's part could not alter the fact that Lehr had chief responsibility for the SRP matter and would not let himself be overtrumped. Supported by steady information from the Office for Protection of the Constitution, the interior minister's officials prepared a nationwide search and seizure operation against the party, as well as against the Communists—and an application to the Constitutional Court to have Remer's basic rights revoked. Numerous informers' reports had in fact by now furnished a very precise picture of the SRP's organizational dynamic and motives. As the office's president Otto John noted with evident satisfaction, a reliable source had been planted directly in the party's directorship.[76] Through that source, fairly complete information was available concerning the right-wing radicals' preparations for their trial in Karlsruhe. Rather than being gripped by panic, the SRP was focusing on the task of clearing away incriminating evidence and laying the groundwork for political activities after a banning. In regard to the latter concern, the focus was less on withdrawing "to the catacombs"[77] as systematically infiltrating "like-minded" parties.[78] It was also the case that the report by the Office of Constitutional Protection pointed to the SRP having its own "source" in Bonn's ministerial bureaucracy—presumably in the justice minister's vicinity, since it was clear that knowledge of his faintheartedness by the party's leadership was not based on contacts between Dorls and Dehler alone.[79]

In the final days of January 1952, following formal acceptance of the government's complaint, the First Panel of the Constitutional Court ordered a large-scale operation to seize evidence from the SRP.[80] Despite the party's intelligence gathering, the cabinet would achieve a surprise strike.[81] Unlike the parallel move against the German Communist Party, which focused solely on its offices, in the case of the SRP the authorities searched private apartments,[82] the Interior Minister's hope being, of course, to find more incriminating material there than in the official headquarters. (Always meagerly equipped, these had long since been cleaned up in readiness for intrusive "visits.")

In the preliminary discussion of the operation with the interior ministers of the Länder and police consultants, Lehr allowed his authoritarian temperament free rein in the presence of two Constitutional Court judges ("earlier on I was police director for many years").[83] When some of the participants expressed doubts—the right of Bundestag delegates to immunity at least needed to be considered, this more frequently the case for the Communists than for the SRP—he called for "extensive interpretation" by the police. An article about Remer in *Reader's Digest* had helped render Lehr furious. "You need always to keep in mind that we're here dealing with enemies of the state, and that if we show excessive timidity we'll be supporting the undermining activities of these enemies.... It's important to read what the Americans are publishing about Remer. You can read and see with what insolence and arrogance this Remer is already confronting the authorities and courts in particular outside and inside the country. Take this as indicating that such creatures shouldn't themselves be confronted all too hesitantly. If we don't seize this radicalism at the right point, it will take cruder forms.[84] Meanwhile its scope has become large enough."

One interchange in particular underscored the interior minister's focus on external opinion in the entire operation (and in this respect his role as the chancellor's faithful follower): his categorical rejection of Otto John's suggestion, formulated merely as a question, that the head of the Allied news agency be notified beforehand so that he had the chance to remove his own informers enough in advance. "What is at issue is an internal German matter, in which our highest court has spoken. We will here not bring in the Allies as a matter of principle." Lehr's added argument that the circle of those initiated had to remain small could not obscure one fact: with this surprise strike, set by him—in a highly personal fashion[85]—for the early morning of 31 January 1952, he intended to demonstrate German initiative to the Allies.

In truth, the campaign against the SRP and its heroes represented a personal need for Lehr—a man with an old-fashioned sense of honor—more than for any other government minister. After having to let himself be reined in by Dehler on several occasions in cabinet meetings, he filed a private lawsuit against Remer in the summer of 1951. In the Lower Saxon electoral contest, the latter had once more calumniated the July Plot's "so-called resistance fighters," explaining that "if someone is ready to commit high treason, the question remains open if high treason is not also treachery against one's country in very many cases. To an extent, these conspirators are national traitors to a high degree, paid from abroad. You can stake your lives that these national traitors will one day have to answer to a German court."[86] As a former member of the Goerdeler circle, Lehr considered himself insulted by these words.[87] His prominence notwithstanding, the state prosecutor's office saw "no sure prospects of success" for the lawsuit and recommended it being withdrawn.[88] But since the Lower Saxon Justice Ministry had asked to be kept continuously informed about the Remer matter, the suit's official notice came to the attention of Fritz Bauer, prosecutor general for the city of Braunschweig.

As a young district court judge in Württemberg, Bauer had been a cofounder of the Association of Republican Judges. He was a Jew, a Social Democrat, and both a former concentration camp inmate and a former emigrant. He had, apparently, been waiting for the proper moment; taking up Lehr's lawsuit, he initiated the proceedings. Bauer made no secret of his political intentions. He was not particularly concerned with Remer, but very much with rehabilitating the July Plotters: explicitly with a "reopening" of the proceedings that had unfolded before hanging-judge Roland Freisler's *Volksgerichtshof*, and perhaps also with correcting the dismal image of the German judiciary emerging from the Hedler trial. That trial had centered, among other things, on the German resistance; in the end, the insults voiced there were not much different from those being confronted by Lehr. Bauer thus decided to look for additional plaintiffs. He also urged Alexander Graf Schenk von Stauffenberg, the brother of Hitler's would-be assassin, whom Bauer knew from his Stuttgart schooldays, to agree to offer testimony. Stauffenberg refused, but by the start of the trial on 7 March 1952, Bauer had assembled a prominent group of witnesses: Otto John, Fabian von Schlabrendorff, Karl Friedrich Bonhoeffer, Minister for Expellees Hans Lukaschek, and others. The new plaintiffs who participated were Marion Gräfin Yorck von Wartenburg, Annedore Leber, Uwe Jessen, and Alexander von Hase; Lehr was represented by his lawyer in the proceedings. Bauer built his case with the help of expert opinions considering the legitimacy of resistance, oath breaking, and tyrannicide from moral-theological, historical, and military perspectives.[89] The media devoted enormous attention to the "Remer trial"—one of the main factors contributing to its emergence as a piece of public pedagogy, indeed as a normative act. It served as a decisive step in the anchoring of the July Plot in the West German republic's historical consciousness. Remer's sympathizers referred to it as a "show trial."[90]

Remer was serving a four-month sentence for defamation and had to be brought to the trial from prison.[91] While his many courtroom supporters continued to find him charming, the press's consistent—and certainly not unbiased—judgment was that both he and his two attorneys cut sorry figures. (One of the attorneys was Erwin Noack, former General Inspector of the Nazi Jurists' Association; he was also responsible for the SRP's reply to the government's submission to the Constitutional Court.) In general, there was correspondingly strong press approval for Bauer's summation—although it is important to note that at the very start Bauer made clear his desire to build bridges and work toward reconciliation.[92] Remer, he explained, was not standing trial for having let the resistance down on 20 July 1944. There was absolutely no desire to reproach those who "for whatever reasons, often surely ethically weighty ones, had not rallied around the flag of freedom and human dignity." Remer was standing trial solely because he had belatedly defamed and reviled the resistors "by calling them high traitors and national traitors." While himself thoroughly open to the idea of a general pardon for the silent and indifferent, Bauer was demanding punishment for the loud and incorrigible—and at the same time a fixing of norms for the future. "What then may have still only been obscurely manifest to many is now more transparent; what then may have been an understandable mistake is now unreasonable defiance, ill will, and conscious sabotage of our democracy."

Bauer was granted full success in precisely this regard: the court affirmed his view of things down to the level of word choice, including "unreasonable defiance" (*unbelehrbarer Trotz*) among the grounds for the three-month sentence. The decision of the Braunschweig judges to incorporate Bauer's definition of the "Third Reich" as an "unjust state"—an *Unrechtsstaat*—into their opinion also served as a signal. On the other hand, they avoided taking a position on one related question that Bauer had also raised: that state's "constitutional legality."[93] Likewise the judges failed to confirm Bauer's thesis that an unjust state like the "Third Reich" "was not subject to high treason in any manner." They simply avoided the question by crediting Remer with having expressed respect for the "high traitors" on other occasions, thus indicating a lack of awareness of his remark's dishonoring character. In this way, the judges also managed to avoid the delicate question of "oath breaking." They did, however, take up Remer's reproach of national betrayal, declaring it as constituting "material factuality," in the sense of the criminal law in force at the time, but not "inner factuality." As the court saw it, the expert opinions and witness testimony had demonstrated "that the men of 20 July 1944, in virtual unanimity, were, precisely, not national traitors."

As opposed to the opinion, the judgment itself took up Remer's charge of payment from abroad, connected as it was with the charge of national treason. The tone of the judgment was more forceful. "Based on the evidence ... there is not a shadow of suspicion attached to any of these men of having been paid from abroad for any action linked to the resistance struggle." And in another passage, the court certified the resistors "as having worked for the removal of Hitler, and thereby of the regime he led, entirely from ardent love of the *Vaterland* and selfless awareness of responsibility to their *Volk* extending to unhesitating self-sacrifice. Not with the intent of damaging the *Reich* or the military power of the *Reich*, but only to help both." All this, of course, was entirely in concord with the emphatic portrait presented by General State Prosecutor Bauer and his witnesses.

In view of the popular critique of the anti-Hitler plotters—as well as of a government with reduced maneuvering room, owing to the rearmament debate and a need for approval from those who both "broke" and "upheld" their "oath"—the Braunschweig judgment was of inestimable past-political significance.[94] It is true that the judgment laid the seeds for a problematic distinction between high treason and national treason,[95] and—even more historically important—for an idealization of the political intentions of the plotters, who in the end emerged as something approaching the fathers of West German democracy.[96] But considering the situation in 1952 Germany, the judgment merits highest praise. What was essential, in the end, was preparing still barren ground for recognizing that resistance to the Nazi regime was just, and in fact was called for.[97] On 20 July 1952, West Germany's newly founded Office of National Service promptly produced a special issue of the weekly *Das Parlament* with the judgment, the expert opinions, Bauer's summation, and additional contributions from prominent resistors (John, Lukaschek, Gerstenmaier, Dahrendorf, and Speidel).[98] This constituted the first official evaluation of the July Plot. Robert Lehr's preface very openly took up the theme Bauer had raised at the start of his summation: the intent was to recall those who had rebelled against "Hitler's *Unrechtsstaat*" with respect and honor, but in doing so there was to be "no establishment of new borders between the men of 20 July and those who could not take their path then."[99]

In any case, the separation from people like Remer was meant to be total. On 11 March 1952, which is to say even before the trial had ended, Lehr had the cabinet approve initiating Constitutional Court proceedings aimed at "removing the basic rights of free expression of opinions, freedom of assembly, and freedom of association from retired Major General Otto Remer for a period to be determined by the Constitutional Court, in accordance with Article 18 of the Basic Law; and for the duration of this period to deprive him of voting rights and freedom and the capacity to hold public office."[100] While Globke, for instance, had recommended that the submission be postponed until the Constitutional Court's verdict regarding banning the SRP had been delivered,[101] a slim majority of ministers—including Dehler—approved Lehr's proposal.[102] Lehr, it was clear, would leave no stone unturned. He had become positively fixated on officially rendering the SRP's big-mouth hero stone dumb—as quickly and enduringly as possible.

The Karlsruhe judges, however, took their time. At the start of January 1952, within the fourteen-day required period, the Socialist Reich

Party's seventy-page response to the government's complaint had been filed; not without finesse, it requested a rejection of the banning request.[103] And at the end of February, the SRP had submitted its own complaints to the court, aimed at the governmental decrees of September 1950 (banning SRP members from public service) and May 1951 (banning the SRP's activist organizations). With the search and seizure measures, the party naturally believed it had a sign that the court's judges considered the available evidence too meager.[104] Even before the measures, Lehr's state secretary, Ritter von Lex, had submitted a "postscript" to the banning application, and a month before the start of the proceedings, he furnished a "new subdivided" version of the "statement of facts." The Constitutional Court had allowed the Interior Ministry's lawyers to study the documents seized in January; these documents had then been handed over to the Office of Constitutional Protection for "safekeeping."[105] On this basis, Lex had once more "widened" the "presentation of evidence." If the SRP attorneys had managed to get hold of the words introducing the new legal brief, they would have discovered a (not wholly inaccurate) confirmation of their view that, at least until then, the complaint from Bonn was resting on wobbly foundations: "The entire material now available clearly shows that to judge by its goals and the behavior of its members, the SRP aims at damaging or doing away with the basic free democratic order or endangering the survival of the German Federal Republic."[106]

Starting on 1 July 1952, the Constitutional Court's First Panel spent two weeks trying to determine if one of the alternatives Lex had offered could be validated. A few days before, the government had handed in two more expert opinions. One of these, written by Social Democratic political scientist Ludwig Bergsträsser, used historical-political examples to again underscore the parallel between the SRP and the Nazi Party; the other, written by Cologne expert in constitutional law Hans Peters, confirmed the applicability of the Basic Law's Article 21 for the purpose of "preventing a return of both the entire National Socialist 'constitutional' system and protecting the German people from similar totalitarian domination by brutal rulers."[107]

The proceedings themselves sometimes had a less academic tenor.[108] At the start, the SRP's newly arrived five-man directorship applied one by one for legal aid, and following the applications' denial, the two attorneys responsible for the complaint response quit after three days' service. From that point on, Dorls, Remer, Gerhard Krüger, Wolf Graf von Westarp, and Fritz Heller acted as both witnesses and lawyers in their own defense. They were not above repeatedly trying harassment tactics. Things came to a head on the ninth day of the proceedings, when the presiding judge, Constitutional Court President Hermann Höpker-Aschoff, denied skillful "party theorist" Krüger permission to hold a transparent "commentary." The party leadership then collectively refused any further testimony, was immediately fined between 100 and 300 marks, and left the proceedings.

Before doing so, however, Krüger succeeded in presenting the new "stab in the back" legend—the July resistors here bearing the guilt for the German defeat—before the court (and before the press). He also succeeded in asserting the accusation that the "defamation" of the German military had recently received the governing parties' approval. Ritter von Lex produced a hasty response, which the Interior Ministry immediately released to the press: "None of the governments in the entire federal region and none of the parties standing behind these governments has disparaged the honor of the German soldier. With approval from all sides, and most emphatically, the Herr Chancellor has repeatedly—namely in the consultations over the law regarding Article 131 of the Basic Law—spoken up for the inviolability of the honor of the German soldier." For this reason, Lex continued, he had to take sharpest exception to "the SRP claiming to uphold the honor of the German soldier for itself alone[!]."[109]

The Karlsruhe judges were distinctly unhappy at the inclination of the Bonn politicians to issue commentaries while the proceedings were unfolding. Halfway through, Robert Lehr could not resist announcing that the "first round" had "clearly gone in the federation's favor." As the *Frankfurter Allgemeine* indicated, Höpker-Aschoff responded with a distinct grumble. "He rather wished that the remarks of Interior Minister Lehr reported in the German newspapers . . . had not been made."[110] The Constitutional Court had been active for less than a year, and the judges were naturally concerned about not being publicly seen as governmental servants. That was all the more the case since no one could accuse the government's representatives in Karlsruhe of being especially brilliant—State Secretary Ritter von Lex's summation on the proceedings' final day, 15 July 1952, was in any case anything but a masterpiece.[111] A good half of his forty-five-minute exposition was devoted to informing the judges about Hitler's program and the history of the Nazi Party, in order to establish parallels with the SRP in a second step. This was unaccompanied by any real intellectual penetration of the SRP's structure and significance—or any convincing account of the danger it posed. According to Lex, in the realm of foreign policy the party pursued goals "showing an absence of all capacity to make judgments informed by *Realpolitik*"; its domestic goals were "irreconcilable with the basic free democratic order of our constitution." The SRP's inner order, he explained, was "authoritarian and undemocratic," thus conflicting with Article 21.1 of the basic law. The party, he continued, offered new ideas beyond those of its Nazi forerunner, using former party members in key positions and "already now" trying "to once more activate" anti-Semitism. In his concluding remarks, focusing on the "state-political significance" of the proceedings, Lex spoke up for the concept of a defensible democracy but also revealed a streak of utilitarianism: "Our *Volk* plunged into this misfortune because it had not yet gained a firm democratic tradition that would have allowed it to clearly distinguish authentic politicians from political adventurers and charlatans.... The indescribably difficult task facing the new state through the reconstruction following the total collapse due to the dictatorship makes it imperative that the organs responsible for the good of *Volk* and state take specially vigilant care that a hopeful beginning is not once more vitiated through the enemies of democracy."

The preceding summation by Horst Pelckmann, an attorney for the government from Frankfurt, was even more pragmatic.[112] Pelckmann did not shy away from somewhat scurrilous images and platitudes. He thus stressed that banning the party on the basis of Article 21 did not require "any demonstration of guilt," since in the end what was involved was not a criminal trial but use of a "highly sensitive instrument for testing the explosive material's 'unconstitutionality.'" Likewise Pelckmann described assertions by members of the SRP directorship that their party disapproved of dictatorship as amounting to "camouflage that we must not be taken in by." But his reasoning in condemning the "amassing of great words" to be found in the party's programmatic writing was more remarkable. With calculated courage of his convictions, Pelckmann recalled "a thought I had during my summation as defense lawyer for the SS at the International Military Tribunal in Nuremberg." He had there spoken up on behalf of individuals who believed it necessary to remain true to Hitler despite his hopeless position and their awareness of the system's criminal nature. "I made these remarks then to demonstrate how, seduced through false ideas, many thousands had been drawn into the fate of a mass organization, without themselves becoming guilty. And for just that reason, I feel dutybound today, six years later—to assist in these proceedings so that the mass of young people will not be plunged into misfortune by unscrupulous *Volk-seducers* who lack a conscience." It was true, Pelckmann noted, that the proceedings had made clear the "full carelessness and untruthfulness of the SRP's propaganda," but a judgment was necessary "that will warn the German *Volk* of its enemies and prevent it from following the Pied Piper tones of its new seducers."

The "warning" could be understood as amounting to necessary protection of the Germans from themselves. And just this warning was delivered by the Constitutional Court's First Panel on the same day. Through a temporary injunction with immediate effect, the Socialist Reich Party and subsidiary organizations were forbidden "any sort of propaganda and publicity in word, sound, image, and writing (including interviews)"; all assemblies were banned, as were all party publications.[113] The accompanying explanation was as follows: In light of the "extensive trial material," it would be a while before the judge's opinion regarding the central issue could be prepared, but this needed to be available in order to pronounce judgment. Meanwhile, the stipulated measures were "urgently requested" on grounds of the "common good." The judges had been above all annoyed by the "large demonstration" the SRP had called for to mark the trial's start in Karlsruhe, various spectacles in Baden-Württemberg, and the behavior of the party functionaries during the proceedings. They thus saw it as incumbent to take steps preventing the SRP "and adherents from continuing to abuse the proceedings before the Constitutional Court for party agitational purposes in the period leading up to the judgment, to already presently throw the still-open decision of the court into public discredit, but also to cause popular unrest through instigative attacks upon governmental agencies."

At this point, the decision was certainly less "open" than the First Panel maintained. And its assertion that the SRP's "existence" and "inner organization" were "not affected" by the directive could not hide the fact that the initial explanation basically served notice of a "final banning" that was on its way—this was, at least, the way Ritter von Lex saw things in the cabinet.[114] The SRP seems to have seen things identically. A few hours before the expected preliminary injunction, the party faction in the Lower Saxon Landtag rechristened itself the "Group of Independent Germans."[115] But this effort to salvage their mandate foundered in the assembly's advisory committee, which denied the name change on the grounds that all delegates were independent.[116]

With by-elections pending in both Schleswig-Holstein and Lower Saxony, the Federal Ministry of the Interior agreed with the Interior Ministries of the Länder on the "most extensive possible" application of the temporary ban; through the press and if need be through posters, the populace was to be informed that "actions aiding and abetting" the SRP were liable to special punishment.[117] But such threats were in fact no longer needed, the party's dissolution process already having begun.[118] Accelerated through quarrels in the leadership, the seemingly tightly organized SRP in fact fell apart in a few weeks, party whip Fritz Heller announcing its immediate "voluntary disbandment" on 12 September 1952. The party had calculated that at least Dorl's mandate could be saved through such a step, along with the Landtag mandates gained over recent years.[119] It had also calculated that, as a result of the new "independent" delegates joining a bourgeois coalition, the Lower Saxon coalition between the Social Democrats and the Union of Expellees and Victims of Injustice might perhaps be overturned. But the party had not taken account of the Constitutional Court. Its judgment, delivered on 23 October 1952, not only declared the SRP to be an unconstitutional organization, but also quashed its mandates, with no possibility of replacement. The judges ordered the party's breakup and the appropriation of its funds for public use. The formation of replacement organizations was also forbidden.[120]

The court's opinion ran to ninety-eight typed pages. The First Panel here thoroughly examined the SRP's history, its ideological and organizational roots, and its program. At the same time, the judges offered a concise disquisition on the role of the parties in the Basic Law and a historical analysis of the German party system's development, with special focus on the right-wing parties since the First World War. The idea behind this was to show how under favorable circumstances (economic crisis, unemployment) the Nazi Party had used an "intentionally unclear party program" and "vague promises" to seize power "with formally democratic means," revealing its "true nature" only afterward, when "inferior persons" had been placed in "leading positions." And as the court saw it, this strategy was still dangerous. "In the modern state, power struggles with the aim of doing away with the existing order are steered in increasingly less open and directly violent a manner; rather they increasingly involve the insidious strategy of inner disintegration. The anticonstitutional goals are seen through openly and with force only once political power has been achieved.... Similarly to the 'cold war,' the modern revolution consists of countless individual hostile acts, each of which seems relatively insignificant and not necessarily against the constitution when considered for itself. The goal of first undermining and then disposing with the existing order becomes clear only through an overview of the many individual acts." With these partly theoretical observations, the Constitutional Court judges had not only developed an argument for banning the SRP that was hard to refute, but they were also looking toward the German Communist Party (its own trial still being several years away).

On the one hand, the court made clear that "in the party leadership, the great majority of positions are filled by former [Nazi] party comrades." On the other hand, it was not impressed by the protest of Dorls and company that the CDU, FDP, and German Party themselves did their best to enroll former Nazis. The SRP, the judges observed, "sets about collecting the truly incorrigible, persons who 'have remained faithful,' not to gain positive potential for democracy, but to preserve and spread National Socialist ideas." In addition, they considered it proven that the party's "leadership principle"—*Führungsprinzip*—was merely a modification of the Nazi "leader principle"—*Führerprinzip*—"through the absence of a *Führer*." They expressed direct indignation at the SRP's anti-Semitism (only hinted at in the government's complaint), as reflected in a cult formed around the executed Landsberg war criminals, including Ohlendorf. "SRP functionaries have designated such a monster in one breath with fallen soldiers from the Second World War as comrades, and glorified them together as martyrs." In the court's opinion, this demonstrated "a horrifying deterioration of ethical concepts, with the murderers being represented as innocent murdered people, the surviving relatives of their victims as guilty of crimes against humanity."

In light of all this, the First Panel saw the Socialist Reich Party's contempt for "basic human rights" as clearly demonstrated—along with its hostility to the multiparty system of free democracies, its structuring along lines of the *Führerprinzip,* and its "essential affinity" with the earlier Nazi Party. It saw the SRP's personal composition and "undisguised glorification of Hitler" as demonstrating that the party considered itself the Nazi Party's successor.

The court declared the annulment of the mandate of SRP members as a direct consequence of the Basic Law's Article 21—albeit in regard to the Bundestag and state parliaments alone.[121] On a community level, it indicated, the situation was different, since decisions of national policy were not made there. In a follow-up meeting with Interior Ministry representatives from the government and Länder, the judges stressed something already implied in their judgment: the SRP's proxy organizations were "to be suppressed by the executive"; additional complaints based on Article 18 of the Basic Law were also permissible.[122] But beyond such a pending "model trial"[123] of Remer—itself to be postponed because of his flight, and then finally quashed in 1960—the government would not consider any further efforts necessary to remove basic political rights from right-wing radicals. The Karlsruhe judgment had sufficed as a desired signal—both to Germans and to those "abroad."

While the court's opinion had carefully avoided any reference to "abroad," politicians and journalists laid rather considerable stress on that perspective. The government's press office produced a comprehensive press review[124] that detailed what the American-controlled

Neue Zeitung had pointed to, with palpable satisfaction, a few days after the judgment: "German press unanimously greets Karlsruhe judgment against the SRP. Only the Communists feel cause for protest."[125] Possibly the most remarkable aspect of the heavy press coverage was the frequent observation that while the cancellation of the SRP-mandates was an important measure, the radical-right functionaries and voters had not simply vanished. *Die Welt,* for example, declared that "we will thus have very good grounds to remain vigilant and, above all, closely observe where these supposedly 35,000 members of the SRP and its voters find their future political home."[126] The *Frankfurter Allgemeine* was even clearer. "In the coming elections, the constitutionally based parties will hopefully be intellectually and morally healthy enough to avoid, say, placing delegates now robbed of influence on their nomination lists for the sake of catching votes, thus speedily bringing about a modern "renazification."[127]

In light of such concerns in the West German press, the view held "abroad" could only be expected: in general, the Constitutional Court's decisiveness was taken as a hopeful development, but in the wake of General Ramcke's appearance before the mass gathering of retired Waffen SS members, there was little outright jubilation.[128] The basic theme was, wait and see. In no more than ten months, with the Bundestag elections, it would become clear whether a high court edict could really banish the neo-Nazi menace. Correspondingly the American High Commission, which had caused displeasure in Bonn with its alarming quarterly report of spring 1951, stuck for now to its cautiously restrained line.[129] But some foreign observes had a sharper view: For example, toward the end of 1952 Fritz René Allemann, a knowledgeable Swiss journalist, contributed a brilliant analysis of the German party system to *Der Monat.* Allemann found it striking "that outside Germany the most known German politician beside Adenauer is precisely Remer." He had meanwhile come to see the "real danger" as stemming, not from that figure, but from the right-wing bourgeois parties. For "at least at present," a "revival of National Socialism in its old form" was not what had to be feared—but rather, far more concretely, the "infiltration of the bourgeois parliamentary right by bearers of a nationalistically colored authoritarian or totalitarian conceptual tradition. Put otherwise, it is not the *renaissance* of National Socialism that we need to view as the grave symptom of disease within the seemingly so vital and unshaken West German political organism, but its democratic *mimicry.*"[130]

In face of events that would galvanize the young republic's political class only a few weeks later, these were prophetic words.

CHAPTER 12

The Naumann Affair and the Role of the Allies (1953)

> I should doubt that in the end a liberal party can be transformed into a Nazi battle group, or that it is possible to act in a greater-German spirit by means of a federalist community; we have, however, to see that it comes to a try.... If there were no FDP already, it would have to be founded now.
>
> —*Werner Naumann in Hamburg, 18 November 1952*[1]

During the night of 15 January 1953, British security officers acting in Düsseldorf, Solingen, and Hamburg arrested six—in part high-ranking—former members of the Nazi Party.[2] According to the occupation authorities, the operation was aimed at the ringleaders of a group, observed for some time, that had formed plans for a Nazi "recapture of power in West Germany." Issued in London, the official communiqué over the action named the individuals and their earlier functions, apparently in a deliberate order: "Dr. Werner Naumann (former state secretary in Goebbels's propaganda ministry; in Hitler's testament, Naumann was specified as Goebbels's successor as Reich propaganda minister); Dr. Gustav Scheel (former Reich student leader and for a time *Gauleiter* of Salzburg. In Hitler's testament, he was earmarked for the post of Reich culture minister); Paul Zimmermann (former SS major general and official in the SS's economic administrative division, which was connected to the concentration camp administration); Dr. Heinrich Haselmayer (tied with Hitler's Munich putsch of 1923, leader of the National Socialist Student Association in Hamburg, published books on 'racial science' and the sterilization of those with hereditary diseases); Heinz Siepen (former Nazi Party local branch leader and chief district officer, now joint proprietor of the Punktal Steelworks in Solingen);

Dr. Karl Scharping (former official in the radio division of the Reich Propaganda Ministry)."[3]

The following day, the list was extended to include the former *Gauleiter* and Reich governor of Hamburg, Karl Kaufmann. Weeks later, Friedrich Karl Bornemann—former regional leader in the Hitler Youth and now head of a Düsseldorf-based information service—who was traveling in the American zone at the time, became the last man on the list.[4] Nearly all those on it were in their mid-forties; all had seen their careers founder through the collapse of the "Third Reich." Immediately after their arrest, the seven individuals were brought to the British military prison in Werl; the sometimes copious documentary material confiscated from their dwellings was transported to Wahnerheide, site of the British High Commission. After weeks of planning, the operation had been ordered by Sir Ivone Kirkpatrick, with Anthony Eden's approval.[5] Its goal was "ascertaining to what extent [the group's] ... activities and their contacts within and without the Federal Republic at present constitute a threat to the security of the Allied Forces."[6] With this formulation, the British were expressly relying on occupation statute; as their High Commissioner explained it, in view of the laws and ordinances that had to be followed in West Germany, its government would not have been in the position to intervene as "decisively and promptly" as the British could, as a result of their "greater authority." In any case, he indicated, the chancellor had been continually informed about the investigation and planned operation.[7]

Kirkpatrick apparently suspected that British motives and German knowledge would be at the center of public attention to the arrests in Germany. And in fact, over the following days the papers were full of speculation about who in Bonn knew how much, and when—and what the real grounds for the spectacular operation were. Hence interest was mainly focused not on the particulars concerning the histories and concrete activities of the arrested men, but basically on one question only: What moved the English to intervene? One example was the *Frankfurter Allgemeine Zeitung* (meanwhile fairly uncontested as the foremost German daily), which devoted a good part of its front-page spread to the Naumann affair over several days, its commentators speculating on all possible motives. In a lead article, Hans Baumgarten advised the British to quickly submit the evidence of a "conspiracy." Paul Sethe already believed the quotation marks justified. In the same edition of the paper, he posed a question with scarcely veiled hostility: "What do they want?" The longer the matter lasted, he suggested, the more ulterior motives would occur to the Germans. "There are thoughts ... of very massive attacks by Francophile English politicians upon German armament.

People have heard that very influential British were extremely unhappy about closer military ties between the United States and West Germany." Naumann was the manager of a German-Belgian export firm founded by one of his earlier subordinates; even the suspicion that commercial interests lay behind the operation was not too grotesque for Sethe's consideration. "England has always had an interest in German exports, as they stood in its way."[8] Two days following Baumgarten's lead article—the arrests had now been completed a week before—Sethe offered one of his own. Its headline was "We Are Still Waiting for an Answer." With undiminished acerbity, he protested the West German government being shoved aside by the British, "in the same way one would doubtless proceed with a colony's self-administrative body." Sethe himself had meanwhile come to a firm conclusion regarding the operation's justification. "In any case Sir Ivone Kirkpatrick has created more neo-Nazis in Germany in eight days than Naumann and Siepen have produced through the sweat of their brows over years.[9]

That the British measure was unjustified, or at least exaggerated, had in fact become more or less common knowledge in Germany after a few days. And yet, in the months before the operation, there had been many worrying symptoms, and many warnings and other statements from Wahnerheide. The source of British attention was by no mean limited to the increasing ventilation in "soldiers' circles" of the idea of "liberating" their "comrades" from the Werl prison,[10] the stir caused by the escape of the two war criminals, or the transparent "Christmas guarantor" propaganda. Kirkpatrick and his secret-service people were also concerned with a separate, more long-term problem: the nature of the direction being taken by members of the Nazi "brotherhood," which had disintegrated in 1951 because of internal quarrels, and by functionaries of the banned Socialist Reich Party—as well as by the right-wing parties and nationalistic movements that were especially popular in northern Germany. The British had repeatedly tried to sensitize their German interlocutors in politics and the Office of Constitutional Protection to such questions.[11] But toward the end of 1952, these efforts had become strained. In the middle of November, fed by British sources, an article in the Stockholm paper *Dagens Nyheter* called very concrete attention to Werner Naumann, to a group of 100 leading Nazis that Naumann dominated—and to the FDP, whose right wing was "well on its way to forming a new Harzburg Front." (The reference here was to the conclave of rightist nationalists, representing politics, the military, and heavy industry and including Hitler, that convened in Bad Harzburg in 1931 to oust Weimar democracy.) The Swedish corespondent did not stint on particulars: "The group's *Spiritus rector* is Landtag delegate Ernst

Achenbach (Düsseldorf). Working in his Office for a General Amnesty in Essen are the former Reich Commissioner in Denmark, Dr. Werner Best, and the former SS Obergruppenleiter Franz Alfred Six. In the realm of foreign policy, the Nazis reject the General Treaty and the European army, since they do not offer Germany sufficient national independence. They desire a reunited Germany with its own army—a Germany capable of exploiting the tensions between East and West for the sake of concessions from both sides. The hope is that all the neutralists and adherents of the 'third way' in Germany can be gathered around this watchword. Naumann and his associates reject anti-Semitism as an element of the coming politics, as this has shown itself to be a bad business."[12]

Two months before the British took action, the name Naumann was thus already familiar in the media, and week by week the indications had been increasing of highly dubious things going on in the environs of people who had first emerged from illegality in early 1950, after the amnesty law's passage. One of the most important such indications was the FDP national convention held in Bad Ems between 20 and 22 November 1952, marked by the effort to push through the highly nationalistic "German program," supported by the right-wing party branches of Hesse and Lower Saxony.[13] Because of the resistance of liberals from Southern Germany, Berlin, and Hamburg, the "program" failed to win out over the relatively moderate "liberal manifesto" and become binding policy. Nevertheless, Friedrich Middelhauve did emerge as acting party chairman and announced a "duty toward the right"; the goal, he explained, was to form a "third block," a "national collective movement" of all forces right of the CDU.

As if to firmly establish the seriousness of this intent, word was let out that Middelhauve—himself not politically incriminated—had chosen to make Wolfgang Diewerge his right hand man.[14] Diewerge had been a highly decorated Nazi Party functionary, an SS *Standartenführer,* and a leading propagandist in Goebbels's ministry.[15] In Middelhauve's circle, praise was now also being bestowed on the well-known Nazi radio commentator Hans Fritzsche[16]—and it had now become clear that the financial strength of Middelhauve's North Rhine–Westphalian party chapter was due not to normal members' contributions, but rather to substantial donations from Ruhr industrialists, in particular Hugo Stinnes Jr. The reaction of figures such as Countess Dönhoff[17] would certainly have been somewhat sharper if they had managed to already learn that two authors of the "German program"—Werner Best and Franz Alfred Six—worked out of the law office of the FDP's foreign affairs speaker, and that both Werner Naumann and Hans Fritzsche had offered their specialists' advice for the draft.[18] But at the time, only the Office of Constitutional Protection and German-based British intelligence had access to such information. With different degrees of success, both tried to interest their guiding political offices in the problem of subversion of the Free Democrats.[19]

On 3 December 1952, the British High Commissioner took the opportunity to engage Otto Lenz, state secretary in the Chancellery, in a detailed conversation about the situation in the FDP. In precise German, Kirkpatrick expressed his "extreme concern" about the party's "penetration" by "radical National Socialist circles." Lenz noted Kirkpatrick's intent to discuss the matter calmly with Adenauer at some point; he added that, "if need be," the British "see themselves forced to take measures and reveal certain connections that gravely implicate the FDP."[20]

Lenz of course immediately informed Adenauer of this overture. A few days later Adenauer informed FDP head Blücher. The latter had himself learned on 3 December, "through conversation," that the North Rhine–Westphalian Office of Constitutional Protection had also "filed a report."[21] Since then, there could be no more doubt concerning the seriousness of the matter; it was also clear that Adenauer—for some time deeply distrustful of any moves toward forming a "large party of the right," whether stemming from Middelhauve or from Hellwege's German Party—found it easier than Blücher to handle the explosive information.[22] He now made use of the freshly delivered arguments with grim satisfaction; to Lenz's consternation, he declared the following in the mid-December meeting of the CDU's directorship: "I've been—just so you see what circumstances we are living in—urgently requested by an external power to see to it that Naumann is arrested as soon as possible."[23] Still deeply annoyed at the humiliation inflicted by the recent unresolved termination of the third debate over the General Treaty, Adenauer added that while he had "no instrument" for such a step, "this is in fact the way the circumstances developing here are being viewed in well-meaning countries."[24]

Later, both Adenauer and Kirkpatrick would explain that they had discussed Naumann's circle on a number of occasions.[25] Even if the chancellor really did not know more at this point than what he was divulging, he at least suspected how alarmed the British were. It was thus only logical for him to broach the matter a few days later in the cabinet, although in that context he had to reckon with indiscretions.[26] It was clear that he was taking precautions, something already making sense on grounds of people other than himself obviously being informed by the British. In any case, two days before Christmas the

SPD's Parliamentary-Political Press Service issued an extended report concerning the "Naumann club." It named names (Scheel, Diewerge, former Düsseldorf *Gauleiter* Friedrich Karl Florian, former Reich student leader Albert Derichsweiler). And it reviewed the "only three" strategic alternatives that, it "seemed to be agreed," were facing the "former ones": "(1) to remain aside; (2) to join the various small clubs and political groups of markedly radical right-wing character; (3) to infiltrate the Union of Expellees and Victims of Injustice.[27]

This information did not reflect the latest developments: looking toward the 1953 Bundestag elections, Naumann's associates had opted for a variation of the third possibility, the FDP now serving as host party.[28] In other respects, the information was quite authentic; as would later become clear, it corresponded in many details with a secret fifty-page British report on the "*Gauleiter* circle." Despite its sweep and the effort to present a "plot"—it was certainly not justiciable in such terms—by pinning down a variety of personal connections, the study did not indulge in panic making. Its gist was this: considered as part of the wider West German political scene, "crypto-Nazism" still represented a "small force, about which it can hardly be said that it already represents a direct threat to the Basic Law's security. If, however, it were to continue developing within the larger right-wing parties and soldiers' organizations in a gradual and unchecked manner, then it could infect increasingly broader and more influential circles with an uncontrolled and uncompromising nationalism. Those supporting such a development are callous realists who, once in power, would not hesitate to move against the entire concept of European unity and Western defense, as long as they saw this as in their interests. The '*Gauleiter* circle' represents a plot against both letter and spirit of the Bonn treaties of 1952."[29]

While without this clarity, the problematic nature of Naumann's activities could also be thoroughly familiar to the politically savvy—at least those located along the Rhine and Ruhr. Shortly before the year's end, a "group of progressive members of the Free Democratic Party in the state of North Rhine–Westphalia" issued an anonymous circular; full of purposive optimism, it announced that the "bitterness against the 'clever men' from the Third Reich, with whom Herr Dr. Middelhauve and Herr Rechenberg have surrounded themselves almost 100 percent, is growing on all sides." The extent to which this "bitterness" actually stemmed from the party's own ranks and not from the British is hard to say. What is clear is the aim of the rhetorical questions with which this odd text confronted the party members: "Do you believe that in the coming Bundestag elections, the FDP will even be able to maintain its share of votes if these types, about whom all of Germany has been speaking with distaste since Ems, are not excluded from all responsible party positions before the next national convention? *Since 1950,* despite the appeal to come together, the North Rhine–Westphalian FDP has not been able to register any *meaningful* election gains!"[30] But it was not only objections bolstered with arguments about future election results that were making the rounds; there was also unhappiness regarding the lack of organizational transparency at the head of the state party chapter, and on 3 January 1953 some thirty representatives of different local chapters met in Cologne with Franz Blücher in order to raise their "serious concern about the influx of radical right-wing elements."[31]

In light of such details, the conclusion seems solid enough that before their strike against the Naumann group the British tried in various ways to move the Germans themselves to take action. It also corresponds to Sir Ivone Kirkpatrick's (certainly rather rough) account of the affair a few years later. Naumann's plan, he explained, had been to "worm his way into" the FDP, but not to play any political role himself at the start. "I saw one of the FDP leaders [Middelhauve] and warned him that if this process continued, I should have to act. My warning had no effect.... I did consider inviting the German government to arrest him, but I discarded the idea because Naumann had agents everywhere and there was a risk that he might be warned in time to destroy his documents.... If Naumann's attempt to enter politics had been an isolated phenomenon I might have taken a different view. But there had been disquieting signs of a resurgence of Nazism.... At the moment power to act resided in the High Commission, and if I failed to use it, we should never be in a position later to complain to an independent German government of tolerance towards a revival of Nazism."[32]

The only questionable aspect of this reminiscence involves knowing whether Kirkpatrick's indication that he had not asked the West Germans to arrest the Naumann group was simply tact. In any case, Adenauer's remarks before the CDU's directorship in mid-December 1952 indicated the contrary; they were, however, uttered in anger. But by the same token, what Adenauer told a group of English journalists four days after the arrests at least left open the possibility of such a previous request on Kirkpatrick's part: the Naumann circle had been observed from both sides for half a year. "Representatives of the Office for Protection of the Constitution and the Secret Service met regularly and exchanged their findings. Even very recently, they shared the view that there was no possibility of taking action. Sir Ivone spoke to me about the Naumann circle two or three times and certainly explained that he considered the matter very important. But he did not offer me any facts that would have furnished the possibility of German officials taking action."[33]

One factor in particular demonstrated the actual negligence—indeed the indifference—of portions of the government, particularly the smaller governing parties, in face of the Nazi potential—and how justified Kirkpatrick's action was from this perspective. This was the political-journalistic commotion breaking out as soon as the first shock was over: a commotion centered on a German "sovereignty" understood as gravely injured by the "intervening of the occupation authorities," albeit such sovereignty actually had a way to go before coming into effect.[34]

The critics spoke up before the English could have had a chance to even sort the confiscated documents, which had been taken away by the truckload.[35] The title, for instance, of the *Frankfurter Allgemeine*'s report over the first reactions from Bonn was "No German Agreement to the Arrests."[36] Very much within his authority as the official responsible for overseeing the Office of Constitutional Protection, Interior Minister Lehr had formed a firm opinion within twenty-four hours: The morning after the arrests he still viewed them as "undertaken properly, since corresponding material is available."[37] He now declared that from the German perspective there had been "no need" for action and that it had been taken despite "the British and German officials doubtless having the same material at their disposal."[38] CDU delegate Gerhard Schröder—nine months later, he would be Lehr's successor—allowed himself to be cited speculating on "a preventive action, only possible under occupation law"—an action that "will no longer be possible after the treaty on Germany takes effect." The "incident," he observed, was thus a demonstration of the necessity of quickly ratifying the treaty.

In line with such a response, the FDP, German Party, and Union of Expellees alliance expressed ample "regret" that Kirkpatrick had identified them as desired objects for Nazi takeover. After all, no party was "responsible for a small circle's plans"; on the weekend of 17–18 January, this sentiment intensified into open rejection of the British action.[39] In his Sunday address, Justice Minister Dehler played the wounded one. That "non-German secret services" would initiate "undertakings" in Germany "that actually should be the prerogative of the Germans" showed no great trust in the Federal Republic. German Party chief Hellwege declared that eight years after the war, "the question of whether neofascist infiltration has occurred has to be clarified by the German *Volk* itself." For his part, with the precarious situation of his FDP laid out before him, Vice Chancellor Blücher was less earnestly indignant in his protests; he was content to call for a speedy review of the evidence, adding that it was "regrettable that such a measure had been taken one-sidedly by an occupying power." Whatever "one-sidedly" was meant to indicate, the matter was understandably unpleasant for all three men.

The chancellor himself was not especially amused by the whole affair; true annoyance set in only with the suspicion that some parties in the American High Commission wished to align themselves with the British action for the sake of influencing public opinion, either to sabotage the treaties with the West or, more probably, to prepare the way for a CDU-SPD coalition through a compromising of the right-wing parties.[40] The source for such suspicions was the latest edition of a regular High Commission opinion poll, completed a few days after the Naumann operation had been completed. Its results then ended up with Drew Middleton, who reported on it at length in the *New York Times.* For a long time now, Middleton had been wholeheartedly disliked in Bonn on account of his critical articles; here again he did full honors to his reputation as an Argus-eyed follower of every neo-Nazi move. Among the mass of data in the eighty-page "Year-End Survey of Rightist and Nationalist Sentiments in West Germany," he laid particular stress on indications of a rise in "pro-Nazi orientations" among eighteen- to twenty-year-olds and FDP members.[41] He placed such findings in the context of reports suggesting that Middelhauve, Achenbach, and a number of other right-wing Free Democrats had had contact with Naumann and other men who were now in prison.[42] The poll also formed the basis for Middleton's report that a majority of Germans believed that Nazism had brought a great deal of good (the poll itself spoke more accurately of a "preponderance" of Germans). In December 1952, 44 percent saw "more good" attached to the recent past; 39 percent more bad." Middleton found it especially vexing that only a fourth of the polled Germans were ready to declare they would do "everything" to prevent the restoration of Nazism.

It is clear that such statistics were in need of interpretation; they were certainly far less sensational than seemed the case in light of recent events. The pollsters—not only American ones—had been coming up with similar numbers for years. Nonetheless, this study—one of 300 such studies originating since 1946 in the offices of the "Reactions Analysis Staff"—had an impact similar to the disclosure of state secrets on many people in Bonn.[43] Headlines the Germans had been hoping for years would never be seen again were now circulating in the international press, and as is often the case in journalistic writing, the degree of precision and sobriety was not especially high. More than a few journalists harbored strong suspicion of German motives; those so inclined interpreted the conjunction between the arrest of newly active Nazis and persistent—indeed apparently rising—esteem for the Third Reich as proof that Western integration and rearmament were disastrous ideas.

Adenauer, who for months had been worried about the fate of the treaties with the West, immediately recognized the potentially explosive nature of the material. On the evening of 19 January 1953 (i.e., four days after the arrests), he spoke up on the radio. This was before he could have access to a more or less full survey of the international press's reaction to the High Commission survey, a reaction that, at least in the American case, would turn out to be relatively moderate.[44] By now, sensing a "plot against Germany and the government," Otto Lenz had furnished the chancellor with such a sharp text that he found it wise to modify much of it.[45] It remained clear enough: the "actually very artificially played up commentaries and hasty conclusions" resulting from the events of recent days stood in contrast to West Germany's political reality. "Ever since this government took office, domestic peace in Germany has been consolidated; and if you, my listeners, think of the domestic turmoil after the First World War, then you will understand how much more stable the Federal Republic's inner political situation is." The Germans, he confirmed, had developed a "healthy skepticism regarding strong slogans from the right and left"; their votes had already made repeatedly clear what they thought about radicalism. He thus would venture on a prediction: "In the coming elections, as well, any party sympathizing in any way with National Socialism, should it in fact come forward, will suffer a complete defeat. In his original version—the basis for the report on the speech in the *Frankfurter Allgemeine*—Otto Lenz had written that it was only necessary "to pose the question of who gained from the campaign to evaluate it correctly." Adenauer, on the other hand, limited himself to a somewhat oracular remark: "I cannot avoid the impression that enemies of European unification and a common defense, who recently found themselves forced to keep silent, have now seized the occasion to check or even destroy this unification, for which the government has worked with all its strength from the start."[46]

On 21 January, date of the first scheduled session of the new year, Adenauer—who was being pressed by the coalition's faction leaders[47]—also made a statement before the Bundestag.[48] Once more, he did not limit his remarks to the arrest of the Naumann group but also confronted the "announcement from the American side," in fact placing his critique of the opinion survey at center stage. As if he were an empirical social researcher by profession, he first found fault with the word choice of the question the surveyed Germans were faced with[49] ("hardly suitable for giving a true picture"), before going on to pick holes in the data's evaluation. "The results of the last opinion survey of December 1952 were the same as the various surveys undertaken by the same authority since September 1951. The percentage of those finding more good in National Socialism was only lower in May 1951. Now in the published report, this low percentage of May 1951 is juxtaposed with the last questionnaire of December 1952, with no consideration of the intervening questionnaire, thus creating the impression of a sudden rise in National Socialist sentiments." The chancellor had been extremely well prepared, probably by Erich Peter Neumann, head of the Allensbacher Institute, whom Lenz had by now elected chief public opinion adviser for the government.[50] Adenauer now presented the group of High Commission public opinion experts with a citation from one of their earlier reports. Here they had indicated that the answer to the question about Nazism's good and bad sides did not reflect a wish to see the "Third Reich" rise again, but simply a "failure to have understood the way the advantages and disadvantages of Nazism were bound up with each other."

Regarding the arrests, Adenauer limited himself to citing the British foreign minister, whose declaration in the House of Commons, he explained, had confirmed his own position.[51] "The activities of a small minority of incorrigible former National Socialists poses no direct danger for the democratic order in Germany." Any additional points would have to be clarified after the investigation's conclusion. But the "citizens of the Federal Republic and everyone abroad" could be sure "that Germany will never return to National Socialism."

During this period, it became increasingly clear that the chancellor harbored more mistrust for the High Commission—apparently rudderless after the resignation of Walter Donnelly, and suspected of Social Democratic sympathies—than for the British.[52] The acting American High Commissioner, Samuel Reber, was furnished with a typed version of Adenauer's sharp remarks on the survey.[53] Kirkpatrick was spared any criticism of the arrests. On 20 January in the cabinet, Adenauer explained that it would simply be necessary to wait for the results of the investigation of Naumann and consorts—which might even clear up the question of possible "relations with the East." In his diary, Lenz further cited Adenauer to the effect that "in any event," the people involved were "old Nazis"; fighting with the occupation authorities for their sake was not in order.[54] Minister of transportation Seebohm likewise noted that "a big commotion is presently uncalled for,"[55] and Lenz, again, registered the fact that Adenauer considered Sir Ivone "a very decent man," whom he believed as little capable as Eden "of wishing to press us into a great coalition."[56]

The guiding spirit behind these remarks—stressing, as they did, the presence or absence of underlying motives—was Vice Chancellor Blücher. Personally above any suspicion, he had every reason to encourage diversions in his role as FDP chief. In general, such remarks showed how little readiness there was in the government to even contemplate the possible political threat of right-wing radicalism. Most cabinet members simply did not wish to believe that the Naumann circle could ever achieve anything—and taken on its own terms, the cabinet members' faith in their own strength, and in the growing strength of the young democracy, was by no means a bad sign. It was only that the ostentatious self-certainty displayed by many political prominents was combined with a sensitivity calling the same certainty into question. The man responsible for inner security, Robert Lehr, offered a good example of this process, declaring at every available opportunity that the government's repute had suffered greatly, "a step on the part of the Allies" thus being urgently needed. Lehr could not be brought around from his idea that "the English measures" had "a political background." He demanded, as it were, satisfaction.[57] But as Adenauer's state secretary observed, the chancellor had only a "very" ironic smile as his response, explaining that "he did not feel himself diminished in reputation. Besides, in a long-term sense he in fact found the plan dangerous enough."[58]

A meeting with Kirkpatrick a few hours later would strengthen his sense of things. The High Commissioner informed the chancellor of "indeed highly incriminating material"—a qualification that Otto John confirmed shortly after.[59] Now less reticent in the company of Otto Lenz, Adenauer explained that he was "not very annoyed at all by the matter, since it involved a discrediting of National Socialist aspirations for all time. The FDP and the German Party will also have to be more careful now."[60] Two days later, before the CDU's directorship, the chancellor was even more straightforward, declaring that if he were a German judge, he would have Naumann "condemned for high treason" on the basis of the documents the British had discovered on him.

Basically Adenauer was very pleased that Kirkpatrick had struck the blow rather than leaving things to the Germans. While seeing the matter with complete sobriety, he did allow himself a dash of election spirits: "I believe this action will really contribute to the suppression of these radical right-wing elements—they would have in any case constituted a certain danger for the FDP in the new Bundestag, and to a lesser extent for the German Party.... Once the Federal Republic has another four years behind it, then I believe that the rudiments of the National Socialist period will be so shriveled that we will have nothing more to fear. Hence this Naumann case promises to also be an action of great inner-political significance for the future."[61]

It would be a long time before the affected parties—especially the Free Democrats—would come to similar conclusions. For the time being, there was recourse to denials, as in the declaration of acting national chairman Friedrich Middelhauve to the press that "there is no relation between the Free Democratic Party and the seven arrested men.[62] With an audacity outdone only by a simultaneous hypocrisy, Middelhauve demanded a "thorough clarification" of what had transpired—events that had "sorely troubled the legal feelings of the German citizen....It fills me with great concern that there has been interference with the legal sphere of a state which the occupying power wished to see at ease with democracy." Regardless of the "incidents," he continued, his party still had "the courage to accept forces from yesterday into its ranks if they are ready for democracy, in order to prevent a strengthening of oppositional circles." But there was "absolutely no danger" of his party being infiltrated. And with the same effrontery, Middelhauve revealed that the British authorities had refused Naumann's lawyer permission to visit him at the Werl prison. The lawyer's name: Ernst Achenbach.

Achenbach had demanded to see his client (and the High Commissioner) a few short hours following the arrests.[63] At that time, he could not yet have been sure that Naumann had been rather careless, both in his telephone calls and elsewhere. "Super-clever Herr Naumann" (Adenauer) had derived great pleasure from urging conspiratorial practices upon his various interlocutors; nevertheless it apparently had never occurred to him that not keeping a day-by-day account of his "reconstruction work" might have been even more clever. But since in Naumann's case intelligence and narcissism were not mutually exclusive, first the British, then the chancellor and the FDP leadership, and finally the German public could read what Goebbels's former state secretary had written on 26 August 1950 concerning the visit of former Ribbentrop-diplomat Achenbach, known to him "from earlier on." The views of the two gentlemen harmonized quickly. "A *Volk* in this situation, without national sovereignty, ruled by High Commissioners, needs Stresemanns."[64] For this reason, Adenauer was "not the worst solution at present." But Achenbach was already thinking ahead, and Naumann noted, "In order to nevertheless enable the N[ational] S[ocialists] to exert an influence on political events under these circumstances, they should enroll in the FDP, infiltrate it, and take over its leadership. With the help of individual examples he explains how easy this would be. With only 200 members, we could inherit the entire state directorship. He wants to engage me as general secretary or something similar! He is so serious about his offer that in the end he means either we accept and support him or he withdraws from politics." Naumann's objection that possibly the "high party leadership" was not as wholeheartedly interested in his collaboration as the Free Democrat's foreign policy speaker led to invective by Achenbach concerning Franz Blücher. Its culmination: "an impossible man, whose sound judgment he doubts."[65]

In view of such citations—making the rounds of the German press in the summer of 1953—it was not surprising that the FDP's directorship tended to assign Achenbach the role of chief guilty party. Meanwhile, Middelhauve's position had started to totter, and not only Blücher would have liked to have seen him fall. Focusing on Achenbach thus also had the advantage of Middelhauve being able to stay, without a public impression setting in that the Free Democrats had drawn no consequences from the Naumann scandal.[66] It remained the case that as the Bundestag elections approached, anyone looking more closely could already see that Middelhauve and his allies in the Rhine-Ruhr region were not willing to have ash strewn on their heads—either by themselves or by others. At the end of April, the national directorship ordered Achenbach to step down as head of the FDP's Committee on Foreign Policy.[67] In contrast, the party expulsion demanded by Dehler (as chairman of a three-man internal investigative committee) did not take place.[68] Instead, against Blücher's bitter resistance,[69] Middelhauve even managed to have Achenbach made eligible to run for the Bundestag in the Essen region. But as he lacked a fixed place on the list, the Landtag delegate would have to wait until 1957 for a Bundestag mandate. In the end, the entire "purging operation" in the FDP's headquarters in Düsseldorf only took in Middelhauve's secretary, Diewerge; the editor of the right-wing nationalist *Deutsche Zukunft* ("German Future"), Carl Albert Drewitz; and Walter Brand, Middelhauve's specialist in communal policies as well as in matters regarding both expellees and officials. All the other former high Hitler Youth and SS leaders doing business there, along with the former Nazi *Kreisleiter*, "*Gau*-judges," and "Reich orators" could stay.[70]

The easy escape of Naumann's partners and protectors in the North Rhine–Westphalian FDP formed a contrast with the fate of their liaison group in the region's German Party chapter, dismissed peremptorily by Hellwege in February 1953.[71] The escape was linked to the favorable turn things had taken for the seven imprisoned men over recent months, a development owing much to Friedrich Grimm's decision to engage himself alongside Achenbach in Naumann's defense. As already in the case of the war criminals, Grimm saw the situation as comparable to the

1923 *Ruhrkampf,* when he had attempted to tear "German men" from the claws of an occupying power.[72]

As a lawyer held in highest esteem by the political right, Grimm received considerable support from the Interior and Justice Ministries. This allowed him and his colleagues responsible for the other cases to set habeas corpus proceedings into play after less than three weeks.[73] Their basis was the fact that the arrests had been carried out without a judge's order and that the accused men had then seen neither a judge nor a bill of indictment. Grimm's strategy was aimed at causing the downfall of the principle of "prime authority" invoked by Kirkpatrick; this was grounded in occupation law, inter alia, but was limited there to situations threatening the occupation authorities. Grimm first received welcome help from Dehler, always ready for a struggle over legal principles. The justice minister not only ordered an international-legal assessment in Göttingen[74] but also raised public objections to Kirkpatrick's sense of law. It could not be the case, he declared, "that all of us stand under the threat of being arrested without a right to constitutional procedure."[75] And on 27 February 1953, while Grimm was pleading before the British superior court in Bielefeld, Dehler even managed to get the cabinet to determine, in Adenauer's absence, that he had issued the declaration in his "official capacity."[76]

But all the pressure coming from Bonn—it was now also being exerted by Carlo Schmid in the SPD's name—and all the efforts of Naumann's defense team—which now included the former lawyer for top English fascist Oswald Mosley—could not prevent the same superior court from throwing out the release petitions and confirming Kirkpatrick's position on 18 March.[77] Meanwhile, however, critics in the United Kingdom had themselves spoken out—their strong doubts centered on the wisdom of Kirkpatrick's decision to treat Naumann and associates for weeks as something like personal prisoners. As a result of the protests, there was increasing sympathy in both London and Wahnerheide for the idea of resolving the problem by handing the prisoners over to the Germans.[78] A contributing factor here was doubtless Kirkpatrick's impression, resulting from a conversation with Adenauer on 2 March 1953, that the chancellor was determined to bring the delinquents before a German court, at least on conspiracy charges.[79]

Ten days later, the two men finally reached an agreement. Knowing from Kirkpatrick that the matter would be decided in the British cabinet, Adenauer furnished the High Commissioner with a well-polished letter proposing that "the investigation and possible prosecution of Naumann and comrades be turned over to the German authorities, [that] the documents be handed over to [Adenauer] for this purpose, and [that] the arrested men be placed at the disposition of the authorized German authorities."[80] In other words, the chancellor himself would decide who would be granted access to the thirty cases of documentary evidence still sitting in London—not, for example, the interior minister, against whose bureau the British harbored justifiable mistrust.[81] And for the time, those awaiting trial would remain in Werl, which along with being a regular prison was in fact already under German administration. Four days later, Kirkpatrick's agreement (under precisely the conditions the chancellor had formulated) lay on the table.[82] In the cabinet, Adenauer declared this to be a "not inessential success." He was careful to stress that Naumann and his accomplices had received money from "French and English nationalists" and "actually had the intention of seizing power in 1957."[83] For over recent weeks, not only Dehler but other government members as well had been expressing rather skeptical views (sometimes internally, sometimes to the public) about the chances of getting the better of the arrested men through the courts. One time Lehr had complained that the available material indicated only a "small conspiracy"; another time Hellwege had criticized the arrested men having to wear "institutional clothing." And there were repeated, occasionally "bitter" debates of principle focused on the justice and justification of the arrests.[84]

In all these discussions, Adenauer defended the British and enjoined his ministers to show restraint. In the process, he regularly reproached the Free Democrats (as Lenz saw it, somewhat exaggeratedly) on account of Ernst Achenbach, whom he had "made a note of" because of his nationalistic critique of the treaties with the West.[85] But also Hellwege found himself warned in a regular cabinet session "to be careful in his statements."[86] In his own special way, Justice Minister Dehler underscored the soundness of Adenauer's judgment. After seeing the British evidence against Naumann, this doubter emerged enlightened, shifted to the chancellor's course, and pleaded emphatically from then on for a condemnation of the entire group. This had little to do with *raison d'état*,[87] very much to do with reason of party. Dehler was in fact horrified by the inroads already made by the Nazis within the FDP.[88]

The hearings by German prosecutors in Werl began on 20 March 1953, three days following Kirkpatrick's letter to Adenauer. On 28 March, the chief public prosecutor issued an arrest warrant against the Naumann group. The corresponding request to open a judicial investigation involved charges of having formed an "anticonstitutional organization," as well as conspiracy (paragraphs 90a and 128 of the Penal Code). According to the prosecutors, both the Hamburg and Düsseldorf circles had the goal of "preserving and developing" Nazi ideas and had

attempted "to gain influence in political parties and other political organizations through 'infiltration,' thus preparing the reestablishment of
National Socialist rule."[89] Following approval of the request by the
investigating judge in the Federal High Court, the accused men were
moved from Werl to Karlsruhe at the start of April. From now on, the
investigation would unfold at a deliberate pace.

Supported by his access (apparently arranged by Adenauer) to the
inculpatory evidence collected by the British, Dehler was now preparing the groundwork for his party-internal investigative report. He was
increasingly consternated at the threat posed by the Naumann group
and the "broadly ramified effects of this conspiracy" within the FDP.[90]
At the same time, the investigating judges were already considering
which arrest warrants could be canceled. Two months following the
start of the investigation, those familiar with the material considered it
highly doubtful that a trial would ever take place. Achenbach had now
withdrawn from Naumann's defense team and had placed himself at the
investigation's disposal (possibly on the same tactical grounds that
would lead him to offer himself as a spy within the Naumann circle to
Otto John[91]). Naturally, his gesture was accompanied by a denial of all
the incriminating passages in the infiltration offer noted by Naumann.[92]

Above all Adenauer and Dehler were alarmed at the increasingly
concrete possibility that at the next remand review Naumann could be
released. At the end of May 1953, Dehler openly indicated in the cabinet that the Federal High Court proceedings were being impaired by
"inadequate experience and limited fitness of the responsible criminal
panel."[93] At the start of June, the chancellor learned through the Office
for Protection of the Constitution that in Karlsruhe the evidence was
considered "insufficient" and the arrest warrants would indeed be canceled.[94] In the presence of his ministers, Adenauer expressed "consternation" at the report and announced his intention to summon chief
prosecutor Carl Wiechmann to Bonn.[95] At the same time, Dehler sent a
personal letter to Hermann Weinkauff, president of the Federal High
Court. Weinkauff's long answer basically amounted to a polite "sorry."[96]
By way of introduction, he explained that after having read the list of
charges, he himself had "no doubt that here was a first dangerous, clever,
and calculated effort to prepare a return of National Socialism." The
specifications of the Penal Code's paragraph 90a were thus "clearly fulfilled," and he would "impose the highest sentence on anyone engaged
in such activities with the best conscience in the world." But this was
nothing other than heavily applied gratuitous courage, meant to somewhat soften the fact that Weinkauff's own view of things was bleak—
and that he had no intention whatsoever to rock the boat through per-

sonal intervention. True, he did claim credit for having convinced the investigating judges not to send the miscreants home—this in "private conversation," through stress on the "extraordinarily heavy responsibility" accompanying the case and its "extraordinary explosiveness" in regard to foreign policy. But, he added, he did not and could not know how the responsible panel would proceed. "No sort of private conversation about this matter is possible with the panel members. The panel president, who is an old friend of mine, let it slip into a conversation with the state prosecutor that until then I had not said anything to him about this matter and certainly would not do so. Among the Federal High Court judges, an extreme touchiness prevails regarding judicial independence. That is, to be sure, no sign of true inner strength; I must, however, take it into account and respect it."

The "touchiness" of the judges was no accident. Whoever had been obliged to pay heed to the intrusive "judges' letters" as little as eight years before—including Weinkauff, former State Court director at the Reich Court—now had to keep anything smacking of political cooption far away from his person. And that person's democratic consciousness could meanwhile have become so firm that he—like Weinkauff—could unhesitatingly write, "until now there has been no interpretation of paragraph 90a of the Penal Code." Naturally this referred not least of all to a certain reluctance to be reminded of the murderously broad interpretation of the regulations concerning high treason and state security typical of the Third Reich. Weinkauff indicated this with the statement that there was evidently a "certain tendency, understandable in itself, to interpret it narrowly. A certain inclination to fall back onto a difference between the matter's legal and political significance seems likewise present, although in my view this matter is also clear-cut in a criminal-legal context. Likewise, there is a certain shyness [*Scheu*] about getting involved in political things in general, and a certain misunderstanding regarding one's own capacity to judge them properly." In the light of the court's judgments regarding communists, its "shyness" unmistakably was connected to a persistent right-eye weakness. Be that as it may, Weinkauff offered the observation that if Dehler wished to avoid such feelings prevailing in the Naumann case, he needed to see to it that the prosecutors proceeded "with the utmost vigor and utmost care." The Federal High Court president had now managed to pass on the dirty work—and to do so in a rather unceremonious fashion.

In any event, over recent weeks the prosecutors had proceeded in a manner leaving themselves open to quite easy attack. Instead of concentrating on the large amounts of incriminating evidence that had been filed, they spent considerable time interrogating the prisoners, who naturally used the opportunity to demonstrate their political harmless-ness.[97] Pleas such as the Düsseldorf and Hamburg meetings having involved simple "get-togethers" of buddies or of a "loose circle of acquaintances" had already made their way onto the provisional charge list, and things were continuing on the same level.[98]

Chief Prosecutor's Wiechmann's visit to the chancellor on 8 June 1953 confirmed the dubious reputation that had started to cling to his troop. As Otto Lenz would hear the next day, Adenauer now learned that, measured against the cleverness of someone like Naumann, the capacities of the "expert" assigned to the case were "completely inad-equate": the man had not even known "what a cover organization was."[99] It may be doubted that Wiechmann would have spoken of a sub-ordinate in just this way, but the chancellor was simply outraged. His indignation may have increased a little later, upon learning of the impression that Wiechmann would then leave with the British. They were obviously eager to learn how things stood with the Naumann case—and found their worst suspicions confirmed. Wiechmann spoke nebulously about "gaps in the evidence" and expressed "doubt" about whether the matter could be pressed forward "with a prospect of suc-cess." Kirkpatrick then delivered a message of complaint to the chan-cellor. "He could not understand how in a political case with such extraordinary significance, it was meant to be impossible for a high judi-cial official to study the material with the necessary thoroughness. He himself had dedicated entire days to the affair." Walter Hallstein took the message; in his response to Kirkpatrick's aide, he could at least invoke the conversation between Adenauer and the chief prosecutor; the chancellor, he indicated, had requested a "thorough and energetic handling" of the case. He had done so "very emphatically," and with an "exhaustive description" of both the case and its political impact. Hall-stein ended by trying to soothe his interlocutor, indicating that a new remand review was only scheduled for August.[100]

In reality, there was no cause to feel soothed. Barely two weeks later a fresh fiasco underscored the fragility of Bonn's entire political struc-ture four years after the republic's founding, at least when viewed by a critical observer from the outside. The justice minister now informed the cabinet of a "grave violation of trust" he had learned of through state prosecutor Max Güde. The latter had been approached by one of Nau-mann's defense lawyers in regard to Adenauer's and Dehler's expres-sion of "disappointment" in the cabinet about the chief prosecutor's lack of "complaisance."[101]

For Naumann's defense team, such undeniable signs of government pressure on the Karlsruhe court to finally begin Naumann's trial, a good two months before the Bundestag elections, was of course worth gold. This was all the more so since the evidence was mounting of activity undertaken by interested parties to make the Naumann group's guilt clearer than previously demonstrated to the public. The *Frankfurter Rundschau* was passed key evidentiary documents that would form the basis for its five-part series "The Grave Diggers Are Among Us," published in the second week of June 1953, and on 9 June 1953 the Northwest German Radio could offer a special broadcast itself based on authentic material.[102] A few days later the daily papers reported that photocopies of documents from the Naumann case were being offered for cash in Düsseldorf.[103]

It is certainly conceivable that the documents were distributed from German quarters—perhaps by Free Democrats like Blücher and Dehler, who felt themselves to be in a bad position within the party.[104] But what became known about Dehler from some of the documents speaks against this theory. Shortly before the arrests, he intended, at Achenbach's bidding, to receive Naumann in his office. Dehler did not dispute Achenbach's offer, but insisted that days before the British action he had already turned it down.[105] It thus seems most probable that the British were doing the disseminating.[106] This is spoken for by the fact that much of the published material was transcripts of Naumann's bugged telephone calls, material that could not be used by German courts but which documented the conspiratorial nature of the Naumann circle in an especially forceful way. Whoever was responsible for the attention-grabbing publications, to the extent that they stemmed from the fragile phalanx of individuals backing a trial, were doing their own cause no good. For not only Naumann's defense attorneys now had welcome cause for indignation; the investigating judge, Scharpenseel, himself felt aggrieved, protesting to his superior, Weinkauff, as well to Dehler. Scharpenseel not only complained about the latest publications but also—another bad omen—took the opportunity to denounce the earlier "statements of different agencies and circles" as "not exactly helpful."[107]

Six weeks later, on 28 July 1953, this phase of the judicial affair was completed. In a remand review arranged earlier than expected, the Second Post Term Criminal Panel of the Federal High Court released Naumann without having to post a bond (it had been offered by his life companion, the owner of the import-export firm he managed). As the three judges explained, at that stage of the investigation there was no longer a pressing suspicion that a "punishable association or union" had existed.[108] A few hours later, Friedrich Karl Bornemann's arrest warrant was also canceled. He was the last member of the Naumann group to have turned himself in to the German authorities, following the freeing, in April already, of some of those originally arrested by the British.

For the West German government, but above all for Adenauer and the FDP's national leadership, the decision of the Karlsruhe judges came as a hard blow. As little as the chancellor or justice minister could actually allow themselves public criticism (thus evoking their premature condemnations of the accused men), they were not willing to forgo all scolding of the judges. "Now as before, I am firmly convinced of Naumann's guilt," declared Adenauer to a correspondent, adding that the democratic parties reacted with "bitterness" to the releases.[109] Dehler merely publicly murmured, "it's horrible."[110] In background conversations, he was more detailed: The judges' decision was "completely incomprehensible," the High Court president himself making no bones about his own disapproval. Under the seal of confidentiality, Dehler now revealed what Weinkauff had already intimated in his June letter: In the future it would be necessary to "make another selection" in appointments to court panels responsible for matters with strongly political implications.[111]

While German public reaction was rather restrained, the response of the foreign press to Naumann's release was predictably critical. Even Basel's reflective *Nationalzeitung* spoke of a *coup de main* (the actual term was *Husarenstück*), and London's *Daily Telegraph* felt itself reminded by the "odd" events in Karlsruhe of "how following the Great War, once time was ripe, a latent aggressive nationalism, in all its fury, saw the light of day."[112]

But the inaccuracy of such remarks did not lie only in the obligatory pessimism they expressed, a stance the newspaper itself seemed to sense would not be substantiated by the pending elections. They also underestimated the enduring impact of the unexpected intervention of the British—who were now refraining from any comments.[113] Namely, starting the spring of 1953, Naumann and his supporters were stigmatized in a manner unheard of until then. While consistently undertaken with a view to foreign opinion, both the previous year's banning of the SRP and efforts to establish past-political norms such as the affairs of Hedler and Remer superficially involved Bonn's initiative alone. In the Naumann case, the latent threat of Allied intervention led to the German government's mobilization. And the most sobering aspect of this development, from the vantage point of directly affected persons like all the former "party comrades" now nurturing their antidemocratic longings, was that the West German government had in the end made common cause with the occupation authorities. Presumably, the fact that this collaboration was not smooth and did not lack differences of opinion actually strengthened its powers of political persuasion. In other words, little room had been left here for notions of a "puppet government." From this perspective, even the Federal High Court decision had a positive aspect, since it clearly demonstrated the independence of the judiciary and seriousness of the principle of democratic separation of powers to the skeptics.

Shortly after his release from jail and under careful observation from the Office of Constitutional Protection,[114] Werner Naumann placed himself at the disposal of the radical right-wing German Reich Party as one of its top candidates. (His colleagues were the retired colonel Hans-Ulrich Rudel, living in Argentina, and the Nazi crown poet Hans Grimm.) Naumann himself would now learn that politics and dispensing justice were separate matters with separate rules. Naumann intended to also run directly in the Diepholz electoral district, until then an SRP citadel. But news of his intention caused a furor,[115] and shortly after the Hamburg senate reacted with a ban on speeches by the candidate, backing it up with a temporary detention.[116] A week later, the North Rhine–Westphalian interior minister, Franz Meyers Naumann, issued a denazification ruling that classified Naumann as "incriminated" (category 2). This meant the end of both active and passive election rights and the end of his candidacy.[117] A hastily issued directive by Kirkpatrick made this massive administrative blow possible; the directive allowed the governments of the Länder to classify people in categories 1 and 2—something previously reserved for the British.[118] In order to avoid new fiascoes, Meyers expressed the "view" to the press that the election officers in the French and American zones respected the classification.[119] The man the radically liberal *Gegenwart* christened "the lion of Diepholz" had roared his last.[120]

In the Bundestag elections of 6 September 1953, Adenauer triumphed, and the radical right suffered a humiliating defeat; the German Rightist Party did not even manage 300,000 votes (or 1.1 percent of the total). In the wake of this development, memory of the Naumann affair had almost faded when, on 3 December 1954, the Sixth Criminal Panel of the Federal High Court finally issued its decision not to open proceedings against Naumann and Bornemann (the chief prosecutor himself had dismissed charges against the others); the entire group was likewise declared "discharged from prosecution." According to the judges, the intention to "reestablish a National Socialist Führer state" was "nowhere clearly expressed" in the talks and statements of the accused men; occasionally, they explained, there was even a word of criticism of individual measures taken by the "Third Reich." And at the same time, the "association" had not even begun to exert "political effect

in the public realm." Although, the court observed, "extreme nationalist" views could hardly be doubted on the part of all the group's members, "they can still not be designated together as former National Socialists, without distinctions." As no suspicion remain in four of the cases,
the court costs and "necessary expenses" were to be covered by the
state.[121] Since Naumann had not been treated so generously, he eventually sued the government for damages but lost the case on appeal at
the end of 1957.[122]

On a federal level, the question of the reorganizational potential of
the former Nazis—a question posed spectacularly by the Naumann
affair—was answered negatively in the second Bundestag elections.
From now on, an independent political representation of such forces,
waning in any case because of the nation's economic success, was
hardly to be feared. Within the right-of-center parties, things were more
complicated; as demonstrated by the fall of the Arnold government in
North Rhine Westphalia and the splitting apart of the FDP's parliamentary faction in 1956,[123] that party's most severe test had only been put
on hold. But what forced that test three years after the Naumann affair
was a quarrel about the party's national profile and policies regarding
Germany: a quarrel receiving important but by no means sole impetus
from Middelhauve's "young Turks," with many of the earlier issues significantly modified and in any case not reducible to the question of Nazi
infiltration.[124] The Nazi problem was solved rather more drastically in
Hellwege's German Party. Like the FDP, the party had to accept some
losses in the second Bundestag elections; now exposed (as was the surprisingly successful All German Block Union of Expellees and Victims
of Injustice) to the Union parties' vortex, they would practically suc-
cumb to that vortex in the third Bundestag elections of 1961.[125]

Looking beyond the power fantasies, destroyed by the British, of a
relatively small group of politically ambitious Nazi functionaries, we
can understand the Naumann affair's deeper, enduring meaning in relation to Germany's traditional "national camp"—as a final parting with
all hopes for a strong political force to the right of the Union. In the fall
of 1953, following the impressive victory of the newly founded, inter-
confessional CDU-CSU, the ground had been removed from under all
efforts at reorganizing the traditional right with inclusion of the Nazi
movement's remaining forces. In the important pre-1950 phase of political rebuilding, the Allied insistence on licensing parties had checked
such efforts. Adenauer's victory confirmed not only his moderate economic and social-political conservatism, but also—what in this context
is decisive—his foreign policy, pointedly nonnationalistic and oriented
toward Western Europe.

Perhaps quite a few people began to understand this connection after the elections. But at the time of the actual confrontation with the Naumann circle and the North Rhine–Westphalian FDP's Nazi infiltration, no leading politician had formulated it more clearly than Adenauer: "I have always said to myself: for our party-political and thus our general German development, it is a great advantage that until now we have not had any strong nationalist party. Think back to Weimar. The German nationalists emerged there and formed a sump for all those who were more or less undemocratic. In saying this I do not want to offend any former nationalists who have joined our ranks. Our great advantage is that we ... have not acquired any major German nationalist party."[126]

By the start of the second legislative period, the new West German state's efforts at past-political integration had essentially been completed (the delayed second amnesty law would follow within a year). But past-political boundaries had also been established—albeit for the time being their locus was far to the right. The Allies had contributed substantially to this process, to be sure never so spectacularly as did the British in January 1953. Looking back on that action, two main figures in its unfolding described it as salutary, and it is interesting to see how similar their judgments were. As Kirkpatrick saw things, "One result of Naumann's incarceration during the summer was to deprive him and his friends of the opportunity of intervening effectively in the autumn general election."[127] And in Adenauer's typically succinct formulation, replying to enthusiastic election congratulations from his Connecticut-based friends Hettie and Dannie Heineman, "I'm especially pleased that the disappearance of the right-wing and left-wing radical parties shows the outside world that Germany is no longer politically threatened.[128]

To a growing degree, satisfaction with West Germany's development, indeed admiration for the chancellor and his policies, had come to characterize the Allies' feelings, particularly those of the Americans. Increasing confidence was also manifest in the foreign media—it was robust enough to cope, as it were, with the neo-Nazi activities and personal-political scandals of the second half of the fifties, especially the West German courts' willful ignorance when it came to prosecuting Nazi crimes.[129] At the end of 1953, *Time* chose Adenauer as "Man of the Year." The September election results were at the top of the list of reasons for the decision: "The West German voters swept all their Communists and Nazis out of national office and overwhelmingly put their faith in the dedicated, firm-handed democrat, Konrad Adenauer."[130]

It is thus apparent that, although many building blocks (especially in the areas of foreign policy and defense) still had to be properly placed, by the mid-1950s the fundamental frame of the new West German house

had been constructed. To that extent, the second Bundestag elections
had acquired even more significance than the first of summer 1949—
something Adenauer tried to impress on his party colleagues, surely for
more than sloganeering reasons.[131] To stay with the construction
metaphor, now it had come to deciding whether to accept or reject the
house; for some time there had been much hope, but little certainty, of
this being accompanied by a brilliant roofing ceremony. Undoubtedly
one basic factor in the ensuing success was the ongoing past-political
program, oriented toward active integration and amnesty and presenting low normative hurdles. Naturally, the individual and collective Nazi burden was immeasurably heavier in West Germany's broad
nonsocialist camp than on the left; within that camp, there were now very
few people who could not see their own past-political interests as being
well taken care of through a continuation of the bourgeois coalition.

The "liquidation of National Socialism in the Federal Republic"—
this also the title of a lengthy paper prepared by the "Working Alliance
of Democratic Circles," at Otto Lenz's initiative, to assist the government[132]—was now well under way. It was being seen through by champions of a policy for the past modeled on pragmatic economic reconstruction, individuals who basically had no real comprehension of
demands that the Nazi burden be dealt with in intellectually and
morally sensitive, introspective fashion. These individuals could meanwhile argue along lines of empirical accomplishment, the "resentment-
Nazis" no longer possessing political weight. "Self-evidently, isolated
deviations are to be accepted. But it was equally self-evident that
decades after Napoleon's death, the French nation included Bona-
partists. Why should Hitlerists die out more quickly?"

The working paper's basic thesis was that the "liquidation of Nazi
ideas" was unfolding more or less automatically and without friction,
thanks to a functioning democracy. As the authors saw things, only the
fact "that foreign circles magnify even the most minor signs of neo-Nazi
life into a state-threatening revolution" had slowed down the process—
although only in inessential ways. Their unstated conclusion was that
in place of "unsuitable advertisements" for the few remaining right-
wing radicals, the "press inside the country and abroad" should cloak
the past in silence. "Remer should not be named a hundred times before
President Heuss is even mentioned once."

At this point, Otto Lenz had been shorn by Adenauer of his historically delicate and all too ambitious plans for an "Information Ministry."
In the winter of 1953 he eloquently encapsulated this process of past-
political social engineering—a process that had increasingly lost any
sight of the perspective held by the victims (collective and individual)

of German violence and terror. "The German *Volk*," Lenz's working paper indicated, "desires work and tranquillity and is engaged in healing the huge damage inflicted by the war. If a Hitler would now make speeches in German cities or Nazi ballyhoo would break out with flags and uniforms, the masses would only react with amusement. Emotion-laden tirades no longer strike the political nerve of the German *Volk*. Former National Socialists can virtually only maintain themselves in areas where the dynamic of reconstruction has not yet taken hold strongly enough."

A half decade before the notion of the "unsurmounted past"—*die unbewältigte Vergangenheit*—became common German currency, many Germans already believed the past surmounted. That such was not the case only began to slowly emerge within German society toward the end of the 1950s, as the central crime of the Nazi period became the object of greater historical-political and criminal-legal focus: the destruction of the European Jews.

CONCLUSION

Three factors characterized the policy for the past developed in Bonn's opening years: a high degree of consensus among those promoting the policy; the sweeping nature of their measures; and the expeditious stringency with which these measures unfolded. From its onset the policy that was to be formulated—amnestying and integrating former supporters of the Third Reich on the one hand, completing a normative separation from Nazism on the other—was undisputed in its premises, generous in its accomplishments, and lasting in its effects. For approximately half a decade it would be a central aspect of legislative and executive action.

In the understanding of German political figures and other contemporaries, the policy was part of the great project of reconsolidation and reconstruction, to which government and parliament gave top priority. As one of the "burdens" resulting from the war (a category to which everything unpleasant from the occupation years was consigned), it basically needed as little justification as did pensions for war victims or assimilation of those expelled from the East. But even when compared to other pressing tasks of the first electoral period, seeing through that policy represented an outstanding challenge. For, numbering in the hundreds of thousands, the army of persons "damaged by denazification" thought of the complete "liquidation" of the hated political purging as a touchstone of the new state's sovereignty. In their view, the state's very legitimacy ought in fact to have hinged upon it.

The virulence of such past-political demands was further intensified by an inclination of great portions of German society to demonstrate solidarity with "the affected ones." A widespread desire to see the purging project's circle of "victims" narrowed to the smallest possible group of "main offenders" corresponded to an increasingly prevalent theory limiting the blame for Nazi crimes to the narrow band of top Nazi leaders. As long, then, as a clean break with the past had not once and for all ended the political purging, people often seemed keen on taking the Allied accusations personally, as a sweeping pronunciation of guilt. In the light of such charges, the democratic parties would seem to have only been voted in on retainer in the fall of 1949; in any event, they were burdened with substantial past-political expectations.

The clear-cut nature of the debt confronting such parties was demonstrated in the series of past-political measures detailed in these pages: the amnesty law already initiated in the first days of Adenauer's government; the generous arrangements made for the "131ers"; the symbolically highly significant settlement of the "war criminal problem"; the extensive amnesty for Nazi criminals, with which the initial legal moves achieved their culmination. Without speedy success in seeing through such measures, the Union would have had to reckon with losses and the Social Democrats with at least stagnation in the next elections. Unmistakable pointers in that direction were regularly offered by the opinion pollsters—and by both the hysteria in the Landsberg marketplace in January 1951 and the solidarity speeches for the Werl escapees in the fall of 1952. The pressure on the CDU-CSU and the SPD to take up past-political populism was all the stronger in that there were plenty of alternatives available: the FDP, the German Party, and the ambitious Union of Expellees and Victims of Injustice, each seeking to profile itself as the voice of those robbed of their "honor."

Up into the period of the second amnesty law's preparation in 1953–54—both amnesty and integration now well under way, with only highly incriminated persons still behind bars—there was no significant principled opposition to the basic West German policy of integration. Insistently manipulated by dubious pressure groups, public opinion had become increasingly radicalized, especially regarding the issue of the imprisoned war criminals; in this context, nothing much was set to change. But the isolated expressions of doubt that had always been formulated by reflective individuals throughout the democratic party spectrum now became stronger and more general, above all in Social Democratic ranks. If the SPD nevertheless ended by approving the second amnesty law, this partly involved confirming a basic past-political goal being practiced by an alliance of left- and right-leaning democratic forces to block the maximalist program of the extremists in the governing coalition's FDP and German parties.

A number of regulations in the second amnesty law had meant many particularly odious so-called end-phase crimes going unpunished. For all the nonincriminated forces in the Union and (even more so) in the SPD, such regulations marked the outer limits of the acceptable, on grounds of both democratic identity and moral self-respect. Going beyond such limits would have involved sparing common killers from punishment—and doing so consciously, and in grand style. The chances of such punishment suffered, in any case, from the high degree of caution being exercised by judges operating in a "clean break with the past" climate. The middle-term and long-term effects of the early West German state's policy toward the past was most clearly manifest in that judicial realm. Until the end of the 1950s, many trials were simply not opened because, in the framework of extremely mild sentencing, a punishment going over the amnesty boundaries "was not to be reckoned with." The establishment in Ludwigsburg of a Central Office for the Investigation of Nazi Crimes at the end of 1958 is usually seen as a response to the "shock" of the Mobile Killing Unit trial in Ulm, but it should, in fact, be tied much more closely to an inactivity of the courts that had lasted for years. This inactivity now seemed to threaten the chances of realizing the superannuation of homicidal crimes set for 1960. Or in any event, one reason for founding the Central Office was to dispense with political reservations regarding the scheduled penalty expiration through reference to the work being done in Ludwigsburg. The calculation turned out to be correct, but five years later, in a context of altered public awareness, the calculation would at least force a suspension of any such expiration for murder. It is in any case clear that the need to continue prosecuting the worst Nazi crimes over the long term was itself the result of the failures of the Adenauer era's early policy for the past.

Many of this study's findings have suggested a close connection, of one particular sort, between West Germany's strong past-political consensus and the enduring presence of the Allies. In the hysteria surrounding the war criminals and other instances, the West Germans presented themselves as a merely mildly secularized *Volksgemeinschaft,* whose thirst for amnesty was inexplicable in terms of the real interests of the large majority. It would not appear far-fetched here to discern, among other things, an indirect admission—confirmed, as it were, through contradiction—of the entire society's entanglement in the Nazi enterprise. Much speaks for understanding that virtually unfettered will to amnesty as an unconscious acknowledgment of the often-cited charge of "collective guilt." Already in 1945, the thesis had encountered a high degree of psychic reception, and a correspondingly vehement rejection; it had never been formulated by the Allies in the manner it was being complained about. But from the beginning, it served the Germans as a welcome reason for feeling unjustly treated.

At the same time, frequently conveying time-tested notions of an "international Jewish conspiracy," the cognitive figure *das Ausland*—that is, "those abroad"—would seem to have formed the sole effective barrier against the resonant demand from right-wing radical and nationalist quarters for a "general amnesty." Consequently, for the heads of the democratic political parties, *das Ausland* served as the *ultima ratio* of past-political debate. In their concern to be accepted as independent representatives of a "sovereign" German politics, these party heads were in fact rather reluctant to draw on that figure. But in case of doubt, they used it to the full.

There has been a widespread tendency by historians to overemphasize the free creative space enjoyed by the Germans, hence by Adenauer; in reality, the latent threat of Allied intervention was inestimably important in the development of the young West German state. The Allied High Commission closely and critically observed the initial round of past-political legislation—naturally legislation regarding the war criminals, but also (and especially) the boundary lines being demarcated, case by case, with a (neo-)Nazism distinctly on the rise since 1950–51. Above all, McCloy—also, of course, first among High Commission equals from the German vantage point—never tired of exhorting his political interlocutors (and occasionally the West German public) to maintain the original anti-Nazi consensus. A highly plausible conclusion is that without such direct Allied control, the past-political boundaries would have been even more amorphous.

Certainly, this did not negate the impact of a realpolitik-induced boundary breakdown by the Allies themselves—most significantly by the Americans, with their pardoning of so many Landsberg prisoners under the sign of "Korea." Nevertheless, without the permanent intervention of the Allies the risk of an organizational merging of nationalist and Nazi political currents would have been far greater. And at the time, no one could say for sure whether the outcome would have been a final brown trickle or a fresh dark fountainhead.

When—as occasionally in the war criminal debate—rational arguments were drowned out by the noise of past-political rabble-rousers, and the heads of the leading parties took recourse to citing "the effect on the *Ausland,*" the admonition did not lack substance—for instance, the sharp reactions in France to the German critique of the treatment of imprisoned SS and Wehrmacht members there. The admonition, however, mainly had a domestic purpose: to avoid taking any position on the correctness of the judgments, even in the case of a crime such as Oradour's. There was a resounding absence of clear, substantive statements to the effect that the "unspeakable" crimes of the Nazi state (a favorite way of putting things) were carried out not only "in the name of Germany" but by German men and even soldiers—and that these persons were rightfully being punished for their crimes. In the face of popular opinion at the start of the 1950s, any such statements would have been paid for with many votes. As demonstrated by the tactics of figures such as Herbert Wehner, Carlo Schmid, and Fritz Erler, this fact weighed hardly less heavily in the SPD than in the Union.

It is precisely the Social Democrats' embrace of such an approach that suggests it would be false to see the democratic parties' very limited argumentative room as having one source alone: imperatives resulting from the German rearmament desired by Adenauer and the Americans. Certainly the former Wehrmacht officers knew how to define the conditions for their cooperation, and the release of their comrades still sitting in Allied "dungeons" was at the top of their list. But much past-political symbolism and (in fact rightfully) damaged feelings of honor were also at stake. In any case, the process involved here was *not* only real-political barter, which as a result of inevitably sweeping demands benefited not only former Wehrmacht members but also incarcerated Nazi functionaries and SS leaders—just the sort of people from whom the former Wehrmacht leaders had the strongest grounds to construct the greatest possible functional and moral distance.

The amnesties for Nazi criminals, the reintegration of the "purging victims," the release of the war criminals, and, not least of all, the depoliticization of officialdom through its material corruption via the "131" law all had effects going far beyond the circle of individuals directly at issue. These measures clearly served to satisfy the collective psychic needs of a society that had gone through an unparalleled political and moral catastrophe in the 1940s, a society whose memory since then concealed deep-seated experiences of disintegration. Here, it would seem, and not only in an asymmetry—palpable on structural, political, and communicative levels—between a majority of fellow travelers and a minority of victims, lay other important grounds for the wide-ranging silence, indeed approval, with which the victims accompanied this course of inner pacification. Its price was living memory. The extent to which the victims suffered from this numbing and ritualization is an open question, perhaps unanswerable in a general manner. What is certain is that the political deactualization of memory thus setting in considerably eased the life of earlier fellow travelers.

At the start of the 1950s, the desire to end the decades of chaos through a deep "clean break," with the prospect of a better future, was deeply anchored in the heads of virtually all Germans. Almost without distinction, these chaotic decades were understood to include the postwar years—in which even Social Democrat Adolf Arndt saw "civil war features." Informing such desire, a need for self-rehabilitation formed one element of the broader, often-described intense need for security characterizing the Adenauer period. A society that had registered its first successes in economic and political reconstruction, but that was still waiting for recognition from guiding nations and neighbors, pardoned, as it were, itself. To this extent, the excessive need for calm and integration was surely also the reflex of a normality being displayed "abroad" and impatiently longed for at home.

In such a context, it perhaps does not go too far afield to see the notorious demands for integration and amnesty as ersatz enactments of a politically corrupted but nonetheless still virulent nationalism that Adenauer had effectively forbidden the Germans. It is a fact that the old nationalist voices and forces flourished on past-political ground better than virtually any other—and that the chancellor, fixated on a fast and firm linkage of the "core state" to the West, often seemed a lonesome preacher, appealing for reason and moderation on account of his central goal.

Adenauer's special role doubtless owed much to the Rhenish-Catholic "Western"-oriented nature of his basic convictions, his distance, charged with experience, from the old nationalist-Protestant elites and the Prussian military. But his unspent capacity to learn was also manifest here—to be sure, under superb pedagogic conditions. No other German politician was offered the chance to familiarize himself with the ideas and approaches of the Federal Republic's Western "guardians" as authentically and continuously as was Adenauer. The basis of this privilege was exclusive access—intended as such by him—to the High Commissioners.

But as we have seen, despite his gifts and special vision, the chancellor not only failed to block the long-term effort to release the war criminals, but himself repeatedly spoke up on their behalf, thus sometimes placing a great strain on his negotiations with the High Commissioners. The question arises of his motives. His usually terse explanations are manifestly tailored to each interlocutor and situation; they generally do not convey the impression that the war criminal issue was of great personal concern to him. This would seem confirmed by his underestimation of the problem in the "General Treaty" negotiations, so that—placed under massive pressure by the FDP and the German Party—he could neutralize it only with very great effort. But in the interests of his paramount goal of Western integration and—as one of its elements—rearmament, no past-political price demanded by right-wing nationalist coalition partners and former Wehrmacht officers was too high to pay. One cynical gesture during the 1953 election battle speaks volumes: his side trip during an appearance at Werl's pilgrimage church to visit the war criminal prison and address the press there.

What may have made such gestures easier for Adenauer was a distinction that not only he soon came to favor: between "real" war criminals, understood as "asocial elements," and the "condemned soldiers," understood as having simply done their duty. Whether Adenauer actually believed in the distinction is hard to say. It is conceivable that even in the case of such an eminent "civilian," the same cognitive mechanisms were at work making it hard for his entire generation to grasp the dimensions of the German war of extermination in the East. In the end we cannot overlook the basic cognitive context. However concrete the facts, brought to light in Nuremberg, of the Wehrmacht's deep complicity in the SS Mobile Killing Unit crimes, as well as of the broad labor investment in the persecution of Jews, cutting across German society, such facts simply stood no chance in German public consciousness of the 1950s. They would remain suppressed for the next few decades.

At the same time, the chancellor was anything but slow-witted; the skill with which he could connect what mattered to him and the Allies is demonstrated most impressively in his approach to the so-called Naumann affair. Adenauer was here the only member of the cabinet to grasp early on how serious the British were in targeting the effort (basically the first since 1931 in Bad Harzburg) at linking the active vestiges of the "old" nationalist right to the remaining "young" Nazi core groups. Naturally he himself had no sympathy for such a scene, finding little to criticize in the imprisonment (based on supra-legal occupation powers alone) of its leaders; he was also not especially bothered by the British interference with a (nonexistent) West German sovereignty—this despite the indignant cries of journalists and cabinet members. To the contrary, for Adenauer, with the second national elections looming, the affair was rather welcome. For it clearly demonstrated that all adventures on the far right faced veto from the occupation powers. At the time, more than a few people were frustrated by the possibilities of the FDP or the German Party under the control of an antinationalist coalition, and more than a few of these had dreams of a "great right-wing party." It would now be clear that such dreams would not be realized. In the same vein, Adenauer viewed his summer 1953 electoral triumph as, in particular, a victory over traditional German nationalism (as well, of course, as a victory over communism).

It is in any case evident enough that the defeat of the extreme parties and resounding victory of the governing coalition was a sign of widespread approval for a basically completed past-political program. At the very least, the ballots cast in the second national elections were also past-political ballots: From now on, radical principles would attract only a minority composed of former perpetrators and "resentment Nazis." These individuals, carrying the same ideological baggage as ever, took their political failure as an excuse to embrace conspiratorial interests; such interests would manage to penetrate the top level of Bonn's ministerial bureaucracy and the justice system, where they would remain effective for years. In contrast, the great majority of fellow travelers had come to see themselves as, in a wider sense, among those *damaged* by Nazism; they now felt sufficiently integrated, even well situated, in a bourgeois republic that acknowledged their self-image. Over the following years, accompanying gradual "completion" of the "131" legislation, such an image would solidify—before, to be sure, starting to evoke increasing objections.

In the Social Democratic camp, circumstances were rather more complicated. The SPD's acceptance of an integration-oriented politics did presume a capacity for self-overcoming on the part of many party members who had risked life and health in resisting the Nazis. These individuals had fought for something other than a democracy that was— at least from their perspective—thoroughly capitalist, and in which the power of the old elites seemed fully restored. It is also the case that both the SPD and the unions were well aware that over the years a fatal attraction for the Hitler regime had also emerged among the workers. Against that backdrop there was little room for rigidly sticking to principles, especially since the working movement's limited political success in the immediate postwar years did not exactly speak for ideological rigidity. It is possible that at the start of the 1950s, a tacit admission of one basic circumstance was not as widespread among the Social Democrats as in the Union—but in the end all the democratic parties knew they had to win their votes from a populace that, in free and fair elections, would have chosen Hitler by an overwhelming majority a mere decade earlier.

A policy for the past that was meant to muster a majority could not ignore this circumstance. But it also had to handle it like a secret. For a portion of the attractiveness of the new mass allegiance to the democratic parties lay precisely in a masking of the historical reality's true, undeniable horror. The partly conscious, partly unconscious need to withdraw from this collective memory defines the *social* function of West German policies of amnesty and integration in the first years following 1949, a function that needs to be considered alongside the *individual* benefits. The measures taken for the sake of normative demarcation served the same collective goal: What both the legislative and judicial branches sanctioned and effectively stigmatized was not, of course, earlier convictions, but continued ideological-political adherence to Nazism, and especially to its crimes. The "right to political error" so effectively postulated by Eugen Kogon in 1947 formed, so to speak, the past-political basic law of the West German republic—a law eminently suited for a policy of wide-ranging integration. Whoever professed "changed convictions" could mostly count on forbearance. It was the "incorrigibles" who faced problems with a judiciary still finding it difficult to focus on the right—those who explicitly refused the anti-Nazi behavioral code, thus troubling, among other things, the general need for quiet.

In such an atmosphere of voluntary silence regarding the individual Nazi past, occasional personal-political turbulence (such as that surrounding Globke) was basically the exception proving the rule. Such turbulence, however, was not subject to systematic instrumentalization. Driven forward by the war criminal debate, an interpretation of the Nazi period took hold that, while not denying the criminal facts, increasingly wove them together with the "horror of modern warfare," the reality of partisan combat, or very generally with the "fog of war." The crimes were thus placed in murky territories "in the East," territories in which real flesh-and-blood Germans could scarcely still be envisioned as perpetrators. In such a context, even a Mobile Killing Unit leader whose mass murder had been proved could be perceived first of all as a former university student or as the son of Württemberg dignitaries. And in such a context, he could count on the intercession of a Theodor Heuss or Carlo Schmid. Major industrial leaders or officials, say Ernst von Weizsäcker, profited from this "neighborly" or "collegial" help to a far greater extent.

We can thus summarize by observing that in the mid-1950s, ascribing the horrors of the Third Reich to Hitler and a small clique of "major war criminals" was a basic element of public West German awareness. In turn, the West Germans accorded themselves, in their majority, the status of politically "seduced" individuals, themselves rendered "martyrs," in the end, by the war and its consequences. At the price of historical reality, the millions of former soldiers had to be granted the possibility of finding a sense in their efforts. The war was thus followed by a battle for memory; there was a suppression of the question of the basic criminal character of the German aggression, its barbarism and madness from the start—a question furnished with a rather clear answer "abroad." This was the source of the stubborn insistence on interpreting the Great War and Second World War as a continuum. It was the source for claiming—partly from ignorance, partly intentionally and with precise knowledge—a "normality" for the latter war that could not *properly* be claimed for the singular crimes of the Germans.

Far into the 1960s, the precarious nature of this interpretive enterprise was not seen as a problem. The reason for this was the quickly realized "hyperstability" (Richard Löwenthal) of the young West German state—a circumstance owing much to its past-political accomplishments. A process of cautious change did begin around 1959–60, at first mainly affecting the scandalously neglected criminal-legal confrontation with Nazism and the no-less-scandalous personal continuity with Nazism inside the judicial system. But as so much characterizing the Adenauer period, this change was primarily induced from "abroad": through Israel, which, as the country of the victims, tracked down Nazi criminals living outside Germany unnoticed by the German authorities, and which managed to arrest Eichmann in Argentina in the spring of 1960; from the states of the Eastern Bloc, which, now that even the most vicious crimes were facing superannuation, began producing documents and former victims of the German quest for "*Lebensraum* in the East"; but above all from the East German state, which since the mid-1950s had been attempting, with great conspiratorial energy, to use the problem of an "unsurmounted past" as a way of destabilizing the Federal Republic.

The departure from the long past-political years of the 1950s had thus slowly gotten started, but it would take more extensive generational changes before a basic change set in, to accompany the incipient student movement. The earlier prevalent interpretations—inspired by totalitarianism theory—of the Third Reich as something like an alien regime descending upon Germany, making use of a small number of "collaborators" and a mass of harmless fellow travelers, now began to fade in conviction. In their place came a growing awareness of the dimensions of the mass crime known as the "Final Solution," along with critical illumination of Nazism's social anchoring, its guiding social strata, and a professional elite that stayed in place after 1945. It is a thought-provoking irony that such a development, the emergence in West German society of a serious and open confrontation with the Nazi past, was made possible only by a very different preceding period—a period of utmost individual leniency, reflecting a policy for the past whose failings would stamp the new state's spirit over many decades.

POSTSCRIPT FOR THE AMERICAN EDITION

Five years have already somehow sped by since the publication of the original German edition of this book in September 1996. In the mid-1990s, part of the discipline of academic history in Germany was in the process of redefining itself as "cultural studies." This was accompanied by a rediscovery of the significance of "collective memory," and to a considerable extent the interest in "overcoming the past" shifted from the arena of practical politics to that of retrospective intellectual evaluation. In other words: the study appeared—unintentionally and despite very different motives—at just the right moment.

I had only decided on designating my basic theme with the term *Vergangenheitspolitik* (eventually emerging as the book's main title) late in the writing process; while the term's mainly positive academic reception has been gratifying, its absorption into journalistic parlance has been completely surprising. As indicated, in this book "a policy for the past" refers rather narrowly—as does its German counterpart—to the process of political interaction between amnesty, integration, and normative demarcation from Nazism unfolding in West Germany during the 1950s. But meanwhile, the term has come to be frequently used in a much wider sense, including in non-German contexts. Very recently I came across an interesting essay on present-day Japanese *Vergangenheits-*

politik regarding Korea. Likewise, the fact that the book's Polish translation already appeared in 1999 (around the time of the paperback German edition) certainly reflects more than a growing Polish interest in recent German history—specifically, the ongoing political debate over how to deal with the communist past.

Against this backdrop, I am especially pleased that my findings will now be accessible to the English-speaking world. Aside from a shorter introduction, with references to a few new publications, the present edition is unabridged. I believe that it may be interesting for readers in (particularly) the United States and Great Britain to see how important the role of both countries was in stabilizing West German democracy in the 1950s. Likewise, as the specific social-political grounding for viewpoints expressed in the key contemporary debates—inside and outside Germany—over Nazism, anti-Semitism, and the Holocaust (most recently: the controversy sparked by the thesis of Hitler's Germany as a nation of accomplices; the polemics surrounding both the exhibit on "crimes of the Wehrmacht" and Berlin's planned Holocaust monument), the history unfolding in these pages may be of some strong interest to a variety of English-speaking readers.

The first word of warm thanks I would like to add here is due Fritz Stern (New York): not only for his generous foreword, but also for his strong support for publication of this English-language edition, and for his helpfulness in finding a title. Michael Brenner (Munich) also furthered the book's seeing print through his own timely prompting, and both Saul Friedländer and Jonathan Petropulous, as well as a number of other American colleagues, offered their aid as well. Many thanks to all these friends and colleagues.

My research assistants in Bochum, above all Thomas Terbeck and Jörg Wolf, helped in the laborious task of locating original citations in English-language books and documents; their efforts have been deeply appreciated. The Institut für Zeitgeschichte (Munich) kindly offered a translation-subsidy from the earnings of the book's original German edition. I would also like to express my gratitude to Peter Dimock at Columbia University Press: in New York last spring, we agreed on the last, salutary steps needed to bring this very long project to a happy end.

But the greatest debt for this American edition is owed to Joel Golb (Berlin and New York), who rendered the far from simple German text into English with precision, inspiration, and great engagement. My thanks to him is bound up with the hope of being able to repeat the very pleasant collaboration in a different context.

Bochum, September 2001, N.F.

ACKNOWLEDGMENTS

Books of this sort are often rather complicated in their realization; but since in the end what matters is the final product, readers can be spared the various obstacles along the way. In contrast, it is important to thank the many friends and colleagues with an important role in the book's inception. Some enriched and clarified my perspective through their readiness to engage in—often extended—discussions. Others read and commented on the manuscript or portions of it; in this respect I would like to express my gratitude to Ulrich Herbert, Bernd Weisbrod, Curt Garner, Christoph Boyer, Lothar Gruchmann—and especially to Hans Woller, whose expert advice, collegial patience, and friendship were and remain inestimable.

The main research for this book was done at the Institut für Zeitgeschichte in Munich. Many individual debts of gratitude naturally accumulate in a research center where one has worked for a long time, and an attempt to settle them in this fashion must necessarily fail. But I will still try: in the Institute's library, more help was offered me than I had a right to expect, and in its archives, I could always rely over the years on the competent assistance of Hermann Weiß and Monika Deniffel. I also benefited from a group of wonderfully reliable research assistants: Thomas Schlemmer, Mathias Rösch, Silke Schumann, Bernd

Wagner, Sebastian Herrmann, and Claudia Moisel. My warmest thanks to all.

Anyone having some acquaintance with the Institut für Zeitgeschichte knows what role has been played there by its administrative director, Georg Maisinger. To say he offered his help when he could might possibly do justice to his modesty, but would still be a drastic undervaluation. In a transitional period for its directorship, his engagement for the Institute and its staff was extremely important. Likewise at the Institute, Renate Bihl contributed substantially to my administrative and editorial responsibilities continuing to proceed apace in periods of concentrated writing. And I have taken considerable pride in Sybille Benker's fidelity to both myself and the manuscript, as expressed in her tireless work on its transcription up to the day of her retirement—and even a bit beyond.

In Rödelheim, Rainer Tiemann—a true artist of word-processing technology—had persuaded me some fifteen years earlier to start using Wordstar; among other achievements, he now saw to my leaving it behind—a task that while necessary, was not easy, but that was still accomplished without loss of data.

I owe a further word of appreciation to archivists in the old West German seat of government in Bonn, in nearby Coblenz, and in other places I visited for research purposes; I will here mention Frau Klimmer from the government's Press and Information Office and Josef Henke from the Federal Archives as representatives of a much wider group.

On 8 May 1991, as part of a lecture series sponsored by the Federal Archives, Friedrich P. Kahlenberg offered me a first opportunity to publicly present some of my findings. At around the same time, I received other forms of much valued support from Kurt Sontheimer, Saul Friedländer, Fritz Redlich, Ian Kershaw, and Hans Mommsen; later from Hans-Ulrich Wehler.

In ways that are not easy to define (but is that what matters?) a number of long-standing friends contributed to this project: Hans Winterberg, Friedrich Lang, Albert Landwehr, Klaus Jancovius, Hans Dräxler, Nada Weigelt, and Sylvia Malzacher and Jean-François Grenon; as well as Gabriele and Karl Bonhoeffer, who invited me to their retreat in Tuscany at the right moment, and Gabriele Jaroschka and Peter Schricker, who invited me to their lakeside house.

Margit Ketterle was present with this project from start to finish; my book is dedicated to her.

The Department of History and Philosophy of the University of Bielefeld accepted the manuscript as a habilitation in the summer semester of 1995. An invitation by the Wissenschaftskolleg in Berlin then facilitated the final editing of the manuscript. But I would be presumptuous to hope that my prose absorbed a little of that wonderful institution's atmosphere, or some of the intellectual stimulus steadily available there from its fellows.

Berlin, fall/winter 1995–96

NOTES

Introduction

1. Dolf Sternberger. "Die deutsche Frage," *Der Monat* 8/9 (1949): 16–21, here p. 17.
2. In the 1980s, a series of political essays preceded the theme's "historicization." The most trenchant of these was probably Ralph Giordano's widely read *Die Zweite Schuld oder von der Last ein Deutscher zu sein* ("Secondary Guilt, or On the Burden of Being a German"); cf. Friedrich, *Kalte Amnestie*; Arnim, *Das Große Schweigen*; Buruma, *Wages of Guilt*. For a methodologically inadequate historian's response to Giordano, cf. Kittel, *Legende von der "Zweiten Schuld"*; for an earlier, more balanced overview, cf. Kielmansegg, *Lange Schatten*. The American and West European perspective concerning West Germany's efforts to "overcome the past" in the 1950s is at the center of Brochhagen, *Nach Nürnberg*. Since the first publication of this book many additional essays and books treating the theme have appeared; I can here cite only a limited selection of the most important, in the order of their appearance: Herf, *Divided Memory;* Schwan, *Politik und Schuld*; Wolfrum, *Geschichtspolitik in der Bundesrepublik Deutschland*; Dubiel, *Niemand ist frei von der Geschichte;* Assmann and Frevert, *Geschichtsvergessenheit-Geschichtsversessenheit;* Moeller, *War Stories;* Marcuse, *Legacies of Dachau*; Reichel, *Vergangenheitsbewältigung* (which contains an up-to-date bibliography).
3. Cf. Dolf Sternberger, "Versuch zu einem Fazit," *Die Wandlung* 4 (1949): 700–710, here p. 701; the comments were prompted by the discontinuation of *Die Wandlung*, which he had edited.

319

4. Lübbe, "Nationalsozialismus."
5. Cf. Kogon, "Das Recht auf den politischen Irrtum."
6. Cf. above all Schwarz, *Ära Adenauer 1* and *2*. Furthermore, Kleßmann, *Die doppelte Staatsgründung*; Kleßmann, *Zwei Staaten, eine Nation*; Doering-Manteuffel, *Die Bundesrepublik Deutschland in der Ära Adenauer*; Weber, *Die Bundesrepublik wird souverän 1950–1955*; Morsey, *Die Bundesrepublik Deutschland*; Birke, *Nation ohne Haus*; Sontheimer, *Die Adenauer-Ära*.

Part I

1. Bundestag-Berichte (BT-Berichte), 1, WP [1st election period], 7 September 1949, p. 1f.
2. The reference is to lesser offenders, "fellow travelers," and exonerated persons.
3. Bundestag-Drucksachen (BT-Drucksachen), 1, WP, no. 1–350, here no. 13, Dringlichkeitsantrag, 8 September 1949.
4. BT-Drucksachen 1, WP, no. 17, 15 September 1949.
5. BT-Drucksachen 1, WP, no. 26, 20 September 1949. On 8 December 1949, the *Süddeutsche Zeitung* observed that the basic approach was completely correct, if hard to realize (p. 3); Ernst Müller-Meiningen Jr. ironically designated Loritz as the "first specialist" in the realm of economic transgressions.
6. BT-Drucksachen 1, WP, no. 27, 21 September 1949.
7. An additional factor for the Christian Social Union (CSU) was its advocacy of the Länder having sole authority in the matter.
8. BT-Berichte 1, WP, 20 September 1949, p. 27. In the cited passages, Adenauer stuck word by word to his draft. In Bundesarchiv (BA), B 136/3769.
9. Schwarz, *Adenauer I*, p. 636, describes its inadequate preparation.
10. Willy Brandt had pressed for this critical point; SPD-Fraktionsprotokolle, vol. I/1, p. 11; on the SPD chairman's reply as well as his general past-political strategy, see Merseburger, *Schumacher*, pp. 453, 494–504.
11. BT-Berichte 1, WP, 21 September 1949, p. 36.
12. BT-Berichte 1, WP, 20 September 1949, p. 27.
13. Thus the critique of Herbst, Einleitung, in Herbst and Goschler, *Wiedergutmachung*, p. 22; cf. Goschler, *Wiedergutmachung*, p. 200f.

Chapter 1

1. Cf. *Die Welt*, 10 September 1949, p. 2; reproduction in Weber, *Bundesrepublik*, p. 121.
2. This is Baring's version, Außenpolitik, p. 17, of a common twist to the biblical citation. (Cf. Thomas Nipperdey, *Deutsche Geschichte 1800–1866* [München, 1983], p. 11: "In the beginning was Napoleon.") Kittel, Legende, p. 387, closes his book with the recommendation to begin a history

of Adenauer-era West Germany with the sentence "In the beginning was 'Vergangenheitsbewältigung' "—"making a clean break with the past."

3. Overview in Vollnhals, *Entnazifizierung*, p. 351ff.

4. Verordnungsblatt für die Britische Zone, no. 7 (1947), p. 68ff.; a list of the amnesties initiated by the Länder is found in *Strafvollstreckung, Strafregister, Gnadenwesen: Sammlung der Bestimmungen über Strafvollstreckung, Strafregister und Gnadenwesen unter Berücksichtigung der Ländergesetzgebung* (Munich and Berlin, 1953), p. 332f.

5. Cf. *Wörtliche Berichte*, vol. 5, printed matter 974.

6. Cf. Protokoll der 2. Sitzung des Juristischen Ausschusses der Ministerpräsidenten, 27 July 1949; the theme had already been addressed in the tenth conference of the justice ministers from the different Länder on 17–18 June 1949 as well as in a meeting of ministerial presidents of the bizone with the military governors on 1 September 1949; *Akten zur Vorgeschichte*, vol. 5, pp. 938, 1094ff.

7. Ibid., p. 1094, n. 25.

8. *Kabinettsprotokolle 1949*, 26 September 1949, pp. 338–41 (following citation from the full minutes; for all later sessions, only the abbreviated minutes are available). For historians, the legal literature on amnesty laws and amnesties in the early West German state is unrewarding; cf., e.g., Marxen, *Grenzen;* Merten, *Rechtsstaatlichkeit;* Schätzler, *Handbuch des Gnadenrechts;* but contrast the succinct overview of Perels, "Amnestien."

9. Copy in BA, B 141/4283. As late as March 1950, Dehler tried to get rid of the self-assured previous director of the bizonal legal office, who had at first been appointed only in a commissarial capacity. Details in Wengst, *Staatsaufbau*, p. 156f.

10. On Dehler's role in the resistance, see Sassin, *Liberale*, pp. 107–14, 223, 242ff., and passim.

11. BA, B 141/4283, Dehler to the justice ministers of the Länder, 3 October 1949.

12. *Kabinettsprotokolle 1949*, 7 October 1949, p. 107.

13. BA, B 141/4283, Müller to Dehler, 8 October 1949.

14. To the annoyance of State Secretary Strauß, the German Press Agency representative had taken part in the session unnoticed and unquestioned regarding his identity; BA, B 141/4283, Notiz Strauß, 18 October 1949; the journalist's report in *Suddeutsche Zeitung*, 19 October 1949, p. 2.

15. BA, B 141/4283, Protokoll des Justizkollegiums, 19 October 1949.

16. *Kabinettsprotokolle 1949*, 18 October 1949, p. 135.

17. Ibid., 28 October 1949, p. 158; BA, B 141/4283, new version of the law draft, 27 October 1949.

18. BA, B 141/4283, Meyer-Abich to Dehler, 3 November 1949.

19. Cf. below, p. 324.

20. Wember, *Umerziehung*, p. 318; on the Spruchgerichte in general, pp. 276–357; cf. Broszat, "Siegerjustiz," p. 517.

21. *Die Welt*, 18 November 1949, p. 2 ("Amnesty of Forgetting: The Federation's Exemption on Punishment Should Be Carefully Weighed").

22. Friedrich Grimm, "Denkschrift über die Notwendigkeit einer General-amnestie (1949)," in BA, B 141/4283; cf. Laak, *Gespräche*, p. 102.

23. Sitzungsbericht des Deutschen Bundesrates (BR-Berichte), 23 November 1949, pp. 68–73; led by Bavaria, the following other Länder voted against recognizing federal authority: Baden, Hamburg, Rheinland-Pfalz, and Württemberg-Hohenzollern.

24. Adenauer's appointments calendar indicates a "cabinet and coalition" meeting of several hours for the afternoon of 29 November 1949; Stiftung Bundeskanzler-Adenauer-Haus (StBKAH), visitors' list Bl. 258.

25. This is the title of the only major contemporary publication on the theme— interestingly written by a member of the Frankfurter Hefte's editorial board: Böttcher, Menschen; cf. *Christ und Welt,* 11 May and 24 August 1950. Researchers began exploring the theme only in the spring of 1995, after it emerged that the longtime rector of the Technische Hochschule in Aachen, Hans Schwerte, had taken this name after the war to shed his previous iden-tity as a member of the SS-*Ahnenerbe;* cf., e.g., *Frankfurter Allgemeine Zeitung,* 6 May 1995, p. 4; for a provisional summary see Karl-Siegbert Rehberg, "Eine deutsche Karriere. Oder: Gelegenheit macht Demokraten. Überlegungen zum Fall Schwerte/Schneider," *Merkur* 50 (1996): 73–80.

26. BA, B 141/4284, Kurzprotokoll der 5. Sitzung des BT-Rechtsausschusses (Auszug), 29 November 1949.

27. BT-Drucksachen 1, WP, no. 251, Adenauer to Köhler, 30 November 1949.

28. *Süddeutsche Zeitung,* 25 November 1949, p. 3 ("A Clean Break Here").

29. BT-Drucksachen 1, WP, no. 251, Adenauer to Köhler, 30 November 1949; this procedure was directly criticized in the Bundestag only by Anton Pfeiffer, a representative of the Bundesrat and director of the Bavarian Chancellery; BT-Berichte 1, WP, 2 December 1949, p. 583.

30. BT-Berichte 1, WP, 2 December 1949, pp. 574, 586.

31. *Kabinettsprotokolle 1949,* 20 September 1949, p. 68.

32. Even the foreign press hardly reacted; the reports in the *Neue Zürcher Zeitung,* a paper markedly critical of Germany, had their usual precision but were completely unspectacular: 15 December 1949, no. 2644 ("Amnesty-Desire for War Criminals"); 21 December 1949, no. 2678 ("Amnesty for Political Prisoners"); and 3 January 1950, no. 13 ("West German Amnesty Law").

33. The following according to BT-Berichte 1, WP, 2 December 1949, pp. 572–87.

34. Cf. below, p. 121–23.

35. The interest, for instance, of the German Communist Party in not allow-ing "brazen racketeers" to get away through an excessively high limit on fines, or that of the Economic Reconstruction Association in sparing innkeepers who had illegally butchered animals to defy price controls.

36. The following according to Bundestag—Parliamentary Archives (BT—PA), Bestand Ausschußprotokolle, Kurzprotokoll der 6. Sitzung des Auss-chusses für Rechtswesen und Verfassungsrecht, 7 December 1949 (also in BA, B 141/4284).

37. On this see below, pp. 21ff.
38. The following according to BT-Berichte 1, WP, 9 December 1949, pp. 651–67; BT-Drucksachen 1, WP, no. 270 and 292.
39. Meanwhile the German Reich Party and National Democratic Party had formed a new Bundestag faction under this name.
40. The following according to BR-Berichte, 9 December 1949, pp. 102–5.
41. The following according to BR-Berichte, 19 December 1949, pp. 119–22.
42. BA, B 141/4284, Blankenhorn to Glain, 20 December 1949.
43. So, e.g., *Frankfurter Allgemeine Zeitung,* 10 December 1949, p. 1 (lead story: "The Bundestag Approves the Amnesty"), and already 3 December 1949, p. 3 ("The Amnesty Even Before Christmas?"); *Suddeutsche Zeitung,* 3–4 December 1949, p. 1 (front-page story: "Federation and Länder Wrestle Over the Amnesty Law"), 10–11 December 1949, p. 1 ("Amnesty Law Passed"), 20 December 1949, p. 1 (front-page story: "Amnesty Law Accepted by the Bundesrat"); for a distinctly different accent see *Die Welt,* 10 December 1949, p. 1 (front-page story: "Reservations of the Bundesrat Concerning the Amnesty Law")—the only major daily to publish the text (p. 5); sarcastically and completely clouding the amnesty plan's political dimension was *Der Spiegel,* 15 December 1949, p. 5.
44. BA, B 141/4284, Brandl to Bergmann, 23 December 1949.
45. BA, B 141/4284, file-note by Thier, 27 December 1949.
46. *Süddeutsche Zeitung,* 29 December 1949, p. 1; after the Allied critique became known, Dehler declared that paragraph 9 had been taken up at the wish of the political center so that "crime in defense of democracy or in the punishment of Nazi crimes could be amnestied. A commentary on p. 3 already was titled "shattered Christmas amnesty"; invoking Ehard, who had referred to the draft as the "most miserable thing that had come his way as legislation," Ernst Müller-Meiningen Jr. spoke of threatening "disgrace."
47. BA, B 141/4282, several unsigned and undated notes, e.g., Bl. 38ff.; the meeting between Strauß and the Allied High Commission is mistakenly given there as 29 December 1949.
48. Political Archives—Foreign Office (PA—FO), exchange of notes with the Allied High Commission, vol. 22, Bl. 191f., Allied High Commission to Adenauer, 29 December 1949 (transl.).
49. BA, B 141/4282, Dehler to Adenauer (telegram), 30 December 1949. Shortly afterward Dehler bitingly justified Adenauer's confirmation of the request as follows: it was all the more defendable "in that neither the High Commission's letter nor the government's explanation has any sort of practical significance." Ibid., Bl. 40 (unsigned and undated).
50. BA, B 141/4282, Adenauer to Allied High Commission, 30 December 1949. The complications concerning the amnesty law had an epilogue in Adenauer's meeting with the Allied High Commission on 12 January 1950. In this venue, the acting British High Commissioner explained that "as you know, the means and ways we made use of to avoid a refusal of the law have been subject to a very severe critique. I hope that in the future we will not face laws that will demand such means from us." Ade-

nauer's response to the additional comment that he would have to admit
that the law had been formulated "very vaguely indeed" was not inaccurate; the blame belonged to the Bundestag committee "in question,"
"since it introduced it there." *Akten zur Auswärtigen Politik,* vol. 1, p. 84f.

51. Bundesgesetzblatt (BGBl) 1949, p. 37f., Gesetz über die Gewährung von
Straffreiheit, 31 December 1949. According to a brochure written upon
Dehler's departure from his post, it also constituted the first law to have
originated with the Justice Ministry; Institut für Zeitgeschichte (IfZ), ED
94/156a, Codex T.D. It was preceded simply by the law concerning the
"Berlin emergency victims." Friedrich, *Kalte Amnestie,* p. 213, oddly terms
the amnesty law "the only amnesty ever issued on political grounds"; his
apparently concrete conclusions are not proven. Müller, *Juristen,* p. 242 is
also inaccurate, especially in his distinction between penalties involving
loss of freedom and those involving prison. Jasper, Wiedergutmachung,
p. 188f. refers to the law; Ratz, *Justiz,* p. 60f. documents it in excerpts.

52. Eugen Gerstenmaier, director of the Evangelical Relief Organization,
looked back on the founding of *Christ und Welt* at the beginning of June
1948 thus: "The starting point was requests for current reading material
coming above all from the camps in which men damned to automatic
arrest were sitting ... . We did not wish ... to be merely friendly depicters
of history." Gerstenmaier, *Streit und Friede,* p. 280ff.

53. Other than was the case regarding punishments pronounced by German
courts on the basis of Control Council law no. 10 of 20 December 1945 on
account of war crimes or crimes against humanity—above all by inquest
courts in the British zone—the amnesty law did not apply to punishments
imposed by the denazification tribunals in the framework of denazification, mainly against major offenders and incriminated persons (cf. p. 329,
n. 37 below).

54. *Christ und Welt,* 12 January 1950, p. 2: "The Little Amnesty."

55. Erich Schmidt-Leichner, "Die Bundesamnestie," *Neue Juristische Wochenschrift* 3 (1950): 41–46, cf. n. 56.

56. Adolf Arndt, "Das Amnestiegesetz," *Süddeutsche Juristenzeitung* 5 (1950):
108–13. The Constitutional Court approved the law in a decision of 22
April 1953; the ruling is documented in *Neue Juristische Wochenschrift*
6 (1953): p. 777f.

57. Cf. Gosewinkel, *Arndt,* esp. pp. 53–63.

58. BA, B 141/4282, Kurzprotokoll der 9. Sitzung des Rechtsausschusses des
BR, 12 January 1950 (excerpt).

59. BA, B 141/4282, Dehler to legal administrations of the Länder, 17 January 1950.

60. BA, B 141/4282, Bowie to McCloy, 6 June 1950, and Dehler to the Chancellor's Office, 4 July 1950; the skeptical inquiry was prompted by three
amnesty cases that are not described further.

61. Claus Seibert, "Zum Begriff der ehrlosen Gesinnung im Amnestiegesetz"
("On the Concept of Dishonorable Intent in the Amnesty Law"), *Neue Juristische Wochenschrift* 3 (1950): 173f.

62. "Rechtsprechung—Entscheidungen," *Neue Juristische Wochenschrift* 3 (1950): 476f.

63. Ibid., p. 318.

64. Schmidt-Leichner, *Bundesamnestie,* p. 46.

65. BA, B 141/4286, Dehler to legal administrations of the Länder, 16 January 1950, with census form example.

66. BA, B 141/4286, Statistische Übersicht zum Straffreiheitsgesetz 1949, undated—the source of the information that follows. Dehler himself spoke later in the Bundestag of 750,000 amnestied persons; BT-Berichte 1, WP, 18 June 1953, p. 13545B. This figure was in line with comparable amnesties. An amnesty on the basis of the law of 20 December 1932 thus benefited 308,000 persons who committed offenses out of economic need; the amnesty law of 7 August 1934 had freed 936,500 persons from sentences up to three months and six months; the laws of 23 April 1936 and 30 April 1938 around 530,000 and 580,000 persons respectively from a maximum sentence of one month. In total, between 1932 and 1938 over 2.5 million perpetrators were amnestied within the Reich. This figure included more than 15,000 persons amnestied with no consideration of the seriousness of their crimes, since they had made themselves liable to punishment out of "excessive zeal for the idea of National Socialism." After 1945, an indictment was possible in such cases only when they involved war crimes, crimes against peace, and crimes against humanity: Control Council law no. 10 of 20 December 1945 did not allow either a limitation-statute or "immunity, pardon, or amnesty issued by the Nazi regime" for such crimes (article II, 5). Beyond this, individuals who had not been criminally prosecuted and amnestied during the Nazi period could also be charged—e.g., those whose deeds followed the last amnesty or whose trial was quashed by Hitler before the indictment. For this reason the "federal amnesty" of 1949 was particularly interesting for Kristallnacht perpetrators. Figures taken from BA, R 22/1221, Bl. 302–6, Gürtner to Lammers, 14 February 1939; Deutsche Justiz 98 (1936), p. 1441, and 100 (1938), p. 1322.—I thank Dr. Lothar Gruchmann for advice and access to the cited documents.

67. BA, B 141/4282, Pressemitteilung des Bundesjustizministeriums, 28 March 1950; a corresponding German Press Agency report in the *Frankfurter Allgemeine Zeitung,* 30 March 1950, p. 4. The press did not show any particular interest in the amnesty for "illegals" either before or after it came into effect. Characteristically, the American German-language *Neue Zeitung* (9 December 1949, p. 1: " 'Illegals' Can Now Become Legal") was one exception; it reported the estimated number of 80,000 "illegals" and indicated that those who had committed crimes before 1945 were not covered. (While this was in fact the case, post-1945 deeds intended to hide such crimes were covered.)

68. BA, B 141/4286, Einzelübersicht zum Straffreiheitsgesetz 1949, 16 February 1951 (figures without Hesse).

Chapter 2

1. BT—PA, Bestand Ausschußprotokolle, Protokolle der 1.-7. Sitzung des Ausschusses für Rechtswesen und Verfassungsrecht, 1, Wahlperiode; BT-Berichte 1, WP, 18 October 1950, pp. 3431–35, report by Menzel. the most important motions: BT-Drucksachen 1, WP, no. 13, motion of the German Party, 8.9.1949; no. 27, motion of the Economic Reconstruction Association, 21 September 1949; no. 97, motion of the FDP, 28 September 1949. Like the motion of the FDP, that of the Bavarian Party, 14 October 1949, no. 99, was linked to the demand for prompt regulation of the legal situation in public service, in line with Article 131 of the Basic Law.

2. *Kabinettsprotokolle 1949,* 11 November 1949, p. 189; cf. Fürstenau, *Entnazifizierung,* p. 152ff., which also treats the Justice Department's guiding principles.

3. BT-Drucksachen 1, WP, no. 482, 31 January 1950.

4. BT-Drucksachen 1, WP, no. 561, 15 February 1950.

5. BT-Drucksachen 1, WP, no. 609, 22 February 1950. The German Party's draft was more complicated and tended to be rather less generous than the FDP's; on the German Party's attitude toward denazification, see Schmollinger, *Deutsche Partei,* pp. 1050ff., 1054; Meyn, *Deutsche Partei,* p. 26.

6. Henke, *Trennung,* pp. 21–83, offers a new assessment of denazification that takes account of the comprehensive literature; for a documentation of all four zones with an introductory overview, see Vollnhals, *Entnazifizierung.*

7. The following is based on BT-Berichte 1, WP, 23 February 1950, pp. 1329–55.

8. Cf. Kogon, *Irrtum.*

9. This the observation of the *Süddeutsche Zeitung,* 24 February 1950, p. 1.

10. He issued the warning to the government—it had a "duty" to take "effective measures" against the development—on the occasion of the opening of the Amerika-Haus in Stuttgart on 2 June 1950. The address (among other loci, in Fischer and Fischer, *McCloys Reden,* pp. 59–69) was connected to McCloy's recent trip to America, during which he repeatedly encountered a public impression of imminent "renazification." His response was, among other things, to remind people soberly of the starting point—i.e., the original intense "nazification" of German society. Cf. Frei, *Renazification,* p. 49ff.; Brochhagen, *Nach Nürnberg,* p. 183f.

11. Schwarz, *Ära Adenauer I,* p. 133, stresses the parties' intention to gain access to a large base of voters through a "speedy and determined" end of denazification.

12. Cf. Kogon, *Irrtum,* p. 655.

13. The development of the constitutional principle of a "defendable democracy" and the founding of a Federal Office for Protection of the Constitution then followed in direct confrontation with the German Communist Party and the neo-Nazi Socialist Reich Party; cf. Doering-Manteuffel, *Bundesrepublik,* pp. 126–32; also Schwarz, *Adenauer I,* p. 131.

14. Cf. *FDP-Bundesvorstand 1949–1954*, p. 34, and Udo Wengst, "Einleitung," in *FDP-Bundesvorstand 1949–1954*, p. xxxiv; Gutscher, *Entwicklung der FDP*, p. 149.

15. The following is based on BT—PA, Bestand Ausschußprotokolle, Entwurf bzw. Sten. Protokoll der 14. Sitzung des Ausschusses zum Schutze der Verfassung, 13 September 1950.

16. The denazification tribunals had imposed serious penalties (fines, property confiscation, work camp sentences, withdrawal of civil rights, etc.) only in cases classified as groups 1 and 2.

17. BT—PA, Bestand Ausschußprotokolle, Sten. Protokoll der 15. Sitzung des Ausschusses zum Schutze der Verfassung, 27 September 1950; also contains information concerning the subcommittee sessions.

18. BT—PA, Bestand Ausschußprotokolle, Sten. Protokoll der 16. Sitzung des Ausschusses zum Schutze der Verfassung, 5 October 1950.

19. According to an Office of Military Government for Germany, United States (OMGUS) survey, at the start of 1949, nearly three-quarters of those polled were more or less dissatisfied with denazification policies; according to Allensbach the figure was around 80 percent in November 1953; cf. A. Merritt, *Germans and American Denazification*, pp. 377, 383.

20. The version agreed on later called for restrictions to be lifted by as early as 1 April 1951, but limited fines not imposed to amounts not exceeding 2,000 German marks; BT-Drucksachen 1, WP, no. 1440 and no. 1658, Mündlicher Bericht des Ausschusses zum Schutze der Verfassung, 6 October and 24 November 1950.

21. BT-Berichte 1, WP, 18 October 1950, pp. 3431–38.

22. The FDP had been able to markedly improve its results throughout the Landtag elections of summer and fall 1950, e.g., in North Rhine Westphalia from 5.9 to 12 percent and in Hesse even from 15.7 to 31.8 percent (there, to be sure, joining forces with the All-German Block-Union of Expellees and Victims of Injustice).

23 The new and—as we have seen—often overtaxed interior minister, Robert Lehr, promptly misinterpreted the ambiguous debate formulation, thus feeling it incumbent to explain to the Bundestag "that concentration camps in this sense do not exist here in the west"; BT-Berichte 1, WP, 15 December 1950, p. 4068C.

24. BT-Drucksachen 1, WP, no. 1658, mündlicher Bericht des Ausschusses zum Schutze der Verfassung, 24 November 1950. In the spring of 1951, the reports requested by the Bundestag were not yet available. Regarding the question of a reparations law, the government expressed the wish to wait for measures by the Länder to unify their laws; BT-Drucksachen 1, WP, no. 2241, Adenauer to Ehlers, 10 May 1951; Goschler, *Wiedergutmachung*, pp. 286–98, depicts the complications involved in the emergence of the first federal indemnity law.

25. BT—PA, Bestand Ausschußprotokolle, Sten. Protokoll der 18. Sitzung des Ausschusses zum Schutze der Verfassung, 23 November 1950.

26. An overview of the termination regulations of the Länder is to be found in Fürstenau, *Entnazifizierung*, p. 235; the Bundestag's termination recommendation is falsely dated there and in Vollnhals, *Entnazifizierung*, p. 353.

27. The following is based on BT-Berichte 1, WP, 14 and. 15 December 1950, pp. 4054f. and 4065–72.

28. Cf. *Süddeutsche Zeitung*, 16–17 December 1950, p. 1 ("Denazification-Debate in Bonn. Critique on Treatment of Main Offenders Splits CDU and FDP"). The report, in the *Frankfurter Allgemeine Zeitung* (16 December 1950, p. 1), even more strongly stressed the "Coming Apart of the Coalition" and the agreement of the CDU and SPD; according to the barely hidden opinion of the reporter, it would have been "logical" to limit the entire denazification process to what was criminally relevant, instead of exempting categories 1 and 2 from the termination. But, he indicates, foreign policy considerations would probably have spoken against that.

29. Encouraged by prison minister Morgenschweis, and with permission to publish from the church, "the Waffen-SS General emeritus" had been able to announce his conversion to Catholicism in the summer, in a 9,000-copy brochure. See Oswald Pohl, Credo, Mein Weg zu Gott, Landshut 1950.

30. Buscher, *Trial Program*, pp. 96, 163, describes the efforts to pardon Pohl; he was one of the seven Landsberg prisoners whose death sentences were not commuted by High Commissioner McCloy and who were executed in June 1951. Cf. also Schwartz, *Begnadigung*, p. 400, and Klee, *Persilscheine*, esp. pp. 104–7.

31. *Frankfurter Allgemeine Zeitung*, 14 December 1950; I thank Dr. Thilo Bode for friendly information offered on 13 June 1993 allowing me to identify the lead article's author ("Bo").

32. BT-Drucksachen 1, WP, no. 1440, mündlicher Bericht des Ausschusses zum Schutze der Verfassung, 6 October 1950; the final version was identical in these points (no. 1658, 24 November 1950).

33. BT—PA, Bestand Ausschußprotokolle, Sten. Protokoll der 16. Sitzung des Ausschusses zum Schutze der Verfassung, 5 October 1950. The committee's reporter, Walter Menzel, had candidly spoken of "domestic and foreign policy reasons" for "emphatically demanding that the Public Prosecutors must persist more than before in their efforts to furnish the necessary evidence when suspicion exists of crimes against humanity." BT-Berichte 1, WP, 18 October 1950, pp. 3434.

34. In response to these points, the only effort at justification (if not at a direct refutation) also came from Euler. He posed the question of "where the public prosecutors were meant to draw their knowledge of those sorts of facts if people no longer file charges. As a consequence of the way it has been executed, denazification has experienced such a derogation in popular awareness that it no longer occurs to anyone to file charges in such cases." BT—PA, Bestand Ausschußprotokolle, Sten. Protokoll der 16. Sitzung des Ausschusses zum Schutze der Verfassung, 5 October 1950, p. 6.

35. When it came to this issue, even critical contemporaries revealed a remarkable amount of confusion. The legal editor of the *Süddeutsche Zeitung,* Ernst Müller-Meiningen Jr., thus on the one hand predicted in 1950 that the remaining proceedings against Nazi criminals would soon be finished—while on the other hand he surmised, in a penetrating commentary on the "normalcy" of the perpetrators, that thousands of murderers certainly still lived "among us with their deeds unexpiated." Müller-Meiningen, *Das Jahr Tausendundeins,* pp. 9 and 32.

36. The authoritative study in this respect, focusing on Bavaria, remains Niethammer's superb book *Entnazifizierung.*

37. Statistics from Fürstenau, *Entnazifizierung,* p. 228ff. By far, most of the classifications in categories 1 and 2 were made in the American zone (1,654 and 22,122 respectively). In the British zone these classifications could be made directly only by the military government; on account of the separate system of inquest courts, the number was very small. Precise statistics were not available for the Bundestag; BT-Berichte 1, WP, 18 October 1950, p. 3432; cf. also Henke, *Trennung,* p. 51.

38. Cf. Fürstenau, *Entnazifizierung,* pp. 237–59.

39. See below, p. 67f. The argument that rejection of denazification also led to deficits in the regular justice system is already found in Jenke, *Verschwörung,* p. 43.

40. *FDP-Bundesvorstand 1949–1954,* 25–26 October 1952, p. 549.

Chapter 3

1. On the following, see the basic study by Wengst (*Beamtentum*); while offering a detailed history of the emergence of Article 131, Basic Law, and the Federal Civil Service Act, to a large extent it neglects the history's past-political dimension. But see now Garner, *Öffentlicher Dienst,* esp. pp. 769–75; idem, *Public Service,* pp. 38–52; and Wunder, *Bürokratie,* pp. 164–68; Langhorst, *Berufsbeamtentum.*

2. Friedrich, *Kalte Amnestie,* p. 273, stresses this as well, but in line with his basically cynical diction, he refers to those who had been excluded as a "group of victims."

3. "Refugees and expelled persons" refers to Germans expelled from Germany's former eastern territories after the defeat.

4. BT-Berichte 1, WP, 13 September 1950, p. 3144.

5. The total number involved included 147,595 "former Wehrmacht members" and 197,332 "forced out" officials, among whom were 33,397 workers and employees, along with 87,379 pensioners and surviving dependents. Around 81,000 rail and post employees with a right to a claim were not considered. These and, unless otherwise indicated, the following statistics are from Statistisches Amt des Vereinigten Wirtschaftsgebietes (ed.), *Statistische Berichte* no. VII/7/2, 10 June 1950 (Verdrängte Beamte und ehe-

malige Wehrmachtangehörige. Statistische Erhebung über den unter Artikel 131 des Grundgesetzes fallenden Personenkreis. Endgültige Gesamtergebnisse für das Bundesgebiet); Archiv für Christlich-Demokratische Politik [ACDP], I-122–087/4. More economically presented than this rich documentation and with slightly different numbers: Wirtschaft und Statistik, Heft 1 (1950), pp. 9–11.

6. The figure offered in Kleßmann, *Staatsgründung*, p. 254, of approximately 150,000 reemployed denazification "victims" is based on a misleading account in Badstübner and Thomas, *Restauration*, p. 386.

7. Cf. *Kabinettsprotokolle 1950*, p. 42 and passim; on Adenauer's illness and subsequent recuperative vacation, see Adenauer, *Briefe 1949–1951*, no. 246–79; StBKAH, 12.19, press report by Martini and Bebber-Buch, 31 May to 1 June 1950.

8. Cf. Wengst, *Beamtentum*, p. 173f., n. 2.

9. BA, B 106/31802, statement by Auerbach before the Committee on Civil Service Law, 15 March 1950.

10. Goschler, *Wiedergutmachung*, pp. 234–41, esp. p. 235.

11. BA, B 106/31802, statement by Schäfer before the Committee on Civil Service Law, 15 March 1950; ibid. for the following citation.

12. Of a total of 240,026 persons included in the statistics for "forced out" officials (including pensioners and surviving dependents), 79 were major offenders and 1,106 were incriminated persons. Among the professional soldiers and their dependents, the proportion was even smaller: of 167,689 individuals, 20 were major offenders and 61 were incriminated persons. Statistische Berichte (see n. 4), tables 1c and 11c.

13. BA, B 106/7558, South Baden chapter of the "Association" to Interior Ministry, 5 August 1950, cited from Wengst, *Beamtentum*, p. 189.

14. Cf. *Kabinettsprotokolle 1950*, esp. pp. 387, 413, 490f.; StBKAH, III/21, Schäffer to Adenauer, 18 September 1950.

15. BT-Berichte 1, WP, 13 September 1950, pp. 3142–46; BT-Drucksachen 1, WP, no. 1306, Adenauer to Köhler, 31 August 1950.

16. Cf. *Kabinettsprotokolle 1950*, p. 413.

17. For details see Wengst, *Beamtentum*, esp. pp. 309–12; Garner, *Schlußfolgerungen*, completes the picture; cf. also Benz, *Versuche zur Reform*.

18. The "Delegation of the Pension Association of Former Professional Soldiers" consisted of Generals Geyr von Schweppenburg, Linde, and Auleb, along with a "younger officer, several noncommissioned officers, one soldier's widow." StBKAH, Adenauer papers, appointment calendar 25 August 1950. After the meeting, Geyr noted that the chancellor "appeared strikingly badly clothed and did not say much. Human interest was not noticeable." IfZ, ED 91/25; cf. also Diehl, *Thanks of the Fatherland*, p. 150ff.

19. BT-Berichte 1, WP, 13 September 1950, p. 3145.

20. Ibid., pp. 3142–61.

21. In the meantime, upon pressure from the FDP, the Bundestag had passed a law concerning immediate measures to find positions for the "131s";

however, it only came into effect in March 1951 and consequently had hardly any practical significance. Cf. Wengst, *Beamtentum,* pp. 201–11.

22. Cf. the reports and opinions in the *Frankfurter Allgemeine Zeitung,* 29 March to 5 April 1951, as well as in *Die Zeit,* 22 February 1951, pp. 3 and 15, and 29 March 1951, p. 1. Adenauer's intensive engagement in the matter became clear in a conversation with journalists to fill in the background on 15 March 1951; Adenauer, *Teegespräche 1950–1954,* p. 54; IfZ, ED 329/3, 16 March 1951. Cf. also Lenz, *Tagebuch,* pp. 64 and 66.

23. Cf. further below, esp. chapter 7.

24. BT-Berichte 1, WP, 5 April 1951, p. 4984. A year and a half later, Adenauer would repeat this declaration of honor before the Bundestag, in the framework of a debate over the General Treaty (see esp. chapter 8) and the European Defense Community. He explained that the government recognized "all those among our *Volk* bearing arms who fought honorably on land, sea, and in the air in the name of high soldierly tradition." Cf. BT-Berichte 1, WP, 3 December 1952, p. 11141.

25. In his 1950 New Year's address, Heuss had declared that "almost four years ago I encouraged the foreign officers to assist in seeing to it that so-called 'discrimination,' the cheap form of collective defamation, be removed from the German professional soldier, who, in the good sort, represented his professional ethos as well as the good sort on the other side" (Heuss, *Politiker,* p. 404); also in: *Neue Zeitung,* 2 January 1951, p. 9.

26. *Frankfurter Allgemeine Zeitung,* 7 April 1951, p. 2.

27. BT-Berichte 1, WP, 6 April 1951, p. 5028.

28. Ibid., p. 5031.

29. Ibid., p. 5032f. The next day the *Frankfurter Allgemeine Zeitung* placed this at the center of its title page report, with the headline "Demands for Courage Are Acknowledged." The failure of additional motions by the SPD parliamentary faction in favor of former noncommissioned officers was not mentioned. On the general topic of the professional soldiers' lobbying and pensioning, see Diehl, *Thanks of the Fatherland,* chap. 6.

30. Cf. BGBl. I 1951, pp. 307–20.

31. Cf. Garner, *Öffentlicher Dienst,* p. 774; idem, *Public Service,* p. 45f.

32. *Der Spiegel* (9 May 1951, p. 5) looks back at the controlled protest against any such move.

33. BT-Berichte 1, WP, 6 April 1951, p. 5037f. Already in presenting the introductory part of the bill Kleindinst had interpreted the addition to its final part as a sort of corrective, making possible consideration of officials and professional soldiers "who have been transferred ex officio to this department and have not made themselves guilty of any crimes"; ibid., 5 April 1951, p. 4987.

34. According to paragraph 67, periods served with the Gestapo, "Research Office," and Waffen SS were not to be considered, but could be in "special exceptional cases." In the first amendment to the "131" law (22 August 1953), this stipulation was more generously formulated: a period with the Gestapo and Waffen SS could now be taken into account when it "appears

justified according to the professional development, the activities, and the personal demeanor of the official." (Exclusion of members of the "Research Office" from the group of those eligible for pensions according to Article 131, Basic Law, was now entirely dispensed with.) Starting with the second amendment (11 November 1957), even promotions with the Gestapo and the Waffen SS could be taken into account, as long as these would also have been achieved in the officials' earlier positions; BGBl. I 1951, p. 318; 1953, p. 988; 1957, p. 1287.

35. Information from Henkys, *Gewaltverbrechen,* p. 210ff., and Jäger, *Strafrecht,* p. 149; Oppitz (*Strafverfahren,* p. 347) speaks of "at least twenty-five" actually condemned Nazi criminals who were active in police service until the start of their investigation; cf. Rückerl, *NS-Verbrechen,* p. 164; Henke, *Trennung,* p. 53.

36. BT-Berichte 1, WP, 6 April 1951, p. 5038f. Miessner had been an official since 1937 and departmental chief in Hannover's board of financial directors since 1946; he then emerged as a driving force behind the first amendment to the "131" law; cf. Wengst, *Beamtentum,* pp. 99 and 241.

37. BT-Berichte 1, WP, 10 April 1951, p. 5097ff.

38. Ibid., p. 5096.

39. Ibid., pp. 5091 and 5090.

40. Cf. the overview of Hockerts, *Sozialpolitische Entscheidungen,* pp. 426–35; with special stress on the integrative function of social policies: idem, *Integration,* p. 44 and passim.

41. Bundestag president Ehlers thus opined "that with this law—concerning which we can ascertain, with much gratitude, that like the federation's other great social laws it was accepted virtually unanimously—great distress and an injustice weighing upon our people have been liquidated" (BT-Berichte 1, WP, 10 April 1951, p. 5110). Langhorst, *Berufsbeamtentum,* p. 64f., also sees a stress on social and financial policies at the expense of the law's political dimensions; Gross, *Phönix in Asche,* p. 87, offers a good example of a purely socio-legal interpretation.

42. BT-Berichte 1, WP, 10 April 1951, p. 5110; after the Bundesrat allowed it through with a slim majority, the law was announced on 11 May 1951, coming into effect retroactively on 1 April 1951 (BGBl. I 1951, pp. 307–20); on the Bundesrat's position, cf. Wengst, *Beamtentum,* pp. 219–22.

43. BT-Berichte 1, WP, 10 April 1951, p. 5110.

44. See Wengst, *Beamtentum,* pp. 222–35; Goschler, *Wiedergutmachung,* pp. 234–41.

45. Thus Goschler, *Wiedergutmachung,* p. 238, with a view to the opening phase.

46. In the second law on the alteration of the "131" law, passed on 11 September 1957, officials were granted an undiminished transitional income for reemployment purposes in paragraph 37—the equivalent of their earned retirement income; in the third alteration, on 6 June 1961, paragraph 37 could be omitted; BGBl. I 1957, p. 1307, and 1961, p. 1586.

47. Cf. Wengst, *Staatsaufbau,* p. 179.

48. *Kabinettsprotokolle 1951,* p. 185; the theme had been on the agenda six times since 25 August 1950.

49. Marburg's chief mayor, Theodor Bleek (FDP), was state secretary in the Interior Ministry. Bleek had joined the Nazi Party in 1942. The same was true for Günther Bergemann, who became state secretary in the Transport Ministry in 1952; this and the following information is from Wengst, *Staatsaufbau,* p. 179f.

50. BA, B 106/7696 and 7738, Übersicht über den Stand der Unterbringung bis März 1952 bzw. Anfang 1953; ibid. for the following statistics, cited from Langhorst, *Berufsbeamtentum,* p. 65f.

51. Cf. the major study by Anikó Szabó, Vertreibung, Rückkehr, Wiedergutmachung. Göttinger Hochschullehrer im Schatten des Nationalsozialismus, Göttingen 2000.

52. This was the repeated critique of the League of Nazi Victims; cf. Wengst, *Beamtentum,* p. 234; Goschler, *Wiedergutmachtung,* p. 241.

53. Concerning Globke, the exculpatory articles by Robert Kempner and Ulrich von Hehl in Gotto, *Staatssekretär.* While seen for Hehl's study (1980) as well as by Schwarz (*Adenauer II*), the Globke papers (ACDP) remain off-limits for open research. On the contemporary SPD criticism of Globke, cf. Gosewinkel, *Arndt,* p. 241ff. For a West German publishing product in the context of the "Globke trial" staged in the GDR, cf. Strecker, *Dr. Hans Globke.* Rich material on the preparation of the various East German anti-Globke campaigns can be found in Institut für Geschichte der Arbeiterbewegung, Zentrales Parteiarchiv, IV 2/2028; JIV 2/2, JIV 2/3; Der Bundesbeauftragte für die Unterlagen des Staatssicherheitsdienstes der ehemaligen DDR, Prozeßakten Globke. As a first sketch of the topic cf. Lemke, *Kampagnen,* esp. pp. 162–70, and idem, *Antifaschismus,* pp. 70–75; cf. also Bästlein, *Nazi-Blutrichter,* p. 413f.

54. A useful collection of relevant material, including the *Frankfurter Rundschau* article, is offered—along with an apologetic interpretation—in Haas, *Beitrag,* esp. pp. 139, 344–63. The confusing linkage of the Foreign Office affair with the placement of the "131ers" is also found in Langhorst, *Berufsbeamtentum,* p. 66f. The Allied position regarding the scandal is touched on in Brochhagen, *Nach Nürnberg,* pp. 191–95.

55. BT-Berichte 1, WP, 22 October 1952, p. 10735f.; italics in original. Similarly already the remarks of the chancellor to a circle of journalists on 1 June 1951; Adenauer, *Teegespräche* 1950–1954, p. 88ff.

56. SPD Press Service, 26 January 1951, cited from Haas, *Beitrag,* p. 160f.; on the ambitions of the chairman of the CDU-CSU faction, Heinrich von Brentano, cf. Schwarz, *Ära Adenauer I,* p. 174. In the summer of 1952, Brentano referred the chancellor to a secret list with names of members of the old Foreign Office thought to be SS security division members. Adenauer remarked curtly that he had "looked through" the list and among the named "personalities no one is now active in the Foreign Service." StBKAH III/38, Adenauer to Brentano, 13 June 1952.

57. Both Kleßmann, *Staatsgründung,* p. 254, and Kielmansegg, *Lange Schatten,* p. 38, convey this impression.

58. These and the following figures from Statistische Berichte (see n. 4), tables 2a and 2b.

59. Henke, *Trennung,* pp. 53, 65.

60. The Social Democrats in the British zone were already concerned with this development at the start of 1949; Archiv der sozialen Demokratie (AdsD), PV-Bestand Heine, Heine to Löwenthal, 25 January 1949. On the basis of a quantitative analysis for Württemberg and Baden, Ruck, *Administrative Eliten,* p. 61ff. and p. 68, concludes that the great proportion of the administrative personnel there had been able to resume careers interrupted in 1945 "long" before the "131" law came into effect.

61. In this regard, Henke, *Trennung,* p. 65, is perhaps too optimistic, owing to an overestimation of the objective significance of an "increasing sensitization of the public" he sees already at work in the mid-1950s.

62. The Mutual Aid Association of Former Combat SS Members (*Hilfsgemeinschaft auf Gegenseitigkeit,* known as HIAG) scored a partial success in its struggle to see all former professional soldiers in the Waffen SS covered by the "131" legislation; cf. Large, *HIAG,* p. 102. According to a memorandum published by the HIAG national directorship, the demands were recognized for 1,500 persons; cf. Die Waffen-SS und das Gesetz gemäß Artikel 131 Basic Law, in Der Freiwillige, Heft 4 (1959), pp. 5–43, here p. 41; Weiß, *Alte Kameraden,* p. 207.

63. *Frankfurter Rundschau,* 25 January 1955 ("Nazi Chief Judge Sues the State of Hesse"); Gruchmann, *Justiz,* p. 272. Scriba's monthly situation-reports on the Provisional Court of Appeal make clear how firmly his general views, and those related to legal policy, were rooted in National Socialism; IfZ, MA 430/2. In a reader's letter (*Frankfurter Rundschau,* 28 January 1955), a former Auschwitz inmate expressed his indignation at Scriba's assertion; on the interned persons' circumstances—there calorie intake was sometimes higher than that of the normal population—cf. Schick, *Internierungslager;* Wember, *Umerziehung;* for an overview, see Knigge-Tesche, Reif-Spirek, and Ritscher *Internierungspraxis.*

64. Woller, *Gesellschaft und Politik,* p. 163; idem, *Deutschland im Umbruch,* p. 109. In the summer of 1959, Scriba would finally accept the settlement he had been offered by Hesse's Verwaltungsgerichtshof at the start of 1955; *Frankfurter Rundschau,* 18 September 1959.

65. Until now, no social-historical study of the effects of the "131" policies has been published; the same is true for an empirically oriented historical analysis of postwar West German officialdom.

66. Exceptionally, Bavarian Radio's chief editor, Walter von Cube, represented a steadfast critical voice regarding the "131" problem and other abuses at the start of the 1950s; cf. the 1956 collection of commentaries and documentary broadcasts, Hammerschmidt and Mansfeld, *Kurs,* esp. p. 49ff, 64ff. Both authors received unusual support from Marcel Schulte, guest commentator for Hessian Radio and chief editor of Frankfurt's *Neue*

Presse; AdsD, Schmid papers 654, Hessian Radio commentary of 16 February 1956.

67. *Der Spiegel,* 20 July 1955, p. 16f. The war victim's pension repeatedly sued for by the widow of the notorious Reinhard Heydrich (*Reichsprotektor* of Bohemia and Moravia, assassinated in Prague in 1942) was a repeated object of commentaries in the Bundestag; BT-Berichte 1, WP, 24 June 1953, p. 13626 and BT-Drucksachen 3, WP, no. 569, Große Anfrage der SPD-Fraktion vom 16 October 1958, and BT-Berichte 3, WP, 22 January 1959, p. 3057, Antwort des Bundesjustizministers. In their final appeal judgment of 27 June 1958, Schleswig's Landessozialgericht ruled against the government and confirmed the decision of 9 February 1953 by the state's Oberversicherungsamt that a "considerable military interest" had existed in "disposing of Heydrich" and that his widow thus qualified for benefits in line with the federal pension; BA, B 141, Ministry of Labor to Ministry of Justice, 24 October 1958. Cf. Bauer, *Im Namen des Deutschen Volkes,* pp. 353–88, esp. p. 364.

68. On 29 August 1957, at the SPD parliamentary faction's initiative, and in response to the bitter complaints of a Jewish widow who had turned to Adolf Arndt on account of a report in an illustrated magazine, the Bundestag—on the second attempt—agreed on Article 135a, Basic Law; it stipulated inter alia that property of Nazis used by direction of the occupying powers to mitigate the suffering of persecuted individuals should not be exempted from the devaluation that was usual in the framework of burden equalization. It had been preceded by a Federal High Court ruling that had recognized the demands for compensation leveled especially against communes by exponents of the Nazi regime. Documents pertaining to the law initiative can be found in AdsD, SPD-Bundestagsfraktion 2/148; BT-Berichte 2, WP, pp. 13279ff., 13350–53, 13522–26; BT-Drucksachen 1956–57, no. 2416, 3623.

69. Cf. Hammerschmidt and Mansfeld, *Kurs,* p. 49; criticism in this regard was on the basis of the pension furnished Freisler's widow: Fränkische Landeszeitung, 10 November 1955, with a reference to the "new legal ordinances and 258 operational orders." The number of orders of execution alone had reached twenty-eight by 1960. For a complaint concerning the "unintelligibility" of the law from a competent source, see the foreword to the synopsis of Wilhelm Kümmel, Bundesgesetz zu Artikel 131 Grundgesetz, Hannover-Döhren 1961, p. 7.

70. BT-Drucksachen 1959, no. 951, 1022, 1085, 1133, 1156 neu, 1215 (interpellations of the SPD and answers of the government); *Im Namen des Deutschen Volkes,* p. 364f.; cf. also the terse biography of Nathans, *Schlegelberger.*

71. The list was published as a supplement to Ephraim, *Der steile Weg.* With the title "And the Persecutors Are Compensated as Follows," the list, furnished with more than two dozen names, pointed to the *actual* ongoing process of *Wiedergutmachung,* thus forming a contrasting conclusion to Ephraim, pp. 351–54.

72. Cited from Bulletin des Presse-und Informationsamts der Bundesregierung (Bulletin BPA [the Federal Government's Press and Information Office]), 28 February 1956, p. 349f. ("Application of Article 18 is necessary. Against abuse of free rights by incorrigible National Socialists").

73. The term *restoration* was coined by Eugen Kogon; in its spirit see, e.g., Carwin's *Unter der Sonne,* a historically grounded critique—published in Kogon's Frankfurter Heften—of the reemployment of the General Director of the Bavarian State Gallery, dismissed in 1945 but regaining his old position in the spring of 1953 following the pensioning of his temporary successor: for Bavaria this was doubtless the "cheapest solution."

74. Cf. in toto Kirn, *Verfassungsumsturz,* and Grawert, *Zusammenbruch.*

75. For this and the following, see Urteil des Bundesverfassungsgerichts vom 17.12.1953, in Entscheidungen des Bundesverfassungsgerichts, vol. 3, pp. 58–162, here p. 58; following citation: pp. 85–89. The court delivered a similar judgment the same day regarding previous public service employees; three additional judgments were delivered regarding communal officials and employees as well as the group of persons circumscribed by the law. Ibid., pp. 162–224.

76. Kreile, *Magna Charta,* p. 85; Kreile's sole critique of the judgment regards the late and insufficiently clear confirmation of the demise of the German Reich; ibid., p. 91.

77. Beschluß des Bundesgerichtshofs vom 20.5.1954, in Entscheidungen des Bundesgerichtshofs in Zivilsachen 13, pp. 265–319; the following citations: pp. 299, 296, 298.

78. The First Panel was headed by the meanwhile deceased first Constitutional Court president, the former Prussian finance minister and FDP politician Hermann Höpker-Aschoff. Social Democrat Rudolf Katz headed the second division, which was generally considered right wing. On the "cattle market" of political nominations to the court, cf. Schwarz, *Adenauer I,* p. 171f.; Wengst, *Staatsaufbau,* pp. 233–44; Billing, *Richterwahl,* esp. pp. 179–89; cf. also Adenauer, *Teegespräche 1950–1954,* p. 385.

79. Beschluß des Bundesverfassungsgerichts vom 19.2.1957, in Entscheidungen des Bundesverfassungsgerichts, vol. 6, p. 132–222; following citations from pp. 143, 145, 180, 195, 176, 198 (italics in original).

80. The decision did, however, leave unmentioned a statement by Otto Koellreutter alluding to the affair surrounding the first president of the Office of Constitutional Protection (a man linked to the July Plot)—that "[Otto] John-types in no way were suitable to be constitutional judges." (Starting in July 1954, John had spent a period in East Germany, where he was presented as a "crown witness" of the Federal Republic's "fascism"; he was condemned for treason in 1955 following his return to the West.) Also unnoted was G. Krauss's assertion that nonjurists, nonspecialists in constitutional law, and emigrants could "not be taken into

account in the question of the moral unanimity of German constitutional doctrine"; cited from Kirn, *Verfassungsumsturz,* p. 208f., nn. 15 and 22.

81. Beschluß des Bundesverfassungsgerichts vom 19.2.1957, in Entscheidungen des Bundesverfassungsgericht, vol. 6, pp. 222–46.

82. *Im Namen des Deutschen Volkes,* p. 368; on the still merely weak reactions to the Gestapo decision, see also Kirn, *Verfassungsumsturz,* pp. 17, 273–76.

83. Kogon, *Beinahe mit dem Rücken,* p. 642; following citation: p. 641.

84. Cf. the *Frankfurter Hefte* article—entirely sharing Kogon's line and terminology—by Karl Otmar Freiherr von Aretin (still full of skepticism in 1958, as a 35-year-old historian from a south German noble family), *Der Erfolgsdeutsche.*

85. Eschenburg, *Rückhalt,* p. 79f.

86. Thus inter alia Wengst, *Beamtentum,* esp. p. 252, 314; recently Sontheimer, *Adenauer-Ära,* p. 176f.; essentially more critical: Mommsen, *Kontinuität.*

87. The examples of narrow-mindedness by courts and bureaus are legion—without the social history of reparations having been researched in detail; for contributions in that direction, see Herbs and Goschler, *Wiedergutmachung* (cf. esp. the articles of Heßdörfer, Jasper, and Spitta); pointedly Pross, *Wiedergutmachung.*

Chapter 4

1. To be sure, Rückerl, *NS-Verbrechen,* p. 121, establishes that in this phase "mainly less serious offenses" were punished, and Kielmansegg, *Lange Schatten,* p. 45, that there can be no talk of systematic legal prosecution—but rather a prevalence of "accusations by chance." Figures from Justice Ministry statistics, reprinted inter alia in Rückerl, *Strafverfolgung,* p. 125.

2. The Justice Ministry would later try to define the source of this weakening in terms of objective circumstances—many perpetrators had already died or had been unreachable; BA, B 305/48, Die Verfolgung nationalsozialistischer Straftaten durch Staatsanwaltschaften und Gerichte im Gebiet der Bundesrepublik Deutschland seit 1945, no year [1961], pp. 14–17.

3. In 1954, 183 investigations were opened. It is certain that no lower figure is available until 1977, but this presumably holds true well into the 1980s. Following a high point of 1,819 persons in 1948, the number of those convicted had sunk continuously and in great leaps since 1949–50. But in the year before the second amnesty law took effect in 1953, it still stood at 123 persons. Cf. Rückerl, *Strafverfolgung,* p. 125, and idem, *NS-Verbrechen,* p. 329.

4. The affair preoccupied the cabinet for years and finally became the focus of a Bundestag investigative committee. The first internal governmental inquiries had already begun at the end of 1949; these were more or less ter-

minated in August 1951. In the spring of 1952, the police investigation led to the provisional arrest of two officials; toward the year's end there were increasing voices favoring an amnesty. Cf. esp. *Kabinettsprotokolle 1949,* p. 232f., n. 25; 1951, p. 625; 1952, p. 72, n. 44; 1953, p. 299, p. 435, n. 2.

5. Details in Schwarz, *Adenauer II,* p. 99; for this reason, a special paragraph was anticipated in the government's draft stipulating a generous amnesty for "calumniations in the context of differing political opinions." BT-Drucksachen 1954, no. 215. Of the more than 500 cases known to the Justice Ministry pending on account of insults to the government, the chancellor, or individual ministers, 80 percent were directed against members of the German Communist Party; the list does not include the accusations against the chancellor. IfZ, ED 94/166b, note, 30 November 1953.

6. BT-Berichte 2, WP, 26 February 1954, pp. 587B, 588D.

7. He meant the question of pardoning the men sitting in Landsberg who had been sentenced in the subsequent tribunals at Nuremberg. Cf. in detail part 2 below.

8. BA, B 141/4340, Kempner to Dehler, 2 May 1952; Kempner had already discussed the matter personally with Dehler in a jurists' conference venue. On the context, cf. Kempner, *Ankläger,* p. 373f., 379ff.; Lichtenstein, Robert M. W. Kempner, p. 29, correctly criticizes the inadequate editorial care in this autobiographical "interview."

9. Exemplary on the situation of the Jewish displaced persons (DPs) in the postwar period is Wetzel, *Jüdisches Leben;* idem, "Mir szeinen doh." Jacobmeyer, "Jüdische Überlebende"; cf. also Königseder and Wetzel, *Lebensmut.* During a first call on the West German president, the board of directors of the newly founded Jewish Central Council had already drawn attention to "certain difficulties" in the organizational integration of around 9,000 Jewish DPs living in Bavaria; BA, B 122/2080, Aufzeichnung Werz, 22 March 1952.

10. BA, B 122/2080, Notiz Marx und Aufzeichnung Werz, 11 and 25 August 1952, along with an unsigned copy. Max Schindler summarizes the sharp internal Jewish critique of Marx in a letter to Lukaschek, 3 April 1950, StBKAH III/21.

11. BA, B 122/2080, Marx to Werz, 22 September 1952, with enclosure.

12. BA, B 141/4380, Levy to Adenauer, 8 December 1952, with enclosure.

13. Possibly the Central Council had been informed that in the context of the reparation negotiations with Israel in March 1952 Finance Minister Schäffer had requested an estimate of West Germany's loss of income owing to Jewish tax and currency exchange transgressions. Following protests within his ministry, Schäffer did not pursue his intentions. Cf. Goschler, *Wiedergutmachung,* p. 201f.; on the "change of climate," pp. 214–24. Cf. idem, "Der Fall Philipp Auerbach."

14. BA, B 141/4380, Strauß to Levy, 9 January 1953.

15. The opening meeting was on 4 October 1951 in Essen's Saalbau. BA, B 305/49, "Aufruf zur Unterstützung der überparteilichen Aktion zur Her-

beiführung der Generalamnestie" ("Call for Support of the Non-Partisan Operation to Bring About a General Amnesty").

16. On the *Weltanschauung* and policing theory of the former "crown jurist of the SS," see Herbert, *Best.*

17. Cf. the unsigned memo concerning "perspectives for liquidating the political criminal cases from a concluded epoch," whose authorship Best claimed in a markedly warm letter to Ernst Kanter, ministerial advisor in the Justice Ministry. In the letterhead, Best named himself *Ministerialrat z. Wv.*—"Ministerial Advisor to be Reemployed." Here he also designated himself editor of the Achenbach-Dehler correspondence. BA, B 141/4338, Best to Kanter, 15 November 1952.

18. On Achenbach's complicity and entanglement in this crime through his subordinate Carltheo Zeitschel, cf. Klarsfeld, *Vichy—Auschwitz,* esp. pp. 24, 32; Hilberg, *Vernichtung,* pp. 646, 1148. In France, Achenbach's former superior, Ambassador Otto Abetz, was condemned as a war criminal to twenty years' imprisonment in 1949 and was released in 1954; Achenbach contributed a foreword to his self-exculpation, appearing in 1951. Indications of a financing of Achenbach's law firm by Ruhr industrialists inter alia are located in *FDP-Bundesvorstand 1949–1954,* p. 916 (information of Dehler); cf. Herbert, *Best,* p. 463f.

19. BA, B 141/4338, Achenbach to Dehler, 3 November 1952 (with an extensive letter to Blücher, concerning the same matter, as an enclosure).

20. BA, B 141/4338, note of Dreher, 6 November 1952; Dehler to Achenbach, 12 November 1952. Since Achenbach was also offering legal assistance to some war criminals in Allied custody, he sometimes had very frequent personal contact with Dehler through the Justice Ministry's Central Bureau for Legal Defense. *FDP-Bundesvorstand 1949–1954,* p. 951 (information of Dehler); IfZ, ED 94, Strauß to Dehler, 4 August 1952.

21. Cf. Udo Wengst, "Einleitung," esp. p. livff., in *FDP-Bundesvorstand 1949–1954;* there pp. 585–676, the minutes of the meetings of the FDP's directorship linked to the party conference. Cf. Gutscher, *Entwicklung der FDP,* pp. 142–48.

22. BA, B 141/4338, Achenbach to Dehler, 8 December 1952, with law bill and justification.

23. BA, B 141/4338, Dehler to Achenbach, 9 January 1953.

24. Regarding the Naumann affair, see chapter 12 below.

25. BA, B 141/4338, Achenbach to Dehler, 20 March 1953. Best had a thoroughly personal interest in the reinstatement of Nazi amnesties (cf. chapter 3 above, p. 325, n. 66) and the "Law Concerning Measures of State Self-Defense" of 3 July 1934, which had been annulled through Control Council Law no. 11, 30 January 1946. In Munich, the public prosecutor's office was investigating him in connection with the blood purge of the SA in June 1934. Through Dehler, Achenbach managed to have these proceedings quashed; cf. Herbert, *Best,* p. 450f.

26. BA, B 141/4338, note of Wahl, 23 April 1953; similarly Jescheck's earlier opinion concerning Best's memo, 27 December 1952.

27. BA, B 141/4338, note of Kanter, 14 February 1953.

28. Dehler reported on this to the party leadership on 25–26 April 1953; *FDP-Bundesvorstand 1949–1954,* pp. 912–21.

29. Archiv des Deutschen Liberalismus (ADL), N 1/834, confidential opinion of Dehler, 27 May 1953; IfZ, ED 329/5, 5 June 1953.

30. At the same time, owing to Blücher's opposition, Achenbach failed in his plan to enter the second German Bundestag through the North Rhine-Westphalian list; details in Udo Wengst, "Einleitung," pp. lxiii–lxvi, lxxxviii, in *FDP-Bundesvorstand 1949–1954.* Cf. *Neue Zeitung,* 1–2 August 1953.

31. The British had already drawn Adenauer's attention to the Naumann group in December 1952. From the start he attributed great significance to the proceedings against the group, considering them justified and—to the surprise of even his confidants—repeatedly stressing the potential danger that the group had made manifest. One of his motives—but not the paramount one—was certainly the opportunity it offered for solid pressure against coalition partner FDP (and to a lesser degree also the German Party); cf. Lenz, *Tagebuch,* esp. pp. 601, 637, 686; *CDU-Bundesvorstand 1950–1953,* pp. 175, 308f., 456, 529.

32. BA, B 141/4338, note of Wahl, 21 July 1953.

33. Interestingly the justification of the relevant paragraphs contained the observation that "very different opinions" were possible regarding the anticipated pardoning of Nazi criminals. Still, it "was undeniable that a large number of these criminal acts had been committed under circumstances and in a time in which legal concepts were confused not only among the broad populace but also among leading individuals." BA, B 141/4342, provisional referee's draft for a second amnesty law, 19 May 1953 (also in: IfZ, ED 94/166b).

34. Preparation of the referee's draft had only started on 16 May; BA, B 141/4342, note of Wahl, 18 May 1953. On 22 May 1953, the Legal Committee already decided to steer the draft of the initiative to the Bundestag for passage; BT-Drucksachen 1953, no. 4428. At this time, Dehler could feel himself in agreement with the cabinet in his rejection of the amnesty for Platow; cf. *Kabinettsprotokolle 1953,* 19 May 1953, pp. 299, 318.

35. BT-Berichte 1949, pp. 13543–50. On 3 July 1953, the Bundesrat had convoked the Mediation Committee "with the goal of a complete elimination of the law"; on 29 July 1953 the Bundestag confirmed the legal resolution with only small changes; BT-Drucksachen 1, WP, no. 4650, and BT-Berichte 1, WP, p. 14270.

36. On 3 August the chancellor's office had fruitlessly requested that Dehler sign the law. In the cabinet session of 25 August 1953, Dehler renewed his reservations. Lehr and Schäffer cautiously agreed with the Justice Ministry, and the matter was postponed until "mid-September" at Adenauer's request. *Kabinettsprotokolle 1953,* p. 435f., n. 2.

37. BA, B 141/4342, note of Dehler, 8 September 1953.

38. In a brief note of 9 September 1953, Dehler maintained that the cabinet had taken up his suggestion "to prepare a general amnesty law." BA, B 141/4342. There is, however, no indication of this in the records of the 8 September 1953 cabinet session; *Kabinettsprotokolle 1953*, p. 449ff.

39. He had already expressed his disappointment with Adenauer in very pessimistic terms in a confidential conversation on 11 August 1953 with Robert Strobel, Bonn correspondent of *Die Zeit*. IfZ, ED 329/5.

40. Schwarz, *Adenauer II*, p. 112ff., holds the West German president and the president of the Constitutional Court responsible for Dehler's fall; they both believed the reforms considered necessary by, in particular, the chancellor were not possible under Dehler; cf. also Ott, *Dehler*, p. 139; Mende, *Freiheit*, p. 248f.; F. J. Strauß, *Erinnerungen*, p. 255f; *FDP-Bundesvorstand 1949–1954*, pp. 1187–93. But it is clear that there was also a strong desire for disposal of the incalculable "rocket" (Brentano) in the Union—and that Adenauer ceded to the desire with pleasure; cf. Lenz, *Tagebuch*, p. 696f., p. 685; *CDU-Bundesvorstand 1953–1957*, 10 September 1953, pp. 7, 34 (Adenauer), p. 21 (F. J. Strauß).

41. BA, B 141/4342, note of Dehler, 9 September 1953. In the following interministerial consultations, Justice Ministry referee Dallinger brazenly asserted that the ministry was not responsible for the plans becoming known.

42. BA, B 141/4342, note of Dallinger, 11 September 1953.

43. The FDP attempted to soften the impact of Dehler's departure from the Justice Ministry by electing him parliamentary faction chairman; the blow nevertheless hit him markedly hard. Cf. Maassen and Hucko, *Dehler*, p. 9. A few months later Dehler became Blücher's successor as chairman of the FDP.

44. For a pregnant overview, see Rückerl, *NS-Verbrechen*, p. 284ff.

45. BA, B 141/4342, confidential transcript of the departmental meeting, 18 September 1953, pp. 10f., 16, 23.

46. BA, B 141/4343, telex of Güde to BMJ, 24 September 1953.

47. One version of the proposed paragraph was especially insidious and very close to what Best wanted. For cosmetic reasons, a first sentence once again exempted persons sentenced to up to two years in prison for deeds committed out of opposition to Nazism. A second sentence then offered unlimited exemption to persons who, "misled by National Socialist doctrines or prompted by an official or service order," had committed deeds that they could not decline "without danger." BA, B 141/4347, Referentenentwürfe zu Paragraph 3a, 21–22 September 1953.

48. BA, B 141/4343, confidential transcript of the meeting with representatives of the judicial administrations of the Länder, 24 September 1953 (draft), citation p. 54.

49. BA, B 141/4347, provisional referees' draft, 8 October 1953, paragraph 9.

50. Cf. p. 339, n. 17. As panel president for the Federal High Court, Kanter was attacked by the GDR in 1958; BA, B 136/1743, Office of Constitutional Protection to Chancellor's Office, 13 September 1958. In his apologetic

"My Experiences as Chief Judge in Denmark," Kanter interprets his 1951 intervention on behalf of an imprisoned Best as fulfillment of a debt of thanks, since at the start of 1945 Best had "perhaps saved my life through his reports to the Foreign Office." IfZ, ZS 1991/I, p. 96f.

51. BA, B 141/4343, confidential transcript of meeting with representatives of the judicial administrations of the Länder, 24 September 1953 (draft), citation p. 52.

52. As was *Referatsleiter* Dr. Dallinger, *Ableitungsleiter* Dr. Schafheutle had been active in the Reich's Justice Ministry; *Unterableitungsleiter* Dr. Kanter and *Referatsleiter* Dr. Dreher had pasts as, respectively, military and special judges—a fact with which they would be confronted some years later in the course of the GDR campaign against "Hitler's blood judges." The past of two occasionally active referees (Wahl, Dr. Meyer) could not be determined; specification of competence in IfZ, Fg 15/3–4, Organisationsplan des Bundesjustizministeriums, 1 February 1953 and January 1954.

53. For the first time in this formulation: see the provisional draft of 19 October 1953; BA, B 141/4347.

54. The committee's chairman, Bonn attorney Hans Dahs, saw to it that the "unanimous" opinion became known to the Justice Ministry. The attorneys rejected only the idea of a general amnesty; punishments that could not be amnestied through the planned law were to be taken care of through individual pardons; BA, B 141/4344, conference minutes, 20 November 1953; italics in original.

55. BA, B 141/4345, secret transcript regarding department meeting, 9 November 1953.

56. BA, B 141/4345, secret transcript regarding meeting with representatives of the judicial administrations of the Länder, 24 November 1953.

57. Cf. *Kabinettsprotokolle 1953*, p. 531.

58. In opposition to the representative of the Bavarian Justice Ministry, Strauß declared deeds committed during the collapse to be "not worthy of amnesty." *Kabinettsprotokolle 1953*, p. 542.

59. BA, B 141/4351, minutes of the session of the Bundesrat Subcommittee on the Amnesty Law, 7–8 December 1953, and of the 127th session of the Bundesrat Legal Committee, 10 December 1953. Position of the Bundesrat in BT-Drucksachen 2, WP, no. 215, appendix 2.

60. BR-Berichte, 18 December 1953, p. 74 (reprint).

61. BR-Berichte, 18 December 1953, p. 71f. (reprint).

62. *Kabinettsprotokolle 1954*, p. 19ff.

63. BT-Drucksachen 2, WP, no. 215, appendix 3.

64. BA, B 141/4351, speech draft of Meyer, 28 January 1954; BT-Berichte 2, WP, 26 February 1954, p. 586ff.

65. BT-Berichte 2, WP, 26 February 1954, p. 593.

66. BT-Drucksachen 2, WP, no. 248, motion of Höcherl, Strauß, Stücklen, and colleagues, 9 February 1954.

67. BT-Berichte 2, WP, 26 February 1954, p. 597. The agreement between CSU and SPD in this point was also revealed in the first consultations over the

law in the Bundestag Legal Committee; BA, B 141/4352, minutes of the ninth session, 16 March 1954.

68. BA, B 141/4352, minutes of the tenth session of the Bundestag Legal Committee, 18 March 1954; ibid. for following citation.

69. BA, B 141/4352, minutes of the twelfth session of the Bundestag Legal Committee, 2 April 1954; ibid. for following citation.

70. BT-Berichte 2, WP, 18 June 1954, pp. 1556–93, ibid. for following citation and the voting results.

71. For more on both the murder and the courts, see Henke, *Besetzung,* chs. III.2 and VII.2.

72. Gesetz über den Erlaß von Strafen and Geldbußen and die Niederschlagung von Strafverfahren and Bußgeldverfahren vom 17.7.1954, BGBl. I 1954, pp. 203–9, here paragraph 9.2.

73. *Süddeutsche Zeitung,* 19–20 June 1954, p. 1 (city edition); according to this report "only something like four" SPD delegates had assented. In its title, the *Frankfurter Allgemeine Zeitung* (19 June 1954, p. 1) referred to "numerous Social Democrats."

74. BT-Berichte 2, WP, 15 July 1954, p. 1925ff.; following citation: p. 1927.

75. *Der Spiegel,* 9 June 1954, p. 4.

76. At the end of 1948 the *Spruchgerichte* had delivered a mere nine sentences of more than five years' prison—or 0.06 percent of their total sentences; cf. the statistical overview in *Die Spruchgerichte* 3 (1949): 85.

77. Walter Becker, "Das Straffreiheitsgesetz 1954," in *Juristische Rundschau* 9 (1954): 321–24, here 324.

78. This and the following information is based on crime statistics up to 31 December 1954 from West Germany's Federal Office of Statistics, in BA, B 141/4357. The statistics were not publicized; cf. the corresponding material in *Wirtschaft and Statistik* 9 (1957): 215, n. 2 ("Rechtspflege"); some general information in *Wirtschaft and Statistik* 8 (1956): 243f.

79. BA, B 141/4339, note of Wahl, 28 November 1952.

80. Among such jokes, for instance, was the play between *Braun-Schweiger* ("the brown [i.e., Nazi] silencers") and the like-named city dwellers, coined by a delegate from the All-German Block-Union of Expellees during the first amnesty debate; BT Berichte 2, WP, 26 January 1954, p. 600. According to a relevant report in the *Frankfurter Allgemeine Zeitung* of 9 September 1952, the Justice Ministry intended to ask the general amnesty lobbyist and international law specialist Friedrich Grimm (cited in the article) "how the estimate of 80,000 was arrived at." Even in the more recent scholarly literature, such exaggerated figures have led to misleading estimates of the significance of the "illegals" amnesty; cf. Rückerl, *NS-Verbrechen,* p. 135; Jasper, "Wiedergutmachung," p. 189.

81. Cf. Rückerl, *Strafverfolgung,* p. 125; the Central Bureau did not extend these statistics past 1978; personal information of Directing State Prosecutor Streim to the author, 19 May and 5 June 1992.

82. BT-Berichte 3, WP, 24 May 1960, p. 6682 (Walter Menzel, SPD); cf. Rückerl, *NS-Verbrechen,* p. 132f.

83. Cf. esp. Erich Schmidt-Leichner, Das Straffreiheitsgesetz 1954, in *Neue Juristische Wochenschrift* 7 (1954): 1265–69; here p. 1266.
84. In this respect see the pathbreaking study of Jäger, *Verbrechen*, pp. 83–160; cf. Buchheim, "Befehlsnotstand."
85. See the interpretation of Becker, *Straffreiheitsgesetz* 1954, p. 323; cf. n. 76 above.
86. *Der Spiegel,* 12 January 1955, pp. 15–21.
87. Bauer, "Im Namen des Volkes," p. 309.
88. BT-Berichte 2, WP, 23 June 1955, p. 5138.

Part II

1. See Jung, *Rechtsprobleme,* esp. pp. 1–6, 107–26, 147–65, 175–81, for a juridical description and evaluation of the legal objections raised by the Germans since the late 1940s—objections discussed in these pages in the context of their contemporary political instrumentalization. Jung's commentary on the two central, repeatedly raised points of criticism—a lack of Allied legal authorization and a violation of the ban on retroactive punishment—leaves no doubt regarding their lack of validity. In addition, Jung points to the same clear conclusion for the charge of a "basically 'unfair trial' " leveled by the defense at the Flick trial (and others) at Nuremberg; ibid., p. 86ff.
2. For an overview of the Dachau trials, see Sigel, *Gerechtigkeit.*
3. For a closer analysis of the figures, see below, p. 346, n. 27.

Chapter 5

1. From a letter to the *New York Herald Tribune,* published on 14 December 1948.
2. Cf. the pointed description of the "road to Nuremberg" in the classic 1981 study by Bradley F. Smith, *The Road to Nuremberg,* as well as idem, *Reaching Judgement,* pp. 20–45; see also Buscher, *Trial Program,* esp. pp. 7–27. The literature on "Nuremberg" and its consequences is vast; for a concise, still suggestive sketch of the historical problems, cf. Gruchmann, "Urteil," along with Erdmann, *Ende,* pp. 98–112.
3. IfZ, MF 1543, U.S. Opinion Concerning Policy Toward Germany, 31 October 1945, p. 3. After the trial's close, the *Chicago Tribune* spoke up once more against the American press's general praise of the proceedings, comparing the International Military Tribunal with "Hitler's court." Ibid., 4 October 1946.
4. Cf the extensive analysis in Bosch, *Judgement,* esp. chapter 5.
5. Cf. Frei, *Lizenzpolitik,* pp. 82–100, esp. p. 95; for a press analysis (sometimes strained in its conclusions), see Jürgen Wilke, "Ein früher Beginn der 'Vergangenheitsbewältigung': Der Nürnberger Prozeß und wie darüber

berichtet wurde," *Frankfurter Allgemeine Zeitung,* 15 November 1995, p. 14.

6. Over the course of the trial (20 November 1945–1 October 1946), the portion of those polled in the American zone who considered it "unfair" was between 4 and 6 percent; the figure rose to 30 percent in 1950. The shift from 78 to 38 percent in those considering it fair was the largest the High Commission opinion experts had observed until then; cf. Merrit and Merrit, *OMGUS Surveys,* p. 33ff., and idem, *HICOG* [Office of the High Commissioner for Germany] *Surveys,* pp. 11, 101.

7. Cf. Woller, *Gesellschaft und Politik,* esp. p. 134f.; on the Evangelical position see Vollnhals, *Evangelische Kirche.*

8. It was above all Bishop Wurm who interceded for Neurath since September 1945; cf. Vollnhals, "Hypothek," p. 60, n. 23.

9. Cf., e.g., the objections to the International Military Tribunal voiced, above all, by Wurm, Meiser, and Dibelius in a meeting of the council of the German Evangelical Church (Evangelische Kirche Deutschlands [EKD]) on 13–14 December 1945. Dibelius expressed himself thus: "That the Russian is appearing there as plaintiff is an unacceptable thought. For this reason Nuremberg is no conscience for the world." *Protokolle des Rates der EKD,* vol. 1, p. 211f.; citation on p. 212.

10. Cf., e.g., the detailed report titled "The German Church View" issued by the United States Forces European Theater, Military Intelligence Service Center, 28 February 1946; IfZ, MF 260, A[djutant]G[eneral] 1945–46/2/4.

11. Wurm to Lawrence, 19 September 1946, cited from Vollnhals, "Hypothek," p. 59.

12. Cf. Spotts, *Kirchen,* pp. 36, 73–78.

13. IfZ, MF 260, Polad 817–7, Offie to Murphy, 7 May 1947.

14. Cf. Vollnhals, "Hypothek," p. 61. The EKD council had already intervened for the interned in a Christmas 1946 message to the *"American Volk":* among the prisoners, the message explained, "alongside a small number of genuine criminals," there was a "great number" of persons finding themselves automatically incarcerated "on grounds of suspicions and slander or as a result of membership in an organization or on account of their position as officials; *Protokolle des Rates der EKD,* vol. 1, p. 717. On 11 February 1948, in his capacity of EKD council chairman, Wurm delivered Clay a detailed "Memo on the Circumstances in the Internment Camps." Wishing to be understood as a "contribution to internal pacification," it pleaded for generous releases and pardons "in view of an extremely tense world political situation" and a "specially hard winter." Transcript in Evangelisches Zentralarchiv (EZA), 2/268.

15. EZA, 2/265, Asmussen to Bell, 14 February 1948 (copy); italics in original.

16. Ibid., Bell to Asmussen, 23 March 1948, along with answers from the general secretary of the Federal Council of the Churches of Christ in America, 1 April 1948, and the president of the United Lutheran Church in America, 10 April 1948.

17. On the following cf. Buscher, *Trial Program*, p. 34ff.; Bower, *Pledge*, pp. 255–58; Schwartz, "Begnadigung," p. 380.
18. *Chicago Tribune*, 23 February 1948; I would like to express warm thanks to the newspaper for allowing generous access to its clipping files.
19. For such an impression, see, e.g., the short biography in the *Neue Zeitung*, 18 September 1948, p. 7.
20. The *Chicago Tribune* naturally made as much capital from this fact as it could. General Clay explained the matter at great length to its correspondents, expressing his formal regret—to be sure also over the isolated case being used to reproach the army with censorship; IfZ, MF 260, AG 1949/75/3, Clay to Foust, 29 March 1948.
21. *New York Herald Tribune*, 24 February 1948.
22. See Smith, *Heimkehr*, esp. pp. 61–81. There was a corresponding committee in the British zone council in Hamburg, but the possibilities available to the Stuttgart counterpart were "greater from the onset, and its range of influence rather wide." BA, B 305/14, Bericht über die bisherige Tätigkeit des Referats "Rechtsschutz für Deutsche im Ausland," 30 June 1950.
23. Cf. from the large amount of—frequently apologetic—literature on this episode: Whiting, *Massacre*. On the following, esp. Weingartner, *Crossroads;* Bower, *Pledge*, pp. 248–71; Buscher, *Trial Program*, pp. 37–40; Mendelsohn, "War Criminal Trials," p. 248f.; also Henke, *Besetzung*, pp. 24–32.
24. Cf. Weingartner, *Crossroads*, p. 184f.
25. Cf. Buscher, *Trial Program*, p. 38.
26. Ibid., p. 93. Cf. Morgenschweis, "Wahrheit," part 4, p. 7.
27. In the Dachau and other American army trials, among a total of 1,672 accused persons, 1,416 were convicted and 426 were sentenced to death. It appears that 268 of such sentences were carried out. In the subsequent tribunals at Nuremberg, there were 184 accused persons, 142 convictions, and 24 death sentences, of which 12 were carried out. Of the 1,085 persons tried before British military courts, 240 received the death sentence (the total number of convictions is not available). The French occupation courts convicted 2,107 persons, 104 receiving the death sentence. According to official Russian statistics of 1990, Soviet military courts condemned 756 persons to death. Between 1945 and 1950, in the Soviet occupation zone, 12,770 persons were transferred to the USSR from the camps run by the Soviet secret police; around 37,600 sentences were reported to have been handed down following the transfers. Figures from Sigel, *Gerechtigkeit*, p. 38f.; Rückerl, *Strafverfolgung*, pp. 28–31; Hermann Weber, Vorwort, in Kilian, *Einzuweisen*, p. 7; Karner, *Archipel*, p. 176. A confidential Justice Ministry report of 1961 estimated the number of total legally sentenced perpetrators as something over 10,000; BA, B 305/48, Die Verfolgung nationalsozialistischer Straftaten durch Staatsanwaltschaften und Gerichte im Gebiet der Bundesrepublik Deutschland seit 1945, undated, p. 22.

28. Cf. the—in any event rather sensational—book by Aarons and Loftus, *Ratlines*, esp. pp. 25–47, and Klee, *Persilscheine*, pp. 25–50; earlier and generally more sober: "Hansjakob Stehle, Pässe vom Papst? Aus neuentdeckten Dokumenten: Warum alle Wege der Ex-Nazis nach Südamerika über Rom führten," *Die Zeit*, 4 May 1984, pp. 9–12 ("Dossier").

29. Cf. Neuhäusler, *Kreuz and Hakenkreuz*, p. 343 and passim; along with this documentation from 1946, cf. idem, *Wie war das im KZ Dachau?* esp. pp. 3–6.

30. In the 1960s it became clear that Neuhäusler did not refrain from falsifying documents for the sake of mitigating the church's stance during the "Third Reich"; cf. Spotts, *Kirchen*, p. 81.

31. IfZ, MF 260, AG 1949/75/3; ibid. for the following citation.

32. In a letter to the director of the Baden-Württemberg military government, 21 May 1948, Wurm confirmed being "informed with precise information by the defense." Ibid.

33. The reference here is to the International Military Tribunal.

34. An illustrative confirmation of this by Hellmut Becker, Ernst von Weizsäcker's defense attorney, in Becker and Hager, *Aufklärung als Beruf*, pp. 35–42.

35. IfZ, MF 260, AG 1949/75/3, LaFollette to Clay, 8 June 1948.

36. Ibid., Clay to Legal Division, 15 June 1948.

37. Ibid., Clay to Wurm, 19 June 1948.

38. The press service for the church of Baden-Württemberg published the letters on 29 June 1948; IfZ, MF 260, 5/344–1/26 The American *Neue Zeitung* and the recently appearing weekly published by the Evangelischen Verlagswerk in Stuttgart, *Christ und Welt*, each published a report with extensive citations (1 July and 4 July 1948, respectively). In both cases, Clay's critique of those sympathizing with individuals who had tormented millions was absent.

39. In self-assured candor, Wurm had already explained to the director of Baden-Württemberg's military government that "from my experience, official petitions do not always manage to reach the crucial departments; they are in the habit of reacting only when the public is brought into play." Ibid., Wurm to LaFollette, 21 May 1948.

40. Cf., e.g., the admiring portrait of Wurm in *Die Zeit*, 13 January 1949, p. 2. Earlier already, albeit emerging self-referentially from the church milieu, *Christ und Welt*, 7 August 1948, p. 2: "Through his tireless intercession on behalf of justice, Bishop Wurm has received a mandate—this the opinion of the 'Evangelische Welt,' rendering him spokesman for the German people, perhaps the only such speaker the German people has today."

41. Internal memorandum, Haefele, 16 September 1948, cited from Buscher, *Trial Program*, p. 99. The observations of the intelligence division of the Bavarian military government, made in the fall and winter of 1948–49, were similarly critical; IfZ, MF 260, 10/88–2/7.

42. Cf. Buscher, *Trial Program*, p. 100.

43. The unusual query of the *Stuttgarter Nachrichten* regarding the extent to which Wurm had considered the effect of his "campaign for fairness and justice" on Nazi circles was promptly parried by *Christ und Welt,* 20 June 1948, p. 2, with the remark that the Länder bishop had here been "misunderstood."

44. Wurm to Kempner, 30 March 1948, cited from the "Sopade" [Social Democratic Party of Germany in exile] Information Service 18 September 1948. An English translation of the letter exchange, which was initially on a personal basis, would be included in an important church memorandum discussed below, pp. 123–26.

45. Wurm to Kempner, 5 May 1948, cited from *Neue Zeitung,* 16 May 1948.

46. Kempner to Wurm, 15 May 1948, cited from the "Sopade" Information Service, 18 September 1948.

47. This was Peter Beauvais, whom LaFollette had brought to Baden-Württemberg in his capacity as theater officer: "I requested Beauvais because he was my chief interrogator. I knew how he thought, and I knew how he conducted his interrogations. I also knew that in every movement that he made in Nuernberg he was conscious of the fact that he had to lean over backward in his treatment of defendants and witnesses in order that no charge could be brought against him personally or against the Nuernberg process generally by reason of any methods which he used. Beauvais is an outstandingly decent honorable young man." IfZ, MF 260, AG 1949/75/3, LaFollette to Clay, 8 June 1948.

48. Ibid.

49. Wurm to Kempner, 5 June 1948, cited from "Sopade" Information Service, 18 September 1948.

50. Cf. *Evangelische Welt,* 1 June 1948, p. 290.

51. Christlicher Nachrichtendienst (Christian News Service [CND]) report, in *Kieler Nachrichten,* 27 May 1948; ibid. for the following citation.

52. Cf. *Neue Zeitung,* 6 August 1948, p. 5.

53. Deutsche Presse-Agentur (dpd) report, cited from *Lüneburger Landeszeitung,* 18 June 1948.

54. Cf. *Die Zeit,* 27 May and 17 June 1948; 14 October and 25 November 1948. Cautious, but also taking Wurm's line, was Ernst Müller-Meiningen Jr. in *Süddeutsche Zeitung,* 22 May and 29 May 1948, both p. 3; Müller-Meiningen had been able to look at the files kept by the Malmédy defense team. Cf. Tüngel's book, published in 1958, meant to settle accounts with the occupation powers: Tüngel and Berndorff, *Auf dem Bauche,* esp. pp. 324–57.

55. Dpd, 12 June 1948, cited from the "Sopade" Information Service, 18 September 1948. *Christ und Welt* (28 August 1948, p. 4) offered a critique of the silence of German politicians that, in light of the paper's usual vantage point, was surprisingly clear and sharp: for the author, these politicians apparently believed "that Nuremberg was the private affair of those arbitrarily accused, and that questions concerning the German people in its entirety are not at stake."

56. IfZ, MF 260, AG 1948/3/1, Frings to Clay, 26 August 1948.

57. Ibid., memorandum J.E.K. to Gailey, 24 September 1948.
58. Cf. Buscher, *Trial Program,* pp. 94 and 110, n. 11.
59. IfZ, MF 260, 5/344–1/26, Office of Military Government for Bavaria (OMGB) Religious Affairs Branch, notes of James Eagar, 1 September 1948.
60. The delegation was composed of Stuttgart High Consistory member Rudolf Weeber; the Landsberg prison minister, August Eckardt; and Weizsäcker attorney Hellmut Becker.
61. IfZ, MF 260, 5/344–1/26, notes of Gauerke, 26 August 1948.
62. Cf. Bower, *Pledge,* p. 260f.; Buscher, *Trial Program,* p. 39f.
63. The *Neue Zeitung* (12 and 16 October 1948, both p. 2) reported the statement of judge Edward LeRoy van Roden, while also including a clarification from the head of the Dachau investigative authority.
64. A considerable number of petitions and copies of letters of reply from Clay in, e.g., IfZ, MF 260, 17/55–1/9, and AG 1949/7.
65. Revealing in this respect is Clay to Royall, 2 October 1948, in Clay papers, p. 889, cf. Clay, *Entscheidung,* p. 254ff. The absence of such concerns is particularly clear in the views expressed by Neuhäusler to the CND, 23 October 1948, in: IfZ, MF 260, 5/344–1/26.
66. On the latter law's interpretation as "supralegal law" in the theoretical sense of Gustav Radbruch, cf. Laage, Auseinandersetzung, esp. p. 414ff.
67. IfZ, MF 260, AG 1948/3/1, Clay to Frings, 25 September 1948.
68. Particulars in IfZ, MF 260, AG 1949/75/5 and 5/344–1/26 (CND-Berichte, 19 and 22–24 October 1948); a part of the responses (Clay for Truman) also in AG 1948/3/1.
69. Cf. *Süddeutsche Zeitung,* 26 October 1948; two days later, the paper published the names of the provisionally spared men.
70. Cf. *Süddeutsche Zeitung,* 30 October 1948.
71. IfZ, MF 260, 5/344–1/26; Neuhäusler to Truman (CND-Bericht, 23 October 1948).
72. Ibid., Wurm to Dulles (CND-Bericht, 22 October 1948).
73. IfZ, MF 260, AG 1949/75/5, Neuhäusler to Clay, 8 November 1948.
74. In December 1948, the papal emissary in Washington delivered a petition for the pardon of those war criminals condemned to death; cf. Clay papers, p. 962.
75. IfZ, MF 260, AG 1949/75/5, Neuhäusler to Clay, 26 October 1948.
76. Ibid., Neuhäusler to Clay, 26 October and 8 November 1948.
77. One example is the affair concerning an Advent wreath that Landsberg's American prison director had gruffly removed from the dining room on account of it being a fire hazard; this prompted Neuhäusler to remark that he had "not even experienced something like that in a concentration camp. In the four Advents and Christmases that I had to spend in a concentration camp, neither Advent wreaths nor Christmas trees were kept from us." Clay had the incident scrupulously investigated, finally justifying the director on the basis of fire regulations. IfZ, MF 260, 1949/75/5, Neuhäusler to Clay, 6 December 1948, and response, 9 May 1949. As *Christ*

und Welt (13 June 1948, p. 6) critically registered, an Advent wreath had already been denied the Nuremberg prisoners in 1947.

78. Cf. Clay papers, p. 1038 and 1062.

79. Clay had reduced the judgment to four years' prison on 8 June 1948. His grounds were that it could not be convincingly shown that Ilse Koch selected camp inmates, and had them murdered, in order to get hold of their tattooed skin, and that her possession of "objects made of human skin" was also not proven. However, news of the shortened sentence only reached the public on 16 September 1948; cf. Smith, *"Hexe" von Buchenwald*, p. 146.

80. Cf. Margret Boveri's clever, measuredly critical report following the Wehrmacht trial sentence announcement in *Die Zeit*, 4 November 1948, p. 3. At the start of August 1948, the Essen city council protested the Krupp trial verdict, and the association of 12,000 Krupp pensioners appealed "in the name of humanity" to the pope, to Clay, and to Eleanor Roosevelt; cf. *Neue Zürcher Zeitung* and *Kieler Nachrichten*, 8. and 12 August 1948, respectively.

81. *Der Spiegel*, 13 November 1948, p. 7f. Cf. the parting letter of a Landsberg prisoner who had been condemned to death in the *Kieler Nachrichten*, 27 November 1948, and the report on the execution of a putatively innocent man in the *Rhein-Echo*, 16 December 1948; the article "Landsberg—Recht oder Macht?" in the *Kölnischer Rundschau*, 11 December 1948, also serves as a prime example.

82. *Neue Zeitung*, 6 November 1948, p. 7.

83. On Manstein see also 144. Cf. Bower, *Pledge*, p. 241. The money collecting was widely registered in the press; cf., e.g., *Neue Zürcher Zeitung*, 11 August 1949. Churchill's first mention of a donation is in a letter to Eden, 13 September 1948; cf. Gilbert, *Churchill 1945–1965*, p. 431.

84. Held from April until June and then in September 1949, the hearings are documented in over 1,500 printed pages. For the following, above all, see U.S. Senate Committee on Armed Services, subcommittee, *Malmédy Massacre Investigation*, 81st Cong., 1st sess., 1949 (hereafter referred to as the Baldwin Report, 13 October 1949); cf. the descriptions, filling in details, in Buscher, *Trial Program*, pp. 40–43, and Bower, *Pledge*, pp. 267–70.

85. Baldwin Report, 13 October 1949, p. 31.

86. Ibid., p. 32.

87. Ibid., p. 33.

88. When it came to solid information on the Baldwin Report, the German press was reticent. Instead of offering such information, the *Süddeutsche Zeitung* "spotlight" column of 19 October 1949 depicted the subcommittee as a hate-twisted, sword-swinging figure of Justice, now commenting with a sense of injury on the plot thesis, "we are one hope poorer." Predictably, *Christ und Welt* (27 October 1949, p. 6) characterized the Baldwin Report as "questionable."

89. *Süddeutsche Zeitung*, 18 October 1949, p. 1; *Neue Zeitung*, 27 October 1949; ibid. for the following citation. Wurm had already expressed his con-

tempt for the "Morgenthau-clique" to the CND; cf. *Süddeutsche Zeitung*, 19 October 1949, p. 2.

90. On the McCarthy link, cf. Weingartner, *Crossroads*, p. 201. Several of Aschenauer's pronouncements saw print; cf., e.g., Rudolf Aschenauer, *Zur Frage einer Revision der Kriegsverbrecherprozesse* ("On the Question of Revising the War Crime Trials") (Nuremberg, 1949) (the brochure was dated 1 September, anniversary of the war's beginning); idem, *Um Recht und Wahrheit im Malmédy-Fall* ("On Right and Truth in the Malmédy Case") (Nuremberg, 1950).

91. A fragment handed down from the OMGB Intelligence Division suggests that at the end of 1948 the circle around Neuhäusler contacted the Americans to propose doing business. In the future the bishop would not publish critical material and if occasion arose would even work against the "national bolshevist" Wurm group. In exchange the Dachau defense team would be given access to the interrogation reports in the Malmédy case and some pilot cases. IfZ, MF 260, 10/88–2/7, Shea to Assistant Land Director, 17 December 1948.

Chapter 6

1. The context of this statement was Servatius's plea for his clients Schumacher and Urmes, in the Luxemburg war crimes trial of former officials in the German civil administration; BA, B 305/16.

2. Cf. the highly factual, lightly malicious report in *Der Spiegel*, 19 May 1949, p. 7ff.

3. IfZ, ED 157/8, conversation transcript, 28 May 1949. The Heidelberg University rector hoped to raise initial funds for a meeting through contributions from the chambers of industry and commerce in Karlsruhe and Mannheim.

4. Copious material in, e.g., BA, B 305/61 and 140.

5. Around at the same time as the founding of the Heidelberg circle of jurists, Aschenauer launched a legal-aid office in Nuremberg supported by both churches and, soon after, a "church committee for prisoners' aid" in Munich; that organization also received (modest) funds from industry by way of a Nuremberg parish; cf. Klee, *Persilscheine*, pp. 78–82.

6. See below, p. 140f.

7. Jung, *Rechtsprobleme*, p. 156ff., particularly criticizes the "position of unincriminated but extremely conservative" Hodenberg regarding a ban on retroactive punishment as "that of a naive political Mr. Clean"; BA B 122/644, Kranzbühler to the office of President von Herwarth, 29 October 1949.

8. Kaufmann was a seventy-year-old emeritus; through his conflict with the generation younger Wilhelm Grewe, head of the delegation seeing to the end of occupation statute, he would be shunted aside politically in 1951; cf. Grewe, *Rückblenden*, p. 132f.

9. Biographical information from EZA, Ranke papers 657/87/7, Evangelischer Pressedienst, Landesdienst Berlin, 4 February 1987.

10. See, in this respect, Buscher, *Trial Program,* pp. 101–4 (with small errors but generally on the mark); less convincing is Klee, *Persilscheine,* pp. 129–32, where the Heidelberg circle is viewed too heavily from the perspective of its concern with fund-raising—and is even in a way prettified as the "quiet help of jurists."

11. See p. 10 above. The agile Achenbach saw to it that the work also circulated in Bonn; a copy is located in the Justice Ministry files (BA, B 141/4283). Tauber, *Beyond Eagle,* esp. p. 524, contains instructive material on Grimm; cf. the apologetic collection published in a radical right-wing context: Grabert, *Friedrich Grimm.*

12. On Achenbach, see above, p. 71ff. One example of his labors is a suggestion to Clay's political advisor Robert Murphy (already known from Paris), made during a trip to the United States in 1949 and contained in a letter that was as audacious as it was mendacious: in the interest of German-American friendship, the war criminal problem might be solved through application of the U.S. parole system and establishment of a pardon commission; IfZ, MF 260, 17/250–2/2, Achenbach to Murphy, undated [before October 1949]; Murphy, *Diplomat,* p. 62, 79f.

13. Vollnhals's account in "Hypothek," p. 63, thus needs correction; unnecessarily dramatic is Klee, *Persilscheine,* pp. 87–93.

14. EZA, 2/264, draft of Ranke, August 1948.

15. EZA, 2/266, folder with excerpts from minutes of interrogations and trials.

16. EZA, 2/261, Kranzbühler to Ranke, 12 July 1949.

17. Cashing in on the promise did, however, take a certain stubbornness on the part of the church's chancellery; EZA, 8/84/Kv/47, Weeber to Ranke, 19 June 1950.

18. Memorandum by the Evangelical Church in Germany on the Question of War Crimes Trials Before American Military Courts; one example inter alia in the Landeskirchlichen Archiv, Stuttgart, Wurm papers, 294; portions of the German draft are in EZA, 2/261.

19. EZA, 2/84/Kv 47, Hartenstein to Ranke, 25 January 1950.

20. Expected to be present, the Evangelical church's council chairman, Dibelius, excused himself on the grounds of ill health, and his deputy, Lilje, did likewise on the grounds of other unavoidable responsibilities; ibid., Ansprache Hartenstein, 21 February 1950.

21. They saw it as the result of a spontaneous invitation by Mrs. McCloy, following an hours-long delay in the scheduled Frankfurt meeting due to a "surprising trip" by the High Commissioner; ibid., confidential transcript (Ranke), undated. But according to his working calendar, on 21 February 1950 McCloy attended an entirely predictable "semi-annual briefing" with General Handy.

22. EZA, 2/84/Kv 47, address of Hartenstein, 21 February 1950.

23. Cited from Schwartz, "Begnadigung," p. 389; for the above and what follows, cf. this excellent essay and ibid., *America's Germany.*

24. For an overview, cf. Jung, "Ius ad bellum," in Niedhart and Riesenberger, Lernen, pp. 262–80.
25. EZA, 2/84/Kv 47, confidential transcript (Ranke), undated; italics in original.
26. It came exactly a day after, with the proviso that McCloy make special arrangements for working with the public; Acheson to McCloy, 22 February 1950, cited from Schwartz, "Begnadigung," p. 388.
27. Ibid., p. 387f.
28. Between 1946 and 1949, German courts in the Western zones and Berlin had imposed 130 death sentences; 24 were carried out, the majority in the British zone (none of these judgments was linked to Nazi crimes); cf. Düsing, Todesstrafe, p. 231f.; 277ff.
29. Cf. Parlamentarischer Rat, vol. 2, p. 575.
30. Cited from Düsing, Todesstrafe, p. 279.
31. Cf. above, p. 346, n. 27.
32. In the second debate's oral justification, Seebohm again expressed his "disgust at the great number of death sentences carried out over recent years," but he no longer referred to a concrete period; cf. Parlamentarischer Rat, Verhandlungen des Hauptausschusses, p. 534 (42nd sess., 18 January 1949).
33. Ibid., p. 670 (50th sess., 10 February 1949).
34. Cf. Düsing, Todesstrafe, pp. 283–86; Doemming, Füsslein, and Matz, "Entstehungsgeschichte," p. 739ff.
35. Cited from Düsing, Todesstrafe, p. 285.
36. The argument still appears in right-wing radical literature; cf., e.g., Franz-Willing, Vergangenheitsbewältigung, p. 10.
37. Parlamentarischer Rat, Verhandlungen des Hauptausschusses, p. 583f. (43rd sess., 19 January 1949).
38. Cf. Doemming, Füsslein, and Matz, Entstehungsgeschichte, p. 169.
39. Christ und Welt, 12 January 1950, p. 2. In 1959 Koch was condemned to death in Warsaw; but—as it was explained—on grounds of health the sentence was commuted to life in prison, where he died in 1968.
40. Die Zeit, 17 November 1949, p. 1 ("The Executioner of East Prussia").
41. Cf. Kölnische Rundschau and Allgemeine Kölnische Rundschau 26 and 27 July 1949, respectively; ibid. for following citation.
42. Cf. Hüwel, Arnold, esp. p. 27–60.
43. Kordt's authorship becomes clear from his correspondence in July and August 1949. In May, he had already prompted Arnold to make a public statement on the trial, without, to be sure, Weizsäcker's name ever being mentioned; IfZ, ED 157/8, Kordt to Becker, 15 May 1949; ibid. for the cited characterization of Arnold.
44. Cf. Blasius, "Patriot," esp. pp. 301–5; see also Döscher, Verschworene Gesellschaft, esp. pp. 69–72 (on Erich Kordt) and p. 110ff. (on Theo Kordt).
45. IfZ, ED 157/48, Weizsäcker to E. Kordt, 21 March 1947; Wein (Die Weizsäckers, esp. p. 324–35) offers a highly informative overview of Weizsäcker's postwar biography.

46. IfZ, ED 157/48, Weizsäcker to E. Kordt, 13 March 1947.
47. IfZ, ED 155, Th. Kordt to Weizsäcker, 11 October 1947.
48. IfZ, ED 157/7, notes of Th. Kordt concerning interrogation on 15–16 October 1947, p. 10f. On the complex details of Weizsäcker's actual role—both his actual efforts to prevent the outbreak of a world war and those on behalf of German hegemony—cf. Blasius, *Großdeutschland*. Weizsäcker would receive a seven-year prison sentence for helping to plan the March 1939 invasion of rump Czechoslovakia and for his bureaucratic complicity in the deportation of many thousands of Jews from France. See further below.
49. While waiting for his judgment in Nuremberg, Weizsäcker included the following in a letter to his wife of 8 March 1949: "Remarkable how the 'resistance' literature can hardly be overlooked anymore. One author already cribs the previous one. It is possible to get a good view of the way historical theses are formed." Cited from Blasius, *Großdeutschland*, p. 157.
50. As, for instance, in the case of the declaration of the former League of Nations commissioner in Danzig, Carl Jacob Burckhardt; cf. Becker's interesting remarks on the question of the authenticity of Burckhardt's published diary: Becker and Hager, *Aufklärung als Beruf*, pp. 36, 38f.
51. Cf. Piontkowitz, *Anfänge*, esp. pp. 57–61.
52. See above, p. 106.
53. IfZ, ED 155, Becker to Richard von Weizsäcker, 12 May 1949.
54. Immediately after the judgment's submission, Becker organized the delivery of excerpts to well over 200 individuals; lists and correspondence in IfZ, ED 155. Regarding his future strategy, Becker expressed himself at greatest length to Robert Boehringer, a friend of Weizsäcker living in Switzerland. Boehringer had financially supported the costly defense, which included the services of American attorney Warren E. Magee; ibid., Becker to Boehringer, 3 May 1949.
55. IfZ, ED 157/8, Becker to Th. Kordt, 21 May 1949. A month later Becker pressed Kordt to let him know "if you consider the entire matter realizable and to what degree you believe that your chief will work for it." He added, "In my view all men sharing our approach and having ties with the West German government have to realize that a West German government capable of action takes on a moral and political burden if it does not energetically speak up against a man like Weizsäcker remaining in jail." Ibid., Becker to Th. Kordt, 22 June 1949.
56. Cf. Wein, *Die Weizsäckers*, p. 329.
57. IFZ, ED 157/8, E. Kordt to Th. Kordt and to Becker, 7. and 8 October 1949, respectively. Soon after, animated by a conversation with two Nuremberg defense attorneys (one being Kranzbühler), the president pressed his party colleague Justice Minister Dehler to seek a conversation with the competent "American expert" in order to help Weizsäcker and others "who we believe have been unjustly condemned." BA, B 122/644, Heuss to Dehler, 29 October 1949.
58. *Kabinettsprotokolle 1949*, 26 September 1949, p. 341 (verbatim session transcript).

59. BT-Drucksachen 1, WP, no. 60, 29 September 1949.

60. BT-Drucksachen 1, WP, no. 165, 4 November 1949; BT-Berichte 1, WP, 1 December 1949, p. 544–48; ibid. for the following citations.

61. Law no. 48–1416 allowed the punishment of all members of organizations declared criminal by the International Military Tribunal on account of collectively perpetrated deeds, as long as the individual members could not produce proof of having been forced to join the organization and of having not participated in the criminal deeds; cf. Lummert, *Strafverfahren*, p. 97.

62. BT-Berichte 1, WP, 1 December 1949, p. 544.

63. Ibid., p. 545f.; ibid. for the following citations.

64. On Oradour, see pp. 139 below. Approximately forty Wehrmacht soldiers were killed during battles between communist partisans and two German companies stationed in Tulle on 7–8 June 1944. The following day, the Second SS Tank Division ("*Das Reich*"), led by General Lammerding and on its way to Normandy, executed at least ninety-nine French hostages. (The same division would be responsible for the destruction of Oradour). For a detailed account—corresponding to the seven condemned war criminals' perspective—of the Ascq episode (false orthography in Bundestag minutes: Asque), in which eighty-six inhabitants of the village were mowed down in revenge for a nearby explosives attack on a train, see *Der Spiegel*, 15 June 1950, p. 11ff. (with interesting readers' letters, 6 July 1950, p. 5f.).

65. BT-Berichte 1, WP, 1 December 1949, p. 547.

66. The influential attorney Behling voiced his support with Dehler for a move to Bonn of Gawlik, former First Public Prosecutor in Breslau's Provisional Court of Appeal. To be sure, he was recommending Gawlic (born in 1904) not to be head of the Central Bureau for Legal Defense, but rather to be the director of the legal aid office of the Evangelical Relief Organization, Flitner, who had suggested himself in conversation with Behling; BA, All. Proz. 21/180, Behling to Dehler, 3 December 1949; Flitner to Behling, 23 November 1949; biographical information on Gawlik in Estate 263/430.

67. In a meeting in Heidelberg on 21 January 1950, lawyer Fröschmann had made a similar request in Gawlik's presence ("Dachau war criminals are poor and cannot pay a lawyer out of their own pockets"); EZA, 8/84/Kv/47, confidential transcript, 30 January 1950.

68. The fact that following its establishment there was little public talk about the activities of the Central Bureau does not justify designating it a "secret department," as does Bower, *Pledge,* p. 364.

69. Dehler was here appropriating Kurt Schumacher's words—forming the basis of the SPD's interpellation, and clearly aimed at the length of sentences imposed in the first postwar trials—in the Bundestag session of 15 November 1949; BT-Drucksachen 1, WP, no. 303, 9 December 1949.

70. Cf., above all, Farmer, *Oradour-sur-Glane.*

71. Both the fact that the trial only began at the start of 1953 and its result showed that there could be no serious talk here of victor's justice: six of the twenty men accused before the military court in Bordeaux were Ger-

mans; all others were Alsatians. One German and one Alsatian were sentenced to death, four Germans received prison terms, and one was acquitted. With the exception of the man sentenced to death, the Alsatians were quickly released because of an amnesty law passed by the National Assembly. In the end both men facing death were pardoned, the last German being freed in 1958. Cf. Farmer, *Oradour-sur-Glane,* chapter 4.

72. BT-Berichte 1, WP, 11 January 1950, p. 781ff.

73. In the cabinet on 22 November 1949, in the absence of the chancellor, Dehler proclaimed his intent of proposing a "Christmas" amnesty. Condemned persons over sixty-five, along with those who were under twenty-one at the time of their deed or had already served a fourth of their ten-year sentence [*sic*] were to be amnestied (as Dehler saw it, the latter group was "in the rule not punishable according to valid German law"). Adenauer apparently did not concur with this proposal to the extent Dehler maintained, since its upshot was a note on 9 December to the French High Commission, which responded on 31 December 1949 that a conditional discharge with good behavior had already been the policy for two years; *Kabinettsprotokolle 1949,* p. 217. This did not prevent Dehler from having his spokesman declare to UPI on 15 December that a corresponding request had already been delivered to McCloy; *Neue Zürcher Zeitung,* 16 December 1949. The German Press Agency report spoke only cryptically of a limited Christmas amnesty by the High Commissioners; *Frankfurter Allgemeine Zeitung,* 16 December 1949.

74. This figure was circulated in the summer of 1949 by pastors for the war prisoners. Confronted with the figure through an inquiry of Eleanor Roosevelt, the OMGUS Administration of Justice Branch indicated it was "quite possible." IfZ, MF 260, POLAD/457/24, memo Sullivan, 8 September 1949.

75. Adenauer to François-Poncet, 6 December 1949, in Adenauer, *Briefe 1949–1951,* p. 142f. Adenauer formulated the request for an acceleration of the proceedings against Germans in France parallel to a letter sent to all three High Commissioners, asking them to work for a release of the German war prisoners being held in Eastern Europe before Christmas; *Kabinettsprotokolle 1949,* 13 December 1949, p. 263f.

76. *Akten zur Auswärtigen Politik,* vol. 1, p. 86. The cabinet met the next morning, the minutes simply referring, in connection with the pending visit of the French Foreign Minister, to Adenauer's remark that François-Poncet showed himself "especially inaccessible" the previous day; *Kabinettsprotokolle 1950,* 13 January 1950, p. 123. Shortly after, in question time devoted to the situation of war prisoners in the Soviet Union and Yugoslavia, Adenauer used the occasion to mention François-Poncet's pledge that the cases still pending in France would be closed during the year; BT-Berichte 1, WP, 27 January 1950, p. 1012.

77. As if acting out in defiance, in an FDP party congress on 22 January 1950 in Hamburg, Dehler demanded full freedom of action for the Federal Republic, along with disposing of the "impediments" of occupation status and

those at work in the Ruhr region. Germany was no aggression-loving state, and Hitler was "to a large extent a result of mistakes in the Versailles Treaty but also, above all, the timidity of France"; cited from *Süddeutsche Zeitung,* 24 January 1950, p. 1 (front-page story: "Gesture of Protest by François-Poncet to Adenauer"). François-Poncet recorded his protest of 12 January 1950 in a letter to Adenauer; Dehler's talk received considerable attention in the international press, and the French commissioner then wrote the chancellor again. A few weeks later, Adenauer mentioned informally to the High Commissioners that had it not been for the two written interventions he would have dismissed Dehler; cf. Brochhagen, *Nach Nürnberg,* pp. 131 and 399, n. 18. Avoiding public discussion was also the gist of a conversation between Adenauer and François-Poncet on 22 March 1950; *Akten zur Auswärtigen Politik,* vol. 1, p. 159.

78. American mistrust becomes very clear in a confidential memorandum of Hans W. Weigert, an old personal friend of Dehler, who as head of the German Justice Branch of the HICOG Administration of Justice Division in Bad Nauheim had already had a precise, critical sense of Dehler's political impact as president of Bamberg's Provisional Court of Appeal; IfZ, MF 260, 17/217–2/2, Weigert to Bowie, 26 April 1950. On McCloy's response, cf. Buscher, *U.S. High Commission,* p. 62, and above, p. 29.

79. Flitner was able to delay the delivery of 2,000 legal cases processed by the Relief Organization for weeks; supported by Gerstenmaier, he expressed only a degree of satisfaction when it was made clear that the organization would be able to retain responsibility for legal aid "toward the east," since a federal department could not be directly active in that realm. Details in BA, B 305/94.

80. As a member of the Bavarian chancellery, Bittner had already gained relevant experience in the War Prisoner Committee of the Stuttgart State Council; as she had not been a Nazi Party member, she appeared a politically opportune appointment in view of the foreign contacts coming with the position. Author's interview with Margarethe Bitter, 19 April 1990.

81. BA, B 305/14, Tätigkeitsbericht des Referats "Rechtsschutz für Deutsche im Ausland," 30 June 1950. For the first quarter of 1950, however, 500,000 marks still appear to have been transferred from the government to the Evangelical Relief Organization; BA, All. Proz. 21/180, Flitner to Behling, 23 November 1949.

82. Central Bureau files make clear that in the view of officials, the compensation of many defense attorneys was disproportionate to services rendered. Relevant details in BA, B 305/13.

83. BA, B 305/14, overview of the period 16 March-30 June 1950.

84. *Süddeutsche Zeitung,* 16 December 1949, p. 3; ibid. for following citation, italics in original.

85. *Frankfurter Allgemeine Zeitung,* 12 December 1949, p. 1.

86. The High Commissioner had received the delegation (Geiler, Hodenberg, Kaufmann, Wahl) on 30 November 1949; IfZ, F 154/1, McCloy's itinerary; cf. Schwartz, "Begnadigung," p. 383; Bird, *Chairman,* p. 330.

87. Details on the establishment of the board—based on recommendations of the Simpson Commission, it also reflected pressure from Congress—in Buscher, *Trial Program*, p. 57ff.; Mendelsohn, "War Criminal Trials," p. 252.

88. Cf. Buscher, *Trial Program*, p. 60; Schwartz, "Begnadigung," p. 385ff.; latter source for the following as well.

89. In a press conference with American journalists on 22 December 1949, McCloy referred to "some general system of parole that would be constantly reviewing the condition of the prisoners." National Archives, Washington, RG 466, McCloy papers D 49/480, HICOG Public Relations Division, 23 December 1949.

90. *Frankfurter Allgemeine Zeitung,* 21 December 1949, p. 3; the *Süddeutsche Zeitung* of the same day included a brief German Press Agency report.

91. For example, an extended program of education, sport, and culture was in place from the start; details in Klee, *Persilscheine,* pp. 76f., 140f.

92. The word circulating in the Heidelberg jurist's circle on 21 January 1950 was that "if possible, a press battle should not be activated." EZA 8/84/Kv 47, confidential transcript, 30 January 1950.

93. *Frankfurter Allgemeine Zeitung,* 7 January 1950, p. 3.

94. Cf. Brochhagen, *Nach Nürnberg,* p. 30f. *Neue Zeitung,* 21 December 1949, p. 1, reported on the German press reaction; this was accompanied by a report on the first releases from Landsberg. The *Tagesspiegel* (Berlin) followed with this succinct comment: "The mildness here seems as surprising as the severity there."

95. AP report, cited from *Frankfurter Allgemeine Zeitung,* 12 January 1950, p. 3.

96. Including, e.g., Cardinal Frings, whom he visited before Christmas 1949, underscoring the necessity of "taking account of the U.S. public." BA, B 141/9576, report of Wahl on a meeting with Knott and Frings, 30 January 1950.

97. Details in Frei, "Renazification."

98. Cf., e.g., his radio address in Washington, 23 January , and his talk in Boston, 26 January 1950, in *HICOG Information Bulletin,* February and March 1950, pp. 15f. and 68–72, respectively.

99. IfZ, F 154/2, McCloy's itenerary, 23 January-2 February 1950.

100. Cf. Buscher, *Trial Program,* p. 62; Schwartz, *America's Germany,* pp. 160–64; ibid. for the following.

101. This above all Bower's argument in *Pledge;* Buscher, *Trial Program,* leans strongly in the same direction.

102. Cited from *Der Spiegel,* 4 May 1950, p. 4; Guderian's further "conditions" were Germany's "equal status in a coalition" and equal participation in an "inter-Allied high command." Meyer (*Situation,* pp. 695–98) cites only comparable formulations for the time "after Korea"; on Wiegand, cf. Tauber, *Beyond Eagle,* p. 1129, n. 43.

103. Cf. *Der Spiegel,* 13 December 1950, p. 4.

104. Cited from *Der Spiegel,* 16 May 1950, p. 3; Kesselring was released in October 1952.

Chapter 7

1. BA, B 122/56.
2. Cf. the excessively sympathetic, at times apologetic account of Meyer, "Situation," along with idem, "Soldaten."
3. On this and the following, see the still valuable, if sometimes superseded, discussion by Baring, *Außenpolitik*, pp. 148–63; see also, above all, Wiggershaus, "Entscheidung," esp. pp. 363–73; Foerster, "Innenpolitische Aspekte"; and Schwarz, *Ära Adenauer I*, pp. 104–18.
4. Cf. Wettig, "Entmilitarisierung," p. 400.
5. The last quotation mark is missing in the draft—apparently a typographical error, as elsewhere there is a reference to the "so-called 'war criminal question.' "
6. The two soldiers being Karl Dönitz and Erich Raeder.
7. Cited from Rautenberg and Wiggershaus, "Himmeroder Denkschrift," pp. 169, 189; italics in original.
8. Security memorandum in Schubert, *Sicherheitspolitik*, pp. 79–83; "Memorandum zur Frage der Neuordnung der Beziehungen der Bundesrepublik zu den Besatzungsmächten" ("Memorandum on the Question of the Reorganization of the Relations Between the Federal Republic and the Occupying Powers") in Adenauer, *Erinnerungen 1945–1953*, p. 358f.
9. Cf. *Frankfurter Allgemeine Zeitung*, 26 August 1950.
10. Adenauer to Arnold, 26 August 1950, in Adenauer, *Briefe 1949–1951*, p. 266 and 539f.
11. In his no less sharp answer, Arnold promptly evoked the right to free expression enshrined in the Basic Law; ibid., p. 540.
12. In the draft, the wording was initially as follows: "The federal government has for months been engaged in difficult negotiations concerning release of our prisoners in France. The government has likewise discussed the question of revising the verdict in the Weizsäcker trial with the American High Commissioner on a number of occasions. There was a prospect of obtaining good results in all these questions. To be sure, a precondition was that they would not be made an object of public discussion, for as you know, just as in America and France we have to reckon with a public opinion interpreting such comments to mean that we are purchasing our cooperation with the other peoples of Western Europe through concessions, and that the desire of the German people for cooperation with the other peoples is based exclusively on getting rid of the burdensome limitations in such a manner." Adenauer changed the entire formulation following "interpreting such comments" to read "to mean that other countries had committed an injustice." Ibid., pp. 266 and 539.
13. IfZ, ED 329/2, 11 August 1950, p. 3, 25 October 1950, p. 3, 2 November 1950, p. 1.
14. *Frankfurter Allgemeine Zeitung*, 16 August 1950, p. 1; ibid. for the following citation.

15. In the heat of polemics, Sethe attributed the Kesselring witticism regarding the jurists as soldiers to Manstein, continuing thus: "Now, keeping in mind that in Korea Americans have to fight against partisans for the first time, and after having read, for instance, Norman Mailer's book *The Naked and the Dead*, we may doubt whether every little lieutenant in Korea regularly consults the legal faculty in Boston."

16. Only the now famous warnings concerning rearmament in the *Frankfurter Heften* were earlier; cf. above all Kogon, "Man braucht Deutschland—auch deutsche Soldaten?"; idem, "Das Gespenst der deutschen Remilitarisierung"; then, "after Korea," idem, "Die Entscheidung auf Leben and Tod."

17. Cf. Dönhoff's title page articles of 13 April, 13 July, 19 October, 23 November 1950.

18. For instance, in the *Südost-Kurier* (Bad Reichenhall), 24 August 1950, where a well-informed article about the Peck Commission—written as the introductory lines put it, from "a special direction"—was titled "Speedy Decision over Landsberg."

19. Cf. *Frankfurter Allgemeine Zeitung,* 23 August 1950, p. 2. According to the later official report, commission member Moran had spoken with every prisoner; HICOG, Landsberg, p. 17. Like the other prominent persons in the Foreign Office trial, Ernst von Weizsäcker had already seen Moran in Landsberg in April and took a liking to him; IfZ, ED 155, Weizsäcker to Becker, 29 April 1950 (with attached material); BA, B 122/644, Becker to Herwarth, undated.

20. Verbatim copy of McCloy's letter to *Aufbau*'s chief editor, Manfred George, in the *Neue Zeitung,* 5 September 1950; there was a report in the *Frankfurter Allgemeine Zeitung* on the same day.

21. Eleven of the men who received early releases had been sentenced in military court proceedings; cf. *Archiv der Gegenwart,* 16 August 1950; *Neue Zürcher Zeitung,* 18 and 28 August 1950.

22. In the original sentence pronouncement, the court had declared that if need be it would accept applications for the correction of errors conceivable in light of the mass of material. On the basis of such defense attorney applications, both Weizsäcker and Woermann were then acquitted of the charge of having planned a war of aggression; Steengracht was acquitted of charges related to the murder and mistreatment of soldiers and prisoners. Unsurprisingly, Hellmut Becker considered these corrections a strong confirmation of his efforts—and as grounds for a search for more exculpations. "What we now need to do is convince the High Commissioner to reduce the last two years even further." IfZ, ED 157/8, Becker to Th. Kordt, 3 February 1950.

23. *Frankfurter Allgemeine Zeitung,* 16 October 1950, p. 1, ibid. for following citation. In an accompanying editorial, the paper declared that with the decision, McCloy had "de facto annulled" the Nuremberg judgment passed on Weizsäcker. "In a juridical sense, it still exists. McCloy cannot pass sentence, but can only pardon. It remains to be wished that those measures of the American legal instances also taking up the flaws in the judgment against

Weizsäcker, as well as of many other men who have deserved it, follow the distinguished conduct of the High Commissioner. Above all, the "unknown Landsbergers," numbering in the hundreds, should not be forgotten. Among them, as well, there are many whose judgments are problematic. They cannot rely on prominent witnesses. They have to wait until right again takes its proper place [bis das Recht wieder seinen richtigen Platz einnimmt]."

24. Among these letters, there may even have been one written by British Foreign Minister Lord Halifax, at the urging of Theo Kordt, to President Truman around the very start of 1950; cf. Döscher, *Verschworene Gesellschaft*, p. 112.

25. Theo Kordt was once again involved in the effort, along with his brother Erich (no longer employed in the Foreign Service), Herbert Blankenhorn, Hans von Herwarth, and Hans Riesser (in the General Consulate in New York)—and Erich Kaufmann. On 24 February 1950, Becker—speaking with Blankenhorn—cited Kaufmann as follows: "it is now established that complicity in bringing about a war of aggression carries a sentence of two years in prison." Becker continued: "Following Weizsäcker's acquittal, the punishment was reduced in this point from seven to five years. I don't believe our American friends have the proper organ to appreciate the involuntarily comic quality at work here." Details in IfZ, ED 157/8.

26. IfZ, ED 155, Trützschler to Becker, 25 February 1950. BA, B 122/644, Becker to Herwarth, 8 April 1950 and undated [end of May 1950]; B 122/648, Weizsäcker to Heuss, 20 October 1950 (handwritten note of thanks); IfZ, ED 157/8, Becker to Th. Kordt, 6 May 1950.

27. In a conversation with Bavarian Radio, Wurm also declared that the Allied judgments were certainly not "mistaken judgments" but that there were indeed "some real judicial murders among them." Cited from German Press Agency, 18 August 1950.

28. Details of HICOG's decision-making process in Schwartz, "Begnadigung," pp. 392–400. At the time of its issuing the commission's report was of course sealed.

29. BT-Berichte 1, WP, 8 November 1950, p. 3563; on the debate in general and its evaluation, cf. Volkmann, "Innenpolitische Dimension," pp. 256–69.

30. An indignant Adenauer suggested as much on 16 November 1950; cf. *Akten zur Auswärtigen Politik,* p. 264.

31. BT-Berichte 1, WP, 8 November 1950, p. 3614; italics in original.

32. Ibid., p. 3591; italics in original.

33. On 9 November , the German Press Agency had reported that McCloy intended to announce his decisions within the next six weeks. "According to reliable information, confirmation of some of the death sentences passed on the sixteen former SS and SD leaders must be expected." Cited from *Frankfurter Allgemeine Zeitung,* 10 November 1950, p. 3 ("Act of Pardon—No General Amnesty").

34. BT-Drucksachen 1, WP, no. 1599, 10 November 1950.

NOTES FOR CHAPTER 7

35. Since 1945, Höfler had been building up the Caritas association for aid to war prisoners, whose purview naturally included war criminals being held abroad. Starting in 1952, Höfler was a delegate of a UN special commission concerned with war prisoner questions; cf. Amtliches Handbuch 2, WP, p. 368.

36. BT-Berichte 1, WP, 14 November 1950, p. 3690ff.

37. *Akten zur Auswärtigen Politik,* vol. 1, 16 November 1950, pp. 264–73; ibid. for following citation.

38. Adenauer reported only on secondary matters the next day in the cabinet session. According to a note of Seebohm's, the ministers only received substantial information in the following session, on 21 November 1950; cf. *Kabinettsprotokolle 1950,* pp. 830 and 839f., n. 32.

39. "I am aware that this entire matter is extremely unpleasant for the Belgian government. Perhaps something can be done on the Allied side to bring this matter to an end. I have heard from the Belgian government to the effect that Belgian legislation does not allow any sort of intervention in a pending court case. But von Falkenhausen can in fact become sick and the proceedings can be broken off. He can be let out on his word of honor. Then what follows will sort itself out." Ibid., p. 271.

40. The chancellor thus also demanded a reinstatement of the radio's pre-1933 legal status; at present, he explained, the "propaganda monopoly" lay in the hands of journalists not accountable to either the legislative branch or the government. *Foreign Relations of the United States (FRUS) 1950,* IV, p. 782.

41. An English translation of the paper in *FRUS 1950,* IV, p. 780ff.

42. Cf. Ibid., p. 782.

43. Cf. Brochhagen, *Nach Nürnberg,* p. 153.

44. *Akten zur Auswärtigen Politik,* vol. 1, 16 November 1950, p. 277.

45. Ibid., p. 274f.

46. Cf. *FRUS 1950,* IV, p. 780, McCloy to Acheson, 17 November 1950.

47. *Akten zur Auswärtigen Politik,* vol. 1, 16 November 1950, p. 277f.

48. This encounter on 15 November 1950 is described in Meyer, "Situation," p. 696, without indication of sources; it is unclear whether it is identical with the night visit of the two men to the home of McCloy's director for political affairs, Samuel Reber, described rather imprecisely in Thayer, *Die unruhigen Deutschen,* p. 251f. (this is assumed by Schwartz, "Begnadigung," p. 395).

49. The *Frankfurter Allgemeine Zeitung,* 15 November 1950, had a three-column front-page report ("Bonn Against Extraditions and Executions. United Declarations of Government and Bundestag"). The single editorial column declared that parliament and government had "spoken to all Germans from the heart, without party distinctions."

50. Evangelische Akademie Bad Boll, Abt. Soldatenfragen, no. 11, Eberbach to the church dean's offices, Oct. 1950; AdsD, Schmid papers, Eberbach to Schmid, 24 October 1950 (Carlo Schmid could not participate in the conference despite his agreement to); cf. Meyer, "Situation," p. 663f.

51. Evangelische Akademie Bad Boll, Abt. Soldatenfragen, no. 11, conversation note of Eberbach, "Soldatentagung" ("soldiers' conference") undated.

52. Evangelische Akademie Bad Boll, Abt. Soldatenfragen, no. 11, Tagungsprotokoll, 22 November 1950.

53. *Stuttgarter Zeitung*, 27 November 1950 ("The Soldiers' Summation").

54. *Frankfurter Allgemeine Zeitung*, 14 December 1950, p. 2; the paper carried three reports on the conference, the last ending with the cited sentence.

55. EZA, 2/84/Kv/41,3, confidential transcript, undated.

56. ADL, N1/2201, Dehler to Klaiber, 27 November 1950; Koch to Dehler, 22 October 1950. The citation was from the judgment against the—acquitted—State Secretary Otto Meißner and was in reference to Hitler's "night and fog" decree; IfZ, Z 2, Weizsäcker trial, p. 460.

57. In Bonn, Erich Kaufmann saw to it that the texts became known in the Justice Ministry and the president's office, among other places; BA, B 122/644, Kaufmann to Klaiber, 5 January 1951, and B 305/93; published English version in EZA, 2/84/6453/11.

58. EZA, 2/84/Kv/41, 3 report of Ranke to Brunotte, 22 January 1950.

59. *Christ und Welt*, 7 December 1950, p. 4. Ingrim had good contacts with Geneva-based Weizsäcker friend Robert Boehringer and with the Weizsäckers themselves; IfZ, ED 155.

60. On the memorandum, see p. 322, n. 22.

61. Mannheimer Morgen, 16 December 1950; Grimm stated there that the general amnesty had "to be as total and radical as the war was total."

62. BA, B 122/644, note of Kaufmann, 20 December 1950. While Heuss did appear before the soldiers, he did not directly address the war criminal question; cf. p. 331, n. 25.

63. *Frankfurter Allgemeine Zeitung*, 27 December 1950; the *Times* (London), 28 December 1950.

64. Cf. Lenz, *Tagebuch*, pp. 45f. 48, 93; Schwartz, "Begnadigung," p. 400.

65. Cf. *Kabinettsprotokolle 1951*, 4 January 1951, p. 33, n. 12; Adenauer, *Erinnerungen, 1945–1953*, pp. 409–13, does not mention this point.

66. Its other members were Bundestag president Hermann Ehlers, Heinrich Höfler, Jakob Altmeier (the only Jewish Bundestag delegate, SPD), Hans-Joachim von Merkatz, and Justice State Secretary Strauß; cf. Kempner, "Ankläger," p. 394; *Manchester Guardian*, 22 January 1951 ("Honourable Men").

67. Schmid had told McCloy that "if the decision of the German people to dispense with the death penalty was good, then the gallows have to be pulled down in Germany, regardless of the monstrosity of past and future crime." Within the SPD parliamentary faction, there was a "long and sometimes turbulent discussion" of this initiative, which had not been agreed on beforehand. Schumacher, Ollenhauer, Wehner, Arndt, Erler and others defended the action, while Greve indicated that if he had known in the Parliamentary Council that doing away with the death penalty

would also be used to spare the Landsberg prisoners, he would have voted against it; *SPD-Fraktionsprotokolle,* 9 January 1951, pp. 226–29 and n. 7. According to the *Süddeutsche Zeitung,* 10 January 1951, p. 3, following the nearly two-hour meeting Schmid had appeasingly indicated "that on the German side, no value is being placed on gaining pardon certificates for specific persons, but that there has simply been a wish to indicate to the High Commissioner that there should be an end to all of that, once and for all."

68. Cited from Schwartz, "Begnadigung," p. 399f. McCloy's PR chief, Shepard Stone, had already argued in similar fashion facing Bonn journalists who had brought up "Korea" in a cocktail party, likewise speaking out against the death penalty. Stone first pointed to the presence of "gangsters" in America as well—those facing death thus not being in that position because they were Germans; he then offered the more stern remark that what the Germans did in Poland was "incomparable," which prompted keen-witted *Zeit* correspondent Strobel to note that Stone "was alluding to Auschwitz." IfZ, ED 329/2, 8 December 1950, p. 1.

69. On 8 January 1951, McCloy received a dubious four-man delegation led by the "President of the Alliance for World Reconciliation," Sigmund-Schulze, for a ninety-minute conversation. One of the main figures in the nascent "Working Alliance for the Rescue of the Landsberg Prisoners"—an organization with changing names including both "Working Ring for Truth and Justice" and "Working Group for Truth and Justice"—was Princess Isenburg, already invited to the McCloys for dinner a few weeks before, after having written Mrs. McCloy "from one woman to another." IfZ, F 154/4, and *Der Spiegel,* 31 January 1951, p. 8ff.

70. In an interview with the correspondent of the Jewish *Daily Forward,* Kurt Schumacher found it worth stressing that none of the Social Democrats who were present spoke. In any event, he confirmed, the SPD was also against the death penalty in cases such as Ohlendorf and Pohl; German translation of the interview in *Neue Zeitung,* 30 January 1951, p. 3. (Information on original interview inaccessible to the author.)

71. Cited from *Kölnischer Rundschau,* 8 January 1951.

72. *Frankfurter Allgemeine Zeitung,* 8 January 1951, p. 3 ("Agitation in Landsberg. Protest Against the Planned New Executions").

73. On Marx, cf. pp. 69–70 above.

74. *Allgemeine Wochenzeitung der Juden in Deutschland,* 12 January 1951, p. 1 ("Three Times Germany"). An unsigned editorial on p. 2 indicated that "in Landsberg, we can observe an effort to fight through to a rehabilitation of the most monstrous mass crimes. On the one hand, the German people reject the idea of a collective guilt, while on the other hand demanding an annulment of the sentences handed out to individually responsible criminals. The intervention of church and politicians for so-called guiltless war criminals has now become risk-free. In a moment when an intervention in the case of the mass killing of innocent people would have been necessary, there was only silence in Germany, icy

silence." From the perspective of local history, cf. *Themenhefte Landsberger Zeitgeschichte* 1 (1993): 13–19.

75. IfZ, ED 94/166b, handwritten conversation note of Strauß, undated.

76. Strauß was accompanied by the Central Bureau referee Bitter; IfZ, ED 329/3, 31 January 1951, p. 3; cf. Bower (*Pledge*, p. 343ff.), who depicts the visit on the basis of American documents (in the process repeating the auditory error "Volheim" for the locus of the Waldheim trials).

77. IfZ, ED 94/166b, handwritten conversation note of Strauß, undated; italics in original.

78. Handwritten note on margin of the carbon: "['discussions'—*Besprechungen*—] should read 'efforts' [*Bestrebungen*]." BA, B 122/644, Heuss to McCloy, 16 January 1951.

79. In mid-January he even withdrew to his Bad Homburg house for a few days with the "flu." IfZ, F 154/4, McCloy's itinerary; Thayer, *Die unruhigen Deutschen*, p. 251ff., depicts the tense atmosphere before this decision; Shuster, *Ground*, terms McCloy's Landsberg decision as the task "burdening him most heavily."

80. BA, B 122/644, McCloy to Heuss, 24 January 1951.

81. AP report, cited from *Frankfurter Allgemeine Zeitung*, 3 January 1951.

82. *Frankfurter Allgemeine Zeitung*, 25 January 1951.

83. EZA, 2/84/Kv/41,3, Meiser to McCloy, 6 January 1951.

84. Ibid., Meiser to Dibelius et al., 29 December 1950.

85. A detailed report on the press conference, in which both Princess von Isenburg and Auxiliary Bishop Neuhäusler participated, appeared in the *Frankfurter Allgemeine Zeitung*, 15 January 1951 ("Finally Reconciliation Instead of Retribution. The 'Committee [*Komitee*] for Truth and Justice' on the So-Called War Criminal Trials").

86. AP report, cited from *Frankfurter Allgemeine Zeitung*, 25 January 1951.

87. *Das Freie Wort*, 19 January 1951.

88. After the visit of the Bundestag delegation to McCloy, Globke had planted appropriate background information; IfZ, ED 329/3, 12 January 1951, p. 3.

89. *Frankfurter Allgemeine Zeitung*, 18 January 1951; ibid. for following citation, italics in original.

90. Cf., e.g., the signatures beneath the published appeal for donations and action, "Weihnachten in Landsberg" ("Christmas in Landsberg"). Calling for protest letters to McCloy and Bonn politicians, the appeal ended as follows: "None of us, and none of the leading men inside or outside the country, will later be able to say 'I knew nothing of this.' " IfZ, MZA 1/169.

91. Isenburg to Wurm, 7 December 1950, printed: ibid., p. 6.

92. The historical literature offers a number of accounts of the meeting; cf. esp. Thayer, *Die unruhigen Deutschen*, p. 249f.; Wettig, *Entmilitarisierung*, p. 401; Meyer, "Situation," p. 700f.; Bird, *Chairman*, p. 344; Brochhagen, *Nach Nürnberg*, p. 196ff. Disquietingly uninformed is Ambrose, *Eisenhower 1890–1952*, p. 503; Abenheim, *Bundeswehr*, p. 45f, is naive and misinterprets the action's purpose.

93. The version coedited by HICOG in Speidel, *Zeit,* p. 285f. Speidel's spare account of the meeting is animated by a pair of digs at Adenauer's inadequate understanding of the significance of the "declaration of honor."

94. Cited from Schubert, *Wiederbewaffnung,* p. 82f.

95. The most widespread version can be found in Rautenberg and Wiggershaus, "Himmeroder Denkschrift," p. 199, n. 162.

96. In any case, writing in the *Frankfurter Allgemeine Zeitung,* 29 January 1951, Paul Sethe showed himself little impressed: "We rule over our own honor" was his basic theme. In his view, the linkage of the demand for release of the war criminals with the "nation's honor" revealed an "overestimation of external honor." Eisenhower, he indicated, had announced his current view, "not the thoughts of his circle from 1945." According to Sethe, the victors had then missed—indeed destroyed—a great opportunity, that for a self-purging of the German people. Sethe's form of nationalism now emerged in its characteristic expression: "We have not been robbed of honor by ourselves or our soldiers having been defined by fools as a mob of gruesome murderers. But we have received dark stains on our national honor through a German government ordering horrifying murders in our name, if not with our will. The group of men who knew of these dreadful deeds or even carried them out was small. But it existed, it belonged to the governing stratum, and that—not the insults—is our burden. This injured honor cannot be repaired from the outside, only we can do so.... To be sure, daily self-reproaches and wild announcements of remorse do not further this goal; neither a person nor a *Volk* can live in such a manner. But certainly the steadfast decision 'never again' belongs here."

97. The statements of McCloy and Handy in HICOG, *Landsberg;* the following information from that source (German versions in Sigel, *Gerechtigkeit,* pp. 176–82).

98. The only "Nurembergers" McCloy did not consider were those whose early release was pending on account of the parole system. At the start of 1951, around 300 Landsberg prisoners were still under the jurisdiction of EUCOM.

99. On Pohl, see p. 36–37.

100. The pardons were received by Ernst Biberstein, Walter Blume, Walter Haensch, Waldemar Klingelhöfer, Adolf Ott, Martin Sandberger, and Eugen Steimle; on their functions, cf. Krausnick and Wilhelm, *Truppe des Weltanschauungskrieges,* p. 644ff.

101. Cf., based on information of the Central Office for the Investigation of Nazi Crimes in Ludwigsburg, Schwartz's overview in "Begnadigung," pp. 406–14, as well as IfZ, Gy 38.

102. Reproduced in Schwarz, *Ära Adenauer I,* p. 137, who flatly defines the Krupp case as a " 'cause célèbre' of Allied retributive justice."

103. BA, B 122/644, Heuss to Adenauer, 16 November 1949; Heuss spoke up for the release request after receiving the president and members of the Board of Industrial Organizations.

104. Details in Schwartz, *America's Germany,* pp. 169–75.

105. In place of many separate citations, see IfZ, MA 1543, Department of State, Division of Public Studies, Weekly Summary of Opinion on Germany, 6 February 1951, p. 1, 5f. The "hostile" reactions lasted weeks; ibid., 13 and 27 February 1951, in both cases p. 6f., 20 February 1951, p. 5f. Cf. Bird, *Chairman,* chapter 18.

106. Cf. Schwartz, "Begnadigung," p. 403.

107. The difference was also revealed in Jewish reactions. On the one hand, in the terminology of the German Press Agency report, the speaker for the "pan Jewish" World Congress criticized the pardons as a "tragic mistake." On the other hand, *Allgemeine Wochenzeitung* editor Karl Marx stated that there was "no cause" to criticize the amnesty; *Frankfurter Allgemeine Zeitung,* 3 February 1951.

108. IfZ, MF 260, 17/245–3/39, HICOG Public Relations Division, "Review of German and Foreign Press Reaction to the Clemency Decisions on Landsberg War Crimes Cases," 10 February 1951; unless otherwise indicated, ibid. for the following.

109. IfZ, ED 329/3, 12. and 24 January 1951, p. 3 and 2, respectively.

110. This was also the opinion of the *Neue Zürcher Zeitung,* 6 February 1951.

111. In contrast, the SPD parliamentary faction preferred not commenting on the sentences' confirmation. Among themselves, individual delegates did speak out strongly against the "murder of defenseless men." *SPD-Fraktionsprotokolle,* 1 February 1951, p. 241f.

112. Cf. *Kabinettsprotokolle 1951,* 9 February 1951, p. 150. On 21 February 1951, the government's press office, citing telegrams and letters mailed to Adenauer "from all parts of Germany," published a sober list of the official steps taken thus far. These included a telegram from Adenauer to McCloy on 15 February 1951 that requested a suspension of the executions in both EUCOM cases until completion of the desired review. IfZ, ED 94/166b, report no. 135.

113. Adenauer complained about "the campaign for the Landsbergers, war criminals condemned to death, that is tumbling head over heals in distortions and misrepresentations." IfZ, ED 329/3, 6 March 1951, p. 2. Cf. Lenz, *Tagebuch,* p. 51, which points to the threatening letters sent to McCloy and his family as particularly incensing the chancellor. "It Is Too Late to Kill!" was the title of *Die Zeit*'s commentary on Landsberg on 8 February 1951, p. 1; the commentary closed with the observation that it was "also too late to kill those who are really guilty." It was left to a local paper to indicate that the agitators were concerned "much less with the prisoners than with rehabilitating the past." *Westfälische Rundschau,* 22 February 1951. *Die Zeit* would alter its position a little on 8 March 1951, when Marion Gräfin Dönhoff conceded that the public widely held the view "that actually aside from Hitler all were more or less innocent and Allied judgments are not at all binding." But, the countess continued, those responsible for the situation were the victors, since they "created new law and promulgated the thesis of the collective guilt of all Germans.

The victims of Nazi rule and opponents of the system thus reappeared suddenly together on the same bench with [the system's] henchmen."

114. *Frankfurter Allgemeine Zeitung,* 2 February 1951, p. 1; I thank Dr. Thilo Bode for attribution of the article (signed "Bo."); personal communication on 13 June 1993.

115. Introduction to the advisory board report in: HICOG, *Landsberg,* p. 18.

116. Ibid., p. 12.

117. Only 31 percent of the urban population considered the decisions correct; in the country the figure was 18 percent (based, respectively, on 80 percent and 64 percent of those who had heard of the matter). A scant 25 percent of the urban residents considered the death sentences justified; cf. Merritt and Merritt, *HICOG Surveys,* pp. 106, 112.

118. German Press Agency Report, cited from *Frankfurter Allgemeine Zeitung,* 13 February 1951 ("The Last Petition for Pardon").

119. AP/German Press Agency Report, cited from *Bonner Generalanzeiger,* 12 February 1951.

120. Cf. *Allgemeine Wochenzeitung der Juden in Deutschland,* 9 February 1951, p. 5 ("Generous Pardoning Policies").

121. IfZ, MZA 1/169, "Noch einmal: Landsberg!" "Dritter Brief" des Arbeitsringes für Wahrheit and Gerechtigkeit ["Once More: Landsberg!" "Third Letter" of the Working Ring for Truth and Justice], 8 February 1951; the pamphlet called for a broad palette of activities, including signature collection, the sending of telegrams to Adenauer and Truman, mobilization of the daily papers' chief editors, and aldermen called to account—all this under the motto "whoever is silent is guilty!"

122. IfZ, MF 260, 17/217–1/14, Dehler to Weigert, 12 April 1950, and 17/217–2/2, Weigert to Bowie, 26 April 1950.

123. *Kabinettsprotokolle,* 9 February 1951, p. 150.

124. IfZ, ED 329/3, 31 January 1951, p. 3f.

125. EZA, 2/84/Kv/40, confidential transcript of the session on 10 February 1951.

126. Ibid., addendum to the transcript.

127. *Kabinettsprotokolle,* 16 February 1951, p. 165.

128. BA, B 122/644, Dehler to Heuss, 22 February 1951; also in: ADL, N1/2201.

129. BA, B 122/644, enclosure (9 February 1951) for Dehler to Heuss, 22 February 1951; ibid. for following citation.

130. Cited from: HICOG, *Landsberg,* p. 21f.

131. The individual who delivered the advice was the German general consul in London, Hans Schlange-Schöningen, who repeatedly tried to bring the negative British reaction to the German Landsberg critique to Bonn's attention; IfZ, ED 329/3, 8. and 16 February 1951, p. 2 and 5, respectively. On the English "consensus about Germany," cf. *Frankfurter Allgemeine Zeitung,* 10 February 1951, p. 3.).

132. Ibid., Heuss to Handy, 23 February 1951; italics in original.

133. Ibid., Handy to Heuss, 13 February and 9 March 1951.

134. This did not preclude isolated extreme statements such as that of CSU Bundestag delegate Hans Schütz: "It is simply sheer madness that soldiers are being hanged from whatever motives at a moment when the German patriot and European politician bleed themselves white in order to overcome the 'not with me' standpoint of German youth and to awaken the readiness for defense. Whoever does not put a stop to this beginning is working for the fifth column of the Bolsheviks.... The Landsberg gallows are a Soviet Russian time bomb in the heart of Germany." Cited from IfZ, MZA 1/169, "Zweiter Brief" des Arbeitsringes für Wahrheit und Gerechtigkeit ["Second Letter" of the Working Ring for Truth and Justice], 23 January 1951, p. 19f. The executions were followed by talk, in the interests of German unity, of the "gruesome game" represented by the long delays that had preceded them: "Guilt? Atonement? Much effort will be required to clear away the heavy psychological burden that Landsberg placed not only on German human beings." Cited from the *Süddeutsche Zeitung*, 8 June 1951, p. 1.

135. BA, B 141/9576, Adenauer to Pius XII., 10 April 1951.

136. Hans-Joachim von Merkatz, the acting chairman of the Bundestag's German Party faction, was still demanding cancellation of the death sentences at the end of May; German Press Agency report, cited from the *Frankfurter Rundschau*, 28 May 1951.

137. The *Frankfurter Allgemeine Zeitung*, 21 May 1951, itself offered one example of this, attesting to Ohlendorf's "eye-striking qualities"—"a distinguished university student with an intelligence far superior to the average. His sympathetic, clever face fascinated the American women sitting in the courtroom. Female reporters and stenographers exchanged their engaging smiles with him: a 'mystical mass murderer' with an engaging, open character that not even his judges could resist." Even the reference to an awakened interest in religious literature—often played on far more crassly in the case of Pohl—is not absent from this account.

138. According to *Der Spiegel*, 31 January 1951, p. 9, even Ohlendorf's defense attorneys ventured in this direction. "But Ohlendorf was not responsible for the murders of his men, Hitler having himself ordered the massacre of the Jews [*das Judenmassaker*] and Ohlendorf having even executed it mildly."

139. IfZ, ED 329/3, 24 May 1951, p. 2.

140. AP report (in German), cited in *Frankfurter Rundschau*, 28 May 1951. From a Swiss perspective, the West German government was even constrained to "take account" of public opinion "to a certain degree." For this reason, the *Neue Zürcher Zeitung* explained on 8 June 1951, Bonn had gone so far as to "sacrifice considerable sums" from its "in any event scant dollar reserves."

141. Above all British justice minister Sir Hartley Shawcross took this line; cf. the *Times* (London), 31 March 1951. Adenauer was well aware of the grounds for which he thanked McCloy—late enough—in the Bundestag for "extreme care and conscientiousness." BT-Berichte 1, WP, 5 April 1951, p. 4984B.

142. IfZ, ED 329/3, 24 May 1951, p. 1.

143. BA, B 122/644, note of Vogel, 22 May 1951.

144. Landsberg's Evangelical prison pastor depicted the dramatic situation in a letter to Länder Bishop Meiser on 27 May 1951. Dehler remarked that the report had "deeply affected" him; he had certainly suspected the torments tied to stopping the execution, but his powers of imagination had still been "too weak." "The rope that was pulled apart several times has been tied once again. It has advanced neither justice nor humanity." EZA, 2/84/Kv/41,2, Dehler to Ranke, 21 June 1951.

145. Cf. *Der Spiegel*, 13 June 1951, p. 13; the magazine's general reporting from Landsberg did not so much reveal a striving for critical enlightenment as a tasteless, eyewitness worm's eye view—and with it, a desire to play up the fascinating criminality of the Third Reich.

146. 28 May 1951 ("When Black Is White: The Landsberg Men").

147. BA, NL 80/300, Bl. 117, statement of 7 June 1951.

148. Benjamin J. Buttenwieser, McCloy's second deputy, used a talk at the Carl Schurz Society in Bremen on 5 March 1951 as an opportunity to offer a certain praise for the German press, along with a direct critique of the politicians' inadequate courage: only "so small a sector"—itself a euphemism—"had been willing to publicly confirm the just fate that finally caught up with these seven mass murderers....Instead of the resoluteness of articulateness, they chose the false haven of silence." Cited from HICOG, 6, *Vierteljahresbericht über Deutschland,* p. 155.

149. *Süddeutsche Zeitung,* 8 June 1951, p. 1.

150. *Frankfurter Rundschau,* 8 June 1951, p. 3. Using the excuse of a procedural motion, Richter had taken the Bundestag floor to declare that the executions violated both the Basic Law and "laws of humanity"; placing the theme on the day's agenda was not allowed. BT-Berichte 1, WP, 7 June 1951, p. 5884.

151. *Hannoversche Presse,* 16 June 1951, p. 2f.

152. *Christ und Welt,* 14 April 1951, p. 1.

153. For example, in Thilo Bode's lead article "And Werl?" 24 April 1951, p. 1.

154. *Frankfurter Allgemeine Zeitung,* 8 June 1951, p. 1 ("Landsberg").

155. Cf. Noelle and Neumann, *Jahrbuch,* p. 358 (survey of September 1951).

Chapter 8

1. BA, B 305/58, appendix (status as of 10 May 1951).

2. BT-Drucksachen 1, WP, no. 2187, 25 April 1951. In part because of pressure from the Central Bureau, the interpellation was not sent on to the Subcommittee on War Prisoners of the Committee on Foreign Affairs.

3. EZA, 2/84/Kv/40/1,2, Wahl to Hallstein, 13 August 1951; here in relation to the " 'war criminals' imprisoned in Germany." On 22 February 1952, journalist Ernst Friedlaender made this usage the subject of one of the columns he wrote for both the *Stuttgarter Nachrichten* and the *Hamburger*

Abendblatt: "We, in contrast, place the word *war criminal* in quotation marks. In doing so, unreasonable people mean that the whole affair is an act of Allied malice and the prisoners are all and sundry innocent people. However, with these quotation marks reasonable people wish to point to the matter being so knotty as a result of the guilty and innocent being thrown together in one concept, so that what counts is, precisely, finally separating them from each other. But once again, people think badly of us abroad because of the imagined and written quotation marks, since they are interpreted in the unreasonable variant [*sic*]."

4. *The Times* (London), 17 December 1951 ("War Criminals of Werl").

5. In September 1951, the—open—question "what do you consider the greatest mistake that the occupying powers have made in Germany since 1945?" was responded to as follows: 11 percent of those queried answered "defamation and unjustified blaming of the Germans"; 8 percent, "the war criminal trials" (doubled responses were possible). The only more frequent responses were the dismantling program (21 percent), unfair treatment by the Russians (15 percent), and unfair intervention by the occupying troops (14 percent). Cf. Noelle and Neumann, *Jahrbuch,* p. 140.

6. BA, B 136/1878, Dehler to Adenauer, 9 February 1952, Vorschlag für die Behandlung des Kriegsverbrecherproblems aus Anlaß der Verhandlungen zur Ablösung des Besatzungsstatuts, enclosure V.

7. If only under their breaths, even the Central Bureau's experts confirmed this to the Bonn press. IfZ, ED 329/2, 11 August bzw. 2 November 1950.

8. The number of Landsberg prisoners had dropped from 549 on 15 December 1950 to 375 on 31 January 1952; in Werl the depletion for the same period was from 238 to 158; in Wittlich from 254 to 154. BA, B 136/1878, Dehler to Adenauer, 9 February 1952, proposal, enclosure V.

9. On Ranke's flight, cf. above, pp. 47f. At the end of 1952, there were approximately 130 prisoners still being held in France without having been sentenced; in Greece there was a single such prisoner. Cf. Bulletin BPA, 6 December 1952, p. 1693.

10. The Evangelical Press Service circulated the report on 26 June 1951 with the title "A General Amnesty—The Hour's Dictate: Reiner Tisch for a New Beginning." EZA, 2/84/Kv/40/1, 2. On the years-long amnesty propaganda of the Sunday paper, cf. Schildt, "Öffentliche Schulddebatte."

11. EZA, 2/84/Kv/40/1, 2, Ranke to Wahl, 14 September 1951.

12. On this and the following, although not always consistent, cf. Buscher, *Trial Program,* p. 102ff., 133.

13. For the report of one of the chief persons involved, cf. Grewe, *Rückblenden,* pp. 138–45.

14. On the negotiations surrounding the treaty, cf. Schwarz, *Adenauer I,* pp. 880–97, 925–55; Maier, *Internationale Auseinandersetzungen,* esp. pp. 52–124; Volkmann, "Innenpolitische Dimension," esp. pp. 283–330.

15. *FRUS 1951,* III/2, pp. 1501–11, here 1509 (HICOM report, 9 August 1951).

16. EZA, 2/84/Kv/40/1, 2, Fehsenbecker to Becker inter alia, 8 August 1951.

17. Ibid., Wahl to Hallstein, 13 August 1951; ibid. for following citation.

18. Ibid., confidential minutes of the session of 17 September 1951.
19. BT—PA, Kurzprotokoll des Unterausschusses Kriegsgefangene, no. 1–11; Gerstenmaier (*Streit and Friede,* p. 382) does mention the subcommittee but does not discuss his own role as chairman.
20. To see conscious deceptive intent at work here, as does Buscher (*Trial Program,* p. 132), involves an underestimation of the conceptual confusion that was then prevalent.
21. BT—PA, Kurzprotokoll des Unterausschusses Kriegsgefangene, no. 13, 17 September 1951.
22. Ibid., no. 14, 8 October 1951.
23. EZA, 2/84/Kv/40/1, 2, document archive to subcommittee, 23 October 1951; along with Wahl, signatories were limited to retired minister president Karl Geiler, High Consistory member Ranke and director Weeber, and the chancellor of the Cologne archdiocese, Knott.
24. BT—PA, Kurzprotokoll des Unterausschusses Kriegsgefangene, no. 15, 26 October 1951.
25. Characteristically it was the Evangelical Press Service that offered the first reference to a connection between the pending treaty negotiations and a "solution to the war criminal question." Cited from *Kölnische Rundschau,* 22 September 1951.
26. The minutes of the meeting between Adenauer and the Allied High Commission on 24 September 1951 can be found in *Akten zur Auswärtigen Politik,* vol. 1, pp. 381–87.
27. Trützschler's Nazi past was the object of research by the Bundestag's recently established Investigatory Committee. In June 1952 it concluded as follows: "A use abroad of the man, who during the entire war participated in the shaping of political propaganda, 'regulating speech' in the Political Section, would damage the image of the Federal Republic. The Investigatory Committee considers it particularly untenable for Dr. von Trützschler to represent the Federal Republic's policies toward Europe as chief referee of the Foreign Office." This verdict caught up with Trützschler in the Hague, where he was serving as acting head of the German delegation in the reparation negotiations with Israel. He was not withdrawn from the post. Cited from Haas, *Beitrag,* pp. 335, 500; cf. Döscher, *Verschworene Gesellschaft,* esp. p. 231ff., 280.
28. Cf. above, pp. 153f.
29. BA, B 305/12, note of Gawlik to Dehler, 29 October 1951 (with attached material).
30. Cf. *FDP-Bundesvorstand 1949–1954,* pp. 250, 258, 275f.
31. One such sarcastic query involved the reference of the chairman of the North Rhine–Westphalian FDP party chapter to rumors indicating Dehler's intent to "henceforth personally take on the Landsberg-Werl complex." BA, B 305/14, Middelhauve to Dehler, 17 October 1951. Complaints were made, for instance, by Catholic ex-priest Franz Ott, who had entered the Bundestag representing an obscure "emergency organization," was now a member of the "German Association" Union of Expellees and Victims of

Injustice faction, and from March 1952 would be an auditor for the German Party. Ott called on Dehler to demand a "tolerable solution" from "the brothers in arms of tomorrow." "In the battle against the world danger of Bolshevism that we all have to engage in at the approaches to the Occident, we simply cannot any longer allow ourselves to passively face such an obvious injustice, should we not wish to abandon the idea of justice and with it one of the few pillars in the fate-laden confrontation." Dehler's response included the observation that there could be no talk of an inhumane treatment of the Werl prisoners—that to the contrary prison conditions deviated positively from the usual. BA, B 305/168, Ott to Dehler, 9 October, response, 22 October 1951.

32. BA, B 305/49, Sander to Gawlik, 13 December 1951, with attached material. The lawyer also made detailed proposals regarding wrongful-imprisonment compensation for the "war criminals" who were to be released—such funds to be demanded from the occupation authorities or to be siphoned from the Marshall Plan.

33. See p. 71.

34. Cf. Rautenberg, "Standortbestimmung," esp. p. 804f.; Schwarz, *Ära Adenauer I*, p. 133f. Working out of the chancellor's office, Otto Lenz tried, with limited success, to keep matters under control; cf. idem., *Tagebuch*, esp. pp. 112–39. A detailed overview of persons, organizations, and political orientation, compiled by the Office of Constitutional Protection, can be found in BA, B 106/15575, John to Egidi, 16 October 1951.

35. BT-Drucksachen 1, WP, no. 2784, 8 November and no. 2829, 15 November 1951.

36. BT-Drucksachen 1, WP, no. 2845, 19 November 1951; this involved a motion by—in this order—the FDP, the CDU-CSU, and the German Party.

37. Cf. below, p. 225.

38. The chairman of the Fulda Bishops' Conference had appealed to the "magnanimity of the powers in question" so that "as many persons as possible be allowed final homecoming to their families." With close consideration it is clear that while not distinguishing between soldiers and Nazi criminals, Frings was in fact speaking only for the first group. "To the extent we are concerned with things for which participants in the war were responsible, things directly connected to the war's events, it seems to me it is time to make a clean break with the past and furnish an appropriate amnesty." UP report, cited from *Kölnische Rundschau*, 4 November 1951.

39. BT-Berichte 1, WP, 5 December 1951, p. 7321f.

40. Cited from *Neue Zeitung*, 24 December 1951.

41. *Die Zeit*, 27 December 1951, p. 1 ("What Those on the Petersberg Do Not Wish to Hear"); similarly on the same day in *Christ und Welt*, p. 6 ("The Lost Year: Revision of the War Criminal Trials Did Not Take Place: Unkept Promises").

42. BA, B 136/1878, Schmid to Adenauer, 15 November 1951. Precisely two months later, Adenauer responded as follows: "You are aware how much

clarifying this complex is personally close to my heart." In his conversations with the Allies, he indicated, the recommendations had already been a "valuable help"; as soon as the conversations had reached a "certain conclusion," he would inform the committee. ACDP, I-237/023–1.

43. *FRUS 1951,* III/1, p. 1280f (notes of U.S. delegation for the fifth meeting, 13 September 1951); cf. Brochhagen, *Nach Nürnberg,* p. 64ff.

44. Cf. Adenauer, *Teegespräche 1950–1954,* p. 161f. In the background conversation on 15 November 1951, Adenauer, referring to the pending negotiations, repeatedly asked journalists "not to carry anything about the matter for now."

45. *Akten zur Auswärtigen Politik,* vol. 1, p. 570 (meeting between Adenauer and Allied High Commission, 14 November 1951, notes of Grewe).

46. *FRUS 1951,* III/2, p. 1591f. (Allied High Commission to Foreign Ministers of the Three Powers, 17 November 1951).

47. Already in the summer Adenauer had urged the Allied High Commission to transfer Neurath to a hospital; *FRUS 1951,* III/2, p. 1857.

48. On 23 August 1951, Adenauer had directly written Schuman and others on the matter, receiving the answer that it would have been "premature and inappropriate to allow the belief to blossom that the table can be immediately swept clean in all points." Adenauer, *Briefe 1951–1953,* pp. 113–17; 522. The chancellor was apparently unaware of the extraordinarily positive report just issued by Karl Roemer, the lawyer he had made responsible for the negotiations in France over the war criminal question. BA, B 136/1878, note of Roemer for Trützschler, 19 November 1951.

49. *Akten zur Auswärtigen Politik,* vol. 1, p. 528 (meeting between Adenauer and Acheson, 21 November 1951); Adenauer, *Erinnerungen 1945–1953,* p. 513f., omits this point from the otherwise extensive verbatim citations from the minutes.

50. In this vein the *Frankfurter Allgemeine Zeitung,* 29 November 1951 ("Is Adenauer Negotiating Over Werl? Review of the Judgments"). The following day the government's Press and Information Office published the translation of a talk by Lord Hankey in the House of Lords on 21 November 1951. Referring to earlier remarks by Churchill and supported by the bishop of Chichester, Hankey had demanded an end to the current British policies regarding war criminals, which, he declared, most likely represented the greatest obstacle for an honest collaboration. The German press naturally eagerly took up Hankey's remarks. BPA, MF 1568.

51. BA, NL 351/9a, Tagebuch Blankenhorn, 6 December 1951. This goes unmentioned in Blankenhorn, *Verständnis,* pp. 128–31, as well as in Adenauer, *Erinnerungen 1945–1953,* who also elided the point in the report on his conversation with Churchill. On the internal British discussion, see esp. Brochhagen, *Nach Nürnberg,* pp. 67–70. On the trip in its entirety, see Schwarz, *Adenauer I,* pp. 894–902.

52. *FRUS 1951,* III/2, p. 1613 (report of Gifford, 11 December 1951); BA, B 141/9576, note of W. Roemer concerning a meeting with Blankenhorn and Hallstein, 5 January 1952, cf. Lenz, Tagebuch, 9 January 1952, p. 192.

53. BA, NL 351/9a, *Tagebuch Blankenhorn*, 6 December 1951. Cf. the extensive hymn for Manstein in *Der Spiegel*, 2 April 1952, pp. 8–14, occasioned by publication of the German edition of the book on the soldier by his defense attorney, Reginald T. Paget (*Manstein: Seine Feldzüge and sein Prozeß* [Wiesbaden, 1952]; English edition: *Manstein: His Campaigns and Jis Trial*, foreword by Lord Hankey [London, 1951]). For an early critique of Manstein's behavior during the campaign in the East, cf. Hillgruber, "Endlösung"; see also Friedrich, *Gesetz*, esp. pp. 655–73; Schneider, "Denkmal."

54. *Frankfurter Allgemeine Zeitung*, 7 January 1952, p. 1; ibid. for following citation.

55. EZA, 2/84/Kv/40/1,2, note of Ranke, 26 January 1952.

56. Two days after the appearance of the *Frankfurter Allgemeine* article, the government's Press and Information Office furnished the press with some information formulated with Adenauer's brevity: "Reports to the effect that the Allied High Commission has demanded a recognition of all the war criminal judgments from the German Federal Government are not based on the truth." BPA, MF 2192, communication no. 31, 9 January 1952.

57. EZA, 2/84/Kv/40/1, 2, note of Ranke, 26 January 1952; alongside Kranzbühler and Wahl, the gentlemen making up the delegation were Hodenberg, Knott, Weber, and Ranke; those sitting alongside Adenauer included Hallstein and Grewe. That the industrious Kranzbühler (and not, say, Wahl) was allowed to present the demands (cf. above, p. 179) was most likely because of his being responsible for the first "resolution" in such a vein (it would be made even sharper on the Central Bureau's advice). BA, B 305/58, Bitter to Kranzbühler, 2 November 1951, with attached material. Following the meeting with Adenauer, Kranzbühler hastened to once more set down the demands. EZA, 2/84/Kv/40/1,2, Kranzbühler to Hallstein, 26 January 1952.

58. BT-Berichte 1, WP, 7 February 1952, p. 8134f.

59. Ibid., p. 8132 C.

60. BT-Drucksachen 1, WP, no. 3078, 8 February 1952.

61. BT-Berichte 1, WP, 8 February 1952, p. 8241f. (statement of Schoettle).

62. Ibid., p. 8244.

63. Cf. *SPD-Fraktionsprotokolle 1949–1953*, p. 336ff.

64. *FRUS 1952–1954*, V/1, p. 88f. (Allied High Commission to Foreign Minister, 12 February 1952).

65. A contributing factor here may have been a correspondence with Ernst Achenbach in the winter of 1951–52. Achenbach had supplied McCloy with brazen proposals for a general "clemency review with neutral or German jurists," adding a confidential threat: "we are reliable friends and, believe it or not, we shall strengthen our influence in the elections of 1953"; ADL, N1/3100, Achenbach to McCloy, 16 February 1952 (copy).

66. *FRUS 1952–1954*, V/1, p. 48f. (minutes of the Acheson-Eden meeting, 16 February 1952); ibid. for the following citation.

67. Ibid., p. 54ff. (Acheson to State Department, 18 February 1952).

68. *Akten zur Auswärtigen Politik,* vol. 2, pp. 317–33 (verbatim minutes of the London Foreign Ministers' conference, 18/19 February 1952); cf. *FRUS 1952–1954,* V/1, pp. 59–64, 66–71 (Laukhuff Minutes, undated).

69. *Akten zur Auswärtigen Politik,* vol. 2, p. 317. At first, McCloy was very enthusiastic about this proposal, initiating appropriate studies and—as he already had pointed to in London—stressing "that guilty military leaders should also be included." *FRUS 1952–1954,* V/1, p. 265 (McCloy to State Department, 28 February 1952). Once the results of an Allied High Commission working group formed to this end were available at the start of June 1952, it was evident that—as was in fact to be expected—hardly any of the condemned war criminals had previously had ordinarily criminal careers. The High Commissioners now dropped the project as counterproductive. Cf. Brochhagen, *Nach Nürnberg,* p. 74f.

70. The American minutes indicate that "the upshot of the discussion was a proposal laughingly proffered by Mr. Eden to use the word *validity* (validité) in English and French and Mr. Adenauer could call it what he liked in German!"; *FRUS 1952–1954,* V/1, p. 68.

71. One of Adenauer's efforts failed completely: moving Schuman, in the presence of Eden and Acheson, to concessions regarding the war criminals incarcerated in France, who were not covered in the agreement under discussion.

72. The final text can be found in *FRUS 1952–1954,* V/1, p. 101f.; German version in BA, B 141/9576.

73. Ibid., p. 82 (Acheson to Truman, 21 February 1952). Cf. Acheson, *Present,* p. 621, where he still retrospectively indicates that "irrelevant obstacles like the Saar and the war crimes sentences had been removed from the stage." Elsewhere (p. 640) Acheson concedes that even after London, the war criminal question counted among "lesser but still troublesome questions."

74. In the cabinet session of 20 February 1952, Adenauer was nevertheless able to convey an impression that the war criminal question had been "satisfactorily resolved." Cf. Lenz, *Tagebuch,* 20 February 1952, p. 259f. On 9 February 1952, in connection with the Transition Treaty, Dehler had sent Adenauer a nearly thirty-page "Proposal for a Concluding Treatment of the War Criminal Problem"; it backed up the demands of the Central Bureau (see above pp. 182–83) with detailed arguments. BA, B 136/1878 and. B 141/9576 (final draft with interesting handwritten corrections). Thilo Bode's lead article of 3 February 1952 was titled "Bastions Such as That in Heidelberg"; Bode here offered a detailed report on the reflections of the jurists' circle, apparently facilitated by Wahl; the title played on the EUCOM legal division in Heidelberg, headed by Col. Damon Gunn and frequently criticized for rigidity.

75. BA, BA 141/9576, Grewe to W. Roemer, 25 February 1952 (secret).

76. Ibid., note of Bitter, 28 February 1952, ibid. for following citation; the draft's German translation: ibid.; the English version can be found in *FRUS 1952–1954,* V/1, p. 101f.

77. BA, B 141/9576, Dehler to Adenauer, 12 March 1952.

78. On the initiative of Hodenberg, Kranzbühler, and Becker, there had even been an agreement to establish their own investigative committee; EZA, 2/84/Kv/40/1, 2, confidential minutes of the session on 9 February 1952.
79. *Welt am Sonntag*, 24 February, *Der Fortschritt*, 28 March 1952; ibid. for following citation and details.
80. Cf. *SPD-Fraktionsprotokolle*, p. 340.
81. For his part, Achenbach tried to "obviate mix-ups and confusion" through systematic work with the press. As a rule, he cited the general invalidity of the "improvement or deterrence theory" as basic grounds for a general amnesty. "Whoever ... acted without personal motive and not to his own advantage—especially following orders—does not need to be improved or deterred, indeed cannot be so." This applied to "practically almost all Germans sentenced as 'war criminals,' since almost all acted only upon orders." *Essener Allgemeine Zeitung*, 1 March 1952 ("Review or Amnesty?").
82. Several citations in Brochhagen, *Nach Nürnberg*, p. 76 and. n. 13, p. 380.
83. The documents on the negotiation process mainly in PA—FO, II/1421; partially also in BA, B 305/60, B 141/9576 and in ADL, N 1/2977.
84. Illustrative here is Grewe, *Rückblenden*, p. 149ff.
85. Cf. the gripping overview in Schwarz, *Adenauer I*, pp. 925–56.
86. *Frankfurter Allgemeine Zeitung*, 24 March 1952 ("The Future of the 'War Criminals': American Statements Regarding the Review Instance in the General Agreement").
87. Cf. the—evidently prompted—article in the *Deutschen* and *Wirtschafts-Zeitung*, 16 April 1952 ("The Walls of Werl: The Anticipated Agreement Over the War Criminals Runs into Reservations"); presuming such an acknowledgment, the author reproduced the constitutional reservations being formulated within the Justice Ministry.
88. BT—PA, stenographic minutes of the Subcommittee on War Prisoners, no. 18, 25 April 1952.
89. ADL, N1/3100, Dehler to Lehmann, 9 April 1952; the one-time ministerial director had furnished Dehler with a report by Bolko Freiherr von Richthofen indicating that Adenauer had not optimally exploited a mood in England favorable to the war criminal cause.
90. There are two summaries of the 25 April 1952 meeting; classified as secret, they are both located in ADL, N1/2977: note of Vogel, 26 April and transcript of Sigrist, 29 April 1952.
91. Ibid., transcript of Sigrist, p. 8, and note of Vogel, p. 6.
92. Ibid., transcript of Sigrist, p. 9ff.
93. In an open letter to General Eisenhower, Admiral Hansen, the league's rather well informed chairman, declared that seven years' "dungeon"—*Kerker*—was enough atonement "where there was something to atone," then addressing the NATO commander in chief as follows: "Bring your entire influence to bear so that a general amnesty is agreed on as the only solution to a question whose solving can, in the near future, turn out to be of decisive significance for the future of the Occidental cultural sphere." Cited from *Deutsche Soldatenzeitung*, 3 April 1952.

94. ADL, N1/2977, transcript of Sigrist, p. 9ff.
95. The actual reason for this was the 25 April 1952 emergence of a coalition in the new federal state of Baden-Württemberg, put together by Reinhold Maier of the Democratic People's Party, comprising the SPD, FDP, and Union of Expellees and Victims of Injustice. This shifted the voting weight in favor of the Länder steered by Social Democrats.
96. *Akten zur Auswärtigen Politik*, vol. 2, p. 126; for the following: p. 133f. (procedural minutes, 28 April 1952).
97. PA—FO, II/1421, Niederschrift über die Sitzung des Unterausschusses für Teil I des Überleitungsvertrages, 29 April 1952.
98. *Akten zur Auswärtigen Politik*, vol. 2, pp. 163–71, cit. p. 164 (minutes 1 May 1952).
99. Cf. *Kabinettsprotokolle 1952*, 29 April 1952, p. 246f.
100. Two reports are available concerning the special committee's fifth session on 30 April 1952: ADL, N1/2977, note of Vogel and short transcript, both 2 May 1952.
101. Cf. *FDP-Bundesvorstand 1949–1954*, 1 May 1952, pp. 288–307.
102. Adenauer had responded on the same day—6 May 1952—to the FDP's extensive requests for alterations; cf. Adenauer, *Erinnerungen 1945–1953*, p. 528ff.
103. On 2 May 1952 in the cabinet, Adenauer posed the reproachful question "How does Achenbach end up in possession of the documents?" Cf. *Kabinettsprotokolle 1952*, p. 248, n. 2.
104. Cf. *FDP-Bundesvorstand 1949–1954*, 8 May 1952, pp. 320–28, cit. p. 328.
105. Thus the reports of the German Press Agency and the UP, cited from *Die Welt*, 3 May 1952. Even before conclusion of the Transition Treaty, the well-informed Thilo Bode reiterated in a 19 May 1952 *Frankfurter Allgemeine Zeitung* lead article that "Justice Makes the Alliance Firmer."
106. Cf. UP report, cited from *Frankfurter Neue Presse*, 5 May 1952 (transcript in BA, B 305/49).
107. On the epilogue to this statement (denied by Mühlenfeld) in the cabinet, cf. *Kabinettsprotokolle 1952*, 2 May 1952, p. 248f., 272.
108. Cf. *FRUS 1952–1954*, VII/1, p. 55f. (McCloy to State Department, 9 May 1952).
109. Cf. *Kabinettsprotokolle 1952*, esp. 10, 12, 14 May 1952, pp. 299ff., 311f., and 322; Lenz, *Tagebuch*, 10, 12, 13, 23 May 1952, pp. 321, 327f., 329ff., and 343.
110. Cf. *Akten zur Auswärtigen Politik*, vol. 2, pp. 193ff. and 217f. (meetings on 13 and 15–16 May 1952). A considerable proportion of the efforts involved the annulment of improvements for the worst, resulting from the retention of Allied custody having to be regulated. BA, B 141/9070, note of W. Roemer, 10, 13, 14, 23 May 1952 (partially secret).
111. Cf. *FRUS 1952–1954*, VII/1, p. 91.
112. *Akten zur Auswärtigen Politik*, vol. 2, p. 356 (minutes of the Bonn conference, part 2, 25 May 1952).

113. The American minutes summarize thus: "The Ministers said that they would bear the Chancellor's remarks in mind." *FRUS 1952–1954,* VII/1, p. 108.

114. *Akten zur Auswärtigen Politik,* vol. 2, p. 357. An initially anticipated dialogue between Adenauer and Schuman in the conference framework, meant to deal with the war criminals imprisoned in France, did not take place. BA, B 141/9070, note of W. Roemer (secret), 26 May 1952 (also in BA, B 305/60).

115. Not in Article 2, treating the Allied rights to reservations, but in Article 8, originally simply presenting the supplementary agreements. Cf. *Bonner Vertrag,* pp. 30, 36.

116. BA, B 141/9070, Adenauer to McCloy, Eden, and François-Poncet, 25 May 1952.

117. Bonner Vertrag, p. 165 (original draft of W. Roemer in: BA, B 141/9070, Roemer to Dehler, 28 May 1952). As of this book's translation, original English-language version of the Transition Treaty was not available.

Chapter 9

1. Cf. below, p. 280.

2. Cf., e.g., the remarkable reflections imparted from his vacation place to the chairman of the North Rhine–Westphalian FDP: Adenauer to Middelhauve, 30 July 1952, in *Briefe 1951–1953,* p. 257f.; cf. also p. 280.

3. Lenz had already lodged a complaint over *Stern's* article on the war criminal theme with the magazine's publisher, Bundestag member Gerd Bucerius, on 24 April 1952. Cf. Lenz, *Tagebuch,* p. 301.

4. IfZ, ED 329/4, 22 May 1952, p. 3; Lenz (*Tagebuch,* p. 342) only reports briefly on the evening meeting in the "press circle of [Alfred] Rapp."

5. Cf. *Die Welt,* 9 June 1952.

6. Cf., above all, the report in the *Deutsche Soldatenzeitung,* spring-summer 1952 (for the sake of political influence, the publication was financially supported by the government). Hansen would complain to a League of German Soldiers colleague that considering its many members, the organization was not appropriately acknowledged. He continued: "In referring to real criminals the chancellor, as well, is unfortunately trying to make excuses." BA, B 136/1881, Hansen to Heye, 17 August 1952 (copy).

7. Cf. German Press Agency report, cited from *Die Welt,* 15 July 1952.

8. See above, pp. 71, 183, 194.

9. BA, B 305/49, circular of Achenbach to newspapers, 30 May 1952. As Best, not without pride, informed the Central Bureau's director, the committee would regularly mail texts of this sort to 600–700 newspapers. Ibid., Best to Gawlik, 10 May 1952.

10. Cf. *Wiesbadener Kurier,* 3 May 1952. In Stuttgart, moderate groups like Caritas, the Women's Service, and State Youth Ring affiliated themselves with a "working group" formed by general amnesty activists. Munich

lawyer Aschenauer was the speaker at a corresponding rally. BA, B 136/1881, note of Gumbel, 1 August 1952.

11. Lenz found no support in the chancellor's office for his suggestion to publicly counter Ramcke's statements. BA, B 136/1881, Ramcke to Adenauer, 7 July, Lenz to Rust, 11 August 1952.

12. Schubert to the contrary in *Wiederbewaffnung*, p. 84.

13. *Freie Demokratische Korrespondenz*, 19 June 1952, pp. 2–6; ibid. for the following citation.

14. Cf. Mende, *Freiheit*, p. 24f.

15. Margarethe Bitter still recalled such an objection in an interview with the author, 19 April 1990.

16. BT—PA, Kurzprotokoll der Sitzung des Unterausschusses Kriegsgefangene, 18.7.1952 (remarks of Höfler).

17. The following is based on Mende, *Freiheit*, p. 215f., himself most likely relying on his diary.

18. BA, B 141/9070, note 24 May 1952.

19. The proceedings against 167 of these 299 prisoners were still pending; 94 of them were former members of the Secret Field Police and the Security Police, and 21 were from the ranks of the Wehrmacht. BA, B 305/49, W. Strauß to Brentano, 13 June 1952.

20. For example, following a session of the Committee on Foreign Affairs, word was issued that only a fourth of war prisoners being held in the West had been Wehrmacht members. The leaders of the Association of Former POWs (more fully, the Association of Repatriated Soldiers, War Prisoners, and Relatives of the Missing) protested by return of post: "Through such a numerical distinction, the impression of a certainly undesired classification must emerge, along with the supposition that with it the weight of special significance is meant to be removed from this tragic problem.... This limitation contradicts all international law in a basic way. Under the sign of modern total warfare, the concept "soldier" can no longer be identified with the classical concept of 1914." ACDP, I-237/023/1, Kießling to Wahl, Material zur Kriegsverbrecherfrage (2), 27 November 1952.

21. Hendrik van Dam voiced an explicit critique of this process in the *Allgemeine Wochenzeitung der Juden in Deutschland*, 25 April 1952. A general amnesty did not involve "only, say, an amnesty for generals, which, if we are to judge by the German illustrated journals, appear to occupy the center of interest. Rather, what is involved here is an amnesty for all war criminals, among whom those guilty of crimes against humanity may be counted."

22. BA, B 305/49, Brentano to W. Strauß and response, 9 and 13 June 1952.

23. In the summer of 1952, the only politically significant papers still willing to come out clearly against a general amnesty were the *Frankfurter Rundschau*, *Stuttgarter Zeitung*, and (American) *Neue Zeitung;* the *Süddeutsche Zeitung*, *Tagesspiegel* (Berlin), and *Hannoversche Zeitung* voiced cautious disapproval. All the other major daily and weekly papers basically embraced the demands for such an amnesty.

24. BT-Drucksachen 1, WP, no. 3477, 21 June 1952; alongside the German Party delegates, a few Free Democrats and the—meanwhile independent—extreme right-wing Adolf von Thadden were signatories.

25. StBKAH 12.29, Hellwege to Adenauer, 15 July 1952, italics in original. The chancellor's terse reply of 22 July referred to the Allies' necessary consideration of "the mood of broader circles in their population." Adenauer, *Briefe 1951–1953*, p. 251.

26. Mende's parliamentary faction colleague Margarete Hütter left no doubt in this regard in the Subcommittee on War Prisoners. BT—PA, abbreviated minutes, 18 July 1952.

27. ADL, N1/3100, Mende to Adenauer, 19 July 1952 (carbon copy for Dehler). IfZ, ED 329/4, 26 June 1952; according to this source, Mende had spontaneously raised the names of Manstein and List with the chancellor.

28. BA, B 136/1881, list (141 names) undated; the press usually referred to 146 names.

29. *Frankfurter Allgemeine Zeitung*, 25 July 1952.

30. ADL, N1/3100, Mende to Adenauer, 19 July 1952.

31. BA, B 305/60, report of Gawlik on the meeting of the Heidelberg circle on 26 July 1952.

32. The German Press Agency placed this point at the start of their report; in *Frankfurter Rundschau*, 17 July 1952.

33. EZA, 2/84/Kv/40/1,1, Wahl to Blücher, 31 July, and circular of Fehsenbecker, 17 August 1952. Walter Strauß, who had accompanied Kranzbühler to a conversation with Blücher, had had the idea of approaching Donnelly via Frings. IfZ, ED 94/210, Strauß to Dehler, 4 August 1952.

34. BA, NL 351/10, note of Noack, 11 June 1952, p. 4; also in: Adenauer, *Teegespräche 1950–1954*, pp. 315–20.

35. BA, B 305/49, Adenauer to Schuman, 14 June 1952 (copy).

36. Cf. Buscher, *Trial Program*, p. 139. Shortly beforehand, Dehler had declared to the Foreign Office that on account of the "standstill" in America's pardoning policy, a new step on the part of the chancellor was "urgently called for." ADL, N1/3100, Dehler to AA, 26 June 1952 (with draft of a letter for Adenauer).

37. BT-Berichte 1, WP, 9-10 July 1952, pp. 9788–923.

38. Ibid., p. 9891f.

39. Ibid., p. 9860 D.

40. Ibid., pp. 9888–91, here p. 9890.

41. *Neue Zeitung*, 9–10 August 1952, p. 5; ibid. for following citation. In his first press conference, Donnelly had stated that the acts perpetrated by the sentenced men spoke for themselves, but that he was ready to consider new evidence. Cf. *Frankfurter Allgemeine Zeitung*, 5 August, and *Süddeutsche Zeitung*, 8 August 1952; Lenz, *Tagebuch*, 12 August 1952, p. 408.

42. Margarethe Bitter contacted, inter alia, lawyers Kranzbühler and Burchard-Motz with the question of what form the assertions in the *Neue Zeitung* could be countered. The answers repeated the usual reproaches: there had been judicial errors and innocent men still sat in prison. Details in BA, B 305/60.

43. Ibid., Hansen to Strauß, 19 August 1952.
44. Cf. *Neue Zeitung,* 16 September 1952, p. 5 ("It must be said once again"); in one part of the press run not until 17 September 1952.
45. BT-Drucksachen 1, WP, no. 3477, 21 June 1952.
46. Cf., to the contrary, Buscher (*Trial Program,* p. 144f.), who to an excessive degree views the debate from new American High Commissioner Donnelly's vantage point.
47. The demands of Rommel's faithful followers even made their way into the *Manchester Guardian,* 15 September 1952, p. 10.
48. Cf. *Kabinettsprotokolle 1952,* 16 September 1952, p. 571f.; we learn from Hallstein that Mende had shown himself to be "exceptionally understanding." The state secretary planned "similar meetings" with delegates Höfler (CDU) and von Merkatz (German Party), two more protagonists in the war criminal issue. Whether the meetings took place before the debate is unclear.
49. BT-Berichte 1, WP, 17 September 1952, p. 10492ff.
50. Ibid., p. 10494ff.
51. Referring to the "growing distress of a broad circle," Achenbach called on the chancellor in a letter of 6 October 1952 to name those "war-condemned" persons "who in your opinion are unworthy of a pardon certificate or are even "asocial elements"; he himself had not been able to find any such persons. After consulting with Central Bureau head Gawlik, who suspected that Best had composed Achenbach's letter and advised not to name names, Lenz responded evasively on 17 October 1952. While incomplete, the available material was sufficient to back up the chancellor's statement, with its citation of the high penalties a certain portion of the sentenced men had also received from German courts. BA, B 136/1881.
52. Diplomatic network, afternoon broadcast for Europe, North and South America, 17 September 1952; Bulletin BPA, 18 September 1952, p. 1261f.
53. BA, B 136/1881, Jahn to Lenz, 4 and 13 October 1952; critically on the Working Alliance now: Stosch, *Adenauer-Legion.*
54. The Foreign Office ordered 2,000 offprints of the text, and the Central Bureau distributed it to cooperating defense attorneys. ADL, N1/3100, note of Bitter, 11 October 1952.
55. BT-Berichte 1, WP, 17 September 1952, p. 10498.
56. Ibid.; on Merten cf. Henkels, 99 Bonner Köpfe, p. 210ff.
57. BT-Berichte 1, WP, 17 September 1952, p. 10504.
58. Ibid., p. 10505. On the occasion of a major interpellation by the German Party and the All-German Block Union of Expellees faction on the theme "German war-condemned in foreign incarceration," Countess Finckenstein could later confirm in relief that "in German usage of the past few years the word *war criminal* has, thank heavens, almost entirely vanished." BT-Berichte 2, WP, 17 February 1955, p. 3382.
59. According to a HICOG survey of August 1952, 59 percent of those asked disapproved of the manner in which the Western powers had handled the war criminal problem, and only 10 percent approved; 63 percent of those

asked believed that most of the sentenced German generals were innocent. Cf. Merritt and Merritt, *HICOG Surveys*, p. 184f.

60. This, e.g., was the tenor of the report in the *Frankfurter Allgemeine Zeitung,* 18 September 1952, p. 1 ("Justice for the 'War Criminals' Demanded. Chancellor and Bundestag for Greatest Possible Number of Releases Before Ratification"). In the accompanying commentary, there was a corresponding indication that "there was no need for a general amnesty in a technical sense," but the practice had to be "fast and thorough." Ibid.

61. The following based on *FDP-Bundesvorstand,* 29 September 1952, pp. 471–86, citations from pp. 472, 474f.

62. Ibid., p. 489.

63. Cf. Schwarz's richly detailed account in, *Adenauer II*, pp. 9–43, 58–65.

64. EZA, 2/84/Kv/40/1,1, circular of Fehsenbecker, 22 December 1952.

65. In a HICOG survey of December 1952, 56 percent of those asked agreed with Ramcke's views, and only 25 percent expressed disagreement; cf. Merritt and Merritt, *HICOG Surveys,* p. 198. Without raising Ramcke's name, Achenbach had 46 percent approval in November 1952 for the following Hiroshima citation; 29 percent of those asked indicated displeasure with the citation, and 25 percent had no opinion. Cf. Noelle and Neumann, *Jahrbuch,* p. 276.

66. PA—FO, III/201–10, reports of the diplomatic missions, 28 and 29 October 1952, and copy for the chancellor, 31 October 1952. Against this backdrop, a British High Commission report to London has a downright comical effect. From "secret sources" it was known that Ramcke had right-wing ties. Public Record Office (PRO) FO 371/97949, Wahnerheide to Foreign Office, 29 October 1952.

67. Cf. *Der Spiegel,* 5 November 1952, p. 8f.; *Archiv der Gegenwart,* 30 October 1952, p. 3718. The piquant aspect of Ramcke's appearance was that since he had not belonged to the Waffen SS he was only meant to offer a word of greeting; the SS strategists had themselves taken pains to avoid any suggestion of betraying the new state. Adenauer addressed the "politically extremely damaging" affair in the next cabinet session; he saw it as evidence that a "German national army" would also be a domestic "misfortune." A request was forwarded to Theodor Blank to let Ramcke know that such remarks "run counter to the interests of those comrades of his still incarcerated by the Western powers." In a letter to the American High Commissioner, Adenauer described the talks as "irresponsible," and speaking to journalists, he made clear his displeasure at the "foolishness" of the general—the government having previously gone all out for his release from French custody (cf. p. 47f above). Finally, the chancellor had Dehler look—fruitlessly—into the possibility of legal measures against Ramcke. Cf. *Kabinettsprotokolle 1952,* 28 October 1952, p. 650f.; Lenz, *Tagebuch,* 28 October 1952, p. 449; Adenauer, *Briefe 1951–1953,* p. 291; idem, *Teegespräche 1950–1954,* p. 401; BA, B 136/1752, Globke to Dehler and response, 5 and 15 November 1952; B 136/1882, Trützschler to Gum-

bel, 25 February 1953. In May 1953, Hesse's interior minister threatened to ban a national gathering of former parachutists, should Ramcke speak there; the 6,000 participants greeted their silent comrade with demonstrative applause. Cf. *Frankfurter Allgemeine Zeitung, 26* May 1953.

68. This from the report in the *Wittlicher Tageblatt,* 5–6 October 1952, transmitted to State Secretary Lenz by acting French High Commissioner Bérard. Adenauer and Lenz indicated that no objections were in order against normal rallies for those "serving time"—but that word had reached the chancellor's office that the leadership of the Association of Repatriated Prisoners had instructed the groups in Wittlich, Werl, and Landsberg to arrange "especially demonstrative" actions. BA, B 136/1881, Lenz to Gumbel, 15 October 1952.

69. Cf. Geile, *Remer-Mythos.*

70. EZA, 2/84/Kv/40/1,1, publication "Recht für die Kriegsverurteilten" ("Justice for the War-Condemned") [November 1952].

71. BT-Drucksachen 1, WP, no. 3826 and 3887, 30 October and 18 November 1952.

72. For example, upon his appearance in Aurich, Reserve Infantry Regiment 79 organized a collection for Kappe's family. Cf. *Die Welt,* 21 October 1952. On 21 September 1952, *Der Stern* published a photo reportage titled "A Letter of Safe Conduct Instead of an Arrest Warrant" (*"Schutzbrief anstelle eines Steckbriefes"*); it was intended as a "warning to all Germans not to become cops for injustice." After that, fugitive Kühn showed up in the editorial offices, "where he was greeted like a repatriated war prisoner." He was able to recount his story over two issues. Citation from ibid., 12 October 1952, p. 10. On 12 December 1952, there was also a major report in the SPD's *Neue Presse* concerning a secret meeting with Kühn ("14 Weeks After the Flight from Werl: Hans Kuhn Rushes from Place to Place").

73. Cf., e.g., *Manchester Guardian,* 27 October 1952 ("Escaped War Criminal a National Hero: Germans Persecute Informer"); correspondent's report in the *Baseler Nationalzeitung,* 14 October 1952 ("Wilhelm Kappe—the 'German man' ").

74. *Der Spiegel,* 8 October 1952, p. 6f.; cf. *Westdeutsche Rundschau,* 17 October 1952 ("Windowpanes Rattled in Aurich: Population Resisted Informer"). *Der Stern* (12 October 1952, p. 10f.) titled its photo story about Heidepeter "The Biggest Rogue in the Entire Country ... That Is and Remains the Informer." The scandalous piece was accompanied by an essay of Ernst von Salomon—former *Freikorps* member and plotter against Walther Rathenau; author of the resentment-laden best-selling *Fragebogen (The Questionnaire)* of 1951—who had sheltered Kühn on Sylt after his escape, and who was pleading for a general amnesty under the motto "take the pot off the fire." Salomon expounded on the "liberation" of the [so-called] "W[ar]C[riminal]s," drawing parallels with the 1920s—without, to be sure, mentioning his involvement in Rathenau's murder. Ibid., pp. 16, 33, 35f.

75. BA, B 136/1882, Egidi to Lenz, 3 January 1953 (with attached material, confidential).

76. When word got out that security measures were being strengthened following the escape of the two war criminals, shrill tones were emitted from, above all, the Association of Former POWs; *Frankfurter Allgemeine Zeitung,* 28 November 1952 ("Stricter Conditions of Imprisonment in Werl"). To this effect, even a year later, see Manstein to Merkatz, 12 October 1953, ACDP, I-148/043/2. From now on the British felt obliged to offer detailed rebuttals; BPA, MF 2192, press statement of the British Information Services, 20 November 1953.

77. *Abendpost* (Frankfurt), 8 November 1952 ("*Abendpost* Hostages turn to Heuss and Adenauer").

78. Kirkpatrick, *Inner Circle,* p. 247. In these terse memoirs, both the "problem of the War Criminals"—described as a "contentious issue which weighed heavily on me"—and, specifically, the guarantor action occupy relatively much space. Kirkpatrick refers to the action as "this ridiculous proposal." Ibid.

79. *Abendpost* (Frankfurt), 10 December 1952.

80. *Abendpost* (Frankfurt), 1 December 1952.

81. Cf. BT-Berichte 1, WP, 3-5 December 1952, pp. 11101–497.

82. Cf. Mende (*Freiheit,* p. 216) who claims memory of "numerous" like-minded "no" votes. Mende's party faction colleague Hütter abstained from voting; for what were acknowledged to be reasons of foreign policy, the FDP's Karl Georg Pfleiderer voted "no." In the German Party, there were three "no" votes. BT-Berichte 1, WP, pp. 11520–27. Shortly before the debate, Mende and Hütter had a conversation with Donnelly—as did Adenauer on the same day; the American raised the prospect of a new Christmas amnesty. Cf. *Kölnische Rundschau,* 29 November 1952; Buscher, *Trial Program,* p. 146f.

83. BT-Berichte 1, WP, p. 11141. Adenauer expressed himself similarly on 6 November 1952 in a conversation with right-wing American journalist Freda Utley; in view of their "resistant" public opinion he spoke up for the Allies, while stressing "that there are no Germans, not even nationalist Germans, who support a release of the real war criminals." Adenauer, *Teegespräche 1950–1954,* p. 354.

84. Bulletin BPA, 6 December 1952, p. 1693 ("On the Question of the 'War Criminals' ").

85. On the background, see Schwarz, *Adenauer II,* p. 35–43.

86. BPA, MF 2192, communication no. 1163, 2 December 1952. BA, B 136/1881, note of Trützschler, 12 December 1952; BA, B 136/1882, Lenz to Hansen, 22 April 1953; Archiv der Gegenwart, 23 October 1952, p. 3708. In September 1952, 65 percent of those polled (76 percent of the men) had indicated that Kesselring was unjustly imprisoned; for Dönitz the figure was 63 percent, for Speer 50 percent, for Heß 43 percent, and for Schirach 38 percent (yes-no question); cf. Noelle and Neumann, *Jahrbuch,* p. 202. A HICOG survey at the end of August 1952 had a similar result: 63 per-

cent of those polled indicated that most of the imprisoned generals were innocent; cf. Merritt and Merritt, *HICOG Surveys*, p. 184f.

87. BPA, MF 2192, press release of the French High Commission, 22 December 1952. The head of the Central Bureau, Gawlik, voiced corresponding satisfaction on an internal basis (the bureau had moved from the Justice Ministry to the Foreign Office on 1 February 1953). EZA, 2/84/Kv/40/2,3, confidential minutes of meeting of the Heidelberg circle in the Justice Ministry, 26 February 1953.

88. BA, B 122/644, notes of Trützschler, 2 February 1953 (copy).

89. Ibid., Heusinger to Klaiber, 31 January 1953; according to Klaiber's handwritten note, Heuss raised the Landsberg theme with Dulles. Already a year before, on 21 January 1952, Heusinger—speaking for Speidel as well—had warned of "extreme psychological difficulties," since the "burning question" of the war criminals was closely connected with the German defense contribution. Ibid.

90. *FRUS 1952–1954*, VII/1, p. 392. The initiative was linked to a peeved chancellor's outburst within the circle of his closest advisers on 15 December 1952—the war criminal question, he exclaimed, had to be resolved "immediately." Cf. Lenz, *Tagebuch*, p. 504.

91. FDP delegate Hütter had explained this development by referring to a nonbinding declaration of HICOG to the effect that an effort was being made to find a solution. BT-Berichte 1, WP, 19 March 1953, p. 12333 (voting results pp. 12363–66).

92. *FRUS 1952–1954*, VII/1, p. 420.

93. *Kabinettsprotokolle 1953*, 27 February 1953, p. 190; to great extent, the six-man list corresponded to the suggestions made by the Heidelberg circle to the Justice Ministry. With one exception, it consisted of jurists who had already been active in the Nazi period: two Provisional Court of Appeal presidents, two Supreme Court of Justice councilors, and a university teacher.

94. Cf., in detail, Adenauer, *Erinnerungen 1945–1953*, pp. 564–89.

95. Ibid., p. 573.

96. *FRUS 1952–1954*, VII/1, pp. 434 and 442ff.

97. The texts are published in Adenauer, *Briefe 1951–1953*, pp. 378–81; on the context, cf. idem, *Erinnerungen 1953–1955*, pp. 209–18; Blankenhorn, *Verständnis*, p. 152ff.

98. *FRUS 1952–1954*, VII/1, p. 468f.

99. Cf. Adenauer, *Erinnerungen 1953–1955*, p. 208; idem, *Teegespräche 1950–1954*, pp. 466f., 469.

100. *FRUS 1952–1954*, V/2, p. 1589.

101. Cf. above, pp. 139f.

102. *FRUS 1952–1954*, VII/1, p. 1629 (McBride minutes, 11 July 1953).

103. The earliest indications came from Blank's department; cf. *Allgemeine Zeitung* (Mainz), 18 July 1953. The AP then furnished strikingly precise details, purportedly thanks to British conference participants. Cf., e.g., *Die Welt*, 21 July 1953 ("War-Condemned Have Grounds for Hope").

104. His position, presented in various SPD newspapers, once again merged those "imprisoned in the West" with the war prisoners being held in the Soviet Union. Cf., e.g., *Lübecker Freie Presse,* 29 July 1953 ("War-Condemned Problem Remains Unsettled. Herbert Wehner: All War Prisoners Must Be Repatriated.")

105. EZA, 2/84/3210-I E/1, Interessenvertretung der im Malmedy-Prozeß Verurteilten ("Interest Representation of Those Condemned in the Malmédy Trial"), circular, April 1953.

106. BA, B 136/3772, Thesen für die Rede des Herrn Bundeskanzlers in Werl am 28 June 1953 ("Theses for the Chancellor's Talk in Werl on 28 June 1953").

107. BA, B 136/1882, Kirkpatrick to Adenauer, 11 June 1953 (he was responding directly to a complaint from Manstein); there were also complaints—especially aggressive in tone—from the president of the Westphalian Evangelical church, Ernst Wilm, 27 December 1951 and 12 February 1952, along with Paul Wartenberg, 29 June 1953.

108. For the latter detail, Cf. AP report, in *Frankfurter Allgemeine Zeitung,* 30 June 1953, p. 3. In general, the visit received scant press coverage; but cf., for an isolated critical voice regarding Adenauer's "handshake" with "Panzer-Meyer," the German Federation of Labor organ *Welt der Arbeit,* 3 July 1953. In 1945, "Panzer Meyer" had been sentenced to death by a Canadian military court on account of the execution of approximately twenty Canadian war prisoners in the area under his command; the sentence was later commuted to life in prison. At the end of 1951 he had been transferred to Werl under British custody. During his visit to Ottawa in April 1953, Adenauer interceded for Meyer with the prime minister. After his release, the former SS general thanked the chancellor for "all sorts of help" offered by the West German diplomatic service—but especially for Adenauer's visit to Werl, which had furnished him with the "firm hope" of being freed in "reasonable time." Details in BA, B 305/169 and 170. Falkenhorst, sentenced to death by a British military court on account of the shooting execution of British soldiers, would be released from Werl in 1953.

109. Cf. *Kabinettsprotokolle 1953,* 30 June 1953, p. 368f.; Lenz, *Tagebuch,* 30 June 1953, p. 659.

110. *Der Spiegel,* 22 July 1953, p. 9. Von Manstein would serve as an adviser in the construction of the Bundeswehr.

111. Transcripts in: BA, B 305/53.

112. In the national elections on 6 September 1953, the CDU-CSU raised their percentage of votes from 31 percent to 45.2 percent. In total, the coalition of CDU-CSU, FDP, German Party, and All-German Block Union of Expellees won 333 of 487 mandates, thus having a two-thirds majority.

113. The only party that was further right, after the banning of the Socialist Reich Party, was the German Party of the Reich, which received approximately 300,000 votes (1.1 percent of the total).

114. This is Herbert's well-chosen term—*Rückkehr in die Bürgerlichkeit*—in *Best,* chapter 4. Achenbach and his "expert" Best indirectly confirmed this

prospect by concentrating above all on having their apologetic theory of the "political offense" (see above, pp. 72f) taken up by the Bonn ministerial bureaucracy responsible for the pardon commissions. BA, B 305/55, Achenbach to Foreign Office, 14 September 1953 (copy). In Achenbach's case, such capacity for conformity led to a remarkable Euro-political career in the 1960s; it was nearly crowned with his appointment as European commissioner in 1970.

115. BA, B 122/645, Trützschler to Heyden, 11 December 1953 (with proposal of the Foreign Office for the president, confidential).

116. BA, B 305/53, circular of Fehsenbecker, 19 September 1953.

117. BA, B 305/55, Gawlik to Höfler, 22 November 1954 (with attached material). Called into question by CDU Bundestag member Höfler, the parole system was expressly defended by Gawlik; he saw it as satisfactory at least until the point when it would be applied to all prisoners—then one would have to see.

118. On 31 March 1954, in the course of commenting on a Foreign Office proposal, Kirkpatrick even remarked that the trials had been "bungled work"; Cf. Brochhagen, *Nach Nürnberg*, p. 104.

119. BA, B 136/1883, preliminary memorandum (strictly confidential), [7 December 1954]. At that point, a further 180 German war criminals were still being incarcerated abroad—109 in France, 53 in Holland.

120. BT-Drucksachen 2, WP, no. 979, 12 November 1954; Adenauer tried to prevent public commentary on the interpellation with a strictly confidential letter to the chairman of the German Party and the All-German Block Union of Expellees parliamentary factions; themes the interpellation covered included the possibility of a general amnesty before ratification of the Paris treaties. BA, B 136/1883, Adenauer to Merkatz, 7 December 1954. The chancellor's admonition was not entirely fruitless, the Bundestag's handling of the interpellation proceeding in a relatively restrained fashion. BT-Berichte 2, WP, 17 February 1955, p. 3382ff.

121. On Pentecost 1955, Hansen wrote the chancellor that if German men were to voluntarily report themselves for a "new defense" with "untroubled hearts and without inner conflicts," then a "solution to the war-condemned problem" was necessary beforehand, along with full maintenance for the old career soldiers, in line with the "131" law. On 11 June 1955, Mende telegraphed Adenauer shortly before his trip to the United States to urge him to intervene for the "war-condemned former soldiers held by the Western custodial powers"; this would be of great "psychological significance" for the "coming defense legislation." Details in BA, B 136/1883.

122. Between the lines, this was even demonstrated by a letter of Blücher to Adenauer on 31 March 1955, in which—in the style of his party colleague Achenbach—the vice chancellor lamented the flawed "pardoning practice of the German state organs," expressing the fear of a "growth in unease and resistance in the population" should a "generous gesture from the custodial powers" not come "soon after termination of the entire ratification process." Hallstein answered for the chancellor on 18 June 1955, offering a

cool review of what had already been achieved and suggesting discretion to the advantage of those concerned. Letter exchange in BA, B 136/1883.

123. A searching study of Adenauer's "triumph," blindly celebrated as it was by the German public, has yet to see print. But cf. Brochhagen, *Nach Nürnberg*, pp. 240–50; Karl-Heinz Janßen, "Heimkehr—fünf Jahre zu spät," in *Die Zeit*, 1 January 1993, p. 9ff. ("Dossier").

124. He was, however, criticized directly for this in the Subcommittee on War Prisoners; BT—PA, session minutes 12 October 1955.

125. Plentiful material on these "prayer weeks," organized mainly in the Evangelical camp between 1946 and 1957 with great expenditure of time and effort, in (among other places) EZA, 2/84/6453/10.

126. Figures according to BT-Berichte 2, WP, 17 February 1955, p. 3383f. (report of Hallstein) and BA, B 305/56, concluding report of the Mixed Board, 21 October 1958; ibid. for the following information.

127. BA, B 136/1882, Ehlers to Adenauer, 25 June 1954; Ehlers relied on information of the Evangelical pastor at Landsberg, Lettenmeyer, in turn furnished by the German Evangelical Church's deputy for war prisoner affairs, Bishop Heckel.

128. According to the summarizing report of Mobile Killing Unit A, in the period from 16 October 1941 to 31 January 1942 Sandberger had reported 5,463 "executions," subdivided into 963 Jews, 4,070 communists, 400 partisans, and 30 others. Cf. Krausnick and Wilhelm, *Truppe des Weltanschauungskrieges*, p. 606f.

129. BA, B 305/147, Heuss to Dehler, 28 November 1949. President Heuss also forwarded the justice minister a letter to his wife from Sandberger's mother with the following words: "Whether the dialogue with the Americans that will certainly start soon can and should be extended to such cases, I cannot determine."

130. Unless otherwise indicated, this and the following information is based on documents in BA, B 122/650, esp. K. Sandberger to Heuss and president's office, 7. and 21 June 1955.

131. Cf. Buscher, *Trial Program*, pp. 37, 166. In 1947, the Republican Langer had maintained in Congress that the International Military Tribunal was modeled on the Moscow show trials; cf. Bosch, *Judgement*, p. 84f. With the Sandberger case, the U.S. pardon lobby turned directly to Truman in May 1949; the president received a family photo of Sandberger with the following accompanying commentary: "Just as you were in World War One an officer in a field artillery unit, so Martin Sandberger was an officer in a German army unit, fighting in Russia during World War Two. By order of a higher authority, he had many unpleasant things to do, including some executions. Some of his decisions must have cost him as much soul torture as your decision to drop the atomic bomb." Cited from Bower, *Pledge*, p. 266 (with mistaken information on Sandberger's Mobile Killing Unit affiliation and activities).

132. BA, B 122/650, Gawlik to Heyden, 30 June 1955 (with excerpts from the trial minutes, 9 April 1948).

133. On Müller, see above, p. 17–18.

134. AdsD, Schmid papers 633, Becker to Schmid, 13 December 1953.

135. But in Schmid, *Erinnerungen,* p. 169, Sandberger is described as responsible for the revocation of a Gestapo summons prompted by Schmid's critique of the doctrine of history as racial conflict, which he termed a "philosophy of cow breeders."

136. AdsD, Schmid papers 635 (copy also in BA, B 122/650).

137. BA, B 122/650, Becker to Heuss, 6 August 1955.

138. Heuss had already revealed himself as specially impressed by the above qualities after—still probing—having asked Becker for his "entirely objective advice." According to the information now at his disposal, Sandberger "behaves in a clearly exemplary manner in prison and has gained great moral and intellectual elasticity in his own continued education and aid offered his comrades in fate. But what he has been reproached with regarding his activities in Estonia and what he has indeed partially admitted (mass executions) is not exactly the sort of thing allowing me to take on such an individual case." (The parenthetical term is crossed out in the draft.) Ibid., Heuss to Becker, 26 July 1955.

139. Ibid., Heuss to Conant, 25 August 1955. On request, Becker received the text of the letter and the American reply—to be sure with the instruction to avoid allowing "Herr Sandberger senior to sense the scruples preoccupying him [Heuss] in this affair"; ibid., Heyden to Becker, 6 September 1955.

140. This was entirely clear to the expert in the president's office. Ibid., note of Heyden, 22 July 1955.

141. Ibid., Dowling to Heuss, 31 August 1955.

142. Cf., e.g., *Stern* 11 (1956): 14–18 ("Still furlough on parole. In the sovereign Federal Republic, 258 Germans are living under American law"). The personnel and maintenance costs for Landsberg (1951) were approximately 3.2 million marks; for Werl (1950), 1.5 million. This prompted the Justice Ministry to consider consolidating the institutions; details in BA, B 141/9576.

143. BA, B 305/55, Höfler to Gawlik, 18 November 1954.

144. Detailed minutes of the regular conferences of the "parole supervisors" in BA, B 305/55.

145. The above in BA, B 305/56, closing report of the Mixed Board, 21 October 1958. The list included in Rückerl, *NS-Verbrechen,* p. 131, indicating that Sandberger is already to be freed in January 1953, is inaccurate; likewise—and with extensive resulting misinterpretations—in Buscher, *Trial Program,* p. 166f.

146. These "war-condemned in the West" received intensive solicitude, not least through Evangelical Church deputy D. Hans Stempel, president of the Speyer churches; BA, B 122/645, Stempel to Heuss, 19 June 1959; IfZ, ED 94/215, Stempel to W. Strauß, 30 September 1959, and additional correspondence (with attached material).

147. When, for example, at the end of 1955 Holland's justice minister declared that there would be no early releases of German war prisoners during his

term of office, the storm of protest was so great that the performance of a Dutch military choir had to be canceled in Bielefeld. German firms threatened their Dutch trading partners with a boycott, and the *Rheinische Post*—a Düsseldorf weekly paper with ties to the CDU—tried to smooth things over with a series of articles (3 and 10 December 1955) that included contributions from Dutch journalists.

148. This is, however, the stance of Buscher, *Trial Program,* esp. p. 159, in relation to the American effort. On the other hand, Clay, *Decision in Germany,* pp. 254–55, is far too optimistic. He retrospectively attributes the criticism to "Communist propaganda" alone, assessing the American capacity for self-correction as "another and valuable lesson in democracy."

149. As the controversy—extending over some years—concerning the exhibition "War of Extinction: Crimes of the Wehrmacht 1941–1945" (opening in 1995) has made clear, this remained the case markedly longer among the general public. In 1999, false interpretations accompanying some of the photos led to further controversy and a temporary closing of the exhibit; this, however, is unlikely to prevent the collapse of the German myth of the "clean" Wehrmacht. Cf. my essay "Faktor 1000: Wehrmacht und Wahrheit in Zeiten der Krawallkommunikation," in *Frankfurter Allgemeine Zeitung,* 2 November 1999, p. 49.

Part III

1. For details see Jenke, *Verschwörung,* pp. 46–73; Tauber, *Beyond Eagle,* pp. 81–116.
2. See Frei, "Renazification," pp. 50–54.
3. Along with the five delegates from the National Right and the two "independents," Dorls and Ott, scattered delegates from the FDP, the Economic Reconstruction Association, the Bavarian Party, and the German Party could be considered part of the radical right-wing spectrum.
4. This did not mean any necessary increase in sensitivity regarding expressions of "everyday" anti-Semitism; on the problem in general, cf. Stern, *Whitewashing.*

Chapter 10

1. BA, B 122/2220, notes of the press chief of Schleswig-Holstein, undated.
2. *Frankfurter Rundschau,* 12 December 1949, p. 2 ("The 'Different Opinion' of a Delegate Concerning the Gassing of the Jews"); Hedler's confirmation in *Neue Zeitung,* 13 December 1949, p. 1f.
3. At this time, the necessary parliamentary motion had not yet been placed on the agenda. Hedler's immunity was lifted two days later by a "huge majority," after a sometimes acrimonious debate. Tellingly, Hedler was supported here not by his own parliamentary faction but by the National

Right and delegate Dorls (for now without a party, later of the Socialist Reich Party). BT-Berichte 1, WP, 14. and 16 December 1949, pp. 716 and 772–78.

4. *Frankfurter Rundschau,* 12 December 1949, p. 2 ("From Hitler to Hedler").

5. Unless otherwise indicated, the following is based on the printed version of the written trial summation (with attached material), 9 March 1950, in (among other places) ADL, N1/1005.

6. Alongside Gustav Dahrendorf and Heinrich Christian Meier, it included relatives of Carl Goerdeler, Friedrich Olbricht, Friedrich Justus Perels, Jens Jessen, Ernst von Harnack, Henning von Tresckow, Adolf Reichwein, Julius Leber, and Adam von Trott zu Solz; as the judgment record put it, it also included "Hans Bernd Gisevius for his dead comrades."

7. On this point in particular, the statements of the chief Social Democratic witnesses were very clear; the continuation of the passage cited in the *Frankfurter Rundschau* was as follows: "With a cynical smile, Hedler asserted that 'I personally doubt that gassing was the proper procedure' (laughter in the assembly). Ibid., appendix II.

8. The summary of the witness testimony conveys this impression; ibid., appendix III. It is confirmed through the report of the Kiel governmental spokesman, who had observed the trial (and had a very negative assessment of the judges' capabilities). The president's office received a copy of the report; BA, B 122/2220, deputy of the state of Schleswig-Holstein to Bott, 15 February 1950, with attached material.

9. Cf. *Frankfurter Rundschau, Frankfurter Allgemeine Zeitung,* and *Süddeutsche Zeitung,* 16 February 1950, pp. 1 and 2 in each.

10. Cf. Meyn, *Deutsche Partei,* p. 32; beyond this, the detailed report in *Die Zeit,* 9 February 1952 ("and stand united behind Hedler. The trial in Neumünster—Judicial Epilogue to a Political scandal").

11. Cf. Jenke, *Verschwörung,* p. 127; Schmollinger, "Deutsche Reichspartei," p. 1175; on the further career of the "150 percent Nazi," cf. Tauber, *Beyond Eagle,* pp. 409, 710, 759, 887, 1306.

12. Cf. *HICOG Information Bulletin,* April 1950, p. 43ff. ("The Hedler Case").

13. Ibid., p. 44.

14. *Frankfurter Allgemeine Zeitung,* 18 February 1950, p. 1 ("Law Stands Over the Party").

15. *Die Zeit,* 23 February 1950, p. 1; on Friedlaender's political biography, cf. my sketch in Frei and Friedländer, *Ernst Friedländer,* pp. 7–33.

16. *HICOG Information Bulletin,* April 1950, p. 43.

17. Once the brochure with the written court opinion was published—the court manifestly made an effort to avoid the most blatant weaknesses of the oral opinion—Sethe once again offered a commentary, defending the judges' arguments more unequivocally than before. *Frankfurter Allgemeine Zeitung,* 12 April 1950, p. 1 ("If You Yourself Were a Judge ... "). Tüngel's impatient, inflexible adherence to the old nationalist model— namely his reference during this period to "dangerous well poisoning"— was aggravated by HICOG's publication of a critical study of German

nationalism, reported on extensively by Drew Middleton in the *New York Times*—that reporter seen as responsible for "extreme anti-German articles" and as supplied with material by "Morgenthau boys." According to Tüngel, the Americans should have gotten their own shop in order, falsely conceived nationalism in the end existing everywhere. *Die Zeit,* 16 March 1950, p. 1. On Middleton's role and self-understanding, see below, p. 284f, and Middleton, *Last July,* pp. 168, 172–76.

18. Circulating in Bonn, this somewhat embarrassing document indicated that the "by no means pro-Jewish" attitude of the accused man had not escaped the presiding judge; but it denied a "pronouncedly anti-Jewish" attitude by referring to the testimony of "witness Schröder, himself a Jewish *Mischling.*" BA, B 122/2220, oral opinion, 15 February 1950, p. 8.

19. Cf. *Frankfurter Rundschau,* 18 February 1950, p. 1; IfZ, Dm 115, Mitteilung des BPA Nr. 43, 17 February 1950. The press announcement had been decided on formally in the cabinet; cf. *Kabinettsprotokolle 1950,* p. 213.

20. Steering a moderate course between left and right as first president of the Weimar Republic, Ebert found himself slandered as a "traitor" in a 1924 court judgment for having taken part in the munitions strike of January 1918.

21. BT-Berichte 1, WP, 16 February 1950, p. 1302.

22. *SPD-Fraktionsprotokolle 1949–1953,* 16 February 1950, p. 100.

23. BT-Berichte 1, WP, 16 February 1950, p. 1302f.

24. Ibid., p. 1305f. On 22 September 1949, the Center Party had already initiated a law for the protection of the federal flag and colors; cf. Schiffers, *Bürgerfreiheit,* pp. 89–94.

25. Ibid., p. 1304.

26. In the course of the trial, it had become clear that Hedler had furnished false information concerning the period of his Nazi Party membership to the denazification authorities; for this reason, he now was facing new legal proceedings.

27. Hugo Stinnes Jr. was a Ruhr industrialist and far-right supporter of the North Rhine–Westphalian FDP; "Schröter" seems to be a reference to Cologne banker Kurt von Schröder, whose villa was the venue for Hitler's secret meeting with Papen on 4 January 1933; a confidant of Adenauer, cofounder of the Rhineland CDU, member of the Frankfurt Economic Council, and Bundestag delegate from 1949 until his death in 1962, Cologne banker Robert Pferdmenge had been briefly arrested in connection with the July Plot.

28. This and approximately 200 additional protest letters, sometimes addressed to *Reichspräsident* Heuss and often with references to Friedrich Ebert ("the first *Reichspräsident,* now dead twenty-five years … cut down by the creeping baseness of political liars and venal slanderers"), are located in BA, B 122/2220. The "organization of the protests," which led to the partial use of preprinted forms, was initiated in the parliamentary faction session of 16 February 1950; *SPD-Fraktionsprotokolle 1949–1953,* p. 100.

29. Details in BA, B 122/2220.

30. *Frankfurter Rundschau,* 17 February 1950, p. 1.
31. Bayerischer Landtag, stenographic minutes, 16 February 1950, p. 796.
32. Cf. *SPD-Fraktionsprotokolle 1949–1953,* 22 February and 10 March 1950, pp. 102 and 108.
33. On the expulsion, cf. BT-Berichte 1, WP, 10 March 1950, p. 1560f. One of Hedler's interlocutors, and a precise witness of the event, was Harold A. Williams, correspondent for the *Baltimore Sun;* I was kindly allowed to examine the paper's byline files ("Alleged Anti-Semitic Deputy Kicked Out of Bonn Bundestag," *Baltimore Sun,* 11 March 1950).
34. From his demonstratively occupied thirty-marks-a-day bed, which he did not leave for three months, Hedler declared, "This propaganda would not be too expensive if it cost 200,000 marks." Cf. *Der Spiegel,* 16 March and 29 June 1950, pp. 3 and 6f. The SPD's legal fight with Hedler would last for years. After the state court in Bonn awarded Hedler damages of 3,000 marks on 10 April 1953, Adolf Arndt filed an appeal that the Cologne Provisional Court of Appeal turned down on 26 July 1956. AdsD, SPD-Bundestagsfraktion, 1, WP/22, 2, WP/41; Arndt papers, vol. 75.
35. Cf. BT-Berichte 1, WP, 22 March 1950, p. 1683f.; *SPD-Fraktionsprotokolle 1949–1953,* pp. 109, 112, 115, 117. The Council of Elders failed in its preceding efforts to convince the Social Democrats not to stage a walkout by pointing to the relatively short exclusion periods. IfZ, ED 329/2, 15 March 1950, p. 2
36. Within the parliamentary faction, this legislative intent had already been discussed on 19 January 1950, hence even before start of the trial; cf. *SPD-Fraktionsprotokolle 1949–1953,* p. 84.
37. BT-Drucksachen 1, WP, no. 563, motion of the SPD parliamentary faction, 15 February 1950.
38. Ibid., no. 564.
39. In a representative survey in June 1951, 40 percent of Germans said they were "for the men of July 20"; 30 percent were against; the remainder either wavering, having no opinion, or being ignorant of the attack on Hitler (11 percent). cf. Noelle and Neumann, *Jahrbuch,* p. 138. Four months later, a HICOG survey produced similar results. Cf. Merritt and Merritt, *HICOG Surveys,* p. 147.
40. BT-Berichte 1, WP, 16 March 1950, p. 1610f., 1617.
41. Ibid., p. 1611ff.; Arndt received a delayed call to order for this.
42. Cf. Gosewinkel, *Arndt,* p. 209; on the relationship between Dehler and Arndt, see esp. pp. 176f., 330–36.
43. Cf. Schiffers, *Bürgerfreiheit,* pp. 39–45.
44. BT-Berichte 1, WP, 16 March 1950, pp. 1593–97; ibid. for following citation.
45. Greve was evidently basing his remarks on an article in the *Frankfurter Rundschau,* 29 December 1949, p. 2, which indicated that Kutscher had already been active for the Frankfurt Economic Council before its committee for political scrutiny denied him his position. In rejecting the reproaches being leveled at Kutscher on the basis of Nuremberg document PS 3319, the Ministry of Economics pointed to his exculpation by a denaz-

ification tribunal. Cf. *Allgemeine Wochenzeitung der Juden,* 6 January and 24 March 1950.

46. A member of the Nazi party from 1933 onward, Kiesinger would be elevated to West German chancellor between 1966 and 1969; during this period, he was subject to heavy criticism on account of his earlier career (both before and during the war, he served as deputy director of the Foreign Office's radio division).

47. BT-Berichte 1, WP, 16 March 1950, p. 1598ff.

48. Ibid., pp. 1602 and 1606.

49. Ibid., p. 1609.

50. Against the agreement between the parliamentary factions, Dehler had used a talk introducing the judicial organization law to inveigh against the condemnation of the Hedler judgments; he revealed himself as utterly uncritical of the judges. Even the president, who had intimated a criticism of the judgment in the Bundestag in connection with a commemorative hour on the twenty-fifth anniversary of Friedrich Ebert's death had to suffer interpretation by Dehler. Ibid., 1 March 1950, pp. 1437–40.

51. BT-Berichte 1, WP, 16 March 1950, p. 1597.

52. For details, see Schiffers, *Bürgerfreiheit;* Gosewinkel, *Arndt,* pp. 208–24.

53. BT-Berichte 1, WP, 12 September 1950, p. 3105.

54. Schiffers (*Bürgerfreiheit,* pp. 204, 342) is highly reticent in this regard and on the following (the book has brief references to Schafheutle's recallable "knowledge"); sharper in judgment is Müller, *Juristen,* pp. 213, 233–36.

55. It is the case that Article 143, Basic Law, had defined high treason as punishable, but an executory law was missing. Cf. Schiffers, *Bürgerfreiheit,* p. 33.

56. Illustrative in this regard is Posser, *Anwalt;* in greater detail, cf., above all, Brünneck, *Politische Justiz.*

57. Cf., beyond the already cited literature, the overview by periods in Bracher, *Diktatur,* pp. 509–20; particularly suggestive is Niethammer, *Angepaßter Faschismus,* pp. 32–55.

58. Some other court cases were also subject to public criticism in the first six months of 1950, including the Hamburg acquittal, confirmed on appeal, of "Jud Süß" director Veit Harlan, accused of having perpetrated a crime against humanity. Cf., in general, the commentary of Ernst Müller-Meiningen Jr., "Attackierte Justiz," in idem, *Das Jahr Tausendundeins,* p. 124ff.

59. Cf. German Press Agency report, cited from *Frankfurter Allgemeine Zeitung,* 23 July 1951, p. 3; *Neue Zeitung,* 21 July 1951, p. 1.

60. Cf. Munzinger-Archiv, 10 January 1953; Tauber, *Beyond Eagle,* p. 1306, n. 78.

61. Kogon, "Fall Hedler," p. 430. The text was originally written for subscribers to the English and French information services of the *Frankfurter Hefte;* authorship indicated only in the volume synopsis. On Kogon's HICOG-financed journalistic activities, see Klaus Körner's informative "Eugen Kogon als Verleger," *Aus dem Antiquariat* 8 (1994): A281–A293.

62. In *Frankfurter Hefte* 6 (1951): 377–82. Ibid. for following citation; italics in original.

Chapter 11

1. In an election rally of the Socialist Reich Party in Melverode; cited from BA, B 141/207, resolution draft, Ministry of the Interior, 2 May 1951.
2. Cf. the summation of Niclauß, *Demokratiegründung*, pp. 111–21.
3. Cf. the introductory description in Jenke, *Verschwörung*, pp. 73–114; a similar contemporary report can be found in BA, B 136/1747, Glaesser to Lenz, 25 April 1951. For a fundamental study of the SRP, based on early access to the archival material, see Büsch and Furth, *Rechtsradikalismus* (the book suffers from an excessively formalized approach and from a penetrating idealization of the democratic "resistance"). Cf. further Tauber, *Beyond Eagle*, esp. pp. 689–725; for a more recent summation, see Schmollinger, "Die Sozialistische Reichspartei."
4. They were mainly academics who, as party bureaucrats, school directors, and writers, had been hit relatively hard by the political purging and were having difficulty reassimilating into bourgeois professions.
5. On the following, along with the works mentioned in n. 3, see Geile, *Remer-Mythos*, esp. pp. 27–37.
6. The SRP would here gain only 1.6 percent of the votes; its direct competition, the German Reich Party, with Wolfgang Hedler, received 2.8 percent. Behind the SPD with 27.5 percent, the second strongest party was— running for the first time—the Union of Expellees and Victims of Injustice (23.4 percent). The other results: CDU 19.7 percent, German Party 9.6 percent, FDP 7.1 percent, Electoral Association of Southern Schleswig 5.5 percent, and German Communist Party 2.8 percent.
7. Geile, *Remer-Mythos*, pp. 87–101.
8. See Schwarz, *Ära Adenauer I*, p. 131.
9. This was in the context of "measures to protect the federation and its democratic institutions," which culminated in preparation of the first law to alter the Penal Code; cf. BT-Berichte 1, WP, 23 February 1950, p. 1338f.
10. Cf. *Kabinettsprotokolle 1950*, 15 and 19 September 1950, pp. 696, 702f.
11. Ibid., p. 703. On the other hand, in a letter to Dehler—not Heinemann— as preparation for the first cabinet session the day beforehand, the chancellor had requested the draft of a proposal regarding "the position of the government in the entire question of communist officials and employees"; this was after he had heard from the Cologne city administration "that these people use their vacations to educate themselves in the eastern zone and then return to continue their agitation work here." Adenauer, *Briefe 1949–1951*, p. 271.
12. Cf. *Frankfurter Allgemeine Zeitung*, 20 September 1950, p. 1 ("No Communists in Federal Service") and p. 4 ("Irreconcilable with Official Duties: The List of Undesired Organizations"); similarly in the *Süddeutsche Zeitung*. In general, the resolution drew little attention.
13. BA, B 141/207, Dorls to Heuss, 21 September 1950 (transcript).
14. Ibid., Heinemann to Heuss, 26 September 1950 (transcript).
15. Ibid., Dorls to Heuss, 11 October 1950.

16. Ibid., note of Dehler, 28 October 1950.

17. Ibid., Dorls to Dehler, 25 October 1950.

18. Ibid., Dehler to Dorls, 20 November 1950. A Constitutional Court review never took place; it is not clear if SRP members were dismissed from civil service because of the decision.

19. Following this, the chairman of North Rhine–Westphalia's right-leaning FDP chapter, Middelhauve, demanded an explanation from Dehler, on the basis of incompatibility between the FDP's plans for an end to denazification and the question of the Nazi pasts of SRP members. ADL, N1/3341, Middelhauve to Dehler and response, 8 and 13 January 1951. Dehler complained to Dorls about the public divulgence of his letter's contents on 15 March 1951 (ibid.), using notable formulations: "From our discussion, you must have gained the conviction of the best will having been shown on my part. I had declared myself ready to intercede in the cabinet for recognition of your party as legal, on the basis of adequate material. In my letter, my main concern was clarifying the structure and total character of your party. I am taken aback by your public distortion of my efforts."

20. Dorl tried to fashion an argument for his party's harmlessness from the fact. In his words to Dehler, "About 75 percent of the SRP are under forty. Only a diminishing fraction of its members stems from the lower or middle leadership ranks of the Nazi Party. The soldierly element is by far the most prevalent. I do not need to especially emphasize that already by nature, there are basic differences between the Nazi Party and ideology and the more soldierly thinking men and their feelings and thoughts." BA, B 141/207, Dorls to Dehler, 25 October 1950.

21. *Kabinettsprotokolle 1951*, p. 126; ibid. for the following information.

22. In spring 1933 they had removed him from his position as chief mayor of Düsseldorf, incarcerating him for some months afterward. Following his release, he sought out resistance circles. Cf. Först, "Lehr," p. 183ff.

23. Many transcripts of local police reports complemented the Federal Office's summaries; also in BA, B 141/210. The membership highpoint (1952) would appear to have been approximately 10,000 overall: 6,500 in Lower Saxony, 1,300 in North Rhine–Westphalia, 800 in Schleswig-Holstein, and 600 in Hesse. Cf., in detail, Büsch and Furth, *Rechtsradikalismus,* pp. 71–93.

24. Cf. *Kabinettsprotokolle 1951,* 30 January 1951, p. 126. The government had decided on the previous charge on 12 December 1950; cf. *Kabinettsprotokolle 1950*, p. 891.

25. For example, he advised against leveling charges against SRP Bundestag delegate Richter (alias Rößler), who had threatened German "collaborators," starting on the day that the illegality of the military laws was determined. Dehler's comment was that the laws were, in fact, strongly "debated from the vantage of international law." BA, B 141/210, Dehler to Lehr and Lenz, 9 March 1951 (secret, final draft; heavy strike-outs in hand).

26. Cf. the summary in Büsch and Furth, *Rechtsradikalismus,* p. 181f.

27. Cf. *Kabinettsprotokolle 1951,* 10 April 1951, p. 293f. and n. 44.

28. Published by the BPA and authored by Raimund Neunteufel; cf. *Kabinettsprotokolle 1951,* 13, 18 April 1951, pp. 309, 321. The SPD and organizations close to the government published similar texts; cf. Büsch and Furth, *Rechtsradikalismus,* p. 177.

29. With Adenauer's knowledge, Feitenhansl received an initial 10,000 marks from the Office of Constitutional Protection; while an additional 25,000 marks were requested, it does not appear that Lenz received that sum from sources set aside for American propaganda. Cf. Lenz, *Tagebuch,* 5, 13, 18, 21, 23, 25 April 1951, pp. 65, 69, 72, 74f.

30. Cf., e.g., SPD Press Service, 24 October 1951, p. 5 ("The Eastern Sources of the SRP").

31. In a letter to the chancellor, the chairman of the "Association of Pension-Entitled Former Wehrmacht Officers and Their Surviving Dependents" reported on a "wave of assemblies" for Remer in Schleswig-Holstein and urged him to send "eloquent speakers," since the "favorable impression that Remer even makes on listeners with a sense of responsibility doubtless produces many new members for the SRP." BA, B 136/1746, Hansen to Adenauer, 6 July 1951.

32. *Kabinettsprotokolle 1951,* 24 April 1951, p. 332ff., cit. p. 333.

33. Cf. this passage in an instructive report from the government's press office strongly alluding to the neutralist rhetoric (hence understood as pro-Soviet) of the SRP: "The danger of the SRP is evident. Above all in rural election districts, the name Remer stirs masses of people. While the government's speakers address 20 to 30 people, 1,000 show up at SRP events. The feeling arises that the SRP is the only party with the ability to fill its assembly places in the smaller cities of Lower Saxony and in the countryside. It becomes evident that the younger farmers are very susceptible here. The SRP has succeeded in running many former "district farmers' leaders" with decisive significance for these election districts. This leads to the conclusion that many members of the SRP come from population strata that would never dream of favoring pro-Soviet policies. But these same strata are angry at Bonn, and Remer pours oil on the fire. This explains how the SRP steadily increases its ranks without even having to mention its own political goals." BA, B 136/1747, Glaesser to Lenz, 25 April 1951.

34. Cf. the interesting after-election poker playing in the meetings of the CDU's directorship on 10 May and 3 July 1951; *CDU-Bundesvorstand 1950–1953,* pp. 29–32, 51ff. The British presented Adenauer with a demand that Hellwege be taken to task for such readiness; presumably the resulting mistrust still played a role in Hellwege's decision, following the British strike against the Naumann group in February 1953 (see chapter 12), to dissolve the North Rhine–Westphalian branch of the German Party on account of right-wing radical infiltration. Cf. Schwartz, *America's Germany,* p. 370, n. 13, and Jenke, *Verschwörung,* p. 135.

35. Cf. Marten, *FDP,* esp. pp. 231–47.

36. BT-Drucksachen 1, WP, no. 2185, 20 April 1951; BT-Berichte 1, WP, 26 April 1951, p. 5488.

37. In this regard, Remer declared "that we can walk down the same road once with political opponents"—and left no doubts about the principles informing his own readiness for defense. "I would say 'yes' to remilitarization if it only involved the German state, but not, as is now the case, if it involves the defense of a Western European border-state formation. We Germans do not wish to be cannon fodder for others and stand in for the Maginot Line in the very first line. For this reason, we are the most unrelenting opponents of remilitarization. (Strong applause.) For this reason, we are no weaklings or cowards. Other people can share such a conviction. For us, what is at stake is life, and we do not want to shoot dead our last substance. But we will defame every German general daring to offer Germans as cannon fodder to the point where no dog would take a piece of bread from him! (Strong applause.)" BA, B 136/1746, stenogram of Remer's talk in Oldendorf, 29 March 1951. On the "Wiesbaden Appeal" cf. Koch, *Heinemann*, pp. 234–51.

38. BT-Berichte 1, WP, 26 April 1951, p. 5498.

39. Reported in the *Frankfurter Allgemeine Zeitung*, 27 April 1951, p. 1 ("Lehr Travels to Lower Saxony: Is Intervention Against the Socialist Reich Party Necessary?")

40. BA, B 136/1746, Lehr to Adenauer, 1 May 1951 (with resolution draft).

41. Ibid.

42. BA, B 141/207, resolution draft for the Ministry of Justice, 2 May 1951.

43. *Kabinettsprotokolle 1951,* 4 May 1951, p. 346ff., cit. p. 347; Lenz, *Tagebuch,* p. 78. The session was interrupted for an hour to reformulate the resolution. Because of what appears to be Lenz's writing error, it is not clear whether Adenauer—back from Strasbourg on the day of the cabinet session—now denied having spoken with Lehr about a banning of the SRP before his trip. What does seem sure is that Adenauer was not consulted during the pause for deliberations.

44. The situation was depicted in a 7 May 1951 *Frankfurter Rundschau* lead article that was quite precisely informed concerning what transpired in the cabinet session. The article indicated that an SRP ban conflicted with Hellwege's ambition to become minister-president; the German Party that the CDU was trying to exclude in Lower Saxony had found a place for an election official by the name of Emil Ehrich, who had to leave Hellwege's Bundesrat ministry after being identified as a former SS *Obersturmführer* and a *Landesgruppenleiter* for the Nazi Party in Rome. The article drew attention in Bonn. BA, B 141/207, note of Dehler, 9 May 1951. Adenauer explained to the High Commissioners that according to Hellwege the reference to Ehrich's Nazi career on an election poster was meant to show "that such an earlier member of the Nazi Party now supported the new state. If I had seen the poster earlier, I would have seen to it that this thought was expressed more clearly." *Akten zur Auswärtigen Politik,* vol. 2, p. 354f. Adenauer was far more critical of Ehrich within the circle of his party col-

leagues; cf. *CDU-Bundesvorstand 1949–1953*, p. 30f. (with a mistaken identification of Ehrich in n. 52). In 1951, Ehrich became a referee in the Lower Saxon State Chancellory; in 1963, he took over the same position in the Lower Saxon Ministry of Culture.

45. IfZ, Dm 115, Mitteilung des BPA Nr. 358/51, 4 May 1951; *Frankfurter Allgemeine Zeitung,* 5 May 1951, p. 1 (front-page story and commentary). Characteristically Dehler indicated to his co-workers only that the cabinet had declined to ban the SRP. BA, B 141/207, note of Dehler, 4 May 1951.

46. The distribution of mandates—both direct and those gained via the *Landesliste*—was as follows: SPD 64, Lower German Union 35, Union of Expellees and Victims of Injustice 21, SRP 16, FDP 12, Center Party 4, German Reich Party 3, German Communist Party 2, German Social Party 1. While the distribution would have statistically allowed formation of a "citizens' block," the SPD quickly reached an agreement on a coalition with the "Alliance" and the Center Party. In contrast to the policy of the German Party and the FDP, collaborating with the SRP was out of the question for the CDU.

47. In American reporting on Germany, the "resurgence of Nazism" grabbed headlines for weeks—this in direct competition with news about the Paris foreign ministers' conference. Drew Middleton (*New York Times*) summarized the situation in the remark that from the perspective of the Federal Republic's relations with the West, the success of the SRP could not have come at a less opportune moment; IFZ, MA 1543, Public Opinion on Germany, 8, 15, 22, 29 May 1951.

48. Without getting into details, Adenauer here evidently drew on information Lenz had gathered from Feitenhansl—and then treated it as established fact.

49. "In the fragile spiritual condition of the German, it is absolutely necessary that he sees power." *Akten zur Auswärtigen Politik,* vol. 1, p. 347ff., cit. p. 348 (verbatim minutes of the session of 5 April 1951).

50. Ibid., pp. 352–68 (verbatim minutes of the session of 9 May 1951); following citations on pp. 352 and 354.

51. Ibid., p. 360. Cf. Schwartz, *America's Germany,* p. 216f. McCloy made the point to Adenauer again after his return from a trip to the United States at the end of June 1951. McCloy reported that Acheson had even asked him "what would happen if the SRP carried out a coup." Adenauer, *Erinnerungen 1945–1953,* p. 457. In his own account (*Present,* p. 556f.) Acheson attributes this pessimism to the French and British alone.

52. *Kabinettsprotokolle 1951,* 8 May 1951, p. 356.

53. StBKAH, 12.49, Mühlenfeld to Adenauer, 11 May 1951; Mühlenfeld added that the threat of a ban had helped the SRP more than damaged it. He had already pointed to the "double-edged" nature of the banning discussion before the election. BA, B 141/207, Mühlenfeld to the "Herr Bundesminister" and to Lehr inter alia, both letters 3 April 1951; italics in original.

54. This was also the gist of a conversation between Adenauer and the Allied High Commission on 25 October 1951; cf. *Akten zur Auswärtigen Politik,* vol. 1, p. 558.

55. BA, B 141/207, note of Dehler, 4 July 1951.
56. BA, B 141/210, Dehler to Lehr, 16 July 1951; italics in original.
57. Ibid., Lehr to Dehler, 2 August 1951 (confidential).
58. Cf. *Kabinettsprotokolle 1951,* 9 October 1951, p. 692.
59. Hence the failure of Otto Lenz's suggestion that the chancellor offer a statement honoring the individuals who resisted Hitler, constantly slandered by the radical right. By the same token, nothing came of the enlightening "Memorandum Concerning the National Socialist Atrocities." Cf. Lenz, *Tagebuch,* 10 May 1951, p. 81; *Kabinettsprotokolle 1951,* 8 May 1951, p. 371, and *Akten zur Auswärtigen Politik,* p. 360f. According to the Justice Ministry, at the start of June 1951 there were no fewer than twenty-five pending cases against the SRP; at the same time, until then there had been only five convictions. Cf. *Kabinettsprotokolle 1951,* p. 420, n. 35.
60. *Teegespräche 1950–1954,* 6 September 1951, p. 145.
61. Hence during the September 1951 Washington foreign ministers' conference and against the explicit backdrop of SRP success, Schuman, Morrison, and Acheson met to discuss the question of future Allied rights of intervention. The foreign ministers ended by agreeing that a " 'threat' to constitutional order" would not yet be present "if Remer picked up five or six additional Parliamentary seats"; *FRUS 1951,* III, p. 1274 (minutes, 13 September 1951; with mistaken variant readings of the editors, who apparently could only imagine a communist threat—from [Max] "Reimann"). In a meeting between Adenauer and the Allied High Commission on 1 October 1951, in connection with the nationalist clamor of the soldiers' organizations, Kirkpatrick spoke concretely of "unfavorable consequences" for the negotiations. This was followed—after some struggle—by the government taking a certain distance from the organizations. Cf. *Akten zur Auswärtigen Politik,* vol. 1, p. 389, and Lenz, *Tagebuch,* 2 October 1951, p. 139.
62. HICOG, "Report über Deutschland," 1 April–30 June 1951, which devoted a chapter to the theme (pp. 32–41) for the first time. The political developments were soberly analyzed—a clear effort being at work to have an impact on an "eagerly" anticipated (p. 40) banning application to the Constitutional Court. A summary of the analysis can be found in *HICOG Information Bulletin,* September 1951, pp. 65–68; cf. Schwartz, *America's Germany,* p. 216 f. A long article by Drew Middleton in the *New York Times Magazine,* 1 July 1951, titled "Neo-Nazism: 'A Cloud Like a Man's Hand.' Revival of Interest in Hitler's Creed Creates Fear of a Future Storm over Germany," caused some stir in Bonn. Likewise, the paper's chief correspondent, Cyrus L. Sulzberger, wrote on 16 July 1951 that although in Germany (as well as Italy) neofascism was still weak, it was on the march. In the French press, there was even talk of Remer as a "new Hitler." BPA, MF 1538.
63. Adenauer, *Briefe 1951–1953,* p. 115 (23 August 1951).
64. Cf. Merritt and Merritt, *HICOG Surveys,* p. 123f. (survey for the second half of May 1951). At the same time 86 percent of the SRP's followers (vs.

34 percent of the population in general) saw more good than bad in National Socialist ideas.

65. For the cabinet session of 30 October 1951, Lenz noted, "Chancellor once more indicated that SRP has extraordinarily disturbing impact on all negotiations. Enforcing the complaint is thus necessary." Lenz, *Tagebuch*, p. 158.

66. BA, B 141/210, Lehr to Dehler, 11 October 1951 (secret).

67. Collected in comprehensive files of the Interior Ministry: BA, B 106/15530–15558.

68. *Kabinettsprotokolle 1951*, 12 October 1951, p. 698.

69. Gone, for instance, was the itself very odd remark, located at the end of a long series of "individual facts," that the "total impression" was the determining factor—and that "a threat of a danger for the maintenance of a basic democratic order" could be determined only "with simultaneous consideration of political experience." BA, B 141/210, proposal, 11 October 1951, p. 32.

70. Ibid., proposal of the Interior Ministry to the Constitutional Court, 10 November 1951, 4. Copy (secret), p. 53f. Significantly this passage was also included in the public explanation of the banning application. Bulletin BPA, 17 November 1951, p. 61. Lehr likewise lay special stress on "unease" abroad; see Lenz, *Tagebuch*, 12 October 1951, p. 148.

71. BA, B 136/1733, note concerning the meeting of the Bundesrat Committee on Inner Affairs, 15 November 1951. Beyond this, the interior ministers recommended that the Länder "regularly exchange ideas with the press in order to avoid articles appearing about neo-Nazi endeavors suitable for use as propaganda for such endeavors."

72. Legal proceedings regarding the communists would begin three years later, in November 1954; thirteen months would pass between conclusion of the submission of evidence and the judgment on 17 August 1956.

73. Cf. *Kabinettsprotokolle 1951*, 16 November 1951, p. 765f.

74. B 141/210, Dehler to Lehr, 19 November 1951 (personal; secret).

75. Ibid., note of Dehler, 27 November 1951.

76. BA, B 141/211, John to Kanter inter alia, 3 March 1952 (secret, with attached material).

77. Cf. Büsch and Furth, *Rechtsradikalismus*, p. 174.

78. BA, B 141/211, Office of Constitutional Protection to Interior Ministry inter alia, 19 January and 3 March 1952 (secret, each with report on the Hannover meeting of the party council and directorship of the SRP, 16 December 1951).

79. BA, B 141/210, Office of Constitutional Protection to Interior Ministry and Justice Ministry, 28 December 1951 (secret, with attached material).

80. BA, B 141/211, Beschlüsse des Bundesverfassungsgericht (1 BvB 1/51), 24 January 1952.

81. Cf. *Kabinettsprotokolle 1952*, 1 February 1952, p. 88.

82. BA, B 141/211, Lehr to Dehler, 31 January 1952 (confidential, with attached material).

83. Ibid., minutes of meeting, 28 January 1952 (secret, 2nd draft).

84. Instead of "cruder"—*gröber*—"more massive"—*grösser*—may in fact be the correct reading here.

85. Even the cabinet only learned about the action when it was a few hours under way; cf. *Kabinettsprotokolle 1952*, p. 84.

86. Cited from the judgment of the state court in Braunschweig, 15 March 1952, in Kraus, *Remerprozeß*, p. 105. Upon learning of Remer's remarks, the cabinet vaguely agreed to examine whether he "should not be criminally prosecuted on account of this insult." *Kabinettsprotokolle 1951*, 8 May 1951, p. 371.

87. A member of the German National People's Party, Carl Friedrich Goerdeler became one of the leading figures in the conservative resistance to Hitler following his resignation as Leipzig's mayor. He was arrested following 20 July 1944 and executed on 2 February 1945.

88. This and the following based on the excellent account in Geile, *Remer-Mythos*, pp. 117–39. Fundamental for the Braunschweig trial of Remer is Wassermann, *Bewertung;* cf. Gress and Jaschke, "Politische Justiz."

89. The expert opinions and judgment are included in Kraus, *Remerprozeß*.

90. Cf. Wassermann, *Bewertung*, p. 77.

91. On 12 November 1951 he had been convicted by the Second Criminal Division of the State Court in Verden on account of his above-mentioned claim that the government had set up London escape quarters; although it was a first offense, the sentence was not suspended.

92. This and the following based on IfZ, Gb 10.03, summation of Bauer, cit. pp. 1, 8.

93. Cf. sentence passed by the State Court in Braunschweig, 15 March 1952, in Kraus, *Remerprozeß*, p. 123; following information and cit. pp. 129, 132, 121.

94. The judgment became binding after a 11 December 1952 decision of the Federal High Court, to which Remer's lawyers had appealed. Remer, however, evaded prison by fleeing to the Middle East in spring 1963. In Egypt he appears to have worked as a military consultant. Following his return to Germany in September 1954, his punishment was reduced to a month remaining time and probation as a corrective to a formal error (the sentence should have been combined with Remer's still uncompleted first sentence to form a single penalty). For details see Geile, *Remer-Mythos*, p. 141ff.

95. On the instrumentalization of this distinction in favor of the radical right, cf. Knütter, *Ideologien*, esp. pp. 137–43.

96. Mommsen ("Geschichte," esp. pp. 3–8) has demonstrated this in penetrating fashion.

97. The extent to which this insight remained fragile two years later, even among university students, is apparent in an interesting survey taken by the Association of Liberal Students. It was sparked by the critique that a representative of the General Students' Organization had offered in an event organized by the "Working Circle of July 20": The "greatest portion" of his colleagues, he had complained, viewed the resistance theme from the van-

tage of high treason, and a "conclusive clarification has ... not yet been achieved." BA, B 168/159, report: "Die Studentenschaft and der 20. Juli."

98. The Office of National Service became the Central Federal Office for Political Education in 1963.

99. Das Parlament, 20 July 1952, p. 1. The main heading of the richly illustrated, thirty-two-page special issue was "The Truth About July 20, 1944— The Brightest and Darkest Day of Modern German History."

100. BA, B 136/1750, Lehr to state secretary of the Chancellor's Office, 29 February 1952 (secret, cabinet matter, with attached material).

101. BA, B 136/1750, handwritten note of Globke (8 March) responding to note of Spieler, 6 March 1952.

102. Cf. *Kabinettsprotokolle 1952*, 11 March 1952, p. 163; in a formal vote, the proposal was approved with seven for and five against.

103. The core of the party's argument involved two points: on the one hand, that there was no law forbidding "the prominent political activities of former National Socialists, as long as they have been fully denazified" (an extensive demonstration of the efforts by the democratic parties to recruit former party members was offered in this context); on the other hand, that the continuation of "organizational forms from the past" was also legal, even when these had been propagated by the Nazi Party. BA, B 141/211, Noack and Schrieber to the Constitutional Court, 2 January 1952.

104. BA, B 141/211, telegram of Richter to Heuss, 2 February 1952 (transcript).

105. Since accepting the banning application, the Constitutional Court approached the proceedings "ex officio"; ibid., Interior Ministry to president's office, 23 February 1952.

106. BA, B 141/212, Lex to Constitutional Court, 16 June 1952.

107. Cited from Büsch and Furth, *Rechtsradikalismus*, p. 185.

108. On the following, ibid., pp. 186–92.

109. BA, B 141/212, communication of the BPA, 10 July 1952.

110. *Frankfurter Allgemeine Zeitung*, 9 July 1952 ("Regret Over Lehr's Statements: Höpker-Aschoff Against Influence on the Trial of the Party of the Reich"); over the preceding days, the Interior Ministry had devoted several press communications to details of the trial.

111. He nonetheless seems to have been very proud of it; BA, B 141/212, Lex to W. Roemer, 14 July 1952, with attached material; ibid. for following citation.

112. Ibid., Pelckmann to Dehler, 22 July 1952, with attached material; ibid. for following citation.

113. *Entscheidungen des Bundesverfassungsgericht*, vol. 1, p. 349ff., ibid. for following citation.

114. *Kabinettsprotokolle 1952*, 25 July 1952, p. 480, n. 29. Lenz registered as a shortcoming the fact that running for the SRP was still allowed; cf. Lenz, *Tagebuch*, 25 July 1952, p. 397.

115. BA, B 141/207, telex of the BPA to the Justice Ministry, inter alia, 15 July 1952.

116. Cf. Jenke, *Verschwörung*, p. 103.

117. Ibid., note of Justice Ministry, 31 July 1952.

118. For details, see Büsch and Furth, *Rechtsradikalismus*, p. 172ff.; Jenke, *Verschwörung*, p. 104ff.

119. The mandate of the second Bundestag delegate to affiliate himself with the SRP (only founded after the Bundestag elections), Franz Richter, had been lost through his arrest in February 1952, following his exposure as Fritz Rößler.

120. Cf. *Entscheidungen des Bundesverfassungsgericht*, vol. 2, pp. 1–79; following citations, pp 20, 39, 65, 68ff.

121. Following changes to the state election law of 1 April 1953, there was a new calculation of the election results in Lower Saxony, producing five additional seats for the German Party–CDU faction, three for the Union of Expellees and Victims of Injustice, two for the FDP, and one for both the Center Party and the German Communist Party. IfZ, Dl, Niedersächsischer Landtag, Tätigkeitsbericht 2, WP, pp. 8, 10. The German Party–CDU failed in its effort to use the altered power balance, with help of the "Alliance," to bring about a change of leadership.

122. BA, B 141/207, minutes of Echterhölter, 28 October 1952.

123. BA, B 136/1750, note of Cramer, 16 July 1953.

124. BPA, MF 2485, Domestic Information Service no. 101/52 and 102/52, 29 October 1952.

125. *Neue Zeitung*, 25 October 1952.

126. *Die Welt*, 24 October 1952 ("The Karlsruhe Ruling").

127. *Frankfurter Allgemeine Zeitung*, 24 October 1952 ("A Heavy Blow").

128. The British press in particular stressed the risk that Nazi adherents would now increasingly spread through other parties. Cf., e.g., *Manchester Guardian*, 27 October 1952 ("Banning of Neo-Nazis May Have Bad Effects"). The U.S. press's reaction conveyed little of significance; IfZ, MA 1543, Public Opinion on Germany, 28 October and 4 November 1952, both p. 4f.

129. This corresponded to the formulation of the summarizing report on McCloy's tenure, which indicated that "although still finding some resonance in certain elements of the German public, Nazism appears to no longer represent a direct menace." HICOG, "Bericht über Deutschland," 21 September 1949–31 July 1952, p. 80.

130. Allemann, "Parteiensystem," p. 382f.; italics in original. Continuation of the analysis may be found in Allemann, *Bonn*, pp. 234–326, here esp. p. 289.

Chapter 12

1. Cited from the original copy of a manuscript confiscated from Naumann by the British, in ADL, N1/817, B1-B30, here B4. The "federalist community [*Gemeinschaft*]" signifies the German Party. In the first part of his five-part series in the *Frankfurter Rundschau* ("The Gravediggers Are Among Us," 9–13 June 1953), Fried Wesemann erroneously read "German Party"—*DP*—for the FDP.

2. Rewarding depictions of the Naumann affair in Horne, *Return*, pp. 160–82 (with some errors of dating); Jenke, *Verschwörung*, pp. 160–84. Brochhagen (*Nach Nürnberg*) fails to examine the matter, which is actually central to his own theme; Kittel (*Legende*, p. 214–48) does not clarify its significance—in particular Adenauer's stance. Most thorough, and unsurpassed in regard to the interaction of the main players, is Tauber, *Beyond Eagle*, pp. 132–46, 891–98. Tauber already had access to the confiscated evidence. Used with the appropriate caution (above all to supplement sometimes distorting cuts in the printed sources), the contemporary apologetic material is also informative: Naumann, *Nau-Nau*; Grimm, *Unrecht*. As a legal "expert opinion" that is both tendentious and, when it comes to the readiness of official international legal experts to serve the goal of the radical right, "completely sundered from its political side": Kruse, *Besatzungsmacht* (cited in the foreword to Kraus, p. 5).

3. Cited here from *Archiv der Gegenwart*, 15 January 1953, p. 3824.

4. Kirkpatrick's public safety adviser and those responsible for the British Intelligence Organization (Germany) had counted on Bornemann's absence. Since they did not want to run the danger of arresting an excessively small group of people for arbitrary reasons, the High Commissioner had, on short notice, approved the arrest of three more suspects from the wider "Gauleiter Circle" who had been under surveillance for some time: Siepen, Scharping, and Alfred Salat, former publishing director of Munich's *Neueste Nachrichten,* which had been part of the Nazi publishing empire. Salat would turn himself in voluntarily and was not incarcerated. PRO, FO 371/103896, Kirkpatrick to Foreign Office (telegram no. 15, top secret), 12 January 1953.

5. Even the anticipated press clarification was carefully agreed on between the Foreign Office and Wahnerheide. From the beginning, Kirkpatrick's goal was to avoid an impression of claiming to move against an immediately pending plot and instead to stress the need for further investigation. The most important documents on the preparation and direct execution of the action are in PRO, FO 371/103896–7.

6. So Eden to his cabinet colleagues. The minutes further indicate that the "arrests had been satisfactorily carried out, and a large number of documents had been seized. Until these had been examined, and further enquiries made on the basis of them, it would not be certainly known how widespread the plot had been or what contacts had been established between this group and agencies in other countries"; PRO, CAB 128/26, 3rd cabinet session, 20 January 1953.

7. Cf. *Frankfurter Allgemeine Zeitung*, 16 January 1953; aside from the lead article, the report on the action occupied the entire front page.

8. *Frankfurter Allgemeine Zeitung*, 20 January 1953, p. 1 ("No Object for Guessing Games"). Sethe's commentary was signed "an."; on deciphering the abbreviation ("Tüngelmann"), cf. Schlumberger, *Adenauer-Bild*, p. 481.

9. *Frankfurter Allgemeine Zeitung*, 22 January 1953, p. 1.

10. Cf. Büsch and Furth, *Rechtsradikalismus,* pp. 146f., 168f. The original goal of the "Preparatory Committee for the Liberation of German Soldiers," emerging in connection with the SRP, had merely been to collect signatures. BA, B 136/1878, Office of Constitutional Protection to the Chancellor, inter alia, 17 November 1951.

11. Kirkpatrick did, in any case, keep conscious distance from the office's president, Otto John, who was denigrated by many in Bonn as a "man of the English." Cf. John, *Zweimal,* p. 244.

12. Cited from the translation circulated as background information by the German Press Agency, 17 November 1952, Inf. 2038, in ADL, N1/830. Various articles by Drew Middleton in the *New York Times* appeared at approximately the same time; e.g., 16 November 1952 ("Old German Nazis Join New Parties: Their Reviving Influence Seen in Right-Wing Groups Which Are Hostile to Adenauer"), and 29 November 1952 ("German Quits Unit Wooing Ex-Nazis"). Cf. Tauber, *Beyond Eagle,* p. 1349, n. 49.

13. Cf. the illuminating convention discussions in *FDP-Bundesvorstand 1949–1953,* pp. 585–676.

14. When it comes to the political self-understanding of a former member of the German State Party, Middelhauve's wordy rebuttal of the charge leveled by the American Jewish Committee in August 1954 that he was a neo-Nazi is of interest. "I was a blunt and open opponent of the Third Reich, remained so in its heyday, and was known as such. I was registered as an enemy of the state in the security service files. Those friends of mine who were forced to join the party were warned to avoid my company by Himmler's bloodhounds. There was no Hitler salute in my business undertakings, no Hitler portrait in my office, although that was mandatory, and all the less so in my house. My children were raised according to my views and kept out of Hitler Youth and the League of German Girls. The Nazis knew that I was their irreconcilable enemy and an unshakable, unbending democrat." In this six-page statement of creed, Middelhauve felt called on to impart the information that despite many "manifestations of degeneration and overproliferation, also lamented by Jews, in German Judaism of the time," he had "always acknowledged [its] mainly valuable contributions to the spiritual and political situation of Germany and the world." ADL, N1/3164.

15. The *Neue Zürcher Zeitung,* 25 November 1952, no. 2637, p. 2, devoted special attention to the new FDP manager on account of his "leading role in the National Socialist polemic against Switzerland" following the murder there of Nazi Party land group leader Wilhelm Gustloff. If, the article observed, Middelhauve saw Diewerge's approach to democracy as positive, this was "hardly an effective justification ... but rather tends to cast an unfavorable light on the acting chairman of the FDP." As a result of his anti-Semitic writings, Diewerge, like Naumann, had gone underground for a while after 1945; cf. Jenke, *Verschwörung,* p. 176.

16. Until his death at the start of 1953, Middelhauve's comrade-in-arms and deputy Baron von Rechenberg was a particular champion of Fritzsche; cf. *Die Welt*, 24 November 1952.

17. Cf. *Die Zeit*, 4 December 1952, p. 1 (" ... and learned nothing new"); Dönhoff did not desire to classify the former Nazi functionaries "in the category of inferior citizens for the remainder of their lives," but believed "they should keep themselves out of public life."

18. Cf. Tauber, *Beyond Eagle*, pp. 134, 142, 892, 1047; Wengst "Einleitung," in *FDP-Bundesvorstand 1949–1953*, p. lxi; a record of the telephone conversation between Diewerge and Naumann tapped by the British on 19 June 1952, in which Middelhauve's secretary announced delivery of the draft program—not for the "old anglers' club"—(the FDP), but on a "wider basis" for everyone "interested in fishery" in ADL, N1/816. Cf. *Frankfurter Rundschau*, 13 June 1953 ("gravedigger" series, part V).

19. Later, a plethora of interesting details would circulate in Bonn's journalistic circles. For instance, Interior Minister Lehr, whose ministry—like the others—was thought to shelter "confidants" of the Naumann group, was said to have directed the Office of Constitutional Protection (activated after the FDP convention in Ems) and its president, John, "not to draw coalition members or those in proximity to the coalition into the investigation." IfZ, ED 329/5, report of 17 January 1953, p. 3. This piece of speculation—denied by the Interior Ministry—(ibid., 20 January 1953, p. 1) might explain Adenauer and Lehr's palpably bad mood in the meeting of the CDU's directorship on 15 December 1952, when Lehr defended the Düsseldorf Industry Club against the chancellor's assertions that Naumann held meetings there. Cf. *CDU-Bundesvorstand 1950–1953*, pp. 175, 196f.

20. Lenz, *Tagebuch*, 3 December 1952, p. 484f.

21. Thus Blücher on 24 January 1953; cf. *FDP-Bundesvorstand 1949–1953*, p. 791.

22. After learning of the "German program" during his vacation in Bürgenstock, Adenauer urgently warned Middelhauve on 30 July 1952 not to risk splitting the FDP and hence ending the governing coalition's majority. "I do not believe that programmatic demands would lead to large numbers of former National Socialists voting for FDP candidates.... In fact, the earlier National Socialists also voted in 1949 and already made their decision then. In general, we can surely say that the German people want nothing to do with right-wing radicalism but are certainly ready to follow a clear, consistent political line." Adenauer, *Briefe 1951–1953*, p. 258. Speaking to English journalists, Adenauer cited this warning after the arrests; cf. Adenauer, *Teegespräche 1950–1954*, 19 January 1953, p. 406. Adenauer's inquiry to Hellwege on 22 September 1952 was equally cool. Adenauer, *Briefe 1951–1953*, p. 277f.

23. Lenz assumed that Adenauer was relying on information he had supplied, thus noting that Kirkpatrick had not spoken of any arrest. Lenz, *Tagebuch*, 15 December 1952, p. 501.

24. *CDU-Bundesvorstand 1950–1953*, 15 December 1952, p. 175.

25. Cf. below, pp. 283f. Kirkpatrick also saw the chancellor directly before the start of the arrests. "He was interested, thanked me for the communication, expressed his approval of the operation and wished me luck. He explicitly promised to tell nobody." PRO, FO 371/103896, Kirkpatrick to Foreign Office (telegram no. 57., secret) 14 January 1953.

26. According to a cabinet note by Seebohm, before taking up the day's agenda, Adenauer addressed, inter alia, the theme of "Ramcke, Naumann-Düsseldorf, etc. abroad." *Kabinettsprotokolle 1952,* 19 December 1952, p. 762, n. 41.

27. *Parlamentarisch-Politischer Pressedienst,* 22 December 1952, with additional documents in AdsD, NL Arndt/158.

28. In Naumann's view, the "Union" had meanwhile passed its apogee, since it was attempting to govern with the SPD (in Lower Saxony) "and had not been able to form a proright movement out of a party for victims of injustice." ADL, N1/817, speech of Naumann, 18 November 1952, here B4.

29. ADL, N1/815, the "*Gauleiter* circle," secret, undated, AD5-AD30. *Der Spiegel* (13 May 1953, p. 5f.) published excerpts from the report ("Nau-Nau. Verschwörung wider den Geist"); the magazine in any event gave the impression that the paper had been written by political advisers of the Land Commissioner in North Rhine–Westphalia after the arrests.

30. ADL, N1/825, circular, end of December 1952; italics in original.

31. *FDP-Bundesvorstand 1949–1953,* p. 792f., cit. n. 2. After disclosure of the Naumann affair, Blücher would be the object of harsh reproaches from the party directorship on account of Middelhauve being been excluded de facto from the assembly; cf. ibid., p. 797ff.

32. Kirkpatrick, *Inner Circle,* pp. 252–53. That Ivone was referring here to Middelhauve would emerge in the cabinet, presumably through Adenauer. According to a note by Seebohm on the cabinet session of 20 January 1953, Middelhauve then urged Kirkpatrick to receive Naumann, since he was "a nice man." Cited from *Kabinettsprotokolle 1953,* p. 125, n. 42.

33. Adenauer, *Teegespräche 1950–1954,* p. 399.

34. According to an Allensbach survey, in February 1953, 47 percent of Germany felt that the arrests should be protested to the English. Only a fifth saw no cause for protest. Cf. Noelle and Neumann, *Jahrbuch,* p. 277.

35. Already in his first report after the action was terminated, Kirkpatrick predicted that in view of the mass of documents ("enough to fill two rooms"), a certain amount of time would be needed for their examination by six staff members of the British Intelligence Organization (Germany). PRO, FO 371/103897, Kirkpatrick to Roberts, 15 January 1953 (top secret).

36. *Frankfurter Allgemeine Zeitung,* 17 January 1953, p. 3.

37. *Frankfurter Allgemeine Zeitung,* 16 January 1953, p. 1 ("British Action Draws Attention in Bonn").

38. *Frankfurter Allgemeine Zeitung,* 17 January 1953, p. 3; ibid. for following citation.

39. *Frankfurter Allgemeine Zeitung,* 19 January 1953, p. 1 ("The initiative was Kirkpatrick's alone. London proceeds more cautiously. Doubts over the political advisability of the arrests.") Ibid. for following citation.

40. For many details on this and the following, see Lenz, *Tagebuch,* 19–21 January 1953, pp. 529–35.
41. Cf. the summary of the survey in Merritt and Merritt, *HICOG Surveys,* p. 197ff.
42. *New York Times,* 18 January 1953, p. 1, 19 ("Rise in Neo-Nazism Is Shown by Survey in West Germany. Big Majority Found Unwilling to Resist Revival of National Socialism—Youth Strongly Share Trend, U.S. Learns").
43. Cf. *Frankfurter Allgemeine Zeitung,* 20 January 1953, p. 1 ("What Do the Americans Want from Bonn? The Links Between the Survey and the Treaties").
44. The State Department's press review confirmed "little disposition to criticize the Adenauer government." In contrast, the argument that Germany's Western integration was the best protection against a revival of Nazism could frequently be found. IfZ, MF 1543, Weekly Summary of Opinion on Germany, 22 and 27 January 1953. A corresponding report of the German General Consulate in San Francisco, 27 January 1953, was similarly undramatic. PA—FO, III 212–02, vol. 3.
45. Cf. Lenz, *Tagebuch,* 19 and 20 January 1995, pp. 529 and 534. On account of a hitch in the government press agency, the *Frankfurter Allgemeine Zeitung* and the *Frankfurter Neue Presse* based their reports on the sharper text.
46. Cited from *Bulletin BPA,* 21 January 1953, p. 97.
47. Cf. Lenz, *Tagebuch,* 21 January 1953, p. 535.
48. BT-Berichte 1, WP, 21 January 1953, p. 11673f.; ibid. for following citation.
49. "Everything taken into account, did the ideas of National Socialism in fact contain more good or bad?"
50. Neumann's detailed analysis of the survey appeared the same day in the *Frankfurter Allgemeine Zeitung* ("The Americans and National Socialism"). He concluded "that the Germans judge National Socialism as it depicted itself from their perspective: as a system of economic and social security with a backdrop of persecution, repression, and war. Every psychologist knows that the broader population does not think in the abstract.... It is thus completely capable of enjoying memories of the carefree economic situation between 1936 and 1937 without thinking about the inner-political terror and bitter aftermath of war in the same breath." To this extent, Neumann indicated, the American survey was "just and reliable." However, in the interest of both sides it was incumbent to ascertain who "wished to poison the well a little" through "consciously falsified conclusions." R. Merritt (*Digesting the Past,* pp. 96–99) offers a thorough summary of the survey results, particularly in regard to the question about the good and bad in Nazism.
51. The declaration had followed intensive discussions with Wahnerheide on 20 and 21 January 1953; details in PRO, RO 371/103897; Parliamentary Debates, House of Commons, Official Report, vol. 510/35, col. 38–42, 207ff.
52. In the cabinet, Seebohm thus noted that "Morgenthau people, who are close to the SPD, tried to poison the atmosphere, very heavy through Nau-

mann and Oradour." *Kabinettsprotokolle 1953,* 20 January 1953, p. 126, n. 42. Luckless Donnelly was considered a man of the democrats; he had announced his departure in connection with the change of administrations at the start of December. In February 1953, Harvard president James Bryant Conant became his successor as High Commissioner (Conant would then serve as ambassador from 1955 to 1957).

53. Adenauer's frosty handwritten letter to Reber closed with the comment that he would "especially welcome ... future communiqués of this sort not being issued without agreement with me beforehand." Reber agreed on this in his answer, which plausibly explained the reasons for the publication: releasing the survey had been decided on in order to avoid speculation after its existence had been divulged to a journalist. PA—FO, II 228, Adenauer to Reber (draft; printed version of the fair copy, 22 January 1953, in: Adenauer, *Briefe 1951–1953,* p. 329f.); replies, 21 January and 4 February 1953.

54. Lenz, *Tagebuch,* 20 January 1953, p. 531.

55. Note regarding the cabinet session on 20 January 1953, cited from *Kabinettsprotokolle 1953,* p. 125, n. 42.

56. Lenz, *Tagebuch,* 20 January 1953, p. 532.

57. Lehr again expressed his demand "that our government receive satisfactory rehabilitation" two days later ("otherwise we will lose too much ground before the elections"). BA, B 136/1754, Lehr to Adenauer, 22 January 1953.

58. Lenz, *Tagebuch,* 20 January 1953, p. 532.

59. Not least of the reasons for Kirkpatrick's intense interest in the discoveries of his evaluation team was to placate the Foreign Office, which was meanwhile being forced to respond to critical inquiries. PRO, FO 371/103898, Kirkpatrick to Foreign Office (telegram no. 83, secret), 21 January 1953.

60. Lenz, *Tagebuch,* 21 January 1953, p. 535.

61. *CDU-Bundesvorstand 1950–1953,* 26 January 1953, p. 308f.

62. Cited from *Frankfurter Allgemeine Zeitung,* 21 January 1953, p. 3 ("Middelhauve Presses for Explanation: English and American Delegates Should Examine the Reproaches"); ibid. for the following.

63. Shortly before the start of the action, Adenauer had urged Kirkpatrick to include Achenbach among those to be arrested. Achenbach now wished to discuss the "wider aspects" of the case, which he referred to as a "fairy tale." In his telephone conversation with Wahnerheide, he cited an early meeting with Dehler. PRO, FO 371/103896, Kirkpatrick to Foreign Office (telegram no. 71, top secret), 16 January 1953.

64. A variant reading (e.g., in *Frankfurter Rundschau,* 9 June 1953, p. 3) was *Strohmänner*—"straw men." Given the first reading, the reference was to Gustav Stresemann, longtime foreign minister during the Weimar Republic.

65. ADL, N1/815, AD1-AD2, transcripts from Naumann's diary; facsimile in Grimm, *Unrecht,* p. 256f. (characteristically, Grimm (p. 202) offers only a palliating summary of the entry, which is hard to decipher).

66. The months-long party controversies are mirrored in detail in the session minutes of the national directorship for 24 January, 28 February, 25 and 26 April, 28 May, and 7 June 1953; pp. 791–849, 870–85, 912–67, 1018–34, and 1044–76; cf. Udo Wengst, "Einleitung," in *FDP-Bundesvorstand 1949–1953*, pp. lx–lxvi; Gutscher, *Entwicklung der FDP*, pp. 151–64; Dittberner, "FDP," pp. 1319–23; the memoirs of Mende, *Freiheit*, pp. 256–60, are inadmissibly palliating in respect to the "liberal concerns."

67. *FDP-Bundesvorstand 1949–1953*, p. 966.

68. The other committee members were minister of housing Fritz Neumayer and the acting chairman of the FDP's Lower Saxon party chapter, Alfred Onnen, himself deeply entangled in the infiltration problem there. On Dehler's critique of Achenbach, see above, p. 74.

69. Cf. *FDP-Bundesvorstand 1949–1953*, esp. pp. 1098–120.

70. Among those spared were Siegfried Zoglmann, now chief editor of the *Deutsche Zukunft*, formerly departmental director in the "Reich Protectorate for Bohemia and Moravia" and an SS *Obersturmführer*, and former career officer Wolfgang Döring, now state party whip for the FDP and soon to emerge as one of the leading speakers for the party's "young Turks." ADL, N1/380, regarding personal data, undated.

71. The weak North Rhine–Westphalian German Party had already entered into negotiations with the FDP in the communal elections of November 1952 and was prepared (not without cash incentive) to support Middelhauve's "collective concept." Cf. Meyn, *Deutsche Partei*, p. 38f.; Jenke, *Verschwörung*, p. 134ff.

72. Cf. Grimm, *Unrecht*, esp. p. 47. Stories from the "Ruhr battle," Grimm's "greatest experience as an attorney in political trials," are to be found throughout his many writings; cf., e.g., idem, *Politische Justiz*, pp. 42–50.

73. On this and the following, see ibid., pp. 40–54.

74. Kruse, *Besatzungsmacht;* cf. the description above, p. 406, n. 2.

75. *Freie Demokratische Korrespondenz*, 26 February 1953, p. 9ff. (Dehler: "the freedom of the individual is inviolable").

76. *Kabinettsprotokolle 1953*, 27 February 1953, p. 194f. and n. 21.

77. On this and the following, see Horne, *Return*, p. 176ff.; court opinion in BA, B 106/15561. At the end of January, Schmid had declared to Bavarian Radio that the arrests were "to be condemned most sharply, not out of sympathy with the arrested men but for the sake of democracy. It is true that every occupying troop has the right to move against acutely dangerous actions, but the impression must not emerge that democracy in Germany consists of what the occupying powers consider compatible with their interests." Schmid would then receive much praise in letters from former party members. AdsD, Schmid papers 633; cf. *Frankfurter Allgemeine Zeitung*, 30 January 1953, p. 1.

78. PRO, FO 371/103904, Kirkpatrick to Eden (top secret), 21 February 1953; Roberts to Kirkpatrick (personal and secret), 25 February 1953; CAB 128/26, 14, 15, and 20, cabinet session, 24, and 26 February , 17 March 1953.

79. Cf. *Kabinettsprotokolle 1953,* 3 March 1953, p. 198, n. 7. During this meeting, Kirkpatrick handed Adenauer transcripts of twenty-five in part extensive incriminatory files. PRO, FO 371/103908, Kirkpatrick to Roberts (secret), 2 March 1953, and FO 371/103907, list of documents.

80. A/AA, II 228, Adenauer to Kirkpatrick, 13 March 1953 (fair draft, supplemented by hand); cf. Adenauer, *Briefe 1951–1953,* p. 349; PRO, FO 371/103908, Kirkpatrick to Foreign Office (telegram no. 277, secret), 12 March 1953.

81. When Adenauer reported on his request to Kirkpatrick in the cabinet, Lehr complained—as Lenz noted—that the material had not yet been made available to him. Adenauer then replied "that he had understanding for this, since a member of the Federal Interior Ministry had entered his name in Naumann's guest book with a Bismarckian dictum and several corps circles. Lehr naturally gets angry and declares that the mistrust is also directed at him, which the chancellor sharply rejects." Lenz, *Tagebuch,* pp. 586, 601; see also *Kabinettsprotokolle 1953,* 13 March 1953, p. 224f.; IfZ ED 329/5, 26 March 1953.

82. PA—FO, II 228, Kirkpatrick to Adenauer, 17 March 1953.

83. *Kabinettsprotokolle 1953,* 27 March 1953, p. 233, and Lenz, *Tagebuch,* 27, 31 March 1953, pp. 600f., 604.

84. Lenz, *Tagebuch,* pp. 547, 573, 582.

85. Adenauer also frequently raised Achenbach with his party colleagues, as on 22 May 1953: "Herr Achenbach is, I believe, a finished man, at least for the next years, since Herr Achenbach is strongly implicated in the Naumann matter. I find it incomprehensible that Herr Achenbach still finds himself walking around free while Herr Naumann has been arrested." *CDU-Bundesvorstand 1950–1953,* p. 529; cf. pp. 537, 550ff., 563.

86. Lenz, *Tagebuch,* p. 586.

87. So Grimm, *Unrecht,* p. 62ff.

88. IfZ, ED 329/5, 16 April 1953.

89. Application of the chief federal public prosecutor, 28 March 1953, cited from Grimm, *Unrecht,* p. 195.

90. Dehler had visited Kirkpatrick in the first half of April; IfZ, ED 329/5, 16 April 1953. Adenauer expressed himself in similar fashion before the CDU's directorship. Cf. *CDU-Bundesvorstand 1950–1953,* 22 May 1953, p. 529.

91. Both the Office of Constitutional Protection and the British believed that Achenbach had simply wished to "cover his back" with this "strange offer." IfZ, ED 329/5, 16 April 1953.

92. Cf. Grimm, *Unrecht,* p. 203.

93. *Kabinettsprotokolle 1953,* 29 May 1953, p. 314.

94. Cf. Lenz, *Tagebuch,* 2 June 1953, p. 637.

95. Cf. *Kabinettsprotokolle 1953,* 2 June 1953, p. 326.

96. ADL, N1/811, Weinkauff to Dehler, 3 June 1953; ibid. for following citation.

97. The evidence included highly revealing texts of Naumann, demonstrating both his tactical caution and essentially Nazi ideas. There was, for

instance, his essay "Where Do the Former National Socialists Stand?" in the (apocryphal) KBI Information Service, 21/1952, edited by accused colleague Bornemann; ADL, N1/821 and PRO, FO 371/103903; partly published in Grimm, *Unrecht,* pp. 239–43.

98. Cf. the documentation in Grimm, *Unrecht,* pp. 195, 203f., 217–22.

99. Lenz, *Tagebuch,* 9 June 1953, p. 641f.

100. PA—FO, II 229, notes of Hallstein for Adenauer, 11 June 1953.

101. The incident served as an occasion to once more extensively discuss how to keep the cabinet consultations secret. One individual present did, in any case, offer a statement that must have caused suspicion: Heinrich Hellwege's assertion that, while knowing Naumann's lawyer from his youth, he had participated in the cabinet session in question (end of May) and had not seen the lawyer "for months." This was possibly a classic denial, since Hellwege's words did not clarify whether, say, he had offered his friend from youth something like an excerpt of the minutes. Cf. *Kabinettsprotokolle 1953,* 23 June 1953, p. 356.

102. Subsequent to the *Frankfurter Rundschau,* the *Stuttgarter Zeitung* produced its own series of articles, and South German Radio also delivered the radio broadcast.

103. Cf. *Frankfurter Allgemeine Zeitung,* 15 June 1953.

104. Following the report of the Dehler-led three-man commission, Blücher offered his own critical depiction of Naumann's infiltration efforts, sending it to a relatively large number of party functionaries. His opponents thus immediately suspected him of having furnished the documents to the press. Blücher's denial of 12 June 1953 in BA, NL 80/299; a fuller version in *Freie Demokratische Korrespondenz,* 17 June 1953.

105. Revealing in this regard is ADL, N1/839, Achenbach to Dehler, 5 June 1953 (copy).

106. This surmise cannot be firmly demonstrated on the basis of the available documents; in any event, there are strikingly many documents stemming from the period of the *Frankfurter Rundschau* publication in the holdings of PRO, FO 371/103913 sealed.

107. Scharpenseel to Dehler, 11 June 1953, cited from Grimm, *Unrecht,* p. 98.

108. Cited from ibid., p. 115; *Frankfurter Allgemeine Zeitung,* 29 July 1953.

109. *Frankfurter Allgemeine Zeitung,* 29 July 1953, p. 2.

110. *Süddeutsche Zeitung,* 30 July 1953, p. 2 ("Naumann's Release Disputed"). The report also cited Interior Minister Lehr to the effect that from the start he believed there were no grounds for an arrest under German law.

111. IfZ, ED 32 9/5, 11 August 1953.

112. Cited from *Frankfurter Allgemeine Zeitung,* 31 July 1953 (selections from the press). Paul Sethe constituted a nigh querulous exception to the predominant German reaction; without wishing to defend Naumann he once again raised sharp principled objections to his premature conviction. Cf. *Frankfurter Allgemeine Zeitung,* 31 July 1953 (lead article: "The Trial Must Come").

113. Naturally in Wahnerheide the German public's reaction continued to be followed very closely. In August 1953, proofs were ready of a "white

paper," prepared weeks before, containing all the basic incriminatory documents and meant to justify the January arrests; by decision of the Foreign Office, they did not go to press. PRO, FO 371/103915–6.

114. BA, B 106/15561, office of John to Egidi, 17 August 1953 (with attached material; copy of Naumann's talk and press conference in Bonn's Citizen's League, 12 August 1953).

115. A summary of the press reaction in *Neue Zeitung*, 15 August 1953: "German press on Naumann's candidacy. Morally and politically unqualifiable—warnings to the democratic parties." The cited opinions did not include any from the *Frankfurter Allgemeine Zeitung*, where shortly before (7 August 1953), Paul Sethe had once more turned on the English—guilty, he indicated, of rendering Naumann "a kind of national martyr."

116. *Neue Zeitung*, 20 August 1953, p. 3.

117. Adenauer praised the decision in the cabinet, observing that the material at hand was "hair raising." In a talk in Munich as late as 31 March 1945, he indicated, Naumann had spoken of a "final victory"—an *Endsieg*—and declared that "not enough blood" had been spilled. Lenz, *Tagebuch*, 25 August 1953, p. 686.

118. PRO, FO 371/103915, Kirkpatrick to Foreign Office (secret), 16 August 1953.

119. Cf. *Neue Zeitung*, 25 August 1953.

120. On the occasion of the Bundestag election, the paper once more warned emphatically against the German Party and the "bankrupters "of yesterday"—this despite "a Herr Naumann" having been stopped at the last moment. The coalition and above all "its underlying pillar, the CDU, should in fact ask how things could have gone so far, and it should also be clear about all those in its ranks who accepted the *Herren* National Socialists as negotiators, allowing them to place—outrageous—demands." *Die Gegenwart* 8 (1953); 545f. and 554–56, citation on p. 546.

121. BA, B 136/1760, decision St E 13/54.

122. Details in BA, B 136/1758.

123. See the summary in Gutscher, *Entwicklung der FDP*, pp. 175–82; Udo Wengst, "Einleitung," in *FDP-Bundesvorstand 1954–1960*, pp. xli–lix. On the end of the CDU-FDP-Koalition in Düsseldorf, cf. Hüwel, *Arnold*, pp. 285–90.

124. That the North Rhine–Westphalian used drastic propaganda to press such an interpretation is a separate matter. Cf., e.g., the reports in *Ruhr-Nachrichten* (Dortmund), 13 February 1956 ("When Naumann Was Exposed") and *Frankfurter Neue Presse*, 22 February 1956 ("Secret Files, Naumann & Co."). Following Arnold's fall on 20 February 1956, Adenauer himself did not tire of warning against the nationalist elements in the North Rhine–Westphalian FDP. In contrast with people like Remer or Thadden, he indicated, those involved were "consequent people who have passed through the National Socialist school, are thoroughly familiar with all the methods of propaganda, and have no scruples." *CDU-Bundesvorstand 1953–1957*, pp. 788–802, 838ff., 930f.; citation on p. 841. Adenauer

returned to the theme in his memoirs as well—the FDP had made use of "certain nationalist currents"—again mentioning Naumann; cf. Adenauer, *Erinnerungen 1955–1959,* p. 107.

125. Already in the third Bundestag the All-German Block Union of Expellees was no longer represented.

126. *CDU-Bundesvorstand 1950–1953,* 22 May 1953, p. 529; similarly 15 July 1953, p. 606; and *CDU-Bundesvorstand 1953–1957,* 10 September 1953, p. 6.

127. Kirkpatrick, *Inner Circle,* p. 253.

128. Adenauer, *Briefe 1951–1953,* 14 September 1953, p. 435. Speaking before the CDU leadership on 10 September 1953, Adenauer began by similarly stressing "that both the radical right and left have been rejected and that we now actually give the impression of being a politically mature people." *CDU-Bundesvorstand 1953–1957,* p. 3.

129. This capacity to take things in stride is evident, for example, in the State Department edited Weekly Summaries of Opinion in Germany; IfZ, MF 1543.

130. *Time,* 4 January 1954, pp. 18–22, citation on p. 18. The American press responded to *Time*'s choice with great approval; IfZ, MA 1543, Weekly Summary of Opinion on Germany, 5 January 1954, p. 4f.

131 Cf. *CDU-Bundesvorstand 1950–1953,* 15 July 1953, p. 606 and passim.

132. BA, B 136/1737, Guhr to Globke, 1 April 1954 (with attached material, ibid. for following citation).

SOURCES AND LITERATURE

This book is based primarily on Bonn sources. Archival material of the German government was central to most chapters—above all holdings of the Justice Ministry, Chancellor's Office, and Interior Ministry (the latter in the Federal Archives in Coblenz; the other holdings still being stored in a provisional archive in Hangelar). The Justice Ministry's terse, traditionally Prussian documentation, organized by Thomas Dehler with the frequent help of suggestive "notes," proved highly valuable. The same can be said for the holdings of the Interior Ministry, steered by Gustav Heinemann and Robert Lehr; their officials also express themselves more self-confidently than do Dehler's, who on account of their pasts leave an all too tentative impression.

By their very nature, documents from the Federal Chancellory are more strongly tied to particular decisions and cases—if also often highly eloquent for just that reason. The same can be said for the (far less comprehensive) documents from the President's Office, and for the Theodor Heuss papers. Along with this archival material from Coblenz, documents there from the Central Bureau of Legal Defense merit special emphasis. First under the Justice Ministry, then the Foreign Ministry, the bureau was responsible for legal assistance to the war criminals incarcerated in West Germany and abroad. These rich holdings (which remain only partially accessible) also contain material from forerunner organizations and lawyers that helps to document the early phase of "the care for war prisoners" and the Nuremberg trials. The main sources for the latter, however, were files of the American military government (microfilm holdings in the Institut für Zeitgeschichte) along with church documents (Evangelisches Zentralarchiv in Berlin).

Among the "Bonn material," as long as it could be seen in Bonn and environs, the holdings of the Political Archives of the Foreign Office and the minutes of the Subcommittee on War Prisoners of the Bundestag Committee on Foreign Affairs deserve special mention. Despite the good will of the archivists, conditions for inspecting the Bundestag documents were not especially propitious. I naturally examined the Konrad Adenauer papers in Rhöndorf, as well as a series of holdings, concerning various figures, in the CDU, SPD, and FDP party archives. The large collection of Dehler papers in the Archiv des Deutschen Liberalismus in Gummersbach proved unusually rewarding, particularly in relation to the Naumann affair—for which I also examined files of the Foreign Office in London.

I made intensive use of Bundestag minutes and printed matter. The (past-)political value of the parliamentary debates in West Germany's first two legislative periods is considerable; it leaves a sense that the frequently palpable scholarly scorn for the legislative branch's deliberations is hardly understandable. The same goes for the large-circulation daily and weekly papers; while their systematic evaluation is certainly a strenuous task, it is unavoidable if a parliamentary democracy's public dimension is to be adequately considered. For the 1950s, use of such sources to that end is rather easier than would be the case for later decades. Television was in its infancy, and newspapers almost always published the radio's occasional critical programs on current affairs. In other words, print almost entirely dominated the media landscape, with illustrated weeklies carrying more and more weight. It is of course sensible to use press-clipping archives (when it comes to the early German Federal Republic, those of the government's Press and Information Office are particularly useful). But such sources cannot replace review of bound newspaper volumes, since that is the only way to see a news item's precise locus—hence to learn something basic about the light in which it was considered.

Finally, much material making the 1950s into Germany's "Adenauer era" is already available in excellently prepared editions and documentary volumes. (We nevertheless need to note a weakness in such texts that is as frequent as it is annoying: truncated lines of continuity in the note apparatus, granting the various personae their biographies until 1933 so long as they are respectably democratic, but leaving out the Third Reich years.) Such material includes Adenauer's letters, "tea-time conversations," and official meetings with the Allied High Commissioners, as well as his remarks before the CDU's national directorship and—most copious by far—his four-volume memoirs, which for long stretches are nothing other than (occasionally, and legitimately, tendentious) documentation. In addition, we have the detailed minutes of the FDP's national directorship and the heavily commentated (if otherwise not notably rewarding) minutes of the SPD party faction.

The published diary of Otto Lenz, Adenauer's illustrious first state secretary in the chancellery, served as a guiding thread through the Bonn hothouse jungle of West Germany's first years. The papers of Lenz's successor, Hans

Globke, whose name is linked to the theme of "overcoming the past" like no other, remain accessible only in the Archives for Christian-Democratic Politics to a few researchers: those approved by Globke's widow after consultation with that foundation.

I. Archival Material

1. Bundesarchiv (BA), Koblenz (Federal Archives, Coblenz)

B 106	Bundesministerium des Innern
B 122	Bundespräsidialamt
B 136	Bundeskanzleramt
B 141	Bundesministerium der Justiz
B 145	Bundespresse- und Informationsamt
B 150	Bundesministerium für Vertriebene
B 168	Bundeszentrale für politische Bildung
B 305	Zentrale Rechtsschutzstelle
NL 80	Franz Blücher
NL 178	Hans Christoph Seebohm
NL 216	Heinrich Lübke
NL 221	Theodor Heuss
NL 253	Kurt Behling
NL 263	Kurt Rheindorf
NL 351	Herbert Blankenhorn
All. Proz. 6	Eichmann-Prozeß
All. Proz. 20	Prozesse gegen Deutsche im europ. Ausland
All. Proz. 21	Prozesse gegen Deutsche im europ. Ausland

Bundesarchiv/Dokumentationszentrale, Berlin (Federal Archives—Central Documentation Office, Berlin)

Z6 NR	Nationalrat der Nationalen Front

2. Politisches Archiv des Auswärtigen Amts (PA/AA), Bonn (Political Archives of the Foreign Ministry, Bonn)
Abteilung II
Abteilung III
NL Wilhelm Haas

3. Parlamentsarchiv des Deutschen Bundestages (BT—PA), Bonn (Parliamentary Archives of the German Bundestag, Bonn)
Sitzungsprotokolle des Unterausschusses Kriegsgefangene, 1. und 2. Legislaturperiode

4. Archiv des Presse- und Informationsamtes der Bundesregierung (BPA), Bonn (Archives of the Federal Office of Press and Information, Bonn)

MF	Zeitungsausschnittsammlungen

5. Archiv für Christlich-Demokratische Politik (ACDP), Sankt Augustin (Archives of Christian Democratic Politics, Sankt Augustin)
   I-026 NL Margot Kalinke
   I-122 NL Wilhelm Laforet
   I-148 NL Hans-Joachim von Merkatz
   I-237 NL Eduard Wahl

6. Archiv des Deutschen Liberalismus (ADL), Gummersbach (Archives of German Liberalism, Gummersbach)
   N1   Nachlaß Thomas Dehler
   Protokolle des FDP-Bundesvorstands

7. Archiv der sozialen Demokratie (AdsD), Bonn (Archives of Social Democracy, Bonn)
   Bestand Erich Ollenhauer
   Bestand Kurt Schumacher
   NL Adolf Arndt
   NL Fritz Erler
   NL Carlo Schmid
   NL Herbert Wehner
   PV-Bestand Fritz Heine
   SPD-Bundestagsfraktion, 1. bis 4. Legislaturperiode

8. Stiftung Bundeskanzler-Adenauer-Haus (StBKAH), Rhöndorf
   NL Konrad Adenauer

9. Archiv des Instituts für Zeitgeschichte (IfZ), München (Archives of the Institute for Modern History, Munich)

Dk 110.001	OMGUS/ICD Opinion Surveys
Dm 115	Pressemitteilungen BPA
ED 91	NL Leo Freiherr Geyr von Schweppenburg
ED 94	NL Walter Strau
ED 155	Sammlung Heinz Förster
ED 157	NL Erich und Theo Kordt
ED 329	Sammlung Robert Strobel, vertr. Informationsberichte
F 154	Itinerar McCloy
Fg 15	Organisationspläne
Gb 10.03	Remer-Prozeß, Braunschweig
MA 430	OLG-Berichte
MA 1543	U.S. State Department, Public Opinion on Germany
MF 260	OMGUS-Akten
MZA 1	Zeitungsausschnittsammlung Wiener Library
Z 2	Weizsäcker-Prozeß
ZS	Zeugenschrifttum
Altregistratur	
Nürnberger Dokumente	

10. Evangelisches Zentralarchiv (EZA), Berlin (Evangelical Central Archives, Berlin)
    Bestand 2 Kirchenkanzlei der EKD 1943–1968
    NL Lothar Kreyssig
    NL Hansjörg Ranke
    Protokolle des Rats der EKD

11. Archiv der Evangelischen Akademie Bad Boll (EA/BB) (Archives of the Evangelical Academy, Bad Boll)
    Bestand Abteilung für Soldatenfragen
    Bestand Tagungen
    Bestand "Aktuelle Gespräche"
    Bestand Direktion Müller

12. Institut für Geschichte der Arbeiterbewegung, Zentrales Parteiarchiv (ZPA), Berlin (Institute for the History of the Workers' Movement, Central Party Archives, Berlin)

IV 2/13/	Abteilung Staat und Recht des ZK der SED
IV 2/902/	Abteilung Agitation beim ZK der SED
IV 2/1001/	Westkommission beim (Politbüro des) ZK der SED
IV 2/2028/	Bereich Agitation und Propaganda beim ZK der SED Büro Norden
JIV 2/2/	Politbüro des ZK der SED, Reinschriftenprotokolle
JIV 2/3/	Sekretariat des ZK der SED, Reinschriftenprotokolle
NL 90	Otto Grotewohl

13. Der Bundesbeauftragte für die Unterlagen des Staatssicherheitsdienstes der ehemaligen DDR (BStU), Berlin (Federal Office for the Documents of the State Security Service of the Former GDR, Berlin)
    Prozeßakten Hans Globke

14. U.S. National Archives (NA), Washington, D.C.

RG 59	State Department
RG 165	War Department
RG 338	European Command
RG 466	Office of the U.S. High Commissioner for Germany

15. Archives of the *New York Times,* New York, New York
    Press-clipping collection
    Byline-files Drew Middleton, Jack Raymond

16. Archives of the *Chicago Tribune,* Chicago, Illinois
    Press-clipping collection

17. Public Record Office (PRO), London

CAB 128	Cabinet Papers, Conclusions

CAB 129   Cabinet Papers, Documents
FO 317   Foreign Office, General Correspondence
FO 1036   Control Council on Germany, British Element

II. Periodicals
Archiv der Gegenwart
Bulletin des Presse- und Informationsamtes der Bundesregierung
Chicago Tribune
Christ und Welt
Frankfurter Allgemeine Zeitung
Frankfurter Hefte
Die Gegenwart
HICOG Information Bulletin
Der Monat
Die Neue Gesellschaft
Neue Juristische Wochenschrift
Neue Zeitung
Neue Zürcher Zeitung
New York Times
Der Spiegel
Die Spruchgerichte
Süddeutsche Juristenzeitung
Süddeutsche Zeitung
Wirtschaft und Statistik
Die Zeit

III. Published Sources and Literature

Aarons, Mark, and John Loftus. Ratlines: How the Vatican's Nazi Networks *Betrayed Western Intelligence to the Soviets.* London, 1991.

Abenheim, Donald. *Bundeswehr und Tradition: Die Suche nach dem gültigen Erbe des deutschen Soldaten.* Munich, 1989.

Acheson, Dean. *Present at the Creation: My Years in the State Department.* New York, 1969.

Adenauer, Konrad. *Erinnerungen.* Vol. 1: 1945–1953; vol. 2: 1953–1955; vol. 3: 1955–1959; Vol. 4: 1959–1963; Stuttgart, 1965–1968.

Adenauer. *Teegespräche 1950–1954, 1955–1958.* Ed. Hanns Jürgen Küsters. Berlin, 1984, 1986.

Adenauer. *Briefe 1949–1951, 1951–1953.* Ed. Hans Peter Mensing. Berlin, 1985, 1987.

Adenauer. "Es mußte alles neu gemacht werden." Die Protokolle des CDU-Bundesvorstandes 1950–1953. Ed. Günter Buchstab. Stuttgart, 1986 (CDU-Bundesvorstand 1950–1953).

Adenauer. "Wir haben wirklich etwas geschaffen." Die Protokolle des CDU-Bundesvorstandes 1953–1957. Ed. Günter Buchstab. Stuttgart, 1990 (CDU-Bundesvorstand 1953–1957).

Adenauer." ... um den Frieden zu gewinnen." Die Protokolle des CDU-Bundesvorstandes 1957–1961. Ed. Günter Buchstab. Düsseldorf, 1994 (CDU-Bundesvorstand 1957–1961).

[Adenauer]. Konrad Adenauer und seine Zeit. Politik und Republik des ersten Bundeskanzlers. Beiträge von Weg- und Zeitgenossen. Ed. Dieter Blumenwitz et al. Stuttgart, 1976.

Adorno, Theodor W. Was bedeutet: Aufarbeitung der Vergangenheit? [1959] In *Gesammelte Schriften,* vol. 10, II. Frankfurt am Main, 1977, pp. 555–72.

Die Ära Adenauer. Einsichten und Ausblicke. Frankfurt am Main and Hamburg, 1964.

Akten zur Auswärtigen Politik der Bundesrepublik Deutschland. Adenauer und die Hohen Kommissare. Vol. 1, *1949–1951.* Vol. 2, *1952.* Ed. Frank-Lothar Kroll and Manfred Nebelin. Munich, 1989, 1990.

Akten zur Vorgeschichte der Bundesrepublik Deutschland 1945–1949. 5 vols. Ed. Walter Vogel, Christoph Weisz, Wolfram Werner, Günter Plum, Hans-Dieter Kreikamp, and Bernd Steger. Munich, 1976–81.

Albrecht, Willy, ed. *Kurt Schumacher. Reden, Schriften, Korrespondenzen 1945–1952.* Bonn and Berlin, 1985.

Allemann, Fritz René. "Das deutsche Parteiensystem: Eine politische Analyse." *Der Monat* 5 (1953): 365–88.

Allemann, Fritz René. *Bonn ist nicht Weimar.* Cologne and Berlin 1956.

Altmann, Rüdiger. *Das Erbe Adenauers.* Stuttgart-Degerloch, 1960.

Ambrose, Steven. *Eisenhower.* Vol. 1, *Soldier, General of the Army, President-Elect, 1890–1952.* Vol. 2, *The President, 1952–1969.* New York, 1983, 1984.

Anfänge westdeutscher Sicherheitspolitik 1945–1956. Ed. Militärgeschichtlichen Forschungsamt. Vol. 1, Von der Kapitulation bis zum Plevenplan. Vol. 2, Die EVG-Phase. Munich and Vienna, 1982, 1990.

Arendt, Hannah. "Organisierte Schuld." *Die Wandlung* 1 (1945–46): 333–44.

Arendt, Hannah. "Konzentrationsläger." *Die Wandlung* 3 (1948): 309–30.

Arendt, Hannah. *Zur Zeit: Politische Essays.* Ed. Marie Luise Knott. Munich, 1989.

Arendt, Hannah and Karl Jaspers. *Briefwechsel 1926–1969.* Ed. Lotte Köhler and Hans Sauer. Munich and Zurich, 1985.

Aretin, Karl Otmar Freiherr von. "Der Erfolgsdeutsche. Studie zu einer beklemmenden Gegenwartsfrage." *Frankfurter Hefte* 13 (1958): 758–64.

Arnim, Gabriele von. *Das große Schweigen. Von der Schwierigkeit, mit den Schatten der Vergangenheit zu leben.* Munich, 1989.

Aschenauer, Rudolf. *Zur Frage einer Revision der Kriegsverbrecherprozesse.* Nuremberg, 1949.

Aschenauer, Rudolf. *Um Recht und Wahrheit im Malmedy-Fall. Eine Stellungnahme zum Bericht eines Untersuchungsausschusses des amerikanischen Senats in Sachen Malmedy-Prozeß.* Nuremberg, 1950.

Aschenauer, Rudolf. *Landsberg. Ein dokumentarischer Bericht von deutscher Seite.* Munich, 1951.

Aschenauer, Rudolf. *Der Malmedy-Fall. 7 Jahre nach dem Urteil.* Munich, [1953].

Aspekte der deutschen Wiederbewaffnung bis 1955. Mit Beiträgen von Hans Buchheim et al. Boppard, 1975.

Assmann, Aleida, and Ute Frevert. *Geschichtsvergessenheit—Geschichtsversessenheit. Vom Umgang mit deutschen Vergangenheiten nach 1945.* Stuttgart, 1999.

Ausschuß für Deutsche Einheit, ed. *Die Wahrheit über Oberländer. Braunbuch über die verbrecherische faschistische Vergangenheit des Bonner Ministers.* Berlin, 1960.

Backes, Uwe, Eckhard Jesse, and Rainer Zitelmann, eds. *Die Schatten der Vergangenheit. Impulse zur Historisierung des Nationalsozialismus.* Frankfurt am Main and Berlin, 1990.

Badstübner, Rolf, and Siegfried Thomas. *Restauration und Spaltung. Entstehung und Entwicklung der BRD 1945–1955.* Cologne, 1975.

Bänsch, Dieter, ed. *Die fünfziger Jahre. Beiträge zu Politik und Kultur.* Tübingen, 1985.

Bästlein, Klaus. "Nazi-Blutrichter als Stützen des Adenauer Regimes." Die DDR-Kampagnen gegen NS-Richter und -Staatsanwälte, die Reaktionen der bundesdeutschen Justiz und ihre gescheiterte "Selbstreinigung" 1957–1968. In *Die Normalität des Verbrechens. Bilanz und Perspektiven der Forschung zu den nationalsozialistischen Gewaltverbrechen,* ed. Helge Grabitz, Klaus Bästlein and Johannes Tuchel, pp. 408–43. Berlin, 1994.

Balfour, Michael. Re-education in Germany After 1945: Some Further Considerations. *German History* 5 (1987): 25–35.

Bar-On, Dan. *Legacy of Silence: Encounters with Children of the Third Reich.* Cambridge, Mass., 1989.

Baring, Arnulf. *Außenpolitik in Adenauers Kanzlerdemokratie. Westdeutsche Innenpolitik im Zeichen der Europäischen Verteidigungsgemeinschaft.* Munich, 1971.

Baring, Arnulf, ed. *Sehr verehrter Herr Bundeskanzler! Heinrich von Brentano im Briefwechsel mit Konrad Adenauer 1949–1964.* Hamburg, 1974.

Bark, Dennis L., and David R.Gress. *The History of West Germany.* Vol. 1, *From Shadow to Substance, 1945–1963.* Vol. 2, *Democracy and Its Discontents, 1963–1988.* Oxford ,1989.

Barnouw, Dagmar. "Konfrontation mit dem Grauen. Alliierte Schuldpolitik 1945." *Merkur* 49 (1995): 390–401.

Barzel, Rainer, ed. *Sternstunden des Parlaments.* Heidelberg, 1989.

Bauer, Fritz. "Die 'Ungesühnte Nazijustiz.' " *Die Neue Gesellschaft* 7 (1960): 179–91.

Bauer, Fritz. *Justiz als Symptom.* In *Bestandsaufnahme,* ed. Hans Werner Richter, pp. 221–32. Munich, Vienna, and Basel, 1962.

Bauer, Fritz. "Im Namen des Volkes: Die strafrechtliche Bewältigung der Vergangenheit." In *Zwanzig Jahre danach,* ed. Helmut Hammerschmidt, pp. 301–14. Munich, Vienna, and Basel, 1965.

Becker, Hellmut. "Gericht der Politik." *Merkur* 4 (1950): 1297–308.

Becker, Hellmut. "Plädoyer für Ernst von Weizsäcker." In *Quantität und Qualität: Grundfragen der Bildungspolitik,* ed. Hellmut Becker, pp. 13–58. Freiburg, 1962.

Becker, Hellmut, and Frithjof Hager. *Aufklärung als Beruf. Gespräche über Bildung und Politik.* Munich and Zurich, 1992.

Bentley, James. *Martin Niemöller: Eine Biographie.* Munich, 1985.

Benz, Wolfgang. "Versuche zur Reform des öffentlichen Dienstes in Deutschland 1945–1952: Deutsche Opposition gegen alliierte Initiativen." *Vierteljahrshefte für Zeitgeschichte* 29 (1981): 216–45.

Benz, Wolfgang. *Die Gründung der Bundesrepublik: Von der Bizone zum souveränen Staat.* Munich, 1984.

Benz, Wolfgang. "Nachkriegsgesellschaft und Nationalsozialismus; Erinnerung, Amnesie, Abwehr." *Dachauer Hefte* 6 (1990): 12–24.

Benz, Wolfgang, ed. *Rechtsextremismus in der Bundesrepublik: Voraussetzungen, Zusammenhänge, Wirkungen.* Frankfurt am Main, 1989.

Bérard, Armand. *Un ambassador se souvient.* Vol. 2, *Washington et Bonn, 1945–1955.* Paris, 1978.

Bergmann, Werner. "Die Reaktion auf den Holocaust in Westdeutschland von 1945 bis 1989." *Geschichte in Wissenschaft und Unterricht* 43 (1992): 327–50.

Bergmann, Werner, and Rainer Erb, ed. *Antisemitismus in der politischen Kultur nach 1945.* Opladen, 1990.

Bergmann, Werner, Rainer Erb, and Albert Lichtblau, eds. *Schwieriges Erbe: Der Umgang mit Nationalsozialismus und Antisemitismus in Österreich, der DDR und der Bundesrepublik Deutschland.* Frankfurt am Main and New York, 1995.

Berthold, Will. *Malmedy. Das Recht des Siegers. Roman nach Tatsachen.* Bayreuth, 1977 (1st ed., 1957).

Bertram, Günter. "Vergangenheitsbewältigung durch NS-Prozesse? Individualschuld im 'Staatsverbrechen.'" In *Das Unrechtsregime: Internationale Forschung über den Nationalsozialismus,* ed. Ursula Büttner, vol. 2, pp. 421–49. Hamburg, 1986.

Billerbeck, Rudolf. *Die Abgeordneten der ersten Landtage und der Nationalsozialismus.* Düsseldorf, 1971.

Billing, Werner. *Das Problem der Richterwahl zum Bundesverfassungsgericht. Ein Beitrag zum Thema "Politik und Verfassungsgerichtsbarkeit."* Berlin, 1969.

Bird, Kai. *The Chairman, John J. McCloy: The Making of the American Establishment.* New York, 1992.

Birke, Adolf M. *Nation ohne Haus. Deutschland 1945–1961.* Berlin, 1989.

Birn, Ruth Bettina. "Die Strafverfolgung nationalsozialistischer Verbrechen." In *Ende des Dritten Reiches—Ende des Zweiten Weltkriegs,* ed. Hans-Erich Volkmann, pp. 393–418. Munich, 1995.

Bismarck, Klaus von. *Aufbruch aus Pommern. Erinnerungen und Perspektiven.* Munich, 1992.

Blanke, Thomas. "Der 'Rechtshistorikerstreit' um Amnestie: Politische Klugheit, moralische Richtigkeit und Gerechtigkeit bei der Aufarbeitung deutscher Vergangenheiten." *Kritische Justiz* 28 (1995): 131–50.

Blankenagel, Alexander. "Verfassungsgerichtliche Vergangenheitsbewältigung." *Zeitschrift für Neuere Rechtsgeschichte* 13 (1991): 67–82.

Blankenhorn, Herbert. *Verständnis und Verständigung. Blätter eines politischen Tagebuchs 1949 bis 1979.* Frankfurt am Main, 1980.

Blänsdorf, Agnes. "Zur Konfrontation mit der NS-Vergangenheit in der Bundesrepublik, der DDR und Österreich. Entnazifizierung und Wiedergutmachungsleistungen." *Aus Politik und Zeitgeschichte* 16–17 (1987): 3–18.

Blasius, Rainer A. *Für Großdeutschland—gegen den großen Krieg. Ernst von Weizsäcker in den Krisen um die Tschechoslowakei und Polen.* Cologne and Vienna, 1981.

Blasius, Rainer A. "Ein konservativer Patriot im Dienste Hitlers—Ernst Freiherr von Weizsäcker." In *Richard von Weizsäcker: Aktualisierte Neuausgabe,* ed. Werner Filmer and Heribert Schwan, pp. 276–306. Munich, 1991.

Boberach, Heinz. "Das Nürnberger Urteil gegen verbrecherische Organisationen und die Spruchgerichtsbarkeit der Britischen Zone." *Zeitschrift für Neuere Rechtsgeschichte* 12 (1990): 40–50.

Bock, Hans Manfred. "Zur Perzeption der frühen Bundesrepublik Deutschland in der französischen Diplomatie: Die Bonner Monatsberichte des Hochkommissars André François-Poncet 1949 bis 1955." *Francia* 15 (1987): 579–658.

Böttcher, Karl Wilhelm. "Menschen unter falschem Namen." *Frankfurter Hefte* 4 (1949):492–511.

Bosch, William J. *Judgement on Nuremberg: American Attitudes Toward the Major German War-Crime Trials.* Chapel Hill, N.C., 1970.

Boveri, Margret. *Der Diplomat vor Gericht.* Berlin and Hannover, 1948.

Bower, Tom. *The Pledge Betrayed: America and Britain and the Denazification of Postwar Germany.* Garden City, N.Y., 1982.

Boyens, Armin. "Das Stuttgarter Schuldbekenntnis vom 19. Oktober 1945. Entstehung und Bedeutung." *Vierteljahrshefte für Zeitgeschichte* 19 (1971): 374–97.

Boyle, Kay. *Der rauchende Berg. Geschichten aus Nachkriegsdeutschland.* Frankfurt am Main, 1991.

Bracher, Karl Dietrich. *Die deutsche Diktatur. Entstehung, Struktur, Folgen des Nationalsozialismus.* Cologne and Berlin, 1969.

Bracher, Karl Dietrich. *Nach 25 Jahren. Eine Deutschland-Bilanz.* Munich, 1970.

Brenner, Michael. *Nach dem Holocaust. Juden in Deutschland 1945–1950.* Munich, 1995.

Brinkley, Douglas. *Dean Acheson: The Cold War Years, 1953–1971.* New Haven, Conn., 1992.

Broch, Hermann. *Briefe über Deutschland 1945–1949. Die Korrespondenz mit Volkmar von Zühlsdorff.* Ed. Paul Michael Lützeler. Frankfurt am Main, 1986.

Brochhagen, Ulrich. "Vergangene Vergangenheitsbewältigung. Zum Umgang mit der NS-Vergangenheit während der fünfziger und frühen sechziger Jahre." *Mittelweg* 36, 5 (1992): 145–54.

Brochhagen, Ulrich. *Nach Nürnberg. Vergangenheitsbewältigung und Westintegration in der Ära Adenauer.* Hamburg, 1994.

Broszat, Martin. "Siegerjustiz oder strafrechtliche 'Selbstreinigung': Aspekte der Vergangenheitsbewältigung der deutschen Justiz während der Besatzungszeit 1945–1949." *Vierteljahrshefte für Zeitgeschichte* 29 (1981): 477–544.

Broszat, Martin. *Nach Hitler. Der schwierige Umgang mit unserer Geschichte.* Munich, 1988.

Broszat, Martin, and Saul Friedländer. "A Controversy About the Historization of National Socialism." *Yad Vashem Studies* 19 (1988): 310–24.

Broszat, Martin, ed. *Zäsuren nach 1945. Essays zur Periodisierung der deutschen Nachkriegsgeschichte.* Munich, 1990.

Broszat, Martin, et al., eds. *Deutschlands Weg in die Diktatur. Internationale Konferenz zur nationalsozialistischen Machtübernahme.* Berlin, 1983.

Broszat, Martin, Klaus-Dietmar Henke, and Hans Woller, eds. *Von Stalingrad zur Währungsreform: Zur Sozialgeschichte des Umbruchs in Deutschland.* Munich, 1988.

Brünneck, Alexander von. *Politische Justiz gegen Kommunisten in der Bundesrepublik Deutschland 1949–1968.* Frankfurt am Main, 1978.

Buchheim, Hans. "Das Problem des sogenannten Befehlsnotstandes aus historischer Sicht." In *Rechtliche und politische Aspekte der NS-Verbrecherprozesse,* ed. Peter Schneider and Hermann J. Meyer, pp. 25–37. Mainz, 1968.

Buchheim, Hans, ed. *Konrad Adenauer und der deutsche Bundestag.* Bonn, 1986.

Buchwald, Frank Andreas. "Adenauers Informationspolitik und das Bundespresseamt 1952–1959: Strategien amtlicher Presse- und Öffentlichkeitsarbeit in der Kanzlerdemokratie." Ph.D. diss., University of Mainz, 1991.

Bude, Heinz. *Deutsche Karrieren. Lebenskonstruktionen sozialer Aufsteiger aus der Flakhelfer-Generation.* Frankfurt am Main, 1987.

Bude, Heinz. *Bilanz der Nachfolge. Die Bundesrepublik und der Nationalsozialismus.* Frankfurt am Main, 1992.

Bührer, Werner, ed. *Die Adenauer-Ära. Die Bundesrepublik Deutschland 1949–1963.* Munich and Zurich, 1993.

Büsch, Otto, and Peter Furth. *Rechtsradikalismus im Nachkriegsdeutschland. Studien über die "Sozialistische Reichspartei."* Berlin and Frankfurt am Main, 1957.

Bundesregierung, ed. *Die antisemitischen und nazistischen Vorfälle in der Zeit vom 25. Dezember 1959 bis zum 28. Januar 1960.* Bonn, 1960.

Burgauer, Erica. *Zwischen Erinnerung und Verdrängung—Juden in Deutschland nach 1945.* Reinbek, 1993.

Buruma, Ian. *The Wages of Guilt: Memories of War in Germany and Japan.* New York, 1994.

Buscher, Frank M. *The U.S. War Crimes Trial Program in Germany, 1946–1955.* New York, Westport, and London, 1989.

Buscher, Frank M. "Kurt Schumacher, German Social Democracy, and the Punishment of Nazi Crimes." *Holocaust and Genocide Studies* 5 (1990): 261–73.

Buscher, Frank M. *The U.S. High Commission and German Nationalism, 1949–52. Central European History* 23 (1990): 57–75.

Buscher, Frank M., and Michael Phayer. "German Catholic Bishops and the Holocaust, 1940–1952." *German Studies Review* 11 (1988): 463–85.

Carwin, Susanne. "Unter der Sonne des Artikels 131." *Frankfurter Hefte* 11 (1956): 789–97.

Clay, Lucius D. *Decision in Germany.* Melbourne, 1950.

[Clay, Lucius D.] *The Papers of General Lucius D. Clay. Germany 1945–1949.* 2 vols. Ed. Edward Jean Smith. Bloomington and London, 1974 (Clay Papers).

Dahrendorf, Ralf. *Society and Democracy in Germany.* London, 1967.

Dam, Hendrik George van, and Ralph Giordano, eds. *KZ-Verbrechen vor deutschen Gerichten.* Vol. 1, *Dokumente aus den Prozessen gegen Sommer (KZ Buchenwald), Sorge, Schubert (KZ Sachsenhausen), Unkelbach (Ghetto in Czenstochau).* Vol. 2, *Einsatzkommando Tilsit. Der Prozeß zu Ulm.* Frankfurt am Main, 1962, 1966.

Danyel, Jürgen. "Die geteilte Vergangenheit. Gesellschaftliche Ausgangslagen und politische Dispositionen für den Umgang mit Nationalsozialismus und Widerstand in beiden deutschen Staaten nach 1949." In *Historische DDR-Forschung: Aufsätze und Studien,* ed. Jürgen Kocka, pp. 129–47. Berlin, 1993.

Danyel, Jürgen, ed. *Die geteilte Vergangenheit: Zum Umgang mit Nationalsozialismus und Widerstand in beiden deutschen Staaten.* Berlin, 1995.

Delmer, Sefton. *Die Deutschen und ich.* Hamburg, 1962.

Deutscher Bundesrat. *Drucksachen.* Bonn, 1949ff. (Bundesrat-Drucksachen).

Deutscher Bundesrat. *Sitzungsberichte.* Bonn, 1949ff. (BR-Berichte).

Deutschkron, Inge. *Israel und die Deutschen. Das besondere Verhältnis.* Cologne, 1983.

Deutschkron, Inge. *Unbequem. Mein Leben nach dem Überleben.* [Köln], 1992.

Diehl, James M. *The Thanks of the Fatherland: German Veterans After the Second World War.* Chapel Hill and London, 1993.

Diehls, Rudolf. *Der Fall Otto John: Hintergründe und Lehren.* Göttingen, 1954.

Diestelkamp, Bernhard. "Kontinuität und Wandel in der Rechtsordnung 1945–1955." In *Westdeutschland,* ed. Ludolf Herbst, pp. 85–116. Munich, 1986.

Diestelkamp, Bernhard, and Susanne Jung. "Die Justiz in den Westzonen und der frühen Bundesrepublik." *Aus Politik und Zeitgeschichte* 13–14 (1989): 19–29.

Diner, Dan, ed. *Ist der Nationalsozialismus Geschichte? Zu Historisierung und Historikerstreit.* Frankfurt am Main, 1987.

Dirks, Walter. "Der restaurative Charakter der Epoche." *Frankfurter Hefte* 5 (1950): 942–54.

Dirks, Walter. "Unbewältigte Vergangenheit—demokratische Zukunft." *Frankfurter Hefte* 15 (1960): 153–58.

Dittberner, Jürgen. "Die Freie Demokratische Partei." In *Parteien-Handbuch,* ed. Richard Stöß, pp. 1311–81. Opladen, 1983.

Doemming, Klaus-Berto von, Rudolf Werner Füsslein, and Werner Matz. "Entstehungsgeschichte der Artikel des Grundgesetzes." *Jahrbuch des öffentlichen Rechts der Gegenwart NF* 1 (1951): vol. 1.

Dönhoff, Marion Gräfin von. *Von gestern nach übermorgen. Zur Geschichte der Bundesrepublik Deutschland.* Munich, 1984.

Doering-Manteuffel, Anselm. *Die Bundesrepublik Deutschland in der Ära Adenauer. Außenpolitik und innere Entwicklung 1949–1963.* Darmstadt, 1983.

Doering-Manteuffel, Anselm. "Konrad Adenauer—Jakob Kaiser—Gustav Heinemann: Deutschlandpolitische Positionen in der CDU." In *Die Republik der fünfziger Jahre: Adenauers Deutschlandpolitik auf dem Prüfstand,* ed. Jürgen Weber, pp. 18–46. Munich, 1989.

Doering-Manteuffel, Anselm. "Strukturmerkmale der Kanzlerdemokratie." *Der Staat* 30 (1991): 1–18.

Doering-Manteuffel, Anselm. "Deutsche Zeitgeschichte nach 1945. Entwicklung und Problemlagen der historischen Forschung zur Nachkriegszeit." *Vierteljahrshefte für Zeitgeschichte* 41 (1993): 1–29.

Doering-Manteuffel, Anselm. "Die Nachwirkungen des Antisemitismus der NS-Zeit im geteilten Deutschland." In *Geschichte und Geist: Fünf Essays zum Verständnis des Judentums,* ed. Franz D. Lucas, pp. 105–26. Berlin, 1995.

Doering-Manteuffel, Anselm, ed. *Adenauerzeit. Stand, Perspektiven und methodische Aufgaben der Zeitgeschichtsforschung (1945–1967).* Bonn, 1993.

Döscher, Hans-Jürgen. *Das Auswärtige Amt im Dritten Reich. Diplomatie im Schatten der "Endlösung."* Berlin, 1987.

Döscher, Hans-Jürgen. *Verschworene Gesellschaft. Das Auswärtige Amt unter Adenauer zwischen Neubeginn und Kontinuität.* Berlin, 1995.

Dreher, Klaus. *Der Weg zum Kanzler. Adenauers Griff nach der Macht.* Düsseldorf and Vienna 1972.

Dubiel, Helmut. *Niemand ist frei von der Geschichte. Die nationalsozialistische Herrschaft in den Debatten des Deutschen Bundestages.* Munich, 1999.

Dudek, Peter. " 'Vergangenheitsbewältigung': Zur Problematik eines umstrittenen Begriffs." *Aus Politik und Zeitgeschichte* 1–2 (1992): 44–53.

Dudek, Peter. "Die Thematisierung der NS-Vergangenheit in der Pädagogik der BRD und der DDR. Eine vergleichende Studie auf der Basis einer systematischen Zeitschriftenanalyse." *Tel Aviver Jahrbuch für deutsche Geschichte* 23 (1994): 371–400.

Dudek, Peter, and Hans-Gerd Jaschke. *Entstehung und Entwicklung des Rechtsextremismus in der Bundesrepublik. Zur Tradition einer besonderen politischen Kultur.* 2 vols. Opladen, 1984.

Düsing, Bernhard. *Die Geschichte der Abschaffung der Todesstrafe in der Bundesrepublik Deutschland.* Offenbach, 1952.

Eberan, Barbro. *Luther? Friedrich "der Große"? Wagner? Nietzsche? ... ? ... ? Wer war an Hitler schuld? Die Debatte um die Schuldfrage 1945–1949.* Munich, 1983.

Ebsworth, Raymond. *Restoring Democracy in Germany: The British Contribution.* London and New York, 1960.

Eckardt, Felix von. *Ein unordentliches Leben. Lebenserinnerungen.* Düsseldorf and Vienna, 1967.

Eckert, Josef. *Schuldig oder entlastet?* Munich, 1947.

Eden, Anthony. *Full Circle.* London, 1960.

Edinger, Lewis J. "Post-Totalitarian Leadership: Elites in the German Federal Republic." *American Political Science Review* 54 (1960): 58–82.

Ehlers, Hermann. *Präsident des Deutschen Bundestages. Ausgewählte Reden. Aufsätze und Briefe 1950–1954.* Ed. Rüdiger Wenzel. Boppard, 1991.

Eisenhower, Dwight D. *Crusade in Europe.* Garden City, N.Y., 1948.

Eisfeld, Rainer, and Ingo Müller, eds. *Gegen Barbarei: Essays Robert M. W. Kempner zu Ehren.* Frankfurt am Main, 1989.

Elm, Ludwig. *Nach Hitler. Nach Honecker. Zum Streit der Deutschen um die eigene Vergangenheit.* Berlin, 1991.

Emrich, Ulrike, and Jürgen Nötzold "Der 20. Juli 1944 in den offiziellen Gedenkreden der Bundesrepublik und in der Darstellung der DDR." *Aus Politik und Zeitgeschichte* 26 (1984): 3–12.

Enders, Ulrich. "Der Hitler-Film *Bis fünf nach zwölf:* Vergangenheitsbewältigung oder Westintegration?" In *Aus der Arbeit der Archive,* ed. Friedrich P. Kahlenberg, pp. 916–36. Boppard, 1989.

Entscheidungen des Bundesverfassungsgerichts. Vols. 1–8. Tübingen, 1952–1959.

Ephraim, Ben. "Der steile Weg zur Wiedergutmachung." In *Juden in Deutschland,* ed. Heinz Ganther, pp. 289–385. Ausgabe, 1958, 1959.

Erdmann, Karl Dietrich. *Das Ende des Reiches und die Entstehung der Republik Österreich, der Bundesrepublik Deutschland und der Deutschen Demokratischen Republik.* Munich, 1980.

"Erinnern oder Verweigern—Das schwierige Thema Nationalsozialismus." *Dachauer Hefte* 6 (1990).

Eschenburg, Theodor. "Der bürokratische Rückhalt." In *Die Zweite Republik: 25 Jahre Bundesrepublik Deutschland—eine Bilanz,* ed. Richard Löwenthal and Hans-Peter Schwarz, pp. 64–94. Stuttgart, 1974.

Euchner, Walter. "Unterdrückte Vergangenheitsbewältigung: Motive der Filmpolitik der Ära Adenauer." In *Gegen Barbarei: Essays Robert M. W. Kempner zu Ehren,* ed. Rainer Eisfeld and Ingo Müller, pp. 346–59. Frankfurt am Main, 1989.

Falter, Jürgen W. "Kontinuität und Neubeginn. Die Bundestagswahl 1949 zwischen Weimar und Bonn." *Politische Vierteljahresschrift* 22 (1981): pp. 236–63.

Farmer, Sarah Bennett. *Oradur-sur-Glane: "Village martyr" in the Landscape of Memory, 1944–1991.* Ann Arbor, 1992.

Faulenbach, Bernd. "NS-Interpretationen und Zeitklima. Zum Wandel in der Aufarbeitung der jüngsten Vergangenheit." *Aus Politik und Zeitgeschichte* 22 (1987): pp. 19–30.

Faulenbach, Bernd. "Eine neue Sicht der Geschichte? Zur Diskussion über die deutschen Vergangenheiten." *Blätter für deutsche und internationale Politik* 37 (1992): pp. 809–17.Faulenbach, Bernd, and Rainer Bölling. *Geschichtsbewußtsein und historisch-politische Bildung in der Bundesrepublik Deutschland. Beiträge zum "Historikerstreit."* Düsseldorf, 1988.

FDP-Bundesvorstand. Die Liberalen unter dem Vorsitz von Theodor Heuss und Franz Blücher. Sitzungsprotokolle, 1949–1954. Die Liberalen unter dem Vorsitz von Thomas Dehler und Reinhold Maier. Sitzungsprotokolle, 1954–1960. 2 vols. Ed. Udo Wengst. Düsseldorf, 1990, 1991.

Felken, Detlef. *Dulles und Deutschland. Die amerikanische Deutschlandpolitik 1953–1959.* Bonn and Berlin, 1993.

Fischer, Erika J., and Heinz-D.Fischer. *John J. McCloy und die Frühgeschichte der Bundesrepublik Deutschland. Presseberichte und Dokumente über den Amerikanischen Hochkommissar für Deutschland 1949–1952.* Cologne, 1985.

Fischer, Erika J., and Heinz-D.Fischer. *John J. McCloys Reden zu Deutschland- und Berlinfragen. Publizistische Aktivitäten und Ansprachen des Amerikanischen Hochkommissars für Deutschland 1949–1952.* Berlin, 1986.

Fischer, Erika J., and Heinz-D.Fischer. *John J. McCloy: An American Architect of Postwar Germany. Profiles of a Trans-Atlantic Leader and Communicator.* Frankfurt am Main, 1994.

Flügge, Horst. "Eine restaurierte Behörde. Der Aufbau des neuen Auswärtigen Amtes in Bonn." *Frankfurter Hefte* 5 (1950): pp. 1244–47.

Först, Walter. "Robert Lehr." In. *Land und Bund,* ed. Walter Först, pp. 169–93. Cologne, 1981.

Foerster, Roland G. "Innenpolitische Aspekte der Sicherheit Westdeutschlands 1947–1950." In *Anfänge westdeutscher Sicherheitspolitik 1945–1956,* ed. Militärgeschichtlichen Forschungsamt, vol. 1, pp. 403–575. Munich and Vienna, 1982, 1990.

Foreign Relations of the United States. Vol. 3: 1951; vols. 5, 7: 1952–54. Washington, D.C., 1981, 1983, 1986 (FRUS).

Foschepoth, Josef. *Im Schatten der Vergangenheit. Die Anfänge der Gesellschaften für Christlich-Jüdische Zusammenarbeit.* Göttingen, 1993.

Foschepoth, Josef. "Zur deutschen Reaktion auf Niederlage und Besatzung." In. *Westdeutschland,* ed. Ludolf Herbst, pp. 151–65. Munich, 1986.

Frankenberg, Günter, and Franz J. Müller. "Juristische Vergangenheitsbewältigung. Der Volksgerichtshof vorm BGH." In *Kritische Justiz* 16 (1983): 145–63.

Franz-Willing, Georg. *Vergangenheitsbewältigung. Bundesrepublikanischer Nationalmasochismus.* Coburg, 1992.

Frei, Norbert. *Amerikanische Lizenzpolitik und deutsche Pressetradition. Die Geschichte der Nachkriegszeitung Südost-Kurier.* Munich, 1986.

Frei, Norbert. " 'Wir waren blind, ungläubig und langsam': Buchenwald, Dachau und die amerikanischen Medien im Frühjahr 1945." In *Vierteljahrshefte für Zeitgeschichte* 35 (1987): 385–401.

Frei, Norbert. " 'Vergangenheitsbewältigung' or ' Renazification'? The American Perspective on Germany's Confrontation of the Nazi Past in the Early Years of the Adenauer Era." In *America and the Shaping of German Society, 1945–1955,* ed. Michael Ermarth, pp. 47–59. New York and Oxford, 1993.

Frei, Norbert. "NS-Vergangenheit unter Ulbricht und Adenauer: Gesichtspunkte einer vergleichenden Bewältigungsforschung." In *Die geteilte Vergangenheit: Zum Umgang mit Nationalsozialismus und Widerstand in beiden deutschen Staaten,* ed. Jürgen Danyel, pp. 125–32. Berlin, 1995.

Frei, Norbert. "Das Problem der NS-Vergangenheit in der Ära Adenauer." In *Rechtsradikalismus in der politischen Kultur der Nachkriegszeit: Die verzögerte Normalisierung in Niedersachsen,* ed. Bernd Weisbrod, pp. 19–31. Hannover, 1995.

Frei, Norbert. "Erinnerungskampf: Zur Legitimationsproblematik des 20. Juli 1944 in Nachkriegsdeutschland." In *Von der Aufgabe der Freiheit: Politische Verantwortung und bürgerliche Gesellschaft im 19. und 20. Jahrhundert,* ed. Christian Jansen, Lutz Niethammer, and Bernd Weisbrod, pp. 493–504. Berlin, 1995.

Frei, Norbert, and Franziska Friedländer, eds. *Ernst Friedländer: Klärung für Deutschland. Leitartikel in der Zeit 1946–1950.* Munich, 1982.

Frey, Herbert. *The German Guilt Question after the Second World War. An Overview.* Ann Arbor, 1979.

Friedländer, Saul. *Reflections on Nazism: An Essay on Kitsch and Death.* New York, 1984.

Friedrich, Jörg. *Freispruch für die Nazi-Justiz. Die Urteile gegen NS-Richter seit 1948. Eine Dokumentation.* Reinbek, 1983.

Friedrich, Jörg. *Die kalte Amnestie. NS-Täter in der Bundesrepublik.* Frankfurt am Main, 1985.

Friedrich, Jörg. *Das Gesetz des Krieges. Das deutsche Heer in Rußland 1941 bis 1945. Der Prozeß gegen das Oberkommando der Wehrmacht.* Munich and Zurich, 1993.

Friedrich, Jörg, and Jörg Wollenberg, eds. *Licht in den Schatten der Vergangenheit. Zur Enttabuisierung der Nürnberger Kriegsverbrecherprozesse.* Frankfurt am Main and Berlin, 1987.

"Die frühe Bundesrepublik und das Erbe des 20 Juli 1944: Eine Denkschrift des britischen Botschafters aus dem Jahr 1955." Ed. Ulrich Brochhagen. In *Mittelweg 36*, no. 2 (1994): 41–49.

Fürstenau, Justus. *Entnazifizierung: Ein Kapitel deutscher Nachkriegspolitik*. Neuwied and Berlin, 1969.

Funke, Hajo, ed. *Von der Gnade der geschenkten Nation. Zur politischen Moral der Bonner Republik*. Berlin, 1988.

Ganther, Heinz, ed. *Die Juden in Deutschland 1951 and 52—5712: Ein Almanach*. Frankfurt am Main and Munich, [1953]. Ausgabe, 1958 and 1959; Hamburg, 1959.

Garbe, Detlef. *"In jedem Einzelfall ... bis zur Todesstrafe." Der Militärstrafrechtler Erich Schwinge. Ein deutsches Juristenleben*. Hamburg, 1989.

Garbe, Detlef. "Äußerliche Abkehr, Erinnerungsverweigerung und 'Vergangenheitsbewältigung': Der Umgang mit dem Nationalsozialismus in der frühen Bundesrepublik." In *Modernisierung im Wiederaufbau: Die westdeutsche Gesellschaft der 50er Jahre,* ed. Axel Schildt and Arnold Sywottek, pp. 693–716. Bonn, 1993.

Garner, Curt. "Der öffentliche Dienst in den 50er Jahren: Politische Weichenstellungen und ihre sozialgeschichtlichen Folgen." In *Modernisierung im Wiederaufbau: Die westdeutsche Gesellschaft der 50er Jahre,* ed. Axel Schildt and Arnold Sywottek, pp. 759–90. Bonn, 1993.

Garner, Curt. "Schlußfolgerungen aus der Vergangenheit? Die Auseinandersetzungen um die Zukunft des deutschen Berufsbeamtentums nach dem Ende des Zweiten Weltkrieges." In *Ende des Dritten Reiches—Ende des Zweiten Weltkriegs. Eine perspektivische Rückschau,* ed. Hans-Erich Volkmann, pp. 607–74. Munich and Zurich, 1995.

Garner, Curt. "Public Service Personnel in West Germany in the 1950s: Controversial Policy Decisions and Their Effects on Social Composition, Gender Structure, and the Role of Former Nazis." In *Journal of Social History* 29 (1995–96): 25–80.

Geile, Dirk. *Der Remer-Mythos in der frühen Bundesrepublik. Ein Beitrag zum organisierten Rechtsextremismus in Niedersachsen*. Unpublished thesis, Göttingen, 1993.

Gellhorn, Martha. *The View from the Ground*. New York, 1988.

Gerstenmaier, Eugen. *Streit und Friede hat seine Zeit. Ein Lebensbericht*. Frankfurt am Main, Berlin, and Vienna, 1981.

Gilbert, Martin. *"Never Despair": Winston Churchill, 1945–1965*. London, 1988.

Giordano, Ralph. *Die zweite Schuld oder Von der Last ein Deutscher zu sein*. Hamburg, 1987.

Glaser, Hermann. *Kulturgeschichte der Bundesrepublik Deutschland*. Vol. 1, *Zwischen Kapitulation und Währungsreform 1945–1948*. Vol. 2, *Zwischen Grundgesetz und Großer Koalition 1949–1967*. Munich and Vienna, 1985, 1986.

Glaser, Hermann. "Totschweigen, entlasten, umschulden. Die Bewältigung der Vergangenheit im Nachkriegsdeutschland." In *Tribüne* 103 (1987): 117–24.

Godau-Schüttke, Klaus-Detlev. "Juristen und Mediziner in Schleswig-Holstein decken den NS-Euthanasiearzt Prof. Dr. Werner Heyde und bleiben straflos." In *Die Normalität des Verbrechens: Bilanz und Perspektiven der Forschung zu den nationalsozialistischen Gewaltverbrechen*, ed. Helge Grabitz, Klaus Bästlein, and Johannes Tuchel, pp. 444–79. Berlin, 1994.

Götz, Albrecht. *Bilanz der Verfolgung von NS-Straftaten.* Cologne, 1986.

Goldmann, Nahum. *Mein Leben als deutscher Jude.* Munich and Vienna, 1980.

Goldmann, Nahum. *Mein Leben: USA, Europa, Israel.* Munich and Vienna, 1981.

Goschler, Constantin. "Der Fall Philipp Auerbach." In *Wiedergutmachung in der Bundesrepublik Deutschland*, ed. Ludolf Herbst and Constantin Goschler, pp. 77–98. Munich, 1989.

Goschler, Constantin. "The Attitude Towards Jews in Bavaria after the Second World War." In *Leo Baeck Yearbook* 36 (1991): 443–58.

Goschler, Constantin. *Wiedergutmachung: Westdeutschland und die Verfolgten des Nationalsozialismus 1945–1954.* Munich, 1992.

Gosewinkel, Dieter. *Adolf Arndt: Die Wiederbegründung des Rechtsstaats aus dem Geist der Sozialdemokratie (1945–1961).* Bonn, 1991.

Gotto, Klaus, ed. *Der Staatssekretär Adenauers: Persönlichkeit und politisches Wirken Hans Globkes.* Stuttgart, 1980.

Grabert, Herbert, ed. *Friedrich Grimm: Ein Leben für das Recht. Erinnerungen an das Wirken eines großen Anwalts und Patrioten.* Tübingen, 1961.

Grabitz, Helge. *NS-Prozesse: Psychogramme der Beteiligten.* Heidelberg, 1985.

Graml, Hermann. "Alte und neue Apologeten Hitlers." In *Rechtsextremismus in der Bundesrepublik: Voraussetzungen, Zusammenhänge, Wirkungen*, ed. Wolfgang Benz, pp. 63–92. Frankfurt am Main, 1989.

Graml, Hermann. "Die verdrängte Auseinandersetzung mit dem Nationalsozialismus." In *Zäsuren nach 1945. Essays zur Periodisierung der deutschen Nachkriegsgeschichte*, ed. Martin Broszat, pp. 169–83. Berlin, 1983.

Grawert, Rolf. "Der Zusammenbruch des Staates und das Schicksal seiner Beamten im Spiegel der Nachkriegsjudikatur." In *Die Wiederherstellung des Berufsbeamtentums nach 1945: Geburtsfehler oder Stützpfeiler der Demokratiegründung in Westdeutschland?* ed. Friedrich Gerhard Schwegmann, pp. 25–46. Düsseldorf, 1986.

Grebing, Helga. *Konservative gegen Demokratie. Konservative Kritik an der Demokratie in der Bundesrepublik nach 1945.* Frankfurt am Main, 1971.

Greil, Lothar. *Die Wahrheit über Malmedy.* Munich, 1958.

Gress, Franz, and Hans-Gerd Jaschke. "Politische Justiz gegen rechts. Der Remer-Prozeß 1952 in paradigmatischer Perspektive." In *Gegen Barbarei: Essays Robert M. W. Kempner zu Ehren*, ed. Rainer Eisfeld and Ingo Müller, pp. 453–78. Frankfurt am Main, 1989.

Grewe, Wilhelm G. *Rückblenden 1976–1951: Aufzeichnungen eines Augen-zeugen deutscher Außenpolitik von Adenauer bis Schmidt.* Frankfurt am Main, Berlin, and Vienna, 1979.

Grimm, Friedrich. *Generalamnestie als völkerrechtliches Postulat.* Cologne and Opladen, 1951.

Grimm, Friedrich. *Generalamnestie. Der einzige Weg zum Frieden.* Freiburg, [1952].

Grimm, Friedrich. *Politische Justiz—die Krankheit unserer Zeit. 40 Jahre Dienst am Recht. Erlebnis und Erkenntnis.* Bonn, 1953.

Grimm, Friedrich. *Gebt die Gefangenen frei!* Freiburg, [1955].

Grimm, Friedrich. *Unrecht im Rechtsstaat. Tatsachen und Dokumente zur politischen Justiz dargestellt am Fall Naumann.* Tübingen, 1957.

Grimm, Friedrich. *Mit offenem Visier. Aus den Lebenserinnerungen eines deutschen Rechtsanwalts.* Leoni, 1961.

Gritschneder, Otto. *Sackgasse Säuberung. Eine kritische Denkschrift zum zweiten Jahrestag des Inkrafttretens des Gesetzes zur Befreiung von Nationalsozialismus und Militarismus vom 5. März 1946.* Privatdruck. Munich, 1948.

Groehler, Olaf. "SED, VVN und Juden in der sowjetischen Besatzungszone Deutschlands (1945–1949)." In *Jahrbuch für Antisemitismusforschung* 3 (1994): 282–302.

Gross, Johannes. *Phönix in Asche. Kapitel zum westdeutschen Stil.* Stuttgart, 1989.

Grosser, Alfred. *Geschichte Deutschlands seit 1945. Eine Bilanz.* Munich, 1974.

Grosser, Alfred. *Ermordung der Menschheit. Der Genozid im Gedächtnis der Völker.* Munich and Vienna, 1990.

Gruchmann, Lothar. "Das Urteil von Nürnberg nach 22 Jahren." In *Viertel-jahrshefte für Zeitgeschichte* 16 (1968): 385–89.

Gruchmann, Lothar. *Justiz im Dritten Reich 1933–1940. Anpassung und Unterwerfung in der Ära Gürtner.* Munich, 1988.

Gutscher, Jörg Michael. *Die Entwicklung der FDP von ihren Anfängen bis 1961.* Meisenheim am Glan, 1967.

Haas, Wilhelm. *Beitrag zur Geschichte der Entstehung des Auswärtigen Dienstes der Bundesrepublik Deutschland.* Privatdruck. Bremen, 1969.

Habermas, Jürgen. *Vergangenheit als Zukunft.* Zurich, 1990.

Habermas, Jürgen. "Was bedeutet 'Aufarbeitung der Vergangenheit' heute? Bemerkungen zur 'doppelten Vergangenheit.' " In *Die Moderne—ein unvollendetes Projekt. Philosophisch-politische Aufsätze 1977–1992,* ed. Jürgen Habermas, pp. 242–67. Leipzig, 1992.

Habermas, Jürgen. "Die Last der doppelten Vergangenheit." In *Die Zeit* 20 (1994): 54.

Haensel, Carl. *Das Gericht vertagt sich. Aus dem Tagebuch eines Nürnberger Verteidigers.* Hamburg, 1950.

Hahn, Erich J. C. "Hajo Holborn: Bericht zur deutschen Frage. Beobachtungen und Empfehlungen vom Herbst 1947." In *Vierteljahrshefte für Zeit-geschichte* 35 (1987): 135–66.

Die Haltung der beiden deutschen Staaten zu den Nazi- und Kriegsverbrechen. Eine Dokumentation. Berlin (Ost), 1965.

Halow, Joseph. *Innocent at Dachau.* Newport Beach, 1993.

Hammerschmidt, Helmut. "Renazifizierung der Bundesrepublik." In *Deutsche Rundschau* 82 (1956): 371–81.

Hammerschmidt, Helmut, and Michael Mansfeld. *Der Kurs ist falsch.* Vienna, Munich, and Basel, 1956.

Hammerschmidt, Helmut, ed. *Zwanzig Jahre danach: Eine deutsche Bilanz 1945–1965. Achtunddreißig Beiträge deutscher Wissenschaftler, Schriftsteller und Publizisten.* Munich, Vienna, and Basel, 1965.

Hankel, Gerd, and Gerhard Stuby, eds. *Strafgerichte gegen Menschheitsverbrechen. Zum Völkerrecht 50 Jahre nach den Nürnberger Prozessen.* Hamburg, 1995.

Hannover, Heinrich. "Zur Beweiswürdigung in Strafsachen gegen NS-Verbrecher." In *Gegen Barbarei: Essays Robert M. W. Kempner zu Ehren,* ed. Rainer Eisfeld and Ingo Müller, pp. 303–23. Frankfurt am Main, 1989.

Hartrich, Edwin. *The Fourth and Richest Reich: How the Germans Conquered the Postwar World.* London and New York, 1980.

Hase, Karl-Günther von, ed. *Konrad Adenauer und die Presse.* Bonn, 1988.

Haug, Wolfgang Fritz. *Vom hilflosen Antifaschismus zur Gnade der späten Geburt.* Hamburg and Berlin, 1987.

Heenen-Wolff, Susann. *Im Haus des Henkers: Gespräche in Deutschland.* Frankfurt am Main, 1992.

Heimannsberg, Barbara, and Christoph J. Schmidt, eds. *Das kollektive Schweigen. Nazivergangenheit und gebrochene Identität in der Psychotherapie.* Heidelberg, 1988.

Henke, Klaus-Dietmar. "Die Grenzen der politischen Säuberung in Deutschland nach 1945." In *Westdeutschland,* ed. Ludolf Herbst, pp. 127–133. Munich, 1986.

Henke, Klaus-Dietmar. "Die Trennung vom Nationalsozialismus. Selbstzerstörung, politische Säuberung, 'Entnazifizierung,' Strafverfolgung." In *Politische Säuberung in Europa: Die Abrechnung mit Faschismus und Kollaboration nach dem Zweiten Weltkrieg,* ed. Klaus-Dietmar Henke and Hans Weller, pp. 21–83. Munich, 1991.

Henke, Klaus-Dietmar. *Die amerikanische Besetzung Deutschlands.* Munich, 1995.

Henkels, Walter. *99 Bonner Köpfe.* Düsseldorf and Vienna, 1963.

Henkys, Reinhard. *Die nationalsozialistischen Gewaltverbrechen. Geschichte und Gericht.* Stuttgart and Berlin, 1964.

Hennig, Regina. *Entschädigung und Interessenvertretung der NS-Verfolgten in Niedersachsen 1945–1949.* Bielefeld, 1991.

Herbert, Ulrich. "Rückkehr in die Bürgerlichkeit? NS-Eliten in der Bundesrepublik." In *Rechtsradikalismus in der politischen Kultur der Nachkriegszeit: Die verzögerte Normalisierung in Niedersachsen,* ed. Bernd Weisbrod, pp. 157–73. Hannover, 1995.

zur Zuwanderung osteuropäischer Juden 1945–1947." In *Geschichte und Gesellschaft* 9 (1983): 421–52.

Jaeger, Hans. "Neo-Faschismus in Deutschland." In *Deutsche Rundschau* 79 (1953): 139–47.

Jäger, Herbert. *Verbrechen unter totalitärer Herrschaft. Studien zur national-sozialistischen Gewaltkriminalität.* Olten and Freiburg, 1967.

Jäger, Herbert. "Strafrecht und nationalsozialistische Gewaltverbrechen." In *Kritische Justiz* 1 (1968): 143–57.

Jahn, Hans Edgar. *An Adenauers Seite. Sein Berater erinnert sich.* Munich, 1987.

Jahntz, Bernhard, and Volker Kähne. *Der Volksgerichtshof: Darstellung der Ermittlungen der Staatsanwaltschaft bei dem Landgericht Berlin gegen ehemalige Richter und Staatsanwälte am Volksgerichtshof.* Berlin, 1986.

Jaschke, Hans-Gerd. "Gewalt von rechts vor und nach Hitler." In *Aus Politik und Zeitgeschichte* 23 (1982): 3–21.

Jasper, Gotthard. "Wiedergutmachung und Westintegration. Die halbherzige justizielle Aufarbeitung der NS-Vergangenheit in der frühen Bundesrepublik." In *Westdeutschland,* ed. Ludolf Herbst, pp. 183–202. Munich, 1986.

Jelinek, Yeshayahu A. "Political Acumen, Altruism, Foreign Pressure or Moral Debt. Konrad Adenauer and the 'Shilumim.' " In *Tel Aviver Jahrbuch für deutsche Geschichte* 19 (1990): 77–102.

Jena, Kai von. "Versöhnung mit Israel? Die deutsch-israelischen Verhandlungen bis zum Wiedergutmachungsabkommen von 1952." In *Vierteljahrshefte für Zeitgeschichte* 34 (1986): 457–80.

Jenke, Manfred. *Verschwörung von rechts? Ein Bericht über den Rechtsradikalismus in Deutschland nach 1945.* Berlin, 1961.

Jescheck, Hans-Heinrich. "Kriegsverbrecherprozesse gegen deutsche Kriegsgefangene in Frankreich." In *Süddeutsche Juristenzeitung* 4 (1949): 107–15.

Jesse, Eckhard. " 'Vergangenheitsbewältigung' in der Bundesrepublik Deutschland." In *Staat* 26 (1987): 539–65.

Jesse, Eckhard. " 'Entnazifizierung' und 'Entstasifizierung' als politisches Problem. Die doppelte Vergangenheitsbewältigung." In *Vergangenheitsbewältigung durch Recht. Drei Abhandlungen zu einem deutschen Problem,* ed. Josef Isensee, pp. 9–36. Berlin, 1992.

Jesse, Eckhard. "Vergangenheitsbewältigung." In *Handwörterbuch zur deutschen Einheit,* ed. Werner Weidenfeld and Hans Rudolf Korte, pp. 715–22. Frankfurt am Main, 1992.

Jesse, Eckhard. " 'Vergangenheitsbewältigung' nach totalitärer Herrschaft in Deutschland." In *German Studies Review* (special issue, 1994): 157–71.

John, Otto. *Zweimal kam ich heim. Vom Verschwörer zum Schützer der Verfassung.* Düsseldorf and Vienna, 1969.

Jung, Susanne. *Die Rechtsprobleme der Nürnberger Prozesse. Dargestellt am Verfahren gegen Friedrich Flick.* Tübingen, 1992.

Just-Dahlmann, Barbara, and Helmut Just. *Die Gehilfen. NS-Verbrechen und die Justiz nach 1945.* Frankfurt am Main, 1988.

Justiz und NS-Verbrechen. Sammlung deutscher Strafurteile wegen nationalsozialistischer Tötungsverbrechen 1945–1966. Ed. Adelheid L. Rüter-Ehlermann and C. F. Rüter. 22 vols. Amsterdam, 1968–81.

Die Kabinettsprotokolle der Bundesregierung. Ed. Ulrich Enders, Konrad Reiser, Ursula Hüllbüsch, Kai von Jena, and Thomas Trumpp. Vols. 1–7, *1949–1954.* Boppard, 1982–93.

Karner, Stefan. *Im Archipel GUPVI. Kriegsgefangenschaft und Internierung in der Sowjetunion 1941–1956.* Vienna and Munich, 1995.

Kasten, Bernd. "Pensionen für NS-Verbrecher in der Bundesrepublik 1949–1963." In *Historische Mitteilungen* 7, no. 2 (1994): 262–82.

Kater, Michael H. "Problems of Political Reeducation in West Germany, 1945–1960." In *Simon Wiesenthal Center Annual* 4 (1987): 99–123.

Kaufmann, Arthur. "Die Naturrechtsdiskussion in der Rechts- und Staatsphilosophie der Nachkriegszeit." In *Aus Politik und Zeitgeschichte* 33 (1991): 3–17.

Kempner, Robert M. W. "Ankläger einer Epoche. Lebenserinnerungen." In *Zusammenarbeit mit Jörg Friedrich.* Frankfurt am Main, Berlin, and Vienna, 1983.

Kempowski, Walter. *Haben Sie davon gewußt? Deutsche Antworten.* Hamburg, 1979.

Kesselring, Albert. *Kesselring: A Soldier's Record.* Trans. Lynton Hudson, introduction by S. L. A. Marshall. New York, 1954.

Kessler, Mario. "Zwischen Repression und Toleranz. Die SED-Politik und die Juden (1949 bis 1967)." In *Historische DDR-Forschung. Aufsätze und Studien,* ed. Jürgen Kocka, pp. 149–67. Berlin, 1993.

Kielmansegg, Peter Graf von. *Lange Schatten: Vom Umgang der Deutschen mit der nationalsozialistischen Vergangenheit.* Berlin, 1989.

Kilian, Achim. *Einzuweisen zur völligen Isolierung. NKWD-Speziallager Mühlberg and Elbe 1945–1948.* Leipzig, 1992.

Kirchheimer, Otto. "The Composition of the German Bundestag, 1950." In *Western Political Quarterly* 3 (1950): 590–601.

Kirkpatrick, Ivone. *The Inner Circle: Memoirs.* London and New York, 1959.

Kirn, Michael. *Verfassungsumsturz oder Rechtskontinuität? Die Stellung der Jurisprudenz nach 1945 zum Dritten Reich, insbesondere die Konflikte um die Kontinuität der Beamtenrechte und Art. 131 Grundgesetz.* Berlin, 1972.

Kittel, Manfred. *Die Legende von der "Zweiten Schuld." Vergangenheitsbewältigung in der Ära Adenauer.* Frankfurt am Main, and Berlin, 1993.

Kittel, Manfred. "Peripetie der Vergangenheitsbewältigung: Die Hakenkreuzschmierereien 1959 and 60 und das bundesdeutsche Verhältnis zum Nationalsozialismus." In *Historisch-Politische Mitteilungen* 1 (1994): 49–67.

Klarsfeld, Serge. *Vichy—Auschwitz: Die Zusammenarbeit der deutschen und französischen Behörden bei der "Endlösung der Judenfrage" in Frankreich.* Nördlingen, 1989.

Klee, Ernst. *Was sie taten—Was sie wurden. Ärzte, Juristen und andere Beteiligte am Kranken- oder Judenmord.* Frankfurt am Main, 1986.

Klee, Ernst. *Persilscheine und falsche Pässe. Wie die Kirchen den Nazis halfen.* Frankfurt am Main, 1991.

Kleßmann, Christoph. *Die doppelte Staatsgründung. Deutsche Geschichte 1945–1955.* Bonn, 1982, 2nd ed. 1991.

Kleßmann, Christoph. *Zwei Staaten, eine Nation. Deutsche Geschichte 1955–1970.* Bonn, 1988.

Kleßmann, Christoph. "Das Problem der doppelten 'Vergangenheitsbewältigung.' " In *Die Neue Gesellschaft* 38 (1991): 1099–105.

Klingenstein, Grete. "Über Herkunft und Verwendung des Wortes 'Vergangenheitsbewältigung.' " In *Geschichte und Gegenwart* 4 (1988): 301–12.

Klönne, Arno. *Rechts-Nachfolge. Risiken des deutschen Wesens nach 1945.* Cologne, 1990.

Knigge-Tesche, Renate, Peter Reif-Spirek, and Bodo Ritscher, eds. *Internierungspraxis in Ost- und Westdeutschland nach 1945: Eine Fachtagung.* Erfurt, 1993.

Knütter, Hans-Helmuth. *Ideologien des Rechtsradikalismus im Nachkriegsdeutschland. Eine Studie über die Nachwirkungen des Nationalsozialismus.* Bonn, 1961.

Koch, Diether. *Heinemann und die Deutschlandfrage.* Munich, 1972.

Koch, Oskar W. *Dachau and Landsberg.* Vol. 1, *Justizmord—oder Mord-Justiz.* Vol. 2, *Amerikas Schande.* Witten, 1974, 1976.

Koebner, Thomas. "Die Schuldfrage: Vergangenheitsverweigerung und Lebenslügen in der Diskussion 1945–1949." In *Deutschland nach Hitler: Zukunftspläne im Exil und aus der Besatzungszeit 1939–1949,* ed. Thomas Koebner, Gert Sautermeister, and Sigrid Schneider, pp. 301–29. Opladen, 1987.

Köhler, Henning. *Adenauer: Eine politische Biographie.* Frankfurt am Main, and Berlin, 1994.

Königseder, Angelika, and Juliane Wetzel. *Lebensmut im Wartesaal. Die jüdischen DPs (Displaced Persons) im Nachkriegsdeutschland.* Frankfurt am Main, 1994.

Koerfer, Daniel. "Ernst von Weizsäcker im Dritten Reich: Ein deutscher Offizier und Diplomat zwischen Verstrickung und Selbsttäuschung." In *Schatten der Vergangenheit: Impulse zur Historisierung des Nationalsozialismus,* ed. Uwe Backes, Eckhard Jesse, and Rainer Zitelmann, pp. 375–402. Frankfurt am Main and Berlin, 1990.

Kogon, Eugen. "Gericht und Gewissen." In *Frankfurter Hefte* 1 (1946): 25–37.

Kogon, Eugen. "Das Recht auf den politischen Irrtum." In *Frankfurter Hefte* 2 (1947): 641–55.

Kogon, Eugen. "Man braucht Deutschland—auch deutsche Soldaten?" In *Frankfurter Hefte* 4 (1949): 18–33.

Kogon, Eugen. "Das Gespenst der deutschen Remilitarisierung." In *Frankfurter Hefte* 5 (1950): 2f.

[Kogon, Eugen]. "Der Fall Hedler." In. *Frankfurter Hefte* 5 (1950):426–30.

Kogon, Eugen. "Die Entscheidung auf Leben und Tod." In *Frankfurter Hefte* 5 (1950): 907–13.

Kogon, Eugen. "Die Wiederkehr des Nationalsozialismus." In *Frankfurter Hefte* 6 (1951): 377–82.

Kogon, Eugen. "Die Aussichten der Restauration: Über die gesellschaftlichen Grundlagen der Zeit." In *Frankfurter Hefte* 7 (1952): 165–77.

Kogon, Eugen. "Beinahe mit dem Rücken an der Wand." In *Frankfurter Hefte* 9 (1954): 641–45.

Kordt, Erich. *Nicht aus den Akten ... Die Wilhelmstraße in Frieden und Krieg. Erlebnisse, Begegnungen und Eindrücke 1928–1945.* Stuttgart, 1950.

Kosthorst, Erich. *Jakob Kaiser: Bundesminister für gesamtdeutsche Fragen 1949–1957.* Stuttgart, 1972.

Kraus, Herbert, ed. *Die im Braunschweiger Remerprozeß erstatteten moraltheologischen und historischen Gutachten nebst Urteil.* Hamburg, 1953.

Krausnick, Helmut, and Hans-Heinrich Wilhelm. *Die Truppe des Weltanschauungskrieges. Die Einsatzgruppen der Sicherheitspolizei und des SD 1938–1942.* Stuttgart, 1981.

Kreile, Reinhold. "Eine deutsche Magna Charta der Selbstbesinnung." In *Frankfurter Hefte* 9 (1954): 83–91.

Kröger, Ullrich. "Die Ahndung von NS-Verbrechen vor westdeutschen Gerichten und ihre Rezeption in der deutschen Öffentlichkeit 1958 bis 1965 unter besonderer Berücksichtigung von 'Spiegel,' 'Stern,' 'Zeit,' 'SZ,' 'FAZ,' 'Welt,' 'Bild,' 'Hamburger Abendblatt,' 'NZ' und 'Neuem Deutschland.' " Diss. Hamburg, 1973.

Kruse, Falko. "NS-Prozesse und Restauration. Zur justiziellen Verfolgung von NS-Gewaltverbrechen in der Bundesrepublik." In *Der Unrechtsstaat: Recht und Justiz im Nationalsozialismus*, pp. 164–89. Frankfurt am Main, 1979.

Kruse, Hans. *Besatzungsmacht und Freiheitsrechte: Rechtsgutachten nebst Anhang.* Göttingen, 1953.

Küpper, Jost. *Die Kanzlerdemokratie: Voraussetzungen, Strukturen und Änderungen des Regierungsstiles in der Ära Adenauer.* Frankfurt am Main, Bern, and New York, 1985.

Laage, Clea. "Die Auseinandersetzung um den Begriff des gesetzlichen Unrechts nach 1945." In *Kritische Justiz* 22 (1989): 409–32.

Laak, Dirk van. *Gespräche in der Sicherheit des Schweigens. Carl Schmitt in der politischen Geistesgeschichte der frühen Bundesrepublik.* Berlin, 1993.

Langbein, Hermann. *Im Namen des deutschen Volkes. Zwischenbilanz der Prozesse wegen nationalsozialistischer Verbrechen.* Vienna, 1963.

Langhorst, Wolfgang. "Berufsbeamtentum und Art. 131 Geschichte und Gesellschaft. Die Rückkehr der NS-Beamtenschaft in die obersten Bundesbehörden." In *Vorgänge* 3 (1989): 60–67.

Large, David Clay. " 'A Gift to the German Future?' The Anti-Nazi Resistance Movement and the West German Rearmament." In *German Studies Review* 7 (1984): 499–529.

Large, David Clay. "Reckoning Without the Past: The HIAG of the Waffen-SS and the Politics of Rehabilitation in the Bonn Republic, 1950–1961." In *Journal of Modern History* 59 (1987): 79–113.

Large, David Clay. " 'A Beacon in the German Darkness': The Anti-Nazi Resistance Legacy in West German Politics." In *Journal of Modern History* 64 (1992): 173–86.

Laurien, Ingrid. "Die Verarbeitung von Nationalsozialismus und Krieg in politisch-kulturellen Zeitschriften der Westzonen 1945–1949." In *Geschichte in Wissenschaft und Unterricht* 39 (1988): 220–37.

Laurien, Ingrid. *Politisch-kulturelle Zeitschriften in den Westzonen 1945–1949. Ein Beitrag zur politischen Kultur der Nachkriegszeit.* Frankfurt am Main, 1991.

Lemke, Michael. "Kampagnen gegen Bonn. Die Systemkrise der DDR und die West-Propaganda der SED 1960–1963." In *Vierteljahrshefte für Zeitgeschichte* 41 (1993): 153–74.

Lemke, Michael. "Instrumentalisierter Antifaschismus und SED-Kampagnenpolitik im deutschen Sonderkonflikt 1960–1968." In *Die geteilte Vergangenheit: Zum Umgang mit Nationalsozialismus und Widerstand in beiden deutschen Staaten,* ed. Jürgen Danyel, pp. 61–86. Berlin, 1995.

[Lenz]. *Im Zentrum der Macht: Das Tagebuch von Staatssekretär Lenz, 1951–1953.* Ed. Klaus Gotto, Hans-Otto Kleinmann, and Reinhard Schreiner. Düsseldorf, 1989.

Lepsius, M. Rainer. "Das Erbe des Nationalsozialismus und die politische Kultur der Nachfolgestaaten des 'Großdeutschen Reiches.' " In *Demokratie in Deutschland: Soziologisch-historische Konstellationsanalysen,* ed. M. Rainer Lepsius, pp. 229–45. Ausgewählte Aufsätze. Göttingen, 1993.

Lessing, Holger. *Der erste Dachauer Prozeß (1945 and 46).* Baden-Baden, 1993.

Leverkuehn, Paul. *Verteidigung Manstein.* Hamburg, 1950.

Lewis, Rand C. *A Nazi Legacy: Right-Wing Extremism in Postwar Germany.* New York, Westport, and London, 1991.

Lichtenstein, Heiner. "NS-Prozesse—viel zu spät und ohne System." In *Aus Politik und Zeitgeschichte* 9–10 (1981): 3–13.

Lichtenstein, Heiner. "Robert M. W. Kempner." In *Gegen Barbarei: Essays Robert M. W. Kempner zu Ehren,* ed. Rainer Eisfeld and Ingo Müller, pp. 20–34. Frankfurt am Main, 1989.

Löwenthal, Richard, and Hans-Peter Schwarz, eds. *Die Zweite Republik: 25 Jahre Bundesrepublik Deutschland—eine Bilanz.* Stuttgart, 1974.

Luchsinger, Fred. *Bericht über Bonn. Deutsche Politik 1955–1965.* Zurich and Stuttgart, 1966.

Lübbe, Hermann. "Verdrängung: Über ein Verhältnis zum deutschen Vergangenheitsverhältnis." In *Der Monat* 2 (1979): 55–65.

Lübbe, Hermann. "Der Nationalsozialismus im deutschen Nachkriegsbewußtsein." In *Historische Zeitschrift* 236 (1983): 579–99.

Lüdtke, Alf. " 'Coming to Terms with the Past': Illusions of Remembering, Ways of Forgetting Nazism in West Germany." In *Journal of Modern History* 65 (1993): 542–72.

Lummert, Günther. *Die Strafverfahren gegen Deutsche im Ausland wegen "Kriegsverbrechens." Rechtsgutachten mit Gesetzestexten.* Hamburg, 1949.

Maassen, Hermann, and Elmar Hucko. *Thomas Dehler, der erste Bundesminister der Justiz.* Cologne, 1977.

Maier, Charles S. "The Unmasterable Past: History, Holocaust, and German National Identity." Cambridge, Mass., and London, 1988.

Maier, Klaus A. "Die Internationalen Auseinandersetzungen um die Westintegration der Bundesrepublik Deutschland und um ihre Bewaffnung im Rahmen der Europäischen Verteidigungsgemeinschaft." In *Anfänge westdeutscher Sicherheitspolitik 1945–1956,* ed. Militärgeschichtlichen Forschungsamt, vol. 2, pp. 1–234. Munich and Vienna, 1982, 1990.

Maier, Reinhold. *Erinnerungen 1948–1953.* Tübingen, 1966.

Manstein, Erich von. *Lost Victories.* Ed. and trans. Anthony G. Powell, foreword by B. H. Lidell Hart, introduction by Martin Blumenson. Chicago, 1958.

Marcuse, Harold. *The Politics of Memory: Nazi Crimes and Identity in West Germany, 1945–1990.* Unpublished ms., 1993.

Marcuse, Harold. *Legacies of Dachau: The Uses and Abuses of a Concentration Camp, 1933–2001.* Cambridge, 2001.

Marten, Heinz Georg. *Die unterwanderte FDP: Politischer Liberalismus in Niedersachsen—Aufbau und Entwicklung der Freien Demokratischen Partei 1945–1955.* Göttingen, Frankfurt am Main, and Zurich, 1978.

Marten, Heinz Georg. *Der Niedersächsische Ministersturz. Protest und Widerstand der Georg August Universität Göttingen gegen den Kultusminister Schlüter im Jahre 1955.* Göttingen, 1987.

Marxen, Klaus. *Rechtliche Grenzen der Amnestie.* Heidelberg, 1984.

Maugham, Viscount. *U.N.O. and War Crimes.* London, 1951.

Maurach, Reinhart. *Die Kriegsverbrecherprozesse gegen deutsche Gefangene in der Sowjetunion.* Hamburg, 1950.

McCloy, John J. "Report on Progress." In *HICOG Information Bulletin* (February 1950): 15–17.

Meding, Holger M. *Flucht vor Nürnberg? Deutsche und österreichische Einwanderung in Argentinien 1945–1955.* Cologne, Weimar, and Vienna, 1992.

Mehlhausen, Joachim. "Die Wahrnehmung von Schuld in der Geschichte. Ein Beitrag über frühe Stimmen in der Schulddiskussion nach 1945." In *... und über Barmen hinaus. Studien zur Kirchlichen Zeitgeschichte.* Göttingen, 1995.

Meier, Andreas. *Hermann Ehlers: Leben in Kirche und Politik.* Bonn, 1991.

Meier, Christian. *40 Jahre nach Auschwitz. Deutsche Geschichtserinnerung heute.* Munich, 1987.

Meiser, Hans. *Der Nationalsozialismus und seine Bewältigung im Spiegel der Lizenzpresse der Britischen Besatzungszone von 1946 bis 1949.* Osnabrück, 1980.

Mende, Erich. *Die neue Freiheit, 1945–1961.* Munich and Berlin, 1984.

Mendelsohn, John. "War Criminal Trials and Clemency in Germany and Japan." In *Americans as Proconsuls: United States Military Government in Germany and Japan, 1944–1952,* ed. Robert Wolfe, pp. 226–30, 247–59. Carbondale, Ill., and Edwardsville, Ill., 1984.

Merritt, Anna J. "Germans and American Denazification." In *Communication in International Politics,* ed. Richard L. Merritt, pp. 361–83. Urbana, Ill., Chicago, and London, 1972.

Merritt, Anna J., and Richard L.Merritt, eds. *Public Opinion in Occupied Germany: The OMGUS Surveys, 1945–1949.* Urbana, Ill., Chicago, and London, 1970.

Merritt, Anna J., and Richard L.Merritt, eds. *Public Opinion in Semisovereign Germany: The HICOG Surveys, 1949–1955.* Urbana, Ill., Chicago, and London, 1980.

Merritt, Richard L. "Digesting the Past: Views of National Socialism in Semisovereign Germany." In *Societas* 7 (1977): 93–119.

Merseburger, Peter. *Der schwierige Deutsche. Kurt Schumacher. Eine Biographie.* Stuttgart, 1995.

Merten, Detlef. *Rechtsstaatlichkeit und Gnade.* Berlin, 1978.

Messenger, Charles. *Hitler's Gladiator: The Life and Times of Oberstgruppenführer and Panzergeneral-Oberst der Waffen-SS Sepp Dietrich.* London, 1988.

Meyer, Georg. "Zur Situation der deutschen militärischen Führungsschicht im Vorfeld des westdeutschen Verteidigungsbeitrages 1945–1950 and 51." In *Anfänge westdeutscher Sicherheitspolitik 1945–1956,* ed. Militärgeschichtlichen Forschungsamt, vol. 1, pp. 577–736. Munich and Vienna, 1982, 1990.

Meyer, Georg. "Soldaten ohne Armee. Berufssoldaten im Kampf um Standesehre und Versorgung." In *Von Stalingrad zur Währungsreform: Zur Sozialgeschichte des Umbruchs in Deutschland,* ed. Martin Broszat, Klaus-Dietmar Henke, and Hans Woller, pp. 683–750. Munich, 1988.

Meyers, Peter. "Vom 'Antifaschismus' zur Tendenzwende: Ein Überblick über die Behandlung des Nationalsozialismus in der historisch-politischen Bildung seit 1945." In *Der Nationalsozialismus in der historisch-politischen Bildung,* ed. Peter Meyers and Dieter Riesenberger, pp. 43–63. Göttingen, 1979.

Meyn, Hermann. *Die Deutsche Partei. Entwicklung und Problematik einer national-konservativen Rechtspartei nach 1945.* Düsseldorf, 1965.

Middleton, Drew. *Where Has Last July Gone? Memoirs.* New York, 1973.

Milan, Max. *Hitler heute. Politik und Propaganda der Nationalsozialisten in der Bundesrepublik.* Frankfurt am Main, [after 1951].

Mitchell, Maria. *Materialism and Secularism: CDU Politicians and National Socialism, 1945–1949.* In *Journal of Modern History* 67 (1995): 278–308.

Mitscherlich, Alexander, and Margarete Mitscherlich. *The Inability to Mourn. Principles of Collective Behavior.* Trans. Beverley R. Placzek. New York, 1975.

Moeller, Robert G. *War Stories: The Search for a Usable Past in the Federal Republic of Germany.* Berkeley, Los Angeles, London, 2001.

Mohler, Armin. *Vergangenheitsbewältigung: Von der Läuterung zur Manipulation.* Stuttgart-Degerloch, 1968.

Mohler, Armin. *Der Nasenring: Im Dickicht der Vergangenheitsbewältigung.* Essen, 1989.

Mommsen, Hans. "Die Last der Vergangenheit." In *Stichworte zur "Geistigen Situation der Zeit,"* ed. Jürgen Habermas, pp. 164–83. Frankfurt am Main, 1979.

Mommsen, Hans. "Die Kontinuität der Institution des Berufsbeamtentums und die Rekonstruktion der Demokratie in Westdeutschland." In *Die Wiederherstellung des Berufsbeamtentums nach 1945: Geburtsfehler oder Stützpfeiler der Demokratiegründung in Westdeutschland?* ed. Friedrich Gerhard Schwegmann, pp. 65–79. Düsseldorf, 1986.

Mommsen, Hans. "Die Geschichte des deutschen Widerstands im Lichte der neueren Forschung." In *Aus Politik und Zeitgeschichte* 50 (1986): 3–18.

[Morgenschweis, Karl.] " 'Für Wahrheit und Gerechtigkeit': Das Bekenntnis des Monsignore Morgenschweis." 9 Teile. In *Der Freiwillige* 18 and 19 (1972–73): Hefte 11–7.

Morsey, Rudolf. *Die Bundesrepublik Deutschland. Entstehung und Entwicklung bis 1969.* Munich, 1987.

Morsey, Rudolf, ed. *Verwaltungsgeschichte: Aufgaben, Zielsetzungen, Beispiele.* Berlin, 1977.

Morsey, Rudolf, ed. *Konrad Adenauer und die Gründung der Bundesrepublik Deutschland.* Stuttgart and Zurich, 1979.

Mosse, George L. *Fallen Soldiers: Reshaping the Memory of the World Wars.* New York and Oxford, 1990.

Müller, Ingo. *Furchtbare Juristen: Die unbewältigte Vergangenheit unserer Justiz.* Munich, 1987.

Müller, Richard Matthias. *Normal-Null und die Zukunft der deutschen Vergangenheitsbewältigung: Ein Essay.* Schernfeld, 1994.

Müller-Hohagen, Jürgen. *Verleugnet, verdrängt, verschwiegen: Die seelischen Auswirkungen der Nazizeit.* Munich, 1988.

Müller-Meiningen, Ernst, Jr. *Die Parteigenossen. Betrachtungen und Vorschläge zur Lösung des "Naziproblems."* Munich, 1946.

Müller-Meiningen, Ernst, Jr. *Das Jahr Tausendundeins: Eine deutsche Wende?* Basel and Frankfurt am Main, 1987.

Müller-Schwefe. *Unbewältigte Vergangenheit: Vom Gestern im Heute.* Wuppertal-Barmen, 1958.

Murphy, Robert. *Diplomat Amongst Warriors.* Garden City, N.Y., 1964.

Im Namen des Deutschen Volkes: Justiz und Nationalsozialismus. Katalog zur Ausstellung des Bundesministers der Justiz. Cologne, 1989.

Nathans, Eli. *Franz Schlegelberger.* Baden-Baden, 1990.

Naumann, Werner. *Nau-Nau gefährdet das Empire?* Göttingen, 1953.

Nemitz, Kurt. "Das Regime der Mitläufer." In *Die Neue Gesellschaft* 2 (1955): 39–45.

Neuhäusler, Johann. *Kreuz und Hakenkreuz: Der Kampf des National-sozialismus gegen die katholische Kirche und der Widerstand.* Munich, 1946.

Neuhäusler, Johann. *Wie war das im KZ Dachau? Ein Versuch, der Wahrheit näherzukommen.* Munich, 1968.

Neumann, Erich Peter, and Elisabeth Noelle. *Antworten: Politik im Kraftfeld der öffentlichen Meinung.* Allensbach, 1954.

Neumann, Franz. *Der Block der Heimatvertriebenen und Entrechteten: Ein Beitrag zur Geschichte und Struktur einer politischen Interessenpartei.* Meisenheim, 1968.

Niclauß, Karlheinz. *Demokratiegründung in Westdeutschland: Die Entstehung der Bundesrepublik 1945–1949.* Munich, 1974.

Niethammer, Lutz. *Angepaßter Faschismus: Politische Praxis der NPD.* Frankfurt am Main, 1969.

Niethammer, Lutz. *Entnazifizierung in Bayern: Säuberung und Rehabilitierung unter amerikanischer Besatzung.* Frankfurt am Main, 1972.

Niethammer, Lutz. "Zum Verhältnis von Reform und Rekonstruktion in der US-Zone am Beispiel der Neuordnung des öffentlichen Dienstes." In *Vierteljahrshefte für Zeitgeschichte* 21 (1973): 177–88.

Niethammer, Lutz. Zum Wandel der Kontinuitätsdiskussion. In *Westdeutschland,* ed. Ludolf Herbst, pp. 65–83. Munich, 1986.

Niethammer, Lutz, ed. *"Hinterher merkt man, daß es richtig war, daß es schiefgegangen ist": Nachkriegs-Erfahrungen im Ruhrgebiet.* Berlin and Bonn, 1983.

Niethammer, Lutz, and Plato, Alexander von, eds. *"Wir kriegen jetzt andere Zeiten": Auf der Suche nach der Erfahrung des Volkes in nach-faschistischen Ländern.* Berlin and Bonn, 1985.

Noelle, Elisabeth, and Neumann, Erich Peter, eds. *Jahrbuch der öffentlichen Meinung 1947–1955* (1957, 1958–1964). *Allensbach 1956* (1957, 1965).

Nolte, Ernst. *Die Deutschen und ihre Vergangenheiten: Erinnern und Vergessen von der Reichsgründung bis heute.* Berlin and Frankfurt am Main, 1995.

Norden, Albert. *Ereignisse und Erlebtes.* Berlin 1981.

Obenaus, Herbert. "Geschichtsstudium und Universität nach der Katastrophe von 1945: das Beispiel Göttingen." In *Geschichte als Möglichkeit. Über die Chancen von Demokratie,* ed. Karsten Rudolph and Christl Wickert. Essen, 1995.

Office of the U.S. High Commissioner for Germany, ed. Report on Germany: September 1949–July 1952. 11 vols. Washington, D.C., 1949–1952.

Oppitz, Ulrich-Dieter. *Strafverfahren und Strafvollstreckung bei NS-Gewaltverbrechen: Dargestellt an Hand von 542 rechtskräftigen Urteilen deutscher Gerichte aus der Zeit von 1946—1975.* Ulm, 1979.

Ostendorf, Heribert. "Die—widersprüchlichen—Auswirkungen der Nürnberger Prozesse auf die westdeutsche Justiz." In *Strafgerichte gegen Menschheitsverbrechen. Zum Völkerrecht 50 Jahre nach den Nürnberger Prozessen,* ed. Gerd Hankel and Gerhard Stuby, pp. 73–97. Hamburg, 1995.

Ott, Gabriel. *Thomas Dehler.* Hof an der Saale, 1985.

Otto, Bernd. *Die Aufarbeitung der Epoche des Nationalsozialismus im fiktionalen Jugendbuch der Bundesrepublik Deutschland von 1945 bis 1980: Ein politikwissenschaftlicher Beitrag zur Jugendbuchforschung.* Frankfurt am Main and Bern, 1981.

Paget, Reginald T. *Manstein, His Campaigns, and His Trial.* Foreword by Lord Hankey. London, 1951.

Pampel, Bert. "Was bedeutet 'Aufarbeitung der Vergangenheit'? Kann man aus der 'vergangenheitsbewältigung' nach 1945 für die 'Aufarbeitung' nach 1989 Lehren ziehen?" In *Aus Politik und Zeitgeschichte* 1–2 (1995): 27–38.

Der Parlamentarische Rat 1948–1949. *Akten und Protokolle.* Vol. 2, *Der Verfassungskonvent auf Herrenchiemsee.* Ed. Peter Bucher. Boppard, 1981.

Parlamentarischer Rat. *Verhandlungen des Hauptausschusses.* Bonn, 1948–49.

Perels, Joachim. "Die Restauration der Rechtslehre nach 1945." In *Kritische Justiz* 17 (1984): 359–79.

Perels, Joachim. "Die schrittweise Rechtfertigung der NS-Justiz. Der Huppenkothen-Prozeß." In *Politik—Verfassung—Gesellschaft: Traditionslinien und Entwicklungsperspektiven,* ed. Peter Nahamowitz and Stefan Breuer, pp. 51–60. Baden-Baden, 1995.

Perels, Joachim. "Amnestien für NS-Täter in der Bundesrepublik." In *Kritische Justiz* 28 (1995): 382–89.

Perels, Joachim. "Die Bewahrung der bürgerlichen Gesellschaft in der Zeit ihres tiefsten Sturzes: Carl Schmitts Positionen nach 1945." In *Recht und Ideologie,* ed. Gerhard Haney, Werner Maihofer, and Gerhard Sprenger, pp. 420–41. Freiburg and Berlin, 1996.

Persico, Joseph E. *Nuremberg: Infamy on Trial.* New York, 1994.

Piontkowitz, Heribert. *Anfänge westdeutscher Außenpolitik: Das Deutsche Büro für Friedensfragen.* Stuttgart, 1978.

Plack, Arno. *Wie oft wird Hitler noch besiegt?* Düsseldorf, 1982.

Plack, Arno. *Hitlers langer Schatten.* Munich, 1993.

Plato, Alexander von. "Eine zweite 'Entnazifizierung'? Zur Verarbeitung politischer Umwälzungen in Deutschland 1945 und 1989." In *Wendezeiten—Zeitenwände: Zur "Entnazifizierung" und "Entstalinisierung,"* ed. Rainer Eckert, Alexander von Plato, and Jörn Schütrumpf, pp. 7–31. Hamburg, 1991.

Pohl, Hans, ed. *Adenauers Verhältnis zu Wirtschaft und Gesellschaft.* Bonn, 1992.

Pollock, Friedrich. *Gruppenexperiment: Ein Studienbericht.* Frankfurt am Main, 1955.

Posser, Diether. *Anwalt im Kalten Krieg: Ein Stück deutscher Geschichte in politischen Prozessen 1951–1968.* Munich, 1991.

Pross, Christian. *Wiedergutmachung: Der Kleinkrieg gegen die Opfer.* Frankfurt am Main, 1988.

Die Protokolle des Rates der Evangelischen Kirche in Deutschland. Vol. 1, *1945 and 1946.* Ed. Carsten Nicolaisen and Nora Andrea Schulze. Göttingen, 1995 [EKD-Protokolle].

Der Prozeß gegen die Hauptkriegsverbrecher vor dem Internationalen Militärgerichtshof: 14. November 1945—Oktober 1946. 41 vols. Nürnberg, 1947–1949.

Quartisch, Helmut. "Über Bürgerkriegs- und Feind-Amnestien." In *Der Staat* 31 (1992): 389–418.

Quartisch, Helmut. "Theorie der Vergangenheitsbewältigung." In *Der Staat* 31 (1992): 519–51.

Raschhofer, Hermann. *Der Fall Oberländer: Eine vergleichende Rechtsanalyse der Verfahren in Pankow und Bonn.* Tübingen, 1962.

Ratz, Michael. *Die Justiz und die Nazis: Zur Strafverfolgung von Nazismus und Neonazismus seit 1945.* Frankfurt am Main, 1979.

Rauh-Kühne, Cornelia. "Die Entnazifizierung und die deutsche Gesellschaft." In *Archiv für Sozialgeschichte* 35 (1995): 35–70.

Rauschenbach, Brigitte, ed. *Erinnern, Wiederholen, Durcharbeiten: Zur Psycho-Analyse deutscher Wenden.* Berlin, 1992.

Rautenberg, Hans-Jürgen. "Zur Standortbestimmung für künftige deutsche Streitkräfte." In *Anfänge westdeutscher Sicherheitspolitik 1945–1956,* ed. Militärgeschichtlichen Forschungsamt, vol. 1, pp. 737–879. Munich and Vienna, 1982, 1990.

Rautenberg, Hans-Jürgen, and Norbert Wiggershaus. "Die 'Himmeroder Denkschrift' vom Oktober 1950: Politische und militärische Überlegungen für einen Beitrag der Bundesrepublik Deutschland zur westeuropäischen Verteidigung." In *Militärgeschichtliche Mitteilungen* 21 (1977): 135–206.

Renger, Annemarie. "Juden und Israel im Deutschen Bundestag." In *Sternstunden des Parlaments,* ed. Rainer Barzel, pp. 139–62. Heidelberg, 1989.

Reichel, Peter. "Zwischen Dämonisierung und Verharmlosung: Das NS-Bild und seine politische Funktion in den 50er Jahren. Eine Skizze." In *Modernisierung im Wiederaufbau: Die westdeutsche Gesellschaft der 50er Jahre,* ed. Axel Schildt and Arnold Sywottek, pp. 679–92. Bonn, 1993.

Reichel, Peter. *Politik mit der Erinnerung. Gedächtnisorte im Streit um die nationalsozialistische Vergangenheit.* Munich and Vienna, 1995.

Reichel, Peter. *Vergangenheitsbewältigung in Deutschland. Die Auseinandersetzung mit der NS-Diktatur von 1945 bis heute.* Munich, 2001.

Richter, Hans Werner, ed. *Bestandsaufnahme. Eine deutsche Bilanz 1962. Sechsunddreißig Beiträge deutscher Wissenschaftler, Schriftsteller und Publizisten.* Munich, Vienna, and Basel, 1962.

Riggert, Ernst. "Zur Lage in den deutschen Soldatenbünden." In *Gewerkschaftliche Monatshefte* 4 (1953): 39–44.

Riggert, Ernst. "Neonazismus in Deutschland: Wirklichkeit und potentielle Gefahr." In *Gewerkschaftliche Monatshefte* 4 (1953): 129–36.

Riggert, Ernst. "Bundestagswahlen und ehemalige Nationalsozialisten." In *Gewerkschaftliche Monatshefte* 4 (1953): 459–62.

Rodnick, David. *Postwar Germans: An Anthropologist's Account.* New Haven, Conn., 1948.

Roellecke, Gerd. "Der Nationalsozialismus als politisches Layout der Bundesrepublik Deutschland." In *Der Staat* 28 (1989): 505–24.

Roloff, Ernst-August. " 'Gewissenhafte Pflichterfüllung zum Wohle der Allgemeinheit?' Ein subjektiver Rück- und Ausblick auf 40 Jahre politische Bildung in der Bundesrepublik Deutschland." In *Aus Politik und Zeitgeschichte* 51 (1988): 3–12.

Rosenthal, Gabriele, ed. *"Als der Krieg kam, hatte ich mit Hitler nichts mehr zu tun." Zur Gegenwärtigkeit des "Dritten Reiches" in Biographien.* Opladen, 1990.

Rothenspieler, Friedrich Wilhelm. *Der Gedanke einer Kollektivschuld in juristischer Sicht.* Berlin, 1982.

Ruck, Michael. "Administrative Eliten in Demokratie und Diktatur. Beamtenkarrieren in Baden und Württemberg von den zwanziger Jahren bis in die Nachkriegszeit." In *Regionale Eliten zwischen Diktatur und Demokratie,* ed. Cornelia Rauh-Kühne and Michale Ruck, pp. 37–69. Baden und Württemberg, 1930–1952; Munich, 1993.

Rückerl, Adalbert. "Probleme der Verfolgung nationalsozialistischer Gewaltverbrechen aus der Sicht der Ludwigsburger Zentralen Stelle." In *Rechtliche und politische Aspekte der NS-Verbrecherprozesse,* ed. Peter Schneider and Hermann J. Meyer, pp. 62–73. Mainz, 1968.

Rückerl, Adalbert. *Die Strafverfolgung von NS-Verbrechen 1945–1978: Eine Dokumentation.* Heidelberg and Karlsruhe, 1979.

Rückerl, Adalbert. "Vergangenheitsbewältigung mit Mitteln der Justiz." In *Aus Politik und Zeitgeschichte* 43 (1982): 11–25.

Rückerl, Adalbert. *NS-Verbrechen vor Gericht. Versuch einer Vergangenheitsbewältigung.* Heidelberg, 1984.

Rückerl, Adalbert, ed. *NS-Prozesse. Nach 25 Jahren Strafverfolgung: Möglichkeiten—Grenzen—Ergebnisse.* Karlsruhe, 1971.

Ruhl, Klaus-Jörg, ed. *"Mein Gott, was soll aus Deutschland werden?" Die Adenauer-Ära 1949–1963.* Munich, 1985.

Rupieper, Hermann Josef. *Der besetzte Verbündete. Die amerikanische Deutschlandpolitik 1949–1955.* Opladen, 1991.

Rupieper, Hermann Josef. *Die Wurzeln der westdeutschen Nachkriegsdemokratie. Der amerikanische Beitrag 1945–1952.* Opladen, 1993.

Sänger, Fritz, ed. *Die Volksvertretung. Handbuch des Deutschen Bundestages.* Stuttgart, 1949.

Salomon, Ernst von, Fragebogen. *The Questionnaire.* Trans. Constantine Fitz-Gibbon, preface by G. Rees. New York, 1955.

Sassin, Horst. *Liberale im Widerstand: Die Robinsohn-Strassmann-Gruppe 1934–1942.* Hamburg, 1993.

Schätzler, Johann-Georg. *Handbuch des Gnadenrechts: Eine systematische Darstellung mit den Vorschriften des Bundes und der Länder.* Munich, 1976.

Schelsky, Helmut. *Die skeptische Generation: Eine Soziologie der deutschen Jugend.* Düsseldorf and Cologne, 1957.

Schenck zu Schweinsberg, Krafft Freiherr von. "Die Soldatenverbände in der Bundesrepublik." In *Studien zur politischen und gesellschaftlichen Situation der Bundeswehr,* ed. Georg Picht, vol. 1, pp. 96–177. Witten and Berlin, 1965.

Schick, Christa. "Die Internierungslager." In *Von Stalingrad zur Währungsreform: Zur Sozialgeschichte des Umbruchs in Deutschland,* ed. Martin Broszat, Klaus-Dietmar Henke, and Hans Woller, pp. 301–25. Munich, 1988.

Schiffers, Reinhard. *Zwischen Bürgerfreiheit und Staatsschutz: Wiederherstellung und Neufassung des politischen Strafrechts in der Bundesrepublik Deutschland 1949–1951.* Düsseldorf, 1989.

Schiffers, Reinhard. "Grundlegung des strafrechtlichen Staatsschutzes in der Bundesrepublik Deutschland 1949–1951." In *Vierteljahrshefte für Zeitgeschichte* 38 (1990): 589–607.

Schildt, Axel. Gründerjahre. "Zur Entwicklung der westdeutschen Gesellschaft in der 'Ära Adenauer.' " In *Blätter für deutsche und internationale Politik* 34 (1989): 22–34.

Schildt, Axel. "Nachkriegszeit: Möglichkeiten und Probleme einer Periodisierung der westdeutschen Geschichte nach dem Zweiten Weltkrieg und ihrer Einordnung in die deutsche Geschichte des 20. Jahrhunderts." In *Geschichte in Wissenschaft und Unterricht* 44 (1993): 567–84.

Schildt, Axel. " 'Jetzt liegen alle großen Ordnungs- und Gesittungsmächte im Schutt': Die öffentliche Auseinandersetzung mit dem 'Dritten Reich' in Schleswig-Holstein nach 1945—unter besonderer Berücksichtigung von Stellungnahmen aus der Evangelisch-Lutherischen Kirche." In *Zeitschrift der Gesellschaft für Schleswig-Holsteinische Geschichte* 119 (1994).

Schildt, Axel. "Solidarisch mit der Schuld des Volkes: Die öffentliche Schulddebatte und das Integrationsangebot der Kirchen in Niedersachsen nach dem Zweiten Weltkrieg." In *Rechtsradikalismus in der politischen Kultur der Nachkriegszeit: Die verzögerte Normalisierung in Niedersachsen,* ed. Bernd Weisbrod, pp. 269–95. Hannover, 1995.

Schildt, Axel. *Moderne Zeiten: Freizeit, Massenmedien und "Zeitgeist" in der Bundesrepublik der 50er Jahre.* Hamburg, 1995.

Schildt, Axel, and Arnold Sywottek. " 'Wiederaufbau' und 'Modernisierung': Zur westdeutschen Gesellschaftsgeschichte in den fünfziger Jahren." In *Aus Politik und Zeitgeschichte* 6–7 (1989): 18–32.

Schildt, Axel, and Arnold Sywottek, eds. *Modernisierung im Wiederaufbau: Die westdeutsche Gesellschaft der 50er Jahre.* Bonn, 1993.

Schlumberger, Frank. *Das Adenauer-Bild in der politischen Publizistik 1949–1955: Die 'Frankfurter Allgemeine' als zeitgeschichtliche Quelle.* Frankfurt am Main, 1991.

Schmid, Carlo. *Erinnerungen.* Bern, 1979.

Schmidt, Ute. "Hitler ist tot und Ulbricht lebt: Die CDU, der Nationalsozialismus und der Holocaust." In *Schwieriges Erbe: Der Umgang mit
Nationalsozialismus und Antisemitismus in Österreich, der DDR und
der Bundesrepublik Deutschland,* ed. Werner Bergmann, Rainer Erb,
and Albert Lichtblau, pp. 65–101. Frankfurt am Main and New York,
1995.

Schmitt, Carl. *Glossarium. Aufzeichnungen der Jahre 1947–1951.* Ed. Eberhard Freiherr von Meden. Berlin, 1991.

Schmitt, Carl. *Das international-rechtliche Verbrechen des Angriffskrieges
und der Grundsatz "Nullum crimen, nulla poena sine lege."* Ed. Helmut
Quartisch. Berlin, 1994.

Schmollinger, Horst W. "Die Deutsche Partei." In *Parteien-Handbuch,* ed.
Richard Stöß, pp. 1025–111. Opladen, 1983.

Schmollinger, Horst W. "Die Sozialistische Reichspartei." In *Parteien-
Handbuch,* ed. Richard Stöß, pp. 2274–336. Opladen, 1983.

Schneider, Christian. "Denkmal Manstein: Psychogramm eines Befehls-
habers." In *Mittelweg* 36, no. 5 (1994): 23–36.

Schneider, Peter, and Hermann J. Meyer, eds. *Rechtliche und politische
Aspekte der NS-Verbrecherprozesse.* Mainz, 1968.

Schollwer, Wolfgang. *Liberale Opposition gegen Adenauer. Aufzeichnungen
1957–1961.* Ed. Monika Faßbender. Munich, 1991.

Schönhoven, Klaus. "Die diskreditierten Deutschen: Reden und Schweigen
über den Nationalsozialismus im Nachkriegsdeutschland." In *Mitteilungen. Gesellschaft der Freunde der Universität Mannheim* (April
1990): 13–20.

Schörken, Rolf. *Luftwaffenhelfer und Drittes Reich: Die Entstehung eines
politischen Bewußtseins.* Stuttgart, 1984.

Schornstheimer, Michael. *Bombenstimmung und Katzenjammer. Vergangenheitsbewältigung: Quick und Stern in den 50er Jahren.* Cologne, 1989.

Schrenck-Notzing, Caspar von. *Charakterwäsche: Die amerikanische
Besatzung in Deutschland und ihre Folgen.* Stuttgart, 1965.

Schröder, Hans-Jürgen. "Die Anfangsjahre der Bundesrepublik Deutschland: Eine amerikanische Bilanz 1954." In *Vierteljahrshefte für Zeitgeschichte* 37 (1989): 323–51.

Schubert, Klaus von. *Wiederbewaffnung und Westintegration. Die innere
Auseinandersetzung um die militärische und außenpolitische Orien-
tierung der Bundesrepublik 1950–1952.* Stuttgart, 1970.

Schubert, Klaus von, ed. *Sicherheitspolitik der Bundesrepublik Deutschland: Dokumentation 1945–1977.* 2 vols. Cologne, 1978, 1979.

Schüle, Erwin. "Die Justiz der Bundesrepublik und die Sühne nationalsozialistischen Unrechts." In *Vierteljahrshefte für Zeitgeschichte* 9
(1961): 440–43.

Schulze, Winfried. *Deutsche Geschichtswissenschaft nach 1945.* Munich,
1989.

Schwab-Felisch, Hans. *Leidenschaft und Augenmaß: Deutsche Paradoxien.* Ed. Olaf Haas. Munich and Vienna, 1993.

Schwabe, Klaus, and Rolf Reichardt, eds. *Gerhard Ritter: Ein politischer Historiker in seinen Briefen.* Boppard, 1984.

Schwan, Gesine. *Politik und Schuld. Die zerstörerische Macht des Schweigens.* Frankfurt am Main, 1997.

Schwartz, Thomas Alan. "Die Begnadigung deutscher Kriegsverbrecher: John J. McCloy und die Häftlinge von Landsberg." In *Vierteljahrshefte für Zeitgeschichte* 38 (1990): 375–414.

Schwartz, Thomas A. *America's Germany: John McCloy and the Federal Republic of Germany.* Cambridge, Mass., 1991.

Schwarz, Hans-Peter. *Vom Reich zur Bundesrepublik: Deutschland im Widerstreit der außenpolitischen Konzeptionen in den Jahren der Besatzungsherrschaft 1945–1949.* Stuttgart, 1980.

Schwarz, Hans-Peter. *Die Ära Adenauer.* Gründerjahre der Republik: 1949–1957. Epochenwechsel: 1957–1963. Stuttgart and Wiesbaden, 1981, 1983 (*Ära Adenauer I, II*).

Schwarz, Hans-Peter. "Modernisierung oder Restauration? Einige Vorfragen zur künftigen Sozialgeschichtsforschung über die Ära Adenauer." In *Rheinland-Westfalen im Industriezeitalter,* ed. Kurt Düwell and Wolfgang Köllmann, vol. 3, pp. 278–93. Wuppertal, 1984.

Schwarz, Hans-Peter. *Adenauer.* Der Aufstieg: 1876–1952. Der Staatsmann: 1952–1967. Stuttgart, 1986, 1991 (*Adenauer I, II*).

Schwarz, Hans-Peter. "Adenauers Kanzlerdemokratie und Regierungstechnik." In *Aus Politik und Zeitgeschichte* 1–2 (1989): 15–27.

Schwarz, Hans-Peter. "Die fünfziger Jahre als Epochenzäsur." In *Wege in die Zeitgeschichte,* ed. Jürgen Heideking, Gerhard Hufnagel, and Franz Knipping, pp. 473–96. Berlin and New York, 1989.

Schwarz, Hans-Peter. "Die ausgebliebene Katastrophe. Eine Problemskizze zur Geschichte der Bundesrepublik." In *Den Staat denken,* ed. Hermann Rudolph. Berlin, 1990.

Schwarz, Hans-Peter, ed. *Die Wiederherstellung des deutschen Kredits: Das Londoner Schuldenabkommen.* Stuttgart and Zurich, 1982.

Schwarz, Hans-Peter, ed. *Konrad Adenauers Regierungsstil.* Bonn, 1991.

Schwegmann, Friedrich Gerhard, ed. *Die Wiederherstellung des Berufsbeamtentums nach 1945: Geburtsfehler oder Stützpfeiler der Demokratiegründung in Westdeutschland?* Düsseldorf, 1986.

Schwibbert, Juliane. "Die Kölner Synagogenschmierereien Weihnachten 1959 und die Reaktionen in Politik und Öffentlichkeit." In *Geschichte in Cologne* 33 (1993): 73–96.

Der schwierige Weg zur Demokratie. Die Bundesrepublik vor 40 Jahren. Ed. der Landeszentrale für politische Bildung Nordrhein-Westfalen. Düsseldorf, 1990.

Segev, Tom. *The Seventh Million: The Israelis and the Holocaust.* Trans. Haim Watzman. New York, 2000.

454 SOURCES AND LITERATURE

Sérant, Paul. *Die politischen Säuberungen in Westeuropa am Ende des Zweiten Weltkrieges in Deutschland, Österreich, Belgien, Dänemark, Frankreich, Großbritannien, Italien, Luxemburg, Norwegen, den Niederlanden und der Schweiz.* Oldenburg and Hamburg, [1966].

Settel, Arthur, ed. *This Is Germany.* Introduction by General Lucius D. Clay. New York, 1950.

Shuster, George N. *The Ground I Walked On: Reflections of a College President.* New York, 1961.

Siepen, Heinz. "Wo stehen die ehemaligen Nationalsozialisten?" In *Nation Europa* 3, no. 4 (1953): 22–25.

Sigel, Robert. *Im Interesse der Gerechtigkeit: Die Dachauer Kriegsverbrecherprozesse 1945–1948.* Frankfurt am Main and New York, 1992.

Simpson, Christopher. *Blowback. America's Recruitment of Nazis and Its Effects on the Cold War.* New York, 1988.

Simpson, Christopher. "Die seinerzeitige Diskussion über die in Nürnberg zu verhandelnden Delikte." In *Strafgerichte gegen Menschheitsverbrechen. Zum Völkerrecht 50 Jahre nach den Nürnberger Prozessen,* Gerd Hankel and Gerhard Stuby, pp. 39–72. Hamburg, 1995.

Smith, Arthur L. *Die "Hexe" von Buchenwald: Der Fall Ilse Koch.* Cologne, 1983.

Smith, Arthur L. "Die deutschen Kriegsgefangenen und Frankreich." In *Vierteljahrshefte für Zeitgeschichte* 32 (1984): 103–21.

Smith, Arthur L. *Heimkehr aus dem Zweiten Weltkrieg: Die Entlassung der deutschen Kriegsgefangenen.* Stuttgart, 1985.

Smith, Bradley F. *Reaching Judgement at Nuremberg.* New York, 1977.

Smith, Bradley F. *The Road to Nuremberg.* New York, 1981.

Smith, Bradley F. *The American Road to Nuremberg: The Documentary Record 1944–1945.* Stanford, 1982.

Soell, Hartmut. *Fritz Erler: Eine politische Biographie.* 2 vols. Berlin and Bonn, 1976.

Söllner, Alfons. "Demokratie als Lernprozeß: Drei Stichworte zur Entwicklung der politischen Kultur in der Bundesrepublik Deutschland." In *Mittelweg* 36, no. 4 (1995): 84–95.

Söllner, Alfons, ed. *Zur Archäologie der Demokratie in Deutschland: Analysen politischer Emigranten im amerikanischen Geheimdienst.* Vol. 1, *1943–1945.* Vol. 2, *1946–1949.* Frankfurt am Main, 1982, 1986.

Sonnenhol, Gustav Adolf. *Untergang oder Übergang? Wider die deutsche Angst.* Stuttgart and Herford, 1984.

Sontheimer, Kurt. *Die Adenauer-Ära: Grundlegung der Bundesrepublik.* Munich, 1991.

Die SPD-Fraktion im Deutschen Bundestag: Sitzungsprotokolle 1949–1957. 2 vols. Ed. Petra Weber. Düsseldorf, 1993 (*SPD-Fraktionsprotokolle*).

Speidel, Hans. *Aus unserer Zeit: Erinnerungen.* Berlin, Frankfurt am Main, and Vienna, 1977.

Spotts, Frederic. *Kirchen und Politik in Deutschland.* Stuttgart 1976.

Steinbach, Peter. *Nationalsozialistische Gewaltverbrechen: Die Diskussion in der deutschen Öffentlichkeit nach 1945.* Berlin, 1981.

Steinbach, Peter. "Zur Auseinandersetzung mit nationalsozialistischen Gewaltverbrechen in der Bundesrepublik Deutschland: Ein Beitrag zur deutschen politischen Kultur nach 1945." In *Geschichte in Wissenschaft und Unterricht* 35 (1984): 65–85.

Steinbach, Peter. "Vergangenheit als Last und Chance: Vergangenheitsbewältigung in den 50er Jahren." In *Die Bundesrepublik wird souverän 1950–1955,* ed. Jürgen Weber, pp. 309–45. Munich, 1986.

Steinbach, Peter. "Mit der Vergangenheit konfrontiert: Vom Erkennen der NS-Verbrechen zur 'Wiedergutmachung.' " In *Tribüne* 97 (1986): 88–179.

Steinbach, Peter. "Die Zeitschrift Tribüne und die Vergangenheitsbewältigung: Zur angemessenen Auseinandersetzung mit der Geschichte." In *Tribüne* 101 (1987): 58–73.

Steinbach, Peter. "Nur äußerlich getilgt ... Vergangenheitsbewältigung zwischen 1945 und 1955." In *Der schwierige Weg zur Demokratie. Die Bundesrepublik vor 40 Jahren,* ed. der Landeszentrale für politische Bildung Nordrhein-Westfalen, pp. 115–44. Düsseldorf, 1990.

Steinbach, Peter. " 'Stachel im Fleisch der deutschen Nachkriegsgesellschaft': Die Deutschen und der Widerstand." In *Aus Politik und Zeitgeschichte* 28 (1994): 3–14.

Steinbach, Peter. "Vergangenheitsbewältigungen in vergleichender Perspektive. Politische Säuberung, Wiedergutmachung, Integration." In *Informationen,* ed. Historische Kommission zu Berlin. Beiheft 18 (1993).

Stephan, Cora, ed. *Wir Kollaborateure: Der Westen und die deutschen Vergangenheiten.* Reinbek, 1992.

Stern, Frank. "The historic Triangle: Occupiers, Germans, and Jews in Postwar Germany." In *Tel Aviver Jahrbuch für deutsche Geschichte* 19 (1990): 47–76.

Stern, Frank. *The Whitewashing of the Yellow Badge: Antisemitism and Philosemitism in Postwar Germany.* Trans. William Templer. Oxford and New York, 1992.

Stöß, Richard, ed. *Parteien-Handbuch: Die Parteien der Bundesrepublik Deutschland 1945–1980.* Opladen, 1983.

Stosch, Stefan. *Die Adenauer-Legion: Geheimauftrag Wiederbewaffnung.* Konstanz, 1994.

Strauß, Franz Josef. *Die Erinnerungen.* Berlin, 1989.

Strecker, Reinhard-Maria. *Dr. Hans Globke. Aktenauszüge—Dokumente.* Hamburg, 1961.

Streim, Alfred. "Zur Legende von der 'zweiten Schuld.' " In *Tribüne* 131 (1994): 129–42.

Streim, Alfred. "Der Umgang mit der Vergangenheit am Beispiel der Zentralen Stelle der Landesjustizverwaltungen zur Aufklärung nationalsozialistischer Verbrechen in Ludwigsburg." In *Formen des Widerstandes im Südwesten 1933–1945. Scheitern und Nachwirken,* ed. Thomas Schnabel, pp. 320–33. Ulm, 1994.

Sühl, Klaus, ed. *Vergangenheitsbewältigung 1945 und 1989: Ein unmöglicher Vergleich? Eine Diskussion.* Berlin, 1994.

Sulzberger, Cyrus L. *A Long Row of Candles: Memoirs and Diaries (1934–1954).* Toronto, 1969.

Tauber, Kurt P. *Beyond Eagle and Swastika: German Nationalism Since 1945.* 2 vols. Middletown, 1967.

Taylor, Telford. *Nuremberg Trials: War Crimes and International Law.* New York, 1949.

Taylor, Telford. *The Anatomy of the Nuremberg Trials: A Personal Memoir.* New York, 1992.

Tetens, Tete Harens. *The New Germany and the Old Nazis.* New York, 1961.

Thayer, Charles W. *Die unruhigen Deutschen.* Bern, Stuttgart, and Vienna, 1958.

Toyka-Seid, Christiane. "Gralshüter, Notgemeinschaft oder gesellschaftliche 'Pressure-Group'? Die Stiftung 'Hilfswerk 20. Juli 1944' im ersten Nachkriegsjahrzehnt." In *Der 20. Juli 1944: Bewertung und Rezeption des deutschen Widerstandes gegen das NS-Regime,* ed. Gerd R. Ueber-schär, pp. 157–69. Cologne, 1994.

Toyka-Seid, Christiane. " 'Nicht in die Lage versetzt, Erbauer eines friedlichen Deutschlands zu sein': Die Vereinigung der Verfolgten des Naziregimes (VVN) in Württemberg-Baden." In *Formen des Wider-standes im Südwesten 1933–1945. Scheitern und Nachwirken,* ed. Thomas Schnabel, pp. 270–83. Ulm, 1994.

Trials of War Criminals Before the Nuernberg Military Tribunals Under Control Council Law No. 10. October 1946—April 1949. 15 vols. Nürnberg, undated.

Truman, Harry. *Memoiren.* 2 vols. Stuttgart, 1956.

Tüngel, Richard, and Hans Rudolf Berndorff. *Auf dem Bauche sollst Du kriechen ... Deutschland unter den Besatzungsmächten.* Hamburg, 1958.

Turner, Ian D. "Denazification in the British Zone." In *Reconstruction in Post-War Germany: British Occupation Policy and the Western Zones, 1945–1955,* ed. Ian D. Turner, pp. 239–67. Oxford, New York, and Munich, 1989.

Ueberschär, Gerd R., ed. *Der 20. Juli 1944: Bewertung und Rezeption des deutschen Widerstandes gegen das NS-Regime.* Cologne, 1994.

Utley, Freda. *The High Cost of Vengeance.* Chicago, 1949.

Verhandlungen des Deutschen Bundestages: Stenographische Berichte und Drucksachen. Bonn, 1949ff. (BT-Berichte; BT-Drucksachen).

Zur Verjährung nationalsozialistischer Verbrechen: Dokumentation der par-lamentarischen Bewältigung des Problems. Ed. Deutscher Bundestag. Bonn, 1980.

Vogel, Georg. *Diplomat unter Hitler und Adenauer.* Düsseldorf and Vienna, 1969.

Volkmann, Hans-Erich. "Die innenpolitische Dimension Adenauerscher Sicherheitspolitik in der EVG-Phase." In *Anfänge westdeutscher Sicher-heitspolitik 1945–1956,* ed. Militärgeschichtlichen Forschungsamt, vol. 2, pp. 235–604. Munich and Vienna, 1982, 1990.

Volkmann, Hans-Erich, ed. *Ende des Dritten Reiches—Ende des Zweiten Weltkriegs: Eine perspektivische Rückschau*. Munich, 1995.

Vollnhals, Clemens. *Evangelische Kirche und Entnazifizierung, 1945–1949: Die Last der nationalsozialistischen Vergangenheit*. Munich, 1989.

Vollnhals, Clemens. "Die Hypothek des Nationalprotestantismus: Entnazifizierung und Strafverfolgung von NS-Verbrechern nach 1945." In *Geschichte und Gesellschaft* 18 (1992): 51–69.

Vollnhals, Clemens. "Zwischen Verdrängung und Aufklärung: Die Auseinandersetzung mit dem Holocaust in der frühen Bundesrepublik." In *Die Deutschen und die Judenverfolgung im Dritten Reich,* ed. Ursula Büttner, pp. 357–92. Hamburg, 1992.

Vollnhals, Clemens, ed. *Entnazifizierung: Politische Säuberung und Rehabilitierung in den vier Besatzungszonen 1945–1949*. Munich, 1991.

Wassermann, Rudolf. "Zur juristischen Bewertung des 20. Juli 1944: Der Braunschweiger Remer-Prozeß als Meilenstein der Nachkriegsgeschichte." In *Recht und Politik* 2 (1984): 68–80.

Wassermann, Rudolf. "Justiz und politische Kultur: Verfolgung nationalsozialistischer Gewaltverbrecher als Herausforderung für Rechtsprechung und Bewußtsein der Öffentlichkeit." In *Recht, Gewalt, Widerstand: Vorträge und Aufsätze,* ed. Rudolf Wassermann, pp. 9–35. Berlin, 1985.

Wassermann, Rudolf. "Vergangenheitsaufarbeitung nach 1945 und nach 1989." In *Jahrbuch Extremismus und Demokratie,* ed. Uwe Backes and Eckhard Jesse, pp. 29–50. Bonn, 1993.

Watt, Donald C. *Britain Looks to Germany: British Opinion and Policy Towards Germany Since 1945*. London, 1965.

Weber, Jürgen. *Gründung des neuen Staates 1949*. Munich, 1981.

Weber, Jürgen. *Die Bundesrepublik wird souverän 1950–1955*. Munich, 1986.

Weber, Jürgen, and Peter Steinbach, eds. *Vergangenheitsbewältigung durch Strafverfahren? NS-Prozesse in der Bundesrepublik Deutschland*. Munich, 1984.

Wehler, Hans-Ulrich. "30. Januar 1933—Ein halbes Jahrhundert danach." In *Aus Politik und Zeitgeschichte* 4–5 (1983): 43–54.

Wein, Martin. *Die Weizsäckers: Geschichte einer deutschen Familie*. Stuttgart, 1988.

Weingartner, James J. *Crossroads of Death: The Story of the Malmedy Massacre and Trial*. Berkeley, Los Angeles, and London, 1979.

Weisbrod, Bernd, ed. *Rechtsradikalismus in der politischen Kultur der Nachkriegszeit: Die verzögerte Normalisierung in Niedersachsen*. Hannover, 1995.

Weiß, Hermann. "Alte Kameraden von der Waffen-SS. Ist die HIAG rechtsextrem?" In *Rechtsextremismus in der Bundesrepublik: Voraussetzungen, Zusammenhänge, Wirkungen,* ed. Wolfgang Benz, pp. 202–12. Frankfurt am Main, 1989.

Wember, Heiner. *Umerziehung im Lager: Internierung und Bestrafung von Nationalsozialisten in der britischen Besatzungszone Deutschlands*. Essen, 1991.

Wengst, Udo. *Staatsaufbau und Regierungspraxis 1948–1953: Zur Geschichte der Verfassungsorgane der Bundesrepublik Deutschland.* Düsseldorf, 1984.

Wengst, Udo. *Auftakt zur Ära Adenauer: Koalitionsverhandlungen und Regierungsbildung 1949.* Düsseldorf, 1985.

Wengst, Udo. "Die CDU and CSU im Bundestagswahlkampf 1949." In *Vierteljahrshefte für Zeitgeschichte* 34 (1986): 1–52.

Wengst, Udo. *Beamtentum zwischen Reform und Tradition: Beamtengesetzgebung in der Gründungsphase der Bundesrepublik Deutschland 1948–1953.* Düsseldorf, 1988.

Wenke, Hans. " 'Bewältigte Vergangenheit' und 'aufgearbeitete Geschichte,' zwei Schlagworte, kritisch beleuchtet." In *Geschichte in Wissenschaft und Unterricht* 11 (1960): 65–70.

Wenzlau, Joachim Reinhold. *Der Wiederaufbau der Justiz in Nordwestdeutschland 1945–1949.* Königstein, 1979.

Wettig, Gerhard. *Entmilitarisierung und Wiederbewaffnung in Deutschland 1943–1955: Internationale Auseinandersetzungen um die Rolle der Deutschen in Europa.* Munich, 1967.

Wetzel, Juliane. *Jüdisches Leben in Munich 1945–1951: Durchgangsstation oder Wiederaufbau?* Munich, 1987.

Wetzel, Juliane. " 'Mir szeinen doh': Munich und Umgebung als Zuflucht von Überlebenden des Holocaust 1945–1948." In *Von Stalingrad zur Währungsreform: Zur Sozialgeschichte des Umbruchs in Deutschland,* ed. Martin Broszat, Klaus-Dietmar Henke, and Hans Woller, pp. 327–64. Munich, 1988.

Wewer, Heinz. "Die HIAG der Waffen-SS." In *Frankfurter Hefte* 7 (1962): 448–58.

Whiting, Charles. *Massacre at Malmédy: The Story of Jochen Peiper's Battle Group.* Ardennes, December 1944; London, 1971.

Widmaier, Benedikt. *Die Bundeszentrale für politische Bildung: Ein Beitrag zur Geschichte staatlicher politischer Bildung in der Bundesrepublik Deutschland.* Frankfurt am Main, Bern, and New York, 1987.

Wielenga, Friso. *Schatten deutscher Geschichte: Der Umgang mit dem Nationalsozialismus und der DDR-Vergangenheit in der Bundesrepublik.* Vierow, 1995.

Wiesenthal, Simon. *Recht, nicht Rache: Erinnerungen.* Frankfurt am Main and Berlin, 1988.

Wiggershaus, Norbert. "Die Entscheidung für einen westdeutschen Verteidigungsbeitrag 1950." In *Anfänge westdeutscher Sicherheitspolitik 1945–1956,* ed. Militärgeschichtlichen Forschungsamt, vol. 1, pp. 325–402. Munich and Vienna, 1982, 1990.

Wiggershaus, Norbert. "Zur Bedeutung und Nachwirkung des militärischen Widerstandes in der Bundesrepublik Deutschland und in der Bundeswehr." In *Aufstand des Gewissens: Der militärische Widerstand gegen Hitler und das NS-Regime 1933–1945.* Herford and Bonn, [1984].

Wiggershaus, Rolf. *Die Frankfurter Schule. Geschichte. Theoretische Entwicklung. Politische Bedeutung.* Munich, 1988.

Wilke, Jürgen. *Holocaust und NS-Prozesse: Die Presseberichterstattung in Israel und Deutschland zwischen Aneignung und Abwehr.* Cologne, Weimar, and Vienna, 1995.

Will, Roland. *Kriegsverbrechen auf dem Weg in die Freiheit: Deutsch-amerikanische Begnadigungspolitik gegenüber Kriegsverbrechern 1948–1958.* Unpublished thesis, Munich, 1990.

Wilmowsky, Thilo Freiherr von. *Warum wurde Krupp verurteilt? Legende und Justizirrtum.* Stuttgart, 1950.

Winkler, Heinrich August. "Nationalismus, Nationalstaat und nationale Frage in Deutschland seit 1945." In *Nationalismus—Nationalitäten—Supranationalitäten,* ed. Heinrich August Winkler and Hartmut Kaelble. Stuttgart, 1993.

Wörtliche Berichte und Drucksachen des Wirtschaftsrates des Vereinigten Wirtschaftsgebietes 1947–1949. Ed. Christoph Weisz and Hans Woller. 6 vols. Munich and Vienna, 1977.

Wolfe, Robert, ed. *Americans as Proconsuls: United States Military Government in Germany and Japan, 1944–1952.* Carbondale, Ill., and Edwardsville, Ill., 1984.

Wolffsohn, Michael. *Ewige Schuld? 40 Jahre deutsch-jüdisch-israelische Beziehungen.* Munich and Zurich, 1988.

Wolffsohn, Michael. "Von der verordneten zur freiwilligen 'Vergangenheitsbewältigung?' Eine Skizze der bundesdeutschen Entwicklung 1955–1965." In *German Studies Review* 12 (1989): 111–37.

Wolffsohn, Michael. *Keine Angst vor Deutschland!* Erlangen, Bonn, and Vienna, 1990.

Wolfru, Edgar. *Geschichtspolitik in der Bundesrepublik Deutschland. Der Weg zur bundesrepublikanischen Erinnerung 1948–1990.* Darmstadt, 1999.

Woller, Hans. *Die Loritz-Partei: Geschichte, Struktur und Politik der Wirtschaftlichen Aufbau-Vereinigung (WAV) 1945–1955.* Stuttgart, 1982.

Woller, Hans. *Gesellschaft und Politik in der amerikanischen Besatzungszone: Die Region Ansbach und Fürth.* Munich, 1986.

Woller, Hans. "Deutschland im Umbruch zwischen Stalingrad und der Währungsreform." In *Der schwierige Weg zur Demokratie. Die Bundesrepublik vor 40 Jahren,* ed. der Landeszentrale für politische Bildung Nordrhein-Westfalen, pp. 101–14. Düsseldorf, 1990.

Wunder, Bernd. *Geschichte der Bürokratie in Deutschland.* Frankfurt am Main, 1986.

Ziesel, Kurt. *Der rote Rufmord: Eine Dokumentation zum Kalten Krieg.* Tübingen, 1961.

INDEX

Abendpost, 218, 219

Achenbach, Ernst, 279–80, 285; on general amnesty for war criminals, 123, 183, 194, 198, 205, 352n12; investigation into the Naumann Affair, 293, 296; as lawyer for Naumann, 289–90, 292, 293, 413n85; release of war criminals before ratification of General Treaty, 215, 383n60; on terminology of war criminals, 213, 382n51

Acheson, Dean, 185, 190, 191, 192, 195, 199, 200

Adenauer, Konrad: during conclusion of the war criminal problem, 204, 206, 207, 208, 210, 212–13, 216, 219, 221, 222, 386n90; election victory of, 224, 310, 387n112; enlisting a commission regarding war crimes and sentencing, 190–92; forming a policy for the past *(Vergangenheitspolitik),* xviii; on German rearmament and restoration of German soldiers,

148–49, 151, 153–55, 169, 171, 359n12; looking at "General Treaty" instead of "general amnesty": 182, 184–186, 188, 190, 191–92, 193, 195, 197–200; during the Naumann Affair, 281, 286–89, 291–93, 295, 297, 300–301; "overcoming" the immediate Nazi past, xvii, 3; "rehabilitation of German soldiers," 95; review and debate around Article 131, 46, 47–48, 53–54, 55; on revised sentencing of war criminals, 135–36, 140, 141; during rise and banning of the Socialist Reich Party (SRP), 253–54, 255, 257, 258–60, 261, 262–63; as *Time's* "Man of the Year," 300; visit to prison in Werl, 223, 309; West German contribution to Western defense, 95; working on the Amnesty Law of 1949, 5, 6–7, 8, 13, 19, 20; working on the Amnesty law of 1954, 68, 75, 76, 338n5

debate around Article 131, 51, 52; during rise and banning of the Socialist Reich Party (SRP), 256, 257; "Working Alliance of Democratic Circles," 213; working on the Amnesty Law of 1954, 86, 91

Christian Social Union (CSU), 3, 8, 16; debate over the General Treaty, 207; discussion about revised sentencing of war criminals, 136; on eliminating/reducing denazification, 28, 29, 30, 33, 34, 38; on a "General Treaty" instead of "general amnesty," 183; position on war criminals and German rearmament, 152–53, 158, 171, 304; review and debate around Article 131, 52; working on the Amnesty Law of 1954, 86

Christlicher Nachrichtendienst, 113

Christ und Welt, 20, 22; article on extradition of war criminals, 129–30; article on general amnesty, 157; commentary on armament and restoration of war criminals, 150; response to sentencing of war criminals, 174

Churchill, Winston, 116, 186, 222

Civil Service Association, 45

Clay, Lucius D., 226; issuing orders of execution, 99, 106, 107, 108, 110, 112, 113, 117, 349–50n77; review of Malmédy trials, 103; submission of anti-Nuremberg petition, 104, 106–7

Cold War, 230, 274

Committee for Foreign Affairs, 157

Committee for Occupation Law and Foreign Affairs, 136, 184, 197

Committee for War Victims and War Prisoners, 181

Committee on Civil Service Law, 49, 50

Committee on Foreign Affairs, 189

Committee on Foreign Policy, 215

Communist Party, 257. *See also* German Communist Party

Conant, James P., 220–21, 222, 228

Constitutional Court: First Panel of the, 265, 270, 273, 274, 275; during the Hedler Affair, 238, 249, 251; inclusion of Article 7.3 of the General Treaty, 216; president of, 271; review and debate around Article 131, 59–60, 64; during rise and banning of Socialist Reich Party (SRP), 255, 258, 259, 261, 262, 264, 265, 269, 270

"Coordination Bureau for the Advancement of Legal Defense for German Prisoners Abroad," 122, 136

Crimea, 144

Criminal-legal norms. *See* Hedler Affair

Dachau: American confrontation of Nazi war crimes at, 103–4; church officials' criticism of trials, 97, 99, 103, 104, 110, 111, 117, 346n27; concentration camp at, 94, 104; trials at, 97, 99, 103, 126, 141, 158

Dagens Nyheter, 279

Daily Telegraph, 297

Dam, Hendrik van, 239

Darmstadt, 116

Darré, Richard Walter, 150

Das Parliament, 269

Dehler, Thomas: on death sentences of war criminals, 153, 156; etiology of the ninth paragraph in the Amnesty Law of 1949, 21, 324n51; on French trials of German war prisoners, 137–40; "General Treaty" instead of "general amnesty," 183, 193–94, 196, 198, 199; on German role in remaining death sentences, 168, 169, 171, 172, 192; on the Hedler Affair, 245–46, 247; "Law for Granting Exemption from Punishment,"

Stinnes, Jr., Hugo, 280
Storch, Anton Labor Minister, 135
Straßer, Otto, 253
Strauß, Franz Josef, 80, 82, 83, 210
Strauß, Justice, 11
Strauß, Walter, 18, 158–59; "Frankfurt
    Plan," 7; on German responsibility
    for sentence enforcement, 196; on
    winding up the war criminal prob-
    lem, 207; work on the Amnesty
    Law of 1954, 80, 81, 82, 83
Strobel, Robert, 172
Stumpff, Hans-Jürgen, 220
Stuttgart, 20
Süddeutsche Juristen-Zeitung, 20
Süddeutsche Zeitung, 12, 141, 142,
    174

Taylor, Telford, 101, 165
Thadden, Adolf von, 35, 37, 247
Thielicke, Helmut, 161
Third Reich, xviii, xix, 39, 42, 53, 60,
    63, 97, 268; Commissioner for the
    Ukraine, 129; crimes of, 145, 230,
    311; end of, 231; "racial" trans-
    gressions by, 6; trials of jurists, 105
Thompson, Dorothy, 98
Times, term of war criminal to "war
    criminal," 177
Toussaint, Hans, 194
Transition Treaty, 195, 196, 198, 201,
    379n117; Adenauer's activities for,
    224; effective date of, 225; and
    Mixed Board review of sentencing
    of war criminals, 212, 221, 228–29;
    signing of, 207; and winding up
    the war criminal problem, 203
Treaty of Westphalia, 139, 194
Truman, Harry S., 113, 169, 172
Tübingen, University of, 226
Tüngel, Richard, 110, 241

Union for Public Services, Transport,
    and Traffic, 43
Union of Expellees and Victims of
    Injustice, 217, 274, 282, 284, 304

United States: American Board of
    Extradition, 154; Armed Services
    Committee, 116; Iowa Supreme
    Court, 100. See also American
    zone of occupation; McCloy, John

van Dam, Hendrik, 239
Vandenberg, Arthur, 124
Vogel, Georg, 172, 173
Volk: guilt on the shoulders of, 1,
    237; the post-Nazi national com-
    munity of, xxi
Volksgemeinschaft, 3, 131, 320n5 (for
    part 1)
Volksgenossen, 4

Waffen SS, 49, 50, 56
Wahl, Alfons, 122
Wahl, Eduard, resolving the war
    criminal problem, 13, 121, 122,
    171, 179, 182, 188–89, 196, 213
Wahnerheide, 278, 279, 291
war crimes: specified definitions of,
    178
War criminals: accomplices of crimes
    of euthanasia, 207; bilateral pardon
    commission decisions, 224–32; as
    'camp-kapos,' 208; changing term
    war criminal to "war criminal,"
    177–78, 370–71n3; church inter-
    vention on behalf of, 97–119;
    clemency reviews by the "Mixed
    Board," 192, 200, 205, 212; and
    Committee for War Victims and
    War Prisoners, 181; and "concen-
    tration camp cases," 207; and
    concept of "binding orders," 206;
    and "Coordination Bureau for the
    Advancement of Legal Defense for
    German Prisoners Abroad," 122,
    136, 138; definition of, 94; as
    "desk murderers," 187, 232; and
    distinction between German sol-
    diers and Hitler's criminals, 164;
    and "General Treaty" instead of
    "general amnesty," 177–201;

NORBERT FREI is professor of modern history at Ruhr-University Bochum. He is the author of many books on twentieth-century German history, including *The Führer State*. He lives in Germany.

JOEL GOLB is a Berlin-based editor, translator and literary historian.